JOSIAH'S PASSOVER

The Bible & Liberation

An Orbis Series in Biblical Studies

Norman K. Gottwald and Richard A. Horsley,
General Editors

The Bible & Liberation Series focuses on the emerging range of political, social, and contextual hermeneutics that are changing the face of biblical interpretation today. It brings to light the social struggles behind the biblical texts. At the same time it explores the ways that a "liberated Bible" may offer resources in the contemporary struggle for a more human world.

Already published:

The Bible and Liberation: Political and Social Hermeneutics (Revised edition), Norman K. Gottwald and Richard A. Horsley, Editors

The Bible & Liberation Series

JOSIAH'S PASSOVER

Sociology and the Liberating Bible

Shigeyuki Nakanose

ORBIS BOOKS

Maryknoll, New York 10545

The Catholic Foreign Mission Society of America (Maryknoll) recruits and trains people for overseas missionary service. Through Orbis Books, Maryknoll aims to foster the international dialogue that is essential to mission. The books published, however, reflect the opinions of their authors and are not meant to represent the official position of the society.

Copyright © 1993 by Shigeyuki Nakanose
Published by Orbis Books, Maryknoll, NY 10545
Scripture quotations, unless otherwise noted, are taken from *The New Jerusalem Bible.*
All rights reserved
Manufactured in the United States of America

Library of Congress Cataloging-in-Publication Data

Nakanose, Shigeyuki.
    Josiah's Passover : sociology and the liberating Bible / Shigeyuki Nakanose.
       p. cm. — (Bible and liberation series)
    Includes bibliographical references and indexes.
    ISBN 0-88344-850-5 (pbk.)
    1. Bible. O.T. Kings, 2nd, XXII, 1-XXIII, 30—Criticism, interpretation, etc. 2. Sociology, Biblical. 3. Liberation theology. 4. Basic Christian communities—Brazil. I. Title. II. Series.
BS1335.2.N35   1993
222'.54067—dc20
                                         93-18286
                                           CIP

To my family:

Masayuki, Sadako,
Masatoshi, Mieko, Seishi,
Akemi, Satoshi, Ayami,
Tikara, Miho, Sadafumi, Miu,
Takashi, Isaya, Keiko,
Yuuka, and Akina

Contents

Foreword

NORMAN K. GOTTWALD

Significant as it is for understanding the religious history of ancient Israel, the value of this book lies not only in its startling conclusions about the ancient biblical religious festival of Passover. Of equal importance is the process of the book's production and consumption within a network of basic ecclesial communities (CEBs), wherein the results of the study are returned to lay Bible readers as a resource in their struggle to reshape their own religious institutions.

In this work, Shigeyuki Nakanose, a leader in the Roman Catholic basic communities of Brazil, presents a critical assessment of Passover — the biblical festival most frequently associated with liberation of the oppressed — in order to determine how it actually functioned in its earliest social settings. His conclusions are subsequently shared with other leaders and lay members in the basic communities as they together explore how Passover, variously understood, assists or obstructs the development of democratic church processes and meaningful improvements in the daily lives of ordinary people.

Because we are accustomed to a radical separation of "academic" and "popular" studies of the Bible, Nakanose's work gives the appearance of being not one but *two* books. Indeed, it is written in such a way that readers who are interested in only one of these two facets of biblical study can use it to great profit. Those who want only to know how the author conceives the history of Passover — and especially the substance and import of Josiah's refashioning of the festival — may simply read chapters 1 through 4 for a self-contained account. On the other hand, those who want chiefly to know how the author's scholarly analysis serves the process of lay biblical interpretation and church renewal can skip directly from chapter 1 to chapter 5. Such single-minded readers may eventually find that they want to read the entire book, but the organization of the presentation leaves that choice to each reader. I will only say enough in this foreword to assist readers in deciding how they want to approach this unusual work.

To my knowledge, Nakanose's study of the biblical Passover is the most thorough social and religious institutional examination of the festival ever undertaken. Only here and there have scholars before him grasped limited

aspects of the comprehensive sociological critique of Passover that Nakanose provides. The author's methods and conclusions bring an entirely new
perspective on the way biblical religious institutions functioned to serve
particular economic, social, political, and ideological ends. He insistently
asks these questions: How do the religious activities in ancient Israel—and
in particular the much-praised Passover—relate to wider social developments? Whose interests are enhanced and whose interests are jeopardized
by these religious acts and institutions? Nakanose is able to demonstrate
that Passover at its inception served the strengthening of the familial and
tribal society of early Israel. Surprisingly, however, he goes on to show how
Passover was eventually coopted by the ruling class of Judah in order to
concentrate wealth and power in its hands and to suppress the autonomy
and vigor of popular Israelite culture and religion. The author makes clear
that religious celebration in the Bible—as in churches today—is never simply what it appears to be: it strengthens some social values and interests
while it weakens others. In his view, the so-called Deuteronomic reform
spearheaded by King Josiah—including a revamped Passover festival as one
of its cardinal features—decisively strengthened the small ruling elite of
Judah to the detriment of the economic, social, political, and religious well-
being of the majority of Israelites.

Similar claims of the oppressive force of various biblical institutions and
practices have of course been advanced by others, often, it must be admit-
ted, so vaguely and imprecisely that they are more a matter of opinion than
of considered argument. On the contrary, the power of Nakanose's hypothesis rests on the great care with which he builds his case, winnowing out
the grain from the chaff in the dominant literary and theological interpretations of Josiah's Passover reform by rooting his analysis in a comprehensive reconstruction of the social history of Israel and Judah. The author
reveals the Passover to have been not simply a "religious" event but at the
same time an economic, social, and political event of unexpected magnitude. Nakanose musters an impressive array of scholarly work in many
branches of biblical studies to focus on the dynamics of religious celebration
as an arena of contest between conflicting social sectors. His treatments of
the social matrix of various types of sacrifices and of the ideological role of
priests and scribes are noteworthy in this regard. In pursuing the inquiry,
the author draws on scholarly resources from Latin America not otherwise
accessible in English. Particularly enlightening is the way Nakanose has
situated Josiah's Passover as the culmination of a long process of tightening
state controls over agriculture, small industry, and trade during the 8th and
7th centuries B.C.E. in response to Assyrian economic and political pressure.
His postulation of a growing pool of surplus landless laborers drawn from
a shrinking independent peasantry as a key factor in the shaping of Josiah's
Passover provides a fresh explanation of many of its features.

In a study of this scope and daring, it is natural that not all of the author's
judgments will be equally convincing to scholars. I myself, for example,

think he underestimates the liberative dimensions in the prophet Isaiah, but this is because I have a different view of the redaction of the prophet's writing. Certainly Nakanose is correct that the book of Isaiah as it has been edited is more supportive of the ruling class than is often recognized. My point here is that Nakanose marshals his categories of evidence and advances his multifaceted argument with a clarity that allows the reader to participate fully in the inquiry, whether agreeing or disagreeing, or simply withholding judgment, either about particulars or with respect to the larger conclusions. All in all, I believe he has given us the proper social historical frame in which to trace a radical transformation of Passover from its "democratized" origins into an "elitist" instrument for the concentration of wealth and power in royal and aristocratic hands. This sharp reversal of a wide consensus among biblical interpreters that Josiah's reform was a liberative one on behalf of the whole people obviously carries far-reaching implications. Some of these implications call for a reevaluation of the Deuteronomic movement in the late monarchy, while others call into question the adequacy of methods and resources normally used in popular study of the Bible.

Had the author ended the book at this point, it would have been enough. Fortunately, he goes on to reflect on the import of his conclusions for Bible study in lay circles and, most importantly, he does this concretely by showing us how his understanding of biblical Passover was shared with leaders and lay participants in Brazilian basic ecclesial communities in and around São Paulo, as well as how they responded to it.

The challenge that Nakanose strives to meet is both hermeneutical and pedagogical. How are social critical understandings of the Bible to be related to Bible reading rooted in the life experience of ordinary people who have not had training in biblical criticism? What happens to popular Bible reading when it is unaware of the social context and import of biblical texts? How can lay groups seeking empowerment in church and society determine when the Bible is liberative and when it is oppressive? How can social critical knowledge of the Bible be made available to ordinary readers as a factor in their own experience rather than one more layer of intellectual oppression in a church where hierarchical experts are generally in charge?

The uniqueness of Nakanose's approach is that he tells us what happened when he shared his discoveries about Josiah's Passover with nine leaders of Brazilian base communities and subsequently with base communities made up of peasants and homeless street people.

The author's basic strategy was to enter a dialogical process in which he first listened attentively to the spontaneous "naive" readings of the biblical text about Josiah's Passover offered by leaders who had little specific knowledge of this aspect of biblical history. In subsequent conversations with these leaders, either singly or in pairs, he learned gradually of their doubts and suspicions about the text. As these difficulties were explored, he introduced his analysis of Josiah's reforms. The group members responded out of their experience of Brazilian society that resonated with Nakanose's social critical reading of Josiah's program. The leaders then prepared various formats, often in storytelling and art work, to translate their emerging social critical view of Josiah into study agendas for the basic communities they led.

Throughout, it is to be noted that Nakanose worked among equals in a common task, privileged only by his specialized biblical training. He was at pains to relate his expertise to the questions emerging in the circle of leaders, generated on the one hand by the biblical text and on the other by their life experience and social understanding. They in turn did the same in the basic community sessions they conducted. Thus, at all levels, the basic community participants shared in "testing the hypothesis" about Josiah's Passover in terms of how it illuminated the Bible and how it bore on their own experience of society.

Perhaps the most important issue Nakanose identifies in using the Bible as a critical resource in church circles is the ingrained tendency of readers to attribute a pious sanctity to whatever the Bible says in the absence of an understanding of the acutal social and religious issues underlying the text. Again and again, Nakanose found that the initial response of church folk—even those most critical of church and society—was to accept the religious claims of the text at face value. Since Josiah is described in the Bible with highest praise as one who followed Yahweh and promoted obedience to the book of the Law, it seemed natural to them to assume that he was a good king who served the people. Only slowly did it become evident to them that religious language in the Bible—including what is said by and about Josiah and his Passover reform—cloaks a variety of social and political interests, and that it is essential to examine the actual life consequences of the ideas and behavior presented in the Bible as "the will of God."

The task that Nakanose formulates, and then vividly illustrates in one instance, is to assist ordinary Bible readers to be as critically aware of social reality in the Bible as they are of social reality in their own life settings. While this sort of lay struggle with the Bible as a critical resource for confronting church and society is prominently exhibited in the basic ecclesial communities of Latin America, it is in practice a world-wide phenomenon emerging among churches engaged in self-examination and renewal as a force in society. For example, just such a burgeoning of lay circles of critical Bible readers, with issues and problems very similar to those grappled with by Nakanose, is occurring in South Africa as that country enters a new era of democratic government. (See Gerald West, *Biblical Hermeneutics of Liberation: Modes of Reading the Bible in the South African Context* [Pietermaritzburg, RSA: Cluster Publications, 1991].) In North America, as progressive Christians struggle to reshape church and society, they too face the need for a social critical understanding of the Bible as a resource for informed reflection and action. In approaching the Bible in this social critical manner, however, these study-action groups enter uncharted territory for which they have had to fashion new instructional methods and create their own study aids.

It seems to me that Nakanose has laid bare a social critical methodology and hermeneutic and a method of teaching them to ordinary Bible readers that is applicable wherever people are striving to use their biblical heritage effectively to bring about progressive changes in church and society. He charts a pathway that follows the hermeneutical circle over its entire course. As we move methodically back and forth between our own life situations and biblical life situations, we become ever more knowledgeable about both settings and—in consequence—more intelligent and committed participants in the events of our time and place. As Nakanose concludes, "How many times do we neglect the fact that it is primarily in the world and not in the Bible that God lives? The biblical Word is our clue to God's presence in the world, rather than God's permanent dwelling place."

Acknowledgments

This project was originally my doctoral dissertation for New York Theological Seminary. I have revised it, endeavoring to avoid technical terms and frequent reference to secondary literature. Since 1978 I have been immersed in daily living with the suffering poor in Brazil and in learning the Bible from their viewpoint. This praxis, while being stimulated and questioned by the faculty and students in the doctoral program, has become a continuing source of additional sociotheological insight and ideas by which this project was nourished. So this project is the creation of every person with whom I have worked, or studied, or from whom I have looked for clues for the reading of the Bible.

Many people have been helpful in this project. Still, certain persons stand out, and these must be given special thanks. I feel a deep debt and gratitude to my doctoral advisers, Dr. Norman K. Gottwald and Dr. T. Richard Snyder, and to my additional readers, Gerson Max and Arthur B. Wyse. They spent many hours going over the manuscript and helped me improve it in innumerable ways. My work with Norman in particular has been a fruitful source of advice and guidance in helping me develop a sociological exegesis of Josiah's Passover.

Because of the loving encouragement and wonderful sense of humor typical of the Brazilian friends with whom I have been privileged to work, special thanks are due to Alice, Arlindo, Carlos, Ércio, Itamar, and Sebastião. They spent many weeks wrestling with the organization of the Bible course described in this project. I would also like to acknowledge my debt to a number of the basic ecclesial community members, who participated in the Bible study meetings with the theme of Josiah's Passover, for their day-to-day struggles in helping me read the Bible through the eyes of the poor.

I must also thank the Christian Brothers with whom I lived during my stay in Harlem, New York, for their hospitality. They cordially received this *padre brasileiro* as their chaplain and broadened my experience of Christian fraternity. It is difficult for me to express properly my appreciation to Br. Henry Otto, CFC. He was the first person to read and discuss my manuscript, providing invaluable redactional assistance. Thanks is also due to Miguel and Edênio, my confreres, who read all or part of my manuscript and provided helpful criticism for its publication. Finally I thank the Society of the Divine Word and New York Theological Seminary for their ideas and financial support, which made my study in New York possible.

But most importantly, I must thank my family in Nagasaki, as well as *minha famlía Verbita* in São Paulo, who strongly supported my work on this project with their words, their acts, and their prayers.

1

Introduction

SOCIOLOGICAL EXEGESIS AND CEB BIBLICAL HERMENEUTICS

This work is an exercise in the sociological interpretation of the Bible and its use in the basic ecclesial communities (CEBs). For several years I have been working among the Brazilian people as a member and pastor of various CEBs, reading the Bible from the perspective of the suffering people in their daily living of the gospel. Such experience leads me to conclude that the Bible is offering critical direction for us today in our struggles for the liberation of our human dignity and status as daughters and sons of God. At the same time, I have also become aware of the further need of "pertinent sociocritical biblical hermeneutics" for Liberation Theology and the CEBs in their use of the Bible. "The liberation theologians," argues Norman K. Gottwald, "are at times working with an older and inadequate biblical exegesis that weakens, or at least fails to do full justice to, their own case" (1989: 251).

Most agree that the historical-critical method is one of the essential and basic tools for modern biblical exegesis. Generally speaking, this method attempts to deal seriously with the prehistory of the text and with the historical setting at work in illuminating the final text. This helps us confront fundamentalist and subjective hermeneutics. By incorporating the full richness and variety of critical tools (e.g., textual criticism, form criticism, and historical criticism), our understanding of the text can be greatly expanded. We acquire a general picture of the society of biblical times, for instance. These insights into the text are incorporated in arguments against fundamentalists, who are generally inclined to read the texts literally, demanding the maintenance of socially and politically conservative values in support of the oppressive situation in Latin America. For example, one can allow for massive public suffering within the theme of Matthew 26:11, "You have the poor with you always, but you will not always have me."

In addition, interpreting the texts within a historical diachronic sequence prevents the exegesis from becoming unduly subjective. It is clear from a

1

study of the Bible that God has been revealed by acting in human history to bring about an integral salvation that is valid in every age (Ex 3:13–15). So, to understand God's messages and acts, one must assume there is a continuity between the historical situation of the people of the Bible and our historical situation today. Knowing the historical situation of the biblical texts, which were originally addressed to the authors' communities in their own historical period, corrects and controls the reading and interpreting of the texts by readers today. There is no way to extract a correct understanding of biblical theology from within the context of the readers alone, which subjective hermeneutics tries to do.

In spite of the fact that it remains impossible for biblical readers today, and particularly for the exegetes, to interpret biblical literature without the historical-critical method, it should be said that this approach has not satisfied exegetical interests and needs in Latin America. The basic methodological problem lies in the fact that this method itself has to avoid two dangers: idealistic and individualistic hermeneutics.

First, the historical-critical method has been directed predominantly toward ideas, and fails to take account of the fact that the biblical texts and the ideas, concepts, and doctrines they contain are themselves the ideological products of a particular sociohistorical setting. Without this hermeneutical perspective, the historical-critical method is not able to recognize that the socioeconomic conflicts in the Bible are actually clues to understanding the same conflicts in our society today.

Also, the historical-critical method has lacked sufficient emphasis on the analysis and interpretation of biblical literature as the product of communal reflection. As a result, the analysis of this method is insufficient and has suffered from the failure to recognize the Bible as emerging out of Israel's collective struggle to oppose oppressive institutional violence from inside or outside its social system. This failure has powerfully supported another alienation, individualism, which is the ideological core of capitalist domination.

CEB biblical hermeneutics has dealt with these problems of individualistic and idealistic hermeneutics to some extent. First, CEB members combat the danger of individualistic hermeneutics by reading the Bible in community and by applying it to their common tasks for liberation. Second, when people introduce their real-community lives and concrete situations into the process of interpretation of the Bible, then the danger of idealistic hermeneutics diminishes.

However, it is also true that CEB pastoral agents and animators may lack information about the material living conditions of the people in the Bible, something the historical-critical method cannot reveal adequately. In this case, they may not lead their community members to interpret the meaning of the biblical texts in a critical way. Lacking this, the Bible can become an oppressive tool rather than a critical one for the people.

For the solution of such problems, biblical scholarship has applied sociology to the study of the Bible, a so-called sociological exegesis (cf. Elliott: 1–13). This method is not incompatible with the historical-critical method, but supplements it in order to reconstruct a "social system" of biblical communities. For a definition of the term *social system,* Gottwald writes,

> The social system of ancient Israel signifies the whole complex of communal interactions embracing functions, roles, institutions, customs, norms, symbols, and the processes and networks distinctive to the sub-systems of social organization (economic production, political order, military defense, judicatory procedure, religious organization, etc.). This social system must be grasped in its activity both in the communal production of goods, services, ideas and in the communal control of their distributions and use (1984a: 27).

Sociological exegesis leads the readers to a critical perspective on the material living conditions (socioeconomic, political, and religious life) of the people in biblical times, and, as well, to a clearer understanding of the concrete demands of social justice today. By using this method, CEB members can critically assess the Bible, particularly its various religious (ideological) roots and uses, "so often used against them, to determine the adequacy of Christian faith and its sources as a contribution to effective liberation from socio-political oppression" (Pixley 1984: 109).

We acknowledge that there has been a significant improvement upon the previous exegesis of Liberation Theology and the CEBs. This improvement has added especially to the biblical aspect of social doctrines, for instance, by the critical study of the prophets in the Old Testament (cf. Gilberto Gorgulho 1985; Milton Schwantes 1986; Severino Croatto 1989). These studies are based on sociological exegesis, and their results have been absorbed by many theologians and pastoral agents in the CEBs. In doing this, the sociological reading of the Bible from the perspective of the poor has enlightened and strengthened CEB biblical movements.

Nevertheless, this improvement has not yet been sufficient, particularly in the sociological interpretation of biblical religious institutions and cultic activites (e.g., the priesthood, the feast, the sacrifice). We must acknowledge a weakness in having to use "an older and inadequate biblical exegesis." As a result, it is difficult for the CEBs to provide an adequate biblical rootage for their grass-roots movements and their religious institutions that have been criticized by conservatives and sectors of the Vatican bureaucracy. (We shall examine these criticisms more fully in chapter 5.) The CEBs have a need to further develop a sociological exegesis that will support the authenticity of their religious institutions and be an asset for their members in using the Bible as a resource for effective liberation from socioeconomic, political, and religious oppression.

The proposal that follows targets sociological exegesis and CEB biblical hermeneutics, focusing especially on the following aspects: research into religious institutions in the Old Testament through sociological exegesis, and the relationship between this research and the awakening of the critical consciousness of CEB members. In doing so, we intend to provide biblical paradigms that support the grass-roots Bible study and religious institutions of the CEBs.

The focal point of this sociological exegesis is the Passover celebration during the period of Josiah's reform:

> The King gave this order to the whole people: "Celebrate a Passover to Yahweh your God, as prescribed in this Book of the Covenant." No Passover like this had ever been celebrated since the days when the judges ruled Israel, nor throughout the entire period of the kings of Israel and the kings of Judah. The eighteenth year of King Josiah was the only time when such a Passover was celebrated in Yahweh's honor in Jerusalem (2 Kings 23:21–23).

I have selected Josiah's Passover as the object of such a sociological-exegetical analysis for several reasons. First of all, the Exodus theme obviously has a strong presence in this issue. Latin American theology stresses an affinity between the current struggles of the suffering masses and the Hebrew people's struggle against the Egyptian tyrant. There is no doubt about the fact that the Passover occupies the central cultic position of the Exodus. Another reason is the consideration of the reforms of Josiah as a centralization of the celebration of the Passover in the national sanctuary in Jerusalem. The reforms consisted of a "Deuteronomistic Movement" in the continuing struggle for control of "Official Yahwism." From this perspective, the study of Josiah's Passover can offer productive insights into the present struggle for control of Latin American Catholicism, mentioned notably in chapter 5, where I will focus on CEB activities.

Research in recent years, especially under the historical-critical method, has produced important new contributions which make it possible to sketch an outline of the Passover. However, it also has been recognized that the conventional method has offered only limited answers to the detailed question as to why King Josiah restored or concentrated the Passover celebration in the Jerusalem Temple. The conventional study of the Passover that follows reinforces this limitation and the necessity of applying sociological exegesis to our research.

SOME ILLUSTRATIVE SKETCHES OF THE PASSOVER

Generally speaking, scholars consider Exodus 12:21–23 as a description of the old Yahwistic ritual (cf. the contrary view that this text stems from the Priestly work, Van Seters). According to the text, the following basic elements characterize the Passover celebration:

1. The Passover is celebrated in the house. Indeed, there is no limitation of worship to determined places or altars. (Haran 1972; 1985: 341–348, argues that the Passover sacrifice in vv. 21–27 should be offered up at one of the houses of God, a temple, as opposed to most critics who view this sacrifice as a family rite.)

2. The presence of the elders: "Moses summoned all the elders of Israel and said to them ... " (v. 21a). It is of interest to note the prominent role of elders in the Passover account. We can most probably detect here the tribal system in which the Passover is celebrated.

3. The narrow choice of the Passover victim: "Go and choose lambs or kids for your families, and kill the Passover victim" (v. 21).

4. The blood ritual: "Then take a bunch of hyssop, dip it in the blood that is in the basin, and with the blood from the basin touch the lintel and both door-posts" (v. 22a–b). The blood ritual is clearly apotropaic – the protective power for the Israelites staying in the house.

5. No one leaves his house all night: " ... then let none of you venture out of the house till morning" (v. 22c).

6. Finally, the Passover celebration in Exodus 12:21–23 is definitely a tribal (family) ritual.

There are some striking similarities between the Passover ritual described above and the sacrifices of the ancient Arabs. De Vaux (1965: 489), for instance, outlines the nature of the sacrifice ritual of the ancient Arabs in the following way: "There is no priest, no altar, and the use of the blood is most important." Accordingly, scholars are inclined to trace the Passover back to the seminomads of pre-Mosaic times. In this period, the religious ordinances are molded as part of the tribal life-style.

However, at the earliest stage in the history of Israel, the agricultural festival had begun to receive important treatment in the socioreligious spheres of Israel. For instance, Exodus 23:14–17 (one of the four Pentateuchal traditions of the cultic calendar), possibly derived from J, mentions the three great annual feasts, i.e., the feasts of Unleavened Bread, of Weeks (the Harvest feast), and of Tents (the feast of Ingathering).

Oddly enough, this ancient religious calendar does not deal with the Passover as an official festival. In other words, the Passover, if it was known to the author of Exodus 23:14–17, was of far less prominence than the festivals mentioned. For Wellhausen (1983: 83–120), the predominance of the agricultural civilization after the People of Israel's settlement in Canaan could not but have far-reaching effects on the worship of Israel. His understanding is only partially correct, however. In fact, the agricultural civilization composes a remarkable cause of change and development in the Passover, but as recent sociological exegesis makes clear, the first Israelites consist of "the vast peasant majority" (Gottwald 1976a: 465), and this concept seems essential in order to understand the predominance of the agricultural festivals in the beginning of the formation of the People of Israel.

Yet such a predominance of the agricultural festivals is understandable because of the fact that these festivals were the annual pilgrimages at the "official level." But that does not constitute an argument against the common view that the Passover may well have been celebrated at the "private family level" in early Israel. The texts Exodus 12:21–23 and 2 Kings 23:22 probably make clear that the Passover as a private family feast was widely celebrated in the period of the Judges and subsequently, however modestly, through the entire period of both the northern and southern kingdoms. Apart from Joshua 5:10–12 (attributed to a P editor), the lack of biblical reference to the Passover as an official festival for this period must be understood within this assumption.

Under these circumstances, one of the most difficult problems arises from the incidental restoration of the Passover ordered by King Josiah. This is all the more surprising because 2 Kings 23:23 makes explicit reference to the novelty of the Passover at the official level of Israelite monarchic history. The account of 2 Chronicles 30:1–27, which states a special observance of the Passover by Hezekiah, can scarcely be historical (cf. Segal: 16–19). What insights can then be drawn from Josiah's Passover being such a novelty at that time? The Bible attests that the restoration of the Passover is connected with the book of law (covenant) discovered in the Temple at that period (2 Kings 23:21). Furthermore, it is generally agreed that this book can be linked to the Deuteronomic phenomenon, specifically as it appears in the Book of Deuteronomy, which also formulates a cultic regulation of the Passover (Dt 16:1–8). To gain better insight into Josiah's Passover, we must turn to a closer analysis of D's Passover. Here a rather clearer and different picture of the Passover emerges.

The best clue we have to understand the Passover material ascribed to the Deuteronomic tradition has to do with the place at which the Passover is celebrated. According to the Deuteronomic purpose of unifying Israel's cultic life, the Passover is attached to a determined place: "You must sacrifice the Passover not in any of the towns given you by Yahweh your God, but in the place where Yahweh your God chooses to give his name a home" (Dt 16:5–6).

Undoubtedly, this radical innovation of Deuteronomy as to the cultic place alters the ritual of the Passover: "Once the Passover was transferred from the home to the sanctuary, the whole ceremony had to be altered. It had to be adapted to the sacral activities of a sanctuary, i.e., in this case to the ritual of sacrifices" (Von Rad 1966: 112). A brief glance at Deuteronomy 16:1–8, which describes the Passover ritual, shows that there were radical changes regarding the ritual. An outline of this text may be useful in gaining a perspective on those ritual elements that differ from those of the Yahwistic source, Exodus 12:21–23:

1. The date of the Passover celebration was fixed: "Observe the month of Abib and celebrate the Passover for Yahweh your God, because it was in the month of Abib that Yahweh your God brought you out of Egypt by night" (v. 1). The Deuteronomist writer gave particular emphasis to the dating of the Passover in harmony with the exodus from Egypt.

2. The Passover would be celebrated "in the place where Yahweh chooses to give his name a home" (v. 2). Repeating the same rule about the place (vv. 2 and 5–6), the Deuteronomic writer puts stress on celebrating the Passover in the place where the house of God is located. In the Deuteronomic tradition, this place, however, is not specified geographically (cf. Cundall: 4–27 on the history of the Central Sanctuary in Israel).

3. The day of the festival of the Passover celebration, the day of sacrifice, is also the first day of the feast of Unleavened Bread, which extends six days thereafter: "You must sacrifice a Passover from your flock or herd for Yahweh your God in the place where Yahweh chooses to give his name a home. You must not eat leavened bread with this; for seven days you must eat it with unleavened bread—the bread of affliction—since you left Egypt in great haste; this is so that, as long as you live, you will remember the day you came out of Egypt" (vv. 2–3).

4. The Passover celebration is one overnight festival: "For seven days no leaven must be found in any house throughout your territory, nor must any of the meat that you sacrifice in the evening of the first day be kept overnight until the next day" (v. 4). After the one-night festival, the pilgrims return to their tent encampments and continue celebrating Mazzot: "You will cook it and eat it in the place chosen by Yahweh your God, and in the morning you must return and go to your tents" (v. 7).

5. The wider choice of the sacrificial victim: "You must sacrifice a Passover from your flock or herd ... " (v. 2).

6. The Passover animal was not roasted, but cooked (boiled): "You will cook it (the Passover)" (v. 7).

7. The blood ritual disappeared.

8. The composite text, vv. 3, 4a, and 8, presents the feast of Unleavened Bread: "You must not eat leavened bread with this; for seven days you must eat it with unleavened bread—the bread of affliction—since you left Egypt in great haste; this is so that, as long as you live, you will remember

the day you came out of Egypt" (v. 3). "For seven days no leaven must be found in any house throughout your territory . . . "(v. 4). "For six days you will eat unleavened bread; on the seventh day there will be an assembly for Yahweh your God; and you must do no work" (v. 8). Thus v. 8 contradicts the Unleavened Bread regulation of v. 3. It suggests that v. 8 is likely a late addition (cf. Mayes 1987: 259, following Halbe 1975a).

In striking contrast to the earlier history of the Passover, the Deuteronomic cultic system removed the Passover from the tribal (family) setting to a national setting (only at the sanctuary), making this cult a pilgrimage feast. That is to say, the Passover with Unleavened Bread was celebrated as one of the three "pilgrimages" at Yahweh's sanctuary. And in defense of this radical innovation, the Deuteronomic writer presents the episode of the Exodus as a vigorous apologetic argument (vv. 1, 3, and 6).

Along with the centralization motif in Deuteronomy 16:1–8 goes a very significant literary device in this text. The device combines the two feasts: the Passover (vv. 1, 2, 4b–7) and the feast of Unleavened Bread—Mazzot (3, 4a, and 8). And in the final text, the two feasts appear, forming one unit of festival regulation. Assuredly it is open to a different perspective from the one in which the Priestly tradition presents the two feasts as distinct and separate (cf. Ex 12:1–20, Lv 23:5–8, and Nm 28:17–25, etc.). Assuming that "Passover and Mazzot are distinct" in other codes, J and P (Driver: 190), it seems highly probable that combining the two cultic regulations may have constituted part of the Deuteronomic work (cf. Childs 1976: 186–89 on the history of Mazzot).

Furthermore, a part of vv. 5–7 refers to a Passover sacrifice regulation concerning the offerer. It should not be taken literally as a reference to the lay offerer, since the Passover was celebrated at the central sanctuary. By the time in which the Book of Deuteronomy was written, the priesthood had been well developed (Dt 18:1–8). The special class that served in the Temple presided over the complex rituals, conducting the sacrificial services. Therefore, the head of the family, mentioned in Exodus 12:21, was not likely to come to perform ritual functions of the Passover at the central sanctuary.

Finally, it also seems clear that the use of the original Canaanite name Abib (Dt 16:1) was typical for the pre-exilic period, and in the old Canaanite calendar "the day of the fall equinox marked the beginning of the new year" (Morgenstern 1924: 64). That is to say, Abib was originally the seventh month of the year. This date of the Passover was designated differently by the Priestly writer, who marked a specific date, "the fourteenth day of the first month," for the feast of Passover according to the spring equinox. As is well-known, this Priestly dating of the Passover was apparently based upon a Babylonian model in which the year began with the spring equinox.

Now the crucial issue at stake is how to understand why the religious reform of Deuteronomy made such radical changes in the Passover rituals.

The problem is made more complex once it is recognized that the authors of Deuteronomy were "attempting to revitalize the nation's religion by making the old traditions alive and relevant for their own time" (Bratcher: 220). Then the question arises, for example, what can one say about a radical change of the Passover rituals departing from its old custom of observing Passover in a domestic setting (a family feast)? Or how is one to explain a sharp break of the D Passover with the traditional procedures? Then what kind of historical and social circumstances made Deuteronomy move toward such changes? Some scholars have tried to understand the restoration of the Passover as an intensely nationalistic, Yahwehistic manifestation against "the constantly growing Canaanization" of Israelite religious institutions (Engnell 1952: 41–43). If so, what can now be said about combining the Passover with the feast of Unleavened Bread, which is generally considered a Canaanite feast? Would it not have been in the interests of the Deuteronomic reform, with its "anti-Canaanization" tendency, to keep and emphasize the traditional rite of the Passover? So it is unlikely that the theory of anti-Canaanization will prove to be of much value for understanding D's program of centralization of worship. Certainly, there is a necessity for further research into who and what stands behind the Deuteronomic phenomenon!

In any case, it is indisputable that there is a historical change or evolution of the Israelite religious institution of the Passover festival in the interval between J and D. In this change, the sanctuary, the Temple, assuredly stands as the most important and central component. It was the Deuteronomic legislator who had altered and adapted the Passover ritual to the sacral activities of a sanctuary. Yet Josiah's reform made the Passover a pilgrimage feast that had to be celebrated only in the Jerusalem Temple. This leads the majority of scholars to conclude that the inspiration of Josiah's Passover is to be found in the Deuteronomic source (Dt 16). The Deuteronomic Law appears to be the ritual backbone of Josiah's Passover celebration, especially in the element of centralizing of worship. However, it is debatable whether Josiah's Passover was carried through wholly according to the Deuteronomic Law.

A comparison of D's Passover and Josiah's Passover shows some divergences. First, according to 2 Kings 22–23 and 2 Chronicles 35:1–19, the Passover is mentioned with special emphasis on the king's central cultic role. This concept hardly comes from Deuteronomy 16:1–8 or elsewhere in the Deuteronomic tradition.

Second, in the Deuteronomic Law, the Levitical priests who came to the central sanctuary would have to be treated equally with the priests of the city in terms of priestly rights and dues (Dt 18:1–8). In contrast, "all the priests of the high places" (the country Levite priests) in Josiah's reform were not permitted to "officiate at the altar of Yahweh in Jerusalem" (2 Kings 23:8–9).

Third, the study of Deuteronomy 16:1–8 pointed out obvious structural features in the relationship between the Passover and Mazzot: they are closely related and constitute a single celebration. Therefore, one could argue, from the omission of the reference to the Unleavened Bread in 2 Kings 23:21–23 (the account of Josiah's Passover), that Josiah's celebration does not agree with the primary form of the Passover Law in the Deuteronomic source. (A commentary that treats the reference to the Unleavened Bread in 2 Kings 23:9 is the one by Jones: 621.)

The divergences above seem to suggest the possibility that, although Josiah's Passover would have contained cultic direction from the Deuteronomic Law, this cultic reform was evidently shaped by the realities of Josiah's time, especially by the royal institutions. This is undoubtedly perceptible in the very active and central cultic role played by King Josiah. Also the official cultic functionaries (the priest in 2 Kings 22–23; the priest and the Levite in 2 Chr 34–35) played very active roles in the celebration of Josiah's Passover. Within this context, one can grasp the gist of 2 Kings 23:21: "The king gave this order to the whole people: 'Celebrate a Passover to Yahweh your God, as prescribed in this Book of the Covenant.' "

Of course the situation in Josiah's time must also be considered in the question as to how the Passover tradition was conceived in Josiah's reform. The vast majority of critical scholars suggest that the Passover tradition had been elaborated and developed in the course of time. In this process, there are strong signs in the Deuteronomic source that the connection of the Passover festival with the event of the Exodus was reinforced and actualized. The Exodus tradition is, in fact, firmly anchored in D's Passover, and is probably presented as an apologetic argument for the celebration of the Passover under Josiah's reform. However, the question as to how and why Josiah presented the Exodus tradition as a vigorous apologetic argument for his Passover celebration is not so easily answered.

Often it has been suggested that it lies in the Deuteronomic spiritual consciousness of a renewal of old traditions. This, in turn, seems to contribute to overstatements of the Exodus experience in the meaning of Josiah's Passover without adequate attention to the reality of Josiah's time. The Passover celebration in Josiah's reform is then understood as a cultic expression of loyalty to the Yahweh of the Exodus. This interpretation has been stressed by T. R. Hobbs:

> Comparison of 2 K 23:21–25 with the parallel account in 2 Chr 35:1–19 reveals the importance of the event of the new Passover for the chronicler. It does not have the same significance for the deuteronomist. For the latter it is important that the event is in accordance with the demands of the book found in the temple. No other motivation is given in the narrative. Therefore the common search for political motives for the move (see the works cited by Montgomery and Gehman: 535–36) is finally fruitless and often speculative. If, as seems likely, the inspiration for the Passover is what is now contained

in Deut 16, then the element of centralization of worship is prominent. However, the original act of worship was also an expression of loyalty to Yahweh, as it brings to mind the Exodus from Egypt (337).

This approach is very idealistic, as though Josiah's Passover was ordered by the very nature of the original Passover tradition, without regard for the social motivations of King Josiah and his priests (officials). For Hobbs, the Passover as a religious phenomenon seems to be unrelated to all other social phenomena. How can one distinguish a religious phenomenon from social realities? Of course, it would be wrong simply to identify the meaning and function of Josiah's Passover with those of the premonarchic Passover. To interpret Josiah's Passover in a sense separated from the existing social system, thereby giving inadequate attention to the significance of that system, would destroy any possibility of doing justice to the whole dimension of Josiah's Passover.

In the course of examining the Passover mentioned above, we have become more and more convinced that Josiah's Passover should be interpreted as a social phenomenon in the sociohistorical situation of Josiah's time. No doubt this requires a critical sociological analysis of the Passover in Josiah's reform. The value of the sociological approach is that it relieves us from the limits of conventional exegesis, which restricts us to ascertaining only what Josiah's Passover was and when and where it was celebrated. It allows us to set out on the search for the specific socioreligious functions that Josiah's Passover was designed to serve.

Among biblical scholars currently interested in sociological exegesis, different steps have been taken and varying approaches employed. The following steps have been set in motion for the present study.

As a starting point proper to a sociological exegesis, our attention must be centered upon a rigorous literary-historical criticism of the texts that will serve as a basis for a careful reconstruction of the contemporary social system. We turn then to a closer study of the social system itself. What conclusions does one draw from the analysis of the social system of the period under study? Analysis certainly leads to socioeconomic, political, and ideological (religious) class struggles reflected in the texts. In itself, therefore, the biblical texts and the ideas, concepts, and doctrines they contain are not neutral and reflect social contradictions and conflicts in process at that time. Because of the structural causes of conflict, historical-material analysis can critically be applied to avoid arbitrary and insupportable reconstructions of the social system, the material living conditions of the people in the Bible. It is precisely this materialistic reading and interpretation of the Bible that is decisive for detecting the "fetish," a false god used to subjugate human beings under the legitimacy of the power of "Surpluses." Moreover, the crucial issue at stake is how to understand what role God plays in combating the fetish for the liberation of God's people. Obviously, this is a process of theological thinking and a task for Christian liberation practice. Finally, it should not be forgotten that all of the exegetical processing is conditioned by social and theological assumptions of the exegetes themselves. In his discussions of exegetical disciplines, John H. Elliott argues:

> the exegete himself and herself, no less than the biblical authors, is conditioned by his or her own social and psychological experience. We bring to the text questions that we have been conditioned to ask, not only theologically but also socially. As the biblical writers wrote, so we exegetes interpret out of self-interest. Our method and presuppositions are also *seins*—and *ortgebunden.* What we see in the text, especially its implications, is what our experience, our gender, our social position, and our political affiliations have prepared us to see (12).

Considering this, it is quite clear that the exegetes involved in CEB activities read and interpret the Bible in association with the sociohistorical context of the suffering masses in Latin America. The scriptural scholars who support the oppressed by enabling them to become emancipated from the oppressive hermeneutics are indeed inspired to use sociological exegesis from the perspective of the poor.

Following these steps of sociological exegesis, Josiah's Passover has been studied and applied to the CEB biblical movements.

THE ORGANIZATION OF THE RESEARCH

The research begins in chapter 2 with a literary-historical criticism of the text of Josiah's reform, 2 Kings 22:1–23:30. The study indicates that the conventional exegesis is very useful in shaping the prehistory of the text, but insufficient as a commentary of the final text. In fact, what is lacking in conventional exegesis is pertinent research into the social dimensions of the period of the texts. In order to attend to such issues, chapter 3 extends the study of the social matrix of the Passover in Josiah's reform. The study is structured and conducted by use of social analysis. Specifically, such an analysis supports this hypothesis: Josiah's reform was imposed as an economic-political-religious system by the dominant social class to extend and legitimize its control over "surpluses." Chapter 4 explores questions concerning the social functions of the Passover as instruments of social forces and social interaction. Here, two areas are of special importance: first, the Passover in the socioeconomic system of exchange and control of surpluses; second, the Passover in the socioreligious system reflecting the conflicts of diverse groups. Finally, chapter 5 focuses upon the role of this sociological exegesis of the Passover in the process of conscientization of CEB members, especially concerning biblical hermeneutics and religious institutions. The sociological exegesis of the Passover will be dealt with during a biblical course for CEB leaders, and will be analyzed seriously in relation to their conscientization about the problems of religious institutions. Later, the basic biblical material studied and used in the course will be treated by the Bible study groups of these leaders. Basically utilizing ethnography, which "means learning from people rather than studying people" (Spradley: 3), I shall demonstrate the process whereby I learn from the CEB members how the sociological exegesis of the Passover helps develop their own hermeneutical skills, incarnated spirituality, and Christian responsibilities.

To the pastoral agents, I have attempted, in this work, to offer "pertinent sociocritical biblical hermeneutics" for their Bible apostolates. Thus I have tried to write a sociological-exegetical commentary on Josiah's Passover in chapters 2–4. Those who may be more interested in CEB biblical hermeneutics and activities may first read chapter 5, and then move to the more detailed biblical arguments in chapters 2–4.

This sociological exegesis of Josiah's Passover is of necessity limited and unfinished. It is limited in certain ways both by the sources available and by the elementary stage of the development of our hermeneutical tools. It is unfinished in the continual development of our CEB biblical movements. Despite these limitations, I hope that this work will help CEB members develop their hermeneutical skills and encourage more openness on the part of non-Latin American readers to the realities of CEB biblical hermeneutics.

2

Critico-Literary Analysis

INTRODUCTION

Over the past 190 years, the critical study of the text 2 Kings 22:1–23:30 has devoted much more attention to evaluating the Deuteronomic phenomenon in the text than many other topics. (Although some church fathers mentioned this theory many centuries ago, it was promulgated by De Wette and reinforced recently by E. W. Nicholson 1967.) The reasons for this concentration of interest are evident. There is general agreement among critical scholars that the Deuteronomistic redaction is present to a large extent in the final text of 2 Kings 22:1–23:30. The text, for instance, consists of the opening and closing Deuteronomistic formulae (22:1–2; 23:28–30). Undoubtedly the final text widely relies on the edition of the Deuteronomistic historical work. Moreover, the book of the law in the Temple (22:8) has traditionally been related to the Book of Deuteronomy, or at least to its legislative section. It would seem therefore that Josiah's reform has commonly been entitled the "Deuteronomic Reformation."

There is, however, considerable disagreement among commentators on the prehistory of the definitive text. In other words, there are several difficulties one encounters when attempting to analyze the various earlier stages of the final text from a literary point of view, in applying a form-critical and source analysis. For example, there is considerable evidence to suggest that the oracle of Huldah (2 Kings 22:15–20) is the result of an amalgamation of two oracles, the first (vv. 16–17) and the second (vv. 18–20). At best a brief summary of some of the traditional questions related to the final text will be treated in terms of background of the later sociological exegesis.

Of course, the aim of this chapter is not to seek to interpret the text or to offer a theological reflection on the text within hermeneutical disciplines of the historical-critical method. Rather, our interest in this chapter centers on shaping the prehistory of the text. In consequence, it is possible for conventional critical studies to assist in recovering the sociological matrix of the final text, thereby avoiding a purely subjective or arbitrary sociological exegesis. This means in practice that we are working with a rigorous literary-historical criticism of 2 Kings 22:1–23:30 that leads to a careful critical reconstruction of the sociohistorical context of Josiah's Passover.

CRITICO-LITERARY ANALYSIS OF 2 KINGS 22:1–23:30

22:1–2

1) Josiah was eight years old when he came to the throne, and he reigned for thirty-one years in Jerusalem. His mother's name was Jedidah daughter of Adaiah, of Bozkath. 2) He did what Yahweh regards as right, and in every respect followed the example of his ancestor David, not deviating from it to right or left.

The vast majority of critical commentators assign vv. 1 and 2 to an introductory Deuteronomistic formula. As is well-known, the phrase v. 2c " ... not deviating from it to right or left" comprises Deuteronomic and Deuteronomistic writing typical of many references found in the Book of Deuteronomy (e.g., Dt 2:27, 5:32, 17:11, 17:20, 28:14) and of Joshua (e.g., Jos 1:7, 23:6). Meanwhile, the presence of "his ancestor David" in the phrase " ... and in every respect followed the example of his ancestor David ... " (2 Kings 22:2) is very common in the form of chronological introduction of a king's reign in Judah: " ... his (Abijam) heart was not wholly with Yahweh his God, as the heart of David his ancestor had been" (1 Kings 15:3), "Asa did what Yahweh regards as right, as his ancestor David had done (1 Kings 15:11)," "He (Amaziah) did what Yahweh regards as right, though not like his ancestor David" (2 Kings 14:3), "He (Ahaz) did not do what Yahweh his God regards as right, as his ancestor David had done" (2 Kings 16:2), and "He (Hezekiah) did what Yahweh regards as right, just as his ancestor David had done" (2 Kings 18:3). Assuredly, it works as a literary device to enhance the role of the Davidic theocracy as a model of God's faithful kingdom.

A remarkable thing in 2 Kings 22:2 is the connection of two phrases: " ... and in every respect followed the example of his ancestor David, not deviating from it to right or left." The connection appears only twice in the Old Testament, in 2 Kings 22:2 and later, as a possible quotation, in 2 Chronicles 34:2.

Perhaps one could argue that the unusual juxtaposition of these two phrases reflects a strong intention of Deuteronomistic writers to present Josiah as a righteous king. It is then possible to understand the superiority of Josiah over other kings of Judah from a Deuteronomistic viewpoint. In this context, vv. 1–2 belong to the edition of the Deuteronomistic historical work.

It is true that under the study of the final redaction, the text 2 Kings 22:1–2 seems to be the opening Deuteronomistic formula. But is that all there is to say? Are there not still deeper questions concerning the prehistory of the text? Are there not some traditions in the text? In this case, one may be a pre-Deuteronomistic tradition that strongly relates to the court: the Jerusalemite and Davidic tradition. The Deuteronomistic authors may have worked over the original and added Deuteronomistic phrases such as v. 2c. Or are there perhaps two different editions of Deuteronomistic historical works, the first appearing to be constructed within the lifetime of Josiah, perhaps by a group from the court (e.g., priests and officers)? Of course, this group plays an important part in Josiah's reform, and its tradition is embodied in the text of the exilic edition of the Deuteronomistic historical work.

This suggestion, the double redaction of vv. 1–2, perhaps assumes even more credibility when we realize that modern scholarship attests a double Deuteronomistic redaction in the Books of Kings. The first edition was produced by the Josianic Deuteronomist (Dtr I) as a programmatic justification of Josiah's reform. In exilic time, it was rewritten and expanded by a later Deuteronomistic editor (Dtr II), whose main concern was to explain the exilic catastrophe, introducing some themes such as "Yahweh's wrath" (cf. Cross 1973: 274–89; R. D. Nelson 1981b).

In sum, vv. 1–2b seems to stem from the work of the Josianic Deuteronomist (Dtr I), who presented King Josiah as another David, a perfect king. The exilic editor added 2c from his historiographic viewpoint. The theory of double Deuteronomistic redaction serves as a basis for the analysis given below of chapters 22–23.

22:3–11

3) In the eighteenth year of King Josiah, the king sent the secretary Shaphan son of Azaliah, son of Meshullam to the Temple of Yahweh. 4) "Go to Hilkiah the high priest," he told him, "and tell him to melt down the silver contributed to the Temple of Yahweh and collected by the guardians of the threshold from the people. 5) He is to hand it over to the masters of works attached to the Temple of Yahweh, for them to pay it over to men working on the Temple of Yahweh, to repair the damaged parts of the Temple: 6) to the carpenters, builders and masons, and for buying timber and dressed stone for the Temple repairs." 7) The latter were not required to render account of the money handed over to them, since they were conscientious in their work. 8) The high priest Hilkiah said to Shaphan the secretary, "I have found the Book of the Law in the Temple of Yahweh." And Hilkiah gave the book to Shaphan, who read it. 9) Shaphan the secretary went to the king, reporting furthermore to him as follows, "Your servants have melted down the silver which was in the Temple

and have handed it over to the masters of works attached to the Temple of Yahweh." 10) Then Shaphan the secretary informed the king, "The priest Hilkiah has given me a book"; and Shaphan read it aloud in the king's presence. 11) On hearing the words of the Book of the Law he tore his clothes.

It has been generally recognized that these verses have a compositional integrity of their own. Indeed, the form-critical analysis suggests that there are two different accounts: Temple repairs (vv. 4–7), and the discovery of the law book (vv. 3, 8, 10–11). Verse 9 serves as a link between two accounts (cf. Jones: 611).

Yet it has long been recognized that there are verbal similarities between vv. 4–7 and 2 Kings 12:9–16, an account of Temple repairs in the reign of King Jehoash (cf. Burney: 356). The term "the high priest" (22:4, 8; 23:4), for instance, is unique to 2 Kings, and appears in 2 Kings 12:11. In view of this it is argued that vv. 4–7 are a Deuteronomistic editorial work based on 2 Kings 12:9–16 (cf. W. Dietrich: 18ff; Montgomery and Gehman: 524).

Hermann Spieckermann, however, argues that vv. 4–7 are not based on 2 Kings 12:9–16, but the reverse is true. It is, therefore, assumed that the text should reliably be a historical narrative. On historical grounds, that Temple repairs were carried out by Josiah is understandable, since the kings in ancient Near Eastern monarchies were responsible for the maintenance of Temples (cf. Frankfort: 265–69).

Unfortunately, the historicity of 2 Kings 22:4–7 does not seem to be easily disentangled by source criticism. The most we can say is that in the account of Temple repairs, the Deuteronomist made use of the earlier documents, perhaps derived from the palace and temple archives (cf. Burney: 355). It is quite possible, too, that vv. 4–7 must be from none other than the Josianic Deuteronomist (Dtr I) himself, who intended to provide a historical setting for the finding of the law book, thus legitimatizing Josiah's reform policies.

Recent studies seem to confirm this mark of Dtr I's work in vv. 3–11. Lohfink (1963, 1978), for example, has pointed out that the pre-form of vv. 3–11 is part of the well-ordered unity, "the short story," which was taken over by Dtr I. "Most characteristic and easy to recognize," he has explained,

> is the short story (*Kurzgeschichte*) concerning the discovery of the Torah and the sealing of the covenant: 22:3–12, 13*, 14, 15–20*; 23:1–3, 21–23. It begins "in the eighteenth year of King Josiah" and ends with a reference to "the eighteenth year of King Josiah." Within the narrative, it is always "the king" who is spoken of. The story unfolds in four separate action units, each of which regularly begins with an initiative of the king (1987: 463–64).

Accordingly, Lohfink provides the following outline of the four separate action units:

I. 22:3   "King Josiah sent"   Temple, book, repentance
II. 22:12 "The king commanded" Prophetic inquiry
III. 23:1   "The king sent"   Covenant-making
IV. 23:21 "The king commanded" Passover in Jerusalem (1987: 464).

Working with this presentation, Dtr I formed the basic structure of his composition of Josiah's reform story. This being so, Lohfink concludes, "the basis for the work of Dtr I consisted of a narrative about the discovery of the Torah (22:3–11), a prophetic inquiry (22:12–20), the sealing of the covenant (23:1–3), and the Passover festival (23:21–23)" (1987: 463). This short-story theory has had its broad outlines accepted and supported by a considerable number of scholars in recent years (cf. Jones 608; Mayes 1987: 88; R. D. Nelson 1987: 253–59).

Behind the critico-literary analysis of vv. 3–11, there remains the difficult question of whether Josiah's reform originated in the discovery of the law book. When does Josiah's reform start? This problem is among the most controversial in Old Testament studies. Commentators stay sharply divided on assuming a definite date of Josiah's reform. One group of scholars (cf. Mayes 1987: 88) argue for 621 B.C.E., giving the account in the Book of 2 Kings for reliability. Another group (cf. Nicholson 1967: 12ff) argues for a much earlier date, possibly 627 B.C.E., following a two-stage reform account given by the Chronicler (2 Chr 34–35): "In the twelfth year he began to purge Judah and Jerusalem of the high places, the sacred poles and the sculpted and cast images" (2 Chr 34:3). On the basis of this Chronicler's dating of the reform, 2 Kings 22:3 becomes the introduction of the second stage of the reform, which follows the discovery of the law book in the eighteenth year of King Josiah.

Viewed on the literary-critical criteria, the earlier group underestimates historical values of the Chronicler's presentation because "the Chronicler was dependent on Kings and did not have any other source at his disposal, a rearrangement of the sequence of the events was the Chronicler's own work" (Jones: 603, following Williamson 1982a). Meanwhile, the latter group links Josiah's reform to a political independence movement from the Assyrian empire, and takes into consideration ancient Near Eastern sources. According to the sources, Ashurbanipal's death is dated 627 B.C.E., the year of Josiah's twelfth year (cf. Saggs 1962: 134ff). It is therefore acceptable that Josiah, taking advantage of the first opportunity to break away from Assyria, may reasonably have started his reforms in 627 B.C.E., purging non-Yahwistic elements from Jerusalem (cf. Oestreicher). The international setting thus contributes substantially to defend the Chronistic dating of Josiah's actions (cf. Cross and Freedman).

The evidence for determining an absolute dating of Josiah's reform remains contested. But at present the studies of scholars have shown a tendency to rely on the sequence of events suggested by 2 Chr 34–35 (cf. Bright: 317–8; Wilson 1980: 221). Besides the international setting, this tendency has been encouraged by several arguments. First, although there is almost no consensus among scholars over historical values of Chronicles as a source, the majority of scholars tend to separate the original cult reform accounts (23:4–20) from the discovery of the book. The account of the cult reform, scholars argue, does not mention the book of the law, and the text mostly stems from the annals of Judah (cf. J. Gray: 714–15). This itself favors the suggestion that the cult reform could already have long been underway before the discovery of the book.

Second, it is, Bright has pointed out, possible to believe that the story of Temple repairs in 2 Kings 22:4–7 itself provides an indirect hint of pre-law book reforms. "The very fact that the Temple was being repaired when the lawbook was found indicates that reform was already in progress, for the repairing and purification of the Temple was itself a reform measure" (Bright: 318; cf. Rowley 1963a: 196).

Third, although the short-story theory underlines "the eighteenth year of King Josiah" as a date of Josiah's reform, it provides no basis for dismissing the suggestion made above that 2 Kings 22:3–11 introduces the second stage of Josiah's reform. In the other words, it may be questioned if it is wise to state that Josiah's reform was due solely to a newly discovered law book and began only after it had been found. On the basis of the short-story theory, G. H. Jones (604–10) supports the Chronistic sequence of events, and argues that the Deuteronomistic historian made the discovery of the law book of primary importance as the impetus for the second stage of the reform, the centralization of all worship in Jerusalem.

For these and other reasons it seems likely that Josiah's actions consist of a two-stage reform, "the exclusive worship of Yahweh" and "the centralization of the cult," respectively. The accounts of the reformation in 22:3–11 would be based on the second stage of Josiah's reform movement. Undoubtedly, the orientation of this redaction, which is a work of Dtr I, consists of presenting Josiah's reform as a consequential action of the discovery of the law book.

22:12–14

12) Then the king gave the following order to the priest Hilkiah, Ahikam son of Shaphan, Achbor son of Micaiah, Shaphan the secretary and Asaiah the king's minister: 13) Go and consult Yahweh on behalf of me and the people about the words of the book that has been discovered; for Yahweh's furious wrath has been kindled against us because our ancestors disobeyed the word of Yahweh by not doing what this book says they ought to have done. 14) The priest Hilkiah, Ahikam, Achbor, Shaphan and Asaiah went to the prophetess Huldah wife of Shallum son of Tikvah, son of Harhas the keeper of the wardrobe; she lived in Jerusalem in the new town. They put the matter to her.

W. Dietrich (13–35) may be correct in suggesting that this section consists of the fragments of a pre-Deuteronomistic source, possibly reflected through the court source. Whatever the source, its present form bears the stamp of the Deuteronomistic editorial work. Accepting Lohfink's insistence on the pattern of the short story in the introductory word, with its reference to the king, v. 12 is the opening of the second action unit in vv. 12–20, "Prophetic inquiry."

Yet v. 13 becomes a contact point between Dtr I and the exile Deuteronomistic writer (Dtr II). On the one hand, v. 13a comes from Dtr I, focusing on Josiah's action. On the other hand, Dtr II skillfully injects his theme of Yahweh's wrath into v. 13b.

Now, what can be said about the *Sitz im Leben* of the traditions and the circle in which the biblical picture of Huldah functioned? The fact that Huldah was an unknown prophetess is more likely to add verisimilitude to her historical involvement in an affair with Josiah's reform. Furthermore, recent research, such as Robert R. Wilson's (1980: 219–223), describes Huldah as a court prophet consulted by the king and his servants. If so, then the biblical picture of the king's servants and Huldah appears to stem from the circle and traditions that arose through reflection on state matters and activities. Then again, it shows that the second stage of the reform would have had its actual historical and sociological root in the court circle.

22:15–20

15) and she replied, "Yahweh, God of Israel, says this, 'To the man who sent you to me say this: 16) Yahweh says this: I am going to bring disaster on this place and the people who live in it—all the words of the book read by the king of Judah. 17) Because they have abandoned me and sacrificed to other gods, so as to provoke my anger by their every action, my wrath is kindled against this place, and nothing can stop it. 18) As for the king of Judah who sent you to consult Yahweh, say this to him: As regards the words you have heard . . . 19) But since your heart has been touched and you have humbled yourself before Yahweh on hearing what I have decreed against this place and the people who live in it, how they will become an object of horror and cursing, and have torn your clothes and wept before me, I too have heard—Yahweh says this. 20) So look, when I gather you to your ancestors, you will be gathered into your grave in peace; you will not live to see the great disaster that I am going to bring on this place.' " They took this answer to the king.

It is not difficult to see in the oracle of Huldah (vv. 15–20) two complete strands, the first oracle (15–17) and the second (18–20). The first oracle announces God's wrath on "this place" (Jerusalem) to "the man who sent you to me," and the second addresses God's promise to "the King of Judah."

The difficult problem, however, turns on the issue of how to explain the incongruity between the first oracle and the second. The apparent tension in the present text has been much discussed (cf. Friedman: 25; Hoffmann: 170–89; Nicholson 1967: 14–15). It has been suggested, for instance, that the promise of Josiah's peaceful death in vv. 19–20a, which theologically and historically diverges from his violent death at Megiddo (23:29), might be considered as part of the original kernel of the prophecy. Then God's wrath on the nation (vv. 16–17) would have been written later, from the historiographic viewpoint of the exilic editor (cf. Montgomery and Gehman: 526).

In contrast, M. Weinfeld argues that the first prophecy about the threat of the divine punishment (vv. 16–17) might have been the original oracle. Secondary to this would be the second prophecy (vv. 19–20), attached by the Deuteronomist to "qualify the threat of the divine punishment" (1972: 25–26).

Actually there seems little point in debating whether vv. 16–17 or vv. 19–20a is the original oracle; the evidence for either one is not likely to be conclusive. These are really two sides of the same coin. Far more important is the fact that both parts themselves appear to focus on the kernel of Dtr I: the cult reform based on Josiah's reading from the law book. It is even possible that by focusing more closely on the organizational structure of the short story taken over by Dtr I, one may identify v. 20c as the conclusion of the second action unit in vv. 12–20, "Prophetic inquiry." Briefly, Dtr II probably reworked and expanded this text. At least, v. 20b, which predicts Judah's destruction under Babylon, seems to stand in the exile Deuteronomistic addition.

It is with this literary-critical criteria that we basically consider the oracle of Huldah as a united story at the Deuteronomistic stage of the history of the account.

23:1–3

1) The king then had all the elders of Judah and of Jerusalem summoned to him, 2) and the king went up to the Temple of Yahweh with all the people of Judah and all the inhabitants of Jerusalem, priests, prophets and the whole populace, high and low. In their hearing he read out the entire contents of the Book of the Covenant discovered in the Temple of Yahweh. 3) The king then, standing on the dais, bound himself by the covenant before Yahweh, to follow Yahweh, to keep his commandments, decrees and laws with all his heart and soul, and to carry out the terms of the covenant as written in his book. All the people pledged their allegiance to the covenant.

There has been a wide consensus for over a hundred years in assigning these verses to the Deuteronomistic source. The reasons for this judgment are presented fully in the older commentaries (cf. Noth 1981: 81ff; Wellhausen 1983: 418ff), and relate to theology and characteristic vocabulary: for example "the Book of Covenant" (v. 2; cf. Dt 5:2–3) and "to keep his commandments" (v. 3; cf. Dt 6:17).

In addition, and perhaps most significant of all, it has long been noticed by literary critics that the section (vv. 1–3) is recognized as the work of Dtr I throughout by content. The text is clearly devoted to the covenant-making ceremony, which is central to the cult reform of Josiah. On the basis of language observations, the text also appears to be from Dtr I. The expression "Judah and Jerusalem" (v. 2), for instance, is commonly identified as late pre-exilic literature (cf. Cogan and Tadmor: 285).

Along with content and language goes a very significant editorial work of Dtr I in vv. 1–3. The opening of the section shows that it is of alternating pattern. In the *New Jerusalem Bible*, the translation of v. 1 is unfortunate (cf. the English translation of this work, p. 21), and perhaps the following translation by T. R. Hobbs offers a better picture of the editorial work of Dtr I: "The king then sent word and all the elders of Judah and Jerusalem were gathered to him" (328). This verb *wayyishlah* "he (the king) then sent" indicates evidence of a direct continuation of 23:1–3 with the narrative of the reign of Josiah in chapter 22. It is quite probable that Dtr I, working with the presentation of the short story, starts the section with a royal initiative, "The king then sent," to serve a definite purpose. Within the framework of the short story and its pattern of alternating sections: "The king sent" (22:3) "The king ordered" (22:12), and "The king sent" (23:1), "The king ordered" (23:21), his purpose is clearly shown to give a central position to King Josiah in the cult reform.

Thus, the Josianic Deuteronomist (Dtr I), who worked in court circles, took over the short story, possibly a royal memorandum or propaganda (cf. Lohfink 1987: 462), and reported the covenant-making ceremony with a strong leadership element by King Josiah. It is basically acceptable to use this text as historical and sociological information about the second stage of the cult reform.

23:4–14

4) The king ordered Hilkiah with the priest next in rank and the guardians of the threshold to remove all the cult objects which had been made for Baal, Asherah and the whole array of heaven; he burnt them outside Jerusalem in the fields of the Kidron and had the ashes taken to Bethel. 5) He exterminated the spurious priests whom the kings of Judah had appointed and who offered sacrifice on the high places, in the towns of Judah and the neighbourhood of Jerusalem; also those who offered sacrifice to Baal, to the sun, the moon, the

constellations and the whole array of heaven. 6) And from the Temple of Yahweh he took the sacred pole outside Jerusalem to the Kidron valley and in the Kidron valley he burnt it, reducing it to ashes and throwing its ashes on the common burial-ground. 7) He pulled down the house of the sacred male prostitutes which was in the Temple of Yahweh and where the women wove veils for Asherah. 8) He brought all the priests in from the towns of Judah, and from Geba to Beer-sheba he rendered unsanctified the high places where these priests had offered sacrifice. He pulled down the High Place of the Gates, which stood at the gate of Joshua, the governor of the city, to the left of the entry to the city. 9) The priests of the high places, however, did not officiate at the altar of Yahweh in Jerusalem, although they did share the unleavened bread of their brother-priests. 10) He rendered unsanctified Tophet in the Valley of Ben-Hinnom, so that no one could pass his son or daughter through the fire of sacrifice to Molech. 11) He destroyed the horses which the kings of Judah had dedicated to the sun at the entrance to the Temple of Yahweh, near the apartment of Nathan-Melech the official, in the precincts, and he burned the solar chariot. 12) The king pulled down altars which the kings of Judah had built on the roof and those which Manasseh had built in the two courts of the Temple of Yahweh, and broke them to pieces on the spot, throwing their rubble into the Kidron valley. 13) The king rendered unsanctified the high places facing Jerusalem, to the south of the Mount of Olives, which Solomon king of Israel had built for Astarte the Sidonian abomination, for Chemosh the Moabite abomination, and for Milcom the Ammonite abomination. 14) He also smashed the sacred pillars, cut down the sacred poles, and covered with human bones the places where they had stood.

The modern form-critical history-of-traditions approach has tended to maintain that a pre-Deuteronomistic source, possibly from the annals of Judah, can be found in the story of reform measures (vv. 4–14). The reason for this argument is evident. First, the text presents a new style of narrative which is quite different from the historical narrative in the preceding sections. Certainly one of the most delightful characteristics is that "the frequent use of 'wāw conjunctive' contrasts with the frequency of 'wāw-consecutive' in the surrounding historical narrative" (Jones: 616). And the story is recounted in a short and abrupt literal form. Scholars incline to attribute these factors to the character of annals. Secondly, in terms of content, there are some sections, such as vv. 11–12, which clearly concentrate on the removal of non-Yahwistic elements from Jerusalem (cf. Hollenstein). These sections seem to reflect the first stage of the reform movement, and as such may be a pre-Deuteronomistic record of the Josianic reform measures in the first phase of the reformation. Thirdly, the account of the cult reform in 22:4–20 does not mention "the book of the

Covenant." And this book, which was mentioned in 23:3, appears in 23:21. It, also, serves to highlight the section (22:4–20) as a preexistence source adopted by the Deuteronomistic writers. Finally, accepting Lohfink's short-story theory, a sequence between 23:4, "The king ordered," and 23:21, "The king ordered," does not follow the starting pattern of "the short story" characterized by an alternating pattern: "the king sent" and "the king ordered" (cf. the previously mentioned outline of the short story, Lohfink 1987: 464). It is reasonable to infer, therefore, that the reform report in vv. 4–14, which was independent in origin, may contain a pre-Deuteronomistic source, possibly derived from the court and temple annals of Judah.

It is also not very difficult to attest the Deuteronomistic editorial work in this reform report. The report begins with the phrase "the king ordered" (23:4). This formula serves the author much in the same way as the phrases "the king sent" (22:3 and 23:1) and "the king ordered" (2 Kings 22:12 and 23:21), to provide an introduction for the reform report in 23:4–20. In this way, the reform report with a royal initiative (23:4–20) is linked to four other reports with a royal initiative, forming the following framework of *the altered short story*:

I.	22:3	"King Josiah sent"	Temple, book, repentance
II.	22:12	"The king ordered"	Prophetic inquiry
III.	23:1	"The king sent"	Covenant-making
IV.	23:4	"The king ordered"	Reform measures
V.	23:21	"The king ordered"	Passover in Jerusalem

Here there is evidence of Dtr I's alteration of the framework provided by the original short story. In the altered short story of Dtr I, the covenant-making (23:1–3) was given a central position. As a result, Dtr I formed his own picture of Josiah with the king's five commands (22:3–23:23) and oriented the basic structure of his text around the covenant-making ceremony in order to present King Josiah as the true cult reformer. Josiah, another David (22:1–2), was vividly portrayed as the righteous and successful king in the carrying through of the demands presented in the discovered law book. In view of this, we must probably believe that the altered short story of Dtr I had been composed within the lifetime of Josiah, as is indicated by the fact that the content of the text is unaware of the sudden and violent death of Josiah at Megiddo.

The other Deuteronomistic editorial work is possibly attested in vv. 8a, 9 throughout by content. These two verses, which give specific details about the fate of the country Levite priests, interrupt the description of the reform at Jerusalem (vv. 6–7, 8b, 10–13). It can be further suggested that this material is based on Dtr I's interest in "cultic centralization" in one place, the Temple in Jerusalem. Also, critical scholars are obviously correct in attributing this factor to a Deuteronomic theology (Dt 12). For this reason, some commentators have considered vv. 8a and 9 an insertion, perhaps derived from the reform measures of the second phase of the reformation or the work of the Deuteronomistic writer himself (cf. Nicholson 1967: 13–14). R. D. Nelson, for example, accepts that 8a and 9 are from Dtr I himself, and argues that the writer is "perhaps imparting some of his own personal knowledge about the Josianic clerical situation" (1981b: 81).

If these conclusions are accepted, then it is clear that Dtr I has adopted and worked over one or more earlier documents, thus composing the accounts of reforms. He has then inserted them between the covenant-making (23:1–3) and the Passover festival (23:21–23), no doubt in order to base Josiah's reforms on the newly discovered law book and the subsequent covenant-making. This would explain the apparent tensions in the narrative presentation and language in 23:4–14, which have been noted by many scholars (cf. Montgomery and Gehman: 528–34; R. D. Nelson 1981b: 79–82).

The fact that Dtr I reflects a large amount of cultural conditioning of the Deuteronomic phenomenon, such as "cultic centralization" and "the law book," should not be misunderstood. A theory that the second stage of Josianic reform stems totally from the discovery of the law book is not justified by this evidence. In other words, it would be rash to identify Josiah's reform simply with the Deuteronomic phenomenon. Rather, a more serious question has to do with the historical and sociological reality of this phenomenon. What did the phenomenon, called "Deuteronomic" by scholars, really mean for Israelite men and women in Josiah's time? Was it only a literary and theological phenomenon that conceptualized and oriented Josiah's cult reform? Who were the writers, the prophets or court intellectuals? Or was there a socioreligious movement of the people or a governmental cultic policy?

Faced with this, we must try to be better informed about Josiah's society before attempting to answer the question of how Josiah's reform relates historically and sociologically to the Deuteronomic phenomenon.

We turn next to the text 23:15–20, which reports the cult reform at Bethel and other Samaritan towns. Some very distinctive features of the Deuteronomistic redaction emerge in the use of actual historical material and prophetic traditions.

23:15–20

15) As for the altar which was at Bethel, the high place built by Jeroboam son of Nebat who had led Israel into sin, he demolished this altar and this high place as well, in the same way, breaking up its stones and reducing them to powder. The sacred pole he burned. 16) On looking round, Josiah saw the tombs there on the hillside; he had the bones fetched from the tombs and burned them on the altar. This he rendered unsanctified, in accordance with the word of Yahweh which the man of God had proclaimed when Jeroboam was stand-

ing by the altar at the time of the feast. On looking round, Josiah caught sight of the tomb of the man of God who had foretold these things. 17) "What is that monument I see?" he asked. The townspeople replied, "It is the tomb of the man of God who came from Judah and foretold what you have done to the altar." 18) "Let him rest," the king said, "and let no one disturb his bones." So they left his bones untouched, with the bones of the prophet who came from Samaria. 19) Josiah also destroyed all the shrines on the high places which were in the towns of Samaria and which the kings of Israel had built to provoke Yahweh's anger; he treated these places exactly as he had treated the one at Bethel. 20) All the priests of the high places who were there he slaughtered on the altars, and on those altars burned human bones. Then he returned to Jerusalem.

The important thing to note in this section is that vv. 16–20 offer a discontinuous account of v. 15 and are not a sequel. The information of vv. 16–18, for instance, shows an apparent discrepancy with v. 15; the altar that is destroyed in v. 15 is still standing in vv. 16–18. The majority of commentators firmly believe that vv. 16–20 have been worked over, being influenced by 1 Kings 12:31–13:32, the story of the cultic institution of the northern kingdom. Indeed these verses record the fulfillment of an ancient prophecy in 1 Kings 13:2ff. Some commentators further assume that vv. 16–20 depend upon the Bethel story of 1 Kings 13, which was the later edition of Kings (cf. Eissfeldt: 579). These items have been classical reasons to attribute vv. 16–20 to the additions to v. 15 made by the exilic editor.

However, there is considerable objection among recent scholars to the theory outlined above. In the first place, it has been affirmed that 1 Kings 12:31–13:32 stand in the first Deuteronomistic level and not in the exile edition. Yet scholars argue that vv. 16–18 should contain a pre-Deuteronomistic oral tradition or narrative (cf. Lemke: 301–26). In view of this, they see in vv. 15–20 the Deuteronomistic work.

R. D. Nelson, for example, suggests that vv. 15–18 are from Dtr I and that vv. 19–20 are an addition to vv. 16–18 attached by the exilic editor. For the scholar, v. 15, which provides the absolutely necessary background for vv. 16–18, may be considered as "the basic annalistic information on Bethel to which the historian attached his further comments in vv. 16–18" (1981b: 82). Meanwhile, vv. 19–20 are additional information on the reform in the former northern kingdom (vv. 15–18); the accounts of the destruction of all the shrines (v. 19) and the bloody elimination of the priests (v. 20) are picked up from 1 Kings 13:32 and 13:2 respectively.

These arguments presented by R. D. Nelson are very plausible. It may be questioned, however, if it is wise to attempt to consider vv. 19–20 as the work of the exilic editor. The fact that vv. 19–20 are almost a duplication of 1 Kings 13 cannot be taken as sufficient evidence to conclude that these verses are a simple copy and are from the later Deuteronomistic redaction.

We would understand, rather, that the earlier stage of vv. 19–20 may be an integral part of the work of Dtr I in vv. 15–20 and serve the author, much in the same way as v. 15, to inform about Josiah's action in the former northern kingdom (cf. Cross and Wright). According to Dtr I, King Josiah extended his cult reform over Bethel and other Samaritan towns under the banner of cult centralization, linked to the promises to the house of David in 1 Kings 13:2–3 and 2 Kings 23:16–18. The altars at Bethel and other Samaritan towns should be condemned because of Dtr I's doctrine that the Jerusalem Temple, the Davidic sanctuary, had been approved as the unique sanctuary for the worship of Yahweh. (For the literature that treats the extent of Josiah's rule in the north, see Alt 1953; Malamat 1973.)

Of course, this explanation of the Deuteronomistic redaction remains largely conjectural. In our judgment, there has been no final solution to these complex literary and theological problems in 23:15–20, since the study of the text continues to be atomized under the varied rubrics of the historical-critical method. In order to rightly understand Josiah's reform activities, it is important to realize that we need to clarify not only the literary and theological but also the sociological dimensions of the biblical texts. What is needed is a means for answering questions about the exact social system under which the text of Josiah's reform was written, and the identity of the Deuteronomistic writers.

Assuredly, the above exegetical tasks are required for answering the specific questions concerning the aims of Josianic actions. One thing can be said immediately in regard to the first stage of the cult reform. Judging by the international setting, the action of "exclusive worship of Yahweh" fundamentally seems to have been related to "Anti-Assyrian movements." This judgment is strongly sustained by the enlightening proposal of Spieckermann (307–70), arguing that the Assyrian cult spread into Jerusalem and Judah through official imposition (cf. the contrary view that Assyrians did not impose their religion on Judah, Cogan 1974; McKay 1973b).

However, with respect to the goal of the action in the second stage, "cult centralization," commentators have not brought forth convincing arguments. Lohfink (1987: 468), for example, suggests that cult centralization is connected originally to the promises to the house of David. This theory is quite plausible, but admittedly it rests basically on general historical inference, starting from the ideological concerns. Still the theory is certainly polemical in tone and must be supported by sociological analysis of Josiah's reform.

It remains for critical scholars to achieve more complete analysis of the sociological matrix of the text 2 Kings 22:1–23:30, especially to reach the kernel of the Passover celebration in 23:21–23.

23:21–23

21) The king gave this order to the whole people: "Celebrate a Passover to Yahweh your God, as prescribed in this Book of the Cove-

nant." 22) No Passover like this had ever been celebrated since the days when the judges ruled Israel, nor throughout the entire period of the kings of Israel and the kings of Judah. 23) The eighteenth year of King Josiah was the only time when such a Passover was celebrated in Yahweh's honour in Jerusalem.

This section, which mentions the book of the covenant, is closely linked to the preceding assembly of 23:1–3. Above all, the section begins with the phrase "The king ordered" and so forms an alternating pattern with "the king sent" (23:1). And this is apparently so obvious prior to literary-critical analysis that the reasons, which support the original short story found in the text 22:1–23:30, come into effect. Thus it is easily conceivable that the great Passover celebration of vv. 21–23 consists of the last part of the covenant renewal ceremony in the original short story.

By placing this Passover episode after the acts of reform (23:4–20), Dtr I transformed the feast into the full concluding ceremony of Josiah's cult reform. Josiah, who was motivated by the Deuteronomic ideal contained in the law book, centralized all worship in Jerusalem, finally reestablishing a Passover of the sort commanded in Deuteronomy 16:5–7. In the altered short story of Dtr I (cf. the previously mentioned outline of the altered short story), the celebration of Passover thus becomes a finishing touch inspired by the newly discovered law book.

Certainly our work is based upon the short-story theory, reinforced recently by Lohfink. By operating with *other* literary-critical criteria, one can provide and attest other hypotheses as to the *Sitz im Leben* of the Passover celebration in 23:21–23. If so, how is one to comment on the biblical text? Does interpretation stem only from literary-critical criteria? It is true that the text of 2 Kings 22:1–23:30 apparently ignores any possible economic or social motives implicit in Josiah's centralized Passover. The text reports the Passover celebration from Yahweh's covenant theology, the kernel of Deuteronomic theology, and presents the feast as a result of Josiah's covenant-making with Yahweh, who requires cultic centralization in Yahweh's chosen city. But is that all there is to say? Are there not still other socioreligious functions that the Passover was designed to serve for Josiah and his kingdom?

Is the exegete content merely to study the ideological (religious) aspects of biblical texts? Or can we neglect the fact that "ideas accompany material reality, in the best of cases guiding and purifying it, and in the worst concealing it" (Pixley 1981: 20)? It is clear from our analysis that, although it remains impossible for modern exegetes to interpret the biblical literature without the historical-critical method, rigorous sociological analyses should be seriously engaged in biblical hermeneutics. Regarding the much-discussed question as to why Josiah centralizes the Passover celebration in the Temple in Jerusalem, we will seek further discussion in later chapters, using "sociological tools."

23:24–27

24) What is more, the spirit guides and mediums, the household gods and idols, and all the abominations to be seen in the country of Judah and in Jerusalem, were swept away by Josiah to give effect to the words of the Law written in the book found by the priest Hilkiah in the Temple of Yahweh. 25) No king before him turned to Yahweh as he did, with all his heart, all his soul, all his strength, in perfect loyalty to the Law of Moses; nor did any king like him arise again. 26) Yet Yahweh did not renounce the heat of his great anger which had been aroused against Judah by all the provocations which Manasseh had caused him. 27) Yahweh said, "I shall thrust Judah away from me too, as I have already thrust Israel; I shall cast off Jerusalem, this city which I have chosen, and the Temple of which I have said: My Name shall be there."

Perhaps more important for exegesis is the recognition that there are several sources within this section which reflect the history of the Deuteronomistic redaction. First of all, the section begins in v. 24 with a reference to the sins of Manasseh (21:5) and with a more extensive reform notice. Josianic reform is nowhere pictured as being widespread with radical actions against "the abominations" in accord with the commands of Deuteronomy (cf. Dt 18:9–12). Since this verse thus contains further elaboration of the reform report, there is the possibility of considering it as a Dtr II addition to vv. 21–23.

In addition, there remains a certain tension in vv. 25–27, which has called forth this discussion. The fact that v. 25 delineates Josiah as an ideal king according to the Deuteronomic theology (cf. Dt 6:5) appears to attribute the verse to the Deuteronomistic work. Nevertheless, commentators stay divided on dealing with the composition of v. 25, namely "double redaction." Because the issue is fully discussed by R. D. Nelson (1981b: 84), interest focuses on our own understanding of the problem. If we recognize the altered short story of Dtr I and its strong concerns with Josianic reform and cult centralization, the following assumption can be made: Verse 25a could have been written by Dtr I to conclude his account of Josiah. That is to say, the end of the reform account composed by Dtr I likely comes with unrestricted praise for Josiah in 25a. At least such a presentation of the verse, the king's royal repentance, can be linked to "his ancestor David" (22:2), thus portraying Josiah as a faithful and righteous king. And verse 25b, which refers to the death of Josiah, probably belongs to the work of Dtr II.

Finally, vv. 26–27 reverse the preceding positive picture of King Josiah, introducing "the motif of Yahweh's wrath." It may be recognized as an exile Deuteronomistic addition, possibly based on 2 Kings 21:10–15; 22:16ff (cf. Jones: 628). In short, the section vv. 24–27 stands in an outstanding example for the theory of "double redaction."

23:28–30

28) The rest of the history of Josiah, his entire career, is this not recorded in the Book of the Annals of the Kings of Judah? 29) In his times, Pharaoh Necho king of Egypt was advancing to meet the king of Assyria at the River Euphrates, and King Josiah went to intercept him; but Necho killed him at Megiddo in the first encounter. 30) His retainers carried his body from Megiddo by chariot; they brought him to Jerusalem and buried him in his own tomb. The people of the country then took Jehoahaz son of Josiah and anointed him, proclaiming him king in succession to his father.

The section begins with a standard concluding formula relating to a king of Judah. Certainly, the reader is at first surprised to find that v. 28 is not only placed before Josiah's death report, but also does not present the "great act" of King Josiah. In the light of these observations, the verse seems unlikely as a part of Dtr I, and is probably to be ascribed to Dtr II.

There can be little doubt that the additional historical statement on Josiah's death at Megiddo (vv. 29–30) appears to be the text of the exilic edition of the Deuteronomistic historical work. It is hardly believed that Dtr I can reconcile the sudden and tragic death of Josiah with "his world view of just retribution; nor could his death be accommodated to Huldah's promise that 'you will be gathered to your grave in peace' (22:20)" (Cogan and Tadmor: 302). Nor can vv. 29–30 be composed by Dtr I.

The fact that 2 Kings 23 omits explanation for the events at Megiddo is an additional warrant for seeing a strong relation between Josiah's death and his tragic encounter with Necho at Megiddo in 609. The tragic statement of vv. 29–30 lies not only in producing a sudden end of the cult reform, but in buttressing the historicity of the altered short story composed by Dtr I shortly after the reform events.

CONCLUSION

In a positive sense, the conventional critical studies have sought to bring together the various literary strands that comprise the present text. Under the historical-critical method (*Textgeschichte, Formgeschichte, Traditionsgeschichte,* etc.), critical scholars shape the biblical text on the oral and literary levels to illuminate its *Sitz im Leben.* As a result of that, the following assumptions can be made in terms of the *Sitz im Leben* of the text 22:1–23:30.

Certainly the critical commentaries are correct in discerning two different redactional works within the present text: the Josianic Deuteronomist (Dtr I) and the exilic editor of the Deuteronomistic historical work (Dtr II). On the one hand, the overwhelming number of critical commentaries judge 22:1–12, 13*, 14, 15–20*; 23:1–23, 25* to be a Dtr I redactional work. On the other hand, 23:24, 26–30 give every sign of being a redactional link from Dtr II. Needless to say, the final text of 22:1–23:30 has been incorporated into the later additional framework.

The crucial issue in studying the redactional framework of Dtr I turns on recognizing the altered short story, highly arranged around Josiah's covenant-making. Furthermore, the altered short story appears to have been composed in a court circle and probably under a strong Davidic theology. Its composition must have occurred shortly after the reform events.

Another important assumption consists of the theory of the "two stage" reform actions. The first stage seems to stem from the anti-Assyrian movement, eliminating the foreign cults in favor of the exclusive worship of Yahweh. The later stage, originated from the discovery of the law book, consists of the centralization of the cult in the Temple of Jerusalem. Gottwald makes this point when he describes the stages of Josiah's reform:

(1) purification of the Jerusalem temple, (2) purification of outlying Judean holy places, (3) discovery/public presentation of the lawbook and a decision to centralize all worship at Jerusalem by closing outlying shrines, and (4) extension of purification and centralization to all the newly controlled territories in the coastal plain and northward into Samaria, and perhaps also into Gilead and Galilee (1985: 371).

At several points in this general survey, it has been clear that the conventional exegesis is very useful, but insufficient as a commentary on the final text. For instance, it seems that whether or not the exegesis is successful can be judged on the literary-critical criteria of each critical scholar. In our judgment, the conventional exegesis has its proper function within exegesis only in illuminating the final text. So it is difficult for the conventional critical scholars to answer the following questions: What kind of historical and sociological reality stands behind the second stage of Josianic reform? Or why did King Josiah centralize the Passover celebration?

Thus further exegetical tasks remain in order to understand the text in its social context. According to George V. Pixley, "We shall not be happy with biblical scholarship until it has learned to read the ideas of the Bible in terms of the historical struggles of flesh-and-blood people" (1981: 20). To pursue this question, we now turn to a full examination of the historical and social context of 22:1–23:30, namely the sociological matrix of the text.

3

Sociological Matrix of Josiah's Passover

INTRODUCTION

The most striking thing that emerges from reading a description of Josiah's cultic reform is a campaign of calculated brutality and vandalism (2 Kings 23:4–20). It is perhaps one of the most brutal actions undertaken in the name of Yahweh reflected in the Old Testament. Especially, "the bloody campaigns to abolish all the local shrines" are seen as a preeminent movement in the history of Israel (Claburn 1973: 12). Within this context, King Josiah inserts the Passover exclusively in a national feast at the Jerusalem Temple (2 Kings 23:21–23).

Very little is known about what exactly happened after the inauguration of cultic reforms, more precisely the Passover. However, it is not likely that the people, particularly in rural circles, fully accepted cultic reform. Certainly M. Weinfeld is correct in seeing the negative effect of the cultic reforms of Hezekiah and Josiah in popular circles:

> For let us bear in mind the far-reaching consequences of this reform: a people who are heart and soul and in every aspect of their daily life bound to the sacral institutions around them (the high places and local sanctuaries), are one day forcibly denied them and are instead presented a single, central sanctuary necessitating pilgrimage which from distant areas was not an easy matter and for some (the aged and infirm) an impossibility. Furthermore, a central sanctuary, for all that it entailed, must by necessity deprive the worshiper of that direct and spontaneous religious experience to which he was accustomed in the local places spread throughout the country (Weinfeld 1964: 202).

In the case of the Passover, which was strongly rooted in homes, it is still more doubtful that the Israelites in rural circles passively accepted Josiah's reform that removed the Passover from their homes to the Jerusalem Temple. The question, then, is: What was Josiah's primary motivation for the violent action of such cultic reforms?

We have already seen an urgent desideratum for answering this question with a sociological approach. What has been lacking is a procedure for examining Josiah's reform as a product of the sociohistorical circumstances of his kingdom. What is needed is a closer analysis of the social system, viewed as a mode of production, under which Josiah's reform, specifically its Passover celebration in the Jerusalem Temple, was carried out. As this analysis provides a pertinent and comprehensive social description of Josiah's society, so we are able to provide the data by which the specific socioreligious function of Josiah's Passover is best examined and clarified.

In this sociological procedure, we are actually using the concept of "mode of production" distinct from the expression of "mode of production of material goods (life)." The former is a theoretic concept and embraces a social system formed by an infrastructural (economic and social instances) and a superstructural level (political and ideological instances). The latter, however, is a descriptive expression and refers only to an infrastructural level (cf. Gebran: 14). According to orthodox Marxists, the economic instance, in the last analysis, determines the social, political, and ideological instances. Recently, neo-Marxists have abandoned this "economic determinism" in making much of Engels' statement: "The economic situation is the basis, but the various elements of the superstructure . . . [constitutions, political theories, religious views, etc.] . . . also exercise their influence upon the course of the historical struggles and in many cases preponderate in determining their form" (Tucker: 760, quoted in McGovern: 33).

Bringing massive Latin American suffering specifically caused by capitalism into the midst of biblical reflections, we are indeed inspired to emphasize the strong effects of economic situations on the history of Israel. So it seems reasonable that a sociological approach to understanding the Passover in Josiah's reform should start with an analysis of the infrastructure of contemporaneous society, particularly to avoid idealistic hermeneutics.

In the Biblical Apostolate in the CEBs, we have come to be aware of a different historical view in which our suffering people read the Bible. For our people, the history of the Bible is the history of heroes and heroines among the people of God, such as Abraham, Moses, and Deborah. The people discover their own immigrant journey in Abraham's life. From the history of Moses, the people talk about their own concrete struggles. Deborah's leadership has a great impact on the prophetic ministry of women in Latin America. The history of the Bible thus circles around the men and women moved by God. Because of this historical view of the people and their sensitivity to human relationships in the Bible, we feature social relations of men and women in the infrastructure at our biblical courses of CEB leaders. This method facilitates a more pertinent understanding of human relationships and subsequent tensions and conflicts within the biblical society, and leads people to "read" their social relations today. By adopting the same method in our study of the infrastructure of Israel's society, we will first analyze the economic situations and later deal specifically with social relations of biblical men and women. Of course, the social relations arise and are shaped by the economic situations. The former cannot be understood except as embodied in the context of the latter. Both of them constitute the same infrastructure.

Likewise, it is almost impossible to divide precisely the historic development and reality of Israel's society into the four separate and abstract instances of the modes of production. They are interrelated, forming a living society (synchronics) in a dynamic history (diachronics). In what follows, there are indeed many social, political, and ideological elements mentioned in the economic analysis because of such dynamics in the social reality. Nevertheless, we stress the importance of structural analysis (analyzing the reality in four separated dimensions), because many people committed to the Biblical Apostolate have neglected to reconstruct the social system of the Bible and have tended even to ignore its infrastructure in concentrating on its historical and ideological significance, the so-called "cultural and theological traditions." This failure to grasp the structural dimensions of the reality can be disastrous, countering the effectiveness of the Biblical Apostolate as a social-change agency. In the absence of a structural analysis of biblical societies, the Bible cannot introduce suffering and marginalized people to a critical outlook of their own society and to a clearer understanding of the concrete demands of social justice. Moreover, we truly need the historical and structural analysis to pinpoint the deepest roots of the crisis in the Israelite society as well as in present-day society.

For that reason, we believe and reinforce the concept that the most important first step we can take for a study of Josiah's Passover in the CEB's context is to begin to analyze the economic situation of Israel's society. We intend to show that a new system of organizing the economic functions of production and distribution initiates and promotes social changes and conflicts in Israelite history.

ECONOMIC ANALYSIS

The Historical Background

The Late Bronze Age saw the emergence of tribal Israel in the Palestinian hill country. The majority of Israel's populace were peasants who revolted and escaped from the tributary control of Canaanite city-states (cf. Mendenhall 1962, 1973; Gottwald 1979). The highlands of Palestine, where the first Israelites had settled, were poor from an ecological viewpoint, having unfavorable topography, climate, soil, and natural resources. Agricultural production, the basis of the economy of these areas, was limited and restricted by semiarid regions and desert areas. The dry, rough lands were indeed adverse natural conditions for the first Israelites, whose agricultural activities would already have been limited by their conflicts with the city-states. As settlers in an already harsh sociopolitical situation, they needed to seek ways of supplying the special conditions of a socioeconomic agricultural system suitable for survival in semiarid areas.

Biblical historians and archaeologists attest that the first Israelites took advantage of the technology recently introduced in the highlands of Palestine, such as terraces, cisterns, and iron implements. By developing and utilizing more complex terraces and cisterns, they gathered and conserved more water and transformed rough and sloping areas into productive farmlands. Specifically, daily water supplied by the cisterns encouraged the peasants to keep herds and flocks in the hill country. Furthermore, "the climatically conditioned crop failures can be balanced more or less by keeping a few cattle" (Lang 1985: 86). By "introducing metals for agrarian use in contrast to their reservation for warfare and luxury within the surrounding statist societies" (Chaney 1986: 53), the first Israelites had made possible "both the extension of the area open to agricultural development through more rapid and more thorough clearing of land of both trees and stones, as well as an increase in agricultural productivity by increasing the amount of land that could be cultivated per unit of human labor" (Frick 1985: 169–170). As a result, the Israelite cultivators were able to establish themselves on relatively productive farms.

Besides the technological factors mentioned above, the harsh sociopolitical situation demanded of the first Israelites a communal economic function of production and distribution. Unlike the Canaanite city-states, whose kings were virtual owners of all the arable land of the states, and who exercised a system of taxation which concentrated the surplus in the central government, early Israel's socioeconomic system was shaped by a tribal mode of production, engaged in a communal type of economy. At its center stood the tribal ownership of land, the principal means of production: "In the intertribal confederacy land had been held in perpetuity by extended families and could not be sold out of the family; protective associations of families guarded the patrimony of each household" (Gottwald 1985: 324). Such tribal treatment of land was one of the most powerful factors in Israel's communal economy and organized their limited arable land and human resources into forces of production as efficiently as possible.

In addition to controlling access to land, the Israelite tribal system regulated the production and circulation of basic resources to provide the entire populace with secure access to an adequate living. In so doing, the first Israelites used and conserved their limited material resources as effectively as possible. The use of "surplus" in this society was determined by the needs of the communal economy. Cults, sacrifices, and feasts, for instance, were a traditional method of storing, socializing, and consuming the surplus in a community. Thus the communal economy aimed at getting rid of waste and misuse of material resources.

In short, Israel's communal economy was one of the best ways the revolutionary peasants found to survive in their "frontier society." What is more, technological advantages, operated efficiently in this communal economy, made it possible for the first Israelites to be engaged in substantial agriculture, based on "regional mixes of grains, wine, oil, and assorted fruits and vegetables, supplemented by small bovine herds and larger sheep and goat herds, only a fraction of which were tended by seasonal nomadic movements into the steppes" (Gottwald 1976a: 466).

At the end of the premonarchic period, this communal economic system unfortunately began to exhibit signs of weakening due to the tendency of a prospering agrarian elite to dominate Israelite economy from within. Frank S. Frick (1985) has suggested that both "techno-environmental and societal aspects" brought about a differentiation of agricultural productivity among the agrarians in the highland areas.

Ecology: The highlands of Palestine offered variability in topographic conditions and soil fertility. The advantage of topographical positions and soil types provided ecological potential for a certain group's agricultural success and gave them more socioeconomic power than others.

Demography: Recent archaeological evidence from some Late Bronze and Iron I sites in the highlands of Palestine indicates the appearance of a number of new walled cities such as Tell en-Nasbeh (Mizpah), a city in the area of Benjamin. This reflects, at least in part, a population growth within certain areas, since the development or expansion of urban centers correlates with demographic growth. Population growth in turn affects the degree of agricultural intensification and production in the communities of this area. As a result, some areas with more population, and consequent human power, became quite productive and wealthy, while others with less population remained much less productive and even poor. We suspect that the population levels of the highland areas were influenced immediately by the numbers of newly arrived immigrants that each area had gradually been absorbing.

Technology: Technology transformed land and human labor into more effective economic potential in the process of agricultural intensification. On the one hand, agricultural terracing, which had gradually developed, was also able to solve problems associated with erosion, rugged soil, and so forth. On the other hand, iron technology in the form of more effective tools enhanced the forces of production. An increasing degree of agricultural technology would have led to a consequent degree of agricultural intensification in each of the area-village communities.

There can be little doubt that agricultural production varied according to local conditions, since all villages were not equally endowed with techno-environmental and societal advantages. This probably set the stage for the emergence of gaps in economic power among the village communities and/ or the tribes. The development of these "gaps" must also be observed in relation to trade. Under the promotion of agricultural surpluses, the sale of valuable agricultural products such as olives and olive oil and grapes and wine enhanced the wealth of rich communities in local and regional commerce. The greed of rich communities had gradually grown and tended toward the destabilizing of Israel's communal economy.

An analysis of the book of the covenant (Ex 20:22–23:33) more specifically indicates such economic procedures privileging a certain group within the same tribe and destroying the communal economy. There is a broad consensus among exegetes today that the book of the covenant was the result of an amalgamation of laws, reflecting the passage of time and the different sociopolitical contexts in which these laws were produced and reproduced. The social settings of Exodus 20:22–23:33 are disputed. But at least the text is instructive enough in showing the social reality of late premonarchic Israel.

Material powers of production: 1. "Oxen" as tractive animals (Ex 21:28–22:31): Holding the larger number of oxen, a group produces more agricultural goods (surpluses) than others. 2. "Hebrew debt-slaves" or "indentured servants" as human labor power (Ex 21:2–21): Their productive output and efficiency increase differentiation among the groups (C. J. H. Wright: 239–65, offers one of the most recent treatments of slavery in Israel).

Master 'adon (a chief of the extended family) in commerce: 1. Buying slaves and women as human labor power (Ex 21:1–11). 2. Selling women as slaves (Ex 21:8). 3. Selling the oxen (their meat) (Ex 21:32–36).

Surplus value: The money (shekels) as an exchange of equivalent things (Ex 21:30–36). This equivalent system produces the basis for reciprocal profit and loss among groups.

In this framework, Israelite society started to witness the dualism of extremes between the rich and the poor, corresponding to increasing breakdowns in the communal economic system. The presence of indebted peasants (Ex 21:2–5) can indicate such contradictions in Israel's tribal economy and the process of socioeconomic change in its society.

By the tenth century B.C.E., this new economic situation forced Israel to adopt a tributary mode of production—namely, monarchy. A bid by the radical agrarian elites to aggrandize their surpluses tended to negate the old social system and pressed for a formation of new modes of production to further the surplus. The poorer agrarians, on the other hand, sought a new, effective institution to protect their property against these radicals (cf. 1 Sm 8:3–5). Additionally, a rapidly increasing Philistine interest in Israelite surpluses and control over the Timna trade route pushed both the poorer and richer agrarians even faster into a state formation to protect their surpluses from foreign interests (cf. 1 Sm 8:19–22). Thus Israelite society's passage from stateless to monarchic peasant society consisted of a combination of internal and external historical causation (cf. Gottwald 1986c: 77–106).

With the rise of the monarchy, the new infrastructure, characterized by "tribute" (tax and corvée), engaged in aggrandizing the surplus in the hands of the monarchic court. In David's reign, his court economy was mostly supported by "foreign income": booty and slaves from consecutive and aggressive campaigns against his neighboring city-states (cf. 2 Sm 12:26–31, etc.), and vassal state tribute paid by his conquered subjects (cf. 2 Sm 8:2, etc.).

International trade must also be considered an important issue in the aggrandizement of surpluses by the court. From ancient times, Palestine was known as an important commercial crossroads: "In the history of Palestine and its various regions the network of roads was of prime importance because of their value as arteries for international commerce in the ancient Near East" (Aharoni 1979: 43). This is one of the main reasons David extended his control to cover Transjordanian and Syrian states such as the Edomite territory (2 Sm 8:13–14). By this move he controlled the Syro-Palestinian corridor, the trade route between Damascus and Ezion-geber, a major source of copper, and secured the commerce with the Phoenicians. The Phoenicians in turn brought the technique of metalworking to Israel in exchange for copper (cf. Harden 1968: 160–83).

Needless to say, David's control over the Transjordanian and Negeb districts brought him agricultural products, such as cereals and raw wool, conducive to an increase in sources of income and produce for import-export trade. Thus David gathered commercial surpluses with a monopoly on trade of the Syro-Palestinian area.

In the above economic picture, David made a satisfactory profit from foreign tribute without relying on tribute from the Israelite peasants. It is, therefore, arguable that David had kept the tribal infrastructure intact. In our judgment, however, the state's ambitious economic moves to increase its surpluses gradually dissolved the tribal infrastructure and deteriorated the peasants' economic situation, even to the point of confiscation of tribal land. There are signs that David seems to have set up these mechanisms of exploitation. His court actually started to abuse the tribal ownership of land. The following example can be cited:

> "My father's entire family deserved no better than death from my lord the king, and yet you admitted your servant to the ranks of those who eat at your table. What right have I to make any further appeal to the king?" The king said, "You need say no more. I rule that you and Ziba divide the property between you." "Let him take it all," Meribbaal said to the king, "since my lord the king has come back home in peace!" (2 Sm 19:29–31).

The story of Meribbaal indeed describes the struggle between the houses of Saul and David over the leadership of the state of Israel. This also illustrates a move of the state engaged in amplifying its power structure by gathering royal retainers (the servant Ziba), to whom the king grants land. We suspect that the property mentioned in this story would be the royal domains of Saul, including the original land of his extended family. If so, King David clearly assumed the right of inheriting the royal domains and of intervening in their distribution.

A comment about the last point might be instructive in understanding the monarchic economy. Apparently no visible system of tribute over the Israelite peasants was instituted to support Saul's court. His basic resources would be the agricultural surpluses of his own royal (tribal) holding land and the foreign tribute from the campaigns against neighboring city-states (1 Sm 15:7–9). In such economic organization, there is a strange text which strikes to the heart of the tribal infrastructure:

> When Saul heard that David and the men with him had been discovered, Saul was at Gibeah, seated under the tamarisk on the high place, spear in hand, with all his staff standing round him. "Listen, Benjaminites!" said Saul to them, "Is the son of Jesse going to give you all fields and vineyards and make all of you commanders of thousands and commanders of hundreds that you all conspire against me?" (1 Sm 22:6–7).

These verses appear to contain a socioeconomic reflection on the ownership of land in the beginning of the united monarchy. What most people ask is: To whom do "all fields and vineyards" belong? Are they a part of the royal land of Saul or the tribal holding land of David's extended family? Actually the point at issue is not simply to distinguish the ownership of these lands. Rather, the point is the problem of the concentration of land in a certain extended family. The question is therefore how such extensive land is concentrated in the court or in the prospering families. Perhaps the campaigns against neighboring city-states reflects the confiscation of their lands, for we read:

> Saul then crushed the Amalekites, beginning at Havilah in the direction of Shur, which is to the east of Egypt. He took Agag king of the Amalekites alive and, executing the curse of destruction, put all the people to the sword (1 Sm 15:7–8).

In the case of David, we also have the similar example:

> David and his men went out on raids against the Geshurites, Girzites and Amalekites, for these are the tribes inhabiting the region which, from Telam, goes in the direction of Shur, as far as Egypt. David laid the countryside waste and left neither man nor woman alive; he car-

ried off the sheep and cattle, the donkeys, camels and clothing, and then came back again to Achish (1 Sm 27:8–9).

It must be emphatically stressed that the Israelite law of inheritance did not apply to these conquered lands. Saul and David possibly appropriated the conquered foreign lands for themselves. Yet the concentration of the original tribal lands within the Israelite society was, in all probability, caused by the indebtedness of the peasants. Crop failures, illness of domestic animals, and so many other small disasters could be balanced by providing the traditional tribal economic supports (the protective association system). If this traditional tribal protection failed because of the greed of prospering agrarian elites, then the poorer peasants ran into debt and became Hebrew slaves (Ex 21:2) or fell among "all those in distress, all those in debt, all those who had a grievance" (1 Sm 22:2). Their lands were, of course, confiscated by the agrarian elites (Saul's family, for one). With this interpretation, the probability is that the land was no longer considered the sacred property of the tribe or extended families (Gn 12:1–3; 15:7), but just negotiable merchandise, at least by the radical agrarian elites in the beginning of the united monarchy. This change would be one of the key dynamics in the emergence of the monarchy, the struggle for the possession of land bringing about fundamental structural changes in the political system of Israel.

In David's administration, there are two points of importance for the study of this indebtedness of the peasants. First, it is certainly abundantly clear that the royal domains in the Palestinian plains and valleys conquered by David yielded a greater and greater proportion of agricultural production. "The land in the plains and valleys," Itumeleng J. Mosala (107) states, "was more fertile, less vulnerable to soil erosion, and because it was on a flat surface, more retentive of water." The sale of these agricultural products in local trade must have created a socioeconomic imbalance in the tribal system of distribution of resources. Apart from the distribution system, David's administration affected the human labor supply in the village agricultural production. Gottwald has proposed that "the twelve-tribe scheme was originated by David for administrative purposes in order to recruit the citizen army or militia, and possibly also to raise taxes and to impose the corvée" (1979: 363). The labor shortage would assuredly have reflected a decline of agricultural intensification and production and have increased risks of poor harvests. As such, the state impoverished the peasants and pushed them into debt on an even greater scale, and their mortgaged lands were indeed confiscated by the agrarian elite and the court (cf. the opposing view that the united court had never confiscated the Israelite tribal land holdings, Mettinger 1971: 80–87).

Linked with the property of Meribbaal discussed above, such a treatment of land has served to reinforce our hypothesis: David confiscated the royal domains of Saul, including the original land of his extended family, to distribute to the royal retainers. The royal retainers in turn profited immensely from these lands (2 Sm 19:31–40). "An officialdom developed in the service of the king in favour of the court, which was responsible for administration and for the produce from the royal domains and from the land in the possession of Israelite tribes and families" (Herrmann: 236). Even the indulgence which the court had granted them increased the wealth of the royal retainers (1 Sm 17:25).

As a result, the Davidic court had been quietly but steadily having its destructive effects on the tribal infrastructure. In particular, the royal ownership of land had been increased, and its distribution and administration represented a fatal attack on the tribal infrastructure.

In Solomon's reign, the threat of the monarchic bid to exploit the peasants apparently expanded and took concrete shape. His economic policy was radically designed to increase the wealth of the court, mainly through international trade (cf. Elat 1979: 527–46), and began to bear fruit in the so-called Solomonic miracle: "The weight of gold received annually by Solomon amounted to six hundred and sixty-six talents of gold, besides what tolls and foreign trade, as well as everything the Arab kings and the provincial governors brought in" (1 Kings 10:14–15).

But this rising tide did not lift all boats. While the ruling elite prospered, the peasants saw their profit shrink, and the old infrastructure of the economy slowly broke down. The roots of this economic contradiction are revealed in the forced and overextended development of the state's infrastructure:

Commercial and military buildup: 1. Equipping a fleet to protect and promote international trade (1 Kings 9:26–28). 2. Building up a force of 1,400 chariots (12,000 horses) to secure the vast nexus of international and interregional trade (1 Kings 10:26–29).

Public construction: 1. The Temple of Yahweh for centralizing the agricultural surpluses of the peasants through feasts (sacrifices), and so forth (1 Kings 6:1–36). 2. The royal palace for the luxurious life of the court members and for the reinforcement (centralization) of the state administration (1 Kings 7:1–12). 3. The storage towns (1 Kings 9:19) such as "House of the Forest of Lebanon" (1 Kings 10:17) to store the state's wealth. 4. The chariot towns to station chariots and cavalry (1 Kings 10:26).

These building programs manifested themselves in a sharp increase in the state's "investments" (the massive explosion of military spending, and so forth). The chariot was, for instance, "imported from Egypt for six hundred silver shekels and a horse from Cilicia for a hundred and fifty" (1 Kings 10:29). This created a staggering deficit in the state's balance of payments and forced Solomon to sell even the royal land: "King Solomon gave Hiram twenty towns in the territory of Galilee" (1 Kings 9:11).

In effect, the state met its financial demands by exploiting the peasants through the strengthening of the taxation system (1 Kings 4:7–19). Also, the sanctuary in Jerusalem helped the court concentrate the agricultural surpluses of peasants. By contrast, the economic resources of the peasants gradually grew more limited, and the situation was aggravated still more by the increase in human labor power absorbed into corvée (1 Kings 5:27). The exploitation of peasants as a cheap state labor force became so extensive that it led to peasant revolts against the king (1 Kings 11:26–40). This economic contradiction between the tribal infrastructure (socialization of goods) and the court (concentration of goods) was a fatal mistake for Solomon, and was an underlying cause for the rupture of his kingdom. The decline was also accelerated by the loss of the Edomite territory (1 Kings 11:21–22, 25b).

What at first was called Solomon's "economic miracle" turned into a mirage. To guarantee available resources to pay for the court consumption, the state had to maintain the maximum in exports and exploit economic resources in the countryside. The peasants, however, could not keep pace with the ambitious economic programs of the state. Shortly after the death of Solomon, we read the following statement of the northern tribes:

> And they [all Israel—the northern tribes] spoke as follows to Rehoboam, "Your father laid a cruel yoke on us; if you will lighten your father's cruel slavery, that heavy yoke which he imposed on us, we are willing to serve you" (1 Kings 12:3–4).

Virtually what faces Rehoboam, Solomon's successor, is an excruciating dilemma. The belt-tightening measures needed to halt the growing court consumption that is wracking the economy would meet with strong opposition from the propertied upper class. On the other hand, the expenditures of the ruling class would exacerbate the social and economic inequities currently threatening to tear apart the rural social fabric. The court members decided to protect and further their interests, and passages in the Book of Kings reflect this:

> King Rehoboam then consulted the elders who had been in attendance on his father Solomon while he was alive, and said, "How do you advise me to answer this people?" They replied, "If you become the servant of this people today, and submit to them and give them a fair reply, then they will remain your servants for ever." But he rejected the advice given him by the elders and consulted the young men in attendance on him, who had grown up with him. He said, "How do you advise us to answer these people who have been saying, 'Lighten the yoke which your father imposed on us'?" The young men who had grown up with him replied, "This is the way to answer these people who have been saying, 'Your father made our yoke heavy, you must lighten it for us!' This is the right thing to say to them, 'My little finger is thicker than my father's loins. Although my father laid a heavy yoke on you, I shall make it heavier still. My father controlled

you with the whip, but I shall apply a spiked lash!' " (1 Kings 12:6–
11).

The passage implies that the economic interest of the court, Rehoboam,
and the young men, outranked the elders as the representatives of the
prominent extended families (cf. Malamat 1965; McKenzie 1959; D. L.
Smith: 94–99). We are to conclude from this that the state's economy had
been deeply involved in efforts to concentrate the surplus in the state treas-
ury and in the hands of the high officials who controlled commerce and
trade as "the king's dealers" (1 Kings 10:28). So, there is the surplus as a
"fetish" that subjugates human beings under the "legitimacy" of the power
of wealth, and even determines a destiny for the united monarchy, leading
to the sociopolitical and religious schism of Israel.

During the three centuries following the division of the kingdom, the
interests of the ruling elite continued to dominate the economy of both the
northern and southern kingdoms. Archaeological evidence from some Iron
Age II sites in Palestine indicates that by the eighth and seventh centuries
B.C.E. there were specialized economic activities taking place in the area:

Industry: 1. Pottery: The archaeological evidence in terms of the pottery
industry shows a certain progress in the production and quality of pottery
in the eighth century B.C.E. In E. W. Heaton's opinion, the improvement
of the techniques of pottery production facilitated "mass-production methods and the employment of unskilled labor" (1968: 37). 2. Woolen textiles:
Excavations in southern Palestine have recovered a number of dye plants
from the eighth to seventh centuries B.C.E.: "There could have been twenty
to thirty dye plants in the town (Debir)" (Silver 1983: 16).

Agricultural Industry: 1. Wine: Wine production was probably the most
important agricultural industry in many of Palestine's cities. Gibeon in Benjamin functioned as the major wine center, and flourished in the eighth to
sixth centuries B.C.E. (Pritchard 1962). 2. Oil: Next to wine, oil is the important product for exportation: "Remains of olive presses from the First Temple period have been found in many sites in Palestine, the most important
being at Shiqmona, Gezer, Beth-shemesh, and Tell Beit Mirsim. They date
from the tenth to the seventh centuries B.C.E." (Stern 1979: 259).

In the background of the development of this mercantilistic economy
lies the strong influence of the state's planning for increasing its income.
First, the tribal infrastructure had been affected by excessive taxation and
corvée and had reached the limits of its capacity for providing further
surplus. This brought the state's taxation system to a standstill. Even the
indulgence which the court had given the royal retainers exerted a limitation on the state's income. In addition, the ruling classes found themselves
forced to strengthen their armaments vis-à-vis their neighboring states such
as Damascus and the great empires, Egypt (1 Kings 14:25–28) and, later,
Assyria. To attend to these internal and external economic demands, the

ruling elite needed a new economic system conducive to a far more abundant flow of surpluses to the court.

Second, under the mercantilistic economy, cash-crop specialized agriculture was more lucrative than the traditional diversified agriculture: "wine and oil were more valuable than most agricultural commodities per unit of weight or volume . . . " (Chaney 1986: 73). While improving the use of the royal domains, the states moved to increase the production of wine and oil for exports, developing a specialized use of agricultural lands. Even the weakness of Damascus and, later, of Assyria, which took place in the first half of the eighth century B.C.E., provided a period of "peace" and the expansion of their territories (cf. 2 Kings 14:23–29, etc.), and could then lead, given the favorable sociopolitical conditions, to an expansion of their foreign market. Of course, under the states' grants and exemptions, their retainers, the merchants and landlords, were integrated into this specialized agricultural system. Archaeological surveys have yielded the following evidence of the proliferation of terraced culture in the eighth to sixth centuries B.C.E.:

> The most trustworthy determination of terrace age has been made by Edelstein and Kislev at Mevasseret Yerushalayim where 8th century pottery from the terraces is plentiful. Another team headed by Edelstein has investigated "farms" in Jerusalem's Rephaim Valley and found one of them, Khirbet er-Ras, complete with terraces, buildings, and assorted agricultural installations, to date from between the 8th and 6th centuries B.C.E. Taken together, the terraced sites of Khirbet er-Ras and Mevasseret Yerushalayim demonstrate the presence of terraced culture in the hills surrounding Jerusalem as early as the 8th century (Hopkins 1983a: 199).

Finally, by controlling the entire economic system—all of the means of production, raw materials, manufacturing, and commerce—the mercantilistic economy could be, for the ruling elite, a more efficient means of producing a larger surplus than the tributary economy ever could have produced by taxation of peasants alone.

To be more precise on the last point, analyzing the economy of the divided kingdoms reveals the fact that the economic moves of these societies were based on their maximizing of surplus labor value. Because of the ruling elite's policy of guaranteeing available surplus for their luxury consumption (cf. Hos 10:1; Is 1:29–30; 3:19–20; Am 6:5) and the military establishment, they promoted the mercantilistic economy in such matters as the royal farms, which produced agricultural products for export. In this process, the successful profit-making economy required the ruling elite to concentrate a cheap labor force and land. The state carried out a policy of obtaining the land of peasants and putting them to work on royal estates. To do this, the state provided more and more cheap labor and farmable land for itself and its retainers. The incident of Naboth's vineyard (1 Kings 21) can illustrate the state's attempt to break "the Israelite law of inheritance" as a strong obstacle in its way:

> This is what happened next: Naboth of Jezreel had a vineyard close by the palace of Ahab king of Samaria, and Ahab said to Naboth, "Give me your vineyard to be my vegetable garden, since it adjoins my palace; I will give you a better vineyard for it or, if you prefer, I will give you its value in money." Naboth, however, said to Ahab, "Yahweh forbid that I should give you my ancestral heritage!" (1 Kings 21:1–3).

Like King Ahab, who acquired Naboth's land by violence (1 Kings 21:4–16), the state forces the concentration of land in the hands of the ruling elite (latifundialization). Besides violence, latifundialization in the rural areas, indeed, makes steady progress by "excessive tribute" and a "rack-rent system" (cf. Am 5:11–12).

In the judgment of most scholars, the use of "rent" played an important role in the exploitation of the poor by the wealthy, leading the former to indebtedness. Frequently, crop failures caused by droughts or pests forced the peasants to incur debts. Specifically, many peasants in the mercantilistic economy were attracted to staple-crop production of wine and olives and abandoned their traditional subsistence agriculture based on crop diversification supplemented by animal husbandry. But the former was easily affected by natural disasters. For instance, olives "can be killed by prolonged frost, and even when they are not killed, cold winter temperatures in general can significantly reduce olive yields" (Frick 1985: 111–112). This accelerated the indebtedness of the peasants. Possibly because of high interest rates, their already mortgaged lands were lost to the landlords or merchants. Thus the independent peasants, already impoverished by the tribute system, became more and more worn down by the rack-rent system, and their lands flowed into the hands of the ruling elite: "The rich lords it over the poor, the borrower is the lender's slave" (Prv 22:7). Indeed, that is a process of latifundialization mirrored by the eighth-century prophets:

> Woe to those who add house to house
> and join field to field
> until there is nowhere left
> and they are the sole inhabitants
>   of the country (Is 5:8).

As a result, the mercantilistic economy drove the small peasants from their land and into two different camps. One group remained in the rural areas and worked as tenant farmers or sharecroppers for the landlords or on royal estates. Another group fled into the cities and worked as unskilled labor for starvation wages. That prosperous regional towns appeared in Palestine in the eighth century B.C.E. attests to the presence of this mercantilistic economy, absorbing the forces of production from the village communities. In regard to Judah, Thomas L. McClellan writes:

> Thus, the urban settlements of 8th century B.C. Judah reveal that there was a high degree of economic specialization by various towns and groups within towns; they were integrated into a regional network in which their surpluses were redistributed. The economic system was organized by the state, under the leadership of the king in his administrative center, Jerusalem (281).

But this prosperity of Judah abruptly ran into grave difficulties. The archaeological evidence indicates the destruction of the regional towns at the same period as the fall of Samaria (722 or 721 B.C.E). Again, McClellan describes:

> However, by the end of the 8th century much of Judah lay in ruins; its urban centers destroyed, and its agricultural system in shambles. The causes for these disasters cannot be precisely identified archaeologically. Historically, the campaign of Sennacherib in 701 B.C. must be looked to as the primary instrument of God's wrath. Sennacherib claimed to have destroyed forty-six towns, most notably Lachish. But it is possible the destruction of some was due to a combination of factors, including the Syro-Ephraimite war of *ca.* 735 B.C., and other events unknown or unsuspected by us, perhaps best described as Acts of God. Whatever the causes, the results were devastating; only Jerusalem stood amidst the desolation of Judah and its once thriving system of urban settlements (281).

Judah indeed suffered serious socioeconomic damage from these "disasters," as well as the Assyrian intervention. First, the destruction of regional agricultural systems brought about a drastic decline in agricultural products, specifically the production of "cash crops" in Judah, and did lead to the consequent loss of domestic and foreign trade. As to domestic trade, the devastated urban centers diminished their regional socioeconomic activities, thus depressing the domestic market. Second, the Assyrian presence not only meant the diminution of geopolitical security for the agricultural activities in Judah, but also made Judah less influential in the control of the Syro-Palestine caravan routes. Third, "the Assyrians probably favored their own newly acquired province of Samaria as the principal producer of wine and oil for Phoenician trade, and Transjordan as the conduit for trade in spices from Arabia, effectively isolating Judah economically" (McClellan: 282). Fourth, after the middle of the eighth century, Judah definitely became a tribute-paying state under the Assyrian empire.

By way of countering the above, Judah began to strengthen even more the centralization of power in Jerusalem. The ruling class had to organize its limited economic structure into efficient production as effectively as possible. The prophet Micah described such practices of the ruling elite who grabbed and concentrated the means of production in their hands:

> Disaster for those who plot evil,
> who lie in bed planning mischief!
> No sooner is it dawn than they do it,
> since they have the power to do so.
> Seizing the fields that they covet,
> they take over houses as well,
> owner and house they seize alike,
> the man himself as well as his inheritance (Mi 2:1–2).

By centralizing economic activities, they directed the maximum amounts of material productivity into their hands. The adoption of this new economic system, a centralized mercantilistic economy, was also designed to promote economic activities through a cheap labor force in Jerusalem. According to Broshi (23), around 700 B.C.E., the population of Jerusalem must rapidly have expanded, and numbered in the area of 24,000 people. This amounted to a doubling of Jerusalem's population, due to the migration from the northern kingdom (2 Kings 17), as well as from the western provinces of Judah, when Sennacherib gave those lands to the Philistines. By buying cheap labor power, the ruling elite was able to maximize its profits. Under the new economic system, the laboring class was, therefore, "condemned never to enjoy the advantages which the system reserves only for the owners of the means of production" (Rius: 95). This economic disadvantage of the populace grew more and more serious for two major reasons.

Military spending: "The period from the fall of Samaria to the end of the eighth century was," Siegfried Herrmann (255) states, "disturbed by a series of rebellions and coalitions hostile to Assyria, in which even Hezekiah of Judah was finally involved." These additional costs (2 Kings 18:14–15, etc.), of course, passed to the populace through tribute.

Migration: The migrants would have depressed still more the labor markets of Jerusalem and others of Judah's cities. Furthermore, the overpopulation in the cities would break the balance of supply and demand, increasing prices of commodities and property (cf. Bardtke).

A greater and greater proportion of the limited national wealth was going to a smaller proportion of the populace. In Chaney's opinion, the richest 2 percent or less of the population controlled half or more of the national income (1986: 55–56).

To summarize, under the tributary mode of production, the old tribal infrastructure was slowly but steadily eroded by the continuing demands of the court, the military, and the developing entrepreneurial interests. In particular, over the centuries of monarchic rule, there were growing economic crises among the peasants, evident above all in the continuing massive hemorrhage of tribute from them to the corrupt ruling elite, the so-called debt crisis of the peasants, and, sequentially, the land monopoly of the ruling elite in the mercantilistic economy.

The Kingdom of Josiah

Zephaniah, a prophet active in the last half of the seventh century B.C.E. in the reign of Josiah, 640–609 B.C.E., condemned rich oppressors in his nation:

> Wail, you who live in the Hollow,
> for it is all over with the merchants,
> all the money-bags have been wiped out!
>
> When that time comes
> I shall search Jerusalem by lamplight
> and punish the men
> stagnating over the remains of their wine,
> who say in their hearts,
> "Yahweh can do nothing,
> either good or bad,"
> For this, their wealth will be looted
> and their houses laid in ruins;
> they will build houses
>   but not live in them,
> they will plant vineyards
>   but not drink their wine (Zep 1:11–13).

One of the most important contributions of Zephaniah 1:11–13 is its evidence that the surplus is controlled by the rich merchants and landowners. In fact, the Book of Zephaniah describes the ruling elite as having reaped a bonanza through the mercantilistic economy and reserving much of that gain for their luxury consumption.

Second Kings 22:3–7, which is part of the account of Josiah's so-called reform, very clearly shows how the ruling elite exploit the populace through economic institutions.

Taxation: "Go to Hilkiah the high priest," he [King Josiah] told him, "and tell him to melt down the silver contributed to the Temple of Yahweh and collected by the guardians of the threshold from the people" (v. 4). This verse, of course, reflects the system of taxation that concentrates the surplus (silver) in the Temple. The Temple, in turn, is clearly involved in the royal system for exploitation of the populace through the feasts and the religious tithe (cf. 2 Kings 18:14–16).

Labor market: "He [Hilkiah] is to hand it over to the masters of works attached to the Temple of Yahweh, for them to pay it over to men working on the Temple of Yahweh, to repair the damaged parts of the Temple: to the carpenters, builders and masons, and for buying timber and dressed stone for the Temple repairs" (vv. 5–6). King Josiah orders the high priest to melt down the silver to pay for materials and the specialized labor of "independent craftsmen" for the Temple repairs (cf. Cogan and Tadmor: 282). This suggests that there are workers who sell their labor to the court, and there is a possibility for reciprocal profit and loss between the ruling elite and the workers. In other words, the rich make a profit from the workers in the reciprocal relation of "rise and fall of wages."

Surplus value: Besides buying labor with money, it has to be taken into consideration that the landless workers may have been forced to subject themselves to the marketplace economy by the necessities of life, such as needing food and clothing. The increase in the value of money produces a profit for the rich and again exploits the poor.

By utilizing the economic institutions above, the ruling elite would efficiently produce and sustain the exploiting society described by the prophet Zephaniah. The Josianic society seemed to be on the same track as the former kingdoms, in terms of the basic economic methods of exploitation. Society was preserved and functioned for the profit of the owners of the means of production, at the expense of the workers.

But the rest of the reform's accounts in 2 Kings 22:8–23:30 proved to be new economic actions on the part of Josiah, with the aim of further concentration of the surplus in the state. According to the account of the reform, Josiah first pushed a religious reform in Judah, purging non-Yahwistic elements and concentrating the religious activities, the feasts and sacrifices, in the Jerusalem Temple: "He [Josiah] exterminated the spurious priests whom the kings of Judah had appointed and who offered sacrifice on the high places, in the towns of Judah and the neighbourhood of Jerusalem" (2 Kings 23:5). He also extended the reform to the territory of the former northern kingdom: "As for the altar which was at Bethel, the high place built by Jeroboam son of Nebat who had led Israel into sin, he demolished this altar and this high place as well, in the same way, breaking up its stones and reducing them to powder" (2 Kings 23:15).

Now is it in fact possible that Josiah's reforms can be understood in terms of religious activities alone? We believe that the answer to this question is emphatically negative. Seen from the above historical reconstruction of the economy of the states of Israel and the situation of world politics in Josiah's time, we can rightly assume that the root of the reforms quite certainly lies in the socioeconomic and political spheres.

As seen in chapter 2, Josiah's reforms were involved as well in the movement of emancipation from Assyria. The probability is that Josiah succeeded in controlling Israelite territory, profiting from the weakened Assyrian empire, a fact which is also attested by 2 Chronicles 34:6–7. By repeatedly referring to rebellions and coalitions hostile to Assyria, the Old Testament conveys the impression that the anti-Assyrian movements of Israel's kings, in which even Josiah was finally involved, were strongly motivated by the attempts to reoccupy positions they had once held. They devoted particular attention to the commercial Syro-Palestinian corridor, which brought huge wealth to David and Solomon. This control over the commercial corridor certainly compelled Josiah to intercept Pharaoh Necho, the king of Egypt who sought to bring the Syrian states under control, at Megiddo.

In this framework, what faces Josiah is an excruciating contradiction. The attempts to rebuild Israel's empire required economic resources, for instance, for an effective military establishment that was highly expensive in itself. Yet the evidence shows the Josianic economy to be limited, because his actual taxation system was in a deadlock due to the ever-widening impoverishment of the populace, and the luxuried life of the ruling elite drained disproportionate resources, as well. Assuredly, Josiah's defeat at Megiddo demonstrated that his kingdom possessed limited military institutions (cf. Soggin 245; Von Rad 1966: 25).

At any rate, to promote and secure his emancipation and reform activities, Josiah would have had to build a strong administrative apparatus. The sources of funds for this consumption would be commerce and taxation. But since more taxation and austerity for the landless workers might well cause a social explosion, he did not face an easy task. On the other hand, there was little possibility of extracting "surpluses" from the ruling elite, the landlords and merchants. Even Josiah's political situation, which had been unstable since his accession to the throne (2 Kings 21:24–26), obliged the king to be chary of touching the wealth of the influential elite. So Josiah had to reconsider raising state taxes.

The last alternative for increasing the state's income would have been to improve somehow the efficiency of extracting "agricultural surpluses" from the peasants. In other words, the court would have to increase the income from the free southern peasants and later reintroduce taxation on northern peasants. From that point on, Josiah undertook his bloody campaign to abolish all the local shrines to which the peasants had been making their offerings and paying the religious tithe. That is also why Josiah destroyed the high place at Bethel, a major sanctuary of the former Northern Kingdom (cf. Am 7:12–13). Consequently, the peasants were forced to bring their surpluses to the Jerusalem Temple.

By our understanding of the economic structure of Judah at that time, this cultic centralization in Jerusalem would have brought about the following economic advantages for the Jerusalemite ruling elite:

Agricultural industry: The increase of agricultural surpluses brought about the much needed "raw materials" vital to the expansion of the agricultural industries in Jerusalem.

Commerce: The flow of pilgrims to Jerusalem resulting from cult centralization was an important factor in causing the capital city to prosper.

Trade: The control over the agricultural product of Samaria made Judah a principal provider of wine and oil for the Phoenician trade, thus expanding its trade with the neighboring states, such as trade in spices from Arabia.

Thus the stage was set for the increase of economic resources in the Josianic kingdom. Surely the process of Josiah's reform, focused on centralization of all worship in Jerusalem, fits well into the centralized mercantilistic economic system that molded the Judean society of that time. Then, it must be said that so far this is a claim that Josiah's reform seemed to be basically projected for aggrandizing the surplus for the state and the ruling elite of Jerusalem.

We believe that this is a convincing explanation for the economic basis of Josiah's reform. It thus becomes clear that, in the time of Josiah, there was a great influx of agricultural surpluses into the city of Jerusalem. In the midst of this, the Passover was celebrated as a national feast. The study of this feast in chapter 4 will necessarily involve a consideration of the enlargement of resources produced by Josiah's reform.

Although we have seen rather broadly how the conflict of classes emerged over the means of production, as well as the distribution of its product in Israelite society, we now must examine the social relations that were articulated and developed in such class struggles. The role the infrastructure plays in the crises of Josiah's kingdom, to which the Passover celebration is a response, will become clearer when we consider further aspects of the social relations of Josiah's society, molded by the ethnic, social, and historical circumstances of Israel's society.

SOCIAL ANALYSIS

The Historical Background

Throughout the Late Bronze Age, the Canaanite city-states experienced a series of social disturbances, evident in the el-Amarna Letters exchanged between Canaanite rulers and the Egyptian court. These texts often mention the *'apiru*, who were recruited as mercenaries by the Canaanite kings in conflicts with their neighboring states. Though scholars disagree on their exact origin, their actual activities, and their precise social status, all do agree that the *'apiru* are a marginal and multiethnic people, and a part of them came from "slaves, abused peasants, and ill-paid mercenaries" who departed from the control of Canaanite city-states (Bright: 139).

The hill regions in Canaan are commonly known as the refuge places for these outsiders. Some scholars argue that the *'apiru* appeared even to succeed in retaining their control upon some cities of the highlands. Behind their success there is the socio-economic decline of the city-states of Canaan in the highlands during the Late Bronze Age. This vacancy provided more space for the *'apiru's* maneuvers.

Yet the social disturbance reflected in the activities of the *'apiru* is deeply rooted in the various crises affecting the Syro-Palestinian underclasses, specifically the peasants. They are struggling to survive, while suffering from the poverty, oppression, and war created by the Egyptian Empire and its subordinate Canaanite city-states. If the peasants continue to be exploited by the tributary rule of their kings, they must either remain working on the royal domains and watch their families slowly starve to death, or they can, like the *'apiru*, escape from the tyrannical rulers. It is thus understandable that the exodus of Canaanite peasants from oppressive tributary rule into the relative freedom of the hill areas is probably a common social movement in the Late Bronze Age.

It is probably this movement that the biblical Israelites, escaping from the slavery of the Egyptian tyrant (Ex 2:23–25), met in Canaan, and to which they joined in such a prominent role, described and often exaggerated in the Bible, for instance by imagining the biblical Israelites as a massed army. The biblical Israelites, with their tribal organization and "praxis" of liberation from Egypt, seemed to be actively and effectively engaged in the class struggle for "survival" in Canaan, and succeeded in organizing a massive revolutionary movement with the Canaanite underclasses. The roots of the first Israelites, therefore, go back to the marginal and depressed underclasses in Syro-Palestine. "More convincing [than conventional scholarly theories]," Gottwald summarizes:

> is the hypothesis that Israel burst into Near Eastern history as an ethnically and socioeconomically heterogeneous coalition of insurgent mercenaries and freebooters (*'apiru*), tribally organized farmers and pastoral nomads (*Shosu*), depressed, "feudalized" peasants (*hupshu*), assorted craftsmen, and renegade priests, all of whom joined in rebellion against the imperial and quasi-feudal sociopolitical structures of Egyptian-dominated Canaan (1976a: 465).

Historically, the revolutionary movement withdrew the oppressed underclasses, with their vast peasant majority, from the Canaanite hierarchical social structure and settled them in a "frontier society" in the Canaanite highlands (cf. Chaney 1983 and Halligan 1983 on ancient Palestinian peasant movements and the formation of premonarchic Israel). This area, which is marked by adverse climatological and topographical conditions, forced the first Israelite peasants to live in a subsistence economy. The recent archaeological evidence from the Late Bronze Age has indicated that the peasants were engaged in such agriculture on a small scale. The majority of the populace in the highlands, Frick describes, "lived in small agricultural settlements like Ai and Khirbet Raddana in the countryside, and archaeologists have now begun to excavate these small, unwalled villages, most of which were five acres or less in size ... " (1985: 142).

At the social level, the subsistence economy in these village communities demanded "economic co-operation" or solidarity among the members. So Israel developed and extended the primitive kinship system (tribal mechanism) that organized the peasants in communal labor, based on tribal ownership of the means of production. By adopting communal labor, the village community was less dependent on professional specialists. Although there was always some differentiation of tasks on the basis of sex and age, most of the members tied by kinship were engaged in the same kinds of tasks. Moreover, the age and sex division of labor might be institutionalized by tribal socioeconomic units such as the extended families, basic units of production, the protective association of the extended families (mutual economic aid), and tribes (regional mutual aid of the extended families). By adopting communal ownership of the means of production, the individual came to be dependent on the village community to produce material resources. These in turn were distributed to all members as equally as possible by the tribal units mentioned above. Thus the tribal system aimed at opposing the attempts of individuals to aggrandize the surplus in their hands.

These two aspects of tribal structures, communal labor and ownership, were doubly helpful for Israel in distancing itself from the Canaanite class society, which was divided between the indigenous populace and the urban professional specialists, and/or between the underclasses and the ruling classes. Furthermore, the social relationship in tribal Israel was based upon "status" in a kinship system. At the top of this society were tribal elders in a patriarchal kinship structure. On the basis of such a social relationship it is obvious that sexism was involved in tribal Israel (cf. Bird; Meyers, 1983, 1984).

However, the "first Israelite free peasants" maintained relatively egalitarian social relations in their village community life, arranged in tribal structures. One of the reasons for the egalitarian society of the first Israelites can be located in their socioeconomic needs, the infrastructure.

As noted in our economic analysis, it was the weakening of this very infrastructure that would eventually promote the collapse of this egalitarian society. The collapse was caused by disparate advantages and the consequent changes in the infrastructure of the highland society. Specifically, the differentiation of agricultural productivity inevitably reflected differentiation in social relationships on the basis of wealth. This does explain why there are two contractive social categories mentioned in the book of the covenant. The covenant exerts discipline over the owners of the men and women (Ex 21:2–4), of the ox (Ex 21:28), of the pit (Ex 21:34), and of the house (Ex 22:7), when these owners are involved in civil or criminal suits. On the other hand, the covenant is concerned with the poor (Ex 23:3, 11), who are suffering from lack of food. The social tendency is thus inclined toward a class society within Israel. Another way of expressing this tendency is to prove that a certain wealthy group has increased agricultural productivity and has departed from the subsistence economy because it is this economy that demands the bonds of social cohesion for the Israelites. Conceivably, the weakened bonds of social cohesion in turn served to promote the emergence of a new class in Israel's society, those squeezed out of their traditional socioeconomic position by new and alien pressures and forced into a catchall position of pauperism. As such, the ability to produce a surplus gradually divided the Israelite society into those who have and those who have not.

Besides the tendency toward class society, the enlargement of economic resources produced a radical change in the life-style of the Israelites. Apparently the wealth can be used to feed an aristocratic class of "noncultivators or leisured class," in the terms of Beattie (186), who live in cities applying their resources in agriculture. Perhaps the employees for the work on their farms can be found among the new-arrived migrants, the indebted peasants, and so forth. The episode concerning Nabal and David in 1 Samuel 25 preserves the memory of how these wealthy Israelites were living:

> Now, there was a man in Maon whose business was at Carmel; the man was very rich: he owned three thousand sheep and a thousand goats. He was then at Carmel, having his sheep shorn. The man's name was Nabal ... David's men went and said all this to Nabal for David, and waited. Nabal retorted to the men in David's service, "Who is David? Who is the son of Jesse? There are many servants nowadays who run away from their masters. Am I to take my bread and my wine and the meat that I have slaughtered for my shearers and give it to men who come from I know not where?" (1 Sm 25:2–3, 9–11).

This text indicates that Nabal is involved in sheep raising with the use of employees (shearers) paid by material resources (meats, and so forth). According to his words, there are masters with a good number of servants, and some of the servants flee from their masters. This reinforces the presence of an aristocratic class and of groups of outsiders at the time when Israel had begun to constitute the tributary mode of production. The probability is that a good number of these wealthy men live in the cities such as Ramah, a city of the wealthy Elkanah (1 Sm 1), and enjoy its conveniences.

With the emergence of such an urban aristocratic class, Israelite social relations gradually became marked by contractual social relations, which form the very foundations of the city life-style. Unlike cooperative social relations, those in contractual relations carry out different kinds of tasks, produce different things, and become professional specialists. Then they reciprocally exchange their tasks and products by "surplus value" to constitute a contractual society. We suspect that the shearers in the story of Nabal (1 Sm 25:11) represent this worker class (paid employees). An important effect of these specialized activities, which essentially involve profit making, is to increase a differentiation of social relations. The exchange of tasks and products is also the basis on which one individual or group more easily exploits others. For instance, the activities of the priest Eli, described in 1 Samuel 1–3, attest to the development of a professional class within Israelite society. By abusing their social advantages of specialization, Eli's sons are able to exploit the populace to concentrate agricultural goods in their own hands (1 Sm 2:12–17). This priesthood surely enriched itself by the promotion of surpluses in Israel and thereby became part of the aristocratic class.

Thus Israel started to face contradictions in its social relations, contradictions between the rich and the poor peasants and between the aristocratic class in the cities and the worker class in both countryside and cities. This second aspect of social relations reflects a state of affairs in which urban concentrations and specialized activities make steady progress in Israel's society. As such, a class society that was actually to come in David's society has already been ripened within tribal Israel.

As is well-known, Israel's society had seen a rapid change in social relations under David, who began to stand out as a leader of the outsiders (1 Sm 22). By adopting contractual relations, he utilized the outsiders as mercenaries and worked even under a Philistine master, Achish son of Maoch (1 Sm 27). Also, it must be pointed out, David was a townsman at heart:

David said to Achish, "If I have won your favour, let me be given a place in one of the outlying towns, where I can live. Why should your servant live in the royal city with you?" That very day Achish gave him Ziklag; and this is why Ziklag has been the property of the kings of Judah to the present day (1 Sm 27:5–6).

These features illustrate how David had kept pace with the social demand of the times: specialized activities and urban concentrations in the contractual society. And that was one of the reasons he was anointed to be the king of Judah and Israel (2 Sm 2:4; 5:1–3). Under the united monarchy, David, as a truly professional king, captured Jerusalem, the Jebusite kingdom, and turned it into the capital of his state. There are strong indications that the occupation of Jerusalem could in fact have been connected with David's sociopolitical plans. Because of its central location in Israel, the city of Jerusalem as a capital provides the best position for David to control the territories of his united monarchy. Yet, with S. Yeivin, it is reasonable to propose that Jerusalem, as an ancient Canaanite city, had a specialized administrative constitution and supplied professional specialists to David, who was eager to set up an efficient administrative apparatus for concentrating resources. "The list of David's ministers," S. Yeivin observes,

> shows quite clearly that he employed non-Israelite officials, who evidently were more expert in the handling of state affairs and administrative routine than his Israelites, so that David made good use of their experience and technical know-how. Suffice it to mention such names as *Shavsha* the Scribe, *Ahithophel* the king's counselor, Jehoshaphat son of *Ahilud* the recorder, *Ittai* the *Gittite* — over the Cherethites and Pelethites, and many of the mighty men of David, including *Urijah* the Hittite. It is quite reasonable to suppose that many, if not all of them, came to him from the civil and military services of the Jebusite kingdom (149–50).

With the Jebusite administrative constitution, Israel witnessed the emergence of quite professional categories, which became a significant factor in the shaping of the Israelite hierarchical structure under the tributary mode of production. Specifically, the officials, involved deeply in the profit-making functions of the court, articulate complex contractual relations inside the Davidic monarchy. The biblical texts 2 Samuel 8:15–18 and 20:23–26, which present the lists of David's principal officials, reveal such social categories in the tributary mode of production:

Military class: 1. A chief commander, Joab, commanding the tribal army recruited from the peasants via the twelve-tribe system (1 Chr 27:1–15). 2. A special commander, Benaiah, commanding the foreign mercenaries (David's bodyguard).

Civil administrative class: 1. A herald, Jehoshaphat, "handling the communications between the king and the country" and taking care of "the ceremonial at the royal audiences" (Mettinger 1971: 61). 2. A chief secretary, Seraiah, working with the royal correspondence and annals. 3. A superintendent of forced labor, Adoram, serving for the raising of the labor force.

Religious class: A chief priest: Abiathar, a Shilonite, was anointed to be a chief priest by David. Later Zadok, who was of "Aaronid pedigree," supplanted Abiathar (Olyan 1983: 183; cf. the different view that Zadok was a Jebusite priest of Jerusalem, Rowley 1939).

From their positions of power, David's ministers and their professional aides served to enhance the court's control over tribute from the Israelite peasants and the conquered city-states, the international trade, and the growing agricultural production in the royal domains. The material resources increasingly available to the court in turn had promoted the royal aristocracy: the king's sons and their wives (2 Sm 3:2–5; 5:13–16), and the royal retainers, the king's friends (2 Sm 19:19, 31–40) and his high officials. Thus it was David who constituted the state bureaucracy as a vehicle for enriching the ruling class and for extracting tribute from the populace.

There is, therefore, no doubt that Israel in David's reign started forming into the class society of the dominant and the dominated. Yet because of the promotion of material resources in the dominant class, Israel faced an internal struggle for the throne (Absalom's and Adonijah's dynastic fights) and for the high official posts (the disputes between Joab and Benaiah and between Abiathar and Zadok). The social relations of this society, of course, assumed contractual and antagonistic aspects.

Apparently David's successor, his son Solomon, came as the end product of this process of internal struggle for control of the state. He was so anxious to raise material resources and maintain his empire that he improved the efficiency of his state's administrative system. Yet most commentators assume that Solomon carried out his administrative reforms under Egyptian influence, as manifested possibly by the presence of Pharaoh's daughter in the court (1 Kings 11:1). There is ample biblical evidence for this administrative improvement:

"Master of the palace" (Ahishar): administering the royal estates (1 Kings 4:6).

"Twelve administrators" effectively extracting tribute from the peasants: "Solomon had twelve administrators for all Israel who saw to the provisioning of the king and his household; each had to provide for one month in the year" (1 Kings 4:7). The list of these administrators reveals the fact that Solomon employed specialized professionals, substituting them for the old tribal chiefs ("List of tribal chiefs" in 1 Chr 27:16–22 seems to be inspired by the "Twelve Administrators" of Solomon).

A remarkable increase in the number of officials: "There were five hundred and fifty officials in charge of the foremen over Solomon's work, who supervised the people employed on the work" (1 Kings 9:23).

New social categories handling trade: "experienced sailors" (1 Kings 9:27); "the king's dealers" (1 Kings 10:28), and so forth.

The royal aristocracy and its retainers had profited immensely from this improvement of the state bureaucracy, as is also evidenced by the repeated references to the multitude of "non-cultivators" (cf. 1 Kings 11). The feeding of this aristocratic class was in the hands of the populace:

> These administrators provided the food for Solomon and for all those who were admitted by him to the royal table, each for the period of a month; they ensured that nothing was wanting. They also provided the barley and straw for the horses and draught animals, where required, each according to the quota demanded of him. The daily provisions for Solomon were: thirty measures of fine flour and sixty measures of meal, ten fattened oxen, twenty free-grazing oxen, one hundred sheep, besides deer and gazelles, roebucks and fattened poultry (1 Kings 5:2–4, 7–8).

The shift in favor of the aristocratic class was not without its equivalent exploitation of the dominated class. The prosperity of the urban nonculti-

vator class was intimately linked to the impoverishment of the rural culti-
vator class. Viewed sociologically, the improvement of the state bureaucracy
by means of the division of labor led to the very class society in which the
ruling class was more easily able to extract the product of the labors of
other classes. As in most class societies, there were the ups and downs of
the social categories. The peasant women who were already victims of the
patriarchal system of masculine hegemony were among the most exploited
categories of the Solomonic society. It is interesting to observe the affliction
of these women in the story of God's punishment on Eve (Gn 3:16), which
probably had its social setting in the united monarchy: "I shall give you
intense pain in childbearing, you will give birth to your children in pain.
Your yearning will be for your husband, and he will dominate you."

The Bible states that the women in the "tributary structure" of the
monarchic state are one of the means of production to supply the official
slaves of the state (1 Sm 8:10–18). Within this social system, the women's
suffering in childbearing seems to express "the women's intense pain" in
losing their children to the official slavery of the state of David and Solomon, instead of having children as their joy and future. The physical dis-
comforts of the birth process should not be considered a punishment of
women. Rather the mental anguish of an oppressive socioeconomic system's
depriving them of normal family life would be the real torment of the
women's suffering (cf. Schwantes 1989b).

To conclude, following the socioeconomic system of the Egyptian Empire
and Canaanite city-states, the Israelite ruling classes developed specialized
activities and urban concentrations, thus maximizing the influx of tribute
from the peasants into the court. Thus the descendants of "the first Israelite
free agrarians," who escaped from the depressed underclass in the tributary
Canaanite city-states, themselves became a class of "tribute-paying peasants" (Gottwald 1986c: 77) and were thrown into a subordinate status.

The social situations of the two rival kingdoms from the mid-ninth to
the seventh century B.C.E. comprise two experiences: specialization of economic activities and the Assyrian intervention. The former set up a more
complex division of labor, elevating contractual and antagonistic aspects of
social relations. The latter produced the Assyrian imperial ruling class,
which subjected Israel to its economic and political domination, and, later,
Judah to excessive taxation. Thus it was, one might say, a time that witnessed the growth of as many social categories as possible. In a broad way,
Mansueto describes these hierarchical social relations as follows:

Ruling class groups: the Israelite royal houses, during the monarchic
period, together with priestly sectors, dependent on taxes and corvées from
the peasant communities; the metropolitan ruling classes of the various
empires which dominated Israel, dependent on tributes levied on the population and collected by the indigenous ruling classes or imperial administrators; and latifundiaries, dependent on rents from more or less private
estates;

Middle layers: craftsmen, functionaries, and lower clergy dependent on benefices which do not provide income sufficient to maintain an aristocratic style of life, and independent craftsmen and merchants;

Exploited classes: two principal kinds of peasantry—peasants protected by redistributional land tenure and other community guarantees—tenant farmers on the estates of latifundiaries, and marginated rural people who have no regular access to the land (34–35).

Within this hierarchical and contractual society, the two kingdoms also witnessed a deplorable proliferation of corruption in the conduct of administrative affairs. The prophets in this period observed that the administrative apparatus was subject to bribes from the wealthy and devoured the poor in both kingdoms: "Your princes are rebels, accomplices of brigands. All of them greedy for presents and eager for bribes, they show no justice to the orphan, and the widow's cause never reaches them" (Is 1:23; cf. Am 2:6–7).

Differences between the two kingdoms' societies are observable, however. When the northern tribes seceded from Davidic rule, Judah remained under the house of David, keeping the same royal retainer families in their high official positions. This provided a way for these families to keep and to increase inheritance of land and other benefits of office, which furthered their wealth. Probably it would be evidenced by the presence of "the people of the land," who were "a political-social element which was loyal to the house of David. This element in the society was the main factor behind the phenomenon of hereditary succession in Judah" (Oded 1977: 458; cf. 2 Kings 11). Also, the country Levite priests derived their living from tithes dependent on the fluctuating economic fortunes of the peasants. Many of them would enjoy the economic stability afforded by a strong monarchy, thus elevating themselves to a much more prosperous level.

Thus the stability of the monarchy in Judah produced prosperous aristocratic classes and maintained relatively stable social relations in the ruling classes. Unlike Judah, Israel witnessed several dynasties, alternately formed and developed by a bloody struggle for the throne. These successive changes of ruling families can certainly be seen as a further indication of the insecurity of the royal retainers, who fought for the right of inheritance. Even Jeroboam's religious politics, which established the two sanctuaries of Bethel and Dan (1 Kings 12:26–33), also inevitably led toward an internal struggle for the post of chief priest and a subsequent instability of the ruling classes. Cross writes:

> We must conclude that Jeroboam carefully appointed two priesthoods for his two national shrines, one of Mushite stock, one of Aaronite ancestry. As we have seen, Jeroboam was in fact no innovator. In his establishment of his cult and cult places he attempted to "out-archaize" David. In the choice of priesthood he also proposed to alienate neither of the rival priestly houses, choosing two national shrines (a

procedure in itself demanding explanation!) and two priestly houses
to serve him. Withal he attempted to strengthen his kingship, as a
usurper must, against the house of David and the great sanctuary of
the Ark in Jerusalem (1973: 199).

This significantly affected the priestly apparatus, thus developing antagonistic social relations in the ruling classes in the history of the northern
kingdom.

In addition to the succession for the throne, the Assyrian expansion at
the end of eighth century B.C.E. brought about a distinctly different effect
on the ruling classes of the two kingdoms. First of all, the capture of
Samaria affected the ruling classes of Israel beyond measure. "The deportations above all," Herrmann writes:

> affected the upper classes. The great mass of the population remained
> to work on the land. According to Judg. 18.30 the priests of the state
> sanctuary of Dan were deported. Amos had already threatened Ama-
> ziah, the high priest of Bethel, with such a fate (Amos 7.17). The
> priests belonged to the upper class as much as the state officials and
> the leading landowners, those who had great estates and those who
> administered royal property. They were replaced by the new settlers,
> who as the privileged class had to make arrangements with those of
> the population who had been left behind (251).

This states that there were non-Israelite priests who profited by the
sacred tribute from the peasants. In contrast, the Israelite priests probably
fled into Jerusalem and were employed, if they were lucky enough, in subordinate functions at the national sanctuary. To be sure, this antagonistic
relationship between the foreign and the Israelite priests would at least in
part trigger the forthcoming Josianic reform.

But the same tragedy did not happen to a similar extent to the ruling
classes of Judah, which remained under its own government in spite of
paying tribute to the Assyrians. During the destruction of some regional
towns, many regional men of power probably disappeared or fled into Jerusalem. Surely the country Levite priests became one of the few aristocratic
or leading classes in the countryside. To be attentive to the continuing
religious activities in the high places and sanctuaries, it must be pointed
out that the country Levite priests maintained their advantageous social
position under the Assyrian hegemony. Faced with the Assyrian pressure,
it seemed to be inconvenient for the Jerusalemite ruling elite to struggle
against the country Levite priests.

In some ways, the weakened regional aristocratic classes would
strengthen the Jerusalemite ruling elite in their administrative center, Jerusalem. To secure their monarchy and their socioeconomic status, they concentrated and exploited the labor classes with their vast migrant labor,

insuring material resources for their relatively luxurious life and tribute for "the metropolitan ruling classes," as alluded to in the preceding economic section. If this is the case, then the step taken by the city of Jerusalem may be explained by the term "tyrannical city" (Zep 3:1) in the truest sense. What faced the populace of Jerusalem at the social level was increasing corruption and a rapidly expanded population that would produce further serious social and economic problems. Specifically, the migrant peasants faced a battle on two fronts. As migrants, they lost bonds of social cohesion and were obliged to find ways to survive in antagonistic social relations. As landless peasants, they lost their free status and had to struggle to avoid actual slavery. Thus the specialized activities and urban concentrations in the contractual society, which David introduced into Israel's society on a large scale, reached their maximum development and fiercely devoured the populace of Jerusalem.

The Kingdom of Josiah

There can be little doubt that the prophet Zephaniah, who worked in the reign of Josiah, had the above in mind when he wrote:

> Disaster to the rebellious,
> > the befouled,
> the tyrannical city!
> She has not listened to the call,
> she has not bowed to correction,
> she has not trusted in Yahweh,
> she has not drawn near to her God.
> The rulers she has
> are roaring lions,
> her judges are wolves of the wastelands
> which leave nothing over
> > for the morning,
> her prophets are braggarts,
> impostors,
> her priests have profaned what is holy
> and violated the law (3:1–4).

We meet here a society in which the ruling elites have abused their privileges, as well as evidence suggesting that the administrative apparatus is subject to bribes. That exacerbates the social and economic inequities and transforms the city of Jerusalem into the "tyrannical city." The crisis of its populace in economic difficulties is intensified, and signs of widespread social pathology flourish.

2 Kings 22–23 more than confirms this antagonistic and hierarchical social formation:

Upper classes: King Josiah, together with his high officials, the high priest Hilkiah, the secretary Shaphan, and the king's minister Asaiah; his friends, Ahikam son of Shaphan and Achbor son of Micaiah; the elders of Judah and Jerusalem (23:1); and the people of the country, possibly prosperous landlords in strong relation with the elders (23:30).

Middle classes: Functionaries (the guardians of the threshold in 22:4), priests (23:2), prophets (23:2), and craftsmen (the masters of work—the carpenters, builders, and masons in 22:6,9).

Underclasses: Those people who were subject to taxation (22:4). They were engaged in two principal kinds of labor: peasants working in their tribal lands or working as "share croppers" for the landlords, and working men and women in cottage or state industries or in construction.

It was noted in the economic analysis that the decline of the Assyrian empire gave opportunities for Judah to begin Josiah's so-called reform. In turning to a close analysis of the sociopolitical situation at that time, the decline of Assyria and its empire was also a turning-point for the upper classes of Judah and of the territory of Israel occupied by Assyrians since 722. The social structure of the two societies under the dwindling Assyrian hegemony comprised two big losers: the country Levite priests in Judah and non-Israelite priests in Israel. The former, who maintained a certain degree of independence under the Assyrian hegemony, became less powerful in relation to the ruling elite in Jerusalem. The latter, who were appointed and settled by the Assyrians, lost their sponsor. No better chance would ever have come to their opponents! Who stood in antagonistic social relation to these two groups of priestly losers?

The first activities of Josiah's cultic centralization were directed toward the high places in Judah. This reform brought the country Levite priests to Jerusalem:

> He [Josiah] brought all the priests in from the towns of Judah, and from Geba to Beersheba he rendered unsanctified the high places where these priests had offered sacrifice. He pulled down the High Place of the Gates, which stood at the gate of Joshua, the governor of the city, to the left of the entry to the city. The priests of the high places, however, did not officiate at the altar of Yahweh in Jerusalem, although they did share the unleavened bread of their brother-priests (2 Kings 23:8–9).

Regarding the status of a priest, the law of Deuteronomy 18:1–8 provided the Levitical priests with the same privileges as the city priests, as we alluded to in the first chapter. Nevertheless, the fact was that "all the priests of the towns of Judah" (the country Levite priests) were employed in subordinate functions at the Jerusalem Temple. This fact suggests that Josiah's reform had a social end in view, not just a change in religious practices. In the history of the united monarchy, one of the more important conflicts was between Abiathar and Zadok, and the main focus of this conflict was the post of chief priest of the royal sanctuary, and the privileges thereof. At the later stages of Judah's history, this dispute probably continued between the two rival levitical groups, the Jerusalemite priests and the country Levite priests. The former, who were of Zadokite descent, controlled the official Yahweh sanctuary and furthered the gathering of their power and wealth. The latter, who performed religious rites in various high places and village sanctuaries, often became local nobility. As noted above, the decline of Assyria made a turning-point in their relationship of power. The time seemed ripe for the Jerusalemite priests to control the entire cult. So, we believe that Josiah's reform in Judah came as the centralization of the cult that involved the dispute between the Jerusalemite priests and the country Levite priests.

The whole of 2 Kings 23 gives us insights into social relations in conflict. We hear in the later activities of Josiah's cultic centralization about a massacre of the priests of the high places in the towns of Samaria:

> Josiah also destroyed all the shrines on the high places which were in the towns of Samaria and which the kings of Israel had built to provoke Yahweh's anger; he treated these places exactly as he had treated the one at Bethel. All the priests of the high places who were there he slaughtered on the altars, and on those altars burned human bones. Then he returned to Jerusalem (23:19–20).

There is no reason to doubt that vv. 15–20 in 2 Kings 23 represent Josiah's political actions to restore the independence of Judah from Assyrian vassalage, and even to extend his control to the former territory of the northern kingdom of Israel. It is fair to observe, however, that these political comments on the reform do not focus enough attention on the historical occasions for particular conflicts between the ruling elite of Judah and the clerical class of Israel. Most commentators assume that Jeroboam's religious reform in 1 Kings 12:26–33 expressed a certain degree of socioeconomic independence from the rival state of Judah. On the other hand, this was also a great blow specifically to the Zadokite priesthood of the Jerusalem Temple, until then the arbiters of the official Yahweh worship, from which they derived sacred material resources. The most significant note is, however, Jeroboam's action in choosing two priestly houses, the Mushite and Aaronite priesthood, vis-à-vis the Jerusalemite priesthood. This inclines us to emphasize the historically increasing hostility between the priesthoods of the two rival states. Even the non-Israelite priests, who were appointed to the priesthood of Israel by Assyrians and probably interfered in the religious activities of Israel, must have deepened the prejudice of Judah's religious classes against them. Finally, an important thing to note, especially regarding the deep prejudice against the non-Israelite priests, is that the deportation of Israelite priests from the former territory of Israel could have promoted the widespread development of "witch-hunting" against the non-Israelite priests.

If this reform is seen, at least in part, in the context of these antagonistic social relations, then we can more clearly understand Josiah's actions punishing the priests in Israel far more cruelly than in Judah. Indeed, the cold-blooded slaughter of the priests in Israel would reinforce the impression that Josiah had a social end in view.

Surely the tragedy of these losers, the country Levite priests and the non-Israelite priests, illustrates the nature of Josiah's reform. They were clearly swallowed up in the waves of development of the centralized mercantilistic economy in Jerusalem. Here the maximizing of surpluses appears to be the chief motivation in human activities. The "reified" surpluses even appear to be real actors in human society, with human beings "running" after them. The surpluses seem to take action, determine, and dictate the social relations in the process of Josiah's reform.

Besides the upper sections of the class structure of the monarchy, this reform also had important impact on the life of the exploited underclasses. In particular, the rural population would become a prominent victim in the reform. First, the centralization of all worship in Jerusalem made religious activities more expensive for them because of their pilgrimage expense in traveling to the capital city. Second, the destruction of local sanctuaries not only meant, for the rural population, a "creation of a religious vacuum in their midst" (Weinfeld 1964: 202–3), but also made a breach in the social life of village communities. Third, some scholars suggest that Josiah adopted "the old method of the levy of the free peasants" (Von Rad 1966: 25). If so, this would have made another serious impact on the social life of the rural population. However, to say this is not to deny that, judging by the erosion of the tribal system of that time, there would have been a need for the state to hire an increasing number of mercenaries for building an effective military establishment.

All of these negative results of Josiah's reform were concealed beneath a pious and exclusive loyalty to Yahweh. In point of fact, the reform represented an attack on the rural population and on many aspects of its social life. Josiah's society appears to be on the track of an urban concentration movement rather than on the track of an egalitarian social movement. The centralization process in Jerusalem, which clearly started with David and developed through the following three centuries, would culminate in Josiah's destruction of local sanctuaries, which represented the bonds of social cohesion for the village communities. It seems likely that the event of the Passover celebration in the Jerusalem Temple must be read on this level as part of the centralizing movement of the urban Jerusalemite patricians against the village communities.

We have now reached the point in the investigation in which we can return to the original question. What kind of historical and sociological reality stands behind Josiah's reform? Does it stem only from a religious intent to centralize the cult in the Jerusalem Temple? It is clear from our continuing analysis of the infrastructure of Josiah's society that the decline of the Assyrian empire provided the ruling elite of Judah with an important opportunity for organizing and establishing a new economic process for production and distribution, namely, a centralized mercantilistic economy in Jerusalem. This promoted change and consequent conflicts in social relations, specifically in the decline and fall of the country Levite priests of Judah and the priests of Israel, thus leading to the decline of the life of village communities.

To be sure, to control or change the social order in any system of human relationships is to affect or redefine political and legal systems. Josiah's politics clearly exemplify this mechanism. We shall turn to this shortly. First, however, we must look at the political developments in the history of Israel that provided the political context of Josiah's reform.

POLITICAL ANALYSIS

The Historical Background

There can be little doubt that the tribal organization, with its assembly and army, was a factor of great historical significance for the political life of early Israel. On the one hand, the tribal assembly, composed of tribal representatives, was a primary entity of political and judicial power over affairs regarding the tribes, and secured social order among them. For example, the assembly of elders, its functions and historical importance, can frequently be seen in the Old Testament (cf. 1 Sm 8:1–9). On the other hand, the tribal army, which was organized by the free peasants, provided cooperative protection for all the tribes of Israel (cf. 1 Sm 13:2). In early Israel, this army had the exclusive function of self-defense against Canaanite city-states and, later, the Philistine league.

While maintaining such a level of cooperation, the village communities or tribes still maintained their own autonomy under the leadership of elders. Indeed, the elders were of basic importance to the political and judicial functions of their autonomous communities. It was by them that tribal levy of troops was determined. Moreover, they were responsible for the jurisdiction of the village courts, as well as for arrangements of "intermarriage among extended families in the same protective association preferred and at times obligatory" (Gottwald 1979: 340).

Thus, unlike the Canaanite city-states, which lived under a state hierarchy and were controlled by the professional army, early Israel established the tribal-system federation and encouraged sociopolitical cooperation and autonomy for the village communities or tribes. Structurally, their political organization was not considered as a centralized unity. In McKenzie's words, "there was no monarchy and no visible central government which could be seen in the sources. 'Israel' as a political unit simply did not exist; there were no agents or channels of political activity for 'Israel' " (1983: 25). However, once the political organization is seen in terms of maintaining social order, then the Israelite tribal federation is an example of a politically uncentralized unity or entity. This unity, indeed, aimed at opposing the attempts of a particular community to build an apparatus of state power. Needless to say, the operation of this tribal federation stood firmly on the self-sufficiency of each village community in the production, distribution, and consumption of goods, as alluded to in our previous analyses of the infrastructure.

Biblical passages that deal with the time of the state's emergence in Israel reveal some disturbance of the public peace, and a subsequent failure of the tribal, uncentralized political unity, as well. The oldest statements against the professional classes' abuse of power (1 Sm 2:12–17; 8:2) come from this period. Externally, the Philistine threat increased (1 Sm 4), so that even the sanctuary of Shiloh was destroyed (1 Sm 5–6). Thus the tendency for some form of a centralized political unit to control these disturbances had grown among the Israelites, and this can be illustrated by the institution of the monarchy in 1 Samuel 8:1–5, 19–20:

> When Samuel grew old, he appointed his sons as judges of Israel. His eldest son was called Joel and his second one, Abijah; they were judges at Beersheba. His sons did not follow his example but, seduced by the love of money, took bribes and gave biased verdicts. The elders of Israel all assembled, went back to Samuel at Ramah, and said, "Look, you are old, and your sons are not following your example. So give us a king to judge us, like the other nations." (1–5) ... They said, "No! We are determined to have a king, so that we can be like the other nations, with our own king to rule us and lead us and fight our battles" (19–20).

So it is not surprising to hear of the consecration of Saul to be a leader of Israel during this period (1 Sm 10). However, the Bible tells us that he was equipped only with an elementary bureaucratic administration and the bare beginning of a professional army (1 Sm 14:52). Also, the consecration of Saul demonstrated a certain ambiguity in that he was presented by Samuel as the leader, rather than as the king: "Samuel took a phial of oil and poured it on Saul's head; he then kissed him and said, 'Has not Yahweh anointed you as leader [*nagid*] of his people?' " (1 Sm 10:1). Joseph R. Rosenbloom's opinion of the consecrations of Saul provides a helpful insight into this ambiguity:

> While the tribal leadership of the Israelites actively sought a monarch and were willing to pay for the anticipated benefits, they were not willing to call upon an individual who would be too powerful for them

to control. So the call went to Saul, from the "least of all the families of the smallest tribe (1 Sm 9, 21)." They wanted a king who would serve them and their interests but not overwhelm them (439).

In fact, Saul, who represented the aristocratic peasants (1 Sm 9; 11:1–11), tried to exercise some political power under the failing tribal political organization. It is understandable that the assembly of elders (1 Sm 15:30) and the tribal judge, Samuel, still held a strong influence in the political sphere. Yet not all of the Israelites were convinced that Saul should reign over them (1 Sm 8:10–18). We suspect that the priesthood, another aristocratic class at that time, would have created some conflict with Saul, possibly resulting in the "massacre of the priests of Nob" (1 Sm 22:6–23). That is, there were internal struggles for building an apparatus of state power. As a result, Saul reigned over Israel with limited resources and public acknowledgment, thus having only a limited ability to control social disturbance and to expand the territory.

We have, then, the disturbed state of the early Israelite monarchy. Besides the Philistine threat, the major social disturbance seemed to lie in the presence of outsiders (1 Sm 22:2), who were composed, in large part, of indebted peasants. They were the fruits of the tribal society's change from a communal and cooperative society into a profit-making and contractual society. This in turn required that Israel pursue economic policies that would satisfy the needs both of the prosperous peasants and of the indebted peasants. As we have seen, the consensus is that Saul, strongly marked by the old tribal system, could not keep pace with this social demand of the times. Most commentators assume that David succeeded in satisfying this demand and reestablishing social order. What kind of economic policies did he execute? One answer comes from focused attention on 1 Samuel 22:1–2:

> David left there and took refuge in the Cave of Adullam; his brothers and his father's whole family heard this and joined him there. All those in distress, all those in debt, all those who had a grievance, gathered round him and he became their leader. There were about four hundred men with him.

The political significance lies precisely in the fact that David built a very professional band of mercenaries who were able to execute successful military campaigns (1 Sm 27:8–9). This mercenary group in turn would attract investment from both prosperous and indebted peasants. The former would invest in protection for their property against internal and external conquerors. The latter would invest their time and energy in a new job category—mercenary—to gain profit and a new social status. The professional army thus would have a positive effect on the well-being and social harmony of the Israelites, and even more on David's political career. In other words,

David's politics were exactly what a growing contractual society wanted to see. Historically, David's military band, benefiting from the socioeconomic and political advantages mentioned above, consolidated his position as the king of Judah (2 Sm 2:1–4) and achieved three further goals: providing a centralized and professional military power, securing political independence from the tribal political leaders, and expanding the area of territorial possessions.

The first goal was achieved in the battle of Gibeon, where David's professional army defeated the tribal army of Israel: "Abner and the men of Israel were beaten by David's retainers" (2 Sm 2:17). Thus David showed the efficiency of a professional army, paving the way for progress to his second goal. This was achieved when David was anointed king of Israel: "So all the elders of Israel came to the king at Hebron, and King David made pact with them in Yahweh's presence at Hebron, and they anointed David as king of Israel" (2 Sm 5:3). This brought about the much-needed political acknowledgment from the tribal leaders of all Israel, which was ratified in a contractual relationship with them, granting political independence from the tribal leaders. Finally, the achieving of these two goals made David less dependent on the tribal system and enabled him to facilitate a smooth operation in establishing a new political system. As soon as he was elevated to be king over Israel, David conquered Jerusalem, using his own band of mercenaries (2 Sm 5:6–8) and designated this city to be his own independent city-state. The independent city-state, in turn, with the Jebusite administrative structure, helped David develop an independent and centralized administrative organization, specifically aiming at aggrandizing the surplus and controlling the resulting political power.

As a result, David constituted the "Israelite State" under the authority of a king both in name and reality. Of course, the surplus "fetish" not only pushed David to consolidate political power inside Israel, but also led him to set stages for his final goal. After establishing Israel's territorial state, David took the step to develop political power in an international context. Weakness in other ancient Near Eastern states, such as Egypt, helped him execute smooth military operations and embark on expansionist policies (cf. Otzen 1979). The Bible reports a series of his successful campaigns against the neighboring city-states in 2 Sm 8:1–14. With the tribute derived from these conquests and the control established over the Syro-Palestinian corridor, the Davidic monarchy came to be a successful empire in the truest sense.

It was not a "successful" empire for all the Israelites, however. Scholars believe that the monarchic system that David set up exercised considerable "favoritism toward Judah" (2 Sm 19:42) in two aspects, military service and the judicial system. The first affected the forces of production of Israelites in the northern state more than in the southern state. The second, in which David failed to be attentive to the tribes of Israel, created discontent among them (2 Sm 15:1–6). The probability is that this favoritism pushed the peasants of the northern tribes to support Absalom's (2 Sm 15:7–18:18) and Sheba's rebellions (2 Sm 20: 1–3). If this is correct, the well-known image of David as an ideal and beneficial king was likely to have been an ideological product on the part of the Davidic retainers. What the peasants of the northern tribes were faced with, in the political sphere, was a central government that started to detach itself from them and even to violate the traditional pact with them.

Under Solomon's reign, a stronger political centralization developed, thus furthering the divergent tendencies between the central government and the peasants. It is interesting to note that Solomon's succession itself took place as a result of internal conflict between two political parties, "the premonarchical elements in Israel-Judah and the bureaucracy created by David" (Cohen 1971: 93). The succession narrative reports the end of this internal conflict with the following passage:

> Whereupon Benaiah son of Jehoiada went out, struck Joab down and put him to death; he was buried at his home in the desert. In his place as head of the army the king appointed Benaiah son of Jehoiada and, in place of Abiathar, the priest Zadok (1 Kings 2:34–35).

It should be noted that the two losers, Joab as chief of the tribal army and Abiathar as a Shilonite (1 Sm 22:20–23), were firmly rooted in the old Israelite tribal order and its traditional bonds. Their removal, therefore, gave opportunities for the new leaders to consolidate their position in the court. Who might these leaders be? By learning the important role performed by Benaiah, the commander of the professional army, we can imagine that they were perhaps rooted in the urban and contractual order and its profit-making bonds. Even the presence of the priest Zadok and the court prophet Nathan in Solomon's sect, who were bureaucratic appointees, affirms the above. With their support, Solomon strengthened his administrative apparatus and the subsequent political centralization and secured its autonomy vis-à-vis the Israelite tribal unit and the external forces. That was a development of the "national security forces" which, according to Chris Hauer, Jr., dominated Solomon's politics: "The passage from the Davidic to the Solomonic administration in ancient Israel was marked by a dramatic change in the basic strategic concept of the national security forces" (1980). During his reign, Solomon took three main measures to develop this national-security aspect of his administration. First, he increased the military power on a large scale (1 Kings 10:26); specifically, he "strengthened his army by developing the chariot arm to an extent never attempted before" (Bright: 213). Second, diplomatic relations were strengthened by his marriage with Pharaoh's daughter and the renewal of alliance with Tyre (1 Kings 5:1–12). Third, Solomon constructed fortifications and other government facilities, and also increased the number of officials such as "twelve administrators," thus keeping strict and permanent watch on potential opponents.

However, this national-security program developed contrary to its purpose by furthering the economic crises alluded to in our analysis of the infrastructure of Solomon's society. The various economic crises brought about the decline of the national-security forces and gave opportunities for opponents, such as Jeroboam, to raise rebellions against the government (1 Kings 11:26–40). When Rehoboam, the son of Solomon, became king, the government could no longer contain the rebellion of the northern tribes. As a result, the united monarchy split into a southern kingdom, Judah, and a northern kingdom, Israel.

To sum up, the politics of the united monarchy represented a rise of the centralized military unit and its progressive detachment from the tribal units in the countryside. The conflict widened between central governments and the peasants in both kingdoms in the following three centuries.

The northern kingdom, the end product of the Israelite tribes' revolts against the Davidic dynasty, more clearly showed the conflict between the monarchy and the tribal units as endorsed by the prophets. According to Cross:

> It is fair to say that the institution of prophecy appeared simultaneously with kingship in Israel and fell with kingship. This is no coincidence: the two offices belong to the Israelite political structure which emerged from the conflict between league and kingdom. While prophecy was not an institution of the league, the charismatic principle of leadership which obtained in the era of the Judges survived in its liveliest form in the office of the prophet (1973: 223).

Because of this "charismatic principle of leadership" (the theory of "the charismatic kingship," which was suggested by Alt 1966, has been challenged by Ahlström 1968; Buccellati: 195–212), the northern kingdom also witnessed a constant change in rule. The Bible tells us that each ruler sought his socioeconomic privileges and political power without any change in the social conditions of the peasants.

Under the Davidic dynasty, the southern kingdom continued to strengthen its centralized power, thus promoting the ambitions of the ruling elite in Jerusalem. Specifically, with the development of the mercantilistic economy and the subsequent emergence of urban-center regional towns, there was a growing wealth and power of urban classes, on the one hand, and a growing number of indebted and landless peasants in the countryside. This was probably the chief cause for the failure of the tribal communal economy and the accompanying weakness of its political power. Even the new courts, which replaced the tribal courts, were subject to bribes from the ruling classes and were compromised by the political centralization of the ruling classes. It is here we find "the nation-state of Judah," which "was organized into a prosperous and complex network of regional towns" (McClellan: 279) in order to impose the centralized economic policy of the ruling elite on the tribal units.

After the decline of regional towns in Judah and the fall of Samaria, political centralization in Judah was strengthened in relation to the centralized mercantilistic economy based in Jerusalem. In fact, the destruction of several important regional towns, which had sustained the power structure outside of Jerusalem, crippled the regional urban elite and their means to power. This provided the conditions for the emergence of "a city-state system" of Jerusalem, replacing "the nation-state of Judah." This dramatic change in Judah, which witnessed a rapid development of a system of fortresses, is generally acknowledged by archaeologists and historians as evidence of the extent of the military and political control of the central government in Jerusalem. McClellan observes this "militarization of Judaean society" in the course of the political centralization:

> In place of regional towns a series of fortresses grew up, for example, Ramat Rahel, Tell el-Ful, and Arad, either by reconstruction on destroyed sites, or by totally new construction (Aharoni 1967; Lapp 1976). The fortresses were garrisoned by soldiery which was presumably under the strict disciplinary control of the higher command in Jerusalem . . . The 7th century B.C. in Judah witnessed a militarization of Judaean politics and society, both by default due to the loss of other segments of society and as a result of the active strengthening of the defenses of Judah by construction of new fortresses (283).

Thus the period between the division of the united kingdom in 931 and the seventh century B.C.E. saw the process of political centralization in full effect and the progressive erosion of the tribal system. We assume that this process would be at its peak in Josiah's time. His policies would appear to represent an attack on the religious autonomy of the provincial cities, which also signified an attack on their political autonomy. The result of this would be the elimination of the priesthood of the provincial cities, enabling the central government to keep a politically tight grip on the rural population. To this phase of Josiah's reformation we shall turn now.

The Kingdom of Josiah

We know that the "succession lists" of royal families can reveal socioeconomic conditions as well as political struggles. The succession of Amon's son Josiah, recorded in 2 Kings 21:23–24, is a splendid example of this fact: "Amon's retinue plotted against the king and killed him in his own palace. The people of the country, however, slaughtered all those who had plotted against King Amon and proclaimed his son Josiah as his successor."

Although he was only eight years old, Josiah thus came to the throne as a result of an internal struggle (2 Kings 21:24–26; cf. Malamat 1953 on the historical background of the assassination of Amon, King of Judah). What is important to note here is that the people of the country (land) exercised political power to maintain the Davidic dynasty and, most importantly, their own wealth and power as Davidic retainer families in Jerusalem. There are grounds to believe that they supported Josiah's political authority, with radical implications, not only for the economy of Judah but also for its internal politics, foreign policies, and social institutions. This meant that the policies of the Josianic administration would appear to represent the power and wealth-seeking interests of the ruling elite. Thus an important political question should be asked: How did Josiah exercise political authority under and/or for the ruling elite in the particular area of his reforms?

It was noted above that the decline of Assyrian power gave opportunities for Josiah to take independent action, evident in the massive removal of foreign cults from Judah and Jerusalem, and in the subsequent purification of the cult in the former northern kingdom. It has often been observed that "there existed in Israel, as elsewhere, a strong interconnection between political dependency and religio-cultural dependency" (Weinfeld 1964: 202). By rejecting the foreign cult, Josiah intended to break away from the yoke of Assyrian servitude. This was particularly shown in the case of the destruction of the shrines in Samaria, with a massacre of the priests appointed by the Assyrians. Historically, Josiah succeeded in restoring the autonomy of Judah and in controlling the former territory of Israel, thus keeping the Assyrians away and protecting the land of the former united kingdom. All this gives a picture of his reform as an anti-Assyrian movement and the subsequent assertion of independence; the impression is confirmed by the two well-known prophets of the time, Zephaniah (Zep 2:13–15) and Jeremiah (Jer 2–4).

What can one say about the primary motivation of this intensely anti-Assyrian movement? Does it merely stem from a resurgence of nationalism among the Israelite populace? It is clear from our socioeconomic analyses that, although Judah was under the oppression of Assyria, the populace could feel more oppressed, impoverished, and marginalized by their own ruling class than by the foreign empire. According to Gottwald:

> So skewed was the socioeconomic structure of Israel and Judah in favor of a rapacious minority—a minority no doubt fully convinced of the wisdom and virtue of their policies in the name of "national security"—that by the time of the culminating Assyrian and Neo-Babylonian interventions in 722 and 587 B.C. the rural population was so demoralized and impoverished as to offer only feeble resistance and, with the connivance of some urban elements, to welcome the conquerors as a possible or probable respite from the unrelenting depredations of their own domestic ruling class (1976a: 466).

To be fair to these social conjectures, it must be pointed out that the anti-Assyrian policy would primarily be shaped and agitated by the ruling elite in Jerusalem (cf. the different view that the growth of a powerful peasant movement for national liberation first offered Josiah an available alternative source of power, Claburn 1968, 1973). By securing the autonomy of Judah and the control of Israel, they intended to promote the centralized mercantilistic economic policy in Jerusalem. So it was with the power- and wealth-seeking interests of the ruling elite in Josiah's reform. We believe that nationalism, the well-known policy of Josiah, came mainly from political propaganda of the ruling elite. Their political gains were skillfully concealed beneath the popular anti-Assyrian policy. It would appear that such a political program was especially manifested in the second stage, where the ruling elite displayed their political power and abilities to the full.

We have noted that the second stage of Josiah's reform was aimed at the centralization of the cult in the Temple of Jerusalem by claiming that the local shrines had performed a more or less contaminated worship of Yahweh. But contaminated worship was the claim of the local shrines against Jerusalem, as well. Was the rural population easily subjected to the imposition of the official Yahweh cult by the ruling elite of Jerusalem? A problem lies in the absence of any reference by Zephaniah or Jeremiah to centralization of the cult in the Temple of Jerusalem (cf. Weinfeld 1964: 209). It is important to consider these aspects of the social context in the second stage of Josiah's reform. His policy, the centralization of the cult in the Jerusalem Temple, would scarcely have had the support of a majority of the populace of Judah. In light of this, it is important to see very carefully how the ruling elite succeeded in carrying out the second stage.

Most scholars agree that the second stage followed the discovery of the law book in the Temple of Jerusalem. "Nothing," Dentan comments, "is told us as to precisely how it was found. It is said only that Hilkiah, the priest in charge of the Temple, announced its discovery to Shaphan the scribe, who then read it before the king" (120–21; cf. 2 Kings 22:3–10). After that, Josiah tore his clothes as a gesture of despair and repentance and gave an order to the court officials to consult the official prophetess, Huldah, about God's intentions (2 Kings 22:11–13). The content of the divine oracle, announced by the prophetess, basically consisted of the judgment of God on the Israelite people for their apostasy (2 Kings 22:14–20). Subsequently, this oracle led the king to call the assembly of the people and to embark on the concentration of the cult in the Jerusalem Temple.

Viewed politically, this decision-making process of the Josianic reform fits well into a centralized political system in which the ruling power has a monopoly of force, as in the exclusive access to the law book. It is interesting to note that "the schematised account in Kings makes the law book of primary importance as the only incentive for the reform" (Jones: 604). But how was this book found? Was it the document of the covenant with Yahweh? This should have been the subject of a lively debate in that time!

Nevertheless, it is said only that the authenticity of the book was validated by a Jerusalemite prophetess, Huldah, who was a court prophet during the reign of Josiah. And the king read out "the entire contents" of this book, and put into effect the reform program set forth in the book (2 Kings 23). Thus the stage for the reform was set by the king and his court officials. The rest of the Israelite population was made up of mere observers in this political process. The erosion of the tribal system, whatever its extent, would surely have contributed to this political neglect of the populace in the shaping of national policy. The political relations among the Israelite people of Josiah's time was, assuredly, based on membership in a centralized and hierarchical political system. More importantly, this political system was the basic structure into which the ruling class incorporated political-economic programs when the centralized administration established the new laws and sanctions.

This was particularly true in the case of the provincial priests who were brought to serve in the Jerusalem Temple. In this case, Josiah appears to have inaugurated measures to put into force the law of Deuteronomy 18: 6–8:

> If a Levite living in one of your towns anywhere in Israel decides to move to the place chosen by Yahweh, he shall minister there in the name of Yahweh his God like all his fellow Levites who stand ministering there in the presence of Yahweh, eating equal shares with them—what he has from the sale of his patrimony notwithstanding.

We have already noted, however, that Josiah in actual practice changed this Deuteronomic law of priestly institutions by force; the city priests set rules governing the behavior of the country Levite priests in the Temple. And it is clear that Josiah did this not so that, by the new law, the country Levite priests "did share the unleavened bread of their brother-priests" (2 Kings 23:9), but so that they were set to "manual labour" (Herrmann: 266). It is evident that the ruling class abused political power in the application of the Deuteronomic laws.

Modern scholarship generally agrees that "the basic form of the book [Deuteronomy] was first composed during the later part of Manasseh's reign or in the early part of Josiah's reign [ca. 650–640 B.C.]. And while no direct evidence exists, it is thought that a group of prophets or priests in Jerusalem was responsible for the collection and ordering of the material of that first edition" (Bratcher: 219). This understanding is only partially correct, however. In fact, the court intellectuals composed the basic form of the book in the last half of the seventh century B.C.E. in the interests of cultic reform, but as de Vaux and Von Rad suggested, the original Deuteronomic tradition had already been edited by the northern Levite priests (de Vaux 1965: 338–9; Von Rad 1966: 23–30). This material was brought to Jerusalem after the fall of Samaria, and served the southern ruling class in their attempts to centralize the kingdom's social activities in Jerusalem, as in the reformation of Hezekiah. In this view the Deuteronomic demands for according the same privileges to Levitical priests as to city priests was the product of the interests of the northern Levite priests.

Judging by the strong centralized political system of Josiah, it is quite probable that the state apparatus, while protecting and furthering the socio-economic interests of the ruling elite, abused political power for its own self-interests in the collecting and ordering of the material from ancient traditions, the original Deuteronomic tradition in particular, and even in the enacting of new laws. While presenting a reform of the fiscal system and a subsequent concentration of the peasantry's agricultural surplus in Jerusalem as the basis of Josiah's reforms, Claburn has isolated three Deuteronomic regulations made for "the feasibility of the new fiscal system." In our judgment, these are more examples of the Deuteronomic laws which were changed to fit into the Josianic ruling class's own interests:

> 1. Those living farthest away would have to be allowed to sell the tithe portion of their grain and bring the easier-to-carry silver to Jerusalem in the assessed amount (Dt 14:24–25);
>
> 2. The peasants would in any case have to be partially compensated for the extra transport costs to themselves by allowing them to deduct their travelling expenses from the amount of the tax due—i.e., to live out of the assessed tithe during the trip (Dt 12:7, 12, 18; 14:23, 26; 16:7–8, 11, 14; 26:11);
>
> 3. The seasonal collection days in the capital would have to be turned into a more impressive celebration than ever before to give the peasants additional positive motivation to go up to the capital to do the king's new thing (2 Kings 23:22–23) (Claburn 1973: 16–17).

By understanding the administrative apparatus of Josiah's time, subject as it was to bribes, this fiscal system would probably aim at the maximizing of surpluses for the ruling elite. (The exploitive effect of this new fiscal system will be discussed in the treatment of Josiah's Passover in the forthcoming chapter.) Then it must be said that what is sought in the practice of these laws is not the protecting of the rural population and the provincial political autonomy, but rather the reinforcing of the centralized political system of the court. Thus the laws were reshaped for further development of the centralized mercantilistic economy in Jerusalem. In line with this policy, it is very probable that the court intellectuals recited the Deuteronomic Law on the old-fashioned form of military organization to draft the free peasants for the reform campaigns.

There is one more important aspect to the political process of Josiah's reform which has to be taken into consideration. It is possible, from 2 Kings 23:1–3, that the landless working class could have been motivated to support the reform. The problem that arises can be put this way: If 2 Kings

23:1–3 does not derive mostly from an ideological product or from simple propaganda on the part of the Josianic court circle, then one must posit that for the landless working people, and in particular the Jerusalemite workers, Josiah's reform would have brought extensive benefits.

As noted, Jerusalem in Josiah's days turned into a so-called tyrannical city, where the majority of the populace were migrants and lived in stark poverty. They were struggling for existence. According to our understanding of this fact, the reform would appear to have brought about the following advantages in the lives of Jerusalemites:

1. The expansion of the Israelite borders could have led to an expansion of a military force, thus increasing the number of mercenaries hired by the Jerusalem court.

2. The reform not only could have brought about an increase in the concentration of the peasants' agricultural surplus in Jerusalem, but also an expansion of the transit trade. This meant that Jerusalem now could become a major agricultural processing center and a major labor market.

3. The tyrannical city, Jerusalem, had witnessed the social and economic inequities threatening to rend the populace. To prevent an explosion, Josiah's government could have embarked on a series of social programs providing welfare, the usual "bread and circuses." The king could most efficiently have obtained the necessary resources by his reforms.

4. The restoration of the territory of the northern state meant an increase of royal land, and could have led to political propaganda for land reform in favor of the landless peasants.

These aspects remain largely conjectural, but the possibility cannot be excluded. The pascal celebration of 2 Chronicles 35:1–18 is, for instance, a literary memory of the probable existence of Josiah's social programs, seen in the distribution of food to the landless workers of Jerusalem.

More importantly, the welfare policies would also serve as the basis for the neutralizing of any "anti-establishment group" (Cohen 1979: 14). While presenting a sociopolitical analysis of the prophetic messages, specifically about the sacrificial cult, Cohen argues:

> Politically, the prophetic message is an anti-establishment message. Regardless of whether the aim of the prophets was reformation or abolition of the sacrificial cult, their indictments certainly challenged and threatened the institutions supporting the cult (1979: 14).

Accordingly, he continues:

For example, there is every reason to suppose, on typological grounds, that large segments of the disadvantaged Israelite populace in the eighth and seventh centuries B.C. remained loyal to the cult as the instrument of their hope, and recoiled angrily at all efforts to link its practitioners to their misfortune. By the same token, there is also every reason to suppose that messages such as those articulated by the prophets were supported by upper class elements, including some on the fringes of authority and power who wished thereby to enhance their political position. Indeed, the occasional suggestion that the prophets themselves may have been, broadly speaking, members of the cultic establishment, is consistent with this possibility. Jeremiah was a priest and, through Anathoth, connected to the Shilonites. Amos in all likelihood was not a humble shepherd and sycamore-dresser (1979: 15–16).

In this political version of the prophetic messages, Zephaniah, who worked in the reign of Josiah, had a general profile on "the fringes of authority and power," while stating his rebuke of court officials (Zep 1:8) and yet maintaining his silence about the king. His messages of justice and humility would be undermined by the government's investment in social programs providing "jobs and food" for the impoverished landless workers.

At any rate, it is important to realize that Josiah's reform does not appear in our social analyses as a social-change program in favor of the rural population. Rather, the reform was produced as a series of socioeconomic programs investing heavily in the development of the centralized mercantilistic economy, as well as in a social program maintaining the landless working class as cheap labor.

This understanding is crucial to our combating the fundamentalist and idealist hermeneutics that have obfuscated the realities of Josiah's reform in cultural and theological traditions for so many years. Formerly, the reform did not represent socioeconomic programs, but was presented as a pious and religious movement that was aimed at purifying the Yahweh cult. In the following section we will examine the ideological and religious dimension of Josiah's reform that reflects the power- and wealth-seeking interests of the ruling class of that time.

IDEOLOGICAL ANALYSIS

The Historical Background

We have seen that the revolutionary peasants, under the leadership of the biblical Israelites, established an "egalitarian society" in the Canaanite highlands. It was a movement of the oppressed classes in Canaan, which focused their hope for liberation from the oppressive tributary rule of the

Canaanite city-states. As such, their communal economic system and tribal organization meant a departure from the socioeconomic and political system of the city-states.

This departure has also been seen in the religious organization and ideology of early Israel. Passages that deal with the time of Israel's emergence in Canaan reveal such religious and ideological departure:

> The men of Israel said to Gideon, "Rule over us, you, your son and your grandson, since you have rescued us from the power of Midian." But Gideon replied, "I will not rule you, neither will my son. Yahweh shall rule you" (Jgs 8:22–23).

The narrative is undoubtedly antimonarchical and throws light on political and religious concepts of that time: early Israel was not living under human rulers but under Yahweh's kingship. So, Yahwism here gave expression to revolutionary Israel's movement against the political domination of tyrannical Canaanite city rulers. How did Yahweh's kingship come to be accepted and developed by the revolutionary peasants who used to worship Canaanite gods such as Baal?

We read in the sources that it was the Levites, with their liberation experience from Egypt, who brought Yahwism into Israel's movement. Yahweh, who accompanied this group in their struggle against the Pharaoh, was against a hierarchical society. Unlike the gods of Israel's neighbors, Yahweh therefore did not provide an ideological support for Canaanite class society, but sought the liberation of its oppressed members. This action and notion of Yahweh assuredly blended well into the ideology and faith of the revolutionary peasants, who were in their struggle against exploitation by the kings of the cities of Canaan.

Thus it came about that the revolutionary peasants formed a covenant with Yahweh and one another to constitute their egalitarian society under Yahweh's kingship. In reality, it was Yahweh's kingship that served as an ideological justification and religious support for the antitributary Israelite society. The issue appears to be indicated by the following main points:

Tribal ownership of land: This practice, which was one of the most important factors of early Israel's communal economy, was fueled by the concept of Yahweh's ownership of land (cf. Lv 25).

Tribal federation and its assemblies: This socio-constitutional organization was underlined by the covenant with Yahweh. There could be no state in early Israel because Yahweh was the true king, thus maintaining a politically uncentralized unit (cf. Dt 33).

Tribal army: This army was commanded by Yahweh, a "warrior" God, whose presence was manifested in the ark of covenant, symbol of Yahweh's throne (cf. Jgs 5; 1 Sm 4:3–5).

Tribal cultic celebrations: There were centralized and localized tendencies in Israel's cultic celebration (cf. Ex 20, 24).

Israel's cultic celebrations thus promoted a confederacy of Israelite tribes, supporting the autonomy of each tribe. Passover was, for instance, celebrated by the extended families, bonding interfamilial relationship. Yet recent critical scholarship argues that the prohibition of divine images in early Israel reflects its refusal to accept the ideology of kingship in the ancient Near East, in which "the king was regarded as the earthly representative of the gods, and as such the image of the god was a symbol of the legitimacy of the earthly king" (Hendel: 380).

In this way the egalitarian tribal social system of Israel was maintained. It is little wonder that early Israel's commitment to a covenant with Yahweh reflected a strong concern with its egalitarian social organization. Unlike neighboring gods, Yahweh was a covenantal partner of the oppressed people, and this covenantal concept of early Israel was developed and maintained by the Levites, represented by the Mushite priesthood of Shiloh and Nob.

Most scholars assume that this covenantal tradition of early Israel, known as the Mosaic covenant tradition, shaped and formed Israel's literature and its theological vision in terms of a God who liberates those who suffer under oppression. In the Mosaic tradition, God's relation to the Israelite community, Brueggemann states, is presented in terms of a tent, asserting "a claim of mobility and freedom for God" (1984: 314). The tent is, in fact, a projection of Israelite tribal egalitarian society in relation to tributary Canaanite society. Accordingly, Brueggemann continues: "The Mosaic tradition tends to be a movement of protest which is situated among the disinherited and which articulates its theological vision in terms of a God who decisively intrudes, even against seemingly impenetrable institutions and orderings" (1984:308).

It was, however, the emergence of monarchy in Israel that allowed a formulation of another major tradition in Israel's literature concerning covenant. Passages that deal with the time of Saul reveal some ambiguity in tribal religious organization and indicate a crisis of tribal Yahwism, for example, with regard to the tribal army,

> Saul then said to Ahijah, "Bring the ephod," since he was the man who carried the ephod in Israel. [Following the Greek text; the Hebrew text reads " 'Bring the ark of God.' For the ark of God was then in Israelite hands."] But while Saul was speaking to the priest, the turmoil in the Philistine camp grew worse and worse; and Saul said to the priest, "Withdraw your hand," Saul and the whole force with him then formed up and advanced to where the fighting was going on: and there they all were, drawing their swords on one another in wild confusion (1 Sm 14:18–20).

The text explicitly states that Saul went out to battle without consulting the oracle of Yahweh, obtained by the ephod. Yet, 1 Samuel 13–15 present

an account of Saul's rejection. At the heart of this narrative, as most scholars recognize, is a conflict between Saul and Samuel, the latter who was
heir to tribal Yahwism, presented in the Mosaic covenant tradition. By
understanding this fact, Saul's action was a statement that the Yahwism of
early Israel could no longer serve as an all-embracing constitutional framework for society. Once the tribal society, with its egalitarian and antiking-
ship bias, was rejected by the class interests of a ruling elite, tribal Yahwism,
which was an ideological product of the tribal society, was also rejected by
them.

There is, therefore, no doubt that the emergence of the Israelite monarchy brought about a change in the religious institutions and ideology of
Israel, thus resulting in the formulation of a new covenant tradition. Actually, this tradition started to take shape during the time of David, who had
the ability to take up the traditional religious organization for his own
political success. The following case can be cited:

> When Abiathar son of Ahimelech took refuge with David, he went
> down to Keilah with the ephod in his hand. When word was brought
> to Saul that David had gone to Keilah he said, "God has delivered
> him into my power: he has trapped himself by going into a town with
> gates and bars." Saul called all the people to arms, to go down to
> Keilah and besiege David and his men. David however, was aware
> that Saul was plotting evil against him, and said to Abiathar the priest,
> "Bring the ephod." David said, "Yahweh, God of Israel, your servant
> has heard that Saul is preparing to come to Keilah and destroy the
> town because of me. Will Saul come down as your servant has heard?
> Yahweh, God of Israel, I beg you, let your servant know." Yahweh
> replied, "He will come down." David then went on to ask, "Will the
> notables of Keilah hand me and my men over to Saul?" Yahweh
> replied, "They will hand you over." At this, David made off with his
> men, about six hundred in number; they left Keilah and went where
> they could. When Saul was told that David had escaped from Keilah,
> he abandoned the expedition (1 Sm 23:6–13).

It is important to recognize that David was able to survive because of
the protection of tribal Yahweh, represented by Abiathar, the priest of
Nob, and the ephod. In practice this meant that David managed to take
advantage of the traditional religious organization to win political and ideological legitimacy from his struggle against King Saul. Unlike Saul, who
struggled against the traditional religious organization (1 Sm 22:6–23),
David thus made this organization a justification for his kingship. Later the
control of Yahwism by David served to legitimatize his united kingdom:
"So all the elders of Israel came to the King at Hebron, and King David
made a pact with them in Yahweh's presence at Hebron, and they anointed
David as king of Israel" (2 Sm 5:3).

All of this should indicate that Yahweh's covenant with Israel was reshaped under David's monarchy. The new covenant, known as the Davidic covenant, laid the political foundation for David's kingdom. Now Yahweh was not a direct covenantal partner of the people of Israel, but of King David. This partnership between Yahweh and David was assuredly enforced by the presence of the ark in Jerusalem, the city of David (cf. 2 Sm 6:1–19). The transport of the ark to Jerusalem with pomp and ceremony tended to justify and support the socioeconomic and political claims of David's group by painting them as true representatives of tribal Yahweh. In practice this ideological justification and religious support would have occurred in the following way:

The royal ownership of land: King David appropriated the Canaanite land by a "holy war" of conquest. We suspect that David, as representative of Yahweh, may also have assumed the right of intervening in the distribution of tribal land that fell vacant (cf. 1 Sm 31; 2 Sm 19:25–31; 21:1–14).

Tribal organization: Under the guarantee of Yahweh, his covenantal partner, King David may have organized "the twelve-tribe scheme" to enforce his tributary system and a subsequent political centralization (cf. 2 Sm 24: 1–9).

Tribal army: King David assumed a territorial command of this army in the cause of aggrandizement of his wealth and security (cf. 2 Sm 8).

National cultic celebration: Jerusalem, the city of David, became a holy city because it was now the resting place of the ark of covenant (cf. 2 Sm 6:16–19).

In the Davidic covenant, Yahweh no longer represented revolutionary Israel's movement, but the power- and wealth-seeking interests of David's monarchy. This was an important turning point in the Yahwist ideology of Israel. What seems clear is that the Davidic group started to foster in Israel a belief that Yahweh legitimated the monarchic system and demanded exclusive loyalty to the king from the people. This royal ideology was further developed and made the dominant covenant tradition during the time of Solomon.

King Solomon, David's successor, who developed the national-security program, took three main measures to provide an ideological justification and religious support for this program. First, King Solomon eliminated Abiathar, an heir of tribal Yahwism, and in his place appointed Zadok, of Aaronite descent, who seemed to be rooted in Hebron and, eventually, in Jerusalem (cf. 1 Kings 2:26–27; Cross 1973; 195–215). The control of Zadok's family over the Jerusalem priesthood enhanced a royal and urban religious activity as the ideological justification of Solomon's economic policy. Second, the Jerusalem Temple was built with architectural roots in the Phoenician city-states (cf. Harden 1968: 89). The Temple, erected on "crown property," was a "royal sanctuary" (Von Rad 1962: 43). By bringing the ark into this Temple, Solomon controlled the mobility and freedom of tribal Yahwism. Third, Solomon, who made a remarkable increase in the number of officials, such as priests and scribes, definitely developed a royal theology in which "the Davidic house now becomes not only historically important but theologically decisive for the future of Israel and all promises and futures are now under the dominance of this institution" (Brueggemann 1984: 314–15).

What we are faced with, in Israel's religious organization and its theological vision, is evidence to show a consolidation of the Davidic covenant tradition during the time of Solomon. There is no doubt that this royal ideology, presented in terms of "house," was committed to the maintenance of the Davidic house and its all socio-constitutional framework, at the cost of the antimonarchic ideology. Does this mean that the government had driven away the revolutionary peasant movement and its Mosaic covenant tradition? The significance of tribal Yahwism that supported the peasants in organizing rebellions against the kings was not to be dismissed lightly, as Sheba's rebellion and Jeroboam's revolt clearly attest. In practice this meant that there was a theological dispute during the time of the united monarchy between two traditions, the Mosaic covenant and the Davidic covenant, reflecting the antimonarchic movement and the maintenance of monarchic order, respectively. This theological dispute can be discerned in developments throughout the following two centuries.

It is clear that the Davidic covenant tradition was a dominant ideological framework, at least in the southern kingdom, which remained under the Davidic dynasty. Furthermore, with a strong tendency to develop a centralized economic policy that favored the Davidic ruling elite at the expense of a depressed underclass, this royal ideology progressed rapidly, thus enhancing the ideological justification of exclusive loyalty of the people to David and his descendants. This can be observed in the rehearsal of the Davidic covenant in Psalm 89:

> "I have made a covenant with my Chosen One, sworn an
>   oath to my servant David:
> I have made your dynasty firm for ever,
> built your throne stable age after age" . . .
> "His dynasty shall endure for ever,
> his throne like the sun before me,
> as the moon is established
> for ever, a faithful witness in the skies" (vv. 3–4, 36–37).

Numerous Psalms intimate this royal ideology that legitimated David as the son of Yahweh and insured the power of the Davidic house over the people. Furthermore, this Davidic king was presented as the great defender of "children of the needy." Psalm 72, dedicated to Solomon, evokes the image of the righteous king:

> God, endow the king with your own fair judgment,
>   the son of the king with your own saving justice,

that he may rule your people with justice,
and your poor with fair judgement.

Mountains and hills,
bring peace to the people!
With justice he will judge the poor of the people,
he will save the children of the needy and
crush their oppressors (vv. 1–4).

It seems likely that the ruling class of that time co-opted such a strong doctrine of Davidic covenant to serve an ideological justification of their own socio-constitutional framework, based on the mercantilistic economy. Needless to say, it was the priests and scribes of the Jerusalem Temple, dependent on benefices of the court, who produced such a royal theology.

Already implied in the foregoing analyses is the remarkable presence of the old tribal tradition in the northern kingdom in the ninth to eighth centuries B.C.E. The significance of the Mosaic covenant tradition that limits and criticizes the institution of kingship is clearly attested to in the phenomenon of prophecy, for example, in Elijah's condemnation against Ahab in 1 Kings 21, as well as in the later confrontation between Amos and Amaziah in Amos 7:10–17. It has often been observed that the "ideology of kingship in Israel, at least in prophetic circles, presumed the conditional and covenantal character of kingship in the north" (Cross 1973: 227). It is, therefore, hardly surprising that the Mosaic covenant tradition, "the patriarchal-Exodus tradition" in terms of Von Rad (1962: 47), is conserved more faithfully in the northern kingdom than in the southern kingdom.

In line with these observations, most scholars argue that the original Deuteronomic traditions, which contain a core of material from the Mosaic covenant tradition, were probably fostered in the northern kingdom. But there is a curious problem about the Deuteronomic laws concerning cultic centralization. Von Rad questioned if these laws "could be understood merely by reference to the situation in Jerusalem at the time of King Josiah" (1966: 27). In fact, according to him and others, the northern Levite priests were, at least in part, responsible for the collection of the material, specifically the sacral and legal traditional material in the Deuteronomic traditions. This may be an explanation for the sociotheological evidence that the demands of cultic centralization may well have been made in the northern Levite priests' circles earlier than the time of Josiah's reform. Sociologically, this hypothesis is supposed to explain the presence of the power struggle of priestly interests in the northern kingdom, particularly between the priesthoods at Bethel and Dan. For these reasons, we believe that the original Deuteronomic traditions contained not only the Mosaic covenant tradition, but such a doctrine of cultic centralization at the national sanctuaries, reflecting the socio-constitutional framework of the northern ruling class of that time. In this version of the original Deuteronomic tradition, we are also in a position to understand the Passover in Deuteronomy 16:1–8, which we studied earlier in chapter 1. The Exodus tradition and the cultic centralization, which are firmly anchored in the D's Passover, would mostly derive from the northern Levite priests.

In some ways the dispute between the antimonarchic and the royal traditions persisted in the ninth to eighth centuries B.C.E., more clearly in the northern kingdom. The revolutionary peasant movement there still appears not to have resigned itself to monarchic subjection. But there was a big turning point. The northern kingdom fell to the Assyrian empire. This led to the deportation of the ruling classes, including the priests of the national sanctuaries. Subsequently, the Assyrians seem to have imposed their imprint on the Israelite religious organization to secure their domination. The fall of Samaria and the continuing Assyrian imperialism also had an important impact on the religious organization of Judean society and its theological vision.

Assyrian imperialism made Judah's social system more centralized in the hands of the Jerusalemite ruling elite, thus encouraging a social pathology. Even the massive migration resulting mainly from the fall of Samaria and the devastation of Judean urban centers exacerbated these socioeconomic inequities in Jerusalem.

The voice of prophetic protest arose in the south. Isaiah, a prophet whose principal message was a purification of the holy city, declaimed against the moral corruption of the ruling elite and preached justice and righteousness as civic virtues. His theological vision, however, drew a distinct line in prophetic interpretation and doctrine. Unlike the northern prophets such as Amos, whose messages were rooted in the Mosaic covenant tradition, Isaiah clearly proposed a social reform within the monarchic social-constitutional framework, rooted in the Davidic covenant tradition. In his theological vision, the royal Yahwist ideology appears to be more sophisticated, and it began to blend into the Mosaic covenant tradition in a way that served the institution of kingship itself. Isaiah announced such a royal ideology:

> A shoot will spring from
>   the stock of Jesse,
> a new shoot will grow from his roots.
> On him will rest the spirit of Yahweh,
> the spirit of wisdom and insight,
> the spirit of counsel and power,
> the spirit of knowledge
>   and fear of Yahweh:
> his inspiration will lie in fearing Yahweh.
> His judgement will not be by appearances,
> his verdict not given on hearsay.
> He will judge the weak with integrity

and give fair sentence
  for the humblest in the land (Is 11:1–4).

There is no doubt that Isaiah described the characteristics of the coming
Messiah under the Davidic covenant tradition. The Messiah, of Davidic
stock, would be filled with the spirit of Yahweh and restore justice in Jerusalem (Is 1:26–27), including punishment against Judah's leaders (Is 22:15–
25). But this restoration deals in-depth with the purification of the Davidic
house itself, securing the continuity of the Davidic dynasty (Is 9:1–6; 11:1–
10). In an ideological context, the egalitarian theology — as an original core
of the Mosaic tradition — was incorporated into the royal ideology to sustain
the Davidic monarchic society. As part of this theological tendency, "the
royal Zion ideology that started during the time of David" (Mosala: 119)
was developed further to legitimize Jerusalem, the city of David, as the
center of the Israelite society. Isaiah announced:

> The faithful city,
> what a harlot she has become!
> Zion, once full of fair judgement,
> where saving justice used to dwell,
> but now assassins!
>
> Your silver has turned into dross,
> your wine is watered.
> Your princes are rebels,
> accomplices of brigands.
> All of them greedy for presents
> and eager for bribes,
> they show no justice to the orphan,
> and the widow's cause never reaches them.
>
> Hence, the Lord Yahweh Sabaoth,
> the Mighty One of Israel, says this,
> "Disaster, I shall get the better
>   of my enemies,
> I shall avenge myself on my foes.
>
> "I shall turn my hand against you,
> I shall purge your dross
>   as though with potash,
> I shall remove all your alloy.
>
> "And I shall restore your judges as at first,
> your counsellors as in bygone days,

after which you will be called
City of Saving Justice,
Faithful City" (Is 1:21–26).

It is not very difficult to observe that this poem reflects the tradition in which Zion was presented as "a city of righteousness." "Staying within the Jerusalem royal theology," Pixley perceptively states, "he [Isaiah] announced a purification of the holy city like the purification of metal to remove impurities, after which the city would truly be a city of righteousness, as the cult practitioners said it was" (1981: 52). Surely Isaiah's messages, messianism, and the Zion traditions, were "an anti-establishment message," threatening the existing ruling officials, but not intending to change the existing social system. The Davidic dynasty and its city, Jerusalem, remained the unchallenged cornerstone of the Judean society.

So there is every reason to suppose, on ideological grounds, that the broad popular humanitarian and eschatological theology in the late eighth to seventh century B.C.E. was strongly rooted in the royal social-constitutional framework, centralized more and more in Jerusalem. All in all, this "Jerusalem theology" took the Mosaic covenant tradition in the royal version of the covenant, the partnership of Davidic kings with Yahweh. As part of this effort, the Mosaic covenant tradition was reproduced, to make it the ideological justification for a royal reform project rather than a peasant revolutionary project. The outstanding example among these royal reform projects was Josiah's reform.

Of course, it should not be forgotten that there is a double Deuteronomistic redaction in the Book of Kings. As attested in chapter 2, the first Deuteronomic or Deuteronomistic theology was most likely composed in a court circle under a strong Davidic theology. Apparently and reasonably, this theology was modified to fit the circumstances of the Babylonian exile. The exilic Deuteronomists were concerned not only with an explanation for the fall of Israel's monarchies but also with the "mechanism for survival" to maintain the Israelite "identity, social structure, and religious/cultural life under stress" (D. L. Smith: 11). In this process, the Mosaic covenant tradition became more and more important, and was blended into the social life of the exilic people. It is likely, therefore, that the Davidic covenant tradition was to be conditioned by the Mosaic covenant tradition in a second and final revision of the Deuteronomistic history.

The Kingdom of Josiah

We have seen that the Josianic reform was engaged in-depth in the power- and wealth-seeking interests of the Jerusalemite ruling elite. The impression is confirmed by Zephaniah's strong indictments against the ruling elite in his nation (Zep 3:1–5). The cultic centralization and subsequent expanding social inequities in Judah were properly the target of bitter criticism from rural circles.

Faced with this criticism, the ruling elite assuredly necessitated a royal propaganda that would sustain the institutional status quo and counteract their opponents. Cohen has a sense for this when, after analyzing the prophetic attacks on the cult, he perceptively describes the reaction of the institutions supporting the cult:

> The cult leaders (the ruling class), we may be sure, indignantly denied the charge of rampant corruption. They categorically rejected the implication of their own involvement in unethical conduct or practice. On the contrary, they no doubt listed a respectable catalogue of their own contributions to the welfare of society. They doubtless credited themselves with unquestioned achievements, including such stability as did exist then and in the past. For the cult leadership, the source of any instability, malaise or corruption could be found in the preachings of opposition spokesmen, whom the cult leadership probably characterized as rabble-rousing demagogues! (1979: 14).

In line with this policy, it is little wonder that the Zadokite priests and scribes of the Jerusalem Temple, who worked with the royal religious organization and its theological production, attempted to justify Josiah's reform. From their viewpoint, Josiah was:

> eight years old when he came to the throne, and he reigned for thirty-one years in Jerusalem. His mother's name was Jedidah daughter of Adaiah, of Bozkath. He did what Yahweh regards as right, and in every respect followed the example of his ancestor David (2 Kings 22:1–2).

In this introduction to the reign of Josiah, the most important character in Josiah's religious organization and its theological vision comes on the scene: his ancestor David. In one stroke, the text confers on Josiah the outstanding virtues of his great ancestor. Within this Davidic tradition, the royal reform implemented by Josiah in his attempt to restore the Davidic empire was officially an execution of Yahweh's justice on earth.

It is not very difficult to establish the main outlines of royal propaganda in support of the reform. King Josiah, of Davidic stock, was presented as a truly Davidic king, a veritable messiah, to establish a neo-Davidic empire. His program of national purification and expansion in the first stage of the reform was possible because of the doctrine that he was the executor of the national liberation movement against the Assyrians. In this royal version of the reform, the liberation theology of the Mosaic tradition was transformed into a royal doctrine that sustained the national consensus of liberation.

The landless peasant phenomenon in Judah may have been an important factor in Josiah's success in promoting this neo-liberation theology. Sociologically speaking, the landless peasants were an uprooted people whose lands were first grabbed by their own rulers and later by the Assyrian policy of deportation. The migrants were seeking the restoration of their lands, and, in this context, the appeal of Josiah to restore the northern territories was brought near enough to win a great degree of support from the dispossessed masses.

Within the Davidic covenant tradition, the court intellectuals also developed royal propaganda for the second stage of the reform, cult centralization — even more than the first stage. First, as is well-known, most scholars have long been aware of the problem of the discovery of the book of the law, and "have spoken of a 'pious fraud' on the part of the Jerusalem priesthood to endorse their own prestige" (Soggin: 244). For instance, according to Gottwald:

> When Deuteronomy is viewed as the end stage of a long process of covenant making and law recitation by a priesthood affected by prophets and collaboration with court officials, its "finding" in the temple in Josiah's reign need no longer be explained as a "pious fraud" to validate Mosaic authorship (1985: 389).

It is little wonder that those court officials recited the Deuteronomic laws concerning cultic centralization in support of the Josianic reform:

> You must completely destroy all the places where the nations you dispossess have served their gods, on high mountains, on hills, under any spreading tree; you must tear down their altars, smash their sacred stones, burn their sacred poles, hack to bits the statues of their gods and obliterate their name from that place. Not so must you behave towards Yahweh your God. You must seek Yahweh your God in the place which he will choose from all your tribes, there to set his name and give it a home: that is where you must go (Dt 12:2–5).

In the Davidic covenant tradition, "Yahweh imposed conditions on himself, namely, eternal and exclusive loyalty to David and his descendants" (Pixley 1981: 47). Yahweh gave the Davidic kingship, so to speak, a monopoly on legitimate religious practice in Israel. Yahweh had manifested himself in the Jerusalem Temple, the city of the Davidic house, which had been approved as the unique sanctuary for the official worship of Yahweh.

This law on the unique sanctuary was certainly a decisive element in the royal propaganda the court intellectuals wanted to create for cult centralization. Along with this propaganda went the legitimacy of Josiah as a true Davidic king. This is particularly clear in the covenant-making ceremony, which was an impressive attempt to make King Josiah into the true Davidic king: "I have made a covenant with my Chosen One, sworn an oath to my servant David" (Ps 89:3). The text of the renewal of the covenant, most of which was composed in the Josianic court circle with skillful use of the Mosaic covenant language, gives direct testimony to the manner in which King Josiah was presented as the direct covenantal partner of Yahweh:

> In their hearing he [Josiah] read out the entire contents of the Book of the Covenant discovered in the Temple of Yahweh. The king then, standing on the dais, bound himself by the covenant before Yahweh, to follow Yahweh, to keep his commandments, decrees and laws with all his heart and soul, and to carry out the terms of the covenant as written in this book. All the people pledged their allegiance to the covenant (2 Kings 23:2b–3).

So it was, to secure the all-important popular support for the court ideology, that the presentation was expressed in terms of the familiar Mosaic language, making it simple for the people to pledge "their allegiance to the covenant," and consequently to King Josiah.

Upon this foundation of Yahweh's covenant with the truly Davidic king Josiah, the priests and scribes of the Jerusalem Temple based their royal propaganda for the legitimacy of King Josiah, "my Chosen One," with elements largely borrowed from the Mosaic covenant tradition. One of the elements of the royal propaganda was probably the humanitarian laws of Deuteronomy (12–26), by which we know of the outstanding virtues of the truly Davidic king who defends the weaker members of the Israelite community. For the landless peasants, the Deuteronomic laws concerning familial property, for instance, deeply moved their sentiments: "You must not displace your neighbour's boundary mark, positioned by men of old in the heritage soon to be yours, in the country which Yahweh your God is about to give you" (Dt 19:14). In this way, Josiah was able to take advantage of the old tribal traditions in responding to the petitions of the landless people to present himself as a successful king, "following the example of his ancestor David."

Passages that deal with the religious reform in Judah reveal another element in the court intellectuals' ideological production to support Josiah's bloody campaign against the local sanctuaries:

> The king ordered Hilkiah with the priest next in rank and the guardians of the threshold to remove all the cult objects which had been made for Baal, Asherah and the whole array of heaven; he burnt them outside Jerusalem in the fields of the Kidron and had the ashes taken to Bethel. He exterminated the spurious priests whom the kings of Judah had appointed and who offered sacrifice on the high places, in the towns of Judah and the neighbourhood of Jerusalem; also those

who offered sacrifice to Baal, to the sun, the moon, the constellations and the whole array of heaven (2 Kings 23:4–5).

According to the classic explanation for the cult in ancient Israel, the worship of Asherah, a Canaanite goddess who was strongly linked to Baal, was non-Yahwist. But this explanation has recently been challenged by Saul M. Olyan, who, after studying all references and alleged references to Asherah and examining epigraphic and archeological data from Israel and from Canaanite religion, concludes that the anti-Asherah polemic is "restricted to the Deuteronomistic History or to materials which betray the influence of deuteronomistic language and theology" (1988: 3). He writes:

The biblical evidence from both the north and the south suggests that the asherah was a standard and legitimate part of the cult of Yahweh in non-deuteronomistic circles, probably even among very conservative groups, as the Jehu traditions and the silence of the books of Amos and Hosea seem to indicate (1988: 9).

Accordingly, he continues:

In the case of the asherah, the deuteronomists associate it with the cult of Baal. Extra-biblical evidence, in contrast, suggests both that the asherah was a legitimate symbol in Yahweh's cult, and that the goddess Asherah was never associated intimately with Baal in Canaanite religion (1988: 73).

Here we have a clear example of theological production of the priests and scribes of the Jerusalem Temple, namely, Deuteronomic invention. Faith in this official Yahweh, whose face had probably started to be created by the court intellectuals of the time of Hezekiah, necessarily entails repudiation and removal of Asherah. The latter, in turn, was "a standard and legitimate part of the cult of Yahweh" among the people on the fringes of power and authority. This is the battle of the gods, that is, the official Yahweh's struggle against the gods of the fringe. In this battle, the official Yahweh of the Davidic kingship becomes one of the "religious weapons of death" (Hinkelammert) with which the Davidic regimes, in particular the Zadokite priests, punished their opponents and destroyed local theologies and cults. The repudiation of Asherah, which had long been underway before the second stage of Josiah's reform, did receive an impetus from the "newly discovered law book" and the subsequent covenant-making.

In this manner, the book of law which was presented to Josiah contained not only the collection of old tribal traditions but also just such a theological invention of the official priests and scribes. They collected and shaped the material of old tribal traditions to favor their own royal establishments. This meant that Deuteronomy, with its persuasive speech patterns, seemed to be a product of royal propaganda in support of the Davidic institutional status quo. Needless to say, Josiah's reform and centralization of the cult was, on ideological grounds, carried out along this Deuteronomic line.

The Passover celebration in the Jerusalem Temple was the result of the Deuteronomic movement. In its propaganda for the reform, the Josianic government implemented Deuteronomic Law on Passover celebrations and held a national festival in Jerusalem. The forthcoming chapter is the story of how this "nationalization" of the Passover festival eventually triumphed, and how the state co-opted the Passover traditions as a core of Exodus to serve its own ideological justification.

CONCLUSION

This concludes our examination of the historical and social context of Josiah's reform in 2 Kings 22:1–23:30. In summary, the sociological exegesis has enabled us to construct a more concrete and complete picture of the Josianic society in which the reform was undertaken and produced. In general terms, Josiah's kingdom was on the same track as the former Davidic kingdoms in terms of basic socioeconomic and political structures. Society served to preserve and enhance the power- and wealth-seeking interests of the Jerusalemite ruling class at the expense of the working people. The decline of the Assyrian empire gave great opportunities for the ruling class to reinforce its centralized mercantilistic economic policy in Jerusalem, thus leading to the so-called Josianic reform.

The reform, which was officially proclaimed to purify and centralize all worship at Jerusalem, abolished all the local shrines and forced the rural population to practice religious activities at the Jerusalem Temple. This gave the ruling class the much-needed "monopoly on socio-economic activities" conducive to the expansion of the centralized mercantilistic economy. By extending cult centralization to the northern territory, the ruling class attempted to expand this economic policy, thus increasing further the state's power and wealth, aiming even at the restoration of Israel's empire over surrounding states.

At the same time, this reform, particularly the destruction of all the local shrines, came as the end product of the power struggle for control of official Yahwism. The reform was, at least in part, designed by the priests of the Jerusalem Temple to control their opponents, the country Levite priests and the non-Israelite priests. The result of this was not only the Zadokite priests' monopoly on legitimate religious practice in Israel, but also a breach in the social life of village communities.

It must be emphatically stressed that Josiah's reform represented an attack on the rural population and on many aspects of their social life. The tribal infrastructure, which had slowly but steadily been eroded by the power- and wealth-seeking interests of the ruling elite since the time of David, suffered a fatal blow in this reform.

All of these negative aspects of the reform were concealed by royal propaganda in the Davidic covenant tradition, produced by the court intellectuals. Officially King Josiah was proclaimed to be a Davidic king and a direct covenantal partner of Yahweh. As a legitimate Davidic king, he led the national liberation movement against the Assyrians to restore the Davidic empire. As a faithful Yahwist, he took actions to wipe out non-Yahwist practices, abolishing all the local shrines. To make this propaganda more credible, the Mosaic covenant tradition was reproduced, to focus upon eulogizing King Josiah as the defender of the impoverished migrants in Judah. As part of this effort, the law on familial property was proclaimed as one of the decisive elements to sustain the apparatus of royal propagation. Thus did the Mosaic tradition become an ideological indoctrination of the Davidic dynasty, which resulted in the so-called pre-exilic Deuteronomic theology.

Within this process of the production of the official theology, Yahwism had increasingly been associated with the power- and wealth-seeking interests of the Jerusalemite ruling class. In other words, its theological doctrine was not determined by the national consciousness, but by the consciousness of the ruling class to obfuscate and reinforce its class interests. Outstanding among these was the anti-asherah theology. Under this official Davidic theology, the country Levite priests were branded non-Yahwist and punished.

More importantly, this official theology or ideology is present in many parts of the Old Testament. Even the prophetic discourses of the southern kingdom in the late eighth to seventh century B.C.E., such as Isaiah and Zephaniah, were strongly based on this Davidic theology. Needless to say, the narrative of Josiah's reform was mostly produced by the priests and scribes of the Jerusalem Temple, who were dependent on benefices of the Davidic house. This masked the reality of the Josianic society, in which the ruling elite reaped a bonanza through the reform.

It is hardly surprising, therefore, that modern fundamentalist and idealist hermeneutics present Josiah's reform as a religious movement under a pious and exclusive loyalty to Yahweh. In the absence of a structural analysis, it is impossible for biblical exegetes to reach an understanding of the real social forces operative in the Josianic society. This hermeneutical failure shows up especially in the interpretation of Josiah's Passover. In order to understand the socioreligious functions of this feast, we must try to penetrate in-depth the biblical social structure and social history of the Passover. To this we shall now turn our attention.

4

Sociological Analysis of Josiah's Passover

INTRODUCTION

As noted in the preceding chapter, the key to our study of the religion of Israel is an understanding of the social situation and social forces operative in Israelite society. By clarifying the process and the context of this society, social analysis helps us see how central a role the economic function of production and distribution, particularly the maximizing of the surplus, played in Israelite history. Having examined the changes of Yahwism in this context, we are now in a position to return to the observation that served as a point of departure for our study. In Josiah's reform, the Passover, originally a family feast, becomes a national pilgrimage feast concentrated in the Jerusalem Temple, and its ritual is redesigned. What social forces are operative in this Passover celebration? To pursue this question, we will turn to a full examination of the role and function the Passover assumed in the Josianic reform. First, however, we must specify in some detail the functions of cultic activities during the pre-Josianic time, that being the direct social context of Josiah's Passover.

In the first chapter we saw that there was a historical change or evolution in the Israelite religious institution of the Passover festival, as reflected in the J and D descriptions of Passover. In this change, the Temple stands as the most important and central component. At this point, it must be emphatically restated that ancient Israel made a radical departure from the Canaanite city-states, and in particular from their cultic activities rooted in the temple service. And so, the important first step for the present study is to begin to characterize the function of the temple in the Egyptian empire and Canaanite city-states. We believe that this function of the royal temple provided the prototypes for the sacral activities of the Jerusalem Temple, to which Josiah adapted the Passover.

THE HISTORICAL BACKGROUND

The important roles the temple played in the Egyptian empire and Canaanite city-states are clearly seen in the sources and are not disputed among scholars; they have recently been discussed and reinforced in the International Conference with the theme of "State and Temple Economy in the Ancient Near East" (cf. Lipiński), and we do no more than recall them here. What is common to the statist societies in the ancient Near East is that the royal temple, which was "a branch of government admin- istration" (Janssen: 509), was not only a religious institution, but equally an economic and political institution.

Apparently, the most immediate factor in the religious dimension that the temple provided was a place for daily offering, yearly festivals, and so forth, serving as the major cultic center. As articulated in the government administration, this religious dimension also served to legitimatize the polit- ical-economic roles of the royal temple. The fact that the cultic activities were completed with offerings suggests that the material goods used in cultic activities would be concentrated in the royal treasuries. This trans- formed the royal temple into "the sacral mechanism that directed via sac- rifice large amounts of material productivity into the control of religious and political hierarchies" (Kennedy: 142).

Royal control over the temple was also the most effective way to secure the support and loyalty of the people to the state. Politically, it should not be forgotten that the Canaanite city-states were "engaged in military com- petition fostered by a chariot-warrior class" (Gottwald 1983a: 25). In this social context, the temple was "a branch of the government with its own function: to guarantee the goodwill of the gods" for the army and the subsequent security and welfare of the people (Janssen: 509). Furthermore, the very fact that the cultic activities, such as the Canaanite fertility cult, were at the center of people's social life, indicates that the royal temple was a strong social force to control and concentrate the national life around the government. Even the temple had an imposing stature as a building, serving as political propaganda for this sociopolitical concentration. According to Carol L. Meyers, "A temple building, as the visible symbol of a god's presence, was the most effective way for the leaders of a country to communicate, in the days before mass literacy and broadcast media, the fact that their god favored the political organization that was being estab- lished" (1985: 1026).

The royal temple was where god dwelt, and its religious power was thus translated into political and economic power for the government's control over the populace. It is of utmost significance that scholars affirm that kings in the ancient Near East were considered "representatives of the gods on earth." Ronald S. Hendel states:

According to Mesopotamian tradition, kingship was lowered down from heaven in the primeval era. In Egypt the king was a god. In Canaan the king was a "son of El," just as the Israelite king of the monarchic era was "son" of Yahweh. This latter usage probably reflects an adoption formula: the king is to be regarded as an adopted son rather than as a natural son, but the bond between king and god is still clear. The close relationship between the king and the gods in the ancient Near East is reflected in the treatment and the ideology of the divine image (379).

The very fact that the bond between king and god was visualized by the cultic images (idols) indicates that idolatry was a fetishism of the ancient Near Eastern religious ideologies, aiding directly in establishing the authority of the royal system, especially its cultic activities. As Gottwald notes,

> Since the idols were focal points of ceremonies in which enormous amounts of foodstuffs and other goods were offered to the gods, thereafter to be turned over to the state and temple officials for consumption or conversion into other forms of usable wealth, it can be said that political and religious hierarchies were directly reproduced and legitimated by idolatry (1986b: 386).

This reinforces the theory that the oppressive reality of the tributary rule of the Canaanite city-states, particularly its ideological order, was legitimated and anchored in the royal temple and its cultic images.

It was from this Canaanite city-state and royal-temple system that the revolutionary peasants made a radical departure, forming "tribal Israel" in the Palestinian hill country. The most important factor in the situation of a "frontier society" of the first Israelites, which prompted a tribal mode of production, was the commitment to socioeconomic egalitarianism, so-called retribalization. Israelite society, loosely linked in an intertribal confederation, provided for "political self-rule, economic self-help, military self-defense, and cultural self-definition" (Gottwald 1983b: 7).

In its cultic constitutions, this tribal society adopted two basic stances: exclusive devotion to Yahweh and rejection of the royal temple. The former led them to exclude cultic images from the religious cult of Israel. The latter encouraged them to promote cultic celebrations that were both centralizing (intertribal cultic activities) and decentralizing (local cultic activities) in their tendencies. It would be unrealistic to claim that early Israel had driven away all of the idols throughout the land. For instance, some Israelites kept their ancestral images in their homes and even made "Yahweh idols" in local cultic activities (Kennedy: 142; cf. Morgenstern 1966; Olyan 1988). On the whole, however, like the royal temple system in the Egyptian empire and Canaanite city-states, this tribal cultic system served not only a religious function but economic and political functions as well.

By rejecting the cultic images, revolutionary Israel attacked the very kernel of the Canaanite city-state system, the fetishism of material and social domination by the rulers. In its place, Yahweh's kingship was established as ideological justification and religious support for the antistatist Israelite society. Apparently this assertion of Yahweh's kingship had strong feedback effects upon the cultic sphere and its socioeconomic aspect. Gottwald argues as follows:

> Renunciation of Idolatry meant, therefore, that precisely in the "religious" act, peasants and herders were simultaneously refusing to reproduce and legitimate the prevailing hierarchies. The "unseen God" of Israel, receiving the "tribute" due, turned it back in large measure to the people who produced it. "Mono-Yahwism" (a less abstract term than "monotheism") was the religious facet of tribal independence turned sharply against idolatry as the religious facet of hierarchic domination (1986b: 386).

By this means, the revolutionary peasants transformed their Canaanite agricultural festivals (cf. Jgs 9:27) into "the feast of Yahweh" (Jgs 21:19) for socializing and for storing or consuming agricultural goods in the community. This also explained why the agricultural festival, which was an annual pilgrimage, received important treatment in the socioreligious spheres of early Israel (cf. Ex 23:14–17; 34:18–23). The Book of Samuel describes such a tribal cultic activity:

> There was a man of Ramathaim, a Zuphite from the highlands of Ephraim whose name was Elkanah son of Jeroham, son of Elihu, son of Tohu, son of Zuph, an Ephraimite. He had two wives, one called Hannah, the other Peninnah; Peninnah had children but Hannah had none. Every year this man used to go up from his town to worship, and to sacrifice to Yahweh Sabaoth at Shiloh. One day Elkanah offered a sacrifice. Now he used to give portions to Peninnah and to all her sons and daughters; to Hannah, however, he would give only one portion: for although he loved Hannah more, Yahweh had made her barren (1 Sm 1:1–7).

There is no doubt that Elkanah made an annual pilgrimage to sacrifice and socialize agricultural goods (cf. 1 Sm 1:24) at Shiloh, a main intertribal shrine, which was the home of the ark in the period of the Judges. A remarkable thing in this story of Elkanah is the use of the verb *zabah* and the noun *zebah*, which referred to "sacrifice": "to sacrifice [*zabah*] to Yahweh Sabaoth" (1:3); "offered a sacrifice [*zabah*]" (1:4); "to offer the annual sacrifice (*zebah*) to Yahweh" (1:21).

It has long been recognized by scholars that the sacrifice (*zebah*), which literally means "slaughtering," was originally incorporated into the cultic activity in tribal social settings, and its important feature was a communal meal. "The sacrifice of a slaughtered animal [*zebah*]," Fohrer describes,

> was a communion sacrifice, for which cattle, sheep, or goats could be used. The animal sacrificed was consumed in a communal meal. The

meat was divided between Yahweh and the worshipers; after some date that can no longer be determined it was also shared with the priest. Yahweh received the most valuable parts of the slaughtered animal, the fat portions, which were burned upon the altar. After he had received his share of the food in this fashion, the actual meal could begin, in the course of which—after the breast and right shank had been removed as the priest's portion—the worshiper, together with his family and invited guests, devoured the meat (1972: 206).

Such a sacrificial meal exactly represented the kind of communal economic system which evolved in early Israel to regulate the production and circulation of basic resources, providing the entire population with secure access to an adequate living. Because of its characteristic feature, the communal meal, the *zebah*, also played a strong role in the context of "pacts" with Yahweh and among the tribes. It is most likely for these reasons that the sacrificial procedure of *zebah* was of prominence in the local and intertribal cultic celebrations.

As is well-known, this sacrificial meal was also found in the private cults of individual or extended families, celebrated in homes throughout the land. Outstanding among these was the *pesah* feast (Passover).

According to Ex 12:21–23, the people slaughtered the Passover victims, lambs or kids, for their families. After roasting, all of the flesh of the animal was to be eaten in a communal meal. Viewed economically, this Passover celebration fits well into the communal economy of early Israel. The first Israelites, whose substantial agriculture was supplemented by keeping a few sheep and goats, and sometimes cows or oxen in lesser numbers, consumed and socialized their pastoral products in private family cultic celebrations. By this manner, the Passover served for getting rid of the attempts of individuals to aggrandize the surplus in their hands at the extended-family level of organization.

On the sociopolitical level, it is important to note the prominent role of elders as celebrants in the sacrificial procedure of the Passover (Ex 12:21). As articulated in the primitive kinship system, the Passover encouraged sociopolitical cooperation and autonomy for the extended family as the basic Israelite socioeconomic and political unit.

On the ideological level, there was the blood ritual. This apotropaic ritual presumed that Yahweh was the king of Israel and, thus, the Passover offered to him was understood to obtain his protective power for the domestic animals and the subsequent welfare of the people. It is possible that the Passover was connected with Exodus tradition in early Israel because of the fact that Israel's cultic tithes were to be given to Yahweh only (cf. Ex 20:3). All in all, Yahweh of the Exodus was the ideological cornerstone of revolutionary Israel's movement. It is doubtful, however, that the cultic actualization and dramatization of the Exodus in the Passover developed to a high level in early Israel. The most we can say is that the connection of the Passover with the Exodus tradition was elaborated and developed in the course of time and definitely reinforced and actualized by Deuteronomic legislation.

From these observations we become more certain that the Passover was commonly celebrated in early Israel. Its sacrificial procedure and particularly the private family setting, was necessarily deeply rooted in the tribal mode of production. The transition from tribal society to royal society, however, would have brought about a major change in the Passover practice.

In short, in the cultic activity of early Israel, as was the case with other Near Eastern peoples, it was common to make pilgrimages and offer sacrifices to God. But the function of the Israelite cult was distinctive, due to its articulation in the tribal mode of production. The significant feature of Israelite cultic activity, which socialized material resources in the community and bonded interfamily or tribal relationships, is clearly attested as being present in the communal meal, in the sacrifice (*zebah*), as well as in the Passover.

By the tenth century B.C.E., Israel experienced a radical change in its social system. Israel's previous stateless society gave way to a monarchic peasant society (a tributary mode of production). Of necessity, this social change brought changes in cultic activity.

The heart of the cultic changes during the consolidation of the monarchic peasant society was the construction of the royal Temple, whose structure and function were extensively borrowed from the Canaanite city-states. Because of its importance, we quote at length from one of the texts that refers to the inauguration and activities of this Temple:

> Solomon then summoned the elders of Israel to Jerusalem to bring the ark of the covenant of Yahweh up from the City of David, that is, Zion. All the men of Israel assembled round King Solomon in the month of Ethanim, at the time of the feast (that is, the seventh month). When all the elders of Israel had arrived, the priests took up the ark and the Tent of Meeting and all the sacred utensils which were in the Tent. King Solomon and all Israel, present with him before the ark, sacrificed countless, innumerable sheep and oxen ... Solomon offered a communion sacrifice of twenty–two thousand oxen and a hundred and twenty thousand sheep to Yahweh; and thus the king and all the Israelites dedicated the Temple of Yahweh. On the same day the king consecrated the middle part of the court in front of the Temple of Yahweh; for that was where he presented the burnt offerings, oblations and fatty parts of the communion sacrifices, since the bronze altar which stood before Yahweh was too small to hold the burnt offering, oblation and the fatty parts of the communion sacrifice. And then Solomon and with him all Israel from the Pass of Hamath

to the Torrent of Egypt—a great assembly—celebrated the feast before Yahweh our God for seven days (1 Kings 8:1–5, 63–65).

Most scholars agree that the Deuteronomistic redaction is present to a large extent in 1 and 2 Kings. The text quoted above is not an exception. The influence of the Deuteronomistic writer is traceable in its literary style, for instance, in the enlargement of the number of oxen and sheep. No doubt this cautions us against building a historical reconstruction of cultic activity in Solomon's time. But at least the text is reliable enough and instructive enough in showing some basic activities of the Jerusalem Temple and its socioeconomic and political functions.

It is hard not to read in the text evidence for a radical departure of the Temple cult from the tribal cultic system. The Temple cult has all the signs of being an important apparatus of the state. This could be true, for as far as the foregoing analysis describes, it is the royal Temple itself that concentrated the surplus. For example, 1 Kings 8:1–4 reveals that the men of Israel came to the royal Temple for the feast, offering sacrifice to Yahweh. This royal cultic activity would immediately be understood as the sacral mechanism by which agricultural goods could be increasingly controlled and concentrated by the central government. It has long been recognized by scholars that the Temple served as a center of commerce (cf. Silver 1983: 67).

Like all temple cultic activities in the ancient Near East, the Israelite Temple cult also had a fetishism to establish its authority as an apparatus of economic stratification. According to 1 Kings 8:5, all Israel sacrificed the pastoral products before the ark of Yahweh. Instead of providing an ideological support for the revolutionary peasants, however, the ark was thus swallowed up in the royal Temple, and became the "fetish" of the material and social domination of the Davidic dynasty.

The transition from the tribal mode of production to the tributary mode of production had an important impact, not only on the way the sacred gifts were collected and distributed, but also on ritual celebrations. The Bible shows us that the following types of sacrifice had become more and more prominent in the Israelite cultic activity during the monarchic period: the offering *minhah*, the burned offering *'olah*, and the peace offering *shelamim*.

In the foregoing chapter we have seen that the years of the Israelite state's consolidation are of the greatest importance for a correct understanding of the monarchic system. If we fail to grasp how the changes really occurred within the cultic system of that time, we shall have failed to grasp the very foundation of the Passover in the royal period. So we must examine in some detail the royal offerings, and especially the peace offering, whose sacrificial meal is similar to the *zebah* and the Passover (cf. de Vaux 1964: 16).

The offering *minhah*, which in the ancient Near East had a broad connotation of gift or tribute given to city gods, was adopted into the tribal mode of production, serving the communal economy (1 Sm 2:29; 3:14). "The Hebrew word *minhah*," G. A. Anderson states, "can mean 'offering' in the generic sense, either animal or vegetable, or as in the case of the priestly writer it can refer specifically to the cereal offering" (27). In the monarchic period, however, this offering was very closely associated with the sacred mechanism of the government to appropriate the surplus from the peasants, that is, "gifts" or "tithes" to the royal Temple. Even the term *minhah* was widely used as tribute in the royal political activity (cf. 2 Sm 8:2; 1 Kings 5:1).

Like the offering *minhah*, the burned offering *'olah*, which is "ordinarily explained by the root *'alah*, 'to ascend' " (de Vaux 1964: 27), was an old "Syro-Palestinian" practice. Unlike the cereal offering, it designated a sacrifice in which an animal victim was slaughtered and entirely burned on the altar. In spite of being found only a few times in the biblical texts from early Israel, the burned offering played a major role in the Temple cult (cf. 1 Kings 9:25). Still, the term *'olah* is a favorite of the Priestly writer. Surely this change reflected Israel's historical and social development, particularly its increasing agricultural productivity. We suspect that the characteristic feature of the burned offering, which was "the objective of evoking an initial response from the deity prior to bringing the primary concerns of his worshippers to his attention" (Levine 1974: 22), was most likely converted into one of the most effective ways to legitimize the royal ideology of the divine image in the king.

The peace offering or the communion sacrifice was brought in the form of an animal, which could be a sheep or a goat, a bull or a cow. The fat and specified parts of the internal organs were burnt on the altar, but, for all the rest, "the worshippers who brought the animal ate the meat in a joyous worship meal, the breast and right thigh being allotted to the officiating priest" (A. C. Myers: 899). Because of its characteristic feature, a common meal, some scholars considered the peace offering identical with the ritual of *zebah* (cf. Charbel 1967: 21; Lach: 191). Many other scholars have observed that both sacrifices originally had different social settings (cf. Rendtorff: 150; Snaith 1957: 314). B. Lang has summarized the matter quite adequately:

> While earlier writers considered *zebhach*, *shelamim*, and *zebhach-shelamim* different terms for one and the same ritual, Rendtorff and Lach have suggested a more differentiated approach: The *zebhach-shelamim* came into being through a combination of the *zebhach* and *shelamim* rituals. In the process, the *zebhach* took on features of the solemn *shelamim* offering, which had previously been exclusively royal and national. The ritual of the *shelamim* offering, however, can be reconstructed only hypothetically. It is always associated with the *'olah*; Rendtorff takes it as the concluding sacrifice of the *'olah* and

leaves open the question whether the sacrificial animal was burned or eaten. Lach, on the contrary, thinks in terms of a sacrificial meal; in his view, the *shelamim* offering was the public counterpart to the *zebhach* (1980: 23).

No doubt this association of the *shelamim* with kingship is clearly attested in the biblical texts related to the years of the Israelite state's emergence. To clarify this royal characteristic feature of the *shelamim*, and its relation with the *zebah*, let us examine these biblical texts, which mention the communion sacrifice:

1. "You [Saul] will then go down, ahead of me, to Gilgal, and I [Samuel] shall join you there to make burnt offerings and to offer communion sacrifices [*zebhe shelamim*]. You must wait seven days for me to come to you, and I shall then reveal to you what you must do" (1 Sm 10:8). The text is clearly a redactional addition in preparation for 1 Samuel 13:8–15, which narrates Saul's rejection. Moreover, the *zebhe* (the pl. construct form of *zebah*), which is a typical Priestly term, is considered as P's addition (cf. Rendtorff: 149–53).

2. "Samuel then said to the people, 'Let us now go to Gilgal and reaffirm the monarchy there.' The people then all went to Gilgal. And there, at Gilgal, they proclaimed Saul king before Yahweh; they offered communion sacrifices [*zebahim shelamim*] before Yahweh, and there Saul and all the people of Israel gave themselves over to great rejoicing" (1 Sm 11:14–15). The text, which proclaims Saul as king, still shares the tribal social reality and its communal meal of the *zebah*. In this sacrificial procedure, Samuel indeed played the major role. The term *shelamim* here was considered P's addition. A major reason for this is an absence of the burnt offering with which the *shelamim* is always associated.

3. "Saul was still at Gilgal and all the people who followed him were trembling. He waited for seven days, the period fixed by Samuel, but Samuel did not come to Gilgal, and the army, deserting Saul, began dispersing. Saul then said, 'Bring me the burnt offering and the communion sacrifices [*shelamim*]'" (1 Sm 13:8–9). In the foregoing chapter we have seen that this text is a part of the narrative of a conflict between Saul and Samuel, thus representing the royal system and the tribal system respectively. Saul's sacrificial procedure was condemned by Samuel because of the fact that Saul was seeking a cultic role.

4. "They brought the ark of Yahweh in and put it in position, inside the tent which David had erected for it; and David presented burnt offerings and communion sacrifices [*shelamim*] in Yahweh's presence" (2 Sm 6:17). The transport of the ark to Jerusalem was a key action of David as an

ideological justification and religious support for his kingship.

5. "David built an altar to Yahweh and offered burnt offerings and communion sacrifices [*shelamim*]" (2 Sm 24:25).

It is hard not to see in these texts evidence for the transition of the tribal society to the monarchic society. Each had its sacrificial procedure of a common meal, the *zebah* on one side and the *shelamim* on the other. (Cf. the different view that the *shelamim* is "a major league institution which the royal interests seek to take over," G. A. Anderson: 49–51. The limit of his position has its premise in his neglect of the researches into the relationship between the *zebah* and the *shelamim*.)

While it played a major role during the tribal period, the *zebah* appeared less frequently in the biblical texts from the early royal period. In the later period, this sacrifice became restricted to the Temple cult and associated definitely with the *shelamim* by the Priestly law (the term *zebah shelamim* in 1 Kings 8:63 is such a Priestly term). Meanwhile, the *shelamim* with the burnt offering was the most common and general sacrifice in the royal period. In the Deuteronomistic history, the *shelamim* offering plays an important role in the national festivals of Israel.

Already implied in the above comment of Lang is the difficulty of grasping in its historical concreteness the origin of the *shelamim*. But recent research has shown that there are strong similarities between the Ugaritic offering *slmm* and the Hebrew *shelamim*. According to G. A. Anderson:

> The similarities are notable. In Ugaritic *slmm* is often paired with the burnt–offering, *srp*. One is reminded of the common biblical pair, *selamim* and *'ola*. In both Ugarit and Israel the *slmm* offering consisted of animals. And, quite possibly, at Ugarit the *slmm* offering was consumed by the worshipers, just as it was in Israel. Finally, the *selamim* offering in the Bible and in Ugaritic has royal characteristics (37).

How did it come about that the *shelamim* became a major sacrifice in the royal period? Why did the state not control and restrict the *zebah* to the Temple cult in the early royal period? Why did the *shelamim* replace the *zebah* in the public cult? The answer to this set of questions cannot be formulated while scholars fail to understand Israelite religion as a social phenomenon. The key to understanding the change in Israelite cultic practice lies in grasping the issues within the social and historical reality of that time.

Probably the original *shelamim*, which may well have been celebrated in the temple cult and absorbed into the royal covenantal ceremony in the Canaanite city-states, was replaced by the tribal sacrifice (*zebah*) in the antitributary Israelite society. We suspect that the *zebah* may well have been celebrated by the pastoral group, who introduced tribal Yahwism into the Israelite revolutionary movement. Quite naturally, the fact that the sacrificial procedure of the *shelamim* was similar to the *zebah* encouraged the revolutionary peasants to neutralize and replace the former with the latter.

Since the late premonarchic period, the elite class indeed had tried to control the *zebah* to appropriate and concentrate the surplus (1 Sm 2:12–17; 1 Sm 15:15). But the Bible tells us that this misuse provoked a strong reaction from the tribal forces (1 Sm 2:17, 22–36). It can be clearly heard in the discourse of Samuel:

> Is Yahweh pleased by burnt offerings
> and sacrifices
> or by obedience to Yahweh's voice?
> Truly, obedience is better than sacrifice,
> submissiveness than the fat of rams.
> Rebellion is a sin of sorcery,
> presumption a crime of idolatry! (1 Sm 15:22–23)

Faced with this indictment, the Israelite ruling elite surely felt the need for a royal sacrifice that would sustain and represent their statehood. It can hardly be accidental that King David twice offered *shelamim* (2 Sm 6:17; 2 Sm 14:24) in the covenantal ceremonies. While taking advantage of the traditional religious organization such as the ark, the king also introduced the royal religious organization represented by the *shelamim* into his governmental apparatus as part of the specialization and urbanization of his administrative constitution. His successor Solomon presented, three times a year, "burnt offerings and communion sacrifices (*shelamim*) on the altar which he had built for Yahweh and set his burnt offerings smoking before Yahweh (1 Kings 9:25). This version of the introduction of the *shelamim* could be quite accurate, because it was during this period that the Israelite state carried out a drastic religious reform: the appropriation of the ark, the replacement of Abiathar by Zadok, the construction of the royal Temple, and the consolidation of the Davidic covenant tradition.

With the arrival of Israelite statehood, and particularly the introduction of the *shelamim*, the *zebah* lost its prominent role in the public cult. Nevertheless, this sacrifice continued to keep its importance in the tribal context. So it was, for instance, that Absalom offered the sacrifices (*zebahim*) in the process of his rebellion against David (2 Sm 15:12). This was a socio-ideological way of solidifying his collusion with the tribal forces. Because of their sociopolitical importance, it became unavoidable for the state to attempt to control the tribal sacrifices.

After its consolidation, the Israelite state developed two major programs for suppressing the tribal cultic practices. First, by absorbing the surplus from the populace, the ruling class gradually disposed of an important source of private family sacrifice. Second, the continuing political central-ization of the urban ruling class insured that cultic practice would be restricted as much as possible to the Temple cult. No doubt the *zebah* was swallowed up in this wave of development of the Israelite statehood.

As a result, it is little wonder that the change in Israel's sacrificial rites was rooted in the transition from the tribal society to the statist society. The royal cult was in fact articulated in the exploitive political economy of the Temple, serving for the ruling class's control over distribution of mate-rial resources. In this context, the tribal cult had been slowly but steadily neutralized by the state and finally restricted to the royal Temple.

As articulated in this Israelite festal practice, the Passover was also fundamentally affected by the social and historical developments of Israel. Because of the centralization of the Passover in the central sanctuary, D's Passover, as appropriated by the Josianic Passover, was in fact the key turning point in this historical change. To illustrate, we will analyze Josiah's Passover in its particular sociohistorical setting and explore the implications of the power- and wealth-seeking interests of the ruling class on religious institutions, especially on the destruction of local religious festivities.

JOSIAH'S PASSOVER

Passages that deal explicitly with the time of Israel's monarchy reveal some ambiguity in the Passover celebration. The first statements about the Passover in this period come from the late monarchic times. We have seen that the Passover texts in 2 Kings 23:21–23 and 2 Chronicles 35:1–19, which contain cultic directions from the Deuteronomic cultic law (Dt 16:1–8), are unanimous in stressing the novelty of the Passover celebration in Josiah's reform. But these passages do not explicitly state that the Passover festival ceased to be celebrated in the pre-Josianic period. The texts are directed primarily toward the Passover as it was celebrated as a national festival, and are silent as to whether it was celebrated as a private family affair in the monarchic period.

Did Israelite religion in the *royal period* know or practice the Passover festival before Josiah's time? Because the festival was deeply rooted in the tribal society and the life of the peasants, it seems reasonable to suggest that it continued to be celebrated at the private family level in the coun-tryside. At the same time, it also seems likely that the Passover celebration became more and more limited due to the ever-widening erosion of the rural society.

Most importantly, the tribal economy, with communal ownership of the land, was eclipsed by the interests of the ruling elite in the mercantilistic economy. The exploited and oppressed peasants were pushed off their land and were forced to work as sharecroppers for rich landowners or to flee into the cities, working as unskilled labor. To be sure, this exodus of the rural poor served as the basis for the decline of tribal festivals, such as the Passover, at the local cultic level. Still, the cultic concentration of Josiah's reform was the fatal blow in this process of neutralizing the local religious institutions and their cultic activities.

But how did it come about that the Deuteronomic legislator came to propose the grafting of a family-festival Passover onto the program of national Temple pilgrimage? How and why did King Josiah carry out this Deuteronomic cultic law? Just what kind of function did Josiah's Passover assume? To these questions we now turn our attention.

In the late monarchic period, Judah experienced the rapacity of those developing the mercantilistic economy. The urban patricians of Jerusalem were making a great effort to maximize the production, circulation, and concentration of material resources to their own advantage. One of the major effects of the mercantilistic economy was the migration of the rural poor to the city of Jerusalem.

Viewed economically, this migration produced the much-needed cheap labor force vital to the expansion of various industries. But whatever industry the ruling elite operated was determined not only by the available labor force, but also by "raw materials," to assure a smooth flow of production. As to agricultural goods, their supply in Jerusalem became ever more scarce, due to the city's rapidly expanding population. The tribute that Judah had to pay to Assyria only worsened the situation.

To guarantee available material resources to supply its overlord, Assyria, its agricultural industries, and its labor force, the state had to maintain the maximum concentration of the country's agricultural goods in its hands. And while the state was truly determined to maintain its retainers' advantages, it ultimately had little choice but to exploit the peasantry's agricultural surplus. The supply of material resources appropriated through the actual fiscal system, however, could not keep pace with increasing demands. The state sought to reorganize its fiscal system in such a manner that the peasantry's agricultural surplus could be brought into the capital as efficiently as possible.

Within this social reality, the court intellectuals drafted the Deuteronomic cultic laws with elements partially borrowed from the former northern kingdom. At the center of this religious reform stands the cult centralization in "the place chosen by Yahweh." By this law, the state aimed at neutralizing the activities of all the religious sanctuaries in the country, with the exception of the royal Temple. This would give the state a monopoly on the peasantry's agricultural surplus, which used to be offered to the local sanctuaries and their Levite priests. The serious need for the surplus not only pushed the state to plan to suppress the local sanctuaries' activities, but also led it to try to control the private cults celebrated in homes.

This was the socioeconomic setting of D's Passover, which later became the ritual backbone of Josiah's Passover festival. The Deuteronomic legislation grafted the family-festival Passover onto one of the pilgrimage festivals, Mazzot, attaching it to the Temple cult. Now the Passover was no longer designed to serve the peasants' socialization of their material resources. Rather, it was absorbed into the sacral mechanism, serving the state's control over the peasantry's agricultural surplus. Thus is also to be explained the wide choice of pascal victims in Deuteronomy 16:2, providing for the state a possibility to control the largest possible portion of the surplus.

But there was a problem. How did the state plan to carry out this economic policy to neutralize the Levite priests of the local shrines, the "semi-independent local dignitaries"? How did the state legitimize this radical innovation in the Passover festival in the face of expected reactions from the traditional tribal forces? Just how did the state administer the Deuteronomic cultic reform?

It should not be forgotten that the religious reform was deeply involved in the national liberation struggle of the Israelite state against the Assyrian hegemony. This was the reason the main ideological support of the Deuteronomic religious reform was the Exodus tradition (Dt 16:1–3), which was now used against Assyrians. All in all, it was the Assyrians who drove the Jerusalemite ruling elite into a tight corner, limiting their profits. Both the national liberation and the cultic centralization could, in fact, lead to situations in which the state could expand its control over both internal and external economic activities.

Religious reform, therefore, played a double role for the patricians of Jerusalem. On the one hand, given the national oppression by the Assyrians, the return to Yahwism, symbolized by the Exodus tradition, could be intended to herald a national liberation that could assist the Jerusalemite ruling elite in the smooth operation of their economic policies. On the other hand, the Deuteronomic legislators in the religious reform, who were the court intellectuals in Jerusalem, produced the royal Yahwism in support of the Davidic institutional status quo. Even more importantly, they provided the unique sanctuary theology that served as an ideological support for the cultic centralization in the royal Temple.

So it was, for instance, that Hezekiah tried to break away from the yoke of Assyrian servitude and to put a religious reform into practice that was most probably a sociopolitical way to expand the Israelite state's control over the production, circulation, and concentration of material resources (2 Kings 18). He failed in his attempt mainly because of the superiority of the Assyrian army. It is understandable, therefore, that the Deuteronomic cultic laws, and in particular the Passover legislation, had a long time to wait for their implementation under the Assyrian hegemony.

Under Josiah, the time had come at last. The decline of Assyria provided space for Josiah's actions to carry out a national liberation movement and the long-delayed religious reform. Specifically, the time was ripe for the urban patricians of Jerusalem to transform the Passover festival into a sacred mechanism of the Temple cult for their own advantages.

Both 2 Kings 23:21–23 and 2 Chronicles 35:1–19 are unanimous in describing Josiah's Passover as a national pilgrimage feast with a great sacrifice in the Jerusalem Temple. It is not difficult to understand the main economic advantages that this Passover pilgrimage could have brought to the ruling elite. First, the pilgrimage insured that the "lucrative business connected with pilgrimages" (Lang 1983: 20) could be prosperous in the capital city. Concerning this matter, there is a Deuteronomic law that expresses and illustrates the sacral mechanism of exploitation:

"Every year, you must take a tithe of what your fields produce from what you have sown and, in the presence of Yahweh your God, in the place where he chooses to give his name a home, you must eat the tithe of your wheat, of your new wine and of your oil, and the firstborn of your herd and flock; and by so doing, you will learn always to fear Yahweh your God. If the road is too long for you, if you cannot bring your tithe because the place in which Yahweh chooses to make a home for his name is too far away, when Yahweh your God has blessed you, you must convert it into money and, with the money clasped in your hand, you must go to the place chosen by Yahweh your God; there you may spend the money on whatever you like, oxen, sheep, wine, fermented liquor, anything you please" (Dt 14:22–26).

What is known generally about the Passover victims of the "herd and flock" would lead us to expect that the Passover pilgrims probably had the same opportunity to sell and buy their offerings as the tithe bearers. Significantly, the fact that the ruling elite controlled the market could lead to an increase in their income through this nationalization of the Passover festival.

Officially, the Passover cultic legislation is silent as to whether the officiating priests receive some portion of the paschal victims or some payment in exchange for their services. It would be unrealistic to assume, however, that they worked for nothing in the royal Temple service. Concerning this, it is certainly significant that the Deuteronomic Passover was accompanied by the sacrificial procedure of the *zebah* (Dt 16:1–7). Even more significantly, the choice portion of the *zebah* fell to the priests, according to the Deuteronomic cultic legislation:

This is what is due to the priests from the people, from those who offer [*zebhe*] an ox or a sheep in sacrifice [*zebah*]: the priest must be given the shoulder, the cheeks and the stomach. You must give him the first-fruits of your wheat, of your new wine and of your oil, as well as the first-fruits of your sheep-shearing. For Yahweh your God has chosen him from all your tribes to stand before Yahweh your God, to do the duties of the sacred ministry, and to bless in Yahweh's name, him and his sons for all time (Dt 18:3–5).

It should not be forgotten that Josiah's cultic reform was, at least in part, designed by the priests of the Jerusalem Temple to monopolize religious practice in their own hands. We also noted that their rapacity for sacred material resources destroyed any opposition in their ranks. It should not surprise us, then, that the officiating priests received substantial payment in exchange for their sacrificial procedure (*zebah*) during the Passover festival.

Another economic advantage that the nationalization of the Passover festival granted to the state was derived from the setting of the date for this festival. "Now the whole people," S. Talmon states, "represented by pilgrims ascending to the temple in Jerusalem from all parts of the country, observed the festival of Passover at one time" (1958: 63). Surely, this concurrent and overwhelming flood of people and sacrificial animals impacted upon the circulation and concentration of material resources in a very significant fashion. At the very least, this served for the state to concentrate the peasantry's agricultural surplus, thus making a substantial profit from controlling the marketplace economy.

And so it was. The centralization of the Passover in the Jerusalem Temple was the result of the state's economic policy to concentrate the largest possible portion of material resources in its hands. In their attempts to rebuild Israel's empire within the mercantilistic economic policy, the Josianic ruling elite were forced to increase the income from the free peasants or lose both their class advantages and the support of the landless working class on which they would become more and more dependent for a source of cheap labor and military contingents. This unstable situation led the ruling establishment to reach out for all existing agricultural surpluses, even those consumed in the private family festival of the Passover. The power- and wealth-seeking interests of the ruling elite had a vital impact on the economic role of this festival.

Of course, this impact was also exerted on the sociopolitical and ideological roles of the Passover. On the social level, it is important to note that the elders lost the role of celebrants in the sacrificial procedure of the Passover festival. In their stead, the priests presided over an elaborate sacrificial procedure according to the Temple cultic law. This priesthood in the service of the Passover sacrifice not only meant a development of specialized professionalism in Israelite society, but also meant an increase in the bureaucratic concentration of power and wealth.

This was exactly the kind of hierarchical social relations that the Canaanite city-states imposed on the people, and why early Israel formed the tribal social relations. With the establishment of the tributary mode of production, and particularly with the gradual movement toward the mercantilistic economy, tribal social relations became less important in economic production and circulation and therefore diminished in social importance.

In this changing social process, the Israelite priesthood became connected with the urban power centers, the royal Temple, and became specialized and centralized. Once such a priesthood was established, society adhered to it in ways that became limiting and oppressive to the cultic role of laymen, the elders in particular. This was especially true with the establishment of the priesthood in the Passover festival, reflecting the erosion of the tribal social relations in Israelite society.

It is important to recognize that this erosion of the tribal socioeconomic system became transformed gradually into a political erosion. In this process, it became more and more possible for the urban patricians of Jerusalem to undertake their oppressive economic policies against the rural populace. The fact that the former tribal cult of Passover became centralized in the royal Temple illustrates a very advanced stage of the statist political domination over the peasants. Viewing Josiah's Passover in terms of these political activities, there is an interesting text that strikes to the heart of the Josianic economic policy:

> For the laity Josiah provided small livestock, that is, lambs and young goats—everything for the Passover offerings for all who attended—to the number of thirty thousand, as well as three thousand bullocks; these were from the king's own possessions. His officials also made voluntary contributions for the people, the priests and the Levites; and Hilkiah, Zechariah and Jehiel, the chiefs of the Temple of God, gave two thousand six hundred lambs and three hundred bullocks to the priests for the Passover offerings; while Conaniah, Shemaiah, Nethanel his brother, Hashabiah, Jeiel and Jozabad, the head Levites, provided five thousand lambs and five hundred bullocks as Passover offerings for the Levites (2 Chr 35:7–9).

As to the Passover offerings, it should not forgotten that the Deuteronomic legislator prescribes a clear law: "You must sacrifice a Passover from your flock and herd for Yahweh your God in the place where Yahweh chooses to give his name a home" (Dt 16:2). Under this law, it is reasonable to assume that the landless working class should have bought their own Passover offerings. But the passage above states that they received the sacrificial animals from the ruling elite.

The question that arises is whether or not the landless working class could afford to buy the Passover offerings. Does the fact that the ruling elite provided the animals indicate a socioeconomic situation of starving tenant farmers and urban working people, as the foregoing chapter suggests? What is the intention of the ruling class in distributing the animals? Were they making any effort to redistribute income in favor of the poor?

Seen from the foregoing sociohistorical reconstruction of the Josianic society, we believe that 2 Chronicles 35:7–9 illustrates that there was no margin for the poor landless working class to buy the sacrificial animals. All in all, there was a stark contrast between rich and poor in the Josianic society. According to one estimate, the richest 2 percent had approximately the same absolute share of the national income as the rest of the population. Unlike the free peasants, the landless working class had almost no possibility of providing the offerings for the pascal sacrifice. By understanding the mechanism of a mercantilistic economy and the importance of a cheap labor force in it, we believe also that the distribution of Passover offerings by the Josianic ruling elite was no doubt a part of their welfare policy, aiming at giving them a symbolic role in the festival as well as at controlling any social explosion.

In contrast to their economic policy toward the landless working class, the ruling elite were ruthless toward the free peasants. By grafting the Passover festival onto the temple cult, the state tried to acquire the surplus of the extended families and to neutralize their sociopolitical cooperation system. It was a function of the mercantilistic system. The erosion of the tribal system could lead, given the control of the entire socioeconomic system to the ruling elite, to an expansion of their profits. Josiah's Passover thus played a double role for the ruling establishment in terms of its economic policy—the welfare policy toward the landless working class, on the one side, and the oppressive policy toward the free peasants, on the other.

This double role of the royal Passover is also visible in the ideological sphere. As any ideology must do, the Passover ideological discourse can function either subversively or hegemonically. In the case of Josiah's ideological indoctrination, the royal Passover that was oppressive in the context of free peasants could become modestly liberating in the context of a landless working class.

Already implied in the above paragraphs is the important role of the Passover festival in bonding the interfamily relationship. In this festival the peasants renewed their covenant with Yahweh and each other to legitimate and reinforce the tribal social system; therefore, the tribal Passover needed to be controlled and dominated by the ruling class.

On the ideological level, it was imperative for Josiah that the Passover be transferred from the home to the royal Temple. Attached to the government festival, the Passover became an effective weapon that sustained the national consensus of religious reform and counteracted the tribal forces or antimonarchical tendencies. As part of this effort, the connection of the Passover with the Exodus tradition was reinforced and actualized, to make the Exodus a national liberation struggle against Assyria.

Once such a national movement against Assyria became established, society adhered to it in ways that became limiting and oppressive to the egalitarian or antimonarchic ideology of the tribal Passover. This was a decisive factor for the ruling class in neutralizing the expected reactions from the traditional tribal forces in centralizing the Passover festival in the royal Temple.

Instead of being oppressive in the tribal context, however, the royal Passover became deceptively liberating in the context of Jerusalemite working people. Apparently there were two main ideological factors that would push the landless working class to adhere to the Passover festival. On the one hand, those who were mostly migrants from the countryside lost bonds of social cohesion or social rooting, and were struggling for their socio-psychological survival. Such a radical need of self-preservation would make the migrants vulnerable to the royal propaganda of the Passover, the religious call of which was still rooted in the consciousness of those former disadvantaged peasants.

On the other hand, Judah, particularly the city of Jerusalem, was on the edge of a social explosion. The socioeconomic difficulties of the populace intensified the sufferings and even threatened the very existence of the poorer classes. One of the results of these social pressures was an increase in religious activities as a "safety valve." This would be another factor that led the landless working class to adhere to the Passover festival.

The royal Passover festival thus played a double role for the Josianic government. On the one hand, it served as an effective religious weapon to control tribal ideological forces through a nationalization of the Exodus tradition against Assyria. On the other hand, given the crisis of the landless working class, the Passover became an effective religious weapon to involve the landless worker in the religious reform. Because of its essential role in the Josianic reform, we suspect that the Passover was highlighted as a distinct pilgrimage feast and was celebrated independently from the feast of Unleavened Bread.

So it was that the Passover festival became identified with the Exodus tradition, expressing a nationalistic and spiritual revival in the struggle against Assyria, thus becoming a centerpiece in the royal propaganda for religious reform. The people, under the strong leadership of the king and priests, celebrated the Passover, "springing from joy over new salvation to be wrought by Yahweh" (Lohfink 1987: 469).

CONCLUSION

Perhaps the most significant point of this study of Josiah's Passover is the understanding of the Israelite religious institutions in terms of their social dynamics. The present study has made it possible to say that there is no historical basis in the pre-Josianic period of Israel's history to support the argument that the religion is not social in its origin or "fundamentally, affected by social developments." Neither is there any historical evidence to support the assertion that "the religion retains an inner ahistorical, asocial integrity all its own which can never be penetrated and illuminated by the unfolding designs of the societal matrix of the religion" (Gottwald 1979: 604). On the contrary, there is ample evidence to suggest that the Israelite religion and its religious institutions were fundamentally affected by the social and historical developments of Israel. More importantly, the tribal religious institutions and traditional cultic activities had been slowly but steadily neutralized by the power- and wealth-seeking interests of the ruling class.

As part of this effect, the Passover festival of the Israelite peasants had been "stolen" by the urban patricians of Jerusalem, and its social power was translated into socioeconomic, political, and ideological power for the ruling elite's control over the populace. Significantly, the ruling elite clashed with the free peasants over the tribal Passover, a local cultic festival that had bonded interfamilial relations and promoted the Mosaic covenant tradition, with its socioeconomic egalitarianism.

With this understanding of religious institutions, we can initiate dialogue with the CEB members, exploring the questions: How does the study of Josiah's Passover help their reading of the Bible? How can they organize their community better, according to the functions of the tribal Passover festival? The process and the result of our dialogue are the issues that will occupy our attention in the following chapter.

5

Sociological Exegesis and CEBs

INTRODUCTION

Two-thirds of the population of Latin America is undernourished, marginalized, oppressed, and victimized by an institutional violence that is produced by capitalist imperialism and supported by multinational corporations and a local oligarchy. In the face of such unjust suffering, one of the most important contributions of basic ecclesial communities (CEBs) is their engagement in the search for the God of life, a God who liberated Israel in the past from its idols and who liberates men and women today from theirs. The God whose action is recognized and recorded in the Bible, insist liberation theologies and CEB members, is the same God whose Word continues to challenge us to work for a fuller participation in Latin American society. Reading the Bible in this way points to the fact that social action is indeed a constitutive dimension of biblical Christian faith.

Assuredly, much of the recent discussion of the CEBs has taken as its starting point this biblical reading from the perspective of the poor. On Monday, April 17, 1987, *L'Osservatore Romano* published an address by Cardinal Ratzinger at the opening of the audience with John Paul II, who received the members of the Pontifical Biblical Commission. In this address, Cardinal Ratzinger, while referring to the problem of biblical hermeneutics, also mentioned the authority of the Pontifical Biblical Commission on biblical hermeneutics in the Catholic Church:

> Certain methods of interpretation of biblical texts are the object of more or less radical criticism; other methods are proposed which open up new horizons, but which also have their limitations. Conscious of its responsibility to the Magisterium and to the whole Church, the Biblical Commission is striving to contribute to the necessary discernment (*L'Osservatore Romano*, 17 April, 1989, 11).

In Brazil, CEB biblical hermeneutics from the perspective of the poor has become the focus of this "radical criticism" from conservatives and

113

sectors of the Vatican. This was directly manifested in 1988 by J. E. Martins Terra, a conservative biblical scholar and an auxiliary Bishop of Olinda and Recife, in his book, *Leitura da Bíblia na Perspectiva do Pobre* (Reading of the Bible from the Perspective of the Poor). The author, by presenting the scholarly works engaged in CEB hermeneutics, argues that the CEB method is a materialistic approach which invalidates an interpretation of the Holy Scripture (cf. Terra 1989).

In late April 1989, the first volume of the Word-Life Project, a Bible study program of CLAR—the Latin American Confederation of Religious—was censored by CELAM—the Latin American Episcopal Commission (cf. a manifesto in "La XXII Asamblea Ordinaria del CELAM"; SEDOC July–August 1989). The volume was written under the influence of Carlos Mesters, widely known in the CEBs for his popular biblical readings. The volume was criticized in part because of its trend of interpreting the Bible from the perspective of the poor. While reporting this affair in the *National Catholic Reporter*, Penny Lernoux writes:

> But neither the Vatican nor CELAM approves of the project, primarily because it reflects the trend among Latin American biblical scholars to interpret the Bible from the viewpoint of the poor. "Poor," according to CLAR's critics, is an ideological word that promotes class conflict, and because "poor" is ideological, a reading of the Bible from the perspective of the poor is likewise. Moreover, such reading starts from the reality of the poor—or the see-judge-act approach of Vatican II—and therefore is contaminated by Marxist analysis, claim the critics (*National Catholic Reporter*, 30 June, 1989, 18).

Accordingly, she continues:

> Censorship of Mesters would send a clear message about Roman power to the Christian Base Communities (CEBs), say church sources, because a denunciation of the theologian would be equivalent to condemning the thousands of Bible-reading circles that depend on his work and are the underpinnings of the communities.

Like Lernoux's report, it is a well-known fact that this struggle for control of biblical hermeneutics reflects a strong tendency on the part of Roman authorities to censor the CEBs as a part of their continuing struggle for control of Latin American Catholicism (cf. Wirpsa). In a real sense, this tendency, states François Houtart, is "a concern to safeguard the exclusivity of those who speak for the magisterium as well as of the controlling function of the hierarchy" (1989: 262).

The CEBs, as we have seen, are under pressure from conservatives and sectors of the Vatican bureaucracy to end the reading and interpretation of the Bible from the viewpoint of the poor. To understand this pressure better, we need to comprehend the ideals and the social history of the CEBs (cf. Teixeira). As part of that larger exploration it will be helpful to examine the institution and activities, as well as the biblical hermeneutics of the CEBs with which I am most familiar, those of the Catholic Church, especially in São Paulo, Brazil.

Certainly one of the most characteristic developments of the Brazilian Catholic Church consists of organizing small communities, officially called CEBs. Although their organization varies from one region to another, each of the CEBs in the city of São Paulo has some five to ten nuclei (smaller groups), where people come together at weekends to celebrate their own lives with God and to work together for their basic needs.

Each nucleus is further organized into reflection groups, or street groups, where the neighboring people get together on weekday nights, normally in one of the members' houses, to pray and reflect on their real-life community and its various concrete situations in the light of the Bible. In the street group, the people give attention to the challenges around them and help one another to cope. When the problem is bigger and more complex, such as a lack of clinics, they try to resolve it through united action with other street groups, other nuclei, and even other CEBs in the area.

One of the results of the small and decentralized organizational form of the CEBs is that people can develop a sense of community more easily. "Our community brings people to pray and work together no matter who they are," one of the CEB members said. The CEBs are, indeed, one of the few social spaces where the suffering get to know one another and build a degree of "solidarity" among themselves. The traditional religiosity of the people's processions, novenas, and devotions honoring patron saints is often the starting point and the motivation of this solidarity.

Besides developing a sense of community, the CEBs also function as educational spaces. Their community meetings help the people confront their social and religious conditions with critical intervention, especially using the see-judge-act method. When participating in this sort of community meeting, the people can perceive their personal and social reality and come to "a new awareness of self, a new sense of dignity." This is what the CEB members call "conscientization."

This conscientization not only leads the people to promote social actions against injustice but also to organize the CEBs differently from the traditional parish churches in terms of having power over the people. Instead of the people going to parish churches, the CEBs now come to them or emerge from them. Instead of a hierarchical church, the CEBs promote a democratic church with a higher degree of participation of the lay people in organizing it.

For example, the training courses, which are organized by the pastoral agents (the clerics, religious, and lay persons involved in the CEB activities), enable the people to develop a sense of Christian responsibility and lead them to assume more leadership in the communities. Thus new ministers (animators) emerge through the CEBs. The church is understood to be not a hierarchical and authoritarian structure selling fatalistic religiosity and legitimatizing the present system of oppression, but rather a community, serving the people by means of critical religiosity incarnated in a search for complete liberation.

Here is where the CEBs meet with severe pressure and criticism from conservatives and sectors of the Vatican. These critics, who seek to restore the old-style parish and hierarchical authorities, see the CEBs as a threat to their power and control. They attempt to maintain a hierarchical church and to reduce the strength of the CEBs as a resource for a democratic church. Two incidents exemplify such attempts. First, in 1989, José Cardoso Sobrinho, who was nominated as Olinda-Recife's Roman Catholic Archbishop, ordered the closing of one liberation theology seminary and one theology school in Recife, where the seminarians were strongly involved in CEB activities. Second, in the same year, the Vatican drastically reduced the size of the Archdiocese of São Paulo, headed by Cardinal Paulo Evaristo Arns, who is well-known throughout the world for his advocacy of human rights and the CEBs. Referring to the last incident, George de Lama, from the *Chicago Tribune*, reported that the Vatican came down strongly on the cardinal, clipping his wings by dismembering the largest Roman Catholic archdiocese. It took away half the cardinal's congregation by dividing the archdiocese into five dioceses and nominating conservative bishops to head the others (cf. *Chicago Tribune*, 28 July, 1989, Section 2, 8).

There can be no doubt that these actions indicate that the Vatican has decided to move into censoring Liberation Theology and the CEBs, restoring orthodoxy to church practices, and struggling to control the direction of the Brazilian Church, the third-world's largest Catholic church.

Within this struggle, the problem of CEB biblical hermeneutics has inevitably arisen, because of its tremendous effect on the conscientization of the CEB members, especially in the street groups raising critical consciousness (awareness of root causes) among the poor. In fact, a major development in the history of the CEBs took place when people came together to reflect on their social conditions, such as housing, health care, and education, in the light of the Bible. By introducing the concrete reality of their own situation into the interpretation of the Bible, the people discover the liberation struggle and praxis of the biblical Israelite communities as their own. The street groups or the biblical reflection groups are rapidly spreading through the suffering masses in slums, leading them to become aware of their oppressive realities and giving orientation on how to deal critically with them.

The conservatives criticize this CEB biblical hermeneutics as a "materialistic reading of the Bible" that foments "communism" among the CEB members and may lead to "disorder" in the church as a result of the participation and influence of the laity. There is no point in detailing or responding to these groundless criticisms. Grass-roots Bible study in the CEBs has played, I believe, a vital role in the Latin American liberation struggle. Above all, reading and interpreting the Bible from the perspective of the poor nourishes the very roots of our exegetical tasks to read the Bible, which has very often been misread by the specific interests and viewpoints of the dominant social classes.

It is appropriate, however, to restate the further orientation of "pertinent sociocritical biblical hermeneutics" for the CEB biblical movement's setting among the Latin American suffering people. For instance, the *Bible—Pastoral Edition* (edited by Bortolini), which was recently published to support and orient the leaders and pastoral agents in CEBs, presents Josiah's reform as a liberation movement against foreign oppression, particularly against the religious and cultural influence of neighboring people. To make this exegesis credible, the commentators of the *Bible—Pastoral Edition* argue that "Josiah is an unique king who receives unconditional eulogies from the biblical author because of the fact that King Josiah attempted to eliminate oppression and corruption, and to reunify the people around the project of Yahweh (cf. Jer 22,15–16)" (428, trans.). Obviously, in this comment on Josiah's reform, they worked with an inadequate sociocritical biblical analysis. For example, the prophecy against King Jehoiakim (Jer 22:13–17), whose text was developed and preseved in Deuteronomistic circles, must be understood in the context of the king's pro-Egyptian socioeconomic policy (2 Kings 23:31–35). This lack of depth in biblical social structure and social history often leads the CEB members to erroneous social and cultural accounts of the biblical Israelite communities, so that their grass-roots Bible study loses its critical function in the liberation struggle today. The CEBs need to further develop a pertinent sociological exegesis.

My chief interest in this chapter is to evaluate this CEB biblical hermeneutics' development by deepening and enriching their sociocritical biblical analysis, and in the process of doing so, to demonstrate that grass-roots Bible study and scientific exegesis supplement each other in the service of social change in the church and society. This process shows up especially in the way that the CEB members discuss their religious institutions, blunting the force of the aforementioned criticism of conservatives and sectors of the Vatican bureaucracy.

During the months of August and September 1990, I had the chance to organize an experimental course for CEB leaders in São Paulo in which the sociological exegesis of Josiah's Passover was treated. Studying and discussing as their major theme Josiah's activities in 2 Kings 21:1–23:30, the leaders became involved in developing hermeneutical skills and critical consciousness to orient their Bible study groups. After the course I also had opportunities to participate in several meetings of the Bible-study groups into which these leaders introduced the theme of Josiah's activities.

This is a chapter about the process of the conscientization of these CEB members with whom I conversed and studied during those two months. It is also about the process of my own conscientization of the problems of the CEB biblical hermeneutics and related institutions.

This attempt to provide information about the Biblical Apostolate in the CEBs relies not only on the evaluation notes of the course and the journals of the Bible study groups, but also relies quite heavily on the results of my conversations with the CEB members, conducted in a form of research known as ethnography (for excellent guidelines for doing ethnography, see Spradley). "An ethnographer," Terry Williams states,

> tries to describe everyday behavior and rituals and, in the process, to reveal hidden structures of power. As this technique requires the researcher to build a close relationship with those being studied, it is necessarily slow: days, sometimes weeks, may pass before the ethnographer can even begin to conduct an interview. These interviews are often "open"; that is, the investigator has key questions in mind, but is willing to let an informant's responses lead into unanticipated areas as these can provide new understandings of the processes under study (2).

This dialogical encounter with others as a basic tool for ethnography has also been a basic tool for the Biblical Apostolate in the CEBs. But we must recognize that the need for producing more pastoral agents and animators in academic forms has often made scripture-study groups dependent on scholars, limiting the dialogical encounters in the Bible courses or schools. To make matters worse, the Bible courses often make some of the participants mini-scriptural scholars or miniclerics in their way of organizing and conducting the meetings of the Bible study groups, which is intimidating to ordinary participants.

To try and avoid this danger of limiting the contribution of the CEB members, the insiders of this study, I did my best to build close relationships with them and to hear their opinions about the issues under study. That is also why I refer to my informants and their communities under assumed names. Remaining anonymous, they were able to speak about the issues more openly.

Through their study of Josiah's Passover, there were many conversations among the participants about their biblical hermeneutics and existing institutions. By presenting the resulting insights, this chapter hopes to describe—as much as possible in their own words—the process by which the CEB members appropriated the sociological exegesis of Josiah's Passover. By doing so, it seeks to understand the CEB biblical hermeneutics and existing institutions from the insiders' points of view.

CONSCIENTIZATION OF CEB LEADERS IN THE BIBLE COURSE

In São Paulo, on the afternoon of August 13, 1990, I started a Bible course for nine pastoral agents and animators. The number of participants was intentionally limited in a way that gave me a greater possibility of developing a close relationship with each of them and getting deep insights into their thoughts (culture). They were not chosen for participation because of anything special about them. Ricardo, a pastoral agent working with the homeless people, and Sonia, an animator of a group of women, were selected simply because I already knew them slightly. Ricardo introduced me to Angieli and Meire, who are helping the homeless people to organize their CEBs in the center of São Paulo. Jair, a pastoral agent working with rural workers, is from a city in the state of Paraná, where I used to work as a pastor. Other participants were introduced to me by my friends. Antonio and Joaquim are animators, leading the CEBs in the South Zone of São Paulo. Ivo and Miguel are lay catechists who are animating the CEBs in the interior of São Paulo.

On the first day we spent time getting to know one another and our communities. Our daily work schedule during the course was worked out as follows:

Morning Prayer	7:30
Breakfast	8:00
Study (three hours with a break)	8:30
Lunch	12:00
Study (three hours with a break)	14:00
Celebration (Mass, etc.)	17:00
Dinner	18:00

The evening was free for recreation, personal study, and interviews.

On the second day I tried to learn from the participants how the CEB leaders would deal with the Bible to prepare their community meetings. They were asked, during the morning study, to read the text of 2 Kings 22:1–23:30 and to present messages that they would like to pass along to their community members. After one and one-half hours of reading and thinking about the text, they assembled to share their messages.

Typical comments were: "What strikes me most is the attitude of King Josiah. The Bible tells us that 'on hearing the words of the Book of the Law he tore his clothes.' After that, Josiah tried to get to know more about the Word of God and to be faithful to it. His honesty and faithfulness is very important for us in organizing our communities" (Ivo).

"King Josiah is a very courageous man. Like his story, we need to hear what the Word of God is saying, and must put it into practice. The story is a good challenge for us to get organized more in the Bible study groups, and celebrating the Passover, the transformation of an old church into a new church" (Jair).

"I read with interest about the destruction of all the shrines on the high places to purify the church of that time. Josiah bravely struggled against idolatry. I hope that we have the same courage and faith in God in difficult times of purification and transformation of our church today" (Sonia).

For most of the participants, the king's faithfulness to the Word of God was the central theme of the text's story. They frequently stated, "What strikes me most is the strong imagery in the passages concerning the king's activities." Such passages, said the participants, were as follows: "He did what Yahweh regards as right, and in every respect followed the example of his ancestor David, not deviating from it to right or left" (22:2). "On hearing the words of the Book of the Law he tore his clothes" (22:11). "The king then, standing on the dais, bound himself by the covenant before Yahweh, to follow Yahweh, to keep his commandments, decrees and laws with all his heart and soul, and to carry out the terms of the covenant as written in this book" (23:3). "As for the altar which was at Bethel, the high place built by Jeroboam son of Nebat who had led Israel into sin, he demolished this altar and this high place as well, in the same way, breaking up its stones and reducing them to powder" (23:15). "The king gave this order to the whole people: 'Celebrate a Passover to Yahweh your God, as prescribed in this Book of the Covenant.' No Passover like this had ever been celebrated since the days when the judges ruled Israel, nor throughout the entire period of the kings of Israel and the kings of Judah" (23:21–22).

These passages surely left an image of a faithful and courageous Josiah in the minds of the participants, and placed the king's activities in the center of their reflections. Because of their intense commitment to the CEBs, it was easy to notice that the participants injected their own concerns about the community activities into these reflections. That is, they were reading Josiah's activities in association with their own lives, resulting in the comments mentioned.

These factors are important in describing the participants' hermeneutics, but the system was a bit superficial. It was the interviews that caused the participants to speak more about the way they were really dealing with the text of Josiah's activities. After lunch, I started conversation-dialogue with the three participants individually (Ricardo, Sonia, and Jair), and also in three combinations (Angieli-Meire, Antonio-Joaquim, and Ivo-Miguel). By listening to the comments on their interpretations of the text, I identified the cultural categories I felt were most important to understand their hermeneutics as a whole. These include *alguma coisa errada* (something wrong), *deve ser* (must be), and *temos que saber* (we must know and/or learn). Let us explore these categories:

Something wrong: "All these destructions Josiah made are very cruel. That was terrible! I can't say exactly what's wrong, but that means *something wrong* to me," Angieli said. This doubt concerning Josiah's violent activities against the shrines emerged first in the conversations with my informants.

"Today we also see such a kind of religious struggle," Angieli added. "You know, I am comparing Josiah's struggle to our struggle in the church between the conservatives and the progressives. I know if we use violent ways like Josiah, things will become worse. He killed the priests? Ah, we never would!"

Besides the destruction of all the shrines, most informants pointed out another *something wrong* in Josiah's activities: his way of decision making. Joaquim said, "Josiah talked to his friends and consulted with the prophetess Huldah about the book of law. Later, he called the people to talk about the book, and then he ordered the reform. You see, the king never consulted with the people about what he should do. I don't know now if it's right or wrong, but I do know how our community members feel about this story in terms of not consulting with 'the base,' and I'm sure that things aren't done the same way."

"Remember what happened to our church!" said Ivo in a pained voice. "Several years ago, the priests took all the images of saints from the church without consulting the people. It was wrong! In the Bible, it's written that 'he [Josiah] did what Yahweh regards as right, and in every respect followed the example of his ancestor David, not deviating from it to right or left.' I don't know for sure if this passage is a lie, but I'm not naive, either. You know what I'm saying? What Josiah did with the priests of the interior was an imposition!"

Certainly it is true that they are very much aware of the relationship between a biblical story and their own real-life situation, and of the importance of reading the Bible in such a social context. By reading the text of 2 Kings 22:1–23:30 in this way, they are able to break fundamentalistic hermeneutics to a certain extent, thus having some doubts as to the correctness of Josiah's activities.

But it is also true that, although they had these doubts, during the morning session, the informants based their comments on the image of a faithful and courageous Josiah. Why did they make comments so inconsistent with their real feelings? What cultural codes influenced their thinking? I asked them several questions to try to find out what was going on in their minds. "Now could you tell me how you can picture Josiah as such a good man?" I began, asking about the informants' inconsistency. The first answer of most of them was, "Well, the king *must be* a good person." The following section will describe the system that serves as hermeneutical regularities for the informants, leading them to say *must be*.

Must be: Miguel said, "Josiah did what the book of the law said." He looked at me with a hesitating smile on his face and continued: "In the name of the Word of God, things *must be* done!"

Without exception, all the informants mentioned Josiah's faithfulness to the book of the law as a reason why he did the right things in the eyes of

God. Miguel's answer to the question, "Could you describe what the book of the law is for you?" was, "Well, it's not the book of paper, but the rules of life, control of life, and after all the Word of God!"

In his turn, Ivo said, "The Bible clearly states that Josiah consulted with Yahweh and followed Him. You see, he executed what Yahweh ordered. The Bible is the book of faith. Looking at Josiah's activities through the eyes of faith, we need to understand what was going on at that time."

For the informants, the term *Yahweh* was a powerful and magical cultural code that directed and held them captive in the fundamentalistic reading of Josiah's activities: "Josiah did what Yahweh was saying." It seems likely that the informants could not adequately deal with the problems of ideological justification occurring in the Old Testament because of a lack of information about the history of Yahwism, such as in the Davidic covenant tradition.

The term *prophetess* was another code word that served to enforce the correctness of Josiah's activities. "Josiah consulted with the prophetess Huldah about the words of the book," Sonia argued. "Huldah was speaking to Josiah's officials in the name of Yahweh, the God of Israel. She prophesied that God would 'bring disaster on this place and the people who live in it.' You see, a prophetess is saying in this way . . . it *must be*! What more can I say? Speaking foolishness, no!"

I believe Sonia and other informants trust the words of Huldah for two reasons. First, they did not have any information about the prophetess except what the Bible told them about her as a messenger of God; second, the figure of prophets such as Amos and Isaiah were very popular among the CEB members as defenders of the poor against oppressors. And so, what the prophetess was saying about Josiah should be considered as the right thing, and consequently silenced their doubts regarding Josiah's activities.

These cultural code words, *Yahweh* and *prophet,* are important not only because of the danger the CEB members face if they do not have the correct information about the historical and social contexts of these terms, but also because this lack of information prevents the members from using their important hermeneutical tool, their own lives and experiences. Let us explain more about the last point.

I insisted with Ricardo, "Wait a minute. I heard you saying that Josiah seemed to be a dictator like our governor. He just commanded the people! But now you're saying that Josiah did the right things in the name of Yahweh and the prophetess Huldah. It's strange?"

Taking a deep breath, he tried to slip away from the question. "Well," he said, "I mean that the words of Yahweh and the prophetess by themselves are good. But it all depends on how the words are put into practice. You understand what I'm saying? Don't you think so? I need to have more information about these guys, Josiah, Huldah . . . "

Like Ricardo, all the informants were confused by the reading of 2 Kings

22:1–23:30. They tried to interpret the text by using their hermeneutical tool, their own lives, and to apply it to the real-life community. Their hermeneutics, however, could not show the informants' real abilities because of their lack of information about social contexts, particularly about Yahwism. What is worse, they could face the danger of subjective interpretation! Antonio underlined, "If the interpretation of the Bible was only dependent on our own experience, it would be dangerous!" I can say that, although they gained wonderful insights into the text by using their own lives and concrete situations, the informants were still slaves to fundamentalism, taking the text literally as it was. In this sense, the lack of information about the text was an important obstacle as the informants tried to interpret Josiah's activities.

"The Old Testament isn't familiar to me," Sonia emphasized this lack of information. "Of course, I know the history of Abraham, Moses, Amos ... But I had never heard the name of Josiah, Huldah, ah, let me see, ah, Hilkiah, Shaphan ... " For the CEB members, the Old Testament is seen as a "difficult book" to read and understand. They stated that they used the Old Testament less than the New Testament when they needed to prepare the community meetings. "It stays half-distant from the people," they said, describing their feelings about the Old Testament.

Ivo mentioned another obstacle. "When I had doubts as to Josiah's activities in the morning, I talked to my companion and we went right to the footnotes in our Bible (the *Bible–Pastoral Edition*). Didn't I, Miguel?" Miguel nodded slightly to me. "According to the footnotes," Ivo added, "Josiah is an excellent king, working hard for the people."

After the conversation with Ivo and Miguel, I spoke again with the other informants about these footnotes in their Bible and came to understand that they also took them into consideration. Here was where another obstacle came into consideration. The informants were pretty dependent on the interpretation of biblical exegetes. I asked Miguel, "Suppose you have different opinions from the footnotes in your Bible. What do you do?"

Without missing a beat, he answered the question. "I think that nobody is the owner of truth," he said. "But you know, as a matter of fact, the doctors [exegetes], bishops, and priests, have the last word in our church. Who is with the Bible every day must know and must give opinions!"

I pressed him, "Does this happen in your community?"

"Ah, yes," he said, "it cannot be in this way. But it happens! And it's better for me to use their opinions than to speak any fooleries. The problem is that I don't have any information about what was really going on in the society of Josiah. I *must know* about that!"

I do not know for sure how many times I have heard this statement: "We *must know* or *learn*." In our conversations, the informants manifested so many times their strong intentions to get information about the text and related issues. Why and what did they want to know? To this we turn now.

We must know: The seeming contradictions that the biblical text reveals were the first target of the informants' curiosity to know. "How do you explain this?" Antonio asked. "The prophetess Huldah said that Josiah would die in peace. But in the end of the story, he was killed in battle. It's strange, isn't it? Huldah prophesied wrongly? Or the Bible must be saying something wrong here?"

Another puzzle was the way in which the book of the law was discovered. Ricardo said, "It's possible that I'm saying fooleries. I'm curious to know why the priests hadn't discovered such an important book for such a long time. And how was it discovered?"

Besides these reasonable questions, the informants were anxious to know what was really happening in Josiah's society. All in all, they cannot really accept the text's story literally as it is presented. Meire stated, "I don't believe that our God ordered Josiah to act in this way. At least the God who I believe in and who I recognize among the homeless people isn't a dictator. This story doesn't sound good! I wanna clarify this."

It seems a major step indeed to suggest that the informants are reading the Bible with a strong faith in the God who acted in the history of Israel and who is working in the midst of present-day suffering. The God whose acts are recorded in the Bible is seen here as the same loving God who is helping the CEB members to organize their communities. With their eyes open to God's action in real-life community, the informants read 2 Kings 22:1–23:30 and came to challenge and question Josiah's activities. In this process of reading the text, they were very much aware of the need for information about Josiah's society in order to understand why God was acting in that way.

In addition, I came to understand that the informants were interested in gaining information about the text more than learning the interpretations of the experts. "I need data," Miguel said. "The names that appear in the text ... If we don't have information about who they are, it's difficult for us to understand why they are acting in that way, and to tell correctly Josiah's 'history' [true story] to our community members."

The informants did not appear to be very much interested in the meaning of the text itself, but they were very much interested in the living actualities of the biblical events that could be applied to their own lives and give meaningful insights into present-day social realities. For the CEB members, there is not much meaning in the text if it is read without association with the real-life community today. The biblical text becomes important and meaningful when it addresses their own lives as a "mirror." They *must know* how to use this mirror rather than research how this mirror was made.

This seems to be true in the CEBs as a whole. The biblical texts that are used at the regular meetings of Bible study groups are selected and prepared by the pastoral agents and animators. They determine directions and guidelines for the reading of these texts. In doing so, they make a "bridge" between the Bible and the real-life community today, helping their members to enter the biblical world. In this role, the CEB leaders are aware of their responsibilities for telling the true stories of the biblical texts in order that their community members may interpret the stories with the deepest possible associations to their actual situations today.

During the second day's discussions, my informants became aware of the danger that their fundamentalistic storytelling of Josiah's activities could become a bridge for further oppression, rather than for liberation. At one point Ivo summed up their feelings as "my understanding about Josiah's history is half-baked and dangerous."

The third day, we started with a review of previous conversations and discussed forthcoming topics and scheduling for the course. By this time we knew one another much better and were more open to one another. For instance, Miguel confessed, "Yesterday night I was concerned about how to explain Josiah's history to my community members. Suppose they ask me about who were the priests killed by Josiah? What shall I say? Suppose I say these priests were conservatives? God forbid! My people would kill me! They would say that these who have been killed in Brazil are progressive priests."

While I was speaking with my informants about how we could organize our course better, I indicated two major things that I would like to learn from them during this course. First, I wanted to know how my informants would read and interpret 2 Kings 22:1–23:30, because they would be gaining information about the social and historical context of Josiah's society. Second, I wanted to see how they would apply the text to their daily lives, especially to their community lives and the church's organization as a whole.

In their turn, the informants restated that they were interested in gaining information about the social and historical context of the people in the Old Testament. "I want to take advantage of this opportunity," Jair said. "How were the communities in the Old Testament organized? Did they have the same problems that we're facing? These are the things that I want to know."

Considering our interests and limited time, the schedule and topics of the course were set as follows:

8/15 – The literal sense of the text and the basic information about the Passover celebration.

8/16 – The socioeconomic context of the Old Testament society before Josiah's time.

8/17 – The socioeconomic context of Josiah's society.

8/18 – 19 – Free days (the informants returned to their communities for the weekend activities).

8/20 – The political context of the Old Testament society before Josiah's time.

8/21 – The political context of Josiah's society.

8/22 – The religious (ideological) context of the Old Testament society before Josiah's time.

8/23 – The religious (ideological) context of Josiah's society.

8/24—The evaluation of the course and the final celebration in the morning.

During the afternoon session of the third day, I spoke with my informants about the writers of 2 Kings 22:1–23:30, as to when and how they wrote. Josiah's court intellectuals, such as the priests, were presented as the main authors of the text.

When they learned about this authorship of the text, it was the beginning of their excited interpretation of Josiah's story. It was like a light flicking on in their minds. "Ah, you see," Sonia exclaimed with a big smile on her face. "Just imagine! They're like those journalists who are flatterers of our government, distorting the news. Now, definitely, I don't feel the need to take Josiah's story literally."

The information about the Passover celebration was more exciting news. The informants, who used to think and talk about this feast in the context of the ideological Passover of Jesus Christ, like a passage to a new life, were surprised by the Passover being so involved with the material living conditions of the people.

For instance, Jair said, "Oh, I know what the Passover seems like. You know, I used to live in a small village in Paraná. The people knew each other like relatives. When some family had a special occasion to celebrate like a marriage, they killed an ox and prepared *churrascada* [social gathering around barbecue].

"After the Mass/celebration, everybody, of course including the priest and the sisters, got together to enjoy *churrascada,* talking, singing, and dancing. I loved to see our old German pastor dancing! Ah, it was a great time, the time of joy and sharing! So, I think that the Passover was like our *churrascada.* The Israelite peasants had the same sort of feast!"

There was a constant flow of such living interpretations during the following days. To this we shall turn shortly. First, however, I must describe in a broad way the method of organizing our discussions about the issues under study, which give the guidelines and features of the course. This method was as follows.

In speaking about the social and historical context of the Israelite people, I tried to use essentially the biblical texts so that my informants could participate more easily in the discussions and discern their own ongoing journey in the lives of the biblical people. In this process, I passed along to them literal and sociological data about the texts when they needed the information.

Reading and interpreting the texts, my informants injected their real-life communities and concrete situations into the reflections. It was in such a *mutirão* (the communal system of working) that each participant had his or her opinion and job, just as in the painting of a huge panel. Jair, Ivo, and Miguel came up with their lives' experiences and struggles for land. The rural economy and various agrarian problems were their strong elements in the "painting" of the collective panel. Talking about their suffering lives on the sprawling periphery of São Paulo, Sonia, Antonio, and Joaquim made important contributions to the interpretation of the actual situations of the Jerusalemite people. The experiences of Ricardo, Angieli, and Meire with the poverty-stricken "street" people gave powerful insights into the understanding of the material living conditions of the biblical people.

In spite of the various and different experiences in their lives, it is obvious that the informants share a sad reality brought about by the same cause. All of them work with or are themselves the victims of the serious agrarian problems in Brazil, whether affecting landless peasants in the countryside or the migrants or homeless people in the city. They are fully aware of the connection between the struggle for justice in the city and of that in the countryside. Because of this, the agrarian problem and the consequent suffering of the people became the major centralizing factor in the informants' reflections on the biblical texts, particularly in Josiah's society.

In this process of Bible study, they also came to understand the importance of structural analysis of society (social analysis), not only because some of them took a course for pastoral agents in learning how to do social analysis, but also because they had learned in their hard lives how the socioeconomic situation affects their entire existence. I heard several testimonies concerning this point during our conversations.

Joaquim said, "Six years ago, I was working as a street sweeper and earning $90 (U.S.) a month. The money wasn't sufficient to sustain my family. We were just able to survive because my wife and eldest daughter worked hard as housekeepers. You know, my wife was already mugged twice. Every day I drank *pinga* [cheap, strong alcohol] and argued with my wife. It was the life of a dog! A religion or church, oh, what about them! These things stayed very distant from me and never came to my mind. Do you think I was a *burro* [donkey in the sense of foolish man]? Maybe or perhaps not? It depends on how you see our society.

"But I confess that it was such a hard situation for me to think or do something, you know. I believe that the people are not 'fools.' They are far smarter than you might think. They're aware of what's going on around them, the manipulation by the government, the rich men, etc. They know that! But they're so oppressed that they look for an easy way to face their harsh realities.

"Some drown their sorrows in drink. Others stay with TV, soccer, etc. And others go after Pentecostal churches, such as the 'Universal Church of the Reign of God' and the 'God is Love Pentecostal Church,' you know that, to get exorcisms and spiritual consolations. It's very hard for them to assume a different and difficult way to struggle against injustice. To participate in community activities, for instance. It's difficult for them to believe in themselves. It's their fault? No, I don't believe it! As *bagunças* [the problems] are so many around the people that it's difficult for them to believe in real changes."

Finally, the entire setting of the meeting was of vital importance to its success. Morning prayers and the celebrations developed a serious religious atmosphere. Role-playing biblical events and preparing artistic presentations (collages, diagrams of various types) heightened the sense of participation in the biblical actualities and made possible a deeper understanding. The association of past events with present actualities became more possible when Angieli and Meire, for instance, copied some pictures from books and made a composite picture of Josiah's society, shown in Illustration I. When the informants communicated with one another and with God through the prayers related to the Josiah story, about their concerns, joys, and sadness in the daily struggle for justice, the Word of God in the Bible was translated into the Word of God today. By studying the Bible in this way, the informants slowly but steadily developed their hermeneutical skills and became more aware of the problems of their communities and the church in general. There was a lot of talking, discussion, and sharing about the Bible and other matters during the course. Let me present some of the comments to describe their conscientization process, following the course schedule.

The fourth and the fifth days (8/16–17): "My God! How crafty this guy Josiah is!" Jair exclaimed. "I suspected the king of doing something wrong, but I never expected that he had such an economic interest behind his reform. Well, well. In this way, I think, I'm probably telling my people a lot of fooleries at the meetings."

Josiah's story, read in the economic context, was big news to most of the informants. "You know what I thought about Josiah's activities?" Jair added. "I thought that Josiah and his priests tried to impose their official religion and power upon the people in the countryside. That is like what's happening here in our church. You know that, don't you? But I had never thought about the interests of these crafty guys who wanted to gather more and more wealth! Look how cunningly they manipulated the Passover celebration. Everyone must come to the city bringing their offerings for the Passover. Josiah was the winner, the real banker!"

It is very interesting to note that, although they already had the habit and skills for doing social analysis in their own lives in their grass-roots movements, the informants were poorly trained for reading the Bible from an economic viewpoint. Their method of interpretation was directed toward the sociopolitical issues, and predominantly ideas. In reading the Bible, they tended to ask who the people in the text were, how they were politically oriented, oppressor or oppressed, and what they were saying. Certainly the economic and materialistic reading and interpretation of the Bible were important hermeneutical skills that they had to develop during the course.

So, at the beginning of our discussion on the socioeconomic context of the Old Testament, it was not easy for my informants to comment on the economic issues, except when the text itself explicitly mentioned some economic activities. But thanks to their own experiences and awareness of the

1. High places of Judah and Jerusalem
2. Prophetess Hulda
3. King Josiah: governs without swaying either from right to left
4. Honesty and work, that is the policy of King Josiah
5. Cashier
6. The book of the Law
7. The Temple

economic problems in their daily struggles, they were quite rapidly developing skills for reading the Bible in the context of the actual material living conditions of the biblical people.

In particular, the experiences with their own agrarian problem helped them to understand deeply "latifundialization" as one of the crucial problems in the real-life community of the Old Testament. "I live in the midst of this struggle for land," Miguel said. "These Israelite peasants would be more oppressed and exploited than I. My Lord, the kings and the big landowners were making every effort to get more land! This way, their union [the tribal organization] didn't have any chance at all to survive. God forbid!"

Another problem that cropped up at the beginning of the study was the lack of information on the part of my informants about the religious institutions and cultic activities of the Old Testament. As to the cultic activities, such as the feasts and sacrifices, their questions were limited to the biblical text as such. There was no hint of problems dealing with socioeconomic issues in their discussions. It also seems likely that the issues of the biblical religious institutions were less interesting for the informants than other matters.

"I don't know anything about the Passover in the Old Testament except that the Israelites celebrated this feast just before getting out from Egypt," said Miguel while studying the Passover. "You, Father, should know about these things that are religious persons' specialties."

"The religious persons! You said?" I asked.

"Yes, Fathers or Sisters should do the talking about these religious things," he replied.

It is very true that the interpretation of some religious issues in the Bible are not popular among the people. Rather these issues are, in a sense, considered as "specialties" of the "experts." This, I believe, seems to reflect the fact that some of the religious institutions and cultic activities are still monopolized by the "specialists." So it is not hard to believe that my informants had a lot of difficulties in interpreting Josiah's story, which contains so many religious elements such as Yahweh, other gods, the covenant, the book of the law, the Jerusalem Temple, the shrines, the priesthood, the prophetess, the cult objects, the sacrifices, and the Passover.

By studying the functions of the religious institutions in the material living conditions of the biblical people (their socioeconomic, political, and religious situations), my informants had slowly overcome these difficulties. They came to understand that the "religious things" in the Bible were affected by the social and historical developments of Israel and should be read in terms of their social dynamics: "These 'things of the church' are not simply holy, and we may deal with them also."

When we were discussing the functions of the Jerusalem Temple, Meire said: "It [the temple] is as our National Bank that sucks our blood [taxes] and makes the *grandes* [the government, politicians, and their friends] more and more grossly fat."

"Yeah, I guess so. But I think that we can also see the Jerusalem Temple today in our church," Ricardo said, in a tone that was almost indignant. "Don't we know how many churches and sanctuaries are gathering wealth in the name of religion? For what? To spend more and more money on material things like Solomon and his friends, isn't it? The people just say 'Amen.' "

Thus the discussions on the socioeconomic context of the Old Testament helped my informants to get closer to the people and to the real-life community of the Bible, and to start their own ongoing journey in Josiah's story.

Angieli said, "My Lord! These people had been exploited by the ruling classes for a long time, like our people, and hadn't any more strength to do something. I believe that it was very difficult for them to organize their communities against Josiah's reform. See these migrants in Jerusalem! Poor sticks! They were the most miserable groups. What could they do? Nothing!

"I think that our homeless people are like these migrants. They are so oppressed that they are easily manipulated by the others. If someone offers *pinga* to them, they will become lambs and say 'Amen.'

"So I can understand very well why the landless workers supported Josiah's reform, like his Passover celebration. What they might lose in this feast was not important. What they felt they needed was just to say 'Amen' and to get the rest of the feast. Just imagine how they could have thought and been concerned with the peasants in the countryside who were major victims of the reform, if they really understood matters. In situations of extreme misery, the people just concerned themselves with their survival.

"You know what I want to say? I'm saying that whoever controls money and power can use other people like dolls. We can see this in the time of elections. The poor people support whom? Josiah is really a cunning guy! He, using these poor workers and homeless people, abused the religious institutions to gather more money. We can see the same thing in Josiah's story in our society today. Unfortunately in the church also."

"What is happening in Josiah's society reminds me of the feast of Our Lady Mary in my hometown parish," said Ivo, who was sitting next to Angieli. "The parish has more than thirty *capelas* [a chapel located in each village]. On the day of the feast, all the people of the villages are invited to participate in the Mass, celebrated in the main church of the city. In fact, they are obliged to come to the main church, because the religious activities in the *capelas* were suspended by the pastor that day.

"After the Mass, the people are also invited to buy barbecue for lunch, and to play bingo. There is a big flow of money into the collection box of the church. The pastor is full of joy on this day. But many people, especially the landless peasants, don't or can't go to the feast. Some don't have transportation. Others don't feel good about the Mass. In fact, the Mass is not like their celebration, which is joyful and spontaneous. Others feel uneasy in being unable to afford barbecue.

"I think that it is good for the people to get to know other communities on this kind of special occasion. It is right for the church to get money through the feast. We need to sustain, for instance, the life of the pastor and the church activities. I can understand these things. What I worry about most is not these things, but what is really done with the money. Most of the money, which the pastor and his friends of the city gather from this big feast, is spent on building a new and splendid church. They spend money on material things, forgetting more important things, such as their economic support for the landless peasant movement and even food for the poor!

"The feast of Our Lady Mary becomes like Josiah's Passover that was a big feast of the people and used by the king and his friends to gather wealth. I believe that Our Lady Mary is not happy with this kind of homage. She wants to see more of her kids living in peace and adequate living conditions rather than a splendid church."

Like Angieli and Ivo, my informants, while discussing the socioeconomic life of Josiah's time, recounted their own history. In a real sense, they are reading their own lives in Josiah's story, and this becomes a source of reflection on their real-life communities and concrete situations. As to the church, most of them complained about the problem of who runs the church and how. "Our church changed a lot, but the same problem is always there."

Jair said he sometimes observed such problems in his pastoral activities. "As you heard, I'm working with the landless peasants in the interior of São Paulo. For example the pastors, who work there, have the last word in the communities. I'm trying to help the peasants to better understand their problems of land and to better organize their communities. My Lord, it's difficult!

"One time I organized a course for the peasants in a certain church. I got sad and worried about it. You know what? Most of the participants were the peasants who had reasonable economic resources. You know, I'm not against their participation. It's very good! But I know that their communities have many poor landless peasants, and some of them are even employees of these participants of the course.

"If these landless peasants get more information and become critical, they will be good animators in their communities and in grass-roots movements. Unfortunately they don't have the money and time for the course. They must work. Of course, their communities have the community boxes, but the money is short. And as always some complain about the use of their money for spiritual things, I mean conscientization, for example, for sending someone to take the course. What really gets me, you know, is that the people still have a mania for electing the richer men to be their representatives."

"The pastor couldn't pay for these poor peasants, could he?" asked Sonia with a strange look.

"Maybe your pastor, Sonia?" replied Jair with a smile on his face. "The pastor is a good guy and isn't against the landless peasant movement. He let us use the church rooms for the course and even offered some cookies and fruit. That's it. He said that each community had to pay for the expenses of the course.

"I don't really know why he can't spend money forming class consciousness among the landless peasants. I know some other pastors in the region who strongly support our landless peasant movement and pay for the courses. Our church still depends very much on each pastor!"

"It's a sad story, the things that are happening to us," said Meire, looking toward Angieli, her partner, "and I even feel ashamed telling it to you. We are working with the homeless people, and, you know, we perceive that there are two different groups of pastoral agents in terms of the ways of dealing with the people. One group treats the people with discipline. They try to keep order in the meetings, for instance. Another group deals with the street people as such. In their meeting, there is not much order and discipline, but much noise and spontaneity.

"About a year ago, the tension between two groups got worse. After a lot of discussions, one from the first group said, 'If someone complains about our policy, why doesn't he seek to form another community somewhere else? We started to organize our community!'

"My Lord! They said 'our community,' becoming a private thing. In fact, you need money to work with the homeless people, for example getting some rooms for the meetings, etc. It's the first group who is getting money and paying us. I don't know from whom and where they are getting things. It's a big secret! Whether you like it or not, they have money and power to impose their policy upon others. Unfortunately, some pastoral agents kept a distance from the groups because of this conflict. We're also uneasy with the situation and don't know how long we can put up with this."

Surely it is true that the reading of Josiah's story in the socioeconomic context served for my informants as a mirror and helped them "see" better their activities and communities. One of the major problems that they saw in that mirror was that their communities still have some features of the old parish church. Jair underlined, "We're trying to form small and democratic communities among the people, like the tribal Israel. But it's not easy for us to get away from an old hierarchical structure. My pastoral activities are very much dependent on the pastor of each parish."

This would mean, I should think, that while the priests keep their socioeconomic power over the lay members, it is difficult for the people to form a real democratic church. The voices of lay persons in running the church, especially in terms of its pastoral strategies, are still limited and under the control of the pastors. This sometimes tends to make the church insensitive to the realities of the poor.

"In our biblical study group, we reflect on the problems around us in the light of the gospel," Ivo said. "We know very well what is going on in our neighborhood. When someone has a problem, we all try to help him or her. But the problem is sometimes so big that our strength alone cannot resolve it.

"For example, the transportation of our bananas to the market. Most of us don't have trucks. The owner of the truck we must use recently increased the transportation fees. We protested against the increase. With the new prices, we can't survive. Some people are suggesting that we need to buy our own community-owned truck.

"Anyway, we need to get organized. We also need a strong union among the communities which have the same problem. If all the small peasants are united, the owners of trucks cannot increase their fees. And we need a little help from the parish and the pastor to get our movement organized. You know what our pastor is saying? He said: 'Wait a moment. I don't like to involve myself too much in these political things. I don't like to see disorder here.' I know that our pastor needs to maintain good relationships with the owners. But I also know that nobody stays neutral, right! I think this pastor must be one of the first to promote the spirit of the Passover!"

There are sighs all around to confirm that the church in Brazil still largely remains a clerical institution. In this context, the CEBs are necessary in order that the lay people, and particularly the oppressed segments of society, may have some decision-making power within the church activities. By hearing the comments given above, I learned that most of my informants are engaged in organizing such CEBs with some resistance from clerical and hierarchical institutions. This resistance was also spoken about in our later discussions of the political and religious life of the Israelite people.

From the sixth to the ninth day (8/20–23): Joaquim said, "I'm impressed with the Israelite people who established a union, a strong union, one that was well organized. Each community had its own autonomy. You see, the lay leaders of communities took care of religious celebrations, such as the Passover.

"I think this is like our celebration that is led by our own people. Every Saturday night we have a celebration in my neighbor's shack. We sing, hear the Word of God, and offer a lot of spontaneous prayers. Almost each member has his or her role in this celebration. You know, my wife is an animator leading the singing."

"Yeah, that's right!" exclaimed Antonio, who participates in the same kind of CEB. "In our community, the animators have celebrated baptisms and marriages. And recently our pastor has invited the people to read together with him part of the eucharistic prayer.

"You know what my people are saying now? They are saying: 'The people can celebrate baptisms, marriages, and even the Mass! What kind of differences are there between the priests and the lay people?' "

"Does your pastor say anything about that?" Ricardo asked. "He said: 'My people are *fogo*' [fire in the sense of radicals]." Antonio replied joyfully, "Of course, he is joking! He always said: 'My role is not to do and say everything in the communities. You have your own animators. My role is to help people become animated and to persevere by understanding better how our God is present with us in our communities and struggles.' We love our Father! He is ours!"

What strikes me most is the level of faith and cooperation among the CEB members. Some of the informants report that their community members share not only the celebration but communal tasks, as well as get money for community activities such as a culinary art cooperative for women. However, the development of such a pastoral strategy, which is decentralizing the church power and its activities, is still very much dependent on each pastor and each bishop. The voice of the laity in choosing their pastors and bishops is not really heard, after all.

"I know that things aren't going well in our neighboring parishes," Antonio reported. "The pastors there just give orders, and as luck would have it, we lost our loving bishop. Last year he was transferred to another region. In his place, the Pope nominated a conservative bishop.

"You know, the people sent several open letters with their signatures to the Pope, asking that he would not do so. But he did. I know very well why he did! The church is returning to the old system. But the people are on firm ground. It is here that the Holy Spirit is at work; and where the Spirit is at work, nobody can stop what happens! Ah, Sonia, you were talking to me about an incident which happened with the new bishop. Please tell us!"

"Yes, it was hard for us," Sonia commented. "Several weeks ago, we had a regional assembly of pastoral activities. The new bishop was there. At the end of our assembly, he announced that he was nominating a sister as the pastoral agent to work with the catechists. You know, we have had a Sister Maria working with us for a couple of years. She speaks our *lingua* [language in the sense that a person knows the reality of the people and shares solidarity with them]. The bishop just said that she was leaving.

"Ah, the people got angry about this nomination. This was very like when Josiah announced the decision of his reform without consulting the people. We knew that the bishop wanted to impose his opinions upon us through his new pastoral agent. We protested against the nomination. We were on firm ground. The bishop couldn't achieve his goal. He needed to learn that he is also a member of our communities and had to talk with us. We're not puppets anymore, like the landless peasants of Josiah's time. We're much more organized and conscious of what is going on in the church."

The story that Sonia told us was not perceived as an isolated incident by my informants, but as part of a broad and consistent attempt by conservatives and sectors of the Vatican bureaucracy to reduce the strength of the CEBs. Josiah's story, read in terms of its social dynamics, was indeed to be of help to them in better understanding their situation under this pressure from hierarchical institutions.

"It's a sin that we pray for vocations [in the sense of candidates for the ministry]," Ricardo said. "I think that the vocations are here and there. God is sending the vocations. But because of the attempt to maintain its interests and status quo, the hierarchical church does not open the door for the lay men and women qualified as ministers.

"Look, what is the Bible telling about the Zadokite family? Once they got an official position in the priesthood, they never gave up seeking more and more wealth and status. In this way, they wiped out their rivals and cut off the *capelas* of the people in the countryside. To make matters worse, they stole a sacred thing from the people! I mean, the priests stole the right of the people to celebrate the Passover, their favorite feast, and monopolized cultic activities in their own hands. They perverted the culture and traditions of the people! This is like what we are seeing in the church today."

"That's true," exclaimed Joaquim, nodding slightly to Ricardo. "You know, my friends, I often ask myself why some priests and bishops don't support our CEBs. Why are they so anxious to secure their things but don't let us organize our church in our way? Why don't they trust us?

"I believe it's because they, like Josiah and his priests, don't live among us and really don't know our reality. They don't understand how important the communities are for us. In the communities, we share our faith, prayers, thoughts, and common tasks to support each other. We share our daily lives and celebrate them in the presence of God. The Bible tells us that we have to struggle not only for ourselves but for everyone, doesn't it? The church is the people who believe in this Word of God and help each other, right?"

Sonia said, "We hear many times that these people, who speak against us, also point out the importance of our role [lay participation] in the church, but their idea of our worth and importance means just within their system and promoting their interests. They see things just from their point of view.

"I bet that they will change their minds if they experience our hard reality. I mean, they don't know how difficult it is to find jobs, to survive on a small salary, to raise our kids with health and education, and—so much! They, like Josiah living in the palace, may know the reality in terms of letters and numbers of newspapers and documents, but not in their flesh and bone. I suppose that 'their God,' as He was, ordered the people just to pray, and let them continue suffering. I believe that 'our God' wants to liberate us from both spiritual and material misery. 'Our God' wants the people to share with each other and to celebrate their Passover with Him."

In our sharing about the political and religious life of Josiah's time, my informants thus talked about the conflict in the church today as well, symbolized by the way in which they referred to God differently: "Our God" and "their God." In a real sense, their comments on Josiah's Yahweh featured "their God" as the God that today stays only in the church building and demands from the people only their prayers and religious sacrifices.

What I presented here is only a portion of our talks about our communities and activities in the light of the Bible. It was a process of mutual evangelization and conscientization. We shared with one another our own histories and our strong faith, which clearly dominated our Bible sharing.

When I explained that the Israelite peasants had been exploited by the urban patricians of Jerusalem and the majority became landless workers suffering from injustice, it was clear that my informants understood from their own experiences and struggles what I was talking about. The way in which these CEB leaders commented on Josiah's story, and particularly on Josiah's Passover, was so concrete and alive that it was clear that they were deeply immersed in the Bible and had come to see their own journey in terms of Josiah's story.

It is also very noticeable from their comments that, although the informants spoke much more about their own lives than Josiah's story itself, the story surely became a stimulus for their discussion and reflection on their pastoral activities. Probably what engaged them most of all was the history of Yahwism, and particularly the ideological justifications used by Josiah and his friends to monopolize the Passover.

While talking with me on the last night of the course, Ricardo said, "I had never thought about the possibility that someone abused God in the name of Yahweh. See the way in which Josiah used the book of the law and the prophetess to justify his reform as the intention of Yahweh! God forbid! How much they manipulated the people in the name of an official Yahweh to monopolize the Passover!

"And how about our church? How many times do we use the Bible and the name of famous theologians to justify our opinions and interests in front of the people? How many times does our church abuse God in the name of 'official Catholic Yahweh' against other religions, other churches, and the laity?"

In this course, I must confess that I did not explain exactly what the sociological exegesis was all about, nor would the explanation have interested my informants. Nevertheless, they adequately understood what kind of biblical hermeneutics they needed to plan the reflection pamphlets and the celebrations for their communities. At one point Sonia summed up this hermeneutics as "the reality of the people in the Bible, the reality of our people today, our real-life community, and our faith in a living God. These are all the tools we use to read the Bible!"

Finally, where my informants were confirmed and improved most in the course was in the sociological reading and interpretation of the Bible, in association with their real-life communities and their concrete situations. Thus they undoubtedly grew closer to the people in the Bible with this course, which has become a source of critical awareness and encouragement in their pastoral activities.

In their evaluation notes, we can see a part of this growth in the informants. For example, Sonia's answer to the question "What does Josiah's story say about your pastoral activities?' is as follows: "With all that is happening in the story, I am most impressed with the danger of 'alienation.' The workers of Josiah's time were very alienated and easily manipulated by the rich. I know if we women only stay watching the soap operas, in the future our kids will be more exploited than we are, and will not celebrate their Passover with dignity."

> Lord, we believe in the power of love and justice.
> We believe in the power of solidarity.
> Lead us from Greed to Sharing,

from Domination to Communion.
Lead us from Grief to Joy,
    from Death to Life.
                    (A spontaneous prayer of Angieli
                        at the final celebration).

CONSCIENTIZATION OF CEB MEMBERS IN THE BIBLE STUDY GROUP

The people who attended the course had come not only from the periphery of the city of São Paulo, but also from its center and the interior of the state of São Paulo. They made a diverse, rich, vital participant body that reflected the different social contexts and struggles of their CEBs. This diversity also appeared in the meetings that these leaders held upon their return to the communities.

Jair held a meeting with the animators of peasant groups, for example. After giving a short report about his experience in the course, he produced, with the help of the animators, a reflection pamphlet on the first meeting about Josiah's story. Second Kings 23:1–3 was selected as a text for the meeting with a theme of "church and participation." The reflection pamphlet is as follows:

Church and Participation

1. A short explanation for the setting of 2 Kings 23:1-3:
    Josiah was the king of the Israelite people. He governed his kingdom with the help of his friends such as Hilkiah. Hilkiah was the most powerful priest who was responsible for the church and religious celebrations of that time.
    One day Hilkiah found an important part of the Bible which contained the Book of the Law. He sent this book to the king through Shaphan, the secretary of the king.
    The king read the book and liked it, but he was not sure about how to interpret the book and the word of God. So he ordered his officials to consult with a court prophetess, Huldah, about the book. Huldah, who was a friend of Josiah and a specialist in the Bible, told them that the word of God suggested a change or reform for the church.
    After getting this answer from Huldah, the king consulted with his friends and officials about how to put the word of God into practice. And they decided to make a big religious reform in the kingdom, according to their interpretation of the book, without consulting the people. For example, in conformity with this reform, the lay people could no more celebrate the religious

celebrations by themselves, nor in their local communities. The celebrations had to be done only by the priests and only in the official church in the Jerusalem City.

After deciding everything about how to do the reform, King Josiah convoked the people for the feast, in which he presented the plan of the religious reform. Let us read the biblical text 2 Kings 23:1–3, which describes this feast!

2. Reading of 2 Kings 23:1–3:

3. Discussion questions:
   a. What about the way Josiah read and put the word of God into practice? Did the decision making about the reform come from the real intention of God and of the People?
   b. In what way would it be correct to read and put the word of God in practice in our community?
   c. What does this Josiah's story have to say about our community activities and our peasant movement?

Like Jair, some of my informants produced similar reflection pamphlets with different topics and different procedures. Other used a storytelling method to introduce the theme of Josiah's story into their community meetings. By using popular terms, they spoke in such a way that their listeners could understand them, and told a certain part of Josiah's story as if the biblical people in the past were explaining their experiences.

Ricardo, who held a meeting in his community of homeless people, was one of those informants using a storytelling method, with songs, pictures, and little plays. Most of his members did not know how to read, but loved to know and hear the words of the Bible.

I now offer a brief outline of how this meeting of the homeless people proceeded. I then present some of their comments on Josiah's story. I present this community meeting for two reasons: first, the Biblical Apostolate among the homeless people is a relatively new pastoral activity and is no easy task; second, this biblical meeting provides an example of how one of the most oppressed segments of society appreciates Josiah's story. Let me present the meeting.

A Meeting in Ricardo's Community

It's about 2:00 Wednesday afternoon. Ricardo's community members come together around a big kettle of stew. Wednesday is their weekly "soup

SE UNE SOFREDOR,
A CIDADE VAI OUVIR O SEU CLAMOR!

1. 12th Mission
2. All those who suffer,
   unite,
   And the city will hear
   your outcry!

day." Since the late morning, the volunteers have been working hard. Some clear up their meeting rooms, which are part of an abandoned government house. Others go to the marketplace, seeking ingredients for the soup. They gather the vegetables, and, if they are lucky enough, find meat and some fish offered by kind marketers. Some others go shopping for bread, butter, and other needs. The money for this shopping is collected from the members, who are normally working as junkmen, shoe-shiners, or whatever! While working cooperatively in groups, they cultivate their sense of responsibility and solidarity.

Some may wonder why I do not start with the description of the biblical meeting itself, but rather with the soup production? The reason is that the soup circle is the most important event in the daily lives of those homeless people, and consequently one of the important tools for talking about the Bible. It was these soup circles that started to gather the homeless people together and even succeeded in forming some communities in the center of São Paulo! So the soup circle became a symbol of the union and the struggles of the homeless people movement, expressed by Picture II.

There are about twenty-five participants in the soup circle this Wednesday. Socially, this gathering is a time for some of them living alone on the streets to meet with and to confirm the survival of other community members, their precious friends in the big and violent city of São Paulo. After this happy communal meal, they naturally move on to their biblical meeting. "Which song can we sing first?" exclaimed Ricardo, inviting the people to gather around and sit. The music sets them dancing, singing, and joining in the gathering.

Some of the songs recount the stories of the Bible, such as the stories of Abraham, Moses, Amos, and others. The song, "The People of God" is a specialty of those suffering people: "The people of God walked through the desert. They were thirsty and tired, but had hope ... We are also the people of God!" Thanks to these songs, they know several stories of the Bible and find their ongoing journey in time.

At this meeting, there are two new participants, Luiz and Alice, who introduce themselves to the others. They, like most of the community members, had abandoned their rural villages for the city because of continuing land conflicts and lack of adequate services.

"I got into São Paulo two years ago," said Alice, recounting her own history. "Just a few days later, I was robbed and lost all my money and documents. And, things are going to get worse and worse ... "

By using Alice's history, Ricardo starts to talk about the realities of the homeless people and gradually moves toward the Bible sharing around Josiah's story, with the use of some pictures. Let us see the point of Ricardo's talk.

Our Reality

Like Alice is saying, it's difficult for the rural people—small peasants, sharecroppers, renters, or day laborers—to live a decent life.

It's true? And why?
—The government gives to the big landowners financial support, but not to the small.
—No land available.
—Much violence over land.
—Police and judges with the big shots.
—The employers pay very little.
—Slave labor, etc.

1. Private

The rural workers have fled into the cities with their dreams to find decent conditions of work, housing, and life.

Now! Are their dreams coming true?

Well, well! What happens to most of the rural workers in the cities?

Is this happening to you?

They do know how to deal with hoes and land, but don't have skills in dealing with machines and money. It takes a while for them to find work in the cities. When they do, they are paid very little.

1. What can we do?

EXPLOITATION ...

So? Who is making money out of their cheap labor?

1. Rich
2. National Congress

What's happening to our society?

The answer ...
    Some want everything for themselves. No sharing! So keeping control over the others! Who are they?

DIVI   SION!

A similar story like this is recounted in the Bible. Let us see!

THE STORY OF JOSIAH

Once upon a time there lived a king in the kingdom of Judah. His name was Josiah. He and his friends lived high and wanted everything for themselves. On the contrary, his people had to pay heavy taxes, and were suffering from extreme poverty. The kingdom was full of the poor landless peasants, living like the suffering people of the street [homeless people].

1. Cashier

To expand their land, wealth, and power, King Josiah and his friends planned to attack and occupy the neighboring kingdoms. For this, they needed to collect for a war chest from the people.

But how did they succeed to get more money for the wars?

Well, . . .
Just look

King Josiah held a secret meeting with his friends and the officials to elaborate a plan for the collection, and decided to use the Bible, which the people loved. The king announced this plan.

Let's hear what the king said, . . .

I, the king of this nation, proclaim: "According to the Bible, our God wants all the people to come to the city Temple and to pay their duties to him: paying the religious taxes, celebrating all the feasts, etc."

Now, the rural people cannot celebrate any longer their feasts by themselves and in their communities. One of these feasts is the Passover, which is like our "soup-circle." In this feast, the peasants share their products and celebrate their union in the name of God.

And whoever was opposed to the king's plan was killed. Of course, the local communities of the people were destroyed and their joyful gatherings were stopped.

TERROR!

What happened to the rural people?

> **MORE EXPLOITATION:** By offering more of their products to the
> king and spending more on travel to the city, the peasants' lives got
> worse and worse, . . . Many of them lost their land!

> **NO UNION:** With the destruction of their communities, the peasants
> lost their places to get together, to talk together, and to pray
> together, . . .

> *Many peasants abandoned their villages and came to live in
> the city, wandering through the streets and begging, . . .*

And what does this story say about our own lives?

I think: "I think . . . ," says Itamar, who is conspicuous among the group
for his chatter, "this king is shameless! It's wrong to close down the communities of the people. Just imagine! If someone closed down our communities and we're not able to come together here . . . I know how these
peasants felt about their lives without the communities."

In his gentle but strong way, Ézio, a thin man, says, "The king is like
our former mayor who used to send his men and police to 'clean up' the

parks and the places under the viaducts. They cleaned up everything and threw our belongings into the trucks. And they, like the soldiers of the king, beat some homeless people who resisted the 'cleaning' and even threw them into prison. One night I got a stroke of the truncheon on my head and felt a dull pain all night."

"Just imagine!" exclaimed Tião, a companion of Itamar, "how much these poor peasants spent on their travels to the city. I think that many of them stayed in the parks and the streets to sleep. I know that! *Que sacanagem* [how filthy]! The king is doing the same thing that is going on around us. The rich want everything for themselves and make plans for this in private meetings."

I hear the homeless people giving such opinions one after another during the meeting. They find their own life process in Josiah's story and identify with the suffering people in the Bible. In a real sense they are living in the same sort of situation: exploitation, misery, and violence.

Probably what strikes me most in the meeting is the level of appreciation for the Bible and their community life among these men and women. Undoubtedly, the most common topic in their Bible reading is their experience told around the soup circle. They look at the tribal Passover in the Bible and give their opinions about their Passover today, summarized in the soup circle. "Look! The people of the Bible also have a joyful gathering," said Maria, sitting next to Ricardo.

"They work together, defend each other, and celebrate the Passover, giving thanks to God for His protection in their lives. Hey! Ricardo! I think this is what you are talking about, the Passover in the Bible, right? This feast says very much about our lives."

(One of the members pictures the soup circle.)

1. Lunch.
2. Collection among the street sufferers

Itamar says, "Like we see in the Bible, we also have our cooperative society. [They keep their collected old papers in the communal storehouse and negotiate together with the junk dealers for the price of the paper.] We support each other. And we have our lunch [soup] and community here."

"Yes, it's true. We have our Passover," said Carlos, who seems to be very much committed to the community. "But, my friends, we need to cooperate more with each other. Many times we see that the same persons are working to prepare our Wednesday gatherings. I know that people are very busy earning their living. But it would be good if more persons participated not only in the gathering but also in the preparation. The Bible is saying that everyone has to help everyone, right!"

Aristeu, one of the oldest members, joins the conversation and says: "I want to talk about our contribution to the lunch. You know that Ricardo sometimes pays for the bread for our lunch because our contributions are small. This is not right! We need to spend more of our money to help the community rather than to buy *pinga* and other things. The lunch is for us. The community is ours!"

(Walking together)

1. Street sufferers unite!
2. Bible
3. Walking together

Thus the homeless people reflect on the community life in the light of the Bible, and even come to make some constructive comments on their community activities, such as the opinions of Carlos and Aristeu. These constructive opinions, I believe, are one of the expressions of their strong appreciation for the community life. It is noticeable that although the community operation is still largely dependent on their pastoral agents, some of the homeless people like Carlos and Aristeu are becoming aware of their own responsibilities for organizing their own communities.

In this process of conscientization, the biblical meeting is doing something else very important. It is translating (introducing) the historical struggles and hopes of the people of God in the Bible into the struggles and hopes of the people of God today. The Bible, read from the viewpoint of both of these peoples in real-life situations, becomes the source of conscientization and union for the CEB members.

The biblical meetings, such as the meeting of Ricardo's community, were observed in the communities that I visited with the other participants in the course. With all that was said in these meetings, I was most excited over their sharing about the Passover. The people reflected on this feast and applied it, as a source of socioeconomic and religious union, to their own daily lives, particularly to their community activities. They were and are following the people of God in the Bible.

CONCLUSION

In this chapter, I have attempted to illustrate the ways in which the sociological exegesis of Josiah's Passover has helped the CEB members develop their hermeneutical skills and critical consciousness, particularly about their church institutions. What lessons can we learn from this particular illustration of sociological exegesis as a tool for the CEB biblical movement?

First, we have to recall that the CEB members are "at times working with an older and inadequate biblical exegesis" that often leads them to face the dangers of fundamentalist, subjective, and idealistic hermeneutics. These methods are inadequate, not only because they cannot offer precise representations of the material living conditions of the people at biblical times, but also because, by presenting the Bible in this way, they can become the exegetical tools of alienation and even of further oppression for the CEB members. So we reconfirm that the task of biblical scholarship and pastoral agents in the CEBs consists of the Bible Apostolate, which supports the people by enabling them to become emancipated from oppressive hermeneutics.

Second, we can appreciate that sociological exegesis is important precisely because it diminishes this danger of oppressive hermeneutics. This method helps the people of the present to grow closer to the actual material living conditions of the people in the Bible, thus becoming a critical tool for the CEB members. As we emphasized in chapters 1 to 4, the sociological method, while supplementing conventional methods, can stimulate a greater understanding of the social situation and of the social forces operative in biblical society. We understand that Josiah's Passover in particular was conditioned by a specific social context, and note that it was translated into socioeconomic, political, and ideological power for the ruling elite's control over the Israelite populace. By introducing such understanding of the Israelite religion and its institutions into their own lives, the CEB members are able to become more aware of the problems of the church today. In the CEBs, sociological exegesis indeed strikes at the roots of the exegetical task of reading the Bible.

Third, through our experience in applying sociological exegesis to CEB biblical activities, we can also come to a better understanding of the importance of both reading the Bible in community and from the perspective of the poor. On the one hand, the reading of the Bible in community frees the people from individualistic hermeneutics. The reading of the Bible through the eyes of the poor, on the other hand, helps the people to grasp more easily the day-to-day struggles of the suffering in the Bible.

But most important, we emphasize that this CEB biblical hermeneutics and sociological exegesis surely supplement each other. It is a process of mutual support. Sociological exegesis provides pertinent sociocritical biblical hermeneutics for the CEBs. CEB hermeneutics in turn prevents sociological exegesis from being overly individualistic in regard to its concern and process. When sociological exegesis is brought into the life of the community or the reality of the people's struggle, then it has "life" and serves the common people, to whom the Bible belongs. In this sense this method really fertilizes the CEB biblical movement, and the Bible becomes a fruitful resource for social change. This fundamental sharing between the grassroots Bible study and scientific exegesis has been aptly described by Carlos Mesters:

> Exegesis is being called upon to concern itself, not with the questions it raises, but with the questions that the common people are raising. In many cases the exegete is like the person who has studied salt and knew all its chemical properties but didn't know how to cook with it. The common people don't know the properties of salt well, but they do know how to season a meal (1984: 132).

"Every method," states John Paul II, "has its limitations; it is necessary to recognize them" (*L'Osservatore Romano*, 17 April, 1989, 11). We appreciate his message. We also appreciate the following message of Dom Hélder Câmara, who really works and lives among the suffering poor: "There is nothing against liberation theology as long as you accept that the eternal liberation of God goes alongside the liberation of human beings from animal-like conditions" (*Chicago Tribune*, 28 July, 1989, section 2, 8).

Assuredly, this message also holds true in the case of sociological exegesis and the CEBs under study. The biblical study groups that I visited during this project research have appropriated and applied the sociological exegesis of Josiah's Passover to their daily lives. This has led to the development of a progressively greater sense of community and has strengthened their liberation movement from socioeconomic, political, and religious oppression. While observing the people sharing their faith and common tasks in the light of the Bible, I have the impression that we are seeing not just the birth of a new kind of decentralized system of the church, but of a new kind of real Christian community.

Let me close with an experience of prayer I had during my visit to one of these communities, Ricardo's group. After their Bible sharing, the group started to play a little game. They sat in a circle and passed a can (one of their soup plates) from hand to hand while listening to the sound of a guitar. The group stopped passing the can whenever the guitarist stopped playing. The person who had the can in his or her hand at that moment had to pay a penalty. For several persons, the penalty was the requirement to perform their specialty, their favorite song or poems, for example, in front of the group.

Arlindo, about thirty years of age, was one of these performers. He arrived in São Paulo about two years ago, coming from the interior of the west-central state of Goiás after losing both his land and his family. With the guitar accompaniment, he passionately sang his favorite song.

I do not remember the title, if it had one, but it was a folk song describing the dream of a loving couple in the countryside. They dream of their peaceful life, surrounded by a small cattle ranch, vineyard, fields, and Mother Nature. I still remember a phrase of the song because it gives a vivid description of this dream. The phrase says, "I just want to live in a small way, in a small house, painted white."

Curiously, although they were a noisy and talkative group, the homeless people fell silent at the song of Arlindo. It was almost as though they were drawn into the dream of rural life described by the song and were meditating upon their memories of past days. They seemed to have a sense of getting back in touch with the way most of the world is supposed to be living. They, like most of the other homeless people, had fled into the city because of poverty and increasing violence over land, and so, I believe, they related to Arlindo's song.

There was, in the middle of the people's circle, a big and much-used Bible, which was set there as a symbol of the presence of God. I gazed at those men and women sitting around the Bible. Their faces were pinched from their harsh daily suffering, and their clothes stank of sweat and poverty. Then my gaze shifted to the Bible, whose story those poor people really loved to hear. I felt the Bible telling me: "If you want to hear the Word of God in me, you must first learn from my people sitting next to you."

How many times do we neglect the fact that it is primarily in the world and not in the Bible that God lives? The biblical Word is our clue to God's presence in the world, rather than God's permanent dwelling place.

Abbreviations

AIR	Patrick D. Miller, Jr., Paul D. Hanson, and S. Dean McBride, ed. *Ancient Israelite Religion.* Philadelphia: Fortress Press, 1987.
AJBI	*Annual of the Japanese Biblical Institute*
AJSL	*American Journal of Semitic Languages and Literatures*
ASTI	*Annual of the Swedish Theological Institute*
BA	*Biblical Archaeologist*
BASOR	*Bulletin of the American Schools of Oriental Research*
BETL	*Bibliotheca ephemeridum theologicarum lovaniensium*
Bib	*Biblica*
BL	Norman K. Gottwald, ed. *The Bible and Liberation.* Maryknoll, N.Y.: Orbis Books, 1984.
BTB	*Biblical Theology Bulletin*
CBQ	*Catholic Biblical Quarterly*
CTM	*Concordia Theological Monthly*
DBS	*Dictionnaire de la Bible.* Supplément, Paris.
EB	*Estudos Bíblicos*
EJ	*Encyclopedia Judaica*, Jerusalem
ET	*Expository Times*
EvTh	*Evangelische Theologie*
Hen	Henoch, Instituto di Orientalistica dell'Università di Torino
HSM	*Harvard Semitic Monographs*
HUCA	*Hebrew Union College Annual*
ICC	*The International Critical Commentary*
IDB	*The Interpreter's Dictionary of the Bible*
IDBSup	*IDB Supplementary Volume*
IEJ	*Israel Exploration Journal*
JAAR	*Journal of the American Academy of Religion*
JANES	*Journal of the Ancient Near Eastern Society of Columbia University*
JAOS	*Journal of the American Oriental Society*
JBL	*Journal of Biblical Literature*
JCS	*Journal of Cuneiform Studies*
JJS	*Journal of Jewish Studies*
JNES	*Journal of Near Eastern Studies*
JQR	*Jewish Quarterly Review*
JSOT	*Journal for the Study of the Old Testament*
LTQ	*Lexington Theological Quarterly*
OTS	*Oudtestamentische Studiën*
PEQ	*Palestine Exploration Quarterly*
PTMS	*Pittsburgh Theological Monograph Series*
RB	*Revue Biblique*
REB	*Revista Eclesiástica Brasileira*
RIBLA	*Revista de Interpretação Bíblica Latino-Americana,* São Paulo
SBL	Society of Biblical Literature

SBLMS	*Society of Biblical Literature Monograph Series*
SBT	*Studies in Biblical Theology*
SEA	*Svensk exegetisk arsbok*
SEDOC	*Serviço de Documentação,* Rio de Janeiro
SJT	*Scottish Journal of Theology*
ST	*Studia Theologica*
StBib	*Studia Biblica et Theologica,* Pasadena
StSem	*Studi Semitici,* Rome
TDOT	G. J. Botterweck and H. Ringgren, ed. *Theological Dictionary of the Old Testament*
VP	*Vida Pastoral: Revista para Sacerdotes e Agentes de Pastoral,* São Paulo
VT	*Vetus Testamentum*
VTSup	*VT Supplements*
WHJP	Benjamin Mazar, ed. *World History of the Jewish People: First Series: Ancient Times.* Jerusalem: Jewish History Publications (Masada Press), 1979.
ZAW	*Zeitschrift für die Alttestamentliche Wissenschaft*
ZDMG	*Zeitschrift der Deutschen Morgenländischen Gesellschaft*
ZTK	*Zeitschrift für Theologie und Kirche*

Bibliography

Abba, R.
1962   "Priests and Levites." *IDB* 3:876–89.
1977a   "The Origin and Significance of Hebrew Sacrifice." *BTB* 7:123–38.
1977b   "Priests and Levites in Deuteronomy." *VT* 27. Fasc. 3:257–67.

Achtemeier, P. J., ed.
1985   *Harper's Bible Dictionary*. San Francisco: Harper & Row.

Ackroyd, P. R.
1974   "An Interpretation of the Babylonian Exile: A Study of 2 Kings 20, Isaiah 38–39." *SJT* 27:329–52.
1978   "The Theology of the Chronicler." *LTQ* 8:103–16.

Aharoni, Yohanan
1967   "Forerunners of the Limes: Iron Age Fortresses in the Negev." *IEJ* 17:1–17.
1968   "Arad: Its Inscriptions and Temple." *BA* 31:1–32.
1979   *The Land of the Bible: A Historical Geography*. 2nd ed. Philadelphia: Westminster.
1982   *The Archaeology of the Land of Israel from the Beginnings to the End of the First Temple Period*. Ed. Miriam Aharoni. Philadelphia: Westminster.

Aharoni, Yohanan, and Avi-Yonah, Michael
1977   *The Macmillan Bible Atlas*. Rev. ed. New York: Macmillan Co.

Ahlström, G. W.
1963   *Aspects of Syncretism in Israelite Religion*. Lund: C. W. K. Gleerup.
1968   "Solomon, The Chosen One." *History of Religions* 8, pp. 94–110. Chicago: University of Chicago.
1982   *Royal Administration and National Religion in Ancient Palestine. Studies in the History of the Ancient Near East 1*. Leiden: E. J. Brill.

Albright, William F.
1957   "The High Place in Ancient Palestine." *VTSup* 4:106–18.
1960   *The Archaeology of Palestine*. Rev. ed. Baltimore: Penguin Books.
1963   *The Biblical Period from Abraham to Ezra*. Rev. ed. New York: Harper & Row.
1969   *Archaeology and the Religion of Israel*. 5th ed. Garden City, N.Y.: Doubleday.
1978   *Yahweh and the Gods of Canaan: An Historical Analysis of Two Contrasting Faiths*. Winona Lake, Ind.: Eisenbrauns.

Alfrink, B.
1934   "Die Schlacht bei Megiddo und der Tod des Josias (609)." *Bib* 15:173–84.

Alt, Albrecht
1953   "Judas Gaue unter Josia." *Kleine Schriften zur Geschichte des Volkes Israel* 2, pp. 276–88. Munich.
1966   "The Formation of the Israelite State in Palestine." *Essays on Old Tes-*

tament History and Religion, pp. 222–309. Ed. Albrecht Alt. Garden City, N.Y.: Doubleday.

Anderson, Bernhard W.
1972   "Introduction: Martin Noth's Traditio-Historical Approach in the Context of Twentieth-Century Biblical Criticism." Martin Noth. *A History of Pentateuchal Traditions*, pp. xii-xxxii. Englewood Cliffs, N.J.: Prentice-Hall.

Anderson, Francis
1978   *The Eighth Century Prophets: Amos, Hosea, Isaiah, Micah.* Proclamation Commentaries. Philadelphia: Fortress.

Anderson, Gary A.
1987   *Sacrifices and Offerings in Ancient Israel: Studies in their Social and Political Importance.* Atlanta: Scholars Press.

Antoniazzi, Alberto
1982   "O Povo e as Traduçães da Bíblia." *VP* (Maio-Junho):15–23.

Aquino, R. S. L.
1980   *História das Sociedades: das comunidades primitivas às sociedades medievais.* Rio de Janeiro: Ao Livro Técnico.

Arnold, W. R.
1912   "The Passover Papyrus from Elephantine." *JBL* 31:1–33.

Assmann, Hugo, and Hinkelammert, Franz J.
1989   *A Idolatria do Mercado.* Petrópolis: Vozes.

Astour, M.
1971   "841 B.C.: The First Assyrian Invasion of Israel." *JAOS* 91:383–89.

Auerbach, Elias
1958   "Die Feste im alten Israel." *VT* 8:1–18.

Auster, Richard D., and Silver, Morris
1979   *The State as a Firm: Economic Forces in Political Development.* Boston: Martinus Nijhoff.

Avigad, N.
1963   "Two Newly-found Hebrew Seals." *IEJ* 13:322–24.
1980   "The Chief of the Corvée." *IEJ* 30:170–73.
1987   "The Contribution of Hebrew Seals to an Understanding of Israelite Religion and Society." *AIR*, pp. 195-208.

Avila, Charles
1981   *Worship and Politics.* Maryknoll, N.Y.: Orbis.

Baly, Denis
1970   "The Geography of Monotheism." *Translating and Understanding the Old Testament: Essays in Honor of Herbert Gordon May*, pp. 253-78. Ed. Harry Thomas Frank and William L. Reed. New York: Abingdon Press.

Banu, I.
1975   "La Formación Social 'Asiática' en la Perspectiva de la Filosofía Oriental Antigua." *El Modo de Producción Asiático*, pp. 297–316. Ed. R. Bartra. México: Era.

Bardtke, H.
1971   "Die Latifundien in Juda während der zweiten Hälfte des achten Jahrhunderts v. Chr. (Zum Verständnis von Jes 5, 8–10)." *Hommages à A. Dupont-Sommer*, pp. 235–54. Paris.

Barnett, R. D.
1981   "Bringing the God into the Temple." *Temples and High Places in Biblical Times*, pp. 10–20. Ed. A. Biran. Jerusalem.

Barrick, W. B.
1980   "What Do We Really Know about High Places?" *SEA* 45:50–57.

Barrois, G. A.
1962   "Trade and Commerce." *IDB* 4:677–83.

Bartra, R.
1978   "Tributo e Posse da Terra na Sociedade Asteca." *Conceito de Mode de Produção*, pp. 157–80. Ed. Ph. Gebran. Rio de Janeiro: Paz e Terra.

Beattie, John
1964   *Other Cultures: Aims, Methods and Achievements in Social Anthropology.* New York: The Free Press.

Beek, M. A.
1972   "The Meaning of the Expression 'The Chariots and the Housemen of Israel' (II Kings ii 12)." *OTS* 17:1–10.

Belo, Fernando
1975   *Lectura Materialista del Evangelio de Marcos.* Estella: Verbo Divino. (English trans.: *A Materialist Reading of the Bible.* Maryknoll, N.Y.: Orbis, 1981.)

Benjamin, Don C.
1983   *Deuteronomy and City Life.* Lanham, Md.: University Press of America.

Berry, G. R.
1920   "The Code Found in the Temple." *JBL* 39:44–51.

Bertholet, Alfred
1926   *A History of Hebrew Civilization.* London: George G. Harrap & Company Ltd.

Betto, Frei
1986   *Introdução à Política Brasileira.* São Paulo: Ática.

Beyerlin, Walter, ed.
1978   *Near Eastern Religious Texts Relating to the Old Testament.* Philadelphia: Westminster.

Bin-Nun, S. R.
1968   "Formulas from Royal Records of Israel and of Judah." *VT* 18:414–34.

Bird, Phyllis A.
1984   "Images of Women in the Old Testament." *BL*, pp. 252–88.

Blenkinsopp, Joseph
1975   "The Quest of the Historical Saul." *No Famine in the Land. Studies in Honor of John L. McKenzie*, pp. 75–99. Ed. J. W. Flanagan and A. W. Robinson. Missoula: Scholars Press.
1983   *A History of Prophecy in Israel.* Philadelphia: Westminster.

Bloch, Abraham P.
1978   *The Biblical and Historical Background of the Jewish Holy Days.* New York: KTAV.

Boecker, Hans Jochen
1980   *Law and Administration of Justice in the Old Testament and Ancient East.* Minneapolis: Augsburg.

Boff, Clodovis
1978   *Comunidade Eclesial – Comunidade Política.* Petrópolis: Vozes.
1979   "A Influência Política da CEBs." *Religião e Sociedade* 4:95–119.
1980a   "Agente de Pastoral e Povo." *REB* 40:216–42.
1980b   "Comunidades Eclesiais de Base e Práticas e Libertação." *REB* 40:596–626.

Boff, C., and Pixley, G.
1989   *The Bible, the Church, and the Poor.* Maryknoll, N.Y.: Orbis.

Boff, Leonardo
1975   "As Eclesiologias Presentes nas Comunidades Eclesiais de Base." *Uma Igreja Oue Nasce do Povo*, pp. 201–9. Ed. Carlos Mesters. Petrópolis: Vozes.

1977   *Eclesiogênese: As Comunidades Eclesiais de Base Reinventam a Igreja.* Petrópolis: Vozes. (English trans.: *Ecclesiogenesis: The Base Communities Reinvent the Church.* Maryknoll, N.Y.: Orbis, 1986).

1982   *Vida segundo o Espírito.* Petrópolis: Vozes.

1990   *Nova Evangelização: Perspectiva dos Oprimidos.* Fortaleza: Vozes. (English trans.: *New Evangelization: Good News to the Poor.* Maryknoll, N.Y.: Orbis, 1992.)

Bokser, Baruch M.

1984   *The Origins of the Seder: The Passover Rite and Early Rabbinic Judaism.* Berkeley: University of California Press.

Bordin, Luigi

1987   *O Marxismo e a Teologia da Libertação.* Rio de Janeiro: Dois Pontos.

Bortolini, J., ed.

1990   *Bíblia Sagrada: Edição Pastoral.* São Paulo: Paulinas.

Brandão, C. R.

1985   *Memória do Sagrado: Estudo de Religião e Ritual.* São Paulo: Paulinas.

Bratcher, Dennis R.

1985   "Deuteronomy." *Harper's Bible Dictionary*, pp. 219–20. Ed. Paul J. Achtemeier. San Francisco: Harper & Row.

Braun, Roddy

1986   *1 Chronicles.* Word Biblical Commentary. Waco, Tex.: Word Books.

Bright, John.

1981   *A History of Israel.* 3rd ed. Philadelphia: Westminster.

Brinton, Crane

1965   *The Anatomy of Revolution.* Revised and Expanded Edition. New York: A Vintage Book.

Brooks, B. A.

1941   "Fertility Cult Functionaries in the Old Testament." *JBL* 60:227–53.

Broshi, M.

1974   "The Expansion of Jerusalem in the Reigns of Hezekiah and Manasseh." *IEJ* 24:2–26.

Brown, Raymond E.

1985   *Biblical Exegesis & Church Doctrine.* Mahwah, N.J.: Paulist Press.

Brueggemann, Walter

1961   "A Form Critical Study on the Cultic Material in Deuteronomy: An Analysis of the Nature of the Cultic Encounter in the Mosaic Tradition." Th. D. dissertation, Union Theological Seminary.

1976   "Yahwist." *IDBSup*: 971–75.

1984   "Trajectories in Old Testament Literature and the Sociology of Ancient Israel." *BL*, pp. 307–33.

Brueggemann, W., and Wolff, H. W.

1982   *The Vitality of Old Testament Traditions.* 2nd ed. Atlanta: John Knox Press.

Buccellati, Giorgio

1967   "Cities and Nations of Ancient Syria. An Essay on Political Institutions with Special Reference to the Israelite Kingdoms." *StSem* 26. Rome: Instituto di Studi del Vicino Oriente.

Budd, Philip J.

1973   "Priestly Instruction in Pre-Exilic Israel." *VT* 23:1–14.

1984   *Numbers.* Word Biblical Commentary. Waco, Tex.: Word Books.

1989   "Holiness and Cult." *The World of Ancient Israel*, pp. 275–98. Ed. R. E. Clements. Cambridge: Cambridge University Press.

Budde, K.

1926   "Das Deuteronomium und die Reform König Josias." *ZAW* 44:177–224.

Buhl, Frantz
1897   "Social Institutions of the Israelites." *American Journal of Theology* 1.

Burney, C. F.
1970   *The Book of Judges and Notes on the Hebrew Text of the Books of Kings (Two Volumes in One).* New York: KTAV.

Butler, T. C.
1983   *Joshua.* Word Biblical Commentary. Waco, Tex.: Word Books.

Carroll, R. P.
1977   "The Aniconic God and the Cult of Images." *ST* 31:51–64.

Catani, A. M.
1981   *O que é o Capitalismo.* São Paulo: Brasilience.

Cazelles, H.
1946   *Études sur le Code L'Alliance.* Paris: Letouzey et Ané.
1979   "The History of Israel in the Pre-exilic Period." *Tradition and Interpretation,* pp. 274–319. Ed. G. W. Anderson. Oxford. Oxford University Press.

Chaney, Marvin L.
1983   "Ancient Palestinian Peasant Movements and the Formation of Premonarchic Israel." *Palestine in Transition,* pp. 39–90. Ed. D. N. Freedman and D. F. Graf. Sheffield: Almond.
1986   "Systemic Study of the Israelite Monarchy." *Semeia* 37:53–76.

Charbel, A.
1967   *Il Sacrificio Pacifico: nei suoi riti e nel suo significato religioso e figurativo.* Jerusalem.
1974   "Posizione degli Shelamim nella Sacra Scrittura." *Salesianum* 36:431–42.
1975   "Origine degli Shelamim in Israele." *Riv. Bibl.* 23:261–78.

Chaui, M.
1986   *O que é ideologia.* São Paulo: Brasiliense.

Childe, V. Gordon
1951   *Man Makes Himself.* New York: The New American Library.
1964   *What Happened in History.* Baltimore: Penguin Books.
1981   *A Evolução Cultural do Homem.* Rio de Janeiro: Zahar.

Childs, Brevard S.
1967   "Isaiah and the Assyrian Crisis." *SBT,* 2nd ser., 3. London: SCM.
1976   *The Book of Exodus: A Critical, Theological Commentary.* Philadelphia: Westminster.
1986   *Old Testament Theology in a Canonical Context.* Philadelphia: Fortress.
1987   *Introduction to the Old Testament as Scripture.* Philadelphia: Fortress.

Chopp, Rebecca S.
1986   *The Praxis of Suffering: An Interpretation of Liberation and Political Theologies.* Maryknoll, N.Y.: Orbis.

Claburn, William E.
1968   "Deuteronomy and Collective Behavior." Ph.D. dissertation, Princeton University.
1973   "The Fiscal Basis of Josiah's Reform." *JBL* 92:11–22.

Clastres, P.
1978   *A Sociedade contra o Estado.* Rio de Janeiro: Francisco Alves.

Clements, R. E.
1965a   *God and Temple.* Philadelphia: Fortress.
1965b   "Deuteronomy and the Jerusalem Cult Tradition." *VT* 15:300–12.
1989   "Israel in its historical and cultural setting." *The World of Ancient Israel,* pp. 3–16. Ed. R. E. Clements. Cambridge: Cambridge University Press.

Cody, Aelred
1965   "Le Titre Égyptien et le Nom Propre du Scribe de David." *RB* 72:381–93.

1969   "A History of the Old Testament Priesthood." *Analecta Biblica* 35. Rome: Pontifical Biblical Institute.

Cogan, Morton D.
1974   *Imperialism and Religion: Assyria, Judah and Israel in the Eighth and Seventh Centuries B.C.E.* SBL Monograph Series 19. Missoula: Scholars Press.

Cogan, M., and Tadmor, H.
1988   II Kings — Commentaries. *The Anchor Bible.* V. 11. Doubleday & Company.

Cohen, Martin A.
1965   "The Role of the Shilonite Priesthood in the United Monarchy of Ancient Israel." *HUCA* 36:59–98.
1971   "The Rebellions During the Reign of David. An Inquiry Into Social Dynamics in Ancient Israel." *Studies in Jewish Bibliography, History and Literature in Honor of I. E. Kiev,* pp. 91–113. Ed. C. Berlin. New York: KTAV.
1979   "The Prophets as Revolutionaries: A Sociopolitical Analysis." *Biblical Archaeology Review* (May/June):12–19.

Collins, John J.
1977   "The Meaning of Sacrifice: A Contrast of Methods." *Biblical Research* 22:19–37.

Comblin, José
1982   "Critérios para um Comentário da Bíblia." *REB* 42. Fasc. 166:307–30.

Coogan, Michael David
1987   "Canaanite Origins and Lineage: Reflections on the Religion of Ancient Israel." *AIR,* pp. 115–24.

Coote, Robert B., and Whitelam, Keith W.
1986   "The Emergence of Israel: Social Transformation and State Formation Following the Decline in Late Bronze Age Trade." *Semeia* 37:107–47.

Couroyer, B.
1955   "L'origine égyptienne du mot 'Pâque.'" *RB* 62:481–96.

Craigie, P. C.
1976   *The Book of Deuteronomy.* The New International Commentary on the Old Testament. Grand Rapids, Mich.: Eerdmans.

Crenshaw, James L.
1986   *Story and Faith: A Guide to the Old Testament.* New York: Macmillan Publishing Company.

Croatto, Severino
1981   *Exodus: A Hermeneutics of Freedom.* Maryknoll, N.Y.: Orbis.
1989   *Isaías. Vol. I:1–39: O profeta da justiça e da fidelidade.* São Paulo: Vozes, Metodista e Sinodal.

Cross, Frank M.
1973   *Canaanite Myth and Hebrew Epic: Essays in the History of the Religion of Israel.* Cambridge, Mass.: Harvard University Press.
1979   "Two Offering Dishes with Phoenician Inscriptions from the Sanctuary of Arad." *BASOR* 235:75–8.
1983   "The Epic Traditions of Early Israel." *The Poet and the Historian,* pp. 13–39. Ed. Richard Elliott Friedman. Chico: Scholars Press.

Cross, Frank M., and Freedman, D. N.
1953   "Josiah's Revolt against Assyria." *JNES* 12:56–8.

Cross, Frank M., and Wright, G. E.
1956   "The Boundary and Province Lists of the Kingdom of Judah." *JBL* 75:202–26.

Crüsemann, Frank
1984   "State Tax and Temple Tithe in Israel's Monarchical Period." Paper presented to the Sociology of the Monarchy Seminar of the Society of Biblical Literature, annual meeting, Chicago, Ill., December 10.

Cundall, Arthur E.
1965   "Sanctuaries (Central and Local) in Pre-Exilic Israel, with Particular Reference to the Book of Deuteronomy." *Vox Evangelica* 4:4–27.

Curtin, Philip D.
1984   *Cross-Cultural Trade in World History.* Cambridge: Cambridge University Press.

da Silva, Antônio Aparecido, ed.
1990   *América Latina: 500 Anos de Evangelização.* São Paulo: Paulinas.

Dalton, George
1980   *Economic Systems & Society: Capitalism, Communism and the Third World.* New York: Penguin Books.

Daly, Robert J.
1978   *Christian Sacrifice: The Judaeo-Christian Background before Origen.* Washington, D.C.: The Catholic University of America Press.

Davidson, R.
1989   "Covenant Ideology in Ancient Israel." *The World of Ancient Israel*, pp. 323–47. Ed. R. E. Clements. Cambridge: Cambridge University Press.

Davies, E. W.
1989   "Land; Its Rights and Privileges." *The World of Ancient Israel*, pp. 349–69. Ed. R.E. Clements. Cambridge: Cambridge University Press.

Déaut, Roger le
1963   *La Nuit Pascale: Essai sur la signification de la Pâque juive à partir du Targum d'Exode XII 42.* Rome: Institut Biblique Pontifical.

de Boer, P. A. H.
1972   "An Aspect of Sacrifice." *Studies in the Religion of Ancient Israel. VTSup* 23, pp. 27–47. Leiden: E.J. Brill.

de Geus, C. H. J.
1975   "The Importance of Archaeological Research into the Palestinian Agricultural Terraces, with an Excursus on the Hebrew Word *gbi.*" *PEQ* 107:65–74.

Delcor, M.
1982   "Reflexions sur la Pâque du temps de Josias d'après II Rois 23, 21–23." *Hen* 4:205–19.

Dentan, Robert C.
1964   *The Layman's Bible Commentary.* Vol 7. *The First and Second Books of the Kings. The First and Second Books of the Chronicles.* Atlanta: John Knox Press.

de Oliveira, M. A.
1989   "As CEBs e os dilemas do processo de democratização." *REB* 49. Fasc. 195:563–72.

de Vaux, R.
1964   *Studies in Old Testament Sacrifice.* Cardiff: University of Wales Press.
1965   *Ancient Israel.* Two vol. Paperback. New York: McGraw–Hill.
1966   "Jérusalem et les Prophètes." *RB* 73:481–509.
1976   *Instituciones del Antiguo Testamento.* Barcelona: Herder.

Dever, William G.
1987   "The Contribution of Archaeology to the Study of Canaanite and Early Israelite Religion." *AIR*, pp. 209–47.

DeVries, S. J.
1978   *Prophet Against Prophet.* Grand Rapids, Mich.: Eerdmans.

De Wette, W. M. L.
1805   "Dissertatio Critica." Reprinted in his *Opuscula*, Berlin, 1833.

Diaz, J. A.
1975   "La muerte de Josias en la redacion deuterónomica de libros de los Reges como anticipación de la teología de libro de Job." *Homenaje a Juan Padro*, pp. 167–77. Madrid: Inst. B. A. Montano.

Dietrich, L. J.
1987   Leitura Sociológica (da Bíblia). Mimeo. São Paulo.

Dietrich, W.
1977   "Josia und das Gesetzbuch (2 Reg. 22)." *VT* 27:13–35.

Dillard, R. B.
1987   *2 Chronicles.* Word Biblical Commentary. Waco, Tex.: Word Books.

Divitçioglu, S.
1978   "Modelos Econômicos a partir do Modo de Produção Asiático." Conceito de Modo de Produção, pp. 89–107 Ed. Ph. Gebran. Rio de Janeiro: Paz e Terra.

Driver, S. R.
1965   *Deuteronomy: Critical and Exegetical Commentary.* Edinburgh: T. & T. Clark.

Dulles, Avery
1987   *Models of the Church.* New York: Doubleday.

Durham, John I.
1987   *Exodus.* Word Biblical Commentary. Waco, Tex.: Word Books.

Dussaud, R.
1949   *Les origines Cananéennes du sacrifice Israélite.* Paris: Leroux.

Dussel, E.
1985   *La Producción Teórica de Marx: un Comentario a los Grundrisse.* México: Siglo Veintiuno Editores.

Eakin, F. E., Jr.
1965   "Yahwism and Baalism before the Exile." *JBL* 84: 407-17.

Eisenstadt, S. N.
1979   "Observations and Queries about Sociological Aspects of Imperialism in the Ancient World." *Mesopotamia*, pp. 21–33.Copenhagen Studies Assyriology. Vol. 7. Ed. Mogens Trolle Larsen. Copenhagen.

Eissfeldt, Otto
1922   "Die Bücher der Könige." *Die Heilige Schrift des Alten Testaments.* Vol. 2, pp. 492–585. Ed. E. Kautzsch. Tübingen: J. C. B. Mohr.

Ekholm, K., and Friedman, J.
1979   " 'Capital' Imperialism and Exploitation in Ancient World Systems." *Mesopotamia*, pp. 41–58. Copenhagen Studies Assyriology. Vol. 7. Ed. Mogens Trolle Larsen Copenhagen.

Elat, Moshe
1975   "The Political Status of the Kingdom of Judah Within the Assyrian Empire in the 7th Century B.C.E." *Investigation at Lachish: The Sanctuary and the Residency (Lachish V)*, pp. 61–70. Ed. Y. Aharoni. Tel Aviv: Gateway Publishers.
1979   "The Monarchy and the Development of Trade in Ancient Israel." *State and Temple Economy in the Ancient Near East.* Vol. 2, pp. 527–46. Ed. E. Lipiński. Louvain: Dept. Oriëntalistiek.

Elliott, J. H.
1981   *A Home for the Homeless.* Philadelphia: Fortress.

Engnell, Ivan
1952   "Paesah-Massot and the Problem of 'Patternism'." *Orientalia Suecana*
              1:39–50.
1967   *Studies in Divine Kingship in the Ancient Near East.* Oxford: Blackwell &
              Mott.
Eph'al, Israel
1979   "Assyrian Dominion in Palestine After the Fall of Samaria." *WHJP* 4/1,
              pp. 276–89.
Epsztein, L.
1986   *Social Justice in the Ancient Near East and the People of the Bible.* London:
              SCM.
Evans, Carl D.
1980   "Judah's Foreign Policy from Hezekiah to Josiah." *Scripture in Context:
              Essays on the Comparative Method*, pp. 157–78. Ed. Carl D. Evans, William
              W. Hallo, and John B. White. *PTMS* 34. Pittsburgh: Pickwick Press.
Evans, William E.
1983   "An Historical Reconstruction of the Emergence of Israelite Kingship and
              the Reign of Saul." *Scripture in Context II. More Essays in Comparative
              Method*, pp. 61–77. Ed. William W. Hallo, James C. Mayer, and Leo G.
              Purdue. Winona Lake, Ind.: Eisenbrauns.
Faleiros, V.
1986   *O que é Política Social.* São Paulo: Brasiliense.
Faur, J.
1978   "The Biblical Idea of Idolatry." *JQR* 69:1–15.
Ferm, Deane William, ed.
1987   *Third World Liberation Theologies.* Maryknoll, N.Y.: Orbis.
Fernandes, F.
1981   *O que é Revolução.* São Paulo: Brasiliense.
Feuer, Lewis S. ed.
1959   *Marx & Engels, Basic Writings on Politics and Philosophy.* Garden City, N.Y.:
              Doubleday.
Fierro, Alfredo
1984   "Exodus Event and Interpretation in Political Theologies." *BL*, pp. 473–
              81.
Finley, M. I.
1973   *The Ancient Economy.* Berkeley: University of California Press.
Fioravante, E.
1978a   "Do Modo de Produção Asiático ao Modo de Produção Capitalista." *Con-
              ceito de Modo de Produção*, pp. 131–55. Ed. Ph. Gebran. Rio de Janeiro:
              Paz e Terra.
1978b   "Modo de Produção, Formação Social Processo de Trabalho." *Conceito
              de Modo de Produção*, pp. 31–41. Ed. Ph. Gebran. Rio de Janeiro: Paz e
              Terra.
Flanagan, James W.
1979   "The Relocation of the Davidic Capital." *JAAR* 47:223–44.
1981   "Chiefs in Israel." *JSOT* 20:47–73.
Fohrer, Georg
1968   *Introduction to the Old Testament.* Nashville, Tenn.: Abingdon Press. Com-
              plete revision of original by Ernst Sellin.
1972   *History of Israelite Religion.* Nashville, Tenn.: Abingdon.
1982   *Estruturas Teológicas Fundamentais do Antigo Testamento.* São Paulo: Pau-
              linas.

Follmann, J. I.
1985   *Igreja, Ideologia e Classes Sociais.* Petrópolis: Vozes.
Foucault, M.
1984   *Microfísica do Poder.* Rio de Janeiro: Graal.
Fraine, J. de
1954   *L'aspect religieux de la royaute Israelite: l'institution monarchique dans l'an-
            cien Testament et dans les Textes mesopotamiens.* Rome: Pontifical Biblical
            Institute.
Frankfort, H.
1948   *Kingship and the Gods.* Chicago: University of Chicago Press.
Freed, A.
1921   "The Code Spoken of in 2 Kings 22–23." *JBL* 40:76–80.
Freedman, David Noel
1987   " 'Who Is Like Thee Among the Gods?': The Religion of Early Israel."
            AIR, pp. 315–35.
Freire, Paulo
1969   *Educação como prática da Liberdade.* Rio de Janeiro: Paz e Terra.
1989   *Pedagogy of the Oppressed.* Thirty-first Printing. New York: Continuum.
Fretheim, Terence E.
1983   *Deuteronomic History.* New York: Abingdon.
Frick, Frank S.
1971   "The Rechabites Reconsidered." *JBL* 90:279–87.
1977   *The City in Ancient Israel.* Missoula: Scholars Press.
1985   *The Formation of the State in Ancient Israel.* Decatur, Ga.: Almond.
1986   "Social Science Methods and Theories of Significance for the Study of
            the Israelite Monarchy: A Critical Review Essay." *Semeia* 37:9–52.
1989   "Ecology, Agriculture and Patterns of Settlement." *The World of Ancient
            Israel*, pp. 67–93. Ed. R. E. Clements. Cambridge: Cambridge University
            Press.
Frick, Frank S., and Gottwald, Norman K.
1984   "The Social World of Ancient Israel." *BL*, pp. 149–65.
Friedman, Richard E.
1981   *The Exile and Biblical Narrative: The Formation of the Deuteronomistic and
            Priestly Works, 1–43.* HSM 22. Chico, Calif.: Scholars Press.
Frost, Stanley B.
1968   "The Death of Josiah: A Conspiracy of Silence." *JBL* 87:369–82.
Füssel, K.
1984   "The Materialist Reading of the Bible: Report on an Alternative
            Approach to Biblical Texts." *BL*, pp. 134–46.
Galbraith, John K.
1980   *The Nature of Mass Poverty.* Harmondsworth, Ind.: Penguin.
Garbini, Giovanni
1988   *History & Ideology in Ancient Israel.* New York: Crossroad.
Garmus, Ludovico
1989   "Imperialismo: estrutura de dominação." *RIBLA* 3:7–20.
Gaster, Theodor Herzel
1953   *Festivals of the Jewish Year.* New York: William Sloane Associates Pub-
            lishers.
1962a   *Passover: Its History and Traditions.* Boston: Beacon.
1962b   "Sacrifices and Offerings, OT." *IDB* 4:147–59.
1969   *Myth, Legend and Custom in the Old Testament.* New York: Harper & Row.
Gebran, Ph.
1978   "Conceito de Modo de Produção—Introdução." *Conceito de Modo de
            Produção*, pp. 13–29. Ed. Ph. Gebran. Rio de Janeiro: Paz e Terra.

Ginsberg, Harold L.
1950   "Judah and the Transjordan States from 734 to 582." *Alexander Marx Jubilee Volume*, pp. 347–68. New York: Jewish Theological Seminary.

Ginzberg, Eli
1932   "Studies in the Economics of the Bible." *JQR* 22:343–408.

Girard, Rene
1986   *Violence and the Sacred.* Baltimore: Johns Hopkins.
1987   *Things Hidden since the Foundation of the Word.* Stanford: Stanford University Press.

Glock, Albert
1970   "Early Israel as the Kingdom of Yahweh: The Influence of Archaeological Evidence on the Reconstruction of Religion in Early Israel." *Concordia Theological Monthly* 41.

Gluckmann, M.
1965   *Politics, Law and Ritual in Tribal Society.* Oxford: Basil Blackwell.

Gnuse, Robert
1985   *You Shall not Steal: Community and Property in the Biblical Tradition.* Maryknoll, N.Y.: Orbis.

Godelier, M.
1978   "Hipóteses sobre a Natureza e a Lei de Evolução do Modo de Produção Asiático." *Conceito de Modo de Produção*, pp. 73–87. Ed. Ph. Gebran. Rio de Janeiro: Paz e Terra.

Goodman, Philip
1961   *The Passover Anthology.* Philadelphia: The Jewish Publication Society of America.

Gordis, Robert
1934/35   "Sectional Rivalry in the Kingdom of Judah." *JQR* 25:237–59.

Gordon, Cyrus
1970   "Cultural and Religious Life." *The World History of the Jewish People.* Vol. 3: *Judges*, pp. 52–68. Ed. Benjamin Mazar. Israel: Jewish History Publications Ltd.

Görgen, Sérgio Antônio
1987   "A Bíblia na Luta dos Sem–Terra." *EB* 5:7–17.

Gorgulho, G.
1985   *Zacarias: a Vida do Messias Pobre.* São Paulo: Vozes, Metodista e Sinodal.
1986   "Promessa ao Rei Davi." *VP* 130: 9–15.
1989a   "Os Salmos do Rei." *EB* 23:9–17.
1989b   "Sofonias e o valor histórico dos pobres." *RIBLA* 3:26–35.

Gorgulho, G., and Anderson, Ana Flora
1987   "A Leitura Sociológica da Bíblia." *EB* 2:6–10.

Gottwald, Norman K.
1959   *A Light to the Nations: An Introduction to the Old Testament.* New York: Harper & Row.
1964   *All the Kingdoms of the Earth: Israelite Prophecy and International Relations in the Ancient Near East.* New York: Harper & Row.
1974a   "Domain Assumptions and Societal Models in the Study of Premonarchic Israel." *VTSup*, pp. 89–100. (Edinburgh Congress Volume.)
1974b   "Were the Early Israelites Pastoral Nomads?" *Rhetorical Criticism: Essays in Honor of James Muilenburg*, pp. 223–55. Ed. J. Jackson and M. Kessler. Pittsburgh: Pickwick Press.
1976a   "Israel, Social and Economic Development of." *IDBSup*:465–68.
1976b   "Nomadism." *IDBSup*:629–31.
1976c   "War, Holy." *IDBSup*:942–44.

1978   "The Hypothesis of the Revolutionary Origins of Ancient Israel: A Response to A. J. Hauser and T. L. Thompson." *Journal for the Study of the Old Testament* 7:37–52.

1979   *The Tribes of Yahweh: A Sociology of the Religion of Liberated Israel, 1250–1050 B.C.E.* Maryknoll, N.Y.: Orbis.

1983a   "Early Israel and the Canaanite Socio-economic System." *Palestine in Transition: The Emergence of Ancient Israel*, pp. 25–37. Ed. D. N. Freedman and D. F. Graff. Sheffield: Almond.

1983b   "Two Models for the Origins of Ancient Israel: Social Revolution or Frontier Development." *The Quest for the Kingdom of God: Studies in Honor of George E. Mendenhall*, pp. 5–24. Ed. H. B. Huffmon, F. A. Spina, and A. R. W. Green. Winona Lake, Ind.: Eisenbrauns.

1984a   "Sociological Method in the Study of Ancient Israel." *BL*, pp. 26–37.

1984b   "The Theological Task after the Tribes of Yahweh." *BL*, pp. 190–200.

1985   *The Hebrew Bible: A Socio–Literary Introduction.* Philadelphia: Fortress.

1986a   "From Biblical Economics to Modern Economies: A Bridge Over Troubled Waters." *Churches in Struggle: Liberation Theologies and Social Change in North America*, pp. 138–48. Ed. W. K. Tabb. New York: Monthly Review.

1986b   "Review of *Ancient Judaism*, by Irving M. Zeitlin." *Religion* 16:383–87.

1986c   "The Participation of Free Agrarians in the Introduction of Monarchy to Ancient Israel: An Application of H. A. Landsberger's Framework for the Analysis of Peasant Movements." *Semeia* 37:77–106.

1989   "The Exodus as Event and Process: A Test Case in the Biblical Grounding of Liberation Theology." *The Future of Liberation Theology: Essays in Honor of Gustavo Gutiérrez*, pp. 250–60. Maryknoll, N.Y.: Orbis.

1993   "A Hypothesis about Social Class in Monarchic Israel in the Light of Contemporary Studies of Social Class and Social Stratifications." *The Hebrew Bible in Its Social World and in Ours (Semeia Studies)*. Atlanta: Scholars Press.

Gray, G. B.
1971   *Sacrifice in the Old Testament: Its Theory and Practice, with a Prolegomenon by B. A. Levine.* New York: KTAV. (Reprint of 1925 edition.)

Gray, John
1970   *I and II Kings.* Old Testament Library. 2nd., fully revised, ed. London: SCM.

Greenberg, Moshe
1950   "A New Approach to the History of the Israelite Priesthood." *JAOS* 70:41–7.

1979   "Religion: Stability and Ferment." *WHJP* 4/2, pp. 79–123

Gressmann, H.
1924   "Josia und das Deuteronium." *ZAW* 42:313–37.

Gudorf, Christine E.
1987   "Liberation Theology's Use of Scripture: A Response to First World Critics." *Interpretation* 1 (Jan.): 5–18.

Gunkel, H.
1928   "Fundamental Problems of Hebrew Literary History." *What Remains of the Old Testament and Other Essays*, pp. 57–68. New York: Macmillan.

Gutiérrez, Gustavo
1987   "Liberation and the Poor: The Puebla Perspective." *Third World Liberation Theologies*, pp. 22–63. Ed. Deane William Ferm. Maryknoll, N.Y.: Orbis.

1988   *We Drink from Our Own Wells: The Spiritual Journey of a People.* Maryknoll, N.Y.: Orbis.

Haag, H.
1960   "Pâque." *DBS* 6:1120–49.

Habel, Norman
1964   *Yahweh versus Baal: A Conflict of Religious Cultures.* New York: Bookman Associates.

Halbe, J.
1975a   "Passa-Massot im deuteronomischen Festkalender, Komposition, Entstehung und Programm von Dtn 16:1–8." *ZAW* 87:147–68.

1975b   "Erwägungen zu Ursprung und Wesen des Massotfestes." *ZAW* 87:324–46.

Haldar, A.
1945   *Associations of Cult Prophets among the Ancient Semites.* Uppsala: Almquist & Wiksells.

1962   "Canaanites." *IDB* 1:494–98.

Halligan, John Martin
1975   "A Critique of the City in the Yahwist Corpus." Ph.D. Dissertation. University of Notre Dame.

1983   "The Role of the Peasant in the Amarna Period." *Palestine in Transition: The Emergence of Ancient Israel*, pp. 15–24. Ed. D. N. Freedman and D. F. Graf. Sheffield: Almond.

Hallo, William W.
1987   "The Origins of the Sacrificial Cult: New Evidence from Mesopotamia and Israel." *AIR*, pp. 3–13.

Halpern, Baruch
1974   "Sectionalism and Schism." *JBL* 93:519–32.

1976   "Levitic Participation in the Reform Cult of Jeroboam I." *JBL* 95:31–42.

1981   "The Centralization Formula in Deuteronomy." *VT* 31, 1:20–38.

1988   *The First Historians: the Hebrew Bible and History.* San Francisco: Harper & Row.

Hanson, P. D.
1977   "The Theological Significance of Contradiction within the Book of the Covenant." *Canon and Authority*, pp. 110–31. Ed. G. W. Coats and B. O. Long. Philadelphia: Fortress.

Haran, M.
1962   "Shiloh and Jerusalem: The Origin of the Priestly Tradition in the Pentateuch." *JBL* 81:14–24.

1972   "The Passover Sacrifice." *Studies in the Religion of Ancient Israel. VTSup* 23, pp. 86–116. Leiden: E. J. Brill.

1985   *Temples and Temple-Service in Ancient Israel.* Winona Lake, Ind.: Eisenbrauns.

Harden, D.
1968   *Os Fenícios.* Lisboa: Editorial Verbo.

Har-El, M.
1981   "Orientation in Biblical Lands." *BA* 44: 19–20.

Hargrove, Barbara
1979   *The Sociology of Religion.* Arlington Heights, Ill.: Harlan Davidson.

Harnecker, M.
1983   *Os Conceitos Elementares do Materialism Histórico.* São Paulo: Global.

Hauer, Chris E., Jr.
1963   "Who was Zadok?" *JBL* 82:89–94.

1969   "The Shape of Saulide Strategy." *CBQ* 31:153–67.

1980   "The Economics of National Security in Solomonic Israel." *JSOT* 18:67– 73.

1982   "David and the Levites." *JSOT* 23:33–54.

Hayes, John H., ed.

1974   *Old Testament Form Criticism.* San Antonio: Trinity University Press.

Hayes, John H., and Holladay, Carl R.

1987   *Biblical Exegesis.* Revised Edition. Atlanta: John Knox Press.

Hayes, John H., and Hooker, Paul K.

1988   *A New Chronology for the Kings of Israel and Judah and Its Implications for Biblical History and Literature.* Atlanta: John Knox Press.

Hayes, John H., and Miller, J. Maxwell

1977   *Israelite and Judaean History.* London: SCM.

1986   *A History of Ancient Israel and Judah.* Philadelphia: Westminster.

Heaton, E. W.

1968   *The Hebrew Kingdoms.* London: Oxford University Press.

1974   *Solomon's New Men: The Emergence of Ancient Israel as a National State.* London: Thames and Hudson.

Hendel, Ronald S.

1988   "The Social Origins of the Aniconic Tradition in Early Israel." *CBQ* 50/ 3:365–82.

Henninger, J.

1975   *Les Fêtes de Printemps chez les Sémites et la Pâque Israélite.* Paris: J. Gabalda et Cie.

Herrmann, Siegfried

1981   *A History of Israel in Old Testament Times.* Second edition, revised and enlarged. Philadelphia: Fortress.

Hindess, B., and Hirst, P.

1976   *Modos de Produções pré-capitalistas.* Rio de Janeiro: Zahar.

Hinkelammert, Franz

1983   *As Armas Ideológicas da Morte.* São Paulo: Paulinas. (English trans.: *The Ideological Weapons of Death.* Maryknoll, N.Y.: Orbis, 1986.)

Hobbs, T. R.

1985   *2 Kings.* Word Biblical Commentary. Waco, Tex.: Word Books.

Hoffmann, H. D.

1980   *Reform und Reformen. Untersuchungen zu einem Grundthema der deuteronomistischen Geschichtsschreibung.* Abhandlungen zur Theologie des Alten und Neuen Testaments 66. Zurich: Theologischer Verlag.

Holladay, John S., Jr.

1987   "Religion in Israel and Judah Under the Monarchy: An Explicitly Archaeological Approach." *AIR*, pp. 249–99.

Holland, Joe, and Henriot, Peter

1983   *Social Analysis.* Revised and enlarged edition. Maryknoll, N.Y.: Orbis.

Hollenstein, H.

1977   "Literarkritische Erwägungen zum Bericht über die Reformmassnahmen Josias 2 Kön. xxiii 4ff." *VT* 27:321–36.

Hollis, F. J.

1933   "The Sun-Cult and the Temple at Jerusalem." *Myth and Ritual*, pp. 87– 110. Ed. S. H. Hooke. Oxford: Oxford University Press.

Hooke, Samuel Henry, ed.

1938   *The Origins of Early Semitic Ritual.* London: Oxford University Press.

1958   *Myth, Ritual, and Kingship: Essays on the Theory and Practice of Kingship in the Ancient Near East and in Israel.* Oxford: Clarendon Press.

Hopkins, David C.
1983a   "The Dynamics of Agriculture in Monarchical Israel." SBL Seminar Papers. Ed. K. H. Richards. No. 22, pp. 177–202. Missoula: Scholars Press.
1983b   "The Emergence of a Royal-Urban Society in Ancient Israel." *HUCA* 31:31–53.
1985   *The Highlands of Canaan: Agricultural Life in the Early Iron Age.* Sheffield: Almond.

Hoppe, L.
1978   "The Origins of Deuteronomy." Dissertation, Northwestern University.

Horsley, Richard A., and Hanson, John S.
1988   *Bandits, Prophets, and Messiahs: Popular Movements at the Time of Jesus.* San Francisco: Harper & Row.

Horst, F.
1923   "Die Kultusreform des Königs Josias." *ZDMG* 77:220–38.

House, Paul R.
1988   *Zephaniah, a Prophetic Drama.* Sheffield: Almond.

Houtart, François
1982   *Religião e Modos de Produção pré-capitalistas.* São Paulo: Paulinas.
1989   "Theoretical and Institutional Bases of the Opposition to Liberation Theology." *The Future of Liberation Theology: Essays in Honor of Gustavo Gutiérrez*, pp. 261–71. Ed. Marc H. Ellis & Otto Maduro. Maryknoll, N.Y. Orbis.

Hummel, Horace D.
1970   "The Influence of Archeological Evidence on the Reconstruction of Religion in Monarchical Israel." *CTM* 41:542–57.

Ianni, O.
1986   *Classe e Nação.* Petrópolis: Vozes.

Ishida, T.
1975   " 'The People of the Land' and the Political Crises in Judah." *AJBI* 1:23–38.
1977   *The Royal Dynasties in Ancient Israel: A Study on the Formation and Development of Royal-Dynastic Ideology.* New York: Walter de Gruyter.

Jacobsen, Thorkild
1987   "The Graven Image." *Ancient Israelite Religion: Essays in Honor of Frank Moore Cross*, pp. 15–32. Ed. Patrick D. Miller, Jr., Paul D. Hanson, and S. Dean McBride. Philadelphia: Fortress.

Jameson, Fredric
1981   *The Political Unconscious: Narrative as a Socially Symbolic Act.* Ithaca, NY: Cornell University Press.

Janssen, J. J.
1979   "The Role of the Temple in the Egyptian Economy during the New Kingdom." *State and Temple Economy in the Ancient Near East* 2, pp. 505–15. Ed. Edward Lipiński. Louvain: Dep. Oriëntalistiek.

Jepsen, A.
1959   "Die Reform des Josias." *Festschrift für A. Baumgartel*, pp. 97–108. Berlin: A. Topelmann. (In *Festschrift Friedrich Baumgartel*. Blangen: Universitätsbund Blangen.)

Johnson, A. R.
1935   "The Role of the King in the Jerusalem Cultus." *The Labyrinth*, pp. 71–111. Ed. S. H. Hooke. London: Oxford University Press.
1962   *The Cultic Prophet in Ancient Israel.* Cardiff: University of Wales.
1967   *Sacral Kingship in Ancient Israel.* Cardiff: University of Wales.

Jones, Gwilym H.
1984   *1 and 2 King. Vols. 1–2.* The New Century Bible Commentary. Grand Rapids, Mich.: Eerdmans.

Kapelrud, Arvid S.
1964   "The Date of the Priestly Code (P)." *ASTI* 3:58–64.
1965   "The Role of the Cult in Old Israel." *The Bible in Modern Scholarship*, pp. 44–56. Ed. Philip Hyatt. New York: Abingdon.
1966   *Israel: From the Earliest Times to the Birth of Christ.* Oxford: Basil Blackwell Mott.

Katzenstein, H. J.
1962   "Some Remarks on the Lists of the Chief Priests of the Temple of Solomon." *JBL* 81:377–84.

Kaufmann, Y.
1972   *The Religion of Israel.* Paperback. New York: Schocken.

Kautsky, John
1982   *The Politics of Aristocratic Empires.* Chapel Hill, N.C.: University of North Carolina.

Keel, Von Othmar
1972   "Erwägungen zum Sitz im Leben des vormosaischen Pascha und zur Etymologie von pesah." *ZAW* 84:414–34.

Kennedy, James M.
1987   "The Social Background of Early Israel's Rejection of Cultic Images: A Proposal." *BTB* 17:138–44.

Kennett, Robert
1931   *Ancient Hebrew Social Life as Indicated in Law, Narrative, and Metaphor.* London: Oxford University Press.

Kenyon, Kathleen
1971   *Royal Cities of the Old Testament.* New York: Schocken.

King, Philip J.
1988   *Amos, Hosea, Micah: An Archaeological Commentary.* Philadelphia: Westminster.

Knight, Douglas A., ed.
1983   "Julius Wellhausen and His Prolegomena to the History of Israel." *Semeia* 25.

Krader, Lawrence
1975   *The Asiatic Mode of Production: Sources, Development and Critique in the Writings of Karl Marx.* Assen (Netherlands): Van Gorcum & Company.

Kraus, H. J.
1958   "Zur Geschichte des Passah-Massot–Festes im Alten Testament." *EvTh* 18:44ff.
1966   *Worship in Ancient Israel. A Cultic History of the Old Testament.* Richmond: John Knox Press.

Krentz, Edgar
1975   *The Historical-Critical Method.* Philadelphia: Fortress.

Kudo, T., and Tovar, C.
1977   *La Crítica de la Religión: ensayo sobre la conciencia social segun Marx.* Lima: Centro de Estudios y Publicaciones.

Külling, S. R.
1964   *Zur Datierung der "Genesis-P-Stücke."* Kampen: Kok.

Küng, Hans
1989   "Küng: Church not so Much Roman as Global." *National Catholic Reporter* 26, no.1 (October 20):10–11.

Kutsch, Von Ernst
1958   "Erwägungen zur Geschichte der Passafeier und des Massotfestes." *ZTK*
            55/1:1–35.

Lach, S.
1969   "Le Sacrifice *zebah selamim*." *Folia Orientalia* 11:187–97.

Lagrange, J. M.
1905   *Études sur les Religions Sémitiques*. Paris: Libraire Victor Lecoffre.

Landsberger, Henry A.
1973   *Rural Protest: Peasant Movements and Social Change*. New York: Harper
            & Row.

Lang, Bernhard
1980   "*zebhack; zebhach*." *TDOT* 4:17–29.
1983   *Monotheism and the Prophetic Minority: An Essay in Biblical History and
            Sociology*. Sheffield: Almond.
1985   "The Social Organization of Peasant Poverty in Biblical Israel." *Anthro-
            pological Approaches to the Old Testament*, pp. 83–99. Ed. Bernhard Lang.
            Philadelphia: Fortress.

Lapp, N.
1976   "Casemate Walls in Palestine and the Late Iron II Casemate at Tell el-
            Ful (Gibeah)." *BASOR* 223:25–42.

Leach, E.
1976   *Culture and Communication*. Cambridge: Cambridge University Press.

Lemaire, A.
1977   "Les inscriptions des Khirbel el-Qon et l'asherah de YAWH." *RB* 84:595–
            608.
1981   *Histoire du Peuple Hébreu*. Paris: Presses Universitaires de France.

Lemke, W.
1976   "The Way of Obedience: 1 Kgs. 13 and the Structure of the Deuteron-
            omistic Historian." *Magnalia Dei*, pp. 301–26. Ed. F. M. Cross. Garden
            City, N.Y.: Doubleday.

Lenski, Gerhard
1966   *Power and Privilege*. New York: McGraw–Hill.
1976   "History and Social Change." *American Sociology* 82:548–64.

Lenski, Gerhard, and Lenski, Jean
1982   *Human Societies: An Introduction to Macrosociology*. 4th ed. New York:
            McGraw–Hill.

Levenson, Jon D.
1985   *Sinai and Zion*. Minneapolis, Minn.: Winston Press.

Levine, B. A.
1971a   "Cult." *EJ* 5:cols. 1155–62.
1971b   "Cult Places, Israelite." *EJ* 5:cols. 1162–69.
1974   *In the Presence of the Lord*. Leiden: E. J. Brill.
1976   "Priestly Writers." *IDBSup*:683–87.

Levine, B. A., and Hallo, W. W.
1967   "Offerings to the Temple Gates at Ur." *HUCA* 38:17–58.

Libânio, João Batista
1989   "VII Encontro Intereclesial das CEBs." *REB* 49. Fasc. 195:515–34.

Lind, Millard C.
1980   *Yahweh Is a Warrior*. Scottdale, Penna.: Herald Press.

Lindblom, J.
1962   *Prophecy in Ancient Israel*. Oxford: B. Blackwell.

Lipiński, Edward, ed.
1979   *State and Temple Economy in the Ancient Near East I and II*. Proceedings

of the International Conference organized by the Katholieke Universiteit Leuven from the 10th to the 14th of April 1978. Louvain: Dep. Oriëntalistiek.

Liverani, Mario
1979   "The Ideology of the Assyrian Empire." *Mesopotamia*, Copenhagen Studies in Assyriology 7, pp. 297–317. Ed. Mogens Trolle Larsen. Copenhagen.

Lochhead, David
1984   "The Liberation of the Bible." *BL* 74–93.

Lohfink, Norbert
1963   "Die Bundesurkunde des Könings Josias." *Bib* 44:261–88 and 461–98.
1976   "Deuteronomic History, The." *IDBSup*:226–32.
1978   "Die Gattung der 'Historischen Kurzgeschichte'." *ZAW* 90:319–47.
1982   *Great Themes from the Old Testament*, esp. pp. 17–37. Chicago: Franciscan Herald/Edinburgh: T. & T. Clark.
1985   "Zur neueren Diskussion über 2 Kön 22–23." *Das Deuteronomium: Entstehung, Gestalt und Botschaft*, pp. 24–48. Ed. N. Lohfink. *BETL* 68. Louvain: Peeters/University Press.
1987   "The Cult Reform of Josiah of Judah: 2 Kings 22–23 as a Source for the History of Israelite Religion." *AIR*, pp. 459–75.

Loisy, Alfred
1920   *Essai Historique sur le Sacrifice*. Paris: Émile Nourry.

Lundbom, J. R.
1976   "The Lawbook of the Josianic Reform." *CBQ* 38:293–302.

Lundquist, J.
1982   "The Legitimizing Role of the Temple in the Origin of the State." SBL Seminar Papers. Missoula: Scholars Press.
1983   "What Is a Temple? A Preliminary Typology." *The Quest for the Kingdom of God. Studies in Honor of G. E. Mendenhall*, pp. 205–19. Ed. H. B. Huffmon, F. Spina, and A. Green. Winona Lake, Ind.: Eisenbrauns.

Maar, W. L.
1982   *O que é Política*. São Paulo: Brasiliense.

Macdonald, J. B.
1986   "A questão do Excedente na Sociedade Primitiva." *Vozes (Revista de Cultura)* 80:590–606.

Macedo, Carmen Cinira
1989   "CEBs: Um Caminho ao Saber Popular." *VP* 146:19–29.

MacKenzie, R. A. F.
1963   "The City and Israelite Religion." *CBQ* 25:60–70.

Maduro, Otto
1980   *Religião e Luta de Classes*. Petrópolis: Vozes. (English trans.: *Religion and Class Struggle*. Maryknoll, N.Y.: Orbis, 1982.)

Mainwaring, Scott
1986   *The Catholic Church and Politics in Brazil, 1916–1985*. Stanford, Calif.: Stanford University Press.

Malamat, Abraham
1950   "The Last Wars of the Kingdom of Judah." *JNES* 9:218–27.
1950–51   "The Historical Setting of Two Biblical Prophecies on the Nations." *IEJ* 1:149–59.
1953   "The Historical Background of the Assassination of Amon, King of Judah." *IEJ* 3:26–29.
1963   "Aspects of the Foreign Policies of David and Solomon." *JNES* 22:1–17.
1965   "The Organs of Statecraft in the Israelite Monarchy." *BA* 28:34–65.
1968   "The Last Kings of Judah and the Fall of Jerusalem." *IEJ* 18:137–56.

1973   "Josiah's Bid for Armageddon." *JANES* 5:267–78.
1974   "Megiddo, 609 B.C.: The Conflict Reexamined." *Acta Antiqua* 22: 445–49.
1979   "The Last Years of the Kingdom of Judah." *WHJP* 4/1, pp. 205–21.
1987   "A Forerunner of Biblical Prophecy: The Mari Documents." *AIR*, pp. 33–52.

Maldonado, L.
1974   *La Violencia de lo Sagrado.* Salamanca: Sígueme.

Mansueto, Anthony
1983   "From Historical Criticism to Historical Materialism." Paper presented at Graduate Theological Union, Berkeley, Calif., May 22.

Marcom, John, Jr.
1990   "The Fire Down South." *Forbes* (October 15):56–71.

Martin, J. D.
1989   "Israel as a Tribal Society." *The World of Ancient Israel*, pp. 95–117. Ed. R. E. Clements. Cambridge: Cambridge University Press.

Martin-Achard, Robert
1974   *Essai Biblique sur les fêtes d'Israël.* Geneva: Labor et Fides.

Marx, Karl
1975   *O Capital.* Rio de Janeiro: Civilização Brasileira.
1983   *Contribuição à Crítica da Economia Política.* São Paulo: Martins Fontes.
1985   *Formações Economicas Pré-Capitalistas.* São Paulo: Paz e Terra.

Matthes, J.
1971   *Introducción a la Sociología de la Religión.* Madrid: Alianza Editorial.

May, H. G.
1936   "The Relation of the Passover and the Festival of Unleavened Cakes." *JBL* 55:65–82.
1937   "Some Aspects of Solar Worship in Jerusalem." *ZAW* 55:269–81.

Mayes, A. D. H.
1978   "King and Covenant: A Study of 2 Kings 22–23." *Hermathena* 125:34–47.
1983   *The Story of Israel between the Settlement and Exile.* London: SCM.
1987   *Deuteronomy.* New Century Bible Commentary. Grand Rapids, Mich.: Eerdmans.
1989   "Sociology and the Old Testament." *The World of Ancient Israel*, pp. 39–63. Ed. R. E. Clements. Cambridge: Cambridge University Press.

Mazar, Benjamin
1960   "The Cities of the Priests and Levites." *VTSup* 4:57–66.
1963   "The Military Elite of King David." *VT* 13:310–20.

McCarter, P. Kyle, Jr.
1987   "Aspects of the Religion of the Israelite Monarchy: Biblical and Epigraphic Data." *AIR*, pp. 137–55.

McCarthy, Dennis J.
1972   *Old Testament Covenant: A Survey of Current Opinions.* Oxford: Blackwell.
1978   *Treaty and Covenant, a Study in Form in the Ancient Oriental Documents and in the Old Testament.* Rev. ed. *Analecta Biblica* 21A. Rome: Biblical Institute.

McClellan, Thomas L.
1978   "Towns to Fortresses: The Transformation of Urban Life in Judah from 8th to 7th Century B.C." SBL Seminar Papers 1: 277–86.

McCurley, Foster R., Jr.
1974   "The Home of Deuteronomy Revisited: A Methodological Analysis of the Northern Theory." *A Light unto My Path. OT Studies in Honor of J. M.*

            Myers, pp. 295–317. Ed. H. N. Bream, R. D. Heim, and C. A. Moore.
            Gettysburg Theo Studies 4. Philadelphia: Temple University Press.
McDonough, Peter
1981   *Power and Ideology in Brazil.* Princeton, N.J.: Princeton University Press.
McGovern, Arthur F.
1987   *Marxism: An American Christian Perspective.* Maryknoll, N.Y.: Orbis.
McKay, John W.
1972   "The Date of Passover and its Significance." *ZAW* 84:435–47.
1973a   "The Horses and Chariot of the Sun in the Jerusalem Temple." *PEQ*
            105:167–69.
1973b   *Religion in Judah Under the Assyrians 732–609* B.C. SBT, 2d series, no. 26.
            London: SCM.
McKenzie, John L.
1959   "The Elders in the Old Testament." *Bib* 40:522–40.
1983   "The Sack of Israel." *The Quest for the Kingdom of God: Studies in Honor
            of George E. Mendenhall*, pp. 25–34. Ed. H. B. Huffmon, F. A. Spina, and
            A. R. W. Green. Winona Lake, Ind.: Eisenbrauns.
McLellan, David
1987   *Marxism and Religion.* New York: Harper & Row.
Meek, Theophile J.
1950   *Hebrew Origins.* Rev. ed. New York: Harper and Brothers.
Meeks, M. Douglas
1989   *God the Economist.* Minneapolis: Augsburg/Fortress.
Melotti, Umberto
1977   *Marx and the Third World.* London: Macmillan.
Mendelsohn, Isaac
1949   *Slavery in the Ancient Near East.* New York: Oxford University Press.
Mendenhall, George E.
1962   "The Hebrew Conquest of Palestine." *BA* 25:66–87.
1973   *The Tenth Generation: The Origins of the Biblical Tradition.* Baltimore:
            Johns Hopkins.
1975   "The Monarchy." *Interpretation* 29:155–70.
1976   " 'Change and Decay All Around I See': Conquest, Covenant and The
            Tenth Generation." *BA* 39:152–57.
1983   "Ancient Israel's Hyphenated History." *Palestine in Transition*, pp. 91–
            103. Ed. D. N. Freedman and D. F. Graf. Sheffield: Almond.
Mesters, Carlos
1971   *Palavra de Deus na História do Homem.* Petrópolis: Vozes.
1975   "O Futuro do Nosso Passado." *Uma Igreja Que Nasce do Povo*, pp. 120–
            200. Ed. Carlos Mesters. Petrópolis: Vozes.
1978–79   "A Brisa Leve, uma Nova Leitura da Bíblia." *SEDOC* 2:733–65.
1984   "The Use of the Bible in Christian Communities of the Common People."
            BL, pp. 119–33.
1987   "Como se faz Teologia Bíblica hoje no Brasil." *EB* 1:7–19.
Mettinger, Tryggve N. D.
1971   *Solomonic State Officials: A Study of the Civil Government Officials of the
            Israelite Monarchy.* Lund: C. W. K. Gleerup.
1976   *King and Messiah: The Civil and Sacral Legitimation of the Israelite Kings.*
            Lund: C. W. K. Gleerup.
Meyers, Carol L.
1982   "The Elusive Temple." *BA* 45/1:33–41.
1983   "Procreation, Production, and Protection: Male-Female Balance in Early
            Israel." *JAAR* 51:569–93.

1984   "The Roots of Restriction: Women in Early Israel." *BL*, pp. 289–306.
1985   "The Temple." *Harper's Bible Dictionary*, pp. 1021–29. Ed. Paul J. Ach-
            temeier. San Francisco: Harper & Row.

Milgrom, J.
1970   "Did Josiah Subdue Megiddo?" *Beth Mirak* 44:23–27.
1976a   *Cult and Conscience*. Leiden: E. J. Brill.
1976b   "Profane Slaughter and a Formulaic Key to the Composition of Deuter-
            onomy." *HUCA* 47:1–17.

Miller, J. Maxwell
1982   "Approaches to the Bible Through History and Archaeology: Biblical His-
            tory as a Discipline." *BA* 45:211–16.

Miranda, José
1974   *Marx and the Bible*. Maryknoll, N.Y.: Orbis.
1986   *Marx against the Marxists*. Maryknoll, N.Y.: Orbis.
1987a   *Communism in the Bible*. Maryknoll, N.Y.: Orbis.
1987b   "Christianity Is Communism." *Third World Liberation Theologies*, pp. 160–
            75. Ed. Deane William Ferm. Maryknoll, N.Y.: Orbis.

Montgomery, James A.
1934   "Archival Data in the Book of Kings." *JBL* 53:46–52.

Montgomery, J. A., and Gehman, H. S.
1976   *The Books of Kings*. ICC. Edinburgh: T.& T. Clark.

Moore, B.
1966   *Social Origins of Dictatorship and Democracy*. Boston: Beacon.

Morgan, L. H.
1976   *A Sociedade Primitiva*. Lisboa: Editorial Presença.

Morgenstern, Julian
1917–18   "Two Ancient Israelite Agricultural Festivals." *JQR* 8:31–54.
1924   "The Three Calendars of Ancient Israel." *HUCA* 1:13–78.
1938   "A Chapter in the History of the High-Priesthood." *AJSL* 55:1–24, 183–
            97, 360–77.
1966   *Rites of Birth, Marriage, Death, and Kindred Occasions among the Semites*.
            Cincinnati, Ohio: Hebrew Union College Press.

Morley, Samuel A.
1982   *Labor Markets and Inequitable Growth: The Case of Authoritarian Capital-
            ism in Brazil*. Cambridge: Cambridge University Press.

Mosala, Itumeleng J.
1989   *Biblical Hermeneutics and Black Theology in South Africa*. Grand Rapids,
            Mich.: Eerdmans.

Myers, Allen C., ed.
1987   *The Eerdmans Bible Dictionary*. Grand Rapids, Mich.: Eerdmans.

Nelson, Glueck
1968   *The River Jordan*. New York: McGraw-Hill.

Nelson, R. D.
1981a   "Josiah in the Book of Joshua." *JBL* 100/4:531–40.
1981b   "The Double Redaction of the Deuteronomistic History." *JSOTSup* 18.
            Sheffield: JSOT Press.
1983   "Realpolitik in Judah (687–609 B.C.E.)." *Scripture in Context II. More
            Essays in Comparative Method*, pp. 177–89. Ed. William W. Hallo, James
            C. Moyer, and Leo G. Purdue. Winona Lake, Ind.: Eisenbrauns.
1987   *First and Second Kings: Interpretation, a Bible Commentary for Teaching and
            Preaching*. Atlanta: John Knox Press.

Netting, Robert McC.
1974   "Agrarian Ecology." *Annual Review of Anthropology* 3:21–56.

Neufeld Edward

1955   "The Prohibitions Against Loans at Interest in Ancient Hebrew Laws."
                HUCA 26:355–412.
1960   "The Emergence of a Royal-Urban Society in Ancient Israel." *HUCA*
                31:31–53.

Neuhaus, Richard John

1990   *The Catholic Moment: The Paradox of the Church in the Postmodern World.*
                San Francisco: Harper & Row.

Newman, Katherine S.

1983   *Law and Economic Organization: A Comparative Study of Preindustrial Soci-*
                eties. Cambridge: Cambridge University Press.

Nicholson, E. W.

1963a   "The Centralization of the Cult in Deuteronomy." *VT* 13:380–89.
1963b   "II Kings xxii. 18 – A Simple Restoration." *Hermathena* 97:96–98.
1967   *Deuteronomy and Tradition.* Philadelphia: Fortress.
1986   "Israelite Religion in the Pre-Exilic Period: A Debate Renewed." *A Word*
                in Season: Essays in Honour of William McKane, pp. 3–34. Ed. James D.
                Martin and Philip R. Davies. *JSOTSup* 42. Sheffield: JSOT Press.

Nicolsky, N. M.

1927   "Pascha im Kulte des jerusalemischen Tempels." *ZAW* 45:171–90 and
                241–53.

Nielson, E.

1967   "Political Conditions and Cultural Developments in Israel and Judah Dur-
                ing the Reign of Manasseh." Fourth World Congress of Jewish Studies I,
                Jerusalem: 103–6.

North, C. R.

1931   "The Old Testament Estimate of the Monarchy." *AJSL* 48:1–19.

Noth, Martin

1960   *The History of Israel.* 2nd ed. New York: Harper & Row.
1966   *The Laws in the Pentateuch and Other Studies.* Trans. by D. R. AP-Thomas.
                London: Oliver & Boyd.
1972   *A History of Pentateuchal Traditions.* Trans. by Bernhard W. Anderson.
                Englewood Cliffs, N.J.: Prentice-Hall.
1976   *El Mundo del Antiguo Testamento.* Madrid: Ediciones Cristiandad.
1977   *Leviticus: A Commentary.* Philadelphia: Westminster.
1981   *The Deuteronomistic History.* Sheffield: *JSOT* Sup Series 15. (Originally
                written in 1957, 2nd ed.)

Oded, B.

1970   "Observations on Methods of Assyrian Rule in Transjordania After the
                Palestinian Campaign of Tiglath–Pileser III." *JNES*: 177–86.
1972   "The Historical Background of the Syro-Ephraimite War Reconsidered."
                CBQ 34:153–65.
1977   "Judah and the Exile." *Israel and Judaean History,* pp. 435–88. Ed. John
                H. Hayes and J. Maxwell Miller. London: SCM.
1979   *Mass Deportations and Deportees in the Neo–Assyrian Empire.* Wiesbaden:
                Harrasowitz.

Oden, Robert A., Jr.

1976   "The Persistence of Canaanite Religion." *BA* 39:31–36.
1987   "The Place of Covenant in the Religion of Israel." *AIR,* pp. 429–47.

Oesterley, W. O. E.

1923   *The Sacred Dance.* Cambridge: The University Press.
1937   *Sacrifices in Ancient Israel.* London: Hodder and Stoughton.

Oesterley, W. O. E., and Robinson, T. H.
1957   *Hebrew Religion: Its Origin and Development.* London: S.P.C.K.

Oestreicher, Th.
1923   *Das deuteronomische Grundgesetz Beiträge zur Förderung Christlicher Theologie* 27/4:37–58. Gütersloh: Bertelsmann.

Ogden, G.
1978   "The Northern Extent of Josiah's Reforms." *Australian Biblical Review* 26:26–34.

Olavarri, E.
1972   "La Celebración de la Pascua y Acimos en la legislación del Antiguo Testamento." *Estudios Bíblicos* 31:17–42 and 293–320.

Olivier, Bernard, and Alberto, Carlos (Frei Betto)
1976   "The Church We Want." *Cross Currents* (Spring) 26, No. 1:1–10.

Olyan, Saul
1983   "Zadok's Origins and the Tribal Politics of David." *JBL* 101:177–93.
1988   *Asherah and the Cult of Yahweh in Israel.* Atlanta: Scholars Press.

Oppenheim, A. L.
1947   "A Fiscal Practice of the Ancient Near East." *JNES* 6:116–20.

Orofino, Francisco R.
1989   "Contigo eu martelei o cavalo e o cavaleiro, o carro e o condutor." *RIBLA* 4:27–35.

Otzen, Benedikt
1977–78   "Israel Under the Assyrians: Reflections on Imperial Policy in Palestine." *ASTI* 11:96–110.
1979   "Israel Under the Assyrians." *Mesopotamia.* Copenhagen Studies in Assyriology. vol. 7, pp. 251–61. Ed. Mogens Trolle Larsen. Copenhagen.

Page, Joseph A.
1989   "Brazil: A Nation in Search of a Miracle." *America* 161/12 (October 28): 273–74.

Panini, Carmela
1990   *Reforma Agarária dentro e fora da Lei.* São Paulo: Paulinas.

Peckham, Brian
1987   "Phoenicia and the Religion of Israel: The Epigraphic Evidence." *AIR*, pp. 79–99.

Pedersen, J.
1934   "Passahfest und Passahlegende." *ZAW* 52:161–75.
1959   *Israel: Its Life and Culture III–IV.* London: Oxford University.

Perdue, L. G.
1983   "The Testament of David and Egyptian Royal Instructions." *Scripture in Context II. More Essays in Comparative Method*, pp.79–96. Ed. William W. Hall, James C. Mayer, and Leo G. Perdue. Winona Lake, Ind: Eisenbrauns.

Petersen, David L.
1975   *Late Israelite Prophecy: Studies in Deutero-Prophetic Literature and in Chronicles.* Missoula: Scholars Press.

Petersen, David L., ed.
1987   *Prophecy in Israel.* Philadelphia: Fortress.

Pfeifer, G.
1969   "Die Begegnung zwischen Pharao Necho und König Josia bei Megiddo." Mitteilungen des Instituts für Orientforschung 15:297–307.

Pixley, George V.
1981   *God's Kingdom.* Maryknoll, N.Y.: Orbis.

178   BIBLIOGRAPHY

1984   "Biblical Embodiments of God's Kingdom: A Study Guide for the Rebel Church." *BL*, pp. 108–18.
1987   *On Exodus.* Maryknoll, N.Y.: Orbis.

Polk, T.
1979   "The Levites in the Davidic–Solomonic Empire." *StBib* 9:3–22.

Priest, J. B.
1980   "Huldah's Oracle." *VT* 30:366–68.

Pritchard, James B.
1962   *Gibeon Where the Sun Stood Still.* Princeton, N.J.: Princeton University Press.
1969   *Ancient Near Eastern Texts Relating to the Old Testament.* 3d ed. Princeton, N.J.: Princeton University Press.

Pszymus, João
1989   "Educação e Poder: A Democracia nas Organizações Populares." Master's thesis, Universidade Federal do Paraná, Brazil.

Rainey, A. F.
1970   "The Order of Sacrifices in Old Testament Ritual Texts." *Bib* 51:485–98.
1971   "Sacrifice." *EJ* 14:cols. 599–607.

Ramalho, J. P.
1989   "Avanços e questões na Caminhada das CEBs." *REB* 49. Fasc. 195:573–77.

Reade, Julian
1979   "Ideology and Propaganda in Assyrian Art." *Mesopotamia.* Copenhagen Studies in Assyriology. Vol. 7, pp. 329–43. Ed. Mogens Trolle Larsen. Copenhagen.

Reed, W. L.
1949   *The Asherah in the Old Testament.* Fort Worth, Tex.: Christian University Press.

Rendtorff, R.
1967   *Studien zur Geschichte des Opfers in alten Israel.* Neukirchen-Vluyn.

Reviv, H.
1979a   "The History of Judah from Hezekiah to Josiah." *WHJP* 4/1, pp. 193–204.
1979b   "The Structure of Society." *WHJP* 4/2, pp. 125–46.

Ribeiro, D.
1985   *O Processo Civilizatório: Etapas da Evolução Sócio-Cultural.* Petrópolis: Vozes.

Richard, Pablo
1987   "Bíblia: Memória histórica dos Pobres." *EB* 1:20–30.
1988   "Leitura Popular da Bíblia na América Latina." *RIBLA* 1:8–25.

Ringgren, Helmer
1966   *Israelite Religion.* Philadelphia: Fortress.
1972   "Israel's Place Among the Religions of the Ancient Near East." *Studies in the Religion of Ancient Israel. VTSup* 23, pp. 1–8. Leiden: E. J. Brill.

Rius (Eduardo del Rio)
1979   *Marx for Beginners.* New York: Pantheon Books.

Roberts, J. J. M.
1973   "The Davidic Origin of the Zion Tradition." *JBL* 92:329–44.
1987   "In Defense of the Monarchy: The Contribution of Israelite Kingship to Biblical Theology." *AIR*, pp. 377–96.

Robinson, J.
1976   *The Second Book of Kings.* Cambridge: Cambridge University Press.
1978   "The Levites in the Pre-Monarchic Period." *StBib* 7:3–24.

Robinson, Theodore H.
1933/34   "Some Economic and Social Factors in the History of Israel." *ET* 45:264–69 and 294–300.

Rolim, F. C.
1980   *Religião e Classes Populares.* Petrópolis: Vozes.

Rose, M.
1977   "Bemerkungen zum historischen Fundament des Josia-Bildes in II Reg 22 f." ZAW 89:50–63.

Rosenbloom, Joseph R.
1972   "Social Science Concepts of Modernization and Biblical History: The Development of the Israelite Monarchy." *JAAR* 40/4:437–44.

Rost, L.
1943   "Weidewechsel und altisraelitischer Festkalendar." *Zeitschrift der Deutschen Palästina-Vereins* 66:205–16.
1965   *Das kleine Credo und andere Studien zum AT.* Heidelberg.
1968   "Josias Passa." *Theologie in Geschiche und Kuntst, Festschrift für K. Elliger*, pp. 169–75. Ed. S. Hermann. Wittenburg: Luther Verlag.

Rostagno, S.
1984   "The Bible: Is an Interclass Reading Legitimate?" *BL*, pp. 61–73.

Rowley, H. H.
1939   "Zadok and Nehushtan." *JBL* 58:113–41.
1963a   *From Moses to Qumran.* New York: Association Press.
1963b   *Men of God.* London: Thomas Nelson & Sons.
1967   *Worship in Ancient Israel: Its Forms and Meaning.* Philadelphia: Fortress.

Rowton, M. B.
1952   "Jeremiah and the Death of Josiah." *JNES* 10:128–30.
1973   "Urban Autonomy in a Nomadic Environment." *JNES* 32:201–15.
1974   "Enclosed Nomadism." *Journal of the Economic and Social History of the Orient* 17:1–30.

Rylaarsdam, J. C.
1962a   "Feasts and Fasts." *IDB* 2:260–64.
1962b   "Passover and Feast of Unleavened Bread." *IDB* 3:663–68.

Saggs, H. W. F.
1962   *The Greatness That Was Babylon: A Sketch of the Ancient Civilization of the Tigris-Euphrates Valley.* New York: Hawthorn Books.
1969   *Assyriology and the Study of the Old Testament.* Cardiff: University of Wales Press.

Sahlins, M.
1974   *Sociedades Tribais.* Rio de Janeiro: Zahar.

Salem, Helena, ed.
1981   *Brasil: A Igreja dos Oprimidos.* São Paulo: Brasil Debates.

Sampaio, Tânia, M. V.
1991   "A desmilitarização e o resgate da dignidade da vida em Oséias." *RIBLA* 8:70–81.

Sawer, Marian
1977   *Marxism and the Question of the Asiatic Mode of Production.* Netherlands: Martinus Nijhoff.

Sawyer, John F. A.
1987   *Prophecy and the Prophets of the Old Testament.* New York: Oxford University Press.

Scharbert, J.
1981   "Jeremia und die Reform des Joschija." *Bibliotheca Ephemeridum Theologicarum Lovaniensium* 54:40–57.

Schauss, Hayyim
1977   *The Jewish Festivals.* New York: Schocken.
Schildenberger, J.
1966   "La Pasqua Ebraica come memoriale." *Parole di vita* 11, no. 2 (Marzo–
            Aprile): 81–101.
Schreiter, Robert J.
1986   *Constructing Local Theologies.* Maryknoll, N.Y.: Orbis.
Schwantes, Milton
1982   *Teologia do Antigo Testamento—Anotações.* São Leopoldo: Polígrafo.
1984   *História de Israel (local e origens).* São Leopoldo: Polígrafo.
1986   *Ageu. Comentário Bíblico.* São Paulo: Vozes, Metodista e Sinodal.
1987   *Amós.* São Paulo: Vozes-Sinodal.
1989a   "Esperanças messiânicas e davídicas." *EB* 23:18–29.
1989b   *Projectos de Esperança: Meditações sobre Gênesis 1–11.* Petrópolis: Vozes.
Segal, J. B.
1963   *The Hebrew Passover.* London: Oxford University Press. (With a full bib-
            liography.)
Segnini, L. R. P.
1984   *O que é Mercadoria.* São Paulo: Brasiliense.
Segundo, Juan Luis
1987   "The Hermeneutic Circle." *Third World Liberation Theologies*, pp. 64–92.
            Ed. Deane William Ferm. Maryknoll, N.Y.: Orbis.
Sekine, M.
1972   "Beobachtungen zu der josianischen Reform." Short Notes. *VT* 22:361–
            68.
Sicre, José L.
1984   "Con los pobres de la tierra." *La justicia social en los profetas de Israel.*
            Madrid: Ediciones Cristandad.
Silveira Leite, Antonio Elias
1990   "Changement Religieux et Migration." Master's thesis, Université Cath-
            olique de Louvain.
Silver, Moris
1983   *Prophets and Markets: The Political Economy of Ancient Israel.* Boston:
            Kluwer-Nijhoff.
1986   *Economic Structures of the Ancient Near East.* Totowa, N.J.: Barnes &
            Noble Books.
Siqueira, Tércio Machado
1987   "A História da Páscoa, memorial da libertação." *EB* 8:6–11.
Smith, Daniel L.
1989   *The Religion of the Landless.* Bloomington, Ind.: Meyer-Stone Books.
Smith, Morton
1987   *Palestinian Parties and Politics that Shaped the Old Testament.* Second, cor-
            rected edition. London: SCM.
Snaith, N. H.
1954   "The First and Second Books of Kings." *Interpreter's Bible.* New York:
            Abingdon Press.
1957   "Sacrifices in the Old Testament." *VT* 7:308–17.
Soares, Sebastião A. G.
1989   "Sofonias, filho do negro, profeta dos pobres da terra." *RIBLA* 3:21–25.
Soares-Prabhu, George M.
1985   "Class in the Bible: The Biblical Poor a Social Class?" *Vidyajyoti* (August):
            322–46.

Sofri, G.
1977   *O Modo de Produção Asiático*. Rio de Janeiro: Paz e Terra.
Soggin, J. Alberto
1985   *A History of Ancient Israel*. Philadelphia: Westminster.
Sorese, Maryann
1987   "The Poor Challenge Brazil." *Maryknoll* 81/8:4–13.
Souza, Marcelo de Barros
1989   "Eu me acuso." *Grande Sinal* 42:387–99.
Spieckermann, H.
1982   *Juda unter Assur in der Sargonidenzeit. Forschungen zur Religion und Liter-
            atur des Alten und Neuen Testaments* 129:30–41. Göttingen: Vandenhoeck
            & Ruprecht.
Spradley, James P.
1979   *The Ethnographic Interview*. New York: Holt, Rinehart and Winston.
Srowr, R. H.
1978   *Modos de Produção: Elementos da Problemática*. Rio de Janeiro: Graal.
Stager, Lawrence, E.
1985   "The Archaeology of the Family in Ancient Israel." *BASOR* 260:1–35.
Stern, E.
1975   "Israel at the Close of the Period of the Monarchy: An Archaeological
            Survey." *BA* 38:26–54.
1979   "Craft and Industry." *WHJP* 4/2, pp. 237–264.
Stinespring, W. F.
1962   "Temple, Jerusalem." *IDB*:534–60.
Talmon, Shemaryahu
1958   "Divergences in Calendar-Reckoning in Ephrain and Judah." *VT* 8:48–
            74.
1967   "The Judeaan 'am ha'ares in Historical Perspective." *Fourth World Con-
            gress of Jewish Studies* 1:71–76. Jerusalem: Magnes Press.
1979   "Kingship and Ideology of the State." *WHJP* 4/1, pp. 3–26.
Teixeira, F. L. C.
1988   *A Gênese das CEB's no Brasil*. São Paulo: Paulinas.
Terra, J. E. Martins
1985   *Origem da Religião*. São Paulo: Loyola.
1988   *Leitura da Bíblia na Perspectiva do Pobre*. São Paulo: Loyola.
1989   "Bíblia: project preocupa Papa e bispos." *Estado de S. Paulo*, April 11.
Tigay, Jeffrey H.
1987   "Israelite Religion: The Onomastic and Epigraphic Evidence." *AIR*, pp.
            157–94
Todd, E. W.
1956   "The Reforms of Hezekiah and Josiah." *SJT* 9:288–93.
Todd, J. C.
1904   *Politics & Religion in Ancient Israel: An Introduction to the Study of the Old
            Testament*. London: Macmillan and Co., Limited.
Tomes, Roger
1971   *The Fear of the Lord: An Introduction to Old Testament Religion*. Heading-
            ton Hill Hall, Oxford: The Religious Education Press.
Torrey, C. C.
1943   "The Evolution of a Financier in the Ancient Near East." *JNES* 2:295–
            301.
Tucker, Robert C.
1978   *The Marx-Engels Reader*. 2nd ed. New York: W. W. Norton.

Van der Leeuw, G.
1964   *Fenomenología de la Religión.* México: Fondo de Cultura Económica.
Van Seters, John
1983   "The Place of the Yahwist in the History of Passover and Massot." *ZAW* 95:167–82.
Vélez, Neftalí
1988   "A leitura bíblica nas Comunidades Eclesiais de Base." *RIBLA* 1:26–43.
Von Rad, Gerhard
1962   *Old Testament Theology.* Vol. I. New York: Harper & Row.
1965   *Old Testament Theology.* Vol. II. New York: Harper & Row.
1966   *Deuteronomy.* Philadelphia: Westminster.
Vriezen, Theodorus C.
1963   *The Religion of Ancient Israel.* Philadelphia: Westminster.
1970   *An Outline of Old Testament Theology.* 2d rev. ed. Oxford: Basil Blackwell & Mott.
Walzer, Michael
1985   *Exodus and Revolution.* New York: Basic Books.
Wambacq, B. M.
1965   "De Sacrificiis." *Instituta Biblica* 1:281–329.
1976   "Les Origines de la Pesaḥ israélite." *Bib* 57:206–24 and 301–26.
1980   "Les Maṣṣôt." *Bib* 61:31–54.
Weinfeld, Moshe
1961   "The Origin of Humanism in Deuteronomy." *JBL* 80:241–47.
1964   "Cult Centralization in Israel in the Light of a Neo-Babylonian Analogy." *JNES* 23:202–12.
1967   "Deuteronomy—the Present State of Inquiry." *JBL* 86:249–62.
1972   *Deuteronomy and the Deuteronomic School.* Oxford: Oxford University Press.
1983   "Zion and Jerusalem as Religious and Political Capital: Ideology and Utopia." *The Poet and the Historian*, pp. 75–115. Ed. Richard Elliott Friedman. Chico: Scholars Press.
1987   "The Tribal League at Sinai." *AIR*, pp. 303–14.
Weingreen, Jacob
1969   "The Rebellion of Absalom." *VT* 263–66.
Weiser, A.
1966   "Die Legitimation des Königs David." *VT* 16:323–54.
Welch, A. C.
1925   "The Death of Josiah." *ZAW* 43:255–60.
1927   "On the Method of Celebrating Passover." *ZAW* 45:24–29.
Wellhausen, Julius
1963   *Die Composition des Hexateuchs.* Berlin.
1983   *Prolegomena to the History of Ancient Israel.* Gloucester, Mass.: Peter Smith. (Originally written in 1878.)
Welten, P.
1969   Die Königs-Stempel. Ein Beitrag zur Militärpolitik Judas unter Hiskia und Josia. Abhandlungen des Deutschen Palästinavereins.
Wenham, Gordon, J.
1979   *The Book of Leviticus.* Grand Rapids, Mich.: Eerdmans.
Whitelam, Keith W.
1979   *The Just King: Monarchial Judicial Authority in Ancient Israel.* Sheffield: Almond.
1986   "The Symbols of Power: Aspects of Royal Propaganda in the United Monarchy." *BA* 49:166–73.

1989 "Israelite Kingship. The Royal Ideology and Its Opponents," in *The World of Ancient Israel*, pp. 119–39. Ed. R. E. Clements. Cambridge: Cambridge University Press.

Wifall, W. R.
1975 "Son of Man—A Pre-Davidic Social Class?" *CBQ* 37:331–40.
1983 "The Tribes of Yahweh: A Synchronic Study with a Diachronic Title." *ZAW* 95:197–209.

Williams, Donald L.
1963 "The Date of Zephaniah." *JBL* 82:77–88.

Williams, Terry
1989 *The Cocaine Kids: The Inside Story of a Teenage Drug Ring.* New York: Addison-Wesley.

Williamson, H. G. M.
1982a *1 and 2 Chronicles.* New Century Bible Commentary. Grand Rapids, Mich.: Eerdmans.
1982b "The Death of Josiah and the Continuing Development of the Deuteronomic History." *VT* 32:242–48.

Wilson, Robert R.
1980 *Prophecy and Society in Ancient Israel.* Philadelphia: Fortress.
1984 *Sociological Approaches to the Old Testament.* Philadelphia: Fortress.

Wirpsa, Leslie
1990 "Latin American Religious in Tug-of-War with Vatican." *National Catholic Reporter* 26, no. 31 (May 25):8.

Wittfogel, K. A.
1957 *Oriental Despotism.* New Haven, Conn.: Yale University Press.

Wolf, Eric R.
1984 *Guerras Camponesas do Século XX.* São Paulo: Global. (Originally written in 1966.)

Wolff, Hans Walter
1982 "The Kerygma of the Deuteronomic Historical Work." *The Vitality of Old Testament Traditions*, pp. 83–120. Ed. W. Brueggemann and H. W. Wolff. 2d ed. Atlanta: John Knox Press.

Wright, Christopher J. H.
1990 *God's People in God's Land.* Grand Rapids, Mich.: Eerdmans.

Wright, G. Ernest
1962 "Cult and History." *Interpretation* 16:3–20.

Würthwein, E.
1976 "Die josianische Reform und das Deuteronium." *ZTK* 73: 395–423.

Wynia, Gary W.
1990 *The Politics of Latin American Development.* Third Edition. Cambridge: Cambridge University Press.

Yadin, Yigael
1949–50 "The Reorganization of the Army of Judah under Josiah." *Bulletin of the Jewish Palestine Exploration Society* 15, 2–4: 86–98. (Summary of a longer article in Hebrew.)
1963 *The Art of Warfare in Biblical Lands.* Vol. 2:275–84. New York: McGraw-Hill.
1976 "Beer Sheba: The High Place Destroyed by King Josiah." *BASOR* 222:5–17.

Yeivin, S.
1953 "Social, Religious and Cultural Trends in Jerusalem under the Davidic Dynasty." *VT* 3:149–66.

Zimmerli, W.
1978 *Old Testament Theology in Outline.* Atlanta: John Knox Press.

Scripture Index

General Index

The Unvarnished Doctrine

The Unvarnished Doctrine

Locke, Liberalism, and the American Revolution

Steven M. Dworetz

Duke University Press   Durham and London

© 1990 Duke University Press
First printing in paperback, 1994
All rights reserved.
Printed in the United States of America
on acid-free paper ∞
Library of Congress Cataloging-in-Publication Data
appear on the last printed page of this book.

Contents

Preface to the Paperback Edition

The Unvarnished Doctrine originally was published in 1990. Reviewers generally treated the book fairly and sympathetically, offering constructive criticism and encouragement. A few were very generous in their assessments. The rare displays of real hostility toward my work were distressing on one level, yet rewarding on another; for the fury of such criticism assured me that I had succeeded in striking vital nerves among the defenders of orthodoxy both in American historiography and in academic political theory.

I continue to view the political thought of the American Revolution as a powerful and humanizing matrix of ideas in which Locke's liberalism, properly understood, constituted one essential, defining, and progressive element. Of course I stressed that element in *The Unvarnished Doctrine* as I sought to initiate a reversal of the deliberalization of eighteenth-century American political thought—a movement informed, on one hand, by a dangerous exaggeration of the desirability of a "politics of virtue" in a diverse society and, on the other, by a failure to understand the inseparable connection between liberalism (its imperfections notwithstanding) and human freedom. John Locke explored and articulated this connection in the seventeenth century, and American Revolutionary thought generally—and often explicitly—understood freedom and the preconditions of freedom in Locke's distinctive terms. The success of the "republican revival," I argued, thus depended in substantial measure on prob-

lematic interpretations of political theory. These failures of interpretation, moreover, generated a one-sided, distorted historiography
that could supply factitious legitimacy to the erosion or subversion of
liberal politics—of freedom—in the present.

Some of the best scholarship since 1990 suggests that, at the very
least, I was on the right track. A number of authors have shown that
eighteenth-century American political thought was broader, more
complex, and more Lockean-liberal in a positive sense than the paradigm depicted in republican historiography. Locke scholarship, too,
has advanced significantly toward the textual redemption of Locke's
philosophy from dogma and obfuscation. Let me mention a few works
that relate in interesting ways to my own.

In his elegant and engaging book, *Republicanism and Bourgeois
Radicalism: Political Ideology in Late Eighteenth-Century England and
America* (Cornell University Press, 1990), Isaac Kramnick maintains
that the historiographic shift away from Locke "has gone too far"
in its treatment of Anglo-American thought in the second half of
the eighteenth century as a paradigm which (as Kramnick quotes
J. G. A. Pocock) does " 'not necessitate reference to Locke at all' "
(pp. 167, 164). Allowing late eighteenth-century figures in England
and America "to speak for themselves," he discovers Locke "very
much alive and well" in their writings and speeches (p. 170). Binding the Revolutionists (and the English radicals and Protestant Dissenters) to classical republican ideology, Kramnick argues, falsely portrays them as "nostalgic defenders of the past, set against modernity
and commerce." In fact, they were "ardent believers in progress and
change" and as such they "relied heavily" on Locke's ideas (pp. 32–
33). If Locke were indeed as irrelevant or hostile to the American
Revolutionary impulse as republican historians claim, why, he asks,
did the Tory and clerical establishment embark on a "crusade to root
out his ideas" (p. 185)? And why did loyalists, such as Josiah Tucker,
denounce the Revolutionists as " 'Mr. Locke's disciples' " (p. 176)?

Ellis Sandoz, in his fascinating and learned study, *A Government of
Laws: Political Theory, Religion, and the American Founding* (Louisiana
State University Press, 1990), understands the founding as an "anti-
modernist embodiment of medieval principles of order" (p. 235), fun-

damentally opposed to "the currents of radical secularist modernity" (p. 85). The founding was, in this sense, reactionary. It looked back for inspiration and guidance, however, not to a sanitized Machiavelli and the secular virtue of republican Rome, but to Biblical religion, classical philosophy (Plato and Aristotle), and medieval theology and political thought. The founding thus represented "a unique anti-modernist rearticulation of Western Civilization . . . profoundly indebted to classical and Christian influences" (p. 25); it was "a great conspiracy of faith and reason" (p. 125). Sandoz acknowledges the presence of other intellectual tendencies, such as liberalism and republicanism, in the founding philosophy, but he asserts nonetheless the determinative preeminence of "classical and Christian thought" in the American Revolution and its constitutional settlement (pp. 100, 83).

One could argue about this estimate of the *relative* importance of classical philosophy and Christian thought (whether or not it was *decisive*) in the philosophy of the American founding, or about the *authenticity* (as distinguished from the *expediency*) of the founders' religious commitments. The inherent methodological limitations of intellectual history allow nothing more than informed speculation in such matters. Moreover, reverence or nostalgia for the classical and Biblical (and republican) traditions ought to be tempered by analysis of the relationships between those traditions and the intolerable forms of oppression they historically defended: for instance, slavery and the domestic subordination of women. Can the traditions be detached, as it were, from those dehumanizing practices and institutions, and reconciled to the demands of justice? Whatever the answer, Sandoz's reaffirmation of the historical and theoretical importance of religion in the American founding stands out as a vital contribution to this field of study.

It is worth noting an ironic link between Sandoz's book and *The Unvarnished Doctrine*. To my horror, Sandoz demonizes Locke, driving the dull stake of "esoteric interpretation" through Locke's covertly Hobbesian heart. Although he insists that "we must deal, of course, with what is said in Locke's books," this turns out to be something other than what Locke himself *actually* says. Indeed, Sandoz explicitly adopts the method of Leo Strauss in *Natural Right and History* (University of Chicago Press, 1953) and thus reads Locke (and apparently only Locke) "with a suspicious eye, as it were, on the assumption that Locke means more or less or something other than simply what he says." This stratagem allows Sandoz to dismiss parenthetically the manifest and essential differences between Hobbes's absolutism and Locke's advocacy of religious toleration and limited government. From the "Straussian viewpoint," as Sandoz calls it, Locke is Hobbes in sheep's clothing—an anti-Biblical hedonist who emancipated the acquisitive instinct from the salutary constraints of classical morality and revealed religion while chattering disingenuously about God and the law of nature. Thus conceived, Locke bears primary guilt for virtually all the great sins of modernity, including "the chronic terror of existence in the shadow of universal barbarism and annihilation" (pp. 58–60, 64–65, 72–73, 82).

Although *The Unvarnished Doctrine* strongly dissents both from this jaundiced reading of Locke and from the capricious method that produces it, I certainly agree with Sandoz when he asserts that such a reading "was simply unthinkable to the American founders," who generally read Locke "as a Christian Whig and an opponent of Hobbes" (pp. 134, 191). Indeed, when Sandoz, after excoriating Locke as a duplicitous Hobbesian heretic, concedes that "Locke may have been read quite *accurately* by Americans . . . as a spokesman for traditional Christian natural law and rights" (p. 191, emphasis added), he ironically confirms a central argument in my book.

In *Algernon Sidney and the Republican Heritage in England and America* (Princeton University Press, 1991), Alan Craig Houston spans two fields—historiography and political theory—with clarity and grace. Confronting the enthusiasm of the "republican revival," Houston reminds us that "the cultivation of civic virtue is an unattractive and impractical ideal for large, complex, and heterogeneous societies" (pp. 3–4). Classical virtue is "a martial ethos that manifests itself in a cult of masculinity and in a glorification of conquest and expansion" (p. 9). His most telling theoretical point in relation to the historiography of the American founding, however, emerges from his interpretation of Locke's contemporary, Algernon Sidney.

The claim that "the defining characteristic of republicanism is a classical theory of virtue, and that the republican language of virtue is distinct from and in tension with the liberal logic of rights and interests" constitutes a central principle of republican historiographers (p. 146); they cite Sidney, moreover, as the quintessential republican and thus the ideological nemesis of Locke. Houston, however, shows that the distinctive feature of Sidney's thought consists not in an advocacy of civic virtue as an alternative to liberal rights and interests, but in a "dramatic reconfiguration" of classical republican themes and the fusion of these transformed themes with those of liberal theory (pp. 157, 166). In Sidney's republicanism, "the language of virtue and corruption was inseparable from the [liberal] logic of rights, interests, laws, and contracts" (p. 169). Indeed, "when attention is restricted to those cases in which the influence of Sidney's ideas" among the American Revolutionary generation "was strongest," we see that "virtually all of the 'republican' principles drawn from Sidney's writings were perfectly compatible with Lockean liberalism." Houston's careful textual analysis thus "casts doubt on the widely held view that there existed a distinct and coherent 'republican' language of politics in Revolutionary America that was distinct from and in tension with Lockean liberalism" (pp. 224–225). This conclusion, which Houston extends to a range of themes, indicates "the need to modify the conceptual framework employed by republican revivalists" (pp. 9, 277).

This emerging critique of the polarity between liberalism and republicanism in the political thought of the American founding is the most noteworthy development in the field over the past three years, and it receives important support from Garrett Sheldon in his excellent study, *The Political Philosophy of Thomas Jefferson* (Johns Hopkins University Press, 1991). Sheldon shows how Jefferson systematically combined elements of both traditions in a coherent and consistent political philosophy. Sheldon's work, like Houston's, thus suggests that historians had actually smuggled into the past the polarity they claimed to have discovered there.

Students of eighteenth-century American political thought can look forward to Jerome Huyler's book on the philosophy of Locke and the American founding (forthcoming from the University Press of

Kansas). Huyler, whose work I have read in manuscript form, argues that the removal of Locke from the philosophy of the founding, as well as the mutual exclusivity of republicanism and liberalism, rest on an inadequate understanding of Locke. He offers a new, sympathetic interpretation of Locke's political philosophy, which he skillfully deploys, planting the flag of Lockean liberalism atop the high moral and ideological ground of the founding of the American Republic and advancing the critique of the polarity that informs the conceptual framework of the republican revival.

Huyler's Locke differs from the Locke portrayed in *The Unvarnished Doctrine*. Both, however, take the side of the angels. Indeed, Locke interpretation remains a growth industry; and the most serious and original scholarship over the past few years continues the liberation of Locke's philosophy from the superficially narrow compass of hostile orthodoxy. The literature is too large to treat here, but I should mention Peter A. Schouls's *Reasoned Freedom: John Locke and Enlightenment* (Cornell University Press, 1992), which is among the best of an outstanding array of scholarly productions.

Schouls's analysis of Locke reveals neither a moral relativist nor a Hobbesian hedonist, but a thinker who "rejects subjectivism about happiness and relativism about the good" and believes that "human beings have no right but to impose upon themselves invariant truth and goodness" (pp. 113, 136–139). How do we know truth and goodness? How do we discover the right way to live? According to Schouls, Locke adopts Descartes's "revolutionary" method: to gain such knowledge, and thus to become "more fully human," people must first "reject *as automatically binding* the principles which their cultural contexts would impose" (p. 44, emphasis added). This method deeply informs Locke's epistemic individualism, producing the view that people "do not become fully human unless they initially reject all prevalent doctrines and opinions *and* accept only such doctrines as can pass a certain test imposed by *each individual's own intellect*" (pp. 28–29, emphasis added). Far from endorsing moral relativism, however, Locke here intends precisely "to *overcome* the relativism of belief conditioned by specific cultural epochs" (p. 35, emphasis added). And he fundamentally rejects any axiomatic identification of the good with the pleasurable. Schouls takes seriously, and as a central element of Locke's philosophy, his explicit insistence that " 'the principle of all virtue lies in a power of denying ourselves the satisfaction of our own desires, where reason does not authorize them' " (pp. 137, 207).

The inalienable obligation to employ one's own reason in pursuit of truth and goodness (or salvation) requires a political form in which religious dogma cannot forcibly be imposed on individuals. Schouls believes that Locke's "methodology and epistemology together [thus] account for the 'revolutionary implications' of his works on politics, on religion, and on education" (p. 22). This indeed is the key to the unity of Locke's thought.

So *The Unvarnished Doctrine* is not—nor did I ever presume it to be—the last word either on the philosophy of John Locke or on the political thought of the American founding. Scholars continue to extend the horizon of our understanding. I would like my book to be read and regarded in the context of, and as a contribution to, this ongoing collective endeavor.

My younger son, Rawley, arrived too late—by a matter of weeks—to join his older brother, Charlie, in the acknowledgments in the first edition. Rawley is here now, offering sympathy and hugs as I growl at the computer. Like his brother, he teaches me something new and important every day.

Steven M. Dworetz
Brookline, Massachusetts

Acknowledgments

Writing a book is, in one sense, a process of accumulating debts that cannot be discharged. They can, however, be acknowledged; and it is indeed a pleasure to do so. Friends, colleagues, teachers, and, above all, my family—there would be no book were it not for their encouragement and forbearance.

I owe a great deal to my teachers: Richard Boris of York College, City University of New York, the friend and teacher who showed me the light; Benjamin Barber and Carey McWilliams of Rutgers University, who taught me what to look for under the light; and Gordon Schochet, also of Rutgers, who taught me to interpret what I found there.

The extraordinary good luck I had with teachers I now enjoy with colleagues at Wheaton College. The political science department has been a repository of goodwill and support. I am also grateful to Kenneth Winston of the philosophy department for reading drafts of various chapters and drawing my attention to a critical question in the methodology of Locke interpretation.

Thanks to the kindness of Professor Thomas Spragens, Jr. of Duke University, my work came to the attention of Reynolds Smith, who became my editor at Duke University Press. I could not have completed this project without his confidence in it and his support.

Several persons read earlier versions of *The Unvarnished Doctrine* during the reviewing process. Their comments and criticisms helped me to prepare the final product. With one exception, they remain anonymous to me, and I must thank them accordingly. The exception is William Bernard Peach, professor of philosophy at Duke University, who read two versions of the manuscript. I am especially pleased to be able to thank Professor Peach by name, since this book has benefited substantially from the suggestions he offered in his wise and constructive critique of the first draft. Needless to say, however, neither he nor anyone else but the author is responsible for defects.

I started reading and writing about Locke, liberalism, and the American Revolution in 1983, when my son, Charlie, was a year old. Nearly all his life Charlie has been waiting for me to finish my book about the Yankees and the British, helping me as only he can. At last I can tell him that the war is over.

Those from whom we receive the most are the most difficult to thank. My wife, Iwona, has been my constant friend and reality check for more than a decade. She has traversed the peaks and valleys of this enterprise with me since its inception. And she has tolerated a good deal of strange behavior from me along the way. She's my absolutely indispensable companion.

This book is for my mother, and in memory of my father.

Steven M. Dworetz
North Attleborough, Massachusetts

The Unvarnished Doctrine

This is Mr. Locke's doctrine,
it is the doctrine of reason and truth,
and it is, sir, the unvarnished doctrine
of the Americans.

—Junius Americanus (Arthur Lee),
Boston Evening Post (May 4, 1772)

1

The Historiographic Revolution: The Rise of "Cato" and the Decline of Locke in American Revolutionary Thought

For any political society the interpretation of its founding ideology is of great significance. The more overtly ideological or theocratic regimes take no chances in this regard. They institutionalize the interpretation of founding doctrine in a high political office. In such systems tinkering with that doctrine is serious political business, never to be undertaken without official approval and supervision; and a fundamental reinterpretation, were it to occur at all, would undoubtedly be a politically revolutionary act.

In contrast, regimes rooted in the liberal-democratic tradition do not appoint a "Secretary for Ideology" to guard, monopolize, and enforce the interpretation of the founding doctrine. In part, this is because liberal-democratic ideology itself includes toleration and free speech among its essential principles and thus precludes the cultivation and enforcement of ideological or religious purity by the state. In these systems, of which the United States is one, the founding doctrine is always, in principle, open to critical review by citizens. Moreover, a reinterpretation need not be the work of political revolutionaries; scholars could do it. But in these matters, even a scholarly revolution can have far-reaching political consequences.

After all, a society's understanding of its founding doctrine is an integral part of its self-consciousness and the ultimate source of its sense of purpose and normative vision. The ideology of the founding furnishes the standards by which citizens evaluate contemporary events, practices, and arrangements. The dominant understanding of the founding doctrine thus reveals something of the political society's moral condition. It also contains prescriptive implications for public policy and constitutes the essential source of historical legitimacy for any general political program.

The contenders in a political-ideological struggle, for example, often seek legitimacy for their agendas in the founding ideology and therefore, consciously or not, selectively interpret that ideology, or selectively appropriate from interpretations developed by others, to accommodate their specific partisan needs. So, while relatively "disinterested" or apolitical scholars may initiate changes in a society's understanding of its founding doctrine, political leaders, parties, and movements will make use of their work—perhaps in ways that the scholars themselves fail to anticipate.

For these reasons a revolution in the historical understanding of the ideology of the founding is very serious—even, and perhaps especially, when it occurs in a society with a liberal-democratic political tradition which is conducive to such a national soul-searching and self-reevaluation. For example, there could be a great deal more at stake than the egos of dueling antiquarians if the reinterpretation of the American founding doctrine calls into question the *historical* significance of the first principles of liberal-democratic ideology itself. Suppose the reinterpreters exclude from the ideology of the American Revolution, or radically demote therein, the one tradition of political thought that *inherently* authorizes religious toleration, constitutional politics (understood as lawful, limited government), and popular revolution against actual or intended tyranny? In effect, the new interpretation would undermine the historical *legitimacy* of toleration, constitutional politics, and popular revolution in the American context. And if that new interpretation were to become the prevailing view, it would permit the critics of those uniquely *liberal* political principles to label them, and those who believe in them, as "un-American."

This turn of events could become life-threatening if the reinterpretation "altogether replaces" liberalism with a "classical republican" political tradition.[1] Civic virtue, the preeminent value in republican ideology, can be incompatible with personal freedom, which only the banished liberalism seems to defend by instinct rather than merely for convenience. Militarism, imposed social and religious conformity, and even American slavery are known to have been justified in the language of civic republicanism.[2] Indeed, although this republican tradition is presumed to be rooted in the ideals of the ancient polis, the acknowledged primary textual source of *American* republicanism too often reads (as we shall see) like a prospectus for the Leviathan.

In any case, with the substitution of republicanism for liberalism in the founding ideology, not only would the one doctrine that innately authorizes constitutional politics and personal freedom be purged from the founding, but its place would be filled by a doctrine that does not inherently preclude, and may in part be inclined toward, the antithesis of constitutional politics and personal freedom, that is, to use the generic term employed by the American Revolutionists, tyranny. And that inclination could become the dominant tendency precisely in the absence of liberal mediation.

In American historiography there has indeed been a fundamental reinterpretation of the founding doctrine—specifically, of the ideology and political thought of the American Revolution—and this scholarly achievement has some serious political implications. Inadvertently, it seems, scholars have cut the historical grounds of legitimacy out from under the defense of constitutional politics by denying that liberalism was an essential ideological component of the founding doctrine; and they have escalated the danger by reinterpreting Revolutionary thought primarily, or even exclusively, in terms of that republican tradition (which is referred to in the literature as classical republicanism, civic republicanism, civic humanism, "country" ideology, the libertarian creed, the commonwealth tradition, etc.). Consider briefly how this historiographic revolution in the study of American Revolutionary thought has transformed our understanding of that chapter of the founding doctrine.

Liberalism once was deemed by scholarly consensus to have held undisputed sway over the political thought of the American Revolution, and historians proclaimed "the Great Mr. Locke, America's Philosopher," as the Revolution's "guide and prophet."[3] From this perspective John Locke's *Two Treatises of Government* looked like "the textbook of the American Revolution" and the source "from which Americans drew the 'principles of 1776.'" Locke's political thought had thoroughly "dominated the political philosophy of the American Revolution," the totality of which could therefore be summarized simply as "an exegesis upon Locke."[4] A few years later Louis Hartz, in his classic study, *The Liberal Tradition in America*, extended Lockean intellectual dominion beyond the Revolutionary period, to the whole of American political thought and behavior.[5] With Hartz (and to Hartz's apparent dismay) the triumph of "Lockean liberalism" was complete.

By the late 1960s, however, a new consensus had begun to emerge. Scholars now criticized the interpretation of Revolutionary thought that comprehended *Locke et praeterea nihil*. They initiated an "essential historical shift away from Locke" and began to develop a new interpretative paradigm to replace what I shall call the Locke model of interpretation.[6]

To these iconoclastic historians Locke appeared as merely "a negligible influence upon American political thought before 1776."[7] Only "in few cases," wrote John Dunn, in an influential essay, could the Revolution "possibly have been thought to have been in any sense about the *Two Treatises of Government* of John Locke."[8] This demotion of Locke was then taken to the extreme by scholars who questioned not only the extent but also the nature of the relationship between his thought and the ideology of the American Revolution. J. G. A. Pocock, a pioneer in the study of the history of political thought and one of the founders of the revisionist movement, led the way by suggesting that we count Locke among the *adversaries* of Revolutionary political thought as this began to take shape within the new interpretative paradigm that Pocock himself was helping to fashion.[9] From this soon-to-be sovereign historiographical perspective, the principles of liberalism appeared to be inconsistent with the "principles of 1776."

As we can see, the interpretation of American Revolutionary thought has shifted dramatically with respect to Lockean-liberal thought. Revisionist historiography has converted the intellectual "guide and prophet" of the Revolution into the Revolution's ideological enemy. *Locke et praeterea nihil* has become *omnia praeter Lockem*, as a new interpretative paradigm—pioneered by Pocock and Bernard Bailyn, often deemed hostile to liberalism, and referred to as the "republican synthesis" or the "republican hypothesis" [10]—has completely replaced the Locke model of interpretation in the study of the founding ideology. Scholars now credit the republican tradition with having furnished the language, the normative concerns, and the inspirational fire of Revolutionary ideology and political thought.

The historiographic radicalism of the republican revision should be carefully considered. It represents a profound and, indeed, unprecedented realignment in the history of political thought. I am not aware of any development in the study of the history of political thought that can match the decline of Lockean theory, and of liberalism in general, and the corresponding rise of civic republicanism in the historiography of the American Revolution. With astonishing speed and thoroughness, scholars have abandoned one interpretation of the founding doctrine in favor of another, apparently antithetical, understanding of Revolutionary ideology.

It is not too difficult to see why, the radical nature and far-reaching significance of the historiographic revolution notwithstanding, the republican synthesis encountered so little resistance in its rapid ascent to the Kuhnian summit. It promised a historical alternative to Hartz's seemingly inescapable Lockean paradigm. Above all, it proclaimed that the Revolutionists fought for virtue's sake and not for "commerce," [11] thus casting a very appealing light upon the motivations of the Founding Fathers. Nevertheless, I feel we have been too hasty and uncritical in accepting both the historical and the interpretative claims of this new account of Revolutionary thought. We should pause to consider what has happened to our understanding of the founding doctrine, how and why it has happened, and what it might mean for American politics now and in the future.

The place to begin is the historiographic revolution itself. That is the subject of this book: a critical examination of the republican revision and a reassessment of the role of Lockean-liberal ideas in the American Revolution. [12] The book is based on historical research, that is, on the writings from the Revolutionary period; and it approaches those writings from the interpretative perspective of political theory, sensitive to the content of the classic texts. It respects the republican revision's many positive contributions to the study of Revolutionary thought (including the debunking of the monolithic Locke model of interpretation). But it criticizes the historical and theoretical distortions of revisionist scholarship and worries about the implications these distortions hold for liberal-constitutionalist politics in America.

The stakes are high, for both citizens and scholars. The historiographic revolution has changed America's historical self-understanding and thus deeply affects the republic as a whole and all of its citizens. On another level it represents a major revision in the history of political thought and thus falls within the jurisdiction of the ivory tower. But as a historical account of Revolutionary doctrine, and with regard to the interpretation of Lockean and republican political theory, revisionist historiography is seriously flawed.

On the one hand, the revision either denies the historical significance of Locke's liberalism or casts it in an anti-Revolutionary light, while proclaiming the decisive importance of republican sources in the formation of American Revolutionary thought. But it will be shown that in relation to the most crucial issues in the Anglo-American dispute (for instance, representation, taxation, consent, religious liberty, the limits of civil authority per se, the right and duty of revolution, and the ultimate sovereignty of the people), the Revolutionists' writings do not support either of these claims. The historical-textual evidence testifies consistently and often explicitly in the language of "Locke on Government." On the other hand, the republican revision rests on specific, unexamined interpretations both of Lockean thought and of the political thought that, the revisionists say, inspired and shaped the development of American republicanism. Yet these interpretations either fail the test of close textual analysis or are historically inappropriate for the period under investigation.

This point about the interpretation of political theory is extremely important. What the republican revision lacks in its most important formative works is, if you will, the interpretative discipline of political theory, born of an intimate acquaintance with the classic texts. As recently noted by Thomas Pangle: "In attempting to assess the merits of this contemporary infatuation with 'classical republicanism,' one cannot avoid being struck by the ignorance its proponents display as regards the original texts of the 'classical republican' philosophers to which they constantly refer. The contemporary scholars of early American history appear to know these texts only casually, or on the basis of secondhand reports."[13] If the goal is to estimate the relative significance of different theoretical traditions in a specific historical context, and to determine the nature of their impact within that context,[14] then a clear, and clearly defined, understanding of those traditions, and of their parent texts, is absolutely essential. It should be obvious that this kind of historical research therefore requires the consistent application of some rigorous standards of interpretation.

For example, the search for Locke in American Revolutionary thought should be informed by an understanding of Lockean thought that satisfies *two criteria of interpretation*. First, the interpretation must be textually sound, or available in Locke's texts; that is, it should be an interpretation that can be legitimately carved out of the Lockean corpus. Second, in developing or choosing a textually sound interpretation of Lockean thought (for there could be more than one textually available Locke), we should try to be sensitive to how Lockean thought most likely would have been interpreted by the contemporaries of the period under investigation. The interpretation, then, must also be appropriate for the Revolution's historical context; that is, it should be an interpretation that most likely *would* have been carved out of Locke's texts by eighteenth-century American readers.

So far, the study of American Revolutionary thought has not satisfied both of these criteria of interpretation with respect to Lockean thought. The seminal works of the historiographic revolution are not adequately informed by the interpretative discipline of political theory thus understood. This book seeks to fill that lacuna in the reinterpretation of the founding doctrine by introducing these elements of political theory into a historical study of Revolutionary thought. A preview of some of the arguments made later in the book provides an indication of what is at stake.

First, consider *Cato's Letters*. We have heard a great deal about this remarkable text, coauthored by John Trenchard and Thomas Gordon in their poignant struggle to retard the rise of modern British politics in the Age of Walpole. In republican historiography "Cato" is reputed to have been "of the utmost importance in the creation of American republicanism."[15] This may be so. But what does that tell us about American republicanism?

The fact is, the revisionists have failed to deliver a credible interpretation of Cato's political thought, leaving us uninformed about some of the sinister possibilities in American republicanism. As the major source of American republicanism (and the principal alternative to Locke), Cato is presumed to have conveyed to the American colonists the civic humanist ideals of citizenship, participation, and virtue (thereby enabling them to resist the so-called Lockean-liberal temptations of unbridled self-interest and capital accumulation). Analysis, however, raises the suspicion that Cato would have found the Leviathan more congenial than the polis. And who is to say that it wasn't the Hobbesian elements in Cato's republicanism that appealed, perhaps intuitively, to the Revolutionists who knew his argument? Would they, indeed, have sought refuge under the Sovereign were it not for their overriding Lockean-liberal commitments to constitutional politics?

With Lockean thought the situation is far more complex, and the implications of the interpretation are absolutely decisive; but three related problems can be previewed easily enough. First, revisionist historians apparently were not sufficiently familiar with Locke's texts. As a result, they failed to recognize, or to interpret correctly, empirical traces of Locke in the Revolutionary writings and, indeed, in *Cato's Letters*. Second, the most influential revisionists failed to grasp the very *basics* of Locke's political theory. Bernard Bailyn, for instance, casually described the justification for resistance to absolute, arbitrary government as an idea which Locke himself would have *opposed*.[16] By thus confusing Locke with Filmer, the republican synthesis identified the Lockean-liberal essence of Revolutionary argument as *anti*-Lockean and *anti*-liberal. The third related problem is the most interesting of all from the standpoint of political theory. In short, the interpretative assumptions that determined the course of revisionist

historiography with respect to Locke and to liberalism closely resembled the conclusions of C. B. Macpherson and Leo Strauss.

I will have more to say about these fascinating, influential, and
curiously convergent interpretations of Locke (especially Strauss's)
later in the book. For the benefit of those who are unfamiliar with the
legends of academic political theory, however, a brief introduction
here will light the way ahead.

The *Two Treatises* emerges from expert Marxist analysis in Macpherson's *The Political Theory of Possessive Individualism* as a book
about property. Macpherson even calls his chapter on Locke "The
Political Theory of Appropriation." Locke's greatest achievement, in
this account, was to transform unlimited appropriation from a moral
disability into a natural right and, indeed, a "positive virtue," and
thus to provide a "moral foundation for bourgeois appropriation,"
i.e., for capitalism.[17] Other aspects of his theory served mainly to
advance this underlying ideological purpose. Accordingly, Macpherson's Locke used natural law as a "facade," to make his theory of
appropriation "more attractive to the taste of his contemporaries."[18]
His political constitutionalism was "essentially a defence of the supremacy of property," a "defence of the rights of expanding property
rather than of the rights of the individual against the state."[19] And he
confined the right of revolution to a majority of a minority, i.e., to a
majority of "the men of substance to whom the security of unlimited
accumulation was of first importance."[20] In short, Macpherson regards property as the core concept in Locke's political theory—the
essential aim of which was to demonstrate, on behalf of the rising
bourgeoisie, the "moral rationality of unlimited appropriation" and
to provide "a positive moral basis for capitalist society."[21]

Leo Strauss's approach to the classic texts is quite different from
Macpherson's,[22] yet he explicitly acknowledges "considerable agreement" between himself and Macpherson on the meaning of Locke's
political philosophy.[23] (Richard Ashcraft thus writes, critically, that
the conception of "Lockean liberalism . . . as the ideology of
the emerging bourgeoisie extends across the political spectrum.")[24]
Strauss identifies Locke's doctrine of property in the *Second Treatise* as "the central part of his political teaching" and "certainly its

most characteristic part." [25] And this doctrine, according to Strauss, aims essentially toward the "emancipation of acquisitiveness" [26]— though Locke attempted to conceal his philosophical radicalism in the "phraseology of the law of nature." [27] Thus, Locke's doctrine of property, which contains the hidden essence of his "hedonistic" political teaching, is in Strauss's view "directly intelligible" to the modern reader "if it is taken as the classic doctrine of the 'spirit of capitalism.' " [28]

In essence, this is the view of Lockean liberalism that informed and guided much of the historiographic revolution (especially where influenced by Pocock). Without directly attributing this view to Strauss or Macpherson, without applying any criteria of interpretation in adopting this view, and without acknowledging the existence of competing, no less credible but less hostile, interpretations of Locke's thought, the revisionists simply took Locke at his *worst*: the possessive individualist, the apologist for bourgeois excess, the corrupt prophet of the "spirit of capitalism." Lockean liberalism thus seemed to be the ideological source of a serious modern problem: the egoistic commercialization of American life. And in order to effect a cure, it would be necessary "to rescue America from liberalism." [29]

For scholars who could translate their social concern into action, two tasks rose to the top of the research agenda. Historiographic redemption of what John Diggins so aptly calls "the lost soul of American politics" from the hedonistic clutches of "Lockean liberalism" would require, first, a radically reduced estimate of Locke's sway over the Revolutionary mind and, on the other hand, the excavation of a distinctively non-Lockean, nonliberal, preferably *anti*liberal tradition of political thought in the ideological foundations of the Revolution. [30] The fall of liberalism and the rise of republicanism in the historiography of the American Revolution—arguably the most stunning reversal in the history of political thought—thus began with a hostile interpretation of Locke and some wishful thinking about Cato.

The time has come to consider this historiographic revolution in detail. A review of some of the seminal literature of the revisionist

movement will set the stage for the critique which follows. This review will conclude with a survey of Pocock's historiography, where an
ironic dependence on the "bourgeois Locke" of Strauss and Macpherson yields an interpretation in which Locke's liberalism is deemed
to be incompatible with, and aggressively hostile to, the dominant,
republican ideology of the American Revolution. This will further
demonstrate the central importance of the interpretation of political
theory in the study of American Revolutionary thought.

Like many revolutions, scholarly or otherwise, the republican revision
began as a revolt against orthodoxy—in this case, the interpretation
of Revolutionary thought which stressed *Locke et praeterea nihil*. To
establish a context for our analysis, let's take a closer look at that
Locke model of interpretation.

Earlier I introduced the Locke model with some representative
statements from that historiographic perspective. Since it was Louis
Hartz who most cogently and comprehensively argued the case for
a Lockean America, his *Liberal Tradition in America* is for us, as it
was for the revisionists, the place to begin. Hartz became famous for
putting the whole of American political and intellectual history into
the framework of "Lockean liberalism," although he spelled it differently, viewed it critically, and took pains to distinguish it from the
teaching of the "actual historic" Locke—an interesting point which
Hartz's critics apparently failed to appreciate.[31] Deemphasizing Locke
in, not to mention excluding him from, the ideological foundations
of the Revolution thus presupposed the refutation of Hartz's thesis or
the development of a more persuasive one.

According to Hartz, American political society is, always has
been, and presumably would continue to be, under the intellectual,
ideological and psychological domination of Lockean liberalism—by
which he meant, among other things, an ethos of individualism, economic self-interest, and materialist values. In thus maximizing the
significance of Lockean liberalism, however, Hartz was not concerned
so much with an explicit phenomenon in the history of ideas as with
the "Lockean" mode of thought and behavior that seems always to

prevail in America at both the individual and the collective-cultural levels. It was in this sense that "Locke has been so basic that we have not recognized his significance."[32]

Only in America has the sway of Lockean liberalism been so ubiquitous, unchallenged, and absolute. And its stranglehold on American intellectual and political life, according to Hartz, can be explained only through a comparative analysis of eighteenth-century social structures in America and in Europe, an analysis which reveals the crucial absence of the "feudal factor" in America's past.[33]

Europeans, in Hartz's account, entered modernity mired in Filmer's feudal patriarchalism and moved, convulsively, to the liberalism of Locke, apparently en route to the socialism of Marx. America, however, was essentially unaffected by the historical dynamics of Western Europe; for these were generated in the feudal system, which America did not share and consequently did not have to overthrow. The original immigrants left this feudal baggage, as it were, on the pier; they did not transport the sociopolitical structures and hierarchies of the Old World to the new. As a result, their descendants, as Tocqueville observed, were "born equal," in a place which Locke himself had cited as an empirical instance of the state of nature. Unlike the Europeans, they did not have to destroy a social system in order to achieve that equality. And this fact, for Hartz (and Tocqueville), explained the singular achievements of the American Revolution—its relatively low level of internal violence and the lack of a Thermidorean reaction—as well as America's enduring, "Lockean" political personality.[34]

In Hartz's view Lockean liberalism in America did not depend upon knowledge of Locke—an argument not without significant methodological implications. Hartz, indeed, explicitly declined to portray the colonists as "splendid citizens" reading Locke and then acting out the revolutionary scenario of the Second Treatise.[35] Locke had merely provided the modern social scientist with categories to describe a mode of behavior which subsequently became virtually universal under specific socio-structural conditions. Those conditions prevailed in the New World, where Lockean liberalism consequently had no "natural enemies" to keep it in check. The social structure did not provide an effective foothold for the forces of Filmer or of Marx. The unique social conditions in colonial America thus allowed Americans to begin with Locke, to stay with Locke, and to develop an "absolute and irrational attachment" for him.[36] As a result, "Locke dominates American political thought, as no thinker anywhere dominates the political thought of a nation. He is a massive national cliché."[37]

Carl Becker was another major proponent of the Locke model of interpretation. More than Hartz, Becker specifically addressed and maximized the influence of Locke upon the American Revolution itself. For Becker, "most Americans" at the time of the Revolution "had absorbed Locke's works as a kind of political gospel."[38] Becker's thesis, like Hartz's, did not depend upon the colonists' having read the *Two Treatises*. The colonists, he argued, could be Lockeans without reading Locke's book because their own governments (which were being threatened by British "innovations") actually conformed, "in a rough and ready way," to the kind of government "for which Locke had furnished a reasoned foundation." "How could the colonists not accept a philosophy . . . which assured them that their own governments, with which they were well content, were just the kind that God had designed men by nature to have! The general philosophy which lifted this common sense conclusion to the level of a cosmic law, the colonists therefore accepted, during the course of the eighteenth century, without difficulty, almost unconsciously."[39] Hence, the strength of the Declaration of Independence, in which "Jefferson copied Locke," was "precisely that it said what everyone was thinking"—even those who had never heard of, let alone read, Locke's *Two Treatises*, but had "absorbed" its enlightened political principles from the prevailing "climate of opinion."[40]

Becker and Hartz interpreted the meaning of Locke's "influence" differently. Hartz used the term "Lockean liberalism" primarily to denote behavior that is animated by materialist values and economic self-interest. Becker, on the other hand, singled out Locke's "natural law and natural rights philosophy" as the decisive, radical element in the political theory of the Revolution.

Despite these differences between them, however, Becker and

Hartz, and the Locke model of interpretation in general, came under the revisionists' fire for basically the same reasons—methodological and substantive. Both scholars, according to their critics, failed to provide, and indeed were not concerned to provide, an adequate textual basis for their arguments; neither drew conclusions chiefly from the political writings from the Revolutionary period; thus, neither took into account what the Revolutionists actually said, the political language they spoke, and whom they quoted in their pamphlets, sermons, and newspaper essays. Becker, in particular, paid dearly for invoking a methodologically problematic "intellectual osmosis" of ideas that were "in the air," and not in available books, to account for the allegedly decisive significance of Locke's ideas.[41]

The methodological critique of the "Locke model" of interpretation was accompanied by vigorous denials of its substantive claims about the predominance of Lockean-liberal ideas in American Revolutionary thought. The revisionists rejected the unverifiable "climate of opinion" as a basis for intellectual history and turned their attention to the actual political writings of the Revolutionary period. There they found very little that could be designated "Lockean." What did emerge from that literature seemed to them very different indeed from the political theory of "Lockean liberalism."

One historiographic alternative to the Locke model, which did not fall within the republican paradigm but should nevertheless be mentioned here, emerged from the research—some would say from the imagination—of Garry Wills. Wills sought to replace Lockean liberalism with the philosophy of the Scottish Enlightenment at the intellectual center of the Revolution. He claimed that Revolutionary thought bore the stamp of a "massive Scottish presence," as exemplified in the writings of Thomas Jefferson. Wills banished Locke to make way for a host of Scottish philosophers, including Adam Smith, David Hume, Thomas Reid, Adam Ferguson, Lord Kames, and, above all, Francis Hutcheson. And according to Wills, these men "stood at a conscious and deliberate distance from Locke's political principles." Wills thus portrayed Jefferson as some kind of communitarian, steeped in the moral philosophy and worldview of the Scottish Enlightenment—the absolute antithesis, it seemed, of a Lockean.[42]

The "blatant errors of fact" and the lack of "scholarly substance" in Wills's major book have already been well documented.[43] They account for his failure to change the way we think about the American Revolution. For this reason, Wills's reinterpretation of Revolutionary political thought should not detain us much longer. We need only pause to note that Wills simply took for granted (and with evident distaste) the bourgeois Locke and to consider how his dependence upon a hostile interpretation of Lockean thought might have influenced his entire project.

The Locke whom Wills enthusiastically dissociated from the Declaration of Independence is casually assumed to be a hedonist in the spirit of Thomas Hobbes. As defined by Wills, "Lockean man" is spurred to action only by the prospect of "immediate gratification," not by any long-range hopes for the "hereafter."[44] Wills's Locke, moreover, is concerned above all with private property. Property is "*the* fundamental right" and "the basis for all other rights in Locke."[45] Finally, Wills did not take seriously Locke's actual definition of property as life, liberty, and estate.[46] Instead, he extrapolated an understanding of Lockean liberalism exclusively from the last item in that formulation. Wills's Locke thus seems close indeed, in his essential concerns, to the Locke of Macpherson and (especially) Strauss. And it is easy to see why Wills wanted to rid the founding doctrine of his grasping, hedonistic presence, even if the purge required "blatant errors of fact."

The republican alternative proved much more effective in transforming historical understanding—and banishing Locke—than Wills's attempt to recast the founding ideology in terms of the philosophy of the Scottish Enlightenment. We can now examine the most important and influential contributions to that successful historiographic revolution.

Bernard Bailyn's *Ideological Origins of the American Revolution* presented the revisionist hypothesis in its seminal and most elegant form. This book was an expanded version of an essay which had originally introduced a collection of political pamphlets from the Revolutionary period in the first, and so far the only, volume of a projected four-volume set.[47] Focusing on these and other "primary" writings,

Bailyn argued that the politics and political thought of the American Revolution had been decisively conditioned and constrained by an essentially non-Lockean ideological tradition.

According to Bailyn, this tradition had originated in the antiauthoritarian writings of Milton, Harrington, and other republicans, or "commonwealthmen," who were active during the tumultuous years of the English Civil War and the interregnum. It was later developed (though never systematized) and utilized by "opposition" theorists, "radical whigs," and "country" politicians and publicists, such as Trenchard and Gordon, Molesworth, and Hoadly (on the "left"), and Bolingbroke (on the "right"), in their losing struggle against Robert Walpole and the "court." In eighteenth-century colonial America, this tradition brought together and harmonized various discordant intellectual themes, only one of which was Lockean. It thereby constituted a comprehensive worldview and an effective revolutionary ideology.[48]

The political ideas of the commonwealth tradition never enjoyed any significant or enduring political success in England. "Country" ideology reflected what Isaac Kramnick calls the "politics of nostalgia"; its political ideals lay in the past; and the evolving structure of British politics stacked the deck in favor of the "court."[49] The transmission of these ideas to colonial America, however, had profound political consequences. "There," Bailyn argued, "an altered condition of life made what in England were considered to be extreme, dislocating ideas sound like simple statements of fact."[50] Transplanted into the sociopolitical context of colonial America, this relatively inconsequential tradition of political thought quickly acquired explanatory salience and explosive ideological power. Through quotation, citation, and plagiarism, the political ideals of this republican ideology, particularly those of Trenchard and Gordon, were incorporated "wholesale" into the Revolutionary writings and thereby came to exercise a decisive—indeed, a determinative—influence upon the minds of the Americans.[51]

It is ironic that here Bailyn offered what was in form, but not content, a Hartzian argument: America served as a unique context —"an altered condition of life"—in which a particular outlook on politics and society assumed ubiquitous and decisive power. For Hartz that outlook was Lockean; for Bailyn, however, it was the commonwealth, or republican, tradition. Indeed, there is even an echo of Carl Becker at this point in Bailyn's analysis. Like Becker, Bailyn attributed a specific ideology's extraordinary influence in America to the uncanny way in which it reflected the experience of colonial politics. But what sounded like "simple statements of fact" to the colonists was, for Bailyn, the commonwealth tradition, whereas for Becker it was the political philosophy of John Locke.

Bailyn, at any rate, argued that the commonwealth tradition had served as the colonists' framework of perception, from which "innovations" in British imperial policy in the 1760s ominously appeared as evidence of a ministerial conspiracy or "design" to extinguish American liberties.[52] He also claimed that "country" ideology had provided the language, concepts, and theoretical concerns of Revolutionary discourse. Thus, "vigilance" was needed to defend "liberty" against the inevitable encroachment of tyrannical "power,"[53] and "virtue"— understood in classical terms as the subordination of particular interests to the general interest or "public good"—was required to stave off the insidious effects of "corruption."[54] England had lost its liberty; she now sought to extirpate liberty in her colonies. The empire had become irredeemably corrupt and seemed determined to export this corruption to America.

Americans, in short, acquired their specific understanding of colonial politics, and of the growing conflict with England, primarily through the interpretative framework of "country" ideology. As Bailyn put it, the "opposition vision of English politics, conveyed through these popular opposition writers [particularly Trenchard and Gordon], was *determinative* of the political understanding of eighteenth-century Americans."[55] That vision, however myopic (and even reactionary) it might have been in its original English environment, became the worldview of the American Revolution.

Bailyn stressed the non-Lockean essence of that worldview as it was transmitted directly to the American colonists through the writings of the "country" ideologues and "radical whigs," particularly Trenchard and Gordon, coauthors of *Cato's Letters* and "the most important of these publicists and intellectual middlemen": "The skeleton of their political thought was Lockean—concerned with inalienable rights and the contract theory of government—but *only* the skeleton. *The flesh, the substance, the major preoccupations and the underlying motivations and mood, were quite different,* as was, of course, the level of discourse."[56]

It was this non-Lockean "substance" that had decisively informed the political thought and inspired the political action of the American Revolutionists. The "specific fears and formulations" of "country" ideology, not "common Lockean generalities," provided the "effective triggering mechanisms" of the Revolution. Virtue and liberty, as distinguished from natural rights (and as opposed to uninhibited capital accumulation), served as the Revolutionists' fundamental normative concerns.[57]

Bailyn thus revealed crucial elements in Revolutionary ideology that previously had been concealed under the false monolithicism of the Locke model of interpretation. And in so doing, he pointed the way toward a historiographic redemption of America's "lost soul." As Bailyn replaced Hartz, Cato replaced Locke; and virtue, in effect, replaced self-interest as the normative priority in the Revolutionary chapter of the American founding doctrine.

John Dunn, a distinguished British scholar and one of the foremost authorities on Locke's political thought, came (ironically, as we shall see) to the aid of the gathering revisionist forces with an important essay on the influence of Locke's political writings in eighteenth-century England and America. Dunn criticized the Locke model of interpretation—he roasted Carl Becker—on methodological grounds and argued that the impact of the *Two Treatises of Government* in colonial America had been grossly exaggerated by scholars who had simply taken Locke's influence for granted.[58] What remained of the Locke model after Bailyn—indeed, even the more moderate claims of a Lockean presence in Revolutionary thought—seemed to collapse under the weight of Dunn's historical argument.

First, Dunn claimed that the *Two Treatises* was scarcely available and seldom read with care before 1750. Hence, direct contact with Locke's political theory was by far the exception, not the rule.

Furthermore, according to Dunn, the *Two Treatises* did not enjoy the prestige and popularity in Europe which might have facilitated the absorption of its ideas, "by a sort of intellectual osmosis," among the American colonists who had never read it.[59] So even if it were methodologically legitimate to establish an interpretative model upon a "climate of opinion," the bibliographical and historical evidence clearly indicated that something other than the "politics of Locke" must have been "in the air" over colonial and Revolutionary America.

Dunn tossed another wrench into the Locke model of interpretation by raising the specter of what might be called the "Tory Locke." Dunn claimed that the American radicals who had studied the *Two Treatises* during the Revolution had approached the book with "gradually consolidated political intentions," in order to find moral and theoretical justification for their actions. Their reading of Locke's text, he argued, had been biased by their political motivations, and they selectively appropriated Locke's ideas—presumably out of context—for their immediate polemical utility.

There was, however, a singular exception—as it were, an objective reader of the *Two Treatises*. Peter Van Schaack, "a close friend of the Revolutionary leaders" and a man who carefully read Locke's book in 1776 with "conscientious indecision" over the question of resistance, concluded that resistance could not be justified on Lockean grounds.[60] And Dunn, in "a wild historical conjecture," suggested that Van Schaack understood the political prescriptions in the *Two Treatises* better than did the radicals who used Locke's arguments for Revolutionary purposes.[61]

Dunn's point here was that the Lockean "influence" on Revolutionary thought was a myth. The "guide and prophet" of the American Revolution was actually an impostor whom the Revolutionists fabricated for partisan political purposes. The "real" Locke would have had nothing to do with the radicals, but instead would probably have supported their Tory adversaries.

Dunn, in any case, explicitly endorsed Bailyn's thesis concerning the ideological origins of the Revolution. He insisted that most educated Americans during the Revolutionary period had absorbed their understanding of politics not from Lockean theory, but from the tradition of political thought which, according to Bailyn, had been engraved in the colonial mind while the *Two Treatises* was still largely unknown in the New World. "For the American population at large," Dunn concluded, the Revolution scarcely had anything to do with the politics of Locke.[62]

Dunn's reputation as a scholar, and as an authority not only on Locke's political philosophy but also on methodological problems in the study of the history of ideas, gave considerable weight to this pronouncement.[63] His essay, moreover, was often cited by less conscientious writers who exaggerated its conclusions in pursuit of a total expurgation of Lockean political thought from the founding ideology.[64] Thus, in only thirty-six pages, Dunn made a significant contribution to revisionist historiography and to the seemingly unlamented decline of "Lockean liberalism."

J. G. A. Pocock is the last major contributor to the republican reinterpretation of Revolutionary thought to receive a detailed treatment in this introductory survey (though there are other important contributors, such as Gordon Wood, whose work is referred to elsewhere in this book).[65] Pocock and Bailyn cofounded this paradigm and have exercised enormous influence on subsequent scholarship. Pocock's work is the more provocative; by itself it is rich and intricate enough to warrant a book-length treatment by a political theorist. The historiography of the American Revolution constitutes only one chapter in the larger history of political thought that unfolds in a series of essays and in *The Machiavellian Moment*. In these works, Pocock aimed at nothing less than a complete revision of late seventeenth- and eighteenth-century Anglo-American political thought in its entirety.

The revision stressed a non-Lockean—indeed, an anti-Lockean—civic humanist or classical republican tradition: "Machiavelli at the expense of Locke." This tradition provided the ideology which, in Pocock's view, Bailyn had correctly perceived as having held an "absolute," "conditioning," and "imprisoning" grip upon the American colonial mind, acting as "a restricting and compulsive force in the approaches to Revolution."[66] Pocock thus endorsed Bailyn's interpretation of Revolutionary political thought, declaring that it "altogether replaces" the interpretative model based upon Locke and associated with Louis Hartz.[67] He also found Bailyn's thesis consistent with John Dunn's devaluation of the role of Locke's political thought in eighteenth-century England and America.[68] Echoing Dunn, he declared that "it is a myth that Locke was an especially authoritative political thinker . . . in eighteenth-century America."[69]

Pocock even went so far as to state, in what he called an "overwhelmingly important" conclusion, that the "predominant language" of the eighteenth-century radicals, in whose ranks stood the American Revolutionists, was one "in which Locke himself did not figure."[70] Thus, understanding eighteenth-century Anglo-American political thought, including the political thought of the American Revolution, "did not necessitate reference to Locke at all"[71]—either for the Revolutionists themselves or, apparently, for those who now study Revolutionary political thought. Pocock's influence in this respect has been decisive. You can see it in the work of scholars who, in examining Revolutionary thought, cite his work and then do not make reference to Locke at all, even when the Revolutionary writings which they analyze contain more explicit and favorable references to Locke than to any other nonbiblical source.[72] Omnia praeter Lockem is truly the offspring of Pocockian historiography.

Pocock set the story told by Bailyn in a much broader context. He extended the commonwealth tradition back through time, backdating its origins to antiquity. The tradition originated with the civic humanism of Aristotle, who stressed citizenship, or active, self-conscious participation in the political community, as necessary for the full development of individual human personality.[73] It then acquired Polybian ideas of mixed government, and the (essentially conservative) notion that, in politics, change necessarily means decline. Retaining these defining characteristics of ancient, preliberal political thought, civic humanism entered the modern world through the Renaissance republicanism of Machiavelli (thereby crosscutting, if you will, the "ancients-moderns" distinction made famous by Leo Strauss). Machiavelli elucidated the essential dialectic of political history in his analysis of virtue and fortuna. Largely for these reasons, he became the central figure in Pocock's historiographical epic.

According to Pocock—and this was a major claim—the "ideas and problems" of civic humanism (which were sharply distinguished from those of liberalism) had "migrated from Italy to England and the American colonies during the second half of the seventeenth and the eighteenth centuries, where they exercised a profound effect on the self-understanding of these . . . societies."[74] First appearing in England during the civil war period, the republican paradigm became a potent ideological force, displacing the monarchical model of descending royal authority with Polybian notions of mixed government, the idea of "balance" between three estates (Crown, Lords, and Commons), and Aristotelian-Machiavellian notions of civic virtue.[75] Then, "a moment of paradigmatic breakthrough" occurred with the publication of James Harrington's *Oceana* in 1656. Harrington's book marked "a major revision of English political theory and history in light of concepts drawn from civic humanism and Machiavellian republicanism."[76] Neville and others then revised Harrington by compounding his ideas about a "balanced" commonwealth of proprietors with the theory of the Ancient Constitution.

"Neo-Harringtonianism," as Pocock labeled the reconstruction of civic humanism at this point in time, established the context in which a theory of "corruption" (meaning economic dependence and demoralization through egoistic or party-spirited behavior) could be substituted for the essentially random notion of *fortuna* in the latter's continuing dialectic with virtue (understood as "balance," "civic personality," and the subordination of private to public interests).[77] The definitive republican philosophy of history began to take shape when corruption, the antithesis of virtue, became associated with "commerce," so that the historical dialectic, in its final form, appeared as the struggle between virtue and commerce.[78] This explanation of history made a great deal of sense, and appealed ideologically, to those fearing the loss of a cherished (and privileged) way of life to the onslaught of capitalism in the eighteenth century. Civic republicanism thus "became an instrument of radical reaction in an era of devastating economic change."[79]

Early in the eighteenth century, Pocock argued, civic republicanism and the dialectic of virtue and commerce served as the conceptual framework and source of ideas for the "country" ideologues who figured so decisively in Bailyn's interpretation of the American Revolution.[80] Trenchard and Gordon (for example) were, in Bailyn's view, the most important transatlantic transmitters of this tradition of political thought. Their collaborations, particularly *Cato's Letters*, "were republished entire or in part again and again, 'quoted in every colonial newspaper from Boston to Savannah,' and referred to repeatedly in the pamphlet literature."[81] Yet Pocock claimed that Cato spoke the paradigmatic language of neo-Harringtonianism in his "critique of corruption and of the republic which is its opposite."[82] Thus, through the influence of Cato (and others like him), political discourse in eighteenth-century America came to be "dominated by neo-Harringtonian conceptual structures," which in the end left the colonists themselves with "no alternative" to "revolutionary action."[83]

Here, as with Bailyn, we can note the ironic reproduction of a distinctively Hartzian characteristic in the republican paradigm: the tendency to make the chosen ideological perspective ubiquitous and inescapable by situating it in a context where all opposing perspectives are objectively suppressed. Hartz cited the absence of a feudal sociological inheritance for having left Locke with no "natural enemies" in America. Pocock substituted civic republicanism for "Lockean liberalism" and asserted that the colonists had no perspective from which to view, explain, and respond to the events leading to 1776 other than the one that was supplied by the republican tradition. " 'Country' ideology ran riot in America" because there was no "court" tradition to hold it in check, "no alternative" to the "neoclassical" tradition "in which to be schooled."[84]

In short, Pocock beat Hartz at his own game. He proposed a historical alternative to Lockean liberalism that would tolerate no historical alternatives. He liberated the American Revolutionists from the Hartzian prison of Lockean liberalism only to reincarcerate them within the paradigmatic walls of republican ideology. And with the Revolutionists objectively committed to virtue, historiographic redemption became a real possibility.

Thus conceived, the ideological situation in colonial and Revolu-

tionary America represented only a slice—albeit an important slice
—of a grand historiographic paradigm which, with the conspicuous
exception of Locke, included virtually every political thinker from
Aristotle to Lenin (hence, *omnia praeter Lockem*).[85] This seemingly
omnivorous republican paradigm stressed other-regarding civic virtue
over self-interest, commerce, and capital accumulation in explicating the political thought of the eighteenth century and beyond.[86] In
Pocock's historical dialectic, virtue and commerce represented the
polar ideological antitheses and the innately incompatible priorities
of contending historical forces. As for Locke, he was "indifferent"
to virtue; and for this reason, he languished alone on the periphery
of eighteenth-century political discourse, speaking a different language entirely (and presumably to himself).[87] Indeed, it was precisely
Locke's alleged indifference to virtue, at a time when everyone else
supposedly was obsessed with the subject, which prompted Pocock to
declare that "Locke himself did not figure" in the political discourse
of the eighteenth century and that, accordingly, understanding the
ideology and political thought of that epoch "did not necessitate
reference to Locke at all."

It is here that the interpretation of Lockean political theory becomes decisive. Nowhere has the implicit dependence upon the bourgeois Locke of Strauss and Macpherson been more consequential than
in Pocockian historiography. The situation is not without irony. In
the very act of warning us against the *historical* distortions of "the
myth of John Locke and the obsession with liberalism," Pocock per-
petuated the *interpretative* distortions of both. He criticized Strauss
and Macpherson for having exaggerated the historical significance
of Locke and liberalism in the eighteenth century; but his paradigm
presumed a bourgeois Locke.[88] In other words, Pocock accepted their
interpretations of Locke's political thought while rejecting the histories of political thought in which those interpretations were, in the
view of their authors, inextricably embedded.[89]

By then assimilating this decontextualized bourgeois Locke, the
ideologue of capitalism, to a history of political thought which he
had redefined as a dialectic between virtue and commerce, Pocock
made the "Lockean paradigm," and liberalism in general, appear in-

nately hostile to the virtue-oriented sources of American Revolutionary thought. Locke thus emerged from Pocockian historiography as a kind of *tory*—the ideological enemy of the Revolution whose "textbook" he once was presumed to have written.[90]

For Pocock, then, it was not enough to portray Locke as harmlessly "indifferent" to virtue and thus irrelevant or neutral in the struggle between virtue and commerce, or merely to conclude that Locke "does not contribute directly" to the tradition which furnished the ideology of the American Revolution. With the bourgeois Locke underpinning the analysis, Pocock thought it best to "allot [Locke] a place, and debate its magnitude, among that tradition's *adversaries*."[91] He thus administered the finishing stroke to the Locke model of interpretation, deliberalized the founding doctrine, and inadvertently demonstrated the decisive significance of the interpretation of political theory in the formulation and revision of historical understanding.

Moreover, by interpreting republicanism as the doctrine of virtue, the antithesis of bourgeois "Lockean liberalism," Pocock delivered precisely the ideology needed to save the soul of the American Revolution. Gordon Wood had described republican ideology as "essentially anti-capitalistic"—hence the source of its great utility in the historiographic crusade and of its seemingly irresistible appeal to many historians and political theorists.[92] Pocock substantially enhanced the value of "anti-capitalistic" (but not quite socialistic) republicanism by developing it, historically and theoretically, into an inescapable, determinative paradigm and imposing it upon the subjects of history. But here, too, as we'll see, the characterization of the ideology, and thus the ideological salvation of the Revolution itself, rested upon a dubious interpretation of political theory—the political theory that the revisionists looked upon as the inspiration for American republicanism.

The preceding survey summarized the principal arguments of the republican revision as these relate, first, to the extent and nature of the role of Locke's political theory in the intellectual and ideological history of the American Revolution and, second, to the tradition of political thought that has displaced Locke's liberalism in that history.

Subsequent chapters will challenge some of those arguments and suggest a new understanding of what I call the Lockean connection in American Revolutionary thought. I would like to employ the remainder of this chapter to preview the interpretation of Locke's liberalism, which will be more fully developed later and which will inform the analysis of the Lockean connection. I shall also try to define further the scope and intention of this book.

Before proceeding to these issues, however, there is one loose end which I should attend to first, and that is John Dunn's "Tory Locke" —that specter raised by his "wild historical conjecture" concerning Peter Van Schaack's decision not to support the Revolutionary movement in 1776. I deal with this here because Dunn himself, as we shall see, has a central—and indeed an ironic—role in the entire affair. His work on Locke is outstanding.[93] And it endures. (Nathan Tarcov, for example, recently credited Dunn with "one of the most sensitive and careful interpretations of Locke.")[94] Yet I will suggest that insofar as Dunn is right about Locke, he is wrong about the role of Locke's ideas in colonial and Revolutionary America.

Dunn's argument about Van Schaack is a classic. His point, again, was that Van Schaack based his opposition to resistance on an accurate reading of the Two Treatises, while the radicals who had read the book and adopted its arguments to justify resistance had misinterpreted Locke's political prescriptions. Dunn, however, left the theater at intermission. Following his arrival in London in 1776, Van Schaack, by his own account of the event, changed his mind, without changing his political principles.[95]

Van Schaack based his initial opposition to the Revolutionary movement on what he himself later deemed inadequate information concerning Parliament's intentions. "From all the proofs I had," he wrote from London, "I could not, on a fair estimate, think them sufficient to establish the fact of an intention to destroy the liberties of the colonies."[96] And only an intention of this sort could have justified resistance according to the political theory of the Two Treatises.[97] Van Schaack therefore allowed the British government the benefit of the doubt; he declined to join the Revolutionary movement and left the colonies for England.

The view from London, however, soon revealed precisely the kind of "design" that justified and, indeed, required resistance on Lockean grounds; and before long, Van Schaack had seen enough to feel himself "totally absolved from all ideas of duty" to the mother country. He then decided to return to America, about which he wrote: "I never can be intimidated from avowing that its welfare was the first object of my [previous] views, however it might be thought that I had erred in choosing the means to promote it."[98] Reflecting upon this "error," and his subsequent decision to support the Revolution, Van Schaack concluded: "[A] man forming his idea of the rectitude of a government from what he knows at the time may change it in consequence of facts coming afterwards to his knowledge, without impeachment of his firmness, *or of the rectitude of his principles*. For what can we reason but from what we know?"[99]

This is the *full* story of Peter Van Schaack and the "Tory Locke," drawn from Van Schaack's own letters and manuscripts. Van Schaack based his original decision to withhold support for resistance not only on Lockean political principles but also, as it were, on insufficient data. Once he had seen the situation at the imperial center, however, those same Lockean principles, by his own account, compelled him to renounce his allegiance to Great Britain and to support his country's armed struggle for independence.

Dunn may have gone too far with his "wild historical conjecture" about Van Schaack, but I think he has found the key that opens the door to Lockean liberalism. I respectfully disagree with Strauss and Macpherson when it comes to Locke. I share Dunn's view, as expressed directly in reference to their interpretations, that the bourgeois Locke is "a lifeless but sinister effigy fit to adorn a crude morality play" (that is, the history of political thought in which it is embedded).[100] I would add that insofar as our efforts to understand the sense of the Revolutionists are informed by this effigy, the event we study tends to assume the appearance of precisely a morality play. In this version, republican virtue triumphs over the venality of "Lockean liberalism." The irony is that Dunn, who probably knows Locke better than anyone does, and whose interpretation so crucially informs this historiographic vindication of Locke's liberalism in the American

Revolution, has done much to advance the fortunes of the republican synthesis.[101]

At any rate, I am persuaded by Dunn and by my own reading of Locke's works, that the "theoretical centrality of Locke's religious preoccupations" is the key to his political philosophy—although (significantly) it is the generally theistic, rather than the specifically Calvinist, nature of Locke's thought that I emphasize in my interpretation. As Dunn puts it, "an extremely high proportion of Locke's arguments [depend] for their very intelligibility, let alone plausibility, on a series of theological commitments."[102]

Locke is a sincere theist whose political theory cannot be detached from his "religious preoccupations" without unhistorically secularizing, and thus distorting, its character. Locke's overriding concern is for the "*eternal* estate," not real estate.[103] His political thought flows from the premise of, and depends fundamentally upon belief in, a benevolent, rational (that is, not arbitrary) God who makes nothing in vain, whose "workmanship" men are,[104] and whose law of nature lays down social and political obligations that are binding upon all individuals, "*legislators* as well as others."[105] Human political arrangements are legitimate only insofar as they accommodate the general purposes of God (for instance, civil government cannot be arbitrary and must always serve the public good). To cite Dunn, "the axiomatic centrality of the purposes of God dominates the entire intellectual construction."[106]

This Locke, moreover, is a political radical, and his radicalism flows directly from his theistic philosophy. To summarize the position that is fully set forth later in the book: The justification for revolution, which is the theme of Locke's *Second Treatise*, involves the emphatic assertion of the people's inalienable right, duty, and competence to judge the conduct of their government and to reassume, when *they* deem it appropriate, the sovereign constituent power. This justification originates simultaneously—and divinely, so to speak—in the suicide taboo and the inseparable moral connection between individual judgment and salvation. With the obligations of the law of nature—which is God's law—incorporated and operationalized in the establishment of civil government, the exercise of individual *political* judgment, culminating in the fateful decision whether to obey or to resist political authority, becomes an essential requisite for salvation.[107]

This is not the place for a detailed account of Lockean thought or a critique of opposing interpretations. But this view of Locke's liberalism can be summarized in Locke's own words, drawn from the *Letter on Toleration*, and, according to Locke, relevant in *every* sphere of human life and association: "The taking away of God, even only in thought, dissolves all."[108] We can borrow a concept from Sheldon Wolin and call this proposition the "notational principle," or "unifying assumption" of Locke's political thought.

> When a unifying assumption [in this case, God] is displaced, the system of ideas is thrown out of balance; subordinate ideas [for instance, property] become prominent; primary ideas recede into secondary importance. This is because a political theory consists of a set of concepts—such as order, peace, justice, power, law, etc.—bound together . . . by a kind of notational principle that assigns accents and modulations. Any displacement or significant alteration of the notational principle or any exaggerated emphasis on one or a few concepts results in a different kind of political theory."[109]

Displacing the notational principle—"the taking away of God"—in Lockean thought converts this "theistic Locke" into the bourgeois Locke, the bane of the republican revision. What the revisionists call Lockean liberalism, however, might be described more accurately as liberalism without Locke's unifying theistic assumption or, if you will, as post-Lockean, secularized liberalism. Their perspective on Lockean liberalism was framed, not by Locke himself, but by three hundred years of post-Lockean history.

The revisionists' fixation on the bourgeois Locke is problematic because it ties their understanding of Revolutionary thought to the unhistorical assumption that eighteenth-century colonists would have developed a twentieth-century interpretation of Locke's seventeenth-century political thought. The more historically credible assumption —one that does not require a time machine—is that the Revolutionists would have understood Locke, as Winthrop Hudson put it, "in terms of his own thought and not in terms of what the rationalists of a much later generation were to make of it."[110] The commitment to hostile and secularized interpretations of Lockean thought, however, has prevented many contemporary scholars from noticing other, more historical, possibilities.[111]

I want to be absolutely clear on this point. As I mentioned earlier, there are two criteria of interpretation which must be satisfied: The interpretation of Lockean thought must be textually sound, that is, available in the Lockean corpus, and historically appropriate, or likely to have been the interpretation developed by the subjects of a historical inquiry. Let's consider the position being advanced here in relation to these two criteria.

I shall construct the theistic Locke by drawing from a wide range of Lockean sources and thus demonstrate that this interpretation is textually sound. Indeed, the theistic origins of Locke's political radicalism, as well as the integral place of his political theory in his overall philosophy, are not likely to appear to readers who consult only the *Second Treatise*. Such essential features of Lockean thought do become clear, however, when the bibliography includes, in addition to the *Second Treatise*, the writings on epistemology, natural law, toleration, religion, and theology; and the reading of Locke that informs this book will be rooted in those texts.

I shall also argue that from the perspective of eighteenth-century colonists, the theistic Locke was most likely to have been *the* Locke —far more likely, in any event, than the bourgeois Locke of Strauss and Macpherson. This is especially so with the New England clergy, whose political teaching we shall examine in detail. The clergy were demonstrably conversant with Locke's writings, and they had similar "religious preoccupations." They openly embraced Locke's political ideas—for example, the justification for revolution, as outlined above —*and* they shared the general philosophical perspective within which those ideas took shape. Moreover, the ministers conveyed the Lockean message, regularly and with great moral authority, to their congregations, by whom they were taken very seriously indeed. The fact that John Dunn, in discounting the role of Locke's political theory in American Revolutionary thought, fails to consider precisely that leading element familiar with and sympathetic to Locke's "theological commitments" reinforces the irony in his association with the republican synthesis.

The theistic Locke, then, is the historically appropriate Locke for an investigation of American Revolutionary thought. The bourgeois Locke, on the other hand, does not satisfy this criterion of interpretation. The eighteenth-century colonists, especially—but not only—the clergy, were not likely to have developed that highly secularized, twentieth-century interpretation of Locke's seventeenth-century political thought. Thus, if we search, as the revisionists have, for the bourgeois Locke in the founding doctrine, we are virtually guaranteed not to find him.[112] And with no conception of the theistic Locke to guide our analysis to the Lockean connection, we would conclude, as the revisionists have concluded, that "John Locke was a negligible influence upon American political thought before 1776." Here again, our historical understanding of the founding doctrine essentially depends upon the interpretation of political theory which informs historical research.

Although I do not wish to get tangled up in the exegetical controversies of what Macpherson dubbed the Locke Industry, I feel obliged to show that, on at least one critically relevant point, the bourgeois Locke fails to meet the other criterion as well—that is, this interpretation is not textually sound. However, the fate of my argument does not depend upon the proposition that the theistic Locke is the *only* Locke available in the Lockean corpus, or even upon denying the textual legitimacy of the bourgeois Locke. It is sufficient to demonstrate that the theistic Locke is textually available, without excluding alternative interpretations, and that this Locke is the most historically appropriate Locke for the task at hand.

In fact, it should be acknowledged (and doing so will not impeach this thesis in the least) that the Locke Industry is, as we might expect it to be, a pluralist enterprise which admits several "Lockes." And although the advocates of each of these Lockes understandably tend to believe that their man is the only authentic one, most—including myself—are liberal enough to resist claiming infallibility and to tolerate other points of view. But while there could be several Lockes available in the Lockean corpus, and the bourgeois Locke might even be one of them, this character is a historically inappropriate choice for an investigation into American Revolutionary thought; and upon reflection, the failure to find the bourgeois Locke in the founding ideology (which the revisionists, of course, regard as a success) should come as no surprise. The theistic Locke, on the other hand, is both textually sound *and* a historically appropriate choice for a study of eighteenth-century thought, especially eighteenth-century New England clerical thought; and this, in sum, is the Locke that informs a crucial manifestation of the Lockean connection in American Revolutionary thought.

I should note here, in defining the scope and intention of this book, that I will be analyzing two kinds of Lockean connections, which I call formal and substantive. The book itself is organized around the distinction between the formal and substantive Lockean connections, so it is important to have a clear understanding of these concepts.

The formal Lockean connection—which is the subject of chapter three—consists in the use of Locke by the colonists (and their allies in Parliament) who *opposed* Great Britain's "innovations" in revenue policy after 1763, as well as the assertion of "illimitable" Parliamentary sovereignty upon which those policies were based. To these Revolutionists, Locke did *not* appear as the ideological enemy. On the contrary, they conceptualized and expressed their opposition to Parliament in distinctively Lockean categories and often in Locke's own words. Moreover, they did so in a way that was faithful to the thrust of Locke's argument. That is, they did not have to twist Locke's political theory, distort his argument, or butcher his sentences, in order to obtain his support for their positions. As we'll see, it was the Tory hard-liners like Joseph Galloway who had to mutilate Locke in order to use him.

I have gathered evidence of the formal Lockean connection from a wide range of primary textual sources—political pamphlets, state papers, and other official documents; newspapers; correspondence; etc. Contrary to the claims of the republican revision, these materials clearly show that on crucial political matters, "Locke on Government" was *by far* the most frequently cited nonbiblical source. They also show that the Revolutionists formulated and expressed their grievances and aims in Lockean-liberal terms and that the essential questions and answers in Revolutionary argument—for instance, "of the extent of the legislative power" and "who shall be judge whether the prince or legislative act contrary to their trust?" (the people)— were the essential questions and answers of Locke's political theory. The analysis of the formal connection will thereby rescue historical understanding of Revolutionary thought from the distorted view that "there was little" in Locke's political theory "to defend the colonists' stand" against Parliament, and from the mystifying claim that "there is absolutely no evidence to suggest that Locke can be singled out above and beyond any other author of the day in support of the colonists' position." [113]

The analysis of the formal connection indeed goes directly to the inspiration for such allegations, calling into question Pocock's "overwhelmingly important" assertion that the language of the Revolution was "a language in which Locke himself did not figure." It also reveals and resolves the confusion underlying Pocock's influential idea that Lockean liberalism was hostile toward the aims and concerns of the American Revolution. This view necessarily presupposes one of two implausible conditions: Either Lockean liberalism is opposed to limited government, consent of the governed, religious toleration, and resistance to actual or intended tyranny, or the Revolutionists themselves rejected these distinctively Lockean-liberal political principles. The first confuses Locke with Filmer; the second confuses Thomas Jefferson with George III. In any case, the analysis of the formal connection will provide historical and interpretative evidence to set the record straight.

It is the emphasis on interpretation that constitutes the distinction between the formal and substantive Lockean connections. The formal connection implies a certain superficiality at the interpretative level. This does *not* imply a misuse or misunderstanding of Locke by the author who cited, quoted, or plagiarized his work. On the contrary, the formal connection implies a correct and legitimate use of Locke in terms both of Locke's theory and of the author's immediate context. An idea which has been appropriated in a formal connection fits consistently or even integrally within the overall structure of Lockean thought; but the formal connection is not concerned with the structure itself. The analysis of the substantive connection, in contrast, probes much more deeply into the realm of interpretation. It identifies affinities between Locke and the author who cited or otherwise used Locke's work in terms of the general philosophical framework within which the appropriated idea is integrally embedded.

Take the doctrine of natural law as an example. A formal connection exists where a Revolutionary author cites Locke as authorizing resistance to magistrates who act, or intend to act, contrary to the law of nature. A substantive connection exists where you can also point to similarities between Locke and that author with respect to (1) the theistic epistemological foundations of natural-law theory, (2) the extension of natural-law obligations into the sphere of civil society, and (3) the corresponding politicization of the divinely appointed duty and right of individual judgment. The substantive Lockean connection thus involves, in this case, not simply the doctrine of natural law, but also a sharing, between Locke and the author who uses Locke, of the general philosophical framework from which that doctrine and its potentially revolutionary political implications emerge.

It is in the analysis of the substantive Lockean connection, then, that the theistic Locke, and what I shall call the political theory of theistic liberalism, come into play. It is here, too, that I focus on the sermon literature of the New England Clergy.

The recovery of the substantive connection in fact takes up two chapters of this book. In chapter 4, I delve further into the role of interpretation in the study of American Revolutionary thought. I examine the revisionists' reading of both Lockean and republican political thought in some detail and in the process raise some questions about the republican paradigm itself; and, applying the two criteria of interpretation that have been set forth above, I begin to develop the interpretation of Lockean thought that informs the substantive connection. In chapter 5, an extensive analysis of the writings of the New England clergy and some further reconnaissance of Locke's philosophy disclose and explain the substantive Lockean connection in the clerical teaching in terms of the political theory of theistic liberalism.

The distinction between the formal and the substantive Lockean connections allows me to organize historical materials in a productive way. But I do not wish to make too much of it. This distinction is not always an empirically unambiguous one; that is, some manifestations of Locke in the Revolutionary writings could fall into either—or both—of these categories. Nevertheless, the formal and substantive connections both have ample text-based support.

To complete this introductory chapter, and before moving on to a discussion of various methodological issues that are involved in a project such as this, I wish to specify the limits of this inquiry as clearly as possible, so that my intentions will not be misconstrued.

First, this book does not pretend to offer a comprehensive and definitive interpretation of Locke's philosophy. That would require a book in itself. This book does, however, examine Locke's thought and attend to his writings far more extensively than does the literature of the republican revision, which seems to rely upon either received opinions or, at best, casual readings of the *Second Treatise*.

On the other hand, the book does not seek to embrace the whole of American Revolutionary thought, enunciating the last word on the founding ideology from an ideologically neutral position.[114] But it does survey a large body of the Revolutionary writings, some of it in considerable depth. And on the basis of that survey, by combining historical research with the interpretative concerns of political theory, the book tempers the extremism of the historiographic revolution and establishes the Lockean-liberal spirit in the Revolutionary chapter of the American founding on firm historical ground.

In no way, however, do I intend to establish a new interpretative paradigm to serve as an explanatory or ideological panacea. On the contrary, I am trying to correct some of the native excesses of paradigmatic analysis, which, as such, tends to generate extreme, distorted interpretations of intellectual history: *Locke et praeterea nihil* or *omnia praeter Lockem*. Disengagement from the republican paradigm therefore entails neither a return to the old Locke model of interpretation

nor the adoption of a new paradigm of "theistic liberalism" which ex-
cludes all other strains of political thought and "altogether replaces"
the republican synthesis. Both Locke and Cato contributed to the
American founding doctrine.

There is, to be sure, a civic purpose behind this historical expedi-
tion. Scholars sometimes overlook the political context within which
they work, as well as the political fallout from their seemingly un-
political research. But by now even the most insulated citizen of the
ivory tower must realize that historians and political theorists are not
the only people who have been bashing liberalism in recent years.
Liberalism also has *political* enemies. Some are highly placed; others
are organized, well-heeled, and connected; many are enthusiastically committed to purging the liberal spirit from American society
—whether or not they realize that by saving the Republic from liberalism, they would also destroy it. By unhistorically purging Lockean
liberalism from the founding doctrine and exaggerating the historical
significance of civic republicanism, the most principled scholars may
inadvertently have helped to prepare the intellectual ground for this
current political assault.

These historical distortions could be politically catastrophic, moreover, if liberalism, whatever its vices, is, as I suspect, the only doctrine that instinctively requires political constitutionalism and the
freedoms associated with it, while civic republicanism, whatever its
virtues, lacks internal theoretical constraints upon the use of political
power. The recovery of Lockean liberalism in American Revolutionary thought, then, could secure a precious source of legitimacy for
the political defense of the liberal spirit.

2

A Discourse on Method

If the experience of writing this book is a reliable indicator, then I am prepared to conclude that all interdisciplinary work, by definition, requires a chapter on method. For some, this is enough to rule out all interdisciplinary work. Unfortunately, surrendering to that impulse would exclude many interesting and important questions from consideration. Not the least of these would be the question of Locke, liberalism, and the American Revolution—a question which I believe can be correctly answered only by combining the virtues of historical research with those of political theory, while avoiding the more egregious vices of both.

This is where the proliferation of methodological problems occurs. The investigator who is compelled, for whatever reasons, to operate in two fields at the same time confronts not only methodological problems peculiar to each field, but also those that arise uniquely from the union of the two. At a general level, he or she has the additional difficulty of addressing two audiences, each with a different set of expectations. Historians, for example, like to see plenty of references to writings from the period in question—in this case, colonial newspapers, pamphlets, correspondence, etc.—but they probably are not much interested in reading a lengthy exegesis on Locke. Political theorists, on the other hand, thrive on the classic texts, but they are likely to have much less enthusiasm for the nitty-gritty of historical research. Special problems of style and organization are thus appended to those of method.

Such problems can overwhelm the best intentions unless they are anticipated and addressed early in the investigation. Hence this chapter on method, in which I shall attempt to spell out rules of procedure that will be acceptable to readers from both fields.

The most contentious methodological questions concern evidence. In seeking to ascertain the extent and nature of the Lockean connection in American Revolutionary thought, what kind of evidence are we going to look for and accept? And where are we going to look for it? An examination of the rules of evidence thus leads into a discussion of the criteria of bibliographic selection.

One form of evidence that seems reliable, and which figured in the early, influential works of the republican revision, is the library catalog. What books did Thomas Jefferson own? Or Harvard? Or Yale? H. Trevor Colburn, an important early contributor to the revision, surveyed the library catalogs of prominent individuals and institutions to obtain "a rough indication of the colonists' common exposure" to various authors and texts.[1] John Dunn also examined library catalogs; and according to Dunn, tracking "Locke on Government" through the libraries of colonial America "certainly calls into severe question the evidential status of the received opinions about the *scale* of the book's distribution and consequent availability."[2]

A library catalog does provide a written inventory of actually available texts; as evidence, however, it is not as unequivocal in its testimony as it first appears. One general problem was recognized by Daniel Boorstin, a distinguished historian, who warned that "one of the commonest and most misleading assumptions of intellectual historians is that in a period like the eighteenth century, the content of a man's library was roughly the same as the content of his mind."[3] Personal book ownership in the eighteenth century did not necessarily imply actual reading of the book, or sympathy for its argument, any more than it does today. Institutional ownership is also a potentially problematic indicator. One book in an institutional library might have been frequently consulted for any number of reasons while another book quietly gathered dust on the same shelf. A single copy of the first book could have been widely circulated among many readers while three copies of the second book were equally ignored. Again, ownership did not imply readership, sympathetic or otherwise. Such information is obviously crucial, but it simply isn't available from the library catalog.

Some specific problems arise in Colburn's analysis of library catalogs. Colburn assembled a "partial survey" of catalogs and book lists and suggested that "there may be special meaning in the frequent priority accorded Sidney's *Discourses* over Locke's *Treatises on Civil Government.*" If, however, in examining Colburn's lists, we count Locke's *Works*, a three-volume set that includes his *Treatises*, a different picture comes into view. Controlling for duplication, so that a catalog which lists Locke's *Works* as well as his *Treatises* receives a score of "one," "Locke on Government" now heads the list, appearing nineteen times, against seventeen for Sidney's *Discourses* and, incidentally, sixteen for *Cato's Letters*.[4]

Moreover, following the same procedure for counting, Colburn's list shows eighteen copies of Locke's *Essay Concerning Human Understanding* (as well as eighteen copies of his *Some Thoughts Concerning Education*). This calls into question the broadly held opinion— Dunn, Pocock, Wills, and others—that Locke was known in colonial America more as a philosopher than as a political theorist.[5] Finally, a similar examination of another study of early American library holdings and booksellers' catalogs by Lundberg and May also reestablishes the priority of Locke's political writings over Sidney's *Discourses* and *Cato's Letters* on the one hand and Locke's own epistemological writings on the other.[6]

In short, library catalogs are useful but not foolproof. The same can be said of virtually all forms of what we shall call empirical evidence. Empirical evidence is textual evidence or evidence drawn from the actual writings from the Revolutionary period. Thus understood, empirical evidence is the substance of this kind of historical research.

The critique of the republican revision and the recovery of the Lockean connection must have a solid empirical—or textual—base, and by this I mean an explicit, identifiable foundation in the political writings from the Revolutionary period. Vague assertions about

a "climate of opinion" may be intuitively correct, but not methodologically sufficient. The republican revision struck precisely at the
empirical weakness of the Locke model of interpretation, denying a
significant textual presence of Locke in the Revolutionary writings;
and the debut of the republican alternative to "Lockean liberalism" in
Bernard Bailyn's introduction to a collection of Revolutionary pamphlets suggested that this new understanding of the founding doctrine
would be anchored textually—or empirically—in the written words
of the Revolutionists themselves.[7]

This book therefore introduces and analyzes a great deal of empirical evidence in support of its underlying thesis—the kind of material
historians rightly expect to see. But the term "empirical" is extremely
vague. Empirical evidence comes in several forms, and there are numerous hidden traps waiting to snare the unwary. Even what appears
to be a methodologically pure datum of empirical evidence—say, an
explicit citation of, or verbatim transcription of a passage from, the
Second Treatise or *Cato's Letters*—can prove only so much; and it is
prudent to specify the limits of even the purest empirical analysis in
advance. Moreover, unless the investigator is *directly* familiar with
the quoted source (especially if the quote is unmarked or unattributed), that piece of evidence is likely to be overlooked entirely. And
without a sound understanding of the political theory in the cited or
quoted work, the evidence could prove precisely the opposite of what
the investigator thinks it proves. This is yet another way in which
the interpretation of political theory figures in historical studies of
political thought.

The following discussion should illuminate methodological pitfalls
such as these. Readers may then determine for themselves the extent
to which investigators—myself included—have managed to avoid
falling into them.

Textual evidence falls into two general categories: external and internal. The most explicit and apparently least problematic form of
external textual evidence is the citation, which is defined here as
"any footnote, direct quote, attributed paraphrasing or use of a name
in exemplifying a concept or position."[8] Another form of external
evidence, one that is not always so easy to detect and may in fact go

undetected by the investigator who is unfamiliar with the source, is an exact, unattributed quotation. Included here, too, and perhaps even more elusive, are passages that are not even wrapped in quotation marks, but are nonetheless verbatim transcriptions from identifiable sources.[9] Plagiarism was not uncommon in the written political polemics of the Revolution; the rules of conventional scholarship simply did not apply under those circumstances. Internal textual evidence, on the other hand, consists of linguistic, theoretical, or doctrinal similarities between a Revolutionary text and, for instance, Lockean theory that are not accompanied by an explicit citation of "Locke on Government." In this category we also include unattributed paraphrasing where there is a reasonable certainty as to the source.[10]

It might seem that external evidence is vastly superior to internal evidence in this kind of historical research, and that internal evidence is too ambiguous to be of much value or simply unnecessary where sufficient external evidence can be adduced. In fact, *both* categories of evidence are valuable and methodologically problematic. My approach to the Revolutionary writings combines both categories in a way that recognizes the advantages and drawbacks of each.

Before exploring the evidential limits of citations, I must say that I have been tempted to rest my case exclusively upon this form of external textual evidence. I have discovered a great many more citations of "Locke on Government" in the Revolutionary writings, clerical and secular, than of any other nonbiblical source. Moreover, the findings of an extensive, ten-year study of the political writings of the founding era—a study which relied exclusively upon citations to assess the "relative influence of European writers" on the political thought of the founding—essentially confirm the results of my own research.[11]

To be sure, the author, Donald S. Lutz, does conclude that "there is still a tendency to overestimate" Locke's importance in early American political thought.[12] This conclusion, however, is based upon a definition of the founding era as the period 1760 to 1805; and within that period, Lutz makes a crucial distinction between the Revolutionary era and the era surrounding the writing, ratification, and implementation of the federal Constitution. The transition from one to the other was marked by a basic shift in the principal concerns of theorization, as the colonists turned their attention from arguments justifying revolution and the right of the people to constitute their own government to disquisitions on the design of governments and constitutions. This transition from the Revolutionary to the Constitutional era seems to have occurred around 1776; and, significantly, it coincided with, and was reflected in, a dramatic decline in Locke's "rate of citation." Lutz thus dates the Revolutionary era from 1760 to approximately 1776—virtually the same parameters established by Bailyn when he opened *The Ideological Origins of the American Revolution* with John Adams's famous observation (in a letter to Thomas Jefferson) that the Revolution "was effected from 1760 to 1775." And if we examine Lutz's findings for this period, we discover that Locke, by a very wide margin, was the most frequently cited author in the American political writings.[13]

On the other hand, the claims put forward by Bailyn and others on behalf of *Cato's Letters* and republican sources in general seem exaggerated in light of the relatively poor showing by Trenchard and Gordon and the other "country" ideologues in Lutz's study. Lutz counted a total of 760 citations in the writings from the Revolutionary era. Of these, "Cato," the highest-scoring "radical whig," collected only nine, while Locke, the highest scorer of all contenders, accumulated sixty-two—that's about one percent for Cato and eight percent for "the Great Mr. Locke." The "right wing" of "country" ideology, represented by Bolingbroke, fared even worse, while "the immortal Sidney," a representative from the "left," whose name we would expect to crop up in many places, was practically invisible. Indeed, Bolingbroke and Sidney both failed to qualify for inclusion in Lutz's table of the twelve "most cited thinkers by decade" for *any* decade during the founding era. Of all the sources of American republicanism, only Trenchard and Gordon earned this distinction—and with little to spare.[14]

Lutz's citation-based findings for the Revolutionary era, then, support the conclusions I have drawn from my own research. First, the revisionists have tended to underestimate the presence of Locke in the Revolutionary writings. I do not understand how anyone who has spent time with these materials can conclude that "there is absolutely no evidence to suggest that Locke was quoted or cited any more than any number of writers."[15] The explicit textual evidence confirms, on the contrary, that Locke was cited or quoted *far* more frequently than any other writers. On the other hand, while this evidence does not imply the restoration of the monolithic Locke model of interpretation, which has been rightly discredited by the republican revision, the low rate of citation of republican sources in the Revolutionary texts hardly justifies the elevation of republicanism to the paradigmatic supremacy once held by "Lockean liberalism."

If citations were as unambiguous as they first appear, we would already be close to our goal. In fact, citations are indispensable tools in this kind of research, but by itself the number of citations to a specific source does not constitute a sufficient index of its historical significance. We can determine who received the most citations, but this will not answer the more intriguing question of *why* the Revolutionists cited one author or text more frequently than others; it doesn't tell us much about the Revolutionists themselves. Counting citations fails to penetrate, theoretically, the relationship between Locke's ideas and Revolutionary theory and practice; it thus goes only part of the way toward establishing the Lockean connection in American Revolutionary thought, as we have defined this concept.

Citation evidence, moreover, is not methodologically pure. The meaning of a particular citation is not always clear. A specific text may have been cited incorrectly, perhaps by design. Misinterpretation of the cited text, innocent or deliberate, by the author who cites it would reduce the citation to a worthless statistic—worse than worthless if the investigator fails to detect the misinterpretation. Some authors simply may have been name-dropping to display their erudition, or to confound their readers, or to satisfy contemporary conventions, when the cited text was actually irrelevant in the author's context. In any case, it is impossible to evaluate accurately the true significance of citation evidence without understanding the text itself and the context within which it was cited.

A text may indeed be cited for a variety of reasons that are unrelated to the extent and nature of the theoretical support it provides for the argument of the author who cites it. One source might be preferred because it is universally respected and therefore "safe," or perhaps even required. Another text could be cited more for its immediate polemical utility than because its author enjoys the polemicist's ultimate intellectual allegiance. In the trenches one grabs whatever weapons are available and effective. Moreover, polemical exchanges tend to involve both parties in a mutual determination of tactics. I might, for example, cite ABC because my opponent also cites ABC, that is, in order to hoist my opponent on his own polemical petard; but I might be secretly convinced that ABC is a dolt and his argument gibberish, and my real intellectual commitments could lie with XYZ, whom I have had neither the occasion nor the audacity to cite. In none of these cases is the citation tantamount to "influence"—a phenomenon in the history of ideas which may in fact be impossible to prove.

The most problematic aspect of citation evidence is its ability to mislead the investigator who is unfamiliar with the cited source and therefore cannot judge whether the author citing that source has done so in good faith or has twisted and distorted its argument for partisan purposes. A most telling example of this can be found in the writings of Joseph Galloway. Galloway had been a member of the Continental Congress who opposed resistance to, and separation from, Great Britain. Failing to stem the Revolutionary tide in America, he chose permanent exile in England. But before leaving, Galloway wrote a pamphlet attacking the Continental Congress in 1775; and in this pamphlet he made explicit use of Locke's arguments, complete with quotations from the *Second Treatise*, to justify submission to Parliament. Perhaps he cited Locke for one of the reasons stated above: His opponents had cited Locke to justify resistance, so the rules of polemics dictated the deployment of Locke to refute those arguments. But whatever the reason, Galloway was no Lockean. His pamphlet reeked of the absolutism of Sir Robert Filmer, Locke's posthumous adversary, and his method of quotation was fundamentally dishonest.

First, Galloway maintained that since America had been discovered and conquered under the authority of the British government, the British government held a lien, so to speak, upon all "the property and territory of America." The colonists claimed Parliament had violated their right to property by levying taxes on them without their consent, but Galloway defended Parliament, and thus condemned the American resistance, by arguing that the "property and territory of America" belonged, as a matter of right, not to the colonists but to the British government itself.[16]

Would a Lockean argue that the right of property originates in conquest and resides in the state? Locke himself went to great pains to refute such claims and to establish the right to property upon an entirely different foundation. We needn't invest in the bourgeois Locke in order to appreciate the discrepancy between Locke and Galloway on the right to property. In fact, Locke's theory, as we'll see in the next chapter, clearly supported the position of the colonists who *opposed* the pretensions of Parliament; and they frequently cited and quoted Locke in their arguments concerning property, consent, taxation, and representation.

Galloway deviated again from Lockean theory, this time directly into the patriarchal politics of Filmer. Galloway charged that in petitioning King George III for relief against Parliament, the colonists had "conveyed to the royal ear nothing but the language of independence." Behind the outward professions of submission and allegiance to His Majesty lay an unspeakable presumption of political equality with the legislative power of England. These petitions, therefore, "were justly treated with neglect." And in Galloway's view, "the reasonable and sensible man" would not "resent a conduct of this kind" on the part of the king; for "the relation between the sovereign authority and its members bears a true resemblance to that between parent and child," and in politics the colonists, by right, ought always to conduct themselves as obedient children.[17]

Galloway thus conceived of political relations in terms clearly more sympathetic to Filmer's patriarchalism than to Lockean constitutionalism. As we know, Locke sought above all to overthrow the principles of Filmer, which had been hauled into service by the Stuart regime in its doomed attempt to establish divine-right absolutism in England. Filmer had tried to "persuade all men that they are slaves, and ought to be so."[18] And Locke's declared purpose in the *Second Treatise* was to provide a conception of political society, of its origin, nature, and end, different "than what Sir Robert Filmer hath taught us." [19] Despite Galloway's appeal to the authority of "Locke on Government," then, he repudiated its essential political principles, preferring instead precisely the principles that Locke had endeavored to refute and replace. In short, Galloway's appeal to the authority of Locke was a clumsy, unscrupulous polemical tactic, which fooled no one at the time, least of all his opponents. [20] But it could fool the uninformed citation-counter into proclaiming the existence of a Tory Locke.

It is not until Galloway actually quotes passages from the *Second Treatise* that we can appreciate the full measure of his mendacity. Galloway quoted two such passages to justify Parliament's illimitable sovereignty over the colonies. In his transcriptions, however, he deleted crucial phrases and truncated the argument, so that Locke's theory lost precisely the radical content which had endowed it with such great contemporary significance. The surgery Galloway performed on these passages in order to adapt them to the Tory position thus brings the ambiguity of the seemingly most unambiguous form of external evidence, as well as the need for familiarity with the quoted text, into the sharpest possible relief. [21]

Let's look first at Galloway's use of §134 of the *Second Treatise*. Here is that passage, reproduced exactly the way Galloway transcribed it in his pamphlet: "The first fundamental positive law of all commonwealths is the establishing of the legislative power. This legislative is not only the supreme power of the commonwealth, but is sacred and unalterable in the hands where the community have placed it." Galloway's punctuation concealed his extension of fragments into whole sentences. The first sentence in this passage, as it actually appears in the *Second Treatise*, is much longer, and reads as follows:

> The great end of men's entering into society being the enjoyment of their properties in peace and safety, and the great instrument and means of that being the laws established in that society; the *first fundamental positive law* of all commonwealths is the *establishing of the legislative power,* as the *first and fundamental natural law,* which is to govern even the legislative itself, is the *preservation of*

the society and (as far as will consist with the public good) of every person in it.

Galloway, as we see, eliminated roughly two-thirds of that sentence in transcription. Natural law—a serious inconvenience for Tory politics—thus disappeared, and with it went a crucial Lockean hedge against the power of the legislature. It is interesting to note that as a member of the Continental Congress in 1774, Galloway, according to John Adams's recollection (and against Adams's own position in the deliberations), insisted on "excluding the Law of Nature" from any official statement concerning the authority of Parliament over the colonies.[22]

To defend further the doctrine of absolute parliamentary supremacy, Galloway also drew from §149, one of the most radical passages in the *Second Treatise*. And on this occasion his exegetical mutilation of Locke's theory was even more extreme. Here is Galloway's transcription: "There can be but one supreme power, which is the legislative, to which all the rest are, and must be, subordinate." This time Galloway punctuated a dependent clause into a complete sentence. And again, a part (which, out of its context, supported Galloway's argument) was made to appear as the whole (which contradicted Galloway's argument). Here is the complete sentence as Locke himself wrote it:

> Though in a constituted commonwealth, standing upon its own basis, and acting according to its own nature, that is, acting for the preservation of the community, there can be but *one supreme power*, which is *the legislative*, to which all the rest are, and must be, subordinate, yet the legislative being only a fiduciary power to act for certain ends, there remains still *in the people a supreme power* to remove or *alter the legislative*, when they find the *legislative* act contrary to the trust reposed in them.

The complete sentence was absolutely central to the argument of the *Second Treatise*, and absolutely fatal to the notorious claim of parliamentary supremacy "in all cases whatsoever." This idea—that there is always "a supreme power" in the people "to remove or abolish" the *legal* sovereign when *they* find that the trust of political authority has been betrayed—is a basic element of Locke's theoretical justification for revolution, and the American Revolutionists used it accordingly in their writings. Galloway, an implacable enemy of the Revolution, cut the heart out of Locke's political theory in the very act of appealing explicitly to its authority.[23]

This analysis alerts us to the potential hazards of citation-hunting and quotation-counting in the study of intellectual history. These forms of external textual evidence are indispensable in historical research; but they can be misleading, and they do not constitute a sufficient basis for evaluating the cross-contextual significance of specific ideas and sources. It is necessary to remember the limits of external evidence, to know the relevant sources, and to cast a wider methodological net over the material.

Internal evidence—the second general category of textual evidence—is no less problematic, and no less indispensable, than its external counterpart. Sometimes the line separating the two categories is as ambiguous as the evidence itself. Paraphrasing without citation, for instance, is counted here as internal evidence since we cannot be certain that a specific text served as the source for the passage in question. Such methodological conservatism may be unwarranted in some cases (for instance, the *Second Treatise* and the Declaration of Independence); but it is better to err on the side of caution in these matters, especially when the evidence as a whole permits the construction of a persuasive argument without subjecting that evidence to speculative modes of interpretation.

Perhaps we can clarify the distinction between external and internal evidence by calling the first objective and the second subjective. A direct quotation or citation is objective in the sense that there are no doubts concerning the source—although, as we have seen, the *meaning* of objective evidence is not unambiguously self-evident. The presentation of data as internal evidence, and the interpretation of that evidence, on the other hand, involve subjective decisions. The investigator must decide whether, for example, the similarity between a passage on the law of nature in a Revolutionary pamphlet and a passage in the *Second Treatise* is (1) a coincidence, (2) a deliberate paraphrase of the *Second Treatise*, or (3) a deliberate paraphrase of a source other than the *Second Treatise*. Locke, after all, was not the only source for Revolutionary ideology who wrote about natural law, or about a number of other "Lockean" concepts; and in the absence of explicit attribution, i.e., objective evidence, we cannot be certain that Locke was in fact the source in a specific case.

There is, then, ample justification for taking a conservative approach and classifying the uncited paraphrase, as well as unattributed similarities of language and doctrine, as internal evidence. The innate ambiguity of such evidence, however, remains; and if we wish to use it, we need to impose some stringent rules for interpretation. There will still be an irreducible element of subjectivity and, thus, uncertainty where internal evidence is concerned (as there is with external evidence, too). But the internal evidence which passes through this methodological filter will constitute a basis for sound inference and reasonable conjecture. In any case, no single category of evidence carries the burden of proof alone. This analysis of the founding doctrine utilizes a combination of internal, external, and other types of evidence, with due regard for the possibilities and limits of each. This applies to the recovery of both the formal and the substantive Lockean connections in American Revolutionary thought.

How can we remove some of the ambiguity from internal evidence and thus qualify it for inclusion in this inquiry? First of all, and this cannot be emphasized too much, we must be familiar with the relevant sources; otherwise, in the absence of attribution, we're going to miss a great deal. (Even when the author does acknowledge the source—as the analysis of Joseph Galloway's pamphlet shows—we are obliged, as it were, to evaluate his scholarship by closely examining the source itself.) With this in mind, and taking uncited paraphrasing or similarity of exposition as an example of internal evidence, a little common sense can go a long way. In the approach taken here, the passage in question must be fairly long, with only slight, inessential deviations from the wording in the proposed source. There are many examples of unattributed paraphrasing of Locke's *Second Treatise* in the Revolutionary writings which meet these criteria.[24]

Another way to qualify internal evidence is to offer a negative argument. In other words, we identify Locke as the source of a particular passage, idea, or doctrine in a Revolutionary pamphlet only after ruling out all sources other than Locke. Of course, it could take forever to perfect this strategy—which means that there is a limit to the degree of certainty it yields. How do we know that, after ruling out all conceivable non-Lockean sources, we haven't missed some inconceivable non-Lockean sources? As with all forms of evidence and argument, "almost certain" is as close to certainty as even full-time negative argument is ever going to come. Nevertheless, the greater the ambiguity of the internal evidence, the more prudent it is to consider other possibilities and the greater the effort that should be expended in that direction.

Negative argument actually produces some interesting situations. Tying methodology to substance for a moment, consider that if Pocock were correct in asserting an antithesis between Locke's liberalism and the republican tradition, and in subsuming *omnia praeter Lockem* within that tradition, negative argument would then be a short and straight avenue to truth. Simply show that the concept or argument conveyed, or language used, in a Revolutionary pamphlet isn't republican, and by definition it must be Lockean. And this is relatively easy to do.

At the conceptual level, for example, the anthropological core of republicanism, as the revisionists understand it, is your basic Aristotle: the individual attains "full humanity [only] through participation or citizenship in a republic,"[25] or, as Pocock puts it, human personality is "perfected in citizenship" (hence, civic humanism).[26] This was not by any means the prevailing view in Revolutionary America. Certainly the clergy did not endow politics, or any other secular pursuit (including capital accumulation), with humanizing, redemptive power; and none of the nonclerical writings that I have examined evince awareness of, much less a pronounced sympathy for, Aristotle's view of man as a political animal, as set forth in his *Politics*. Indeed, even "Cato," the alleged inspiration for American republicanism, found the Leviathan more congenial than the polis.[27]

In any case, since the civic humanist conception of human nature does not inform Revolutionary ideology to any discernible extent, and the Pocockian choice is between Locke and *omnia praeter Lockem,* the founding doctrine must be Lockean and, indeed, *Locke et praeterea nihil.* The use of negative argument on the Revolutionary writings, in the context of Pocockian historiography, thus restores the monolithic Lockeanism that the republican revision claims to have overthrown. Aside form the inadequacy of the Locke model of interpretation as a guide to American Revolutionary thought, the fact that in this case certainty regarding internal evidence *is* achieved through negative argument is enough to trigger profound suspicion—not about negative argument, of course, but about Pocock's historiographic paradigm.

I do use negative argument to rule out republicanism as a source for language, doctrine, and concepts found in the Revolutionary writings; it is especially useful at the conceptual level, which is where the most interesting arguments transpire; but since I reject Pocock's division of the ideological universe into two hostile camps, Locke and the civic republicans (i.e., everyone else), the effects of negative argument in my analysis are much less explosive than in the scenario outlined above.[28] As I indicated earlier, I employ negative argument to clarify the more ambiguous samples of internal evidence, and in conjunction with other forms of evidence, and then weigh the cumulative effect. At the risk of turning a chapter on method into a chapter on substance, I offer two examples of how this approach illuminates the Lockean connection in critical areas of Revolutionary thought.

In demonstrating the substantive Lockean connection (as defined in chapter 1) in the political thought of the New England clergy, a good deal of significance will be attributed to the Lockean doctrine of natural law in the ministers' writings. Now Locke, of course, was neither the only nor the first philosopher to contemplate the law of nature. How can we be reasonably certain—the highest level of certainty to which this work aspires—that the clerical doctrine of natural law was Lockean?

First, I use negative argument to rule out, on conceptual grounds, civic republicanism as a possible source of the clerical doctrine of natural law. Second, I point to both internal and external evidence of similarities between Locke and the ministers with respect to the theistic epistemological foundations of natural-law theory as well as to the extension of natural-law obligations into civil society and the consequent politicization of the right and duty of individual judgment. It is not simply the doctrine of natural law, but also the general philosophical framework from which that doctrine and its political implications emerge, that constitute the substantive Lockean connection in American Revolutionary thought. Finally, I offer what might be called "circumstantial" evidence: James Otis explicitly designated Locke as the Revolution's authority on natural law. Otis, to be sure, was not a man of the cloth. But he did have close ties to some radical and influential ministers—close enough for one prominent Tory to identify him as the driving force behind the notorious "Black Regiment" of seditious preachers. Thus, Otis could have served as a kind of link between Locke and the ministers in this regard.[29]

Alone, none of these three steps would take us far enough to establish the existence of the substantive Lockean connection. Together, however, they constitute a persuasive argument.

The second example of how diverse forms of evidence are assembled and presented, with cumulative impact, in subsequent chapters concerns what I will call the ministers' Lockean exegesis of the "politicks of St. Paul." St. Paul's Thirteenth Letter to the Romans ("The powers that be are ordained of God. . . . [T]hey that resist shall receive to themselves damnation," etc.) was easily the ministers' favorite text. Locke, too, had subjected Romans 13 to careful exegesis. Both Locke and the ministers, moreover, offered the same surprising interpretation. They turned the Apostle on his head, so to speak, deriving a morally compelling demand for political resistance from this apparently unequivocal prescription for universal and unlimited obedience. It is true that the ministers, so far as I know, did not explicitly cite Locke's *Paraphrase and Notes on the Epistle of St. Paul to the Romans* in this specific context.[30] Nevertheless, the evidence, as a whole, points convincingly to a Lockean connection in the "politicks of St. Paul".

First, on the basis of comparative textual analysis, it is clear that Locke and the clergy developed essentially similar interpretations of Romans 13. This can be classified as internal evidence, though (as we shall see) there is very little, if any, ambiguity involved. Second, through similar reasoning, Locke and the ministers derived (or rationalized) from Romans 13 the same theory of politics; that is, the relation between theology and political theory in both Lockean and clerical thought is virtually the same. Here, again, the evidence is internal insofar as there is no explicit Lockean citation or transcription specifically tying theology to political theory; still, the similarities revealed through comparative analysis are distinctive and unmistakable. Third, a negative argument can be made effectively eliminating republican political theory, with its essentially secular orientation, as a source for clerical thought in this regard. Fourth (and here we begin to reduce significantly the possibility that these similarities are merely coincidental and unrecognized by the ministers themselves), the political theory in the sermon literature is sewn together with numerous explicit citations of "Locke on Government"—external evidence to satisfy the most empirical scholarly appetite, yet unreported in the authoritative revisionist account of clerical thought.[31] Finally, there is a telling piece of circumstantial evidence. Ezra Stiles, a prominent clergyman writing as president of Yale in the critical year 1775, noted "Mr. Locke's . . . exceedingly high" reputation as a "Scripture commentator" among his clerical colleagues and the public.[32] The ministers, then, were aware of, and in sympathy with, Locke's exegesis of Romans 13—an important slice of "Lockean liberalism" which I do not believe has surfaced in the revisionist literature.

Again, no single link in this chain is strong enough to carry the argument. It is the cumulative effect of various forms of evidence —internal, external, circumstantial—with some reinforcement by negative argument that establishes the Lockean connection in the "politicks of St. Paul."

I feel this lengthy discussion of evidence has been necessary to clear the air of methodological confusion. However, so much talk about the relative value and cumulative impact of different forms of evidence in identifying sources may have created the impression that the identification of sources is my principal concern, when in fact this is not the case. As I have been arguing, sources cannot be identified with certainty. A citation written in blood would not prove beyond doubt that the argument served by that citation had been inspired by the cited source, be it "Locke on Government," *Cato's Letters*, or any other text.

Moreover, I am not out to show that an idea, argument, or doctrine in a sample of Revolutionary writing came from Locke, but that it is *distinctively Lockean* (that is, consistent with the spirit of Lockean liberalism, which is understood in terms of a textually sound, historically appropriate interpretation of Locke's thought). For example, I try to show, especially in relation to New England clerical thought, that both the political ideas *and* the general philosophical structure within which those ideas are *integrally* embedded are characteristic of Locke's liberalism (as I will define that doctrine). This is the essence of the substantive Lockean connection; it has textual roots in both the writings of Locke and the writings of the American Revolution; but it is not wholly dependent upon the identification of sources. It is neither possible nor necessary to prove that the clergy *learned* theology, epistemology, "Scripture commentary," and political theory from reading Locke's texts in order to achieve this aim.

In sum, empirical—or textual—evidence, both internal and external, is necessary and important, but, in a sense, only instrumentally so. That evidence does mitigate the unhistorical extremism of the republican revision. It clearly shows, for instance, that the Revolutionists formulated and presented their arguments for resistance in the vocabulary, and often in the actual words, of the *Second Treatise*. No other source came close to "Locke on Government" in this regard. And it is important to show this in light of the prevailing tendency to write about Revolutionary ideology as if Lockean-liberal thought were irrelevant or hostile in relation to the discourse and objectives of the Revolution itself. However, the critique of the republican revision and the recovery of the Lockean connection also have a conceptual dimension. Simply put, there are important elements in Revolutionary ideology—elements without which no understanding of the founding doctrine is complete—that do not fit within the republican paradigm but which are essentially consistent with Lockean-liberal thought. Empirical evidence, which has been methodologically processed in the manner set forth above, testifies persuasively to the existence of these elements. It is political theory, however, that endows them with meaning.

Having considered the nature of evidence in a historical study of political thought, we can turn to a second area of methodological importance: selecting the sources of evidence. The purpose of this study sets the general bibliographic requirements with respect to primary literature, both Lockean and Revolutionary, but it also imposes some limitations.

Concerning Locke, the issue is relatively simple. The emphasis I place upon the interpretation of Locke's thought mandates an examination of a broad range of Lockean texts. This must extend at least to the writings on politics, toleration, religion, theology, and epistemology—in other words, those works to which we know that many members of the New England clergy were exposed, and from which an understanding of Locke's "theistic liberalism" could emerge.[33] For the Locke scholar this might not be enough to constitute an authoritative, comprehensive account of Lockean thought. But it is not my purpose to provide such an account; and the fact that I am equally concerned, in the same book, with American Revolutionary thought makes it virtually impossible to satisfy the established criteria for scholarly works devoted exclusively to Lockean thought. In short, I have not read the entire Lockean corpus—every letter, every journal entry, etc.; nor have I utilized everything that I have read. Nevertheless, given the nature and purpose of this inquiry, the reader, I trust, will conclude that my coverage of the Lockean corpus has been sufficient, that more than enough textual support for the "theistic Locke" has been adduced, and that far greater attention has been paid to the works of Locke, and to the content of his thought, in this book than in the literature of the republican revision.

Life becomes rather more complicated when we ponder the writings from the Revolutionary period. In Neil Postman's words, this was Typographic America—public discourse through the medium of print. And the Revolutionary generation was indeed a prolific one; by any standards, their literary output was enormous. It is necessary, then, to make some practical distinctions within that mass of writings. An overview of the Revolutionary literature can help to put the problem into a perspective from which I can explain some of the bibliographic decisions I have made in the course of my research. Here, too, the nature of this inquiry has guided those decisions.

The first print medium to consider is the political pamphlet. The eighteenth century, like the seventeenth, has been described as "a great age of political pamphleteering."[34] And pamphlet production during the Revolutionary period was "very considerable."[35] Scholars estimate that between four hundred and twelve hundred political pamphlets dealing with the Anglo-American controversy were published in the colonies from 1764 to 1776.[36] "The world and his wife, if we ignore the illiterate masses, were not only reading but writing pamphlets."[37] And these pamphlets were frequently read aloud to the "illiterate masses" in churches, at town meetings, and in taverns.[38] For historians, pamphlets reveal "the bent and genius of the age."[39] For the contemporaries of that age, however, they served as effective tools of political education and propaganda—the "instruments of immediate popular influence."[40]

Attesting to the strategic importance of political pamphlets is a resolution that was issued by the North Carolina Provincial Council, a proresistance organization, on December 24, 1775. Governor Josiah Martin, a Loyalist, had distributed "great numbers of Tory pamphlets" in the parts of the province where "the people" were "not well informed." The Provincial Council therefore "Resolved, that the Continental Delegates from this Province be immediately informed thereof," and that they be urged "to procure the best pamphlets that can be had for the true information of the people, to counteract and frustrate the wicked and diabolical stratagems of Governor Martin and other tools of a corrupt ministry." The special significance of this call for propaganda lies in the fact that, of a series of resolutions issued that Christmas Eve, it was the only one that did not deal directly with urgent military necessities. The other resolutions concerned recruitment, military intelligence, and ammunition of a more material nature.[41]

Political pamphlets were not of a single kind. The great majority of pamphlets were written by members of the educated elite. But within this group, styles and opinions varied considerably. And in most cases the writings could be categorized according to the kind of education and subsequent professions of the authors. Regional differences, too, were very salient.

On the whole, leaders from the central colonies, such as John Dickinson and Daniel Dulany, had been trained as lawyers at English law schools (the Temple, or at Lincoln's Inn). They expressed their opposition to Parliament in the 1760s and early 1770s in legal and constitutional arguments that were designed primarily "to convince those who had control of the government that they were exceeding their authority or that their acts were wholly unjustified by the English theory of Colonial law or by the precedents and practice under it." [42] In other words, they argued from precedent, not nature. A great many pamphlets of this type appeared throughout the Revolutionary period.

In contrast, the intellectual elites from New England usually received their education at Harvard or Yale (where Locke's writings had graced the library shelves, and fortified the curriculum, since early in the eighteenth century). [43] Moreover, these schools had been established primarily "to insure the continuance of a learned and orthodox ministry"; and until 1778, more graduates from these institutions entered the ministry than into any other profession. [44] Indeed, every annual Massachusetts Election Sermon from 1710 to 1776 was delivered by a Harvard graduate, while all of the ministers who delivered the Connecticut Election Sermons each year for the same period had been graduated either from Harvard or Yale. [45] And the preachers of election sermons, though constituting only a small fraction of all the New England clergy, were sociologically representative of the entire group. [46]

John Adams noted in February 1776 that liberal political ideas "have been long in contemplation and fully understood by the people at large in New England, but have been attended to in the Southern colonies only by gentlemen of free spirits and liberal minds, who are very few." [47] And both friends and foes of the Revolution itself, as well as generations of the Revolution's historians, have ascribed the advanced political thinking of the people of New England to the influence of their religious leaders.[48] While the lawyers from the central colonies led their people in what was "at the beginning a constitutional resistance within the lines of the English law," the (non-Anglican) clergy "directed the course of the movement" in New England and led their people in what was "a revolutionary resistance at all times." Uninspired by the learned but tame legalistic arguments from positive law favored by their more conservative countrymen to the south, the leaders in New England—clerical and secular— insisted that "their rights rested upon something above and beyond English law." They sought their political precedents in God, scripture, and the law of nature.[49]

We thus have (at least) two distinct, general orientations in the pamphlet literature—two categories for sorting out that literature. Seeking the more radical elements in Revolutionary thought, and those elements most likely to be in tune with Locke's "religious preoccupations" and "theological commitments," I have devoted a large portion of my research to the second, that is, to the writings of the leaders of New England, the clergy.[50] There are, in fact, several good reasons for focusing upon the sermon literature, independent of my interpretation of Locke. Not the least of these is my desire to understand the ideological preparation of a religious people for revolution. And it is precisely the ministers' great prestige and influence in their communities which make their sermons such promising material for this kind of inquiry. Only the clergy enjoyed regular strategic access to the minds of the common people of New England, people for whom "religion was not a mere Sunday ritual," but "an enveloping influence seven days of the week."[51] On the whole, eighteenth-century New Englanders took their ministers very seriously indeed.

A study of the clerical writings thus sheds some light upon the ideological dynamics of the American Revolution by addressing the crucial but neglected question of how the people were induced to act—indeed, to take violent, courageous, dangerous action. One of the most curious features of Bernard Bailyn's interpretation of the ideological history of the Revolution is that the event seems to have occurred in the heads of the authors whose pamphlets he considers important. Bailyn's elites may well have influenced one another by debating the fine points of the English constitutional and common law. But is this the stuff of which revolutions are made? Were the people who fought and died for the cause merely acting on the advice of lawyers citing Judge Blackstone? Or did they risk everything because, as believers, they listened to their religious leaders, who for decades prior to the Stamp Act crisis had been preaching that those who do not resist tyranny "will receive to themselves damnation"? [52]

No doubt the majority of pamphlets selected by Bailyn were not without some popular influence—though not as much as one might expect. [53] But, as C. H. Van Tyne put it, "the historical muse has been too much of a worldling"; we should remember that "the pulpit was in that day the most direct and effectual way of reaching the masses." [54] And from the pulpit, the ministers (often with the help of "Locke on Government") "carried the people" of New England, "whose leaders they were, very far beyond the ideas of resistance which prevailed elsewhere." [55] The many sermons which were published in pamphlet form thus provide us with a perspective on the Revolutionary ideological education of the common people which simply is not available from the perspective of Dickinson's "Pennsylvania Farmer."

Bibliographic decisions obviously affect the outcome of the inquiry. This is the main reason why I am concerned to spell out and defend the criteria governing my choices. By the same token, the republican hypothesis has been shaped by bibliographic decisions, too. Jesse Lemisch claims that Bailyn's influential conclusions about the American Revolution "arose directly out of his choice of sources, not necessarily out of reality." [56] Lemisch's judgment is severe, but not entirely unreasonable. We can assume, at the very least, that Bailyn's account of the Revolution was heavily informed by his reading of the seventy-two pamphlets he selected for a four-volume collection. As of today, only one volume, containing fourteen pamphlets, has been published; but the existing volume includes tables of contents for the unpublished ones, so Bailyn's opinion concerning the most important American writings is known. [57] And the criteria governing Bailyn's selection of pamphlets need to be examined.

Bailyn applied two criteria in selecting pamphlets: "contemporary fame" and "representativeness." He was not very specific about the first of these criteria, and his choices here were, in fact, somewhat questionable in quantitative terms. Thomas R. Adams, a noted bibliographer of seventeenth- and eighteenth-century pamphlet literature, has compiled a list of the twelve pamphlets which, from 1764 to 1776, appeared in the greatest number of American editions, printed in the most American cities. Of Bailyn's complete list of seventy-two pamphlets, all of which were selected in part for their contemporary fame, only six appear on Adams's list of twelve.

For example, James Otis's *Rights of the British Colonies* appeared in Bailyn's first volume; Thomas Jefferson's *Summary View of the Rights of British America* (1774), James Wilson's *Considerations on the . . . Authority of the British Parliament* (1774), and the Tory pamphlets of Samuel Seabury, Thomas Bradbury Chandler, and Joseph Galloway were slated to appear in the projected volumes. On the basis of Adams's research, however, generous assumptions about the "contemporary fame" of these pamphlets are not warranted, since none of them earned a place on his list of twelve "best-sellers." "Printers were also businessmen," Adams observes; and it is unlikely that they would have continued to turn out new editions of a pamphlet "unless they thought the public would buy them."[58] Colonial printers, it seems, were not so different from the media chieftains of the 1980s; they, too, operated on the principle of supply and demand.

Bailyn's other main criterion of selection, "representativeness," is also problematic. Representative of what? Representative of whom? Perhaps the pamphlets were selected because they represented the republican worldview. But to what extent was the republican worldview, as set forth in these pamphlets, representative of Revolutionary thought as a whole? It certainly did not represent the whole of Revolutionary thought. On the other hand, what elements of Revolutionary thought are not represented in Bailyn's sources (or in his interpretation of those sources)?

By no means am I saying that Bailyn's pamphlets were irrelevant, or that republican thought was an inessential ingredient in the founding ideology. And I am not claiming to have constructed a bibliography that expresses the whole of Revolutionary thought. I simply believe that my bibliographic choices, particularly with regard to the sermon literature, illuminate other essential—but neglected—elements in Revolutionary doctrine. In referring to his list of pamphlets, Bailyn wisely acknowledges that "no two people making such a selection would agree on all the items to be included; the present choice, like any choice, may be open to criticism."[59] Needless to say, his caveat applies to my choices, too.

Of course, my sources are not limited to sermons preached in New England and published in pamphlet form. The analysis of the formal Lockean connection presents evidence collected from colonial newspapers,[60] broadsides, correspondence, formal resolutions and official state papers,[61] as well as from "secular" political pamphlets; and it does not favor one region over another. The bibliography as a whole thus includes numerous selections from all the major forms of political writing from throughout the colonies, as well as enough sermons to save even the most endangered soul.

Just as the Locke scholar might have reservations about the bibliography of Locke's works (which is quite extensive but not all-inclusive), the historian might wish for even greater coverage of American materials. In fact, the Locke scholar might say, "Too much American history," and the historian might respond, "Too much Locke." Such are the perils of writing a book for two demanding audiences. But just as I do not pretend to have written a comprehensive, authoritative account of Locke's philosophy, I am not trying to establish a new paradigm for the study of American Revolutionary thought. The bibliography of Lockean and American sources strongly supports the critique of the republican revision where Locke is concerned and firmly establishes the Lockean connection in American Revolutionary thought. And that is my main objective.

There is one other item in the bibliography, which does not fall into the categories described above: *Cato's Letters.* In the republican synthesis, this remarkable early-eighteenth-century English text is said to have been "of the utmost importance in the creation of American Republicanism."[62] But "Cato's" republicanism has a dark side, about which his new friends have thus far been silent. In chapter four, we'll resurrect some of the hidden content of American republicanism—and consider the theoretical foundation of the republican paradigm—through the medium of Cato's political thought. That analysis should reaffirm my basic point: It is both interesting and desirable to combine the virtues of historical research with those of political theory in the study of the American founding doctrine.

In this chapter I have tried to shed or preempt the methodological vices which could disturb that happy union. We can now look at what the American Revolutionists and their friends in Parliament thought about tax reform in the 1760s.

3

The Lockean Response to British

"Innovations"

As Gad Hitchcock stepped up to the pulpit to deliver the annual Massachusetts election sermon in 1774, this was the situation: Ten years
had passed since the Stamp Act Crisis had, in the words of another
minister, "shaken the very foundations of government."[1] When the
foundations shake, the people feel it, especially when their preachers sound the alert. And once the people are agitated, the entire
structure begins to crumble. In the decline of empires and political
systems, this is the point of no return.

That point in the dissolution of political ties between England
and her American colonies was probably already history by the time
Hitchcock looked down upon his distinguished congregation. The
days of British America were numbered. Blood ran through the streets
of Boston. Lexington and Concord were around the corner.

In those days preachers gave the state of the union address—
not as public officials, or as leaders of government, but as the conscience of the community. (They knew that the voice of conscience
is always compromised in possession of government power.) The election sermon was that kind of event.[2] Thus, the political leaders of
the Commonwealth were there. And so were the king's men, including the new military governor, General Thomas Gage, who had
been recently entrusted by His Majesty George III to put out the fires
of rebellion in Massachusetts. This made for a tense situation, but
Hitchcock rose to the occasion. He threatened the crown with the

ultimate weapon: "The people . . . are the only source of civil authority on earth." And he made sure the general was fully briefed on
the situation. "Our danger," he warned, "is not visionary, but real.
Our contention is not about trifles, but about liberty and property,
not ours only, but those of posterity."[3]

Throughout that year the situation continued to deteriorate. Parliament had injected overt religious controversy into the political
dispute with the ill-timed Quebec Act, part of a legislative package
known in the colonies as the Intolerable Acts, or Coercive Acts.
The Quebec Act, which recognized Catholicism as the "official" religion in that province, may have made sense in Quebec, with its
largely Catholic population; but to restless and suspicious New England Protestants, it "established popery" in the British Dominions
and thus constituted a direct and lethal threat. A great many colonists, the proud descendants of Laudian refugees who had given sanctuary to regicides, never shed their fear and loathing of "prelatical
tyranny." To these people (for whom Anglicanism was simply another
form of "popery"), it seemed "very clear that the Stuart family" had "a
hand in the whole scheme," hoping to settle some old scores with the
dissenters who had managed to escape. They interpreted the Quebec
Act as a plan "to keep a large body of Popish Canadians in terrorism"
against Protestants in America.[4]

The rhetoric was excessive, revealing a vicious strain of bigotry and
paranoia in Revolutionary culture, even among men of the cloth.
(Back then it was Catholics sweeping down from the north; today it's
Communists surging up from the south or liberals subverting the Republic from within; but the self-righteous intemperance is essentially
the same.) Even those who could control their hyperbole, however,
still viewed the legislation with alarm. To the Reverend William
Gordon, establishing "popery" meant "the reestablishment of arbitrary power and a despotic government" right next door, with "the
base, diabolical design of procuring the assistance" of the inhabitants
of Quebec "in quelling the spirit of freedom" in America. In the unlikely event that Gordon's congregation had forgotten what the spirit
of freedom, and the conflict with England, were about, the preacher

offered this emphatic reminder: "It is not conquest, but *liberty and property* that are at stake!"[5]

The Tories took a hard line on Gordon's sermon, denouncing it as "treasonable," a doctrine of "sedition, rebellion, carnage and blood."[6] But Gordon's message about liberty and property, like Hitchcock's, was conventional wisdom throughout the Revolutionary years (and for nearly a century prior to the Stamp Act). From the outset the colonists' troubles with Parliament revolved around the "inseparable" issues of "liberty and property."[7]

This chapter will show that the colonists' analyses of these problems were distinctively and often explicitly Lockean. It will also show that when the British government, in effect, asserted its right to abolish liberty and property in America, the Revolutionists articulated the Lockean-liberal theoretical response to political absolutism: there are some things that civil authority, as such, cannot do. Contrary to the claims of the republican revision, then, Locke's theory supported the cause of the Revolutionists, not the designs of Parliament, on the issues the colonists cared about most. We will see that the Revolutionists—and their allies in Parliament—correctly used Locke's ideas and language (or at least the ideas and language that Locke himself used), and often his very words, to formulate and express their arguments on these crucial issues. This will establish the formal Lockean connection in American Revolutionary thought and thereby correct a serious distortion of history—a distortion which effectively suppresses the political theory of constitutional politics and limited government, as well as the justification for popular revolution, in the founding doctrine.

Perhaps I should state two obvious points here. First, establishing— or recovering—the Lockean connection neither includes nor requires a demonstration of Locke's "influence" upon American Revolutionary thought. I do not know how to measure influence; in fact, I doubt that it can be measured at all; and after having devoted a chapter to the avoidance of methodological pitfalls, I have no desire to step into a black hole. Furthermore, the point is not who influenced whom, but that Revolutionary thought was of a certain character. Judging

by the concerns and positions in Revolutionary thought, a vitally important element in that character was Lockean-liberal. "Influence" is
strictly an academic concern and ultimately a futile one. But we can
show that the American Revolutionists held liberal ideas about politics; and this could prove to be very useful indeed when the defenders
of constitutional politics in modern America start looking around for
a source of historical legitimacy.

The second point is that I do not attribute causal significance
to Lockean political theory with respect to Revolutionary politics.
Unlike some of the proponents of the republican revision, I am not
making causal claims for any political theory, ideology, or language.[8]
One of the most convincing explanations of the causes of the Revolution that I have encountered is rooted more concretely in politics. It
asks the critical yet often neglected question: What were the *political*
stakes? This explanation reminds us that some highly placed individuals had a great deal to lose if Parliament were to prevail in its
attempt to exercise legislative sovereignty (which included the power
to tax) over the colonies. The hard-won power of the colonial legislative assemblies, and of the men who sat in them, hung in the balance.
While this book is not a history of the American Revolution, a moment's reflection here will help to illuminate the dynamics of the
formal Lockean connection in American Revolutionary thought.

This account of the causes of the Revolution regards the extension of local legislative power at the expense of the royal authority
and executive prerogative as "the most notable political development
in the empire during the eighteenth century."[9] In securing the exclusive power to tax during the century prior to the Revolution, the
colonial assemblies had scored substantial political gains against their
rivals for power, the royal governors—a pattern that paralleled the
development of Parliamentary supremacy and the decline of the royal
prerogative in England.[10] Those most immediately damaged by the
growth of local legislative power, the royal governors themselves,
attested to these developments.

Governor Samuel Shute of Massachusetts, for example, complained directly to the king in 1723 that "the House of Representatives is in a manner the whole legislative, and in a good measure the

executive power of this province," and "has for some years past been
making attempts upon the few prerogatives that have been reserved
to the Crown."[11] Shute's successor, Jonathan Belcher, in a letter to
the Board of Trade in 1732, accused the Massachusetts House of Representatives of "continually running wild," and of attempting to take
"the whole legislative, as well as the executive part, of the government into their own hands."[12] And things were not much different
down south. "Little by little," wrote Governor James Glen of South
Carolina in 1743, "the people have got the whole administration in
their hands . . . . The whole form of government is unhinged," he
warned, "and the governor divested of his power."[13]   .

C. H. Van Tyne is one of those historians whose work, which was
published in the early part of the twentieth century, seems to have
been overlooked in the historiographic revolution. But his analysis stands the test of time. Van Tyne concluded that "no cause of
the final rebellion was more profound, perhaps, than this nagging
conflict" between the provincial assemblies and the royal governors.
"The whole center of gravity of the colonial administration shifted
gradually from London to the capitals of the American provinces," he
writes.[14] The result was the rise of an indigenous and increasingly en-
trenched political elite, based in the colonial legislative assemblies.
This development virtually guaranteed that the revenue measures
which Parliament introduced in 1764 would be vigorously opposed as
usurpation. Political careers, and the power structure itself, were at
stake. As another historian, Jack Greene, has more recently observed:
"The British challenge after 1764 threatened to render [the] accom-
plishments [of the provincial representative assemblies] meaningless
and drove them to demand autonomy in local affairs and eventually
to declare their independence. At issue was the whole political structure forged by the lower houses over the previous century. In this
context the American Revolution becomes in form, if not in essence,
a war for political survival. . . ."[15]

Thus, by 1764, the provincial representative assemblies had already
become the dominant centers of political power, in which the careers
of the most talented and ambitious colonial leaders were based; and
the exclusive power of taxation constituted the foundation of the

entire political structure. Parliament now threatened to undermine that structure by claiming the power of taxation, or at least a share of that power, for itself. This is why the Stamp Act Congress, in its Petition to the King, complained that the colonial legislatures (and, of course, the colonial legislators) would be, "in effect, rendered useless by the late Acts of Parliament."[16] Both King and Parliament severely underestimated the lengths to which the colonial political elites would go in order to avoid being reduced to that pitiful condition. Apparently, it was not until 1774 that Lord North realized the necessity of using force " 'to take the executive power from the hands of the democratic part of the government.' "[17] And that meant war.

In any case, Lockean theory did not cause the American Revolution. By the same token, an "imprisoning" and "conditioning" republican ideology did not act "as a restricting and compulsive force in the approaches to revolution," leaving the colonists with "no alternative" to "revolutionary action."[18] Lockean theory, however, did supply the concepts and categories in which the Revolutionists articulated their deepest concerns about liberty and property. Moreover, although some historians and political theorists may dream about the "anticapitalistic" nature of civic republicanism in the American Revolution, this doctrine also placed a high premium on liberty and property.[19] Nevertheless, republican ideology could not furnish effective theoretical shelter against Parliament's new economic policies or, for that matter, against the dangerous principle of illimitable parliamentary sovereignty upon which those policies were based. To defend liberty and property, then, the opposition to Parliament enlisted the services of Locke, not "Cato."

On the other hand, it should be noted that in establishing the Lockean-liberal defense of liberty and property, the Revolutionists drew not at all from chapter 5 ("Of Property") of the Second Treatise, but primarily from chapter 11 ("Of the Extent of the Legislative Power"). The issue in dispute was not the right of the subject to appropriate from nature, but the right of the government to expropriate the subject. Accordingly, the Revolutionists did not call upon the "bourgeois Locke" to justify unlimited appropriation; they used Locke's political theory to do what it does best, that is, to define the inherent moral limits of civil authority with respect to liberty (civil as well as religious) and property and to justify resistance and revolution when government exceeds, or threatens to exceed, those limits. The formal Lockean connection, then, was not an ideological rationalization for unlimited capital accumulation; it was, instead, a demand for constitutional politics and limited government; and when England failed to honor that demand, it became a justification for armed resistance and revolution.

The offensive "innovations" in Great Britain's colonial policy began in 1763, taking the initial form of Parliamentary measures "for the purpose of raising a revenue" in the colonies.[20] These measures constituted an assault on liberty and property because they disrupted a special relationship between taxation and consent, a relationship that had been institutionalized in colonial politics through the mechanism of representation. Basically, the political equation looked like this: Liberty and property are inseparable; one cannot endure without the other. Consent, moreover, is the sine qua non of property; if you do not control the disposal of an object by granting or withholding consent, it is not your property in the first place. In a large political community, however, where the population is dispersed over extensive territory, representation becomes the necessary institutional mechanism for registering consent. Without representation, then, there is no consent and, therefore, no liberty and no property.

For the colonists, the institutional framework for liberty and property was not an ideal to be strived for; it was a system they wished to preserve. They did not object strenuously to taxation per se. On a house call to Westminster, Dr. Franklin informed the Lords that the colonists already paid, without serious protest, "many and very heavy taxes."[21] But these taxes always had been self-imposed, so to speak, through enactment by the provincial representative assemblies. By 1764 "no taxation without representation" had been a fact of political life in the colonies for nearly one hundred years.[22] But the new revenue policy changed all that; it involved the imposition of taxes upon the colonists by a distant legislative body in which they were not, and by all accounts could not be, represented.[23] This threatened an existing condition of self-government, in which the colonists actually enjoyed the "essential British right that no person shall be subject to any tax but what in person or by his representative he hath a voice in laying."[24] The revenue measures (particularly the Stamp Act, which affected the press) thus roused the British colonies in North America from the long slumber of "salutary neglect" and occasioned the first concerted political challenge to the authority of Parliament.[25]

The ideological sanctity of colonial political institutions had been firmly established by the highest moral authorities in the colonies long before Prime Minister Grenville tried his hand at tax reform. For one hundred years before the Revolution, the New England clergy had been insisting that the liberty and property of the people were inviolable under God's law; only governments and political arrangements that respected and preserved liberty and property could legitimately lay claim to the obedience of the people.[26] This principle enjoyed the status of fundamental law; not even kings could violate it with impunity. Thus, in a sermon that later earned the title of the "morning gun of the Revolution," Jonathan Mayhew declared that Charles I *deserved* to go to the scaffold in part because he levied taxes without consent.[27] By the time Thomas Jefferson leveled the same accusation against George III in the Declaration of Independence, the illegitimacy of the king's conduct could be taken for granted.

Just as the colonists had an ideologically sanctioned political tradition of liberty and property to defend, they also had (at least in New England) a revolutionary tradition to defend it with. This tradition originated with an incident that came to be known as the "Glorious Revolution in America." James II, shortly before his own deposition, had commissioned his "trusty and well-beloved Sir Edmund Andros" to be his "captain-general and governor-in-chief" of all the New England provinces and of "New York and East and West Jersey."[28] But Andros proved to be a political bungler second only to his royal master, whom he soon joined in forced retirement. By 1691, the ex-king's governor had committed two unpardonable sins. First, he offended and frightened New Englanders with his "Episcopalian zeal," allowing only Anglican ministers to perform marriages and publicly proclaiming the "martyrdom" of Charles I.[29] Second, Andros and his associates had "made laws for the levying of monies without the consent of the people either by themselves or by an assembly."[30] The authors of a pamphlet entitled *The Revolution in New England Justified* accused them of making "laws destructive to the liberty of the subjects, . . . for they made what laws they pleased without any consent of the people, either by themselves or representatives, which is indeed to destroy the fundamentals of the English . . . government."[31]

The authors then stated that this form of oppression, against which a revolution was justified and had in fact been carried out, had never been experienced anywhere in the English colonies except "where Sir Edmund Andros hath been governor."[32] This suggests that as far back as 1691, the principle of "no taxation without representation" was already institutionalized *throughout* the colonies, and that it was a principle which the colonists themselves, even then, were willing and able to defend against "innovations." As for Andros, he was returned to England in chains.

The Andros incident became a fertile historical source of legitimacy for the American Revolutionists. If an assault on liberty and property (and the threat of Anglican imposition) had justified a successful revolution in 1691, why not eighty years later, when the danger was so much greater and the stakes so much higher? The Boston radicals certainly recognized the educational value of New England's "revolutionary tradition." They reprinted and distributed the pamphlets from the Andros controversy in 1773 in order to remind the public of the historical continuity between New England's "glorious," revolutionary past and the "second revolution" now under way. The clergy, too, invoked the memory of the infamous "Sir Edmund Andros—a name never to be forgotten." The political moral of the story was that Andros and his government "had trampled upon all our laws and rights," but the people rose to the just defense of their liberty and property.[33]

Benjamin Wright observed that "in the relatively crude productions of 1689–91, one can discover many of the seeds which were to bear fruit after 1760."[34] The political writings from the Revolutionary period also addressed liberty and property, as well as the essentially connected issues of taxation, representation, and consent. They did so, however, with far greater theoretical sophistication. During the "second revolution," of course, the revolutionists had the opportunity to consult "Locke on Government," and this contributed a great deal to the improvement in their political theory.

Indeed, by 1747 "Locke on Government" was already being cited to justify organized and even violent political protest. In East New Jersey, "land-rioters," known also as the "Jerseymen," challenged the power of the large proprietors who had benefited from the contradictory seventeenth-century grants issued by the House of Stuart. The Jerseymen constituted a large, well-armed, organized movement whose activities included a serious attempt to set up a "counter-government." Since the existing laws and institutions of the province, as well as the official voice of London, favored the large proprietors, they saw no alternative to such radical action. When charged by their adversaries with "libel," "sedition," and "inbred malice to authority," the Jerseymen (who were hardly anarchists) sought legitimacy in "Locke on Government." In a lengthy written justification, they explicitly invoked the authority of Locke on the relationship between property and government; to drive the point home, they transcribed word for word twenty-five lines from sections 138 and 139 of the *Second Treatise*.[35]

In sum, by the 1760s, the colonists already had a revolutionary tradition rooted in concerns about liberty and property, taxation, representation, and consent. They enjoyed political institutions which embodied those concerns. And there had been at least one "local" historical episode in which Locke's theoretical formulations had actually been cited to justify revolutionary political action on behalf of liberty and property. Let us look now at the way those formulations figured in the continental protest that began in 1763.

In Revolutionary political thought the term "property" denoted a relationship between an individual and some object, not the object itself. That is, X becomes my property—or, I have property in X—only if I alone control the disposal of X. This control over the disposal of X can be called my liberty (or right or power) to dispose of X as I please, and in this sense liberty itself is involved in the definition of property. The right of disposal constitutes the defining condition of property and, indeed, the "substance of liberty." By 1767 this was said to have "fled to a distant country."[36]

The colonists and English politicians who opposed Parliament's "innovations" in revenue policy established their arguments on this conception of property. Property, as such, necessarily implied an "exclusive right of disposal. Property without this is but an insignificant name."[37] And here, at the very foundation of the central argument in Revolutionary polemics, the opposition adopted Locke's distinctive language and appealed directly to his authority. At the very least, the Revolutionists used the language that Locke had used, in order to make arguments that were essentially consistent with the arguments in the *Second Treatise*.

John Dickinson, in his celebrated *Letters from a Farmer*, borrowed "the words of Mr. Locke" from section 140 of the *Second Treatise* to ask the question that had captured the political attention of the colonists: "What property have they in that which another may, by right, take when he pleases to himself?"[38] "Hampden," in one of his broadsides, asked precisely this question, attributing it to "Mr. Locke."[39] "A Virginian" repeated the question, verbatim, in a letter to the *Pennsylvania Gazette*.[40] The same question (in quotes, but unattributed) opened an important official communication from The Sons of Liberty of New York.[41] William Hicks quoted these words from "Locke on Government" in his pamphlet, *On the Nature and Extent of Parliamentary Power*,[42] as did John Lathrop in a sermon preached nearly ten years later, in 1774.[43] And in a speech that was reprinted in several colonial newspapers, Charles Pratt, First Baron Camden, read these (and other) "words of that consummate reasoner and politician, Mr. Locke," before the House of Lords to support the colonists in their opposition to parliamentary taxation.[44]

The Revolutionists and their friends also favored section 138 of the *Second Treatise* because it, too, went straight to the heart of the matter. This section begins with Locke's insistence that "the supreme power cannot take from any man any part of his property without his own consent." And it includes the statement that "no body hath a right to take their substance or any part of it from them, without their own consent; without this, they have no property at all. For I have truly no property in that which another can by right take from me, when he pleases, against my consent."

The opening lines from section 138 appeared, with attribution, in a letter to the *Pennsylvania Gazette*.[45] Other lines from this section found their way into an issue of the openly seditious, widely circulated *Massachusetts Spy*; a footnote directed readers to "Locke on Government."[46] The manifesto which marked the establishment of the Boston Committee of Correspondence in 1772 also included an exact transcription of lines from section 138. Recognizing this external textual evidence of the Lockean connection in that important historical document requires close and active familiarity with the *Second Treatise* itself, since the author(s) neither cited Locke nor enclosed the transcribed passage in quotation marks.[47]

There's more. For example, an anonymous author who signed his work "From the County of Hampshire" praised the "immortal Mr. Locke" and then transcribed the first seventeen lines of section 138, calling them "lines which ought to be written in letters of gold and sunk to the center of every man's heart."[48] John Allen, in a pamphlet entitled *The American Alarm*, closely paraphrased this passage from "the great Mr. Locke."[49] And Camden, America's champion at Westminster, reminded the Peers of the essential limits of the legislative power by reading aloud the first two lines of this section during the debate on the Declaratory Act.[50]

An observer of this historic debate recorded Lord Mansfield's reply to Camden, in which Parliament's right to tax the colonies was forcefully asserted. "As to Mr. Locke," Mansfield argued, "though he had said that money could not be raised in a free government without your own consent, yet it was no more than a general proposition never intended to extend to all particular circumstances whatever."[51] Nevertheless, Locke certainly intended for this general proposition to extend to, and even to define, "free government" as such. In fact, he presented it as a moral limitation on "the legislative power of *every* commonwealth, in *all* forms of government."[52] And with respect to particular circumstances, Camden reminded the Lords that Locke's proposition was "drawn from the heart of our constitution, which he thoroughly understood, and will last as long as that shall last."[53]

Both Camden and the Declaratory Act which he opposed figure prominently in our story. The latter, which we will consider later in this chapter, is especially important, since it lay at the heart of the constitutional issue that had come between the colonies and the mother country after 1764, namely, defining the limits of the legislative authority. Camden himself, according to Samuel Adams, thoroughly understood the Lockean nature of that issue. In a letter to Camden in 1768, Adams praised him for his "great knowledge of the constitution and the law of nature, of the extent of parliamentary authority and the rights of British subjects."[54] Camden had furnished plenty of evidence of this knowledge in his eloquent speeches on behalf of the colonists. Speaking for the first time before the House of Lords on February 3, 1766, Camden cited Locke and issued this warning: "The sovereign authority, the omnipotence of the legislature, my lords, is a favorable doctrine, but there are some things they cannot do."[55]

This may be the most concise statement of the constitutional principle in the written record of the American Revolution. On the basis of this statement, Randolph G. Adams, writing in 1922, described Camden as "one Englishman who had read his Locke . . . and who seems almost like a voice crying in the wilderness of parliamentary sovereignty and supremacy."[56] Ernest Barker, too, called Camden "a solitary figure in England, however much his view," which "corroborated" Locke's, "might be acclaimed across the Atlantic."[57] Finally, Van Tyne noted that "men who thought with Lord Camden . . . were in the minority in England, while those who agreed with [Samuel] Adams were in the majority in America."[58] This suggests that Locke's political theory was more highly esteemed and indeed more relevant in Revolutionary America than in his native land.

In Revolutionary America the colonists embraced the distinctively Lockean conception of property insofar as it essentially contained the notion of consent. I have no property in X—no control over the disposal of X—if "another" can take X from me "when he pleases," that

is, without my consent. Locke himself had expounded this notion of
the relationship between property and consent in section 139 of the
Second Treatise. "The prince or senate . . . can never have a power
to take to themselves the whole or any part of the subjects' *property*,
without their own consent. For this would be in effect to leave them
with no *property* at all." Locke reaffirmed his position in section 193,
where he held it to be in the nature of property that "without a man's
own consent, it cannot be taken from him." Transposing this formulation into the American Revolutionary context, Joseph Warren asked
how the colonists in North America could "be said to have property"
if the British government could, whenever it pleased, take all or any
part of it from them "without even asking their consent?"[59] From
the colonists' Lockean theoretical perspective, this was a rhetorical
question; no satisfactory answer could be found.

Consent, in any event, provided the only legitimating connection
between taxation and property. Parliament, however, severed that
connection when it enacted the new revenue measures. As the Connecticut House of Representatives complained in its Resolves of 1765,
"The consent of the inhabitants of this colony was not given to the
said Act of Parliament."[60] In its petition to the King, the Stamp Act
Congress objected to "statutes by which your Majesty's Commons in
Britain undertake absolutely to dispose of the property of their fellow subjects in America without their consent."[61] And in Parliament
itself, Lord Chatham (Pitt, the Elder) demanded that "the sacred-
ness" of the colonists' property "remain inviolable." It should be "tax-
able only by their own consent, given in their provincial assemblies;
else it will cease to be property."[62]

We should not underestimate the significance of consent in the
colonists' argument. "The consent of the people is the only foundation" of civil government; "therefore, every act of government . . .
against or without the consent of the people is injustice, usurpation,
and tyranny." Thus spoke the Massachusetts General Court (in words
attributed to John Adams) in January 1776 in a proclamation that was
read aloud in churches, courts, town halls, and taverns throughout
the Commonwealth.[63]

Property, moreover, required consent; and the person without property was nothing more than a slave. Property was "inconsistent" with slavery—at least one colonial writer actually quoted Locke on this point.[64] Locke himself had described the person who was "not capable of property" as "being in the *state of slavery*."[65] And for the colonists, "liberty, which distinguishes a free man from a slave, implies some sort of right and/or property of his own, which cannot be taken from him without his consent."[66] Consent creates, or at least preserves, property and thus stands between liberty and slavery. A government that takes an individual's property without his consent "commits a robbery" and "destroys the distinction between liberty and slavery."[67] As John Tucker put it, in an election sermon, liberty demands that "no man shall have his property taken from him, but by his own consent." Otherwise, Tucker asked, citing "Locke on Government," "what is he . . . but a perfect slave?"[68]

With this in mind, we should be careful not to misconstrue an early and representative description of the Stamp Act as "that mark of slavery" as simply a piece of rhetorical hyperbole or as a literary manifestation of some generalized paranoia that was distorting the colonists' political perception.[69] From the Lockean theoretical perspective of the colonial opposition, this described precisely the inescapable consequences of Parliament's revenue initiative. Silas Downer, a Rhode Island Son of Liberty, eloquently summarized the position in a few lines; and the Lockean thrust of the argument is unmistakably clear.

> The common people of Great Britain very liberally give and grant away the property of the Americans without their consent, which if yielded to, must fix us in the lowest bottom of slavery; for if they can take away one penny from us against our wills, they can take all. If they have such power over our property, they must have a proportional power over our persons; . . . hence . . . they can take away our lives whensoever it shall be agreeable to their sovereign wills and pleasure.[70]

Unless political practice incorporated the principle of consent, liberty would give way to slavery and life itself would be insecure. Par-

liament's "innovations" in revenue policy thus struck directly at the
indivisible Lockean triad of life, liberty, and property (estate).

From here we can put the issue of representation into perspective. The familiarity of the slogan "no taxation without representation" suggests that this was the focus of Revolutionary agitation.
Representation was undeniably important (especially to the representatives). In Revolutionary political theory, however, representation
was merely the institutional mechanism through which the people
could register their consent to the taxes they were expected to pay.
As such, it did not enjoy the status of a "first principle." The Massachusetts House of Representatives clearly recognized the *derivative*
nature of the right of representation while upholding the *fundamental* principle of consent in its Resolves of 1765: "No man can justly
take the property of another without his consent. . . . Upon this
original principle, the right of representation in the same body which
exercises the power of making laws for levying taxes . . . is evidently
founded." Thus when the House spoke of "certain essential Rights
. . . which are founded in the Law of God and Nature, and are the
common Rights of Mankind," this meant, in the first place, the "inherent" right to consent to the disposal of one's property. No man
could be deprived of this right by any "Law of Society . . . consistent with the Law of God and Nature." The right of representation,
on the other hand, did not usually receive authorization at the very
highest level.[71]

Though secondary to consent in this strict theoretical sense, representation for the colonists was indeed a non-negotiable political
demand. "Representation . . . in our constitution," wrote "Junius
Americanus" (citing "Mr. Locke's doctrine"), is "the mode of giving
consent." Thus "representation and taxation are constitutionally inseparable," and there must be no taxation without representation.[72]
Camden went even further than this, actually bestowing upon representation the theological sanction that the Massachusetts House
of Representatives reserved only for the "*original* principle" of consent. He maintained that "taxation and representation are inseparably united; God hath joined them, [and] no British Parliament can

separate them." He then stated that "this position is founded on the laws of nature," and "is itself an eternal law of nature."[73]

Nevertheless, it was tradition and necessity, and not theology or metaphysics, that made representation the constitutional "mode of giving consent" and thus gave it such a visible and important role in Revolutionary argument. On the one hand, representation was already a cherished institution in American politics by 1760. The tracts from the Andros affair show that, as early as 1691, representation was already deemed an institution worth fighting for.[74] On the other hand, although only a mechanism, representation was nonetheless the only mechanism, practically speaking, through which consent could be given to proposals affecting a great number of widely dispersed people. Self-government on a scale larger than that of the small town absolutely depended on it. Thus, in their separate declarations of 1765, the colonial legislatures of South Carolina and New Jersey, as well as the Stamp Act Congress, spoke literally as one: "It is inseparably essential to the freedom of a people, and the undoubted right of Englishmen, that no taxes be imposed on them but with their own consent, given personally, or by their representatives."[75]

Though Locke himself did not have a "political theory of representation," he continued to furnish the Revolutionists with the means of expression by including the concept of representation in his formulations on property, taxation, consent, and the limits of legislative authority per se. In enumerating those essential limits in the *Second Treatise*, he stated in section 142 that the legislative "must *not raise taxes* on the property of the people, *without the consent of the people,* given by themselves or their deputies." Locke recognized the need for taxation in civil society. But "the preservation of property being the end of government, and that for which men enter into society,"[76] consent constitutes an indispensable condition for legitimacy in the transfer of property from individuals to the government (though apparently not "for the regulating of property between the subjects one amongst another").[77] Thus he maintained in section 140: " 'Tis true, governments cannot be supported without great charge, and 'tis fit everyone who enjoys his share of the protection should pay out of his estate his proportion for the maintenance of it. But still it must be with his own consent, i.e., the consent of the majority, giving it either by themselves, or by their representatives chosen by them." Without consent, taxation "invades the *fundamental law of property*, and subverts the end of Government." Consent, however, can be given through representatives freely chosen by the people. The people have "reserved to themselves the choice of their *representatives*, as the fence to their properties."[78] Representation is therefore consistent with civil society, whose chief end is the preservation of property (understood not merely as material possessions or "estate," but as "life, liberty, and estate").[79]

The Revolutionists took a distinctively and often explicitly Lockean approach to this vital issue of representation. At the very least their approach was consistent with the basic tenets of Locke's political theory. In addition to some of the passages from the Revolutionary writings already cited in this chapter, consider a few more of the prominent but essentially representative expressions of the colonists' position. In a petition to Parliament protesting the proposed Stamp Act, the Virginia House of Burgesses declared: "It is essential to British liberty that the laws imposing taxes on the people ought not to be made without the consent of representatives chosen by themselves."[80] James Otis, the Boston radical, insisted that the British government had no right to levy taxes on the colonies unless the colonists were represented in Parliament.[81] According to Dr. Franklin, it was the "opinion" of the colonists that their property "ought not to be given away without their consent, by persons at a distance, unacquainted with their local circumstances and abilities."[82] Camden formulated his defense of the colonies around the same argument, with explicit appeals to Locke.[83] And the keynote speaker at the annual meeting of merchants in Philadelphia in 1768 quoted Locke's passages on representation directly as the most succinct way to state the theme of his address.[84]

The issue of representation took a peculiar form during the early stages of the controversy over the new revenue measures, as the debate turned to the notion of "virtual representation." The colonists, of course, demanded representation in the making of any laws that affected them. Supporters of the Stamp Act, on the other hand, argued that the colonists were represented in Parliament, virtually if not actually, that is, even though they did not elect and send representatives to Parliament; the colonies therefore could not claim exemption from parliamentary taxation on the grounds of representation. Although neither side took the notion of virtual representation seriously after the initial flurry of polemical exchanges, it still consumed a great deal of literary energy during the Stamp Act crisis. The debate therefore deserves some attention in this discussion of representation, particularly insofar as it can be related to Locke.

It should be noted, first, that while the colonists rejected the notion of virtual representation, they did not demand actual representation *in Parliament*. Quite the contrary. The Massachusetts Resolves of 1765 declared that representation in Parliament "is *impracticable* for the subjects in America." The New Jersey Resolves of 1765 stated that "the people of this colony are not, and from their remote situations cannot be, represented in the Parliament of Great Britain." The Stamp Act Congress reaffirmed this principle in its Declarations, as well as in its Petition to the House of Commons.[85] In fact, the colonists would have flatly rejected an offer to send representatives to Parliament since that would only "secure to the Parliament the right they claim to tax us." Actual representation in Parliament, then, would "annihilate effectually the power of our assemblies."[86] And as we have seen, the determination to preserve that power was a fundamental factor in bringing about the American Revolution.

Nevertheless, some of the defenders of the new revenue measures at first asserted that the colonies, like certain boroughs in England which did not elect members to the House of Commons, enjoyed a virtual representation in Parliament. Thomas Whately, for instance, insisted "that the colonies are represented in Parliament. They do not indeed choose members of that assembly," he conceded; but neither do "nine-tenths of the people of Britain." Each member of the House of Commons represents "all the commons of Great Britain," and not simply his electoral constituency. All are represented; all are therefore obliged to submit to Parliament.[87] Soame Jenyns, who also invoked the doctrine of virtual representation to defend the Stamp Act, wanted to know why this system of representation did not "extend to America as well as over the whole island of Great Britain." If Manchester and Birmingham can be represented in Parliament without electing members, Jenyns asked, "why are not the cities of Albany and Boston equally represented in that assembly?"[88]

The colonists attacked the doctrine of virtual representation from two directions; and the differences between these approaches reflected the regional differences, as well as the corresponding differences in theoretical orientations, that were discussed in the previous chapter.

James Otis of Boston expounded the more radical position. Otis rejected virtual representation per se, offering this political prescription: "To what purpose is it to ring everlasting changes to the colonists on the cases of Manchester, Birmingham, and Sheffield? If those now so considerable places are not represented, they ought to be."[89] For Carl Becker, Otis's "'ought to be' is the fundamental premise of the whole colonial argument"—the essentially revolutionary normative impulse.[90] This impulse explains, and is expressed in, the colonists' ultimate recourse to Lockean abstractions of natural law and natural rights; for "the 'ought to be' is not ultimately to be found in positive law and custom, but only in something outside of, beyond, above the positive law and custom."[91] As Benjamin Wright observed, "an appeal from that which is legally established to that which should be established almost invariably involves the assertion of principles of a higher validity than those made by human legislatures."[92] And for the colonists, the "principles of a higher validity"—the principles from which the fundamental norms of the Revolution were drawn—were the principles of God, divine law, the law of nature.

Otis's preferred source on the law of nature, moreover, was John Locke. He explicitly recommended Locke's ideas over those of the Scottish Enlightenment philosophers, Hugo Grotius and Samuel Pufendorf, precisely on this crucial subject. John Dunn, in his influential essay discounting the significance of Locke's political theory in Revolutionary thought, claims that in America, his *Two Treatises* "never held the unimpeachable eminence of the works of Grotius and

Pufendorf."[93] According to Otis, however, the latter made it "their constant practice to establish the matter of right on the matter of fact"—here Otis cited with approval Rousseau's critique of Grotius. He then directed his readers to those "purer fountains" of natural-law theory, "particularly Mr. Locke."[94] Here, in Locke's doctrine, Otis discovered the norms that would animate Revolutionary political thought. It was essentially a Lockean "ought to be" that served as the "fundamental premise of the whole colonial argument."

Daniel Dulany of Maryland, in contrast to Otis, produced a legalistic refutation of virtual representation based, as it were, upon a study of comparative politics. Dulany did not reject virtual representation as such; but he did show that the "notion of a virtual representation *of the colonies* . . . is a mere cobweb, spread to catch the unwary and entangle the weak."[95] Dulany argued that virtual representation, to be consistent with liberty, presupposed an identity of interests among everyone involved in the political system—the electors, nonelectors, and representatives. "The security of the non-electors against oppression is that their oppression will fall also upon the electors and the representatives."[96] There may indeed have been such an identity of interests in England, Dulany allowed, where a system of virtual representation could thus be justified. But a "total dissimilarity of situation" subsisted between the mother country and the colonies. "There is not that intimate and inseparable relation between the electors of Great Britain and the inhabitants of the colonies which must inevitably involve both in the same taxation."[97] A virtual representation of the colonies in Parliament, then, would not be consistent with liberty. Dulany concluded that the principle of the Stamp Act had to be "given up as indefensible on the point of representation, and the validity of it rested upon the power which they who framed it have to carry it into execution."[98]

Resting the case for the Stamp Act on the theory of virtual representation turned out to be a strategic blunder of the first magnitude. A thin theory such as this could not bear the heavy burden of justification which the proponents of the Stamp Act had imposed upon it. And the theory's implied negation of existing political practice in the colonies ensured a prompt and vigorous response from that quarter. This defense of the Stamp Act thus provided an easy and irresistible target for the opponents of that legislation.

Moreover, as a justification for taxation, the theory of virtual representation contained a crucial concession to the colonial opposition insofar as the theory made its stand on "the point of representation"; for this presupposed that the power to tax depended upon representation per se, and that taxation was therefore the prerogative of some kind of representative assembly.[99] In short, only representation, as a mechanism of consent, could make taxation legitimate. This concession was all that remained of the theory of virtual representation by the time the opposition writers had put it out of its misery. But this was enough to turn the tables and put "propriety" on the American side of the argument.[100]

How did Lockean theory fit into the debate over virtual representation? On the Tory side, not well at all. Locke insisted that the majority must give their consent to taxation "either by themselves, or by their representatives chosen by them."[101] He did not say that the majority could give their consent through *representatives chosen by others for them*. Locke's argument, then, was friendly to the Revolutionists and hostile to the proponents of virtual representation. Perhaps for this reason, I have failed to find a single appeal to "Locke on Government" for the purpose of justifying parliamentary taxation of the American colonies on the grounds of virtual representation— though Soame Jenyns, the defender of virtual representation, *attacked* Locke's theory of government.[102]

But Locke did have something to offer the Revolutionists (as the passage just quoted clearly suggests). In addition to Otis's important reference to Locke's theory of natural law in a pamphlet attacking virtual representation, Dulany's argument also followed the Lockean line on a crucial point. Dulany made an identity of interests between electors, nonelectors, and representatives the precondition for liberty in a system of virtual representation; a system without that identity of interests would necessarily become oppressive. Locke, on the other hand, warns against governments that "think themselves to have a distinct interest from the rest of the community, and so will be apt to increase their own riches and power by taking what they think fit from the people." [103] Locke's argument seems essentially consistent with the central point in Dulany's refutation of virtual representation.

Dulany himself did not mention Locke. But Locke's warning about a "distinct interest" is from the often-quoted section 138 of the *Second Treatise*, so the odds are that Dulany had encountered it before, if not in the *Second Treatise* itself then in the writings of his contemporaries. In fact, at least one Revolutionary author actually repeated Locke's warning, in Locke's own words, precisely in this context. "A Virginian" wrote to the editors of the *Pennsylvania Gazette*, referring to Locke as a "great philosopher and statesman" and offering several passages from the *Second Treatise* to support the colonists on a number of issues; and his inventory of Lockean passages included section 138, which he aimed specifically at the theory of virtual representation. [104] But even if Dulany had neither read the *Second Treatise* nor learned about it from his contemporaries (two very slim possibilities), his argument could hardly be regarded as one which Locke would have opposed. Locke, indeed, would have stood with both Dulany and the more radical Otis against the theory of virtual representation.

Let's consider the analysis to this point, in terms of the methodological categories developed in the previous chapter. In sum, there is sufficient textual evidence, both internal and external, to establish the formal Lockean connection with respect to these central issues in American Revolutionary thought. This connection does not depend entirely, or even primarily, upon the identification of sources in the Revolutionary writings. The purpose here is not to show that an idea, argument, or doctrine in a sample of Revolutionary writing came from Locke (which would be impossible to prove with regard to *any* source, even in the presence of the most explicit external evidence), but that it is distinctively Lockean (or consistent with the Lockean-liberal spirit, which is understood in terms of a textually sound, historically appropriate interpretation of Locke's thought). In this case, internal and external textual evidence supports the conclusion that the fundamental Revolutionary argument was essentially consistent with integral parts of the liberal political theory of the *Second Treatise*.

Could the Revolutionists have obtained their Lockean arguments about consent, taxation, representation, and property from a "Lockean" source other than Locke himself? This is certainly a possibility. If so, however, it would not make the arguments any less Lockean, or any less liberal; it would not make Locke's political theory any less congenial to the Revolutionary position; and there is still the fact that in terms of external evidence, Locke is by far the most visible source.[105] In any case, it is impossible to rule out all sources other than Locke; and since the identification of sources is not our primary concern, it is not necessary to do so. Nevertheless, it would be interesting to see how some of these pivotal issues are handled in *Cato's Letters*, the principle "non-Lockean" source of Revolutionary thought.[106]

"Cato" establishes his position in his ninety-seventh Letter: "The first care which wise governors will always take is to prevent their subjects from wanting and to secure them in the possession of their property, upon which everything else depends."[107]

This passage is interesting for two reasons. First, Cato's position is hardly antithetical to Locke's "bourgeois" argument that the chief end of government is the protection of property. We somehow expect something different from this major source of "essentially anticapitalistic" American republicanism (though perhaps not from the spokesman for "extreme libertarianism," as Bailyn once characterized Cato).[108] Indeed, Locke's position is, as it were, less bourgeois than Cato's insofar as Locke includes life, liberty, and estate in his definition of property while Cato seems to mean estate only.[109] On the other hand, Cato is supposed to have been the voice of Aristotelian civic humanism in the eighteenth century; but his idea of what should constitute the "first care" of the magistrate is a far cry from Aristotle's demand "that the legislator should make the education of the young his chief and foremost concern."[110] Modern politics could use some civic humanism in this regard, but it will have to come from a source other than Cato's political doctrine.

Cato was closer to Locke than to Aristotle in defining the pri-

orities of government, but he still wasn't close enough for the purposes of Revolutionary argument. Consider the guidelines by which
Cato's "wise governors" will formulate revenue policies: "They will
raise no taxes but what the people shall see a necessity for raising;
and no longer than that necessity continues: and such taxes ought
to be levied cautiously, and laid out frugally." [111] Prudent advice indeed. And, again, there is nothing here with which Locke would
have quarreled. Neither Locke nor the American colonists, however,
would have accepted such taxation as legitimate. Cato did not mention consent; he did not mention representation. In short, Cato had
little to offer the Revolutionists on these crucial issues. Their argument required the language of consent and representation, woven
into a political theory of limited government, with a moral justification for revolution to give it teeth. This is why they turned most often
to "Locke on Government," and adopted the distinctively Lockean-
liberal position, in their hour of need.

The Revolutionists, of course, did not read "Locke on Government" and consequently decide that representation was a good idea.
It was the century of pre-Revolutionary political experience that
pushed representation into the forefront of Revolutionary argument
and endowed Locke's political theory with such great contemporary
significance. Here it is worth recalling Carl Becker's explanation of
Locke's appeal to the Revolutionists: They turned to Locke because
their own governments actually conformed, "in a rough and ready
way," to the kind of government "for which Locke had furnished
a reasoned foundation." Locke's political theory "assured them that
their own governments, with which they were well content, were just
the kind that God had designed men by nature to have!" [112]

Sir Ernest Barker called this synthesis of Lockean theory and colonial political experience "the essence of the American Revolution." [113]
Quoting Locke's chapter "Of the Extent of the Legislative Power,"
Junius Americanus (Arthur Lee) captured the spirit of this synthesis
(and provided the title for this book) in 1772:

"[T]he prince or senate . . . can never have the power to take to
themselves the whole or any part of the subjects property without

their consent." Here the American line seems fairly drawn. . . .
Representation being in our constitution the mode of giving consent, representation and taxation are constitutionally inseparable.
This is Mr. Locke's doctrine, it is the doctrine of reason and truth,
and it is, Sir, *the unvarnished doctrine of the Americans.*[114]

Given the established political tradition in the colonies, as well as
the influence of the colonial representatives whose power was directly
threatened by Parliament's "innovations," it is difficult to imagine
the Revolutionists taking the non-Lockean, or anti-Lockean, position which revisionist historians have attributed to them. Indeed,
what *is* the non-Lockean, or anti-Lockean, position on representation, consent, and the limits of governmental authority? To find out,
let's return to the Declaratory Act, the target of Camden's eloquent
Lockean polemics in the House of Lords.

The Declaratory Act asserted the unlimited sovereignty of Parliament over the people of North America. Hardly anyone paid much
attention to the act when news of it first arrived in the colonies.[115]
It had been passed as a corollary to the Repeal of the Stamp Act in
1766, on the same day (March 18), and the general rejoicing over
that apparent victory for liberty and property temporarily drowned
out its ominous message, which was essentially a promise to abolish
both: "the King's Majesty, by and with the advice and consent of
the Lords Spiritual and Temporal, and Commons of Great Britain, in
Parliament assembled, had, hath, and of right ought to have, full
power and authority to make laws and statutes of sufficient force and
validity to bind the colonies and the people of America, subjects
of the crown of Great Britain, *in all cases whatsoever.*"[116] Parliament
wanted the colonists to know that it was repealing a *particular* tax
law without in any way surrendering its claim to the *right* to resume
taxation at its exclusive discretion.

But the Declaratory Act went much further than that. It had the
stink of real despotism about it. The British government did not
restrict its claim of legislative authority to economic policy but im-
modestly extended it to "all cases whatsoever." Taxation was only one
form of legislation. In fact, following the repeal of the Townshend

Act in 1769, taxation ceased to be much of an issue. The Intolerable Acts, which propelled England and the colonies into armed conflict, had little to do with taxation. In short, the Act proclaimed Parliament's right to do anything it wished with respect to the people of America, even that which they feared most.

John Adams clarified the issue and linked the colonists' greatest fear to the chilling implications of the Declaratory Act. Adams recognized the centrality of the Act's underlying principle in the Anglo-American dispute. He called the "authority of Parliament . . . the essence of the whole controversy," and referred to "the power of Parliament" as "the secret, latent principle upon which all encroachments against us are founded." Most fearsome of these was the encroachment upon religious liberty. "If Parliament could tax us," Adams wrote, "it could establish the Church of England" in America. And he knew that *nothing* served to mobilize Revolutionary political thinking more than the dreaded prospect of an army of Anglican bishops landing in America to reimpose the religious tyranny from which the colonists' ancestors had fled in the first place.[117]

Some very astute people actually believed this to be Parliament's secret intention. Jonathan Mayhew, the influential clergyman who liked to cite Locke and who had close ties to James Otis,[118] warned that "the stamping and episcopizing of our colonies are only different branches of the same plan of power"; the revenues that Parliament hoped to obtain through the stamp tax were "partly intended to maintain a standing army of bishops" in the American colonies.[119] The Stamp Act had been defeated, but the lethal principle behind it had been enlarged and affirmed, not simply to preserve the honor of Parliament, but to pave the way for a total assault on liberty (civil as well as religious) and property in America.

With so much at stake, it is not surprising that the Declaratory Act and the "annihilating words" of its underlying principle—"in all cases whatsoever"—soon became the "foundation of all our complaints," the "bone of contention" and the "source of all these unhappy differences" between England and the colonies.[120] The colonists understood that "the present dispute . . . turns on the question of Parliamentary power," at the heart of which is Parliament's claim to bind

the colonies " 'in all cases whatsoever.' " [121] This "fatal edict" guaranteed "endless and numberless curses of slavery upon us, our heirs, and
their heirs forever." [122] It was "so subversive of liberty and so destructive of property" that it indisputably promised "to reduce Americans
to the most abject slavery." [123] Concede anything to Parliament on
this issue and we might as well "give up the matter and submit to
slavery at once." [124]

The colonists did not concede. They made repeal of the Declaratory Act a precondition for reconciliation with the mother country. [125]
And when Parliament refused to comply, they took up arms "not . . .
merely to drown a chest of tea, but to oppose the dangerous authority"
which Parliament had "usurped, pretending a right to bind us 'in all
cases whatsoever.' " [126]

The centrality of the principle of the Declaratory Act in the conflict between England and the colonies meant that the theoretical
question of the American Revolution was, fundamentally, a *Lockean* question: "the extent of the legislative power." [127] Locke provided
not only the question but the answer, too—to paraphrase Camden
(who would still be a maverick at Westminster), there are some things
that Parliament, or *any* civil authority, cannot do. Parliament had
claimed that its authority over the colonists was "not only supreme
but illimitable." [128] Far from supporting the illimitable sovereignty of
Parliament, however, Lockean political theory does precisely the opposite. For Locke, the legislature is the supreme organ of government,
but its supremacy is contingent; it is neither absolute nor unlimited;
and the last word always belongs to the people.

First, there is "natural law, which is to govern even the legislative itself," and which "stands as an eternal rule to all men, *legislators*
as well as others." [129] Second, legislative power is "only a fiduciary
power," which has been established by the people only "to act for certain ends." Yet "there remains still in the people a supreme power to
remove or alter the legislative, when they find the legislative act contrary to the trust reposed in them." [130] It should be noted, moreover,
that the very things Parliament was attempting to do—for instance,
taking property without the consent of the people—were specifically

proscribed in the *Second Treatise* by both natural law and the fiduciary nature of civil authority.[131]

In short, the *Second Treatise* establishes "the *Bounds* which the trust that is put in them by the Society, and the Law of God and Nature, have *set to the Legislative* Power of every Commonwealth, in all Forms of Government."[132] Lockean constitutionalism, which we may call the liberal doctrine of limited government, thus directly contradicts the absolutist position staked out by Parliament in the Declaratory Act.

Locke's argument in the *Letter on Toleration*, which was highly esteemed in New England, is also relevant in this context.[133] Locke's constitutionalism and Lockean toleration converge when Locke declares that "the care of souls cannot belong to the civil magistrate," and that the civil power "neither can nor ought in any way to be extended to the salvation of souls";[134] for this, in essence, is to impose yet another strategic restriction upon the legislative power (and perhaps the most important one of all). The Declaratory Act, however, did not recognize this restriction, either. "In all cases whatsoever" extended in principle to the soul as well as to the purse. This is precisely why people like Adams and Mayhew were so upset. The Declaratory Act only reinforced the already formidable alliance between the politicians and the clergy, since both would be "rendered useless," if not worse, in the new era of parliamentary sovereignty.

The Revolutionists, at any rate, found Locke to be an indispensable ally in opposing the principle of the Declaratory Act. *They* knew that the question before them was a Lockean question and that Locke had furnished the only answer consistent with liberty. " 'But,' says the famous Mr. Locke, 'whenever a power exists in a state over which the people have no control, the people are completely enslaved.' If this be the case, what shall we say to the claim of Parliament to legislate for us 'in all cases whatsoever'?"[135] The Revolutionists and their friends in Parliament frequently turned to Locke on this vital issue— sometimes in arguments that attacked the Declaratory Act by name, elsewhere in arguments that challenged its underlying principle of illimitable legislative sovereignty. Some of these arguments were explicitly Lockean, others distinctively so. In terms of our methodological categories, the evidence here is both external and internal, and it points unmistakably to a Lockean connection of high significance.[136]

To say that Locke had nothing to offer the Revolutionists in their theoretical struggle against the principle of the Declaratory Act,[137] or that Locke's arguments supported Parliament's position in that struggle,[138] accomplishes three things. First, it betrays an astonishing failure to recognize the very basics of Locke's political theory. It is hard to believe that Locke's spirited advocacy of limited, as explicitly opposed to unlimited, government would be missed by anyone even remotely familiar with his name or work, but apparently this is the case.

Second, these claims deprive the Revolutionists of their theoretical voice on the fundamental issue of the Revolution itself. Here, however, the claims are simply unhistorical, since the colonists did cite Locke, and did make distinctively Lockean arguments, to challenge the "fatal edict." They used Locke *correctly*, too. Indeed, as seen from the analysis of Joseph Galloway's pamphlet in the previous chapter, extreme forms of textual mutilation were required to bring Locke into line with the Tory position.

Finally, and perhaps most serious of all, these claims do more than betray theoretical confusion and unhistorical interpretation. Denying that Locke's liberal doctrine of limited government played an important and positive role in the founding ideology destroys the essential source of historical legitimacy for the defense of constitutional politics in the modern age. What other political theory *inherently* imposes limits on political power, in both temporal and spiritual affairs? An American Revolution without Lockean liberalism appeals to those who think of Lockean liberalism only as an apology for bourgeois excess; but an American Revolution without Lockean constitutionalism could have a steep political price in the struggle against new "encroachments" upon civil and religious liberties in America.

We have established the formal Lockean connection in American Revolutionary thought with respect to the Revolutionists' defense of liberty and property and their demand for constitutional politics and limited government. Although this goes a long way toward correct-

ing some of the excesses of revisionist historiography, it does not by
any means exhaust the topics upon which the Revolutionists turned
to Locke more frequently than to any other secular source. Some of
these topics will be covered in depth in subsequent analyses of clerical thought in New England. But the external evidence clearly shows
that the "secular" authors also called upon Locke to support their
views on a variety of issues (and in many ways their arguments echoed
the clerical teaching).

For example, these authors trusted Locke to elucidate the revolutionary "politicks of St. Paul" and the distinction between tyrants
and magistrates.[139] They often invoked the authority of Locke on the
fiduciary nature of civil authority, the "dissolution of government,"
and the political judgment and ultimate sovereignty of the people.[140]
The opposition writers also recommended Locke as a source of wisdom on prerogative,[141] tyranny,[142] toleration,[143] liberty,[144] the proper
end of government,[145] independence from Great Britain,[146] and other
topics.[147] Conspicuously absent from this list, however, were the characteristic concerns of the "bourgeois Locke": possessive individualism, uninhibited accumulation, hedonism, the "spirit of capitalism."
In short, the Revolutionists did not cite Locke's notorious chapter
"Of Property." They cited Locke as an authority on constitutional
politics and revolution.[148]

Internal evidence also supports the formal Lockean connection
over a wide range of topics in the secular writings from the Revolution. Here again, the theoretical concern was not to excuse bourgeois appropriation, but to specify the extent and nature of civil
authority and to justify resistance and revolution where civil authority had exceeded, or intended to exceed, the bounds of legitimacy. Many authors—some of whom cited Locke elsewhere, on these
and other matters—wrote in Lockean terms and Lockean language
about life, liberty, and property, and the end of civil government.[149]
They offered distinctively Lockean formulations on power-as-a-trust,
popular political judgment, and the "dissolution of government" and
reversion of the supreme constituent power to the people.[150] Their
arguments for the right and duty to resist closely paralleled those in
the Second Treatise.[151] They tacitly invoked the combined authority of

Locke and St. Paul to set forth the "political maxims of America."[152] Like Locke himself, these authors made the crucial distinction between tyrants and magistrates,[153] condemning the former as rebels who ought to be resisted and overthrown.[154] And they voiced distinctively Lockean misgivings about the union of church and state.[155]

On all of these vitally important issues, the very least that can be concluded on the basis of the internal textual evidence of the formal connection is that in terms of language, theory, and prescription, American Revolutionary thought differed in no essential way from Lockean-liberal political theory. Yet even this unnecessarily modest conclusion calls into severe question the now-orthodox assertion that the language of the Revolution was "a language in which Locke himself did not figure,"[156] not to mention the suggestion that Locke should be counted among the "adversaries" of the ideology of the American Revolution.[157] Take into account the external textual evidence and some of the extreme pronouncements of the historiographic revolution retreat entirely from history into the realm of fiction.[158]

The formal connection, supported as it is by internal and external evidence, stands as a historical-textual refutation of these and other attempts to rid the founding doctrine of its Lockean-liberal elements. While the formal connection does not imply a return to the exclusivity and monolithicism of the Locke model of interpretation, it does restore some historical balance to our understanding of American Revolutionary thought.

Yet this is only the formal connection. For all its importance, it touches only the surface of Lockean thought. The analysis of the substantive Lockean connection in the political thought of the New England clergy will probe much more deeply into the realm of interpretation in order to establish more fundamental affinities between Lockean thought and the political thought of the American Revolution. To prepare for this analysis, we first need to consider how the interpretation of political theory, both Lockean and republican, affects our understanding the founding doctrine.

4

Historiography and the Interpretation of

Political Theory

Of all the lessons that could be drawn from the historiographic revolution in the study of American Revolutionary thought, perhaps the most important is this: We need to incorporate a more demanding standard for interpreting political theory into the methodology of historical research.

As it has evolved from a rebellion against Hartz into orthodoxy, the republican revision of American Revolutionary thought has tended to neglect the interpretation of political theory. In happily proclaiming the historical triumph (and normative superiority?) of civic republicanism over Lockean liberalism, too much has been taken for granted about both. Lockean liberalism, to the extent that it is said to stand for anything, represents the bourgeois ethos—hedonism, materialism, self-interest. This generally corresponds in spirit to the unfriendly interpretations of C. B. Macpherson and Leo Strauss.[1] Republicanism, on the other hand, is uncritically hailed, by political theorists as well as historians, as the civic humanist alternative to Lockean liberalism, the doctrine of virtue offering ideological salvation for "the lost soul of American politics."[2] Building upon these interpretative assumptions, the revision portrays the development of the founding doctrine as a kind of morality play in which civic virtue (republicanism) triumphs over commerce and corruption (liberalism) in the American Revolution.

A morality play is immensely satisfying (if your side wins); but it is also an extreme abbreviation—and in that sense a serious distortion—of history. Ironically, this criticism of the republican revision offers the well-intentioned friends of "Cato," who may become disenchanted with their champion after reading a bit further, a chance to reconsider their commitments. The rise of Cato and the decline of Locke would be a setback for liberty if, as an examination of the relevant texts suggests, this means the elevation of Hobbes disguised as a "republican" and the suppression of the liberal-constitutionalist essence in the founding doctrine. Unmediated by Lockean liberalism, American republicanism might be more than the revisionists anticipated. It is fortunate, then, and not unexpected in the Revolutionary context, that, as shown in the previous chapter, the Revolutionists took the Lockean-liberal alternative to political absolutism and obedience "in all cases whatsoever" as the "unvarnished doctrine of the Americans." The historical path leads back to Locke, but to Locke properly understood.

"Properly understood" implies that there is a great deal more to Lockean liberalism than the caricature that generally informs revisionist historiography. The *Second Treatise* may indeed look like "bourgeois ideology" to some modern interpreters (from both the left and the right), but the "spirit of capitalism" is neither the only nor the most important quality that it conveys. And in all events, the many Revolutionists who admired Locke and regarded him as their foremost theoretical ally against the forces of political despotism did not see him in that light. For them, "Mr. Locke's doctrine" was essentially the doctrine of consent, lawful and limited government, toleration, and resistance to tyranny. But in dismissing Lockean thought as insignificant, irrelevant, or antagonistic in relation to the ideology of the American Revolution, the revisionists have inadvertently thrown the precious babies of political constitutionalism out with the bath water of bourgeois ideology. The founding doctrine consequently loses its intrinsic justification for liberal politics. This is not a matter to be taken lightly.

The previous chapter sought to inject some history and political theory into the morality play and to repair, thereby, some of the damage that has been inflicted upon the founding doctrine by the excesses of the historiographic revolution. Drawing from a wide range of Revolutionary writings, it demonstrated the textual existence of the formal Lockean connection with regard to the vital issues in Revolutionary argument, while abolishing the idea of a "Tory Locke." We proceed now with a more concentrated focus in the Revolutionary writings (the sermons of the New England clergy), a more extensive consideration of Lockean thought (the "theistic Locke"), and some critical commentary on the revisionists' political theory. The interpretation of political theory thus becomes even more important as this study of American Revolutionary thought continues.

This chapter prepares the ground for that analysis. We begin by examining how the revisionists have fared in the field of interpretation with respect both to Lockean thought and to the political thought which, they say, most heavily influenced the creation of American republicanism. This will raise some interesting questions about the theoretical structure and coherence of the republican paradigm itself. We then turn to the interpretation of Lockean thought that informs the analysis of the substantive Lockean connection. The legitimacy and use of this interpretation will be established and justified in terms of the two criteria of interpretation that were defined in chapter one— viz., textual availability and historical appropriateness. We'll also consider the "bourgeois Locke" in relation to these criteria.

This chapter thus serves simultaneously as a critique of revisionist historiography from the interpretative perspective of political theory and as a link between the analyses of the formal and substantive Lockean connections in American Revolutionary thought. In short, it offers additional evidence of the crucial role that the interpretation of political theory plays in the formulation and revision of historical understanding.

In approaching the issue of interpretation as it involves the republican revision, *Cato's Letters*, the early-eighteenth-century collaboration by John Trenchard and Thomas Gordon, serves well as a point of departure. American republicanism may have had many sources. But the most authoritative voices in the revisionist movement proclaim *Cato's Letters* to have been "of the utmost importance in the creation of American republicanism."[3] It was primarily from Cato that Americans received the non-Lockean teaching that supposedly became the worldview of the American Revolution. It was through Cato's "country" ideology that Aristotle, Polybius, Cicero, Machiavelli, Harrington, Neville, etc., collectively captured the American Revolutionary mind, saving it from the corruption of liberalism by endowing it with a civic humanist, or republican, personality.

A closer look at Cato, however, reveals a startling discrepancy between what he actually says and the ideas which the republican revision has attributed to him and, by extension, to American republicanism. And in some cases, the differences involve very basic yet fundamentally important points of political theory. For example, according to the quasi-official, frequently cited chronicle of the revision, Cato "believed that all men are naturally good and that citizens became restless only when oppressed."[4] Cato himself, however, says precisely the opposite.

For openers, Cato believes in original sin.[5] So, perhaps it is the devil who brings out the Machiavelli in him. Indeed, it seems impossible to reconcile Cato's alleged belief in innate human benevolence with the textually authentic Machiavellian nature of his political anthropology. Machiavelli characteristically eschews theological rationalizations and thus declines to discuss original sin. Nevertheless, his verdict on human nature is quite severe. "Men are more prone to evil than to good," he says. In fact, they "never do good unless necessity drives them to it." Machiavelli's prince legislates and rules, survives and prospers on the assumption that "all men are wicked and that they will always give vent to the malignity that is in their minds when opportunity affords."[6] And as for Cato, he also insists that "the making of laws supposes all men naturally wicked."[7]

In noting this apparent disregard for the reality of the text, we are also obliged to inquire how a central figure in the Machiavellian-republican paradigm could ever be expected to believe that "all men are naturally good." That statement about Cato should have immediately aroused suspicion. Even the casual reader of Machiavelli's political theory knows that the assumption of human benevolence tends to shorten the tenure of the prince. Perhaps a reflexive association of the "negative" view of human nature with the despised "liberal para-digm" has tempted the revisionists to read their alternative to Locke through rose-colored glasses and to overlook the substance of Machia-velli's political teaching. Whatever the reason, their interpretation of Cato on the fundamentally important question of human nature pre-cisely contradicts the text and, indeed, is conceptually unintelligible in the context of a Machiavellian-republican paradigm.

This reference to Machiavelli in the context of interpreting the sources of American republicanism points to a theoretical problem deep within the Pocockian paradigm. The problem involves Pocock's understanding both of Machiavelli and of Locke, as well as the ironic relationship between the epic historiographies of Pocock and Strauss. Ultimately, it is the paradigmatic antithesis between republicanism and liberalism—a hallmark of revisionist extremism—which is at stake. And the outcome depends upon the interpretation of political theory.

Pocock's antithesis between liberalism and republicanism has al-ready been questioned by some astute critics. Jeffrey Isaac, for in-stance, suggests that the languages of liberalism and republicanism, "far from being mutually exclusive, are mutually interdependent com-ponents of the discourse of liberal capitalist society."[8] John Diggins believes that the ethos of "private interest" motivates behavior even when it wears the "public face" of republican rhetoric.[9] Like Isaac, Diggins sees a common reality underlying the apparently antithetical languages of liberalism and republicanism. I wish to suggest that the antithesis itself rests, at least in part, upon Pocock's tacit acceptance of the Strauss-Macpherson interpretation of Lockean liberalism.[10] If this is true, however, then Pocock wishes to have his cake and eat it too, by ordering à la carte, as it were, off Strauss's menu—a practice which Strauss himself would resist and which breaks the very rules of paradigmatic analysis upon which Pocock's own historiography operates.

Strauss and Pocock seem to agree on the meaning of Locke's thought (though not about its historical importance). And they both regard Machiavelli as the decisive figure in the history of political thought. But the two scholars are miles apart in defining Machiavelli's historical function. Pocock's Machiavelli served as the filter through which the civic humanism of Aristotle, Polybius, and Cicero passed into the modern world. For Strauss, Machiavelli was responsible for the great schism, not continuity, between ancients and moderns, between classical and modern political philosophy.[11]

The differences between Strauss and Pocock are most consequential, however, with respect to the nature of Machiavelli's teaching and to the relationship between Machiavelli and Locke in the history of political thought.[12] Pocock's Machiavelli is a hero. He describes Locke, on the other hand, as, at best, "no kind of classical or Machiavellian republican," and he offers an interpretation of American Revolutionary thought that "stresses Machiavelli at the expense of Locke," indeed, to the exclusion of Locke.[13] He even casts the bourgeois Locke as the chief (if not the only) ideological adversary of the republican principles championed by Machiavelli and, later, by the Revolutionists who had inherited them (primarily through Cato).

But Strauss does not see any antithesis between the republican Machiavelli and the liberal Locke; nor does he confer any honors upon the Florentine Secretary. Quite the contrary. First, Strauss's Locke perfected what Strauss's Machiavelli had begun. Machiavelli became "victorious" through Locke. Locke is thus the completion, and not the negation, of Machiavelli.[14] Moreover, these gentlemen were partners in crime. Machiavelli taught corruption, not virtue; above all, he was the "teacher of evil," not the benevolent medium for Aristotelian civic humanist ideals.[15] Machiavelli and Locke contribute to the same pathology in Strauss's history of political philosophy; and Machiavelli, indeed, is the source of the contagion.

It is worth noting why Strauss treats Machiavelli like the plague, suppressing much that is positive and poignant in his political thought.[16] Strauss does this largely because his account of the history of political thought requires a prince of darkness to subvert the "Great Tradition" (a role he had originally assigned to Thomas Hobbes but later transferred to Machiavelli). As John Gunnell observes in his penetrating analysis of Strauss's paradigm, "interpretations of particular works are viewed principally as a means of reconstructing the tradition as a whole."[17] In this way, Strauss's historiography also demands the services of the bourgeois Locke to complete the devil's work initiated by Machiavelli, thus contributing to the fall of Western political philosophy.

Pocock's problem arises from the assumption that he can appropriate one integral component of Strauss's paradigm and plug it into his own. But Strauss's subjects derive their essential meaning primarily from the parts they play in his "dramaturgical account of the corruption of modernity" and from their relationships to the other dramatis personae.[18] The bourgeois Locke becomes unintelligible without the "teacher of evil" and the Great Tradition which these two villains helped to overturn. Pocock, however, tears the bourgeois Locke from his essential historiographical context, leaving behind his inseparable companion. He takes Strauss's Locke without Strauss's Machiavelli and without Strauss's history of political thought. But Strauss does not offer one without the others: It's all or nothing. Indeed, "all or nothing" is the Fundamental Law (and the Fundamental Flaw) of Paradigmatic Analysis, be it Straussian, Pocockian, or Hartzian.

Centering his paradigm on Machiavelli, then, Pocock confronts the following alternatives: First, he could adopt a Locke other than the one fashioned by Strauss, i.e., other than the bourgeois Locke. He could thereby withdraw from the untenable (and dangerous) antithesis between republicanism and liberalism. Second, he could continue with the bourgeois Locke and, obeying the Fundamental Law of Paradigmatic Analysis, redefine Machiavelli in Straussian terms, i.e., as the "teacher of evil." The "Machiavellian moment" would then mark the genesis of pathology and corruption, rather than the renascence of civic virtue, in the modern world.

Needless to say, the second option would not please the historians and political theorists who, on the advice of Pocock, invested heavily in "Machiavelli at the expense of Locke." They might well conclude that even the bourgeois Locke offers a better deal than Machiavelli. The first alternative, on the other hand, would temper the unhistorical extremism of the revisionist paradigm and allow for consideration of a different interpretation of Locke—one that is textually legitimate, less hostile to liberalism, and historically appropriate for the study of eighteenth-century intellectual history. Before exploring the possibilities that lie in that direction, however, we should return to the textual inspiration for American republicanism and see how Cato has been treated by his janissaries.

Perhaps the most remarkable oversight with respect to the interpretation of political theory in the historiographic revolution has been the failure to detect, or to explain satisfactorily, the ominous presence of Thomas Hobbes at the heart of Cato's "republican" political thought. Consider only three of the many "Hobbesian moments" in *Cato's Letters.*

> Between subject and subject, and between magistrates and subjects, concord and security are preserved by the terror of the laws and the ties of mutual interest; and both interest and terror derive their strength from the impulses of self-love.[19]

> We do not expect philosophical virtue from [the people], but only that they follow virtue as their interest, and find it penal and dangerous to depart from it. And this is the only virtue that the world wants, and the only virtue that it can trust to.[20]

> Nothing but fear and selfish considerations can keep men within any reasonable bounds; and nothing but the absence of fear can set men at defiance with society, and prompt them to oppress it.[21]

Echoes of Hobbes reverberate through Cato's political doctrine. Laws, Cato declares, "are intended for terror and protection."[22] "Fear" and the "terror of the laws" are needed to restrain "the unruly and partial appetites of men," and to produce, thereby, a distinctively Hobbesian kind of virtue—virtue that completely lacks a positive, participatory content. The aggressively, relentlessly acquisitive nature of man makes him innately incapable of anything more.[23] Men, it seems, will become restless precisely when they are *not* oppressed, or at least, as Hobbes puts it, where there is "no visible power to keep them in awe." And like Hobbes himself, Cato derives this "knowledge of politics" from "knowledge of the passions."[24]

The kind of virtue which Cato expects from the people, as well as his reliance on "fear and selfish considerations" as the principal determinants of political behavior, call into question the authoritative account of Cato's thought in the republican synthesis. Since Pocock defines republican virtue as "active," "participant civic virtue," he is obliged to find such virtue in *Cato's Letters*. Yet the Hobbesian spirit in Cato's politics will not be denied.[25]

Pocock knows that the Leviathan is an inappropriate context for republicanism. He cites Harrington, that quintessential English republican, as criticizing Hobbes for having substituted "private and voluntary subjection for public and active virtue."[26] On the other hand, Pocock does acknowledge the presence of Hobbes in *Cato's Letters*. But he insists that "the ideal of civic virtue is not abandoned" by Cato. Virtue appears as "the passion for pursuing the public good."[27] It seems clear, however, in the passages quoted above that Cato himself does not expect such public-regarding behavior from the people without some potent Hobbesian incentives. Moreover, the fear-induced "civic virtue" sought by Cato could hardly be considered "active" or "participant"; it resembles, on the contrary, that characteristic political passivity of the obedient Hobbesian subject. Pocock scores, of course, if public apathy, silence, and obedience—all passionately pursued—procure the public good. But this is a far cry indeed from the classical republican ideals of virtue, citizenship, and participation.

Cato's economic policy also demands attention. The republican revision seems desperate to believe that his republicanism is "essentially anti-capitalistic"—the doctrine of virtue ready to do ideological battle against the selfish, demoralizing commercial instinct of "Lockean liberalism" (though certainly not from the proletarian perspective).[28] Yet the laissez-faire capitalists and market zealots who nowadays wave the banner of libertarianism have named their think-tank, The Cato Institute, after the "essentially anti-capitalistic" hero of the republican synthesis. While the republican Cato defends virtue against commerce, his libertarian alter ego does precisely the opposite. Will the real Cato please stand up?

For the textual Cato, and for American Revolutionary thought in general, no less than for Locke, liberty and property were inseparable.[29] Moreover, as Jeffrey Isaac notes, there are significant "individualist features of republicanism, particularly with regard to private property." Republican ideology condemned luxury, not accumulation. "Industry" and "frugality" were essential attributes of republican man. But as Isaac observes, "this is, in one sense, Hartz's Lockean man" (though I hasten to emphasize "in one sense," for there is a great deal more to Lockean man than Hartz's "Lockean liberalism"). It was, at any rate, "the stock market and the corruption of the court, not commerce itself," which prompted the neo-Harringtonian critique.[30] Cato himself neither repudiated nor surrendered to capitalism. In fact, he recommended "'honest commerce,'" which implies neither hostility to capitalism nor devotion to laissez-faire (though he was considerably closer to the commercial republic than to the classical republic of virtue).[31]

Such misconceptions about Cato raise questions about the ideological identity of the authors who spoke through him. The republican credentials of Trenchard and Gordon seem to have been taken for granted in the republican synthesis. Yet the collaborators themselves explicitly repudiated republicanism—and they didn't mince words about it, either. This suggests, again, that wishful thinking rather than close textual analysis has facilitated the rise of Cato in the historiography of the American Revolution.

Gordon said of Trenchard, in a preface to an edition of *Cato's Letters* published after Trenchard's death: "He was not for a commonwealth [a republic] in England. He neither believed it possible, nor wished for it." Trenchard, in fact, was as a champion of the status quo, conservatively opposed to political innovation. "Fearful of trying experiments upon the constitution," he "thought that we were better as we were than any practicable change could make us."[32] Trenchard, in other words, embraced the British constitution, which Thomas Paine would later condemn for incorporating "the base remains of two ancient tyrannies," monarchy and aristocracy, suppressing the "new republican materials."[33] Indeed, as Cato, Trenchard called that constitution "excellent," and he insisted that "liberty may be better preserved by [England's] well-poised monarchy than by any popular [or republican] government." "The phantom of a commonwealth must vanish," he warned, "and never appear again but in disordered brains."[34]

As it was said of Trenchard in the *Dictionary of National Biography*, he was "by no means a republican, as his opponents wished to consider him."[35] It is likely that the author of this description was thinking of Gordon's comments, as well as of the biting criticism leveled by Cato himself against all arguments for "any popular government" or "utopian commonwealth."[36] Nowadays, it's Cato's friends who wish to make him into something he was not. His declared antipathy for republican ideals has neither deterred them from extolling his political thought as the principal source of American republicanism nor alerted them to the darker tendencies that could be lurking within that doctrine.

At a higher level of abstraction, Cato's Hobbesian problem becomes more acute and, indeed, we can see serious theoretical and historical discrepancies between Bailyn and Pocock, cofounders of the republican synthesis who are generally presumed to see eye-to-eye on the Revolution.

By comparing the Revolutionary texts with *Cato's Letters* and other sources of American republicanism, Bailyn identified the essence of the Revolution's "theory of politics": the antithesis between liberty and power. Liberty requires power; but power, because of man's instinctive and relentless pursuit of it, has the natural advantage and tends to destroy liberty.[37] This does sound like Cato, and it echoes through the Revolutionary writings. But to call this theory of politics "republican" (not to mention "nonliberal"), we must try to imagine Hobbes in a toga; for the underlying conception of human nature is straight from the *Leviathan*—the "perpetual and restless desire of power after power that ceaseth only in death."[38]

Even more problematic in this regard is that what Bailyn seems to view as the essence of American republicanism, Benjamin Barber, in *Strong Democracy*, understands as the "characteristic dilemma" of liberalism. "Liberty cannot survive without political power," says Barber, "but political power extirpates liberty." This is the "chief dilemma of polarized liberalism" and the source of liberalism's "defining ambivalence."[39] Barber's critically conceived paradigm of liber-

alism thus includes, as an integral and defining component, the republican theory of politics as it was defined by Bailyn himself in the
seminal text of the republican synthesis.

What is at stake here is not simply the question of who has the
bigger paradigm, Bailyn or Barber—both are very impressive. The
point is that Barber's political theory implicitly calls into question
the theoretical coherence of the republican synthesis. How can the
"characteristic dilemma" of liberalism reside at the core of the republican paradigm's nonliberal—or, as Pocock sees it, antiliberal—
theoretical structure? That genius Hartz, wherever he is, may yet have
the last laugh.

Barber is on a different quest, but he brings us within range of a
contradiction in the foundation of the republican synthesis. By citing
Pocock for assistance in explicating the " 'story of liberalism' " and the
generation of its "characteristic dilemma" of liberty and power,[40] Barber is, in effect if not by design, citing Pocock against Bailyn, and thus
the republican synthesis against itself. The problem here is theoretical: "Liberty versus power" is not the same theory of politics as "virtue
versus commerce." But the root of the problem is historical: Tracing the "ultimate origins" of American Revolutionary ideology back
to the "radical social and political thought of the English Civil War
and Commonwealth period" (Bailyn) is not the same as tracing those
origins back to "Aristotle, Polybius, and Cicero" (Pocock).[41] Pocock
endorses, and draws upon, Bailyn's reading of American Revolutionary thought as if their two perspectives on that subject were entirely
congenial.[42] And much of the authority of the republican paradigm
rests upon the same unwarranted assumption.

The problems of interpretation with respect to Cato's political theory
raise serious questions for the republican revision of American Revolutionary thought. A movement which redefines the founding doctrine and, in effect, rewrites a chapter in the history of political
thought ought to be able to distinguish between the low road to the
Leviathan and the high road to the polis. Moreover, if the revision
fails to deal adequately with a minor thinker like Cato, what should
we expect when it ventures into the Pantheon to tangle with a heavy-

weight like Locke? After all, Cato's doctrine is relatively straightforward; you only have to follow the signs, which are there for all to see. Locke, however, is one of the people who put those signs on the road in the first place. He is a pathfinder, an innovator; his work therefore must be read with greater-than-average care.

Indeed, we should read Locke carefully if only to sharpen our view of Cato and of American republicanism. Those who are actively familiar with Locke's writings will recognize that when Cato does move away from Hobbes and Machiavelli, he heads not toward Athens, but in a distinctively Lockean direction. His polemical salutes to individual liberty, the limits of governmental power, and the right of resistance are close enough to passages from the *Two Treatises* to qualify as paraphrase, either of the *Two Treatises* itself or of whatever sources Locke might have been paraphrasing when he wrote it.[43] But Cato's political liberalism seems ad hoc—not an integral part of his doctrine, as it is for Locke's. The ideas that could offset the Hobbesian tendencies in Cato's doctrine do not, in his case, seem to be grounded in a philosophy that could justify them under pressure. At best, Cato is caught in a tug of war between Hobbes and Locke. At worst, he leans toward Hobbes—pulled by his anthropological assumptions, pushed by his conservative dread of change. In either case, or anywhere in between, it is knowledge of Locke that helps us to identify these parameters of American republicanism through the prism of Cato's political theory.

Recognizing Locke in Cato is important, but the main objective here is to recognize Locke in American Revolutionary thought and to understand the importance of interpretation to that end. In fact, we've already seen problems with Locke interpretation in the analysis of the formal connection. For example, the assertions that Locke had nothing to offer the colonists in their struggle against parliamentary despotism, and that Locke's arguments favored the despot, not only fly in the face of the historical record; these assertions also betray a failure to grasp the very basics of Locke's political theory. How could the Lockean-liberal doctrine of limited government and resistance to tyranny be antithetical to the ideology of the American Revolution? Insofar as the Revolutionists preferred constitutional politics to political absolutism, the claim stands only if one overlooks, suppresses, or radically misconstrues the very substance of Locke's political theory. But the republican revision of the founding doctrine was undertaken and carried through by some of the finest scholars in the field. How, then, could it have fallen so wide of the mark in a matter of such consequence?

To a great degree the problem lies in the interpretation of political theory—or the lack thereof. Locke's thought has been stereotyped and taken for granted in one of two ways: in vaguely "neutral" (Bailyn) or in hostile (Pocock) terms. Either way there has been too much trust placed in received opinions about Locke and too little, if any, actual engagement with Locke's texts. Yet it is only by actually reading Locke's books that one becomes familiar enough with their contents to recognize certain inexplicit forms of textual evidence (such as unattributed quotations, especially those that are not set off by quotation marks) and to evaluate the significance of direct citations in the Revolutionary writings (e.g., Joseph Galloway's). Even at the relatively "superficial" level of the formal connection, then, this kind of historical research absolutely requires direct familiarity with the relevant sources of political theory. In addition to the examples from previous chapters that support this view, consider how taking Locke for granted (in "neutral" terms, that is, not as the bourgeois Locke) rather than working with a clearly defined, textually informed interpretation of Locke's thought has led Bernard Bailyn astray on two occasions.

First, Bailyn asserts that Locke's "ideas would scarcely have supported" the Reverend Jonathan Mayhew's argument in his *Discourse Concerning Unlimited Submission* (1750).[44] We'll take a long look at Mayhew's sermon (which served as a model for patriotic sermons during the Revolutionary years) in chapter 5 and see that he developed his argument in substantively Lockean terms; that is, he derived his Lockean political prescriptions from specific theistic principles and arguments to which Locke himself had subscribed. But we already know enough about Lockean thought to appreciate the problem with Bailyn's position.

Mayhew vigorously denounced the doctrine of unlimited submission and proclaimed the people's right and duty to resist tyrants—this was the theme of his sermon, which was delivered to commemorate the execution of Charles I as an act of justice. Bailyn thus implies that Locke would have supported unlimited submission and rejected the notion of legitimate resistance. I doubt that Bailyn would want to attribute such views to Locke, but he can't have it both ways; he cannot maintain that Locke's "ideas would scarcely have supported" Mayhew's argument without turning Locke into Filmer, that is, into a proponent of despotism and obedience "in all cases whatsoever"; and there is no way to reconcile that conversion either with the political theory of the Second Treatise or with what the Revolutionists themselves thought about "Mr. Locke's doctrine." Bailyn might have avoided this difficulty had he treated Locke's thought with a little more care.

The second episode concerns Bailyn's dismissal of a Locke citation in an important sermon delivered by Simeon Howard in 1773, as a result of which he failed to recognize a significant instance of the substantive Lockean connection in clerical thought. Howard's footnote—"see Locke on government"—supports his description of liberty in the state of nature. Natural liberty, according to Howard, is not "licentiousness," insofar as "the law of nature which bounds this liberty forbids all injustice and wickedness, allows no man to injure another in his person or property, or to destroy his own life."[45] Bailyn treats Howard's appeal to Locke in this context as one of those "times when he is referred to in the most offhand way, as if he could be relied on to support anything the writers happened to be arguing." He thus implies that Howard cited Locke merely to dress up an argument that was not necessarily or essentially "Lockean."[46]

But Howard's citation of Locke was not "offhand." The position it supported—the understanding of natural liberty—was distinctively Lockean. The distinction between liberty and license was an essential one for Locke (as it was for the authors of other important sermons and political pamphlets in colonial and Revolutionary America).[47] "Freedom is not [as Filmer or Hobbes would have it] a liberty for every man to do what he lists."[48] The law of nature governs the state of nature, and that law, which "obliges everyone," sets moral limits upon natural liberty. So although the state of nature is a "state of liberty, yet it is not a state of license." There are some things which men, in or out of the state of nature, cannot do. For example, as "the workmanship" and therefore the "property" of God, all men live at God's pleasure, not at their own or at that of any other man. The law of nature thus decrees that "no one ought to harm another in his life, health, liberty, or possessions." And since man is the "property" of God, he "has not liberty to destroy himself," either. No one, according to Locke, may "quit his station willfully"[49]—a sentiment explicitly endorsed by Simeon Howard.

Bailyn misses the point of Howard's citation, apparently because he is unaware of the supreme significance of this divine injunction against suicide in Locke's political theory: it is part of the basis for the doctrine of limited government and for the justification of revolution.[50] For Locke, since a man, as the "workmanship" and therefore the "property" of God, "cannot take away his own life, neither can he give another power to take it."[51] The right of self-preservation therefore "must be understood primarily as a duty towards God."[52] And it is precisely this duty to preserve one's life that delegitimizes absolute, arbitrary power and makes political freedom, which implies limited government, a moral imperative.

The argument goes like this: Locke says that freedom is "not to be subject to the inconstant, uncertain, unknown, and arbitrary will of another man,"[53] and he calls this the indispensable "fence" to preservation.[54] "Freedom from absolute, arbitrary power is so necessary to, and closely joined with, a man's preservation that he cannot part with it, but by what forfeits his preservation and life together."[55] Hence, "reason bids me" to regard "as an enemy to my preservation" whosoever "would take that freedom away"[56]—an enemy, moreover, whom it is lawful for me to "kill . . . if I can," regardless of his station.[57] And since tyranny, which is the negation of freedom and therefore of life itself, can be more easily avoided than overthrown, the duty of self-preservation authorizes and, indeed, requires a preemptive revolution against perceived tyrannical intentions.[58]

Howard makes essentially the same argument as Locke. The law of nature prohibits suicide. The principle of self-preservation, understood by Howard primarily as a duty to God, "allows of everything necessary to self-defence, opposing force to force, and violence to violence."[59] "Men are bound to preserve their own lives as long as they can." To do otherwise would make one a "criminal in the sight of God." Whoever loses his life "by neglecting to oppose the violent attacks of wicked men" should not be sanguine about the hereafter.[60] Howard thus concludes that "it is not only the right but the duty of men" to preserve themselves and "to defend that liberty with which providence has made them free." Neglect of this "high obligation" dishonors God.[61] The innocent, moreover, "are not always obliged to receive the first attack," but should instead "act upon that ancient maxim of prudence" by forcibly opposing "the first unjust demands of an encroaching power"—that is, a preemptive strike.[62]

In sum, Howard cited Locke to support the divinely imposed natural-law limitations (this is a substantive connection) on liberty, which included the prohibition of suicide. From the suicide taboo both Locke and Howard derived a repudiation of arbitrary power and a moral justification for revolution. If Bailyn's reading of Locke were up to par, he would not have dismissed Howard's citation of Locke in this matter as "offhand" or implied that Howard's argument was not Lockean. But as it turned out, a superficial reading of Locke transformed an important manifestation of the Lockean connection into an occasion for further belittling the significance of Locke in American Revolutionary thought. To appreciate the full extent of the damage, moreover, Bailyn's massive influence on subsequent scholarship must be taken into account. For example, if Bailyn, as a leader of the historiographic revolution, had not erroneously dismissed this citation, Nathan Hatch might at least have mentioned it in a crucial reference he made to Howard's sermon in his revisionist analysis of the clergy.

Citing the authority of Bailyn, Hatch declares it "evident that . . . the real center of New England's intellectual universe had become the ideals of liberty defined by the eighteenth-century Real Whig tradition." The clergy, he says, absorbed from that "Real Whig" or "country" ideology "a particular definition of political liberty." Liberty, thus defined, is "that capacity to enjoy one's own public and private life within limits set by defined law rather than by the arbitrary will of those in power."[63] It is not clear why we should consider this a distinctively "republican" conception of liberty, since it is virtually indistinguishable from Locke's "liberal" definition of liberty in the *Second Treatise*.[64] But Hatch does not mention Locke—even though his primary source cites Locke, and only Locke, precisely in this context.

In fact, Hatch's footnote here contains three references. One is to Bailyn (an "Ibid." from the previous note); the second is to the editor's introduction to an abridged collection of the writings of Trenchard and Gordon; and the third (which is the only reference to primary material in this context) is to Simeon Howard's sermon from 1773.[65] But on the page of Howard's sermon cited by Hatch, Howard himself refers to "that natural liberty which has been mentioned" on the previous page.[66] And there, unacknowledged by Hatch, the only citation that Howard offers to support his definition of liberty is "see Locke on government"[67]—precisely the citation casually dismissed by Bailyn as "offhand" and insignificant.

Taking Locke for granted has taken its toll in historical research. Taking the bourgeois Locke for granted, however, has made matters much worse; for this is a hostile interpretation which reduces Lockean thought to a corrupt ideological rationalization for uninhibited capital accumulation, in part by suppressing Locke's liberal-constitutionalist politics (not to mention the theistic philosophical context for his politics).

Here the major culprit is Pocock. However much he eschews the historiographies of Macpherson and Strauss, it is still the bourgeois Locke who informs his famous antithesis between republicanism (virtue) and liberalism (commerce). It is this understanding of Locke which helped to launch the historiographic crusade against Lockean liberalism in the first place. And one may safely conclude that it has been at least partly responsible for generating accounts of American Revolutionary thought that, following Pocock, "did not make reference to Locke at all" when the Revolutionists themselves were referring precisely to Locke far more than to anyone else; for the preponderance of citations of "Locke on Government" in the Revolutionary writings—indeed, the centrality of Lockean liberalism in Revolutionary argument—cannot be easily accommodated in an account of intellectual history wherein Locke represents only the "spirit of capitalism" and the Revolution symbolizes the triumph of virtue over commerce.

In following Pocock, revisionists seem to have tacitly received the bourgeois Locke as gospel, the last exegetical word, without recognizing the existence of competing interpretations of Locke's writings. And so they have sealed Locke's great fall in the American Genesis. But there are textually sound, Lockean alternatives to the bourgeois Locke. There are Locke scholars who do not regard Locke as one of the bad guys (and political theorists who do not view liberalism as a liability for Western civilization). Indeed, the seemingly innate pluralism of what Macpherson called the Locke Industry needs to be acknowledged in light of the unexamined consensus that prevails in the historiographic revolution. Locke scholars are by no means united in declaring the meaning of Lockean thought. Is this because, as Locke scholars, they are too liberal to think they know the truth, and to proclaim it, when they see it? Hardly. This wouldn't be very Lockean, anyway, since Locke, in the final analysis, was a believer.

So whence the pluralism? In fact, the potentially befuddling multiplicity of Lockes originates in the richness and complexity of Lockean thought itself, in its insights, ambiguities and contradictions, in the scope and level of analysis, as well as in the high secrets and deep mysteries that attracted Locke's uncommon intelligence. For these reasons there is little consensus and a great deal at stake, ideologically and philosophically, in the interpretation of Locke's thought. But republican historiography seems unaware both of the "epic" nature of Locke's thought (to borrow Sheldon Wolin's term) and of the consequent diversity of opinion concerning its meaning; and this shuts the door to some interesting possibilities. Committed to the overthrow of the bourgeois Locke, the revisionists have little reason to suspect that there is more to Locke than "the spirit of capitalism" and even less incentive to seek it—either in Locke's books, in alternative interpretations of Locke's books, or in the founding doctrine.

Nathan Tarcov identifies the problem and points toward a solution.

"Finding nothing decent or inspiring in the interpretations of Locke that are offered to them, students of our political culture have gone off seeking 'non-Lockean' elements in our heritage. They should discover, instead, the 'non-Lockean' elements in Locke."[68] What follows is one definition of some of the important " 'non-Lockean' elements in Locke." These are elements of Locke's theistic liberalism. They are constituent elements in the substantive Lockean connection in American Revolutionary thought.

If relying upon received opinion—especially hostile opinion—about Locke has obscured the formal Lockean connection in American Revolutionary thought, it has pushed the substantive Lockean connection altogether out of sight. The idea of a substantive Lockean connection implies that some Revolutionary authors, particularly the New England clergy, recognized and sympathized with the general philosophical framework within which the distinctively Lockean-liberal political principles—toleration, limited government, the right of resistance, etc.—were integrally embedded. One must go through and beyond the *Second Treatise* to see that framework and to understand the place of Locke's political theory within it. Moreover, the interpretation that emerges from this reading of Locke's works contradicts some key points in the interpretations of Macpherson and, in particular, Strauss. In other words the theistic Locke must replace the bourgeois Locke en route to the substantive Lockean connection in American Revolutionary thought.

Instead of switching Lockes arbitrarily (which seems to be how the bourgeois Locke was adopted by the republican revision in the first place), let's consider this situation in light of the two criteria of interpretation that were defined in chapter 1. First, the interpretation of Locke that guides this study of eighteenth-century thought must be available in the Lockean texts, i.e., an interpretation that can be legitimately carved out of the Lockean corpus. Second, in developing or choosing a textually sound interpretation of Lockean thought, we should try to be sensitive to how Lockean thought most likely would have been interpreted in the period under investigation. The interpretation, then, must also be historically appropriate or an interpretation that most likely would have been carved out of Locke's texts by eighteenth-century American readers. In sum, the study of American Revolutionary thought should be guided by the interpretation of Locke which best satisfies both of these criteria.

Of course, the pluralism of Lockes in the Lockean corpus means that both the bourgeois Locke and the theistic Locke could meet the first criterion. Therefore it is not necessary (and not within the scope of this book) to mount a comprehensive critique of the bourgeois Locke on exegetical grounds. It is sufficient to demonstrate that the theistic Locke is textually sound, without excluding alternative interpretations, and that this Locke is more appropriate than the bourgeois Locke for a historical study of eighteenth-century thought. Generally, this is the course I follow.

Nevertheless, as we examine the textual roots of the theistic Locke, we will encounter one critically relevant point where the theistic Locke and the bourgeois Locke take mutually exclusive positions. In particular, the relationship between reason and revelation in Lockean thought is centrally important in Professor Strauss's interpretation. And on this vital issue, the theistic Locke and the bourgeois Locke are inherently incompatible. The point is crucial for two reasons. First, the clerical view of the relationship between reason and revelation is identical to the position of the theistic Locke. Second, both Locke and the clergy referred to this relationship when seeking epistemological grounds for their similar political prescriptions. "Theistic epistemology" thus constitutes a key element in the substantive Lockean connection in clerical thought, and the textual credentials of the bourgeois Locke on this topic must be carefully considered.

The theistic Locke begins to come into view when we recognize what John Dunn called "the theoretical centrality of Locke's religious preoccupations" as the key to understanding Lockean thought. According to Dunn, "an extremely high proportion of Locke's arguments [depend] for their very intelligibility, let alone plausibility, on a series of theological commitments."[69] We need to identify some of those commitments and determine how they inform Locke's political theory; this will give us a textually sound model of Locke's "theistic liberalism." We'll begin here and look even further into Locke's thought in chapter 5, where applying the same procedure to the sermons and other writings of the New England clergy and comparing the results to the analysis of Locke will illuminate the substantive Lockean connection in American Revolutionary thought.

Begin with the foundation of any theistic philosophy: God. Locke was "distinctively a Biblical Christian."[70] He believed that the existence of God "is so fundamental a truth, and of that consequence, that all religion and genuine morality depend thereon."[71] Hence, "no general ethical theory could be stated unless the idea of God were included as the most important constituent."[72] For Locke, belief in God is "the foundation of all morality" and, moreover, that alone which makes men capable of "all society."[73]

It is a strange kind of secular rationalism that regards belief in God as a precondition for ethics and social existence, but this is indeed Locke's view. Civil society presupposes that all its members recognize their mutual obligations and respect the sanctions behind them, and this requires belief in God; for "what duty is cannot be understood without a law, nor a law be known without a lawmaker, or without reward and punishment."[74] God is the lawmaker; the law of nature is "the decree of the divine will discernible by the light of nature," that is, by reason (while Scripture, we shall see, is the same divine law made known through revelation); and it is the belief in the pleasures of heaven and the pains of hell that encourages us to fulfill our obligations.[75] The function of the law of nature, then, is social and political—to show men their duties in relation to one another. "Without this law men can have no social intercourse or union among themselves."[76]

The belief in heaven and hell is also essential here. A few might grasp the intrinsic superiority of living according to the law of nature, but it is only the certainty of divine and everlasting reward or punishment that can furnish the greater part with a compelling reason to obey the moral law. Locke invokes this theological sanction in several key places in his works. In *The Reasonableness of Christianity*, for instance, he asserts that: "The view of heaven and hell will cast a slight upon the short pleasures and pains of this present state and give attractions and encouragements to virtue, which reason and interest, and care of ourselves, cannot but allow and prefer. Upon this foundation, and upon this only, morality stands firm and may defy all competition." [77] Locke offers the same argument in his *Essay Concerning Human Understanding*. "When the eternal state is considered in but its bare possibility, which no man can make any doubt of," men will order their preferences and regulate their actions "not according to the transient pleasures or pain that accompanies or follows them here, but as they serve to secure that perfect durable happiness hereafter." [78] The "true ground of morality," he argues, "can only be the will and law of a God, who sees men in the dark, has in His hand rewards and punishments, and power enough to call to account the proudest offender." [79] To know that "God had given a rule whereby men should govern themselves," and that "He has power to enforce" this rule "by rewards and punishments, of infinite weight and duration, in another life," is to apprehend "the true touchstone of moral rectitude." [80]

It is fair to say that in this area Lockean morality is vulnerable to John Stuart Mill's critique of Christian morality in general. "It holds out the hope of heaven and the threat of hell as the appointed and appropriate motives to a virtuous life." It thus falls "far below the best of the ancients," giving to morality "an essentially selfish character." [81] In this sense Locke's morality is hedonistic. But it is not, as Leo Strauss and Garry Wills would have it, the materialistic hedonism of Hobbes. (If it were, there would be no essential difference between Hobbesian and Lockean politics, that is, between despotic and constitutional government.) Hobbes has little faith in the efficacy of the "Spirits Invisible" for securing human covenants. He trusts only the fear of the violent death that awaits those who are remiss in their obligations; he does not speculate about eternity. Locke's hedonism, in contrast, was a "Christian hedonism," in which the ultimate rewards and punishments of this world paled in comparison to those of the next. [82]

In any case Locke has a short supply of sympathy for nonbelievers. He believes that "the taking away of God" destroys the prospects for a liberal polity, leaving the grim Hobbesian extremes—as Gerald

Runkle puts it, life in a jungle or life in a cage—as the only possible alternatives.[83] Atheism thus constitutes "a crime which, for its madness as well as guilt, ought to shut a man out of all sober and civil society," and atheists are excluded from the general toleration.[84] Here, too, Locke is subject to criticism by Mill, who extends the blessings of liberalism to nonbelievers.[85] And the difference between Locke and Mill, like the difference between Locke and Hobbes, originates in Locke's "theological commitments."

Toleration, in fact, is a most interesting area in which to expound the theistic Locke. Locke's liberalism is the locus classicus of the separation of church and state and, as such, the object of neotheocratic vexation. All the more ironic, then, to discover that the Lockean argument, in both its moral and prudential dimensions, is embedded in theistic justification.

Locke's dualism is reflected in his attempt to accommodate both the spiritual and physical aspects of human existence. To this end, in the fourth and definitive *Letter on Toleration*, he declares that it is "necessary above all to distinguish between the business of civil government and that of religion, and to mark the true bounds between the church and the commonwealth."[86] He defines a commonwealth as "a society of men constituted only for preserving and advancing their civil goods." Civil power consists only of outward force; and the legitimate use of force "belongs wholly to the civil magistrate," who may apply it only "for the safety and security of the commonwealth, and of each man's goods."[87] A religious society, on the other hand, aims at "the gaining of eternal life" through the public worship of God. A church therefore does nothing (or ought to do nothing) which "relates to the possession of civil goods."[88]

Two conclusions follow from this comparative analysis of civil and ecclesiastical concerns. First, the civil power, which "consists wholly in compulsion," is essentially unsuited for the promotion of salvation; hence "the care of souls cannot belong to the civil magistrate."[89] On the other hand, "no force is to be employed [in the church] for any reason whatever." The church can have "no compulsive power"; for the use of such would be in direct contradiction to its essential mission, that is, the promotion of salvation. The church must instead rely on "exhortations, admonitions, and advice" to keep its members "within their duty." The severest sanction available to the church is reserved for incorrigibles: they "should be separated and cast out from the society."[90] In short, the church and the commonwealth have different ends and therefore must make use of different means to attain those ends. The two societies are functionally distinct.

This is at root a moral argument. For Locke, "true and saving religion consists in the inward persuasion of the mind, without which nothing has any value with God."[91] Physical force saves no one. Whether applied by political or by religious authorities, it creates only hypocrites, for which God rewards neither the "converted" nor the ones who turn the screw. Only autonomous choice based upon uncoerced subjective conviction can affix a moral status to an individual's conduct and thus render him eligible for salvation.[92] Locke's commitment to the "eternal estate" thus ordains three distinctively liberal political ideas: liberty (both civil and religious), the secularization of politics, and putting the tools of coercion beyond the reach of religious institutions—in sum, the separation of church and state.

Locke adds prudential considerations to the moral argument. Social peace depends upon the recognition, in practice, of the essential differences between "the business of civil government and that of religion." In Locke's view, most of the wars between the European states had been fought to impose one religion or another. Moreover, political turmoil and violence within states generally arose in response to the "refusal of toleration to people of diverse opinions"; for "there is only one thing which gathers people for sedition, and that is oppression."[93] Elsewhere Locke says that "to settle the peace of places where there are different opinions in religion, two things are to be perfectly distinguished: religion and government."[94] This concern for social peace reinforces the functional distinction Locke posits between church and state; it prompts him to warn that "he mixes heaven and earth together . . . who confuses these societies, which in their origin, their end, and their whole substance are utterly and completely different."[95]

Locke emphatically concludes that "the whole power of civil government is concerned only with men's civil goods, is confined to the care of things of this world, and has nothing whatever to do with the world to come."[96] The civil power "neither can nor ought in any way to be extended to the salvation of souls."[97] For that matter, the civil power should not concern itself with the cultivation of virtue either. Here Lockean liberalism stands in sharp contrast to the republican tradition—not, as Pocock believes, because Locke is "indifferent" to virtue (which is the central ideal of civic republicanism), but because for Locke the cultivation of virtue is not, as it were, a police matter.[98] He does believe that God, "by an inseparable connexion, [has] joined virtue and publick happiness together, and made the practice thereof necessary to the preservation of society."[99] But he insists that only nonpolitical institutions such as the church and the family can raise people to virtue through an "education for liberty."[100] Neither salvation nor virtue can be promoted by the keeper of the sword.

So "the lawmaker," according to Locke, "hath nothing to do with moral virtues and vices," and "nothing to do with the good of men's souls, or their concernments in another life."[101] The fundamental limit to civil authority thus emerges from the secularization of the state and the depoliticization of virtue: Civil government, which "is concerned only with men's civil goods" and not with the cultivation of virtue or, in particular, with "the salvation of souls," is, by definition and not merely by preference, less than absolute.

The irony of it is that Locke secularizes the state (and depoliticizes virtue) because in his view God wants it that way. The distinction between civil and ecclesiastical jurisdictions is itself theologically defined. Mutual toleration in matters of religion, which presupposes the separation of church and state, "is so agreeable to the Gospel and to reason that it seems monstrous for men to be blind in so clear a light."[102] It is not indifference to the soul (or to virtue) which underlies secular politics. On the contrary, politics must be secular precisely because the condition of the "eternal estate" is of paramount importance. For Locke "man's first care should be of his soul" and of its immortal destiny "in the world to come."[103] But "regarding his salvation, every man has the supreme and final power of judging for himself," and "the care, therefore, of every man's soul belongs to himself, and is to be left to him"—not to the political authorities.[104] The use of civil power (which "consists wholly in compulsion") where the soul is concerned serves more to obstruct than to clear the road to salvation.[105]

Even the prudential arguments about social peace—the arguments that are agreeable to reason—are indebted to divine purpose. The law of nature "orders . . . the keeping of public peace," and therefore toleration and the separation of church and state; and the law of nature, like revelation, is an expression of the divine will.[106] In sum, God's exile from the Lockean polity is, as it were, self-imposed. The moral and prudential arguments for toleration, which is a cornerstone of Lockean-liberal politics, can be traced back to the "religious preoccupations" of the theistic Locke.

This point about the law of nature being an expression of divine will raises the question of the relationship between reason and revelation—that is, between the law of nature, which reason apprehends, and the law revealed in scripture—in Locke's thought. The position being advanced here is that Lockean epistemology is essentially theistic: Locke regards natural and revealed law as mutually consistent, equally valid, and originating from the same divine source.[107] As indicated above, theistic epistemology constitutes a vitally important element in the substantive Lockean connection in the political thought of the New England clergy, and it is also a point on which the textual basis for the bourgeois Locke, whom Strauss views as a kind of deist, must be critically examined.

First of all, Locke was not a deist or a rationalist in the modern sense of the term. Seventeenth-century deism was known for its total dependence upon reason in ethical theory and its "definite rejection of Scripture as a guide to morals."[108] But we know that Locke saw things differently. Belief in God, and in eternal retribution (one way or the other), was the elemental constituent in the Lockean worldview. It served as "the true touchstone of moral rectitude," the "foundation of all morality," and the fixed prerequisite for "all society."[109] Yet the necessary religious convictions were, for Locke, "purely matters of faith." They were "above reason," "beyond the discovery of reason," and thus made known to men only through revelation. Where reason could "reach no higher than probability, faith gave the determination" and "revelation discovered on which side the truth lay." [110] It is hard to see much support for deism here.

Indeed, however much Locke celebrated and exemplified the power and glory of reason, he declined to join the deists in proclaiming its moral sovereignty. On the contrary, he categorically denied that "unassisted reason" could "establish morality in all its parts upon its true foundation, with a clear and convincing light." [111] To Locke this was dangerous nonsense. "A full knowledge of true morality" could be found "in no other book than the New Testament." [112] Revelation, not reason (though not in opposition to reason), constituted the original and only source of a complete ethical doctrine. [113] Far from endorsing the deists' rejection of revelation, then, Locke reminded them of its necessity. He had the deists specifically in mind when he wrote, in *The Reasonableness of Christianity*, that "many are beholden to revelation, who do not acknowledge it." [114]

There were other important issues on which Locke and the deists of his day did not see eye to eye. Not the least of these concerned the deists' belief in innate ideas. Locke, of course, is famous for his attack on the doctrine of innatism in the *Essay Concerning Human Understanding*. He could no more accept the deists' innatist epistemology than their denial of revelation in favor of a purely rationalist approach to morality. There are, then, at least two substantive philosophical subjects in relation to which Lockean thought must be fundamentally distinguished from deism. [115]

So how has Locke come to be associated with deism? First, though Locke was "active in the controversy against the deists," [116] he did sympathize with their "liberal program" and even expressed the hope that *The Reasonableness of Christianity* would be "useful to the deists" in their efforts to refute "a host of speculative dogmas that were being more and more questioned by educated men." [117] Deists, on the other hand, made use of Lockean epistemology, and this, too, laid him open to the charge of deism. Yet as John Yolton observes, the deists' application of Locke's work was "flashy and superficial" while traditional theologians were "much more penetrating, perceptive, and positive" in appropriating Locke's ideas for their purposes. "The most careful applications of the Lockean epistemology are to be found among the theologians who were seeking to undermine deism . . . in the name of tradition."[118] And of this Locke himself undoubtedly would have approved; for he feared the growing influence of radical deism more than the waning influence of orthodox Anglicanism.[119]

Establishing Locke's relationship to seventeenth-century deism does not settle the question of the relationship between reason and revelation within Lockean thought itself (which later will be shown to correspond to that found in New England clerical thought). Here we must engage Strauss's bourgeois Locke on textual grounds; for on this crucial point, the bourgeois Locke and the theistic Locke take mutually exclusive positions. To be sure, the methodology of Locke interpretation adopted in this book generally allows—as other approaches do not—more than one "textually sound" interpretation of Locke, Strauss's included. Nevertheless, the point in contention is an important one, and the texts here are with the theistic Locke, for whom reason and revelation jointly express a single idea.

Strauss attempts to establish an antithesis between the law of nature and revealed law in Locke's philosophy. He contends that the law of nature, as Locke understands it, does not originate in the will of God and thus is not a "law of nature in the proper sense of the term."[120] The Lockean law of nature, moreover, differs from revealed law not only in origin but in content. For Strauss, Locke's law of nature prescribes an uninhibited Hobbesian hedonism and is thus fundamentally opposed to the teaching of the Gospel.[121] He thus implicitly joins Locke to the deists in rejecting revelation as a source of ethics. At the same time, however, he makes Locke more radical (and more "modern") than the deists in positing an opposition between the teachings of natural and revealed laws in Locke's thought. Strauss's Locke believes that "the law of reason [i.e., the law of nature], which obliges man as man, and the law revealed in the gospel, which obliges Christians," are essentially different and, in fact, irreconcilably opposed in terms of their respective prescriptions concerning the right way to live.[122]

Strauss himself seems to believe that the two teachings can never be reconciled. In fact, this is a major philosophical theme in Strauss's interpretation of the history of political thought. The one thing required by biblical religion is the opposite of the one thing required by philosophy: "a life of obedient love versus a life of free insight." One or the other, revelation or reason, must be sacrificed in any attempt to achieve a synthesis or harmony between them.[123] Between "Jerusalem and Athens" lies "a tension that can never be resolved."[124] This, of course, is a legitimate philosophical view and not a very extraordinary one in the modern age; it might even be correct. But I think Strauss is wrong to impute this view to Locke.

To support the claim that Locke has only a " 'partial law of nature,' " which is not consistent with the "clear and plain teaching" of revelation (and in fact contradicts the biblical prescription), Strauss offers this passage from Locke's *Second Vindication of the Reasonableness of Christianity*: "As men, we have God for our king, and are under the law of reason; as Christians, we have Jesus the Messiah for our king, and are under the law revealed by him in the gospel. And though every Christian, both as a deist and a Christian, be obliged to study both the law of nature and the revealed law. . . ."[125]

But as John Yolton points out, this is one of those occasions when Strauss ends quotations at midsentence, "using a frequent device of dots" to eliminate "inconvenient statements" (shades of Joseph Galloway and the Tory Locke!). Here, in speaking of natural and revealed law, the uninterrupted Locke goes on to say "that in them he may know the will of God, and of Jesus Christ, whom he hath sent; yet in neither of these laws is there to be found a select set of fundamentals, distinct from the rest, which are to make him a Deist or a Christian."[126] As we can see, the complete passage denotes an understanding of the relationship between reason and revelation in Locke's thought that is precisely the opposite of the view which Strauss's abbreviation of the passage is intended to support.

An opposition between reason and revelation in Locke's thought would constitute a denial of Locke's theism. Yet there is a great deal of textual evidence which is difficult to reconcile to Strauss's interpretation. For example, in addition to the above citations attesting to the essential place of revelation in Locke's philosophy, there are at least two more occasions when Locke himself explicitly affirms that the law of nature and the revealed law represent harmonious expressions of the divine law, that is, of the will of God.

In his *Essays on the Law of Nature*, Locke argues that revealed law (or what in this context he calls the "positive divine law") and the law of nature are distinguished "only in method of promulgation and in the way in which we know them." This is the only difference between them. Revealed law "we apprehend by faith"; the law of nature "we know with certainty by the light of nature and from natural principle" (or reason). Both laws, however, come from the same source and impose the same kind and measure of obligation. "If natural law is not binding on men, neither can positive divine law be binding, and that no one has maintained. In fact, the basis of obligation in both cases is the same, i.e., the will of a supreme Godhead." [127]

In the *Essay Concerning Human Understanding*, Locke describes the divine law as "that law which God has set to the actions of men, whether promulgated to them by the light of nature or the voice of revelation." "Reason is natural Revelation"; "Revelation is natural Reason"; and both come from God, who is "the eternal fountain of light and the father of all knowledge." [128] Here again, the only difference between the natural and revealed laws is in the way in which they are "promulgated" by God to mankind.

These passages cast doubt upon the claim that Locke has a "secularized" natural-law theory, one that is independent of and opposed to the teaching of biblical religion. [129] The law of nature and the law revealed in scripture are complementary, harmonious, and mutually reinforcing expressions of divine will. They differ neither genetically nor substantively—neither in origin nor in content—but "only in method of promulgation."

If Locke were to regard reason and revelation as conveying mutually exclusive laws, he would not invoke them simultaneously as grounds for supporting or opposing a particular argument. Yet in *The Reasonableness of Christianity*, for instance, he claims that revelation contains "a full and sufficient rule for our direction, and conformable to reason." Reason and revelation "both together" affirm that the precepts of the New Testament "come from God." [130] In the *First Treatise*

Locke asserts that neither "reason nor scripture," both of which declare what "may be said to be by God's appointment," support Filmer's
scheme of the sovereignty of Adam or the absolutist doctrine of the
divine right of kings.[131] In the *Second Treatise* Locke describes the
agreement between the law of nature and scriptural precept as "the
voice of reason confirmed by inspiration."[132] And in the *Letter on Toleration*, as we have seen, gospel and reason jointly prescribe mutual
toleration in matters of religion.[133]

Explicit textual evidence presents a serious challenge to the bourgeois Locke in this regard. But Strauss has a patented response—one
that not only prepares Locke for his role as a villain in the epic tale of
the decline of Western political thought, but also insulates the interpretation from substantive criticism. Strauss claims that Locke, like
all the great writers in the Pantheon of political philosophy, feared
persecution for propounding the unconventional; so he deliberately
concealed his true intention and conveyed the essence of his teaching "about all crucial things . . . exclusively between the lines" of his
texts.[134] And that is precisely where we find the bourgeois Locke, the
Locke who offered (among other things) a Hobbesian law of nature
antithetical to the teachings of revealed religion. The interpreters
who fail to make this discovery, or who put more stock in Locke's
actual words than in his esoteric communications, are dismissed a
priori on methodological grounds, without due consideration of their
views. They simply don't know how to read the Great Books.[135]

Strauss's method has prompted a great deal of controversy. (Even
Pocock has complained about "methodological assumptions that tend
to place Strauss's procedure beyond the reach of criticism—which
is, of course, to make it critically worthless.")[136] To be sure, Strauss
does cite passages from *The Reasonableness of Christianity* that seem
to warrant the esoteric approach to Locke's texts. Yet there are even
more passages (*Conduct of the Understanding, Essay Concerning Human
Understanding, An Essay for the Understanding of St. Paul's Epistles*)
where Locke insists, to the contrary, that writers should strive to be
clear and candid in writing about philosophical topics and that readers, for their part, should concentrate on plain language and logical
argument and not read their own views into the works of past philoso-

phers.[137] The key point concerning the esoteric method, however, is that it allows the interpreter to disregard the passages which call into question the method itself as well as the interpretation it yeilds. This is how the esoteric method tends to immunize itself against methodological as well as substantive criticism.

Martin Seliger has analyzed the convergence of substance and method in Strauss's interpretation of Locke—on the one hand, the discovery of the "Lockean" antithesis between reason and revelation (and the preference for the former), and on the other hand, the dismissal of a preponderance of explicit textual evidence to the contrary in favor of this esoterically conveyed teaching. Seliger shows how, in Strauss's interpretation, "the esoteric intention of the *Treatises* proceeds from the irreconcilability of a natural law of hedonistic self-preservation with the natural law which agrees with scriptural principles," an irreconcilability that Strauss reads unhistorically back into Locke's thought.[138] Locke thus becomes "softer" and more marketable, but no less "hedonistic," than Hobbes.

> Mainly on the basis of stipulating an unbridgeable gulf between a naturalistic and a religiously-founded conception of morals and politics, Strauss finds that Locke expressed his inclination towards a purely Hobbesian conception in one set of statements which is irreconcilable with Locke's more frequently stated views. According to the esoteric method, the inoffensive views must be cancelled; they are intended to mislead the censor and protect the writer.[139]

In other words, Strauss begins with an idea which must be attributed to Locke if Locke is to play his appointed role in the history of political philosophy. He then applies the esoteric method, which delivers the necessary interpretation. John Gunnell's comment on Strauss's work is worth repeating here: "Interpretations of particular works are viewed principally as a means of reconstructing the tradition as a whole." Seliger, at any rate, declines to follow Strauss in dismissing Locke's many "attempts to reconcile his concessions to hedonistic naturalism with an enlightened belief in Christianity" as red herrings planted by the philosopher to mislead unenlightened censors.[140] Instead, he takes Locke at his word.

To be sure, Locke did perceive some kind of tension between the teaching of Biblical religion and that of philosophy. The dilemma, as Strauss puts it, between "a life of obedient love versus a life of free insight" is reflected in Locke's concern over the apparent contradiction between the omnipotence and omniscience of God on the one hand and human freedom—and thus, for Locke, morality itself—on the other.[141] Locke, however, did not see this as Strauss does, that is, as an inherently unresolvable dilemma. He simply doubted his own ability to resolve it. Writing to Molyneux about certain revisions in the *Essay Concerning Human Understanding*, Locke spoke candidly on this crucial point.

> I own freely to you the weakness of my understanding, that though it be unquestionable that there is omnipotence and omniscience in God, our maker, and I cannot have a clearer perception of any thing than that I am free, yet I cannot make freedom in man consistent with omnipotence and omniscience in God, though I am as fully persuaded of both, as of any truths I most firmly assent to. And, therefore, I have long since given off the consideration of that question, resolving all into this short conclusion, that if it be possible for God to make a free agent, then man is free, though I see not the way of it.[142]

Locke's private remark to Molyneux, a friend, reveals a deeply held philosophical view that is essentially consistent with the many explicit statements attesting to his own belief in the truth of, and harmony between, reason and revelation in the books he published. It is, however, essentially inconsistent with the rejection of revelation and the preference for an anti-scriptural, Hobbesian-hedonistic natural-law doctrine that Strauss reads "exclusively between the lines" of those books.

In sum, Locke did not hold the opinion that Strauss attributes to him, and that esoteric interpretation claims to discern behind the explicit textual evidence to the contrary. Strauss's interpretation assumes that there can be no synthesis or harmony between reason and revelation, between philosophy and religion. This might be true. But "*Locke*'s assumption is that any rift between scriptural principles and the dictates of reason is purely fortuitous; there is none whatsoever between God's righteous law and reason."[143] Locke's seventeenth-century assumption about the relationship between the prescriptions of biblical religion and the philosophical way of life is not the twentieth-century assumption of Professor Strauss. On this crucial point, then, the bourgeois Locke fails to satisfy the first criterion of interpretation. The texts favor the theistic Locke.

Locke's theism inspires the secularization of politics in his political theory. Since the law of nature, which we know by reason, is indeed an expression of divine will, God remains essentially, although not explicitly, within the Lockean polity; for, as Locke says, "the obligations of the Law of Nature cease not in society but only in many cases are drawn closer, and have by human laws known penalties annexed to them to enforce their observation"; and "the municipal laws of countries . . . are only so far right as they are founded on the Law of Nature, by which they are to be regulated and interpreted."[144] All "social intercourse and union" among men depend upon the law of nature, which "God hath given to be the rule betwixt man and man, and the common bond" of "fellowship" and social existence. Moreover, "the law of nature stands as an eternal rule to all men, legislators as well as others." God's law thus defines the "extent of the legislative power," just as God ultimately judges the moral status of resistance in particular cases.[145]

Resistance to the exercise of arbitrary power is itself rooted in a theistic context: our duty to the Creator, whose "workmanship" and "property" we are, to preserve ourselves. This we observed in the analysis of the Lockean connection in Simeon Howard's sermon. Arbitrary power must be resisted because, as it negates freedom, which is the "fence" to preservation, it is life-threatening and therefore illegitimate by definition. The divine prohibition of suicide thus has revolutionary political implications. And as for the fateful decision whether or not to make a revolution in a specific situation, Locke's argument, which again flows from his "theological commitments," is more radical still; for God assigns to "the people"—and, indeed, to "any single man"—the responsibility for judging whether or not government follows the "law antecedent and paramount to all positive laws," and for obeying or resisting that government accordingly; and this is a "judgment they cannot part with." The exercise of sound, socially responsible political judgment is a requisite for salvation.[146]

These and other theistic intimations of divine will in Locke's political theory are examined in the sermonology of chapter 5. But let us note for now that in Locke's political theory, God essentially informs the secular political order even though—and precisely insofar as— He is absent from it. For modern interpreters, this may seem like a paradox. But it is a paradox "of the interpreters' rather than of the philosopher's making."[147]

For better or for worse, Locke's "religious preoccupations," which John Dunn properly emphasizes in his account of the *Two Treatises*, are certainly not the preoccupations of twentieth-century liberalism. To be a Lockean liberal in the full sense of the term means to be concerned above all with one's "eternal estate."[148] Lockean individualism, for example, emerges from the individual's relationship with God; its basis is the individual's responsibility—Locke calls it his "duty and interest"—to judge for himself in matters pertaining to his own salvation.[149] In contrast, modern individualism is secular, acquisitive, materialistic, and essentially unconstrained by considerations of duty to God or anything else. This is not a way of life that could be justified in the framework of Locke's theistic liberalism.

So how did Lockean liberalism become the "Lockean liberalism" which revisionist historians, political theorists, and critics of modernity love to hate? Perhaps Locke's theistically inspired secularization of politics has somehow interacted historically with social, economic, and technological changes to produce the more radical secularization, personal and political, which characterizes modern Western life. The dynamics remain unclear. But we do know that the theistic foundation of Lockean individualism—indeed, of Lockean liberalism —has evaporated; and as Locke himself warns, "the taking away of God, even only in thought, dissolves all."[150] The duties which arise from each individual's relationship to a common creator no longer carry much weight in Western political theory. Twentieth-century observers may applaud or regret this development; but in either case they should stop trying to attribute it to Locke. Lockean liberalism may have become "bourgeois" as it lost its grounding in a theistic worldview, but it did not start out that way. Nor was it perceived in such a light by the American Revolutionists who proclaimed it their "unvarnished doctrine."

This recalls the question of historical appropriateness—the second criterion of interpretation. Should we expect twentieth-century scholars and eighteenth-century colonists to read a seventeenth-century text in the same way? Even if Locke's political teaching were, as Strauss says, "directly intelligible today if . . . taken as the classic doctrine of the 'spirit of capitalism,'"[151] it seems unlikely, historically speaking, that eighteenth-century colonists would have understood it, or desired to use it, as such. It is true that the economic changes that were to transform pious Puritans into capitalist yankees were already under way in New England society before the trouble with Great Britain had begun.[152] But the bourgeois Locke would have been unintelligible, or a pariah, in Revolutionary America.

In any case, the theistic Locke is more historically appropriate than the bourgeois Locke for a study of American Revolutionary thought. It is much more likely that the American colonists who read Locke's books understood him—and understood him sympathetically—"in terms of his own thought and not in terms of what the rationalists of a much later generation were to make of it." As Winthrop Hudson observed in a priceless but neglected article on Locke and the American Revolution, modern interpreters seem unable to avoid unhistorically secularizing Locke's political thought, reading it as a kind of reflection of contemporary liberalism; but "certainly the 'pietists' of the Revolutionary generation in America . . . would not have read Locke in this way."[153] This applies especially to the clerical "vanguard" in New England. The ministers hailed Locke as "*a defensor fides*" and as a "Scripture commentator."[154] They shared his overriding concern for the "eternal estate." And like Locke himself, the ministers "formulated their political theories with one eye on God and the other on man."[155]

Indeed, the American Revolutionists—clerical and "secular"—neither read nor cited the "bourgeois Locke."[156] Nor did they share the modern intellectual historians' and political theorists' secular de-

tachment from Locke's "religious preoccupations." The pervasive-
ness of religion in the daily lives of the colonists suggests, on the
contrary, that they would have appreciated these fundamental concerns of Locke's philosophy, that they would have understood Locke
"in terms of his own thought" and not in the categories of distinctively modern interpretations. The difference between Locke and the
American Revolutionists was less than one hundred years. The difference between the political writings of the American Revolution
and the modern interpreter is two hundred years and a worldview.
The recovery of the Lockean connection in American Revolutionary thought depends in part upon the recognition of these crucial
historical differences.

It also depends upon emphasizing the interpretation of political
theory in historical research and developing a better understanding of the political theories that constitute American Revolutionary
thought. Taking Locke and Cato for granted has helped to generate
some dangerous distortions in the historical record of the founding
doctrine. Taking them seriously provides compelling incentives as
well as the means for setting the record straight.

5

Theistic Liberalism in the Teaching of the New England Clergy

Carl Becker was not so far from the truth as his critics contend when he suggested that "most Americans had absorbed Locke's works as a kind of political gospel."[1] Actually, most Americans before and after 1763, and especially in New England, "absorbed" Lockean political ideas *with* the Gospel. Moreover, they did not have to read Locke to be so informed, because many of their religious leaders had read, understood, and sympathized with Locke, and had been preaching the fundamentals of Lockean political theory—thereby establishing the substantive Lockean connection—for many years before Parliament tried its hand at tax reform; and eighteenth-century New Englanders tended to take their ministers seriously.[2] As Clinton Rossiter put it, the New England ministers, who "gave the first and most cordial reception" to Locke's arguments, regularly fed their congregations "doses" of Locke's political theory in a "scriptural spoon." As a result, "Locke rode into New England on the backs of Moses and the Prophets."[3]

But why Locke (and not "Cato")? Why did the clergy take Locke so seriously? Why did they cite Locke, and cite him favorably, far more frequently than any other nonbiblical source? I believe that the reasons for the ministers' peculiar affinity for Locke lie on a deep interpretative level, in the realm of Locke's theistic liberalism. The Lockean connection in clerical thought originated in a foundation of shared "religious preoccupations" and "theological commitments,"[4] from which Locke and the ministers derived essentially similar ideas about civil government, with the ministers often citing Locke to make their political points. This common theistic ground has been neither explored nor (as far as I can tell) even recognized by students of clerical thought, regardless of whether their orientations have been *Locke et praeterea nihil* or *omnia praeter Lockem*. But it helps to explain the clergy's obvious affection for Locke's political theory.

The recovery of the substantive Lockean connection in the political thought of the New England clergy thus requires the excavation of that common theistic foundation. We need to trace the derivation of Lockean-liberal political ideas from theistic notions and principles. To do this properly we must analyze the ministers' ideas and arguments, comparing them to those of Locke. There is a great deal of material to cover. These events transpired in what Neil Postman has dubbed the Age of Exposition—making this chapter a long one. A road map should help to keep us on track.

I have divided the chapter into four sections. Each section identifies a theistic concept shared by Locke and the ministers and traces the movement of the idea from theology to political theory in Lockean and clerical thought. First, we shall examine clerical epistemology, in terms of the relationship between reason and revelation. Locke's position on this issue was discussed in chapter 4, so there is already a basis for comparison (though Locke's view will be examined further). Next, we shall see that Locke and the clergy interpreted the nature of God in essentially the same terms. This shared understanding of the deity, which the ministers liked to justify with simultaneous appeals to reason and revelation, had as its political reflection the liberal idea of limited—or constitutional—government.

Theology and political theory openly converged in the clergy's interpretation of chapter 13 of St. Paul's Epistle to the Romans—the subject of the third section. The ministers cited this scriptural passage far more frequently than any other source, biblical or secular,[5] and in so doing they turned an apparent demand for universal and unlimited passive obedience into a morally compelling justification for

revolution, drawing a right and even a *duty* to resist certain kinds of
civil rulers from "the politicks of St. Paul." Yet, as we shall see, Locke
himself had interpreted Romans 13 in the same way. Indeed, the liberal constitutionalism of the *Second Treatise* seems like the Lockean
exegesis of "the politicks of St. Paul" in the form of political theory.
And it is significant that the ministers knew of, and greatly admired,
Locke's "scripture commentary."[6]

The fourth theological commitment shared by Locke and the New
England clergy is the most important topic in this sermonology,
namely, the belief in the prime necessity of individual judgment in the
pursuit of salvation. The clergy initially confined this individualism to
the realm of religion. But theory and experience soon persuaded the
ministers to follow Locke by irrevocably extending individual judgment into the political sphere. Hence the revolutionary assertion of
the right, duty, and competence of the people to judge the conduct of
their governors, and to obey or to resist them accordingly, came down
from the New England pulpit as early as 1736. That this was a decisive step in the ideological preparation of the people who would fight
for the Revolution attests to the vital importance of the substantive
Lockean connection in American Revolutionary thought.

At the risk of reawakening the methodological demon, let me conclude this introduction by recalling a point from earlier in the book.
The substantive Lockean connection in clerical thought implies that
in clerical thought, both the political ideas and the general philosophical structure within which those ideas are integrally embedded
are characteristic of Locke's theistic liberalism. Did the ministers
learn all this from Locke? No one can say; "influence" is impossible
to prove. But the ministers knew of, and shared, Locke's "theological commitments"; moreover, they drew essentially the same political
inferences from this theistic framework as Locke did, and they cited
and otherwise employed "the great Mr. Locke" far more than any
other "secular" source in the process. Whether they *learned* epistemology, theology, scriptural interpretation, or political theory from
Locke, then, is irrelevant. What matters is that, on the basis of the
internal and external evidence in the clerical writings, the clergy's

teaching across these categories was, for the most part, faithful to the spirit of Locke's liberalism.

I. Reason and Revelation:
Theistic Epistemology in Clerical Thought

Any analysis of New England theology or, for that matter, of the political theory of the clergy immediately encounters the epistemological question of how, according to the ministers, men know the nature of God, or what God intends for or requires of them. An appropriate place to begin this sermonology, then, is with the ministers' conception of the relationship between reason and revelation, the two possible sources of all knowledge.

There were numerous theological divisions within New England Protestantism, sometimes within a single denomination. Doctrinal controversy was the rule, not the exception; it fed some of the most heated polemical exchanges of the day. Yet, in general, the ministers across denominations tended to treat natural and revealed law as two consistent, complementary, and interdependent expressions of a single divine will. Whether addressing the relationship between revelation and reason directly, or in seeking epistemological support for a different, and often a political, point, they often reaffirmed their belief in the common derivation of natural and revealed law from the will of God. Indeed, this theistic epistemology was a distinguishing characteristic of Puritan thought. As Perry Miller said of New England clerical thought in general, "there was no intention to discredit either source [of knowledge], but rather to integrate the divine and the natural, revelation and reason, into a single inspiration."[7] And as we saw in chapter 4, the same could be said of "Mr. Locke's doctrine."

Let us begin in 1717. That year witnessed the publication of John Wise's *Vindication of the Government of the New England Churches*. Wise had resisted Andros in New England's "glorious revolution" almost thirty years earlier, serving time in prison for his political activities prior to Andros's fall. Now he sought to defend religious liberty against the proposed establishment of a synod in Massachusetts (which he felt would impose conformity). Wise offered "a striking argument for democracy in church and state," reminiscent of Lockean social-contract theory. He rested his case in part on the claim that the ecclesiastical constitution of 1648 had been drawn up by men according to the principles of "right reason." But "whether we receive it directly from Reason or Revelation," Wise argued, "it is agreeable that we attribute it to God"; for each of these, reason and revelation, "is equally an emanation of His wisdom."[8] The constitution, therefore, ought not to be changed in any fundamental way.

Jared Eliot, who perhaps was the first minister to cite "Locke on Government," shared Wise's view of the singular origin of reason and revelation.[9] In 1736 Eliot proclaimed the "great usefulness both of reason and of divine revelation in religion" and warned, "Let not these which God hath joined together, be by any man under any pretence put asunder." Directing his arguments to those who "represented" reason "as useless and dangerous" and "not to be considered in religion," so "that they might do the greater honor to divine revelation," Eliot defended reason as "a strong evidence for religion and one of its great supports." Those who condemn reason "undervalue the most noble faculty of our soul, slay one of the witnesses, promote *enthusiasm*, and deprive religion of one grand support."[10] This argument calls to mind Locke's warning that "he that takes away *reason*, to make way for *revelation*, puts out the light of both."[11]

John Barnard invoked theistic epistemology in a political context in his 1734 Massachusetts Election Sermon. To the royal governor, lesser magistrates, and the people's representatives, he presented "the council of God . . . as collected from the dictates of right reason and revelation." Discussing "kings and the thrones which they sit on" in terms of "what ought to be" rather than of "what they always are," he declared that "the original of government is from God, who has taught it to mankind by the light of natural reason and plainly required it in His Word" (i.e., Scripture). The dictates of reason, moreover, are "no other than God speaking to his rational creatures by the inward sentiments of their own minds." Thus, both reason and revelation come from God and together teach a single theory of government. Barnard actually described reason in words that Locke himself had used in the *Essay Concerning Human Understanding*, calling it "the candle of the Lord which He hath set up in us."[12]

The ministers appealed simultaneously to reason and revelation to support their arguments concerning the origin of civil government. Unanimously, it seems, they agreed that civil government came "ultimately" from God—Romans 13 was the usual scriptural source of this information—but that it came "immediately" from man. "The general institution of it is of Him, but the particular constitution of it of man—the special mode or form of government not being determined from above." And they deemed this "the dictate of reason as well as the voice of scripture."[13]

On this and other subjects the ministers frequently appealed to reason or the law of nature as the law, will, or voice of God—something which Locke himself had done in the *Two Treatises*.[14] Charles Chauncey, an influential Bostonian who actively supported the patriots' cause all through the Revolutionary years, argued in 1747 that as civil government "originates in the reason of things, 'tis at the same time founded on the will of God; for the voice of reason is the voice of God."[15] Andrew Eliot made the same argument in 1765, during the Stamp Act crisis; he, too, concluded that "the voice of reason is the voice of God."[16] And John Tucker used almost the same words in a similar context in his 1771 Connecticut Election Sermon (which contained three citations of "Locke on Government").[17] Finally, Samuel West made the case for civil government in 1776 from "reason, which is the voice of God." Whatever reason requires, West maintained, "is as much the will and law of God as if it were enjoined us by an immediate revelation from heaven, or commanded in sacred Scriptures."[18]

This formulation, as well as the simultaneous appeal to scripture, was also invoked when the discussion turned to the key issues of submission and resistance. In 1769 one clergyman, with a reference to Galatians, called upon his congregation to "stand fast" in the "liberties wherewith Christ hath made us free," in the "rights founded in the law of nature, which is the law of God, eternal and immutable."[19] And shortly before the fateful skirmishes at Lexington and Concord,

Peter Whitney warned that should rulers "enjoin or require things of their subjects contrary to the laws of nature, which are the laws of God, and contrary also to the Christian religion," then "we must obey God rather than man, and stand fast in that liberty wherewith Christ hath made us free."[20] As we shall see, Whitney made judicious use of the *Second Treatise* in this sermon.

Theistic epistemology informed some of the most characteristic and distinguished disquisitions on the subject of resistance to civil authority. In his celebrated *Discourse Concerning Unlimited Submission*, Jonathan Mayhew vigorously denounced passive obedience and nonresistance, doctrines that "are fetched neither from divine revelation nor human reason." Since Mayhew recognized no other source of knowledge, it did not matter "from whence [these doctrines] come or whither they go." What counted for Mayhew was that "neither the law of reason nor of religion requires that any obedience or submission should be paid" to civil rulers who "abuse their trust and power." On the contrary, both reason and revelation require that such rulers "should be totally discarded, and the authority which they were before vested with transferred to others."[21]

Daniel Shute also attacked passive obedience and nonresistance on theistic epistemological grounds. These doctrines, he argued, "can be supported neither by reason nor by revelation." Thus they "came not from above," but in fact "may be urged . . . by the rulers of darkness." Shute, like Mayhew and others, saw reason and revelation pointing people away from unlimited submission. If "laws made by civil rulers" do not "answer to the great end" for which they exist, then subjects "may be morally obliged to resist them, as it must ever be right to obey God rather than men."[22]

The right and duty to oppose a tyrannical exercise of power frequently received the dual sanction of scripture and reason. Charles Turner spoke about the duty of the people to oppose rulers who violate the public good, the end of all government. That duty "arises from the regard they owe to the great immutable law of self-preservation" and from the obligation "every person in society is under to all the rest . . . by the law of Christian charity." And in Turner's view, these principles were "perfectly consonant to right reason and to the word of God." (He traced their historical legitimacy to the Revolution of 1688.)[23] John Lathrop found gospel "agreeable to the dictates of reason," especially on the subject of self-defense. For further illumination he directed his readers to the discussion of the state of war in "Locke on Government."[24] Samuel West "confirmed from reason and Scripture" that the same principles that require us to obey lawful magistrates "also require us to resist tyrants." In an election sermon delivered less than two months prior to the Declaration of Independence (and in which he cited "Locke on Government"), West aggressively reiterated this theme. "Reason and revelation do both teach us that our obedience to rulers is not unlimited, but that resistance is not only allowable, but an indispensable duty in the case of intolerable tyranny and oppression."[25]

We will return to the theory of resistance later in this chapter. For now it suffices to note how for the clergy, tyranny had no foundation in either reason or revelation. On the other hand, the right and duty to resist tyrants were said to be consistent with reason and the law of nature on the one side and the law revealed in scripture on the other. On this crucial issue, then, the ministers adopted the epistemological view of the relationship between revelation and reason, and of their shared generation from the will of God, that we find throughout Locke's philosophy. And the political prescriptions which the ministers justified on theistic epistemological grounds were essentially consistent with those found (and similarly justified) in the *Two Treatises*. For example, Locke's famous attack on Filmerian absolutism included the accusation that Sir Robert's doctrine, which "denied Mankind a Right to Natural freedom" and demanded universal submission, was without foundation in "Scripture or Reason."[26]

Another subject to consider in this discussion of clerical epistemology is religious toleration. Here the clerical teaching reads, on the whole, like a paraphrase of Locke and actually contains quite a few citations to what one commentator called Locke's "unanswerable *Letter of Toleration*." The *Letter*, in fact, was the first American edition of a Lockean text—the work of the senior class at Yale in 1742.[27]

For Locke, as we saw in chapter 4, mutual toleration in matters of religion "is so agreeable to the Gospel and to reason that it seems

monstrous for men to be blind in so clear a light."[28] Some of the
ministers who argued for toleration in Lockean terms also sought to
derive it jointly from these sources. Charles Chauncey, in 1739, based
his argument on the belief that "the use of force in matters of religion and conscience" contradicted "the example of Christ and the
precepts of his Gospel" as well as "the nature and reason of things."[29]
Moses Dickinson, writing in 1755, enjoined civil magistrates from
punishing subjects "for their religious principles, provided they don't
disturb the civil peace." Dickinson's position and the way in which
he supported it were quintessentially Lockean. All men, he argued,
have a "right . . . as moral agents and accountable creatures to think
and act for themselves in those things that relate to their own eternal salvation." Moreover, neither reason nor Gospel permitted us to
draw any other conclusion. "All persecution merely upon account of
religion is an unmerciful violation of the law of nature and of the law
of Christ."[30]

Another example of the clerical understanding of the relationship
between reason and revelation comes from Thomas Foxcroft's *Seasonable Thoughts on Evangelical Preaching*, which was published in Boston
in 1740. Historically, the most intriguing feature of this sermon is
the epigram, in which the author quoted a passage from Isaac Watts's
Humble Apology. "You are not to stand up here as a professor of ancient or modern philosophy, nor as an usher in the school of Plato,
Seneca, or Mr. Locke, but as a teacher in the school of Christ." This
suggests that Locke was already a known and controversial figure in
clerical debates as early as 1740.

Foxcroft, in any case, seems to have read Locke carefully enough
to reject Watts's opinion that Christ and Locke taught in different
"schools" (an opinion that might have put Locke on the side of the
deists). The minister declared that "the doctrine of providence is a
dictate of reason as well as revelation, though the glories of this provi-
dential domain are veiled to the eye of natural reason."[31] Foxcroft's
argument was both epistemologically and theologically significant,
and it varied in no essential way from what Locke himself maintained
in his *Essay Concerning Human Understanding*. Reason, Locke argued,
leads men to certain knowledge of the existence of God. However,

the fundamental precepts of Christianity become known to men only through revelation and are therefore matters of faith. For instance, the idea "that the dead shall rise and live again" is "beyond the discovery of reason."[32] Knowledge of this and other principles of Christianity—indeed, "a full knowledge of true morality"[33]—must depend upon revelation, and belief in them therefore must be a matter of faith.

The indispensability of revelation is, of course, the other side of Locke's theistic epistemological coin. And just as the ministers agreed with Locke's view of reason as an essential support of religion,[34] they likewise concurred with his rejection of the deistic doctrine of "natural religion," precisely because it depended exclusively upon reason for its ethical teaching and regarded revelation as irrelevant or impossible. As we saw in chapter 4, it was with specific, critical reference to natural religion that Locke, in *The Reasonableness of Christianity*, maintained that human reason alone, "unassisted" by divine revelation, could not "establish morality in all its parts, upon its true foundation, with a clear and convincing light."[35] Natural religion was not false, except insofar as it claimed to be sufficient. Revelation, on the other hand, compensated for the various essential deficiencies of natural religion, but it did so without ever contradicting the principles of reason.[36]

Samuel Johnson, who had introduced the study of Locke to students at Yale in 1716,[37] offered a discourse on *The Necessity of Revealed Religion* in 1727. He claimed that "true knowledge of God" by "the mere light of nature" was attainable, if at all, only by "extraordinary geniuses" who "had singular leisure and advantages for such speculations." But "the generality of men entertained but the darkest and grossest apprehensions of the Deity." "The improvements of the natural light could never extend very far in the reforming of mankind. . . . And therefore a divine and supernatural revelation . . . would certainly be the most compendious and expeditious method of bringing mankind in general to a just sense of God." Johnson concluded that "the general state and condition of men" morally precluded them from obtaining "any tolerably right apprehensions of the divine nature without supernatural revelation."[38]

Johnson's arguments seemed to echo those in Locke's *Reasonable-ness of Christianity*. The New Testament, according to Locke, was "designed by God, for the instruction of the illiterate bulk of mankind, in the way of salvation."[39] Although it spoke "ever so clearly to the wise and virtuous," reason "had never authority to prevail on the multitude."[40] Immediately following a critical reference to "natural religion," Locke suggested that

> it is at least a surer and shorter way to the apprehensions of the vulgar, and mass of mankind, that one manifestly sent from God, and coming with visible authority from him, should, as a king and lawmaker, tell them their duties, and require their obedience, than leave it to the long and sometimes intricate deductions of reason, to be made out to them. Such trains of reasoning the greatest part of mankind have neither leisure to weigh nor, for want of education and use, skill to judge of.[41]

Here and elsewhere in this text, Locke recommended revealed religion in part because it extended the teaching of reason, in a clear and compelling way, to the masses.[42]

As we have seen, Locke wrote *The Reasonableness of Christianity* partly to chastise, and partly to aid, the deists. Locke's insistence upon the need for revelation and his epistemological critique of innatism put him squarely outside the deists' camp. Yet he sympathized with their opposition to the "speculative dogmas" of the day. So it was with the deists in mind that he gently rebuked the "many [who] are beholden to revelation, [but] who do not acknowledge it."[43]

Now we can note that many New England ministers made the same kinds of arguments against the deistical tendencies in natural religion. John Bulkley, for instance, spoke up for "the usefulness of revealed religion, to preserve and improve that which is natural." Revelation, he argued, provides knowledge which is of great service to natural religion, but "which nature makes no discovery of." The deists' rejection of revelation, then, was inconsistent or insincere.[44] Like Bulkley, Gad Hitchcock made a Lockean "appeal to the deists, who . . . had themselves profited by the revelation which they repudiated."[45] Natural religion, he believed, is aided, and not contradicted, by revelation. The "great aim and tendency" of the revealed law is to give individuals "more just and enlarged notions of the principles, and more strongly to oblige them to the duties, of natural religion."[46]

Also worth noting is Jonathan Dickinson's appeal to revelation as "the means to restore unto *reason* the empire of the mind, and to reduce the exorbitancy of the *passions* and appetites." Dickinson's book, which included a preface by Thomas Foxcroft, used Lockean arguments (or arguments that Locke himself had used) to attack the kind of radical deism that was found more often in England than in America—the deism which had troubled Locke. And Dickinson even called his book *The Reasonableness of Christianity.*[47]

Another of Locke's arguments for revelation held that "knowledge of morality, by mere natural light, makes but a slow progress and little advance in the world."[48] Immediately before calling attention to the deists' unacknowledged debt to revealed religion, Locke observed that we take a great many things "for unquestionable obvious truths, and easily demonstrable, without considering how long we might have been in doubt or ignorance of them had revelation been silent."[49] Turning now to the clerical writings, we find that at least two ministers—Gad Hitchcock and Samuel Langdom—believed, as Locke did, that "achievement of correct religious ideas would have been much delayed if man had received no divine aid."[50]

It bears repeating that the problem with natural religion, according to Locke and the ministers, was its deistic tendency to deny the relevance or even the possibility of revelation. It was, in other words, a part of the truth falsely presenting itself as the whole truth. By no means, however, was the *substance* of natural religion—the teaching of reason—considered false in itself, in any way incompatible with the teaching of revealed religion, or expendable in social and religious life. As one minister put it, "[It is] the excellency of natural religion that it hath its foundation in the rational nature of man, and is therefore stable, fixed and indispensable. . . . it is fundamental to all civil order, the welfare of society and the laws of government." Nevertheless, he continued, "the mere religion of nature," by itself, could not obtain for man "the great end of all religion," which was "the guiding of men to God as their ultimate supreme happiness."

For conducting men to this "great end," natural religion alone was "insufficient."[51] As Locke himself had argued in his *Reasonableness of Christianity*, reason left virtue "unendowed" by the promise of immortality and final reckoning. Thus, "human reason unassisted failed men in its great and proper business of morality." Revelation, however, made virtue "visibly the most enriching purchase, and by much the best bargain," by providing the "view of heaven and hell," and of everlasting rewards and punishments, which in turn served as the only "foundation" upon which "morality stands firm."[52]

For Locke and the ministers, the "sufficient rule for our direction" was received from revelation but was always "conformable to that of reason."[53] Revealed truths were invariably "found to be agreeable to reason."[54] Reason, on the other hand, was the indispensable "judge" of the authenticity of revelation and thus necessary for religion itself.[55] Reason served as "one grand support" of religion.[56] As Locke put it, "he that takes away *reason*, to make way for *revelation*, puts out the light of both."[57] Echoing Locke's argument from the *Essay Concerning Human Understanding*, Charles Chauncey of Boston inquired: "If we give up our understandings, how shall we be able to ascertain the sense of any text of scripture?"[58]

The ministers, in short, recommended precisely the kind of balance between reason and revelation—between the interdependent and harmonious expressions of God's will—that Locke himself had prescribed. As Jared Eliot warned in 1736, "we should have a just value for *reason* and *revelation*. Let not these which God has joined together, be by any man under any pretense put asunder."[59] Or to cite Samuel West, a minister whose own citations confirm his familiarity with Locke: Relying only upon reason leaves us "destitute of piety," whereas we tend "to run into enthusiasm" by relying exclusively upon the doctrines of revealed religion. In West's liberal view, "a true gospel minister should seek to avoid both extremes."[60]

The clerical writings thus show that the ministers, like Locke, consistently believed that God is "the Father of light and the fountain of all knowledge," disclosing His will through the interdependent media of natural and revealed law.[61] Reason is "the candle of the Lord," which illuminates natural law; Revelation is His word;

and both are indispensable for social and religious life. This common theistic epistemological ground, where, for the ministers and for Locke, the most important things were at stake, constitutes a crucial element in the substantive Lockean connection in American Revolutionary thought. Theistic epistemology helps to explain why the New England clergy (to quote Rossiter again) "gave the first and most cordial reception" to Locke's ideas. The "high degree of correlation" that Pocock observed between eighteenth-century republicanism and deism,[62] on the other hand, further explains why it was Locke, and not Cato, who "rode into New England on the backs of Moses and the Prophets."

II. The Theistic Basis for Political Constitutionalism: The Limited Sovereignty of God

We can now consider a specifically theological concept and see how it was incorporated or reflected in political theory. Our subject is Locke's and the ministers' interpretation of the nature of God, which theistic epistemology helped to define. We begin by formally introducing some important but neglected scholarship that deals with this very issue.

Alice Baldwin's *The New England Clergy and the American Revolution*, originally published in 1928, remains the most meticulous and enlightening treatment of clerical thought.[63] Baldwin's sermonology reveals a "direct line of descent from seventeenth-century political philosophy to the doctrines underlying the American Revolution." She notes, in particular, the empirical and the conceptual preeminence of Locke's ideas—ideas drawn from "his essays on religious toleration and human understanding as well as [from] those on government"—in the clerical writings. "[Locke] was quoted by name as early as 1738, but his influence is to be seen in earlier works. Especially after 1763, the references to him are numerous, not only by the more prominent ministers of the larger towns but by those of country villages as well. And in many works in which no direct reference is made one finds his theories, sometimes his very phrases, and this is true for years before 1763 as well as afterwards."[64] Measured by actual citations as well as by the recurrence of distinctively Lockean language and arguments in relation to crucial points of political theory, Locke emerged from Baldwin's study as the most important "secular" source in the sermon literature before and during the Revolutionary years.[65]

Baldwin's work is invaluable for our purposes. She provided the initial focus on "the analogy between theology and political theory" in the clerical teaching, and to this she attributed the clergy's notable fondness for Locke. The general interpretation of Biblical doctrine concerning the origin, nature, and end of civil government, Baldwin argued, was "identical" with the political theory of the *Two Treatises*. In the context of our current subject, the ministers' understanding of the nature of God made the political constitutionalism in the *Two Treatises* irresistible.[66]

While essentially correct, Baldwin's insight into the relationship between Lockean and clerical thought can be enlarged. That is, Baldwin apparently did not recognize the analogy between theology and political theory in *Locke's* teaching. This applies not only to the theological question of the nature of God, but also to her interpretation of clerical epistemology. She correctly defined the relationship between reason and revelation in clerical thought; but she seemed to suggest that the ministers subscribed to this view *in spite of* their conspicuous devotion to Locke's political theory.[67] In either case, the analyses offered in this chapter should strengthen, not undermine, Baldwin's general thesis. The Lockean connection in clerical thought was more deeply rooted than even she suspected.

The concept of "limited sovereignty" seems like an oxymoron. How can a power be supreme and at the same time be subordinate to something which imposes limits upon it? Indeed, sovereignty is by definition unlimited, or it simply isn't sovereignty (and by the same token, "absolute sovereignty" is redundant). Historically, this logical problem took a political form. As expressed on one side by Governor Thomas Hutchinson in his warning to the Massachusetts legislature, and affirmed on the other side by patriots such as Benjamin Franklin and James Wilson, there could be no middle ground between the sovereignty of Parliament and the independence of the colonies.[68] Sovereignty was a kind of zero-sum political game.

Yet the contradictory notion of limited sovereignty—what logic could not resolve and what in Anglo-American politics culminated in the War of Independence—held the status of a theological first principle among many New England ministers. The concept of God that informed the clerical teaching in general could be expressed by the paradox of omnipotence that is limited by its own perfection. God's power was absolute and indivisible, but not arbitrary. "God by the perfection of his own being was limited by [his own] inviolable law."[69] God was "limited," too, by his own benevolence. "God's sovereignty is limited by wisdom, justice, and mercy."[70] Finally, it was essentially in God's nature to keep his word. Covenant theology absolutely presupposed a deity bound by its own promises.[71]

The ministers thus seemed unperturbed by the logical difficulties that arose from combining omnipotence with constraint in the nature of God. They also seemed eager to draw a potentially explosive and distinctively Lockean-liberal *political* inference from this theological concept: the idea that arbitrary, illimitable civil power—the kind that could "bind . . . the people of America . . . in all cases whatsoever"—was morally repugnant.

Clerical writings from early in colonial history to 1776 bear this out. In 1692 one minister argued that civil rulers must be subject to law. "God Himself (with reverence be it spoken) cannot punish his own creature without a law broken"; so "he that governs without or against law arrogates a higher prerogative than God doth."[72] "Unaccountable will" and "inconstant humor," said another in 1710, "are imperfections that God's nature cannot suffer." God, therefore, governs only "by stable measures."[73] Or as John Bulkley wrote three years later, "the divine government is managed by fixed and steady rules."[74] And as an anonymous clerical author put it in 1747, the way of God is to act, and to dispose of all things, "according to the strictest rules of infinite and inviolable justice."[75]

Jonathan Mayhew moved from theology to political theory specifically in the context of a theory of resistance. His great polemic against unlimited submission was based fundamentally upon the proposition that "God Himself does not govern in an absolute, arbitrary and despotic manner." Even God's power "is limited by law." Hence the power of the civil magistrate, precisely because it comes ultimately (though not immediately) from God, cannot exceed the power of God Himself. Civil power can never be arbitrary; it must always be subject to law.[76] Throughout his public life Mayhew maintained that "in all free constitutions, law, and not will, is the measure of the magistrate's power."[77] We can now see how Mayhew's theory of government—a theory which augurs the spirit of American constitutionalism—rested on a specific theological idea.[78]

The most prominent preachers from the Revolutionary period often based their justifications for resistance on the argument that Parliament's attempt to assert "illimitable" sovereignty over the colonies assumed "a higher prerogative than God." John Tucker, for instance, joined theistic epistemology with the notion of God's limited sovereignty and, with an explicit appeal to "Locke on Government," arrived at a moral justification for revolution.

Tucker began by asserting that "principles of reason and equity" are consistent with the "peculiar laws of Christianity" because "intimations from the all-perfect mind cannot be contradictory." That is, since natural and revealed laws both come from God, they *must* be consistent, since God does not, or cannot, issue contradictory decrees. This involuntary exclusion of contradiction from the nature of the deity yielded the proposition that "even the supreme Ruler of the world is not a despotic, arbitrary monarch," but is instead a kind of limited sovereign. His "sacred laws are wisely adapted to the human system, and calculated for its good." God therefore does not require our obedience to "mere authority," that is, to arbitrary or lawless power, but only to *lawful* authority. Tucker then summoned "the great and judicious Mr. Locke" to illuminate the difference between the lawful magistrate and the tyrant, that is, between civil power that we ought to obey and civil power that we have a right to resist: "'Wherever law ends, tyranny begins. . . . And whosoever in authority exceeds the power given him by law . . . ceases in that to be a magistrate: and acting without authority, may be opposed as any other man who by force invades the right of another.'"[79]

John Lathrop, another noted member of the notorious "Black Regiment," cited the same passage from "Locke on Government" in arguing that "the laws of every well-constituted society, nation, or state are above kings."[80] Lathrop, for whom true revelation was always "agreeable to the dictates of reason," believed that if God must act within law, then so must kings and legislatures. The Revolutionary roots of American constitutionalism, understood in the Lockean-liberal sense of lawful and therefore limited government, were thus intertwined with theology in clerical thought.[81]

Samuel West's fiery election sermon of 1776 sheds further light upon the theistic origins of political constitutionalism in clerical thought. It also reveals the underlying connections between epistemology, theology, and political theory. West put it all together, combining the exclusion of contradiction from the divine essence with the idea of the limited sovereignty of God in the context of theistic epistemology; and his understanding of the nature of God closely resembled his understanding of the nature of civil government. Like Locke (whom he cited),[82] West believed that natural and revealed laws can never contradict each other, since they come from the same source—a source incapable of contradiction. "[Any] revelation, pretending to be from God, that contradicts any part of the natural law, ought immediately to be rejected as an imposture; for the Deity cannot make a law contrary to the law of nature without acting contrary to himself—a thing in the strictest sense impossible, for that which implies contradiction is not an object of the divine power."[83] The law of nature and the law of the Gospel both come from God, and the omnipotence of God does not include the power of self-contradiction. Epistemology and theology were thus like two sides of the same coin. The epistemological consistency between reason and revelation implied, or presupposed, a deity constrained by law. West then moved easily from the notion of God as "a constitutional monarch superbly limited by the law which He had created" to the political doctrine of limited government.[84]

If the deity was itself constrained by law, and thus prohibited by its own nature from acting in an arbitrary way, then the civil magistrate, who received his authority ultimately from God (though immediately from the people), was bound by that same law and, indeed, by the very principle of rule by law. Rule without or against law lacked the divine sanction and was therefore illegitimate. And since "civil government . . . was ordained of God," its purpose and end was like that of "the government of Christ and God Himself," namely, "the good of the people." Civil rulers had to rule for the good of the people in order to retain the divine sanction for, and thus their subjects' submission to, their governments. Baldwin suggests that this "analogy between theology and political theory" in the clerical teaching explains the ministers' high regard for the *Two Treatises*, for Locke claimed "that governments are limited by the purpose for which they were founded, viz., the good of the people"; and this argument was essentially consistent with the ministers' theologically derived conception of politics.[85]

Baldwin is basically correct; but like the republican revisionists who have rejected her "Lockean" interpretation of clerical thought (without either confronting it or offering a textually credible alternative), she does not probe very deeply into Locke's thought. Familiar Lockean aphorisms taken out of context are about as far as she or her critics have gone. (Some of the critics haven't gone even that far.) But while the revisionists thereby overlook or deny the significance of Locke, Baldwin, writing before Strauss and Macpherson developed the "bourgeois Locke," and thus unencumbered by the revisionists' anti-Lockean sentiments, confirms the existence of an important Lockean connection. My argument is that Baldwin's thesis would be even stronger if it were informed by the "theistic Locke." *Lockean* liberalism did not emerge from some kind of secular vacuum. It was shaped and inspired by "religious preoccupations" and "theological commitments" similar to those of the New England clergy— as with the relationship between reason and revelation, so too with the nature of God.

Like the ministers, Locke envisaged God as a limited sovereign. For evidence, I offer, first, this passage from the *Essay Concerning Human Understanding*. "God Himself cannot choose what is not good. The freedom of the Almighty hinders not his being determined by what is best." For Locke it is no paradox to combine freedom with determination in the divine nature insofar as the aim of such determination is happiness. We do not count the "constant desire of happiness and the constraint it puts upon us to act for it" as "an abridgment of liberty, or at least an abridgment of liberty to be complained of." Thus the determination or necessity to seek happiness is fully consistent with freedom and, in the case of the deity, omnipotence. "God Almighty Himself is under the *necessity* of being happy."[86]

Bibliographic context is important here. The fact that these remarks appear in the chapter "Of Power" underscores Locke's strong philosophical commitment to the ideas they express. According to Professor Yolton, most of Locke's substantive revisions and additions for the fourth and fifth editions of the *Essay* occurred precisely at this point in the text; so it is highly likely that these arguments received careful scrutiny by an author deeply "interested in the posthumous fate of his books."[87] We may therefore view them as indicative of Locke's true feelings on this very sensitive subject.

Moreover, this was not the only time that Locke treated God as a kind of constitutional monarch, suggesting that there are some things that even God cannot do. Further along in the *Essay*, in speaking "Of Faith and Reason" (and apparently tying theistic epistemology to speculations about the nature of God), he declared that God "cannot lie"; He "cannot err and will not deceive."[88] In the *Two Treatises* Locke twice stated that God is bound by his own promises.[89] And in *The Reasonableness of Christianity*, he rejected the idea that God could act arbitrarily in relation to individual souls. "[I]t is impossible that [God] should justify those who had no regard to justice at all, whatever they believed. This would have been to encourage iniquity, contrary to the purity of his nature. . . ."[90] The "Christian hedonism" we spoke of in the previous chapter evidently presupposes justification by works, not by faith. Be that as it may, the limited sovereignty of God is the underlying theological concept.

In sum, Locke and the ministers shared essentially the same conception of the deity, and they drew similar political conclusions from that theological position. In their view arbitrariness and contradiction are not part of God's nature. There are some things which even divine omnipotence cannot do. Theistic epistemology converges with this interpretation of God's nature, as reflected in the necessary consistency between the natural and revealed laws, both of which come from a source that is incapable of contradiction. And we have seen how, for the ministers, God's "lawfulness" means that arbitrary civil power is illegitimate, and that civil rulers are bound to the principle of rule by law. We also mentioned the content of the law which morally binds all magistrates: political sovereignty must be limited by the end for which civil power, as such, is established, namely, the good of the people.[91] In the following section, we shall examine the scriptural basis for this political doctrine, both in clerical thought as well as in Locke's "secular" political theory.

III. The Lockean Exegesis of the "Politicks of St. Paul"

Basing a revolutionary teaching on the scriptural authority of chapter 13 of St. Paul's Epistle to the Romans must rank as one of the greatest ironies in the history of political thought. This passage, proclaimed by George Sabine as "the most influential political pronouncement in the New Testament," served as the touchstone for passive obedience and unconditional submission from Augustine and Gregory to Luther and Calvin.[92] "Let every soul be subject unto the higher powers, for there is no power but of God: The powers that be are ordained of God. Whosoever therefore resisteth the power, resisteth the ordinance of God; and they that resist shall receive to themselves damnation. For rulers are not a terror to good works, but to the evil. . . . For he is the minister of God to thee for good. . . ."[93]

The medieval church fathers as well as the reformers and counter-reformers of the sixteenth century all invoked this doctrine in denouncing disobedience and resistance to civil authorities. To them it seemed absolutely unequivocal. If civil rulers, as such, "are ordained of God," then resistance is in all cases a sin and, indeed, as Luther put it, "a greater sin than murder, unchastity, theft, and dishonesty, and all that these may include."[94] In sum, Romans 13 easily earned its reputation in the history of political thought as "the locus classicus of passive-obedience theory."[95]

Nevertheless, it was precisely from the "politicks of St. Paul" that

the New England ministers drew a scriptural justification for political
resistance. They invoked St. Paul's doctrine against itself and thus,
so to speak, converted the Apostle from "a friend to tyranny and
arbitrary government" to "a strong advocate for the just rights of
mankind."[96] The principal scriptural authority for political theory remained constant, but a change in the interpretation of this passage
transformed the duty of passive obedience and nonresistance to all
civil rulers into the duty to resist, "to the utmost of our power," certain kinds of civil rulers.[97] The Apostle's argument, as the ministers
generally interpreted it, made the doctrine of unlimited passive obedience "most shocking to a Christian ear" and submission to tyrants
"highly criminal in the sight of Heaven."[98]

The clergy did not treat St. Paul as a radical simply as a matter
of Revolutionary exigency. Jonathan Mayhew in 1750, and Samuel
West in 1776, offered the same "liberal" interpretation of Romans 13.
Even before Mayhew this interpretation appeared in a number of
pamphlets and sermons, while, as far as I have been able to determine, no one invoked his "authoritarian" alter ego to support the
doctrine of passive obedience.[99] And from 1750 on this passage served
as the perennial "favorite" of ministers writing about government,
the limited nature of obligation, and the right or duty of resistance.[100]
Indeed, by 1761, three years before the Stamp Act crisis, Benjamin
Stevens "thought it needless" to explain Romans 13 in his *Election
Sermon*, since that passage had already been "so fully vindicated by
so many able writers from the unjust interpretations of the friends of
slavery and the abettors of tyranny."[101]

The "liberal" reading of Romans 13 was not, in fact, an American
innovation. Quentin Skinner traces the prototype to John Colet, a
fifteenth-century English humanist—and, in a way, Skinner's methodological ancestor. Colet took a historical approach to scripture in
his *Exposition of St. Paul's Epistle to the Romans*. According to Skinner,
he attempted "to elucidate St. Paul's meaning by examining the precise historical context in which his words were originally uttered."
Colet believed that the "prevailing political conditions in Imperial
Rome" compelled the Apostle to " 'act circumspectly' " in addressing
the Romans and to enunciate a doctrine for the times, not for all

time. And no general principle of unconditional subjection should be drawn from injunctions so constrained by historical particularities. Colet thus explained—and explained away—the seemingly unqualified demand for political passivity, concluding that St. Paul did not intend to be understood as the author of passive-obedience theory.[102]

For our purposes it is interesting to see that, like Colet, both Locke and Mayhew took a historical approach to the interpretation of Romans 13 (though, as we shall see, they went much further than Colet toward a radical reading of this passage). Locke felt that ignorance of "the particularities of the history in which these speeches are inserted" constituted an obstacle in the way of our understanding the doctrine of St. Paul.[103] Moreover, changes in the meaning of words and phrases over time had made the meaning of the Epistles difficult to apprehend. Thus, "many things . . . lie concealed to us, which, no doubt, they who were concerned in the letter understood at first sight."[104] Mayhew, for his part, called attention to the Apostle's actual, historical audience. St. Paul addressed recent converts to Christianity, many of whom believed that their new religion entitled them to a complete exemption from obedience as such. Mayhew, as we shall see, did not rely primarily upon this historical argument in refuting the "slavish" reading of Romans 13; but he did refer twice to the anarchistic inclinations of the Apostle's audience as a way to explain the stringency of his language.[105]

Colet, in any case, did not go so far as to extract a theory of resistance from Romans 13. He could argue against the Epistle being read as a universally valid political prescription for unconditional passive obedience, but his methodological step fell short of transforming it into a justification for revolution. This required a new reading of the content of the passage—a shifting of interpretative emphases.

The full "vindication" of the Apostle began in Europe during the 1550s. Skinner uncovered "the earliest systematic statement" of the new interpretation and of "its implications in Protestant political thought" in the works of Ponet and Goodman. These Marian exiles "abandoned the cardinal Augustinian assumption that, even if our rulers fail to discharge the duties of their offices, we must still regard them as powers ordained of God." A ruler who does not uphold the laws of God is not "ordained of God" and thus is not entitled to our obedience under St. Paul's injunction. Moreover, when the Apostle says "there is no power but of God," he " 'does not here mean any other powers but such as are orderly and lawfully instituted of God.' " One cannot argue otherwise without embracing the morally repugnant, blasphemous notion that God necessarily ordains and approves " 'all tyranny and oppression.' " According to Skinner, this position was "of course revolutionary" for a Protestant in those days.[106]

Ponet did not dispute the conventional view of tyranny as divine punishment for sin; but he profoundly radicalized Protestant political theory when he asserted that "we can only return to God by getting rid of the tyrant."[107] From this perspective passive obedience merely compounds the sins for which tyranny has been inflicted upon us. Redemption is obtained only by actively resisting and actually deposing the tyrant. Tyranny is at once divine retribution for sin and God's compelling summons to political action. Revolution becomes a "fallen" people's avenue to salvation.

This radicalization of the Pauline doctrine actually predates the initial colonization of North America. It was in the colonies, however, that the revision was perfected in theory and practice. Given the independent spirit of New England Protestantism, which Burke called "a refinement of the principle of resistance,"[108] as well as the specific causes and circumstances of the original migration, the "authoritarian" Apostle, the patron saint of passive obedience, could not gain a foothold in that part of the continent. His fate, and that of his doctrine, might even be described as a Hartzian exclusion of liberalism's "natural enemies": Like Filmer and his patriarchal absolutism, they could never succeed in the New World.[109]

Consider the following. New Englanders demonstrated their unequivocal contempt for passive obedience by overthrowing the Andros administration in 1691 (an episode discussed in chapter 3). A tract that had been written to defend this "Glorious Revolution in New England" proclaimed that "the doctrine of passive obedience and non-resistance is by means of the happy Revolution in these nations now exploded, and the assertors of it become ridiculous."[110] A contributor to the *New England Courant* in 1722 denounced passive obedience as a doctrine that would "destroy the world itself." [111] This was a theory fit "for Turks and Indians," said the editors of the *New England Weekly Journal* in 1731, but not for a free people. It persuades princes that they are above the law [112]—that they are, in other words, entitled to "a higher prerogative than God." Five years later Edward Holyoke confirmed this opinion in an election sermon, calling passive obedience "a doctrine calculated for none but a nation of slaves." [113]

The New England ministers continued to denounce the doctrine of passive obedience throughout the Revolutionary period, referring to it as "absurd," "long-exploded," the cause "of fatal convulsions when promulgated amongst a vital people," and "a doctrine of iniquity and the grand support of misrule and tyranny." [114] One "Lockean" preacher in the midst of the Stamp Act crisis spoke for the clergy at large in rejecting passive obedience as "a doctrine of rebellion," thus hoisting the Tories on their own petard. As the House of Hanover owed its place on the throne of England to the right of resistance and the Glorious Revolution of 1688, this doctrine, though it appears to demand universal submission, actually denies the legitimacy of that Revolution and thus "breaks up our allegiance to King George III." [115]

Moreover, as we have seen, passive obedience was deemed contrary to both reason and revelation. Many ministers, like Locke, were quite explicit on this point, while some even ascribed authorship of that epistemologically discredited doctrine to the "rulers of darkness." [116] Finally, we should recall that Samuel West established the connection between the nature of the deity and the consistency between revelation and natural law precisely to refute passive-obedience theory. Had the theistic principles "been properly attended to and understood," that is, had it been understood that the exclusion of contradiction from the divine essence meant that no true revelation could possibly contradict "any part of natural law," then "the doctrine of non-resistance and unlimited passive obedience to the worst of tyrants," because it was "contrary to natural law," would "never have found credit among mankind." [117]

The repudiation of passive obedience was often woven into and justified by the clergy's characteristic explication of "the politicks of

St. Paul." The ministers read a kind of teleology in the Apostle's view of government and civil magistracy by emphasizing the ends for which these institutions were "ordained of God." They stressed the first sentences of the third and (especially) the fourth verses of Romans 13. "Rulers are not a terror to good works, but to evil. . . . He is the minister of God to thee for good." On the one hand, "thee" usually received a plural construction and thus referred to mankind, society, or the community.[118] On the other hand, insofar as God and Christ governed for the good of mankind, it was inconceivable that any divinely appointed institution could be intended for any other purpose. Thus, "the sense of the sacred writer we judge to be that civil magistracy is *designed* of God for good to the governed"; "the end of all human authority is the good of the public"; God has appointed civil magistrates for no other reason but "to be his ministers *for good to the public.*"[119]

At this point Romans 13 underwent a profound transformation from a conservative to a radical teaching. There is evidence of this momentous change in the clerical writings from the first half of the eighteenth century—and at least one piece was heavily laced with quotations from the "celebrated Mr. Locke."[120] But the most eloquent and certainly the most influential systematic statement of the "liberal" interpretation of St. Paul appeared in Jonathan Mayhew's *Discourse Concerning Unlimited Submission and Non-Resistance to the Higher Powers* in 1750—the sermon Thornton called "the morning gun of the Revolution." "Its effect on the public mind was decided and permanent. From this moment—the dawn of independence—the spirit of the people was aroused, ever gathering force and intensity, ever narrowing and concentrating in the idea of *resistance.*"[121]

Taking Romans 13 as his text, and indeed as his authority, Mayhew demolished the doctrine of passive obedience and expounded a theory that treated active resistance in certain cases not only as a right but as a duty. This was the theory that would inform the teaching of the New England clergy throughout the Revolutionary period. In turning to Mayhew's *Discourse*, then, one heeds the advice of John Adams, who recommended it to those who "really wish to investigate the principles and feelings which produced the Revolution."[122]

Yet the *Discourse* itself conveyed nothing contrary to the conventional wisdom of its day. It was "Mayhew's renown as a young, radical preacher" and above all his "vigorous language," not a new political theory, which thrust this sermon into the spotlight.[123] When Mayhew expressed the same ideas, but in cooler language, in his 1754 Massachusetts Election Sermon, not even the Royal Governor flinched (though he might have privately dissented).

Mayhew prefaced his *Discourse* with the hope that it would serve "to keep up the spirit of civil and religious liberty" against the "tory-spirited" Church of England, which had been preaching passive obedience and nonresistance in commemorating the "martyrdom" of Charles I. He tackled the issue directly by seeking "to ascertain the sense of the Apostle" in Romans 13. Did St. Paul, as some insisted (anticipating by sixteen years the language of the Declaratory Act!), "make resistance to princes a crime in all cases whatsoever"? Did he actually maintain that the civil ruler, as such, has "God's authority and commission to bear him out in the worst of crimes so far that he may not be withstood or controlled"? Or could the Apostle be taken to mean that disobedience and resistance were justifiable in certain situations? Mayhew's "main design" in the *Discourse* was to answer these questions in the light of Romans 13.[124]

As we have seen, Mayhew attacked the "authoritarian" interpretation of Romans 13 on historical-contextual, theological, and epistemological grounds. St. Paul's use of seemingly unconditional language was forced upon him by the nature of his actual audience. Mayhew also invoked the idea of God as a "limited sovereign." A deity limited by law (albeit its own law) and hence not arbitrary did not sanction arbitrary rule in civil society. A civil ruler thus retained divine sanction only so long as his government conformed to the ways of God, i.e., so long as he ruled within and according to law. Passive-obedience theory was weakened even further in Mayhew's eyes by the fact that it had no epistemological foundation either in natural or revealed law. Hence, Mayhew argued, it did not come from God and ought not to have been regarded as a sacred, moral, or prudent teaching.[125]

But what *did* come from God? What exactly was the scriptural prescription concerning political obligation? Here we come to the "politicks of St. Paul" according to Mayhew and the direct extrapolation of a theory of resistance from the "locus classicus of passive-obedience theory."

Mayhew imposed "utilitarian" conditions upon obedience by emphasizing verses three and four and interpreting them in the manner indicated above: "Rulers are not a terror to good works, but to evil . . . . He is the minister of God to thee *for good.*" Here, according to Mayhew, the Apostle argues "explicitly" what is implicit throughout his "politicks": "The sole end of all government" is "the happiness of society" and "the good of society"; and "the end of magistracy is the good of civil society, *as such.*"[126] Rulers, to be sure, are "ordained of God," but they retain their commission, that is, they are to be deemed magistrates and therefore obeyed, only so long as "they do not grossly abuse their power and trust, but exercise it for the good of those that are governed." As Mayhew read St. Paul, we do not owe submission "to all who bear the title of rulers in common"; we must obey only those "who actually perform the duty of rulers by exercising a reasonable and just authority for the good of human society."[127]

The Apostle's message is clear, according to Mayhew. Obedience is a Christian duty. Christians are obliged to render obedience to all civil magistrates.[128] But a ruler who acts out of the "character" of a magistrate—a ruler, that is, who uses his power to pursue his own particular good at the expense of the governed and against the good of society—*ceases to be a magistrate* and therefore need not be obeyed. "When once magistrates act contrary to their office and the end of their institution—when they rob and ruin the public instead of being guardians of its peace and welfare—they immediately cease to be the ordinance and ministers of God, and no more deserve that glorious character than common pirates and highwaymen."[129] Rulers who attempt to exercise power above or without the law suffer the same loss of legitimacy. "As soon as a prince sets himself up above the law, he loses the king in the tyrant. He does, to all intents and purposes, unking himself." And tyrants cannot claim the people's obedience based on the Apostle's teaching. Resisting the tyrant "is no more rebellion than to resist any foreign invader."[130]

According to Mayhew, St. Paul's argument "in fact proves the contrary" of a duty to submit to oppressors and tyrants. The "utilitarian" reading of Romans 13 elicits from that text a *duty to resist* such rulers. "The Apostle's argument is so far from proving it to be the duty of people to obey and submit to such rulers as act in contradiction to the public good, and so to the design of their office, that it indeed proves the direct contrary." [131] The tyrant must not be obeyed, but "totally discarded"—and for exactly the same reason that the civil magistrate is to be obeyed. Obedience to civil magistrates and resistance to tyrants and oppressors are duties which arise from a single source, the "regard for the public welfare," which subjects *and* sovereigns "are indispensably obliged to promote, as far as in them lies." [132]

Mayhew framed this "utilitarian" argument in the strong language of duty in order to convey the sense of St. Paul. The "apparent usefulness of civil authority" to society is the "motive and argument for submission" to civil magistrates. Submission to tyrants, however, implicates subjects in crimes against the public welfare and in the destruction of civil society, and this cannot be reconciled with God's will as revealed in Romans 13. "If it be our duty, for example, to obey our king merely for this reason, that he rules for the public welfare, which is the only argument the Apostle makes use of, it follows, by a parity of reason, that when he turns tyrant, and makes his subjects his prey to devour and destroy, instead of his charge to defend and cherish, we are *bound* to throw off our allegiance to him, and to resist; and that according to the tenor of the Apostle's argument in this passage." [133]

St. Paul makes our duty to promote "the common safety and utility" the "only rational ground for submission" to civil government. And "if, in any case, the common safety and utility would not be promoted by submission to government," but the contrary would be effected, we would then be equally obliged to resist. "By grounding his argument for submission wholly upon the good of civil society, it is plain he implicitly authorizes *and even requires* us to make resistance, whenever this shall be necessary to the public safety and happiness." [134] Resistance to "a reasonable and just authority" is indeed, according to Mayhew, resistance to the will of God, and thus a guarantee of "damnation." But when tyranny holds sway, submission contributes to the ruin of society, and "*they that do not resist will receive to themselves damnation.*"[135]

This was the essence of the "politicks of St. Paul." The scriptural foundation of passive-obedience theory had been transformed exegetically by Mayhew into the foundation of a revolutionary doctrine. Under the right conditions Romans 13 would henceforth serve in the same way that the *Second Treatise* itself was intended to serve, that is, as Peter Laslett put it, "as a demand for a revolution to be brought about."[136] An examination of the sermons from the Revolutionary years will bear this out.

In the midst of the Stamp Act crisis, Andrew Eliot reminded whoever might be tempted to invoke Romans 13 to justify submission to Parliament that St. Paul's argument actually proved the contrary of nonresistance. "St. Paul very plainly teaches us how far subjection is due to a civil magistrate when he gives it as a reason for this subjection, 'for he is the minister of God to thee for good.' The end for which God has placed men in authority is that they may promote the public happiness. When they improve their power to contrary purposes, when they endeavor to subvert the constitution and to enslave a free people, they are no longer the ministers of God." In other words, they "cease to be magistrates." And in that case, said Eliot, when they "pervert their power to tyrannical purposes, submission is so far from being a duty that it is a crime." Eliot drove the point home in the unequivocal language of religious duty. Submission to tyrants "is an offence against God . . . who has appointed government for the welfare and happiness, and not for the destruction, of his creatures."[137]

Other sermons from this period contained the same kind of "inversion" of St. Paul's doctrine. Stephen Johnson, for instance, declared that God (according to St. Paul) had not ordained tyranny or oppression, but "civil government, which is mercifully erected for the protection and preservation of the fundamental liberties and rights of mankind."[138] Johnson grounded his rejection of passive obedience in the "politicks of St. Paul," offering three citations of "Locke on

Government" for emphasis and illustration. Obedience was due only to rulers who acted "within the bounds of the law of God." Arbitrary and unlawful acts "dissolve the government and the subjects' obligation of obedience." Such acts initiate a "state of war with the people," who may then "reassume their natural rights and defend themselves with all the power God has given them." [139] Johnson also cited Locke to show that this power should be used "in a way of prevention," before the doors of the dungeon swing shut. [140]

In his Massachusetts Election Sermon of 1773, Charles Turner took the crucial fourth verse of Romans 13 as his text—"he is the minister of God to thee for good." Turner laid down what in Revolutionary New England was the standard interpretation of this passage. God "appoints" civil rulers "to be his ministers *for good to the publick*." He has "designed" civil magistracy "for good to the governed." The decision between obedience and resistance belongs to the people and depends upon their judgment of the conduct of the magistrate. If the ruler acts as a magistrate in "the sense of the sacred writer," then submission is a duty. If, however, he uses his power to feather his own nest, and his actions undermine rather than promote the public welfare, then his subjects are obliged to resist. According to Turner, this was the doctrine of the Glorious Revolution of 1688; and it was, as we have seen, "perfectly consonant to right reason and the word of God" and therefore justified on theistic epistemological grounds. [141]

Peter Whitney's "fast day" sermon from 1774 provides another example of an overt alliance between Locke and the Apostle for Revolutionary purposes. It also delineates the connection between theology, epistemology, and political theory. Revelation, Whitney argued, concurs with reason in declaring that the civil ruler is the minister of God "for *good* to the public." Therefore, the civil magistrate ought to be obeyed. But if rulers "forsake their proper sphere, thwart God's design in ordaining them, disserve the people, and take measures which tend to ruin them, the Apostle's ground of the people's subjection ceases; and, indeed, *submission becomes a fault, and resistance a virtue*." [142] Precisely at this point in his sermon Whitney called upon "the great Mr. Locke" to illuminate the difference between the magistrate (who must be obeyed) and the tyrant (who must be opposed). He cited section 202 of the *Second Treatise* (a favorite with Revolutionary authors): "Wherever law ends, tyranny begins"; the ruler who acts without or against law "ceases in that to be a magistrate" and by this change in "character," makes himself legitimately subject to forcible resistance. Whitney, like a number of his clerical colleagues, explicitly supplemented the "politicks of St. Paul" with Locke's political theory in an effective, radicalizing sermon.[143]

In 1776 Samuel West rehearsed the arguments that Mayhew and others had made over the previous twenty-six years. West acknowledged that St. Paul's doctrine had served as the "great anchor and main support" for passive-obedience theory. But he denounced this "slavish" interpretation of Romans 13 as a perversion of sacred scripture. "This text is so far from favoring arbitrary government that, on the contrary, it strongly holds forth the principles of true liberty."[144] The *correct* interpretation starts out from the proposition that God ordained civil magistracy "for the preservation and safety of civil society." Rulers are the ministers of God, and therefore must be obeyed, *only* "while they act up to the end of their institution." Resistance, however, "ceases to be criminal" when rulers "cease being the ministers of God, i.e., when they act contrary to the general good and seek to destroy the liberties of the people."[145] The language is very familiar. The Apostle, according to West, affirms that when rulers "act contrary to the end and design" of civil government, "they cease being magistrates" and thus forfeit their claim to the subject's obedience.[146]

West traced every important step in the radicalization of St. Paul. All men, he argued, are principally obliged "to promote the public good." Hence arises the duty to obey the civil magistrate, who is "a terror to evil works" and the minister of God for good. But this "regard for the public" is also the source of our duty to oppose "every exertion of arbitrary power" that, as such, is "injurious" to the public good. The character of magistracy and the determination of political obligation are thus inseparably linked through the concept of the public good in the "politicks of St. Paul." "Whenever rulers pursue measures directly destructive of the public good they cease being God's ministers, they forfeit their right to obedience from the subject, they become the pests of society, and the community is under the strongest obligation of duty, both to God and to its own members, to resist and oppose them." [147] Subjects have an "indispensable duty" to oppose rulers who have exchanged the character of the magistrate for that of the tyrant by "subverting the public happiness," and to oppose them without reservation. [148]

West's summation of Romans 13 is worth reproducing at length. It was representative of clerical thought in general and, as such, it captured a most radical element of American Revolutionary thought in 1776.

> If the apostle, then, asserts that rulers are ordained of God only because they are a terror to evil works and a praise to them that do well; if they are the ministers of God only because they encourage virtue and punish vice; . . . if the sole reason why they have a right to tribute is because they devote themselves wholly to the business of securing to men their just rights, and to the punishing of evil doers—it follows, by undeniable consequence, that when they become the pests of human society, when they promote and encourage evil-doers, and become a terror to good works, they then cease being the ordinance of God; they are no longer ministers of God; they are so far from being the powers that are ordained of God that they become the ministers of the powers of darkness, and it is so far from being a crime to resist them, that in many cases it may be highly criminal in the sight of heaven to refuse resisting and opposing them to the utmost of our power. . . . The same reasons that require us to obey the ordinance of God, do equally oblige us, when we have power and opportunity, to oppose and resist the ordinance of Satan. [149]

In this way the New England clergy "vindicated" the Apostle, presenting him not as "a friend to tyranny and arbitrary government," but as "a strong advocate for the just rights of mankind." [150] The ministers thus drew a revolutionary doctrine, proclaiming a *duty* to resist tyrants in the compelling terms of religious obligation, from the "locus classicus of passive-obedience theory." And the sermons we have examined in this section reflect the consensus across a large body of clerical writings.[151]

As I noted above, the ministers frequently fortified their "liberal" interpretation of Romans 13 with citations of "Locke on Government" as they sought to establish beyond dispute the right and duty of resistance. The textual evidence clearly supports Baldwin's claim that "often 'the great Mr. Locke' was cited in proof of the duty as well as the right to resist tyranny."[152] Yet Locke himself had derived the same unequivocal refutation of passive obedience from Romans 13 in his lengthy exegesis and paraphrase of St. Paul's Epistles. And although this literary testimony to Locke's "religious preoccupations" earned high marks in clerical circles, neither Baldwin nor the republican revisionists mention it.[153]

Locke undertook his exegesis of St. Paul for personal religious reasons. "I have, for my own information, sought the true meaning" of St. Paul's Epistles. Constitutionally incapable of accepting "the pope's interpretation of sacred scripture," he deemed it his "duty and interest, in a matter of so great concernment" to him as a Christian, to search the scriptures for himself, to "study the way to salvation in those holy writings, wherein God has revealed it from heaven."[154] This project thus symbolized Locke's personal commitment to a position he had set forth earlier, in the *Letter on Toleration*: "Regarding his salvation, every man has the supreme and final power of judging for himself."[155] And though his exegesis was not directly tied to his explicitly political work, his "liberal" interpretation of Romans 13 complemented the arguments of the *Two Treatises* (as well as the arguments that Mayhew would make, and other ministers in Revolutionary New England would echo, many years later).

According to Locke, St. Paul said that God ordained civil magistracy "only for thy good." The "end of Government, and the business of the magistrate," are "to cherish the good and punish ill men." Obedience to civil rulers is of course a Christian duty, and Christians ought not, "by any means, to resist them."[156] Locke, however, referring to the third verse, elicited from the Apostle a crucial limiting condition on obedience: "It seems that St. Paul meant here magistrates having and exercising a lawful power."[157] Moreover, the determination of whether the rulers "in being" were in fact "lawful" magistrates, "and consequently were, or were not, to be obeyed," was not "the distinct privilege" of Christians alone. Moving beyond the parochialism of the *Letter on Toleration*, he stated that this determination, from which a revolution could legitimately ensue, was the "common right" of all men.[158] Locke thus interpreted St. Paul as a "constitutionalist," in much the same way as did Mayhew and the New England clergy; and he extended the *inalienable* right of *political judgment* to all men.[159]

Locke's emphasis on the "publick good" in the *Two Treatises* as the objective that defined legitimate government conformed to the relationship he outlined between obedience and the end of civil government in his analysis of Romans 13. Section 92 of the *First Treatise*, for example, contained unmistakable traces of the "liberal" Apostle intertwined, so to speak, with some "typical" Lockean observations concerning government and property. The right to property originated in the right of self-preservation (which was, in the first place, a duty to God).[160] Moreover, "government, being for the preservation of every man's right and property," exists only "for the good of the governed." According to Locke, the sword was given to the civil magistrate "for a *terror to evil doers,*" and to uphold "the positive laws of the society, made conformable to the laws of nature, for the public good." The sword was "not given to the magistrate for his good alone."[161]

We find this concern for the public good throughout the *Second Treatise*, and though the connection with scripture here is not so readily apparent, there is no departure from Locke's interpretation of the "politicks of St. Paul." It is true that Locke limited government to the preservation of property, which, we should remember, included life, liberty, and estate.[162] Yet in several places and in various contexts, he also identified the end of government, and of its institutions, as the public good. Indeed, for Locke, the public good *was* the preservation of property (broadly understood).

In the beginning of the *Second Treatise*, Locke defined political

power as "*a right* of making laws with penalties of death, and consequently all less penalties, for the regulating and preserving of property, and of employing the forces of the community, in the execution
of such laws, and in the defense of the commonwealth from foreign
injury, and all this only for the publick good."[163] Laws "ought to be
designed for no other end ultimately but *the good of the people*"; for the
"foundation and end of all laws," as such, is "the publick good."[164] As
for the supreme governmental institution, the legislative, its power,
"in the utmost bounds of it, is *limited to the publick good* of the society."
The legislative therefore "can never have a right to destroy, enslave,
or designedly impoverish the subjects."[165] The power of the legislature, or even of the society that has constituted the legislature, can
never "be supposed to extend farther than the common good." Civil
Government "is to be directed to no other *end* but the *peace, safety,*
and *publick good* of the people."[166] The "end of government itself . . .
is the publick good and preservation of property."[167]

In the footnotes to his exegesis of Romans 13, Locke wrote that,
according to St. Paul, obedience should be rendered only to rulers
"having and exercising a *lawful* power" (my emphasis).[168] Rule by law,
for the public good, distinguishes the civil magistrate, who ought
to be obeyed, from the tyrant, who ought to be resisted.[169] St. Paul
thus supports a key argument from the *Second Treatise*, an argument
that not only sounds like Mayhew's exegesis of Romans 13—Bernard
Bailyn to the contrary notwithstanding[170]—but also was cited in
many of the sermons and "secular" writings from the Revolution:
"Wherever law ends, tyranny begins, if the law be transgressed to
another's harm"; and tyranny must be resisted. "Whosoever in authority exceeds the power given him by the law . . . ceases in that
to be a magistrate." He loses his authority—or, as Mayhew said, he
"loses the king in the tyrant"—and thus becomes as subject to legitimate forcible resistance "as any other man who by force invades the
right of another."[171] For Locke, a civil magistrate—that is, a ruler
who is ordained of God and whom we therefore ought to obey—
always "makes the laws the bounds of his power and the good of the
publick the end of his government." The tyrant, however, "makes all
give way to his own will and appetite" and thereby forfeits his com-

mission along with his claim to our obedience.[172] (No wonder the ministers liked to cite " 'the great Mr. Locke.' ")

To be sure, tyranny is not only rule without law and "the exercise of power beyond right"; it is also the "use of the power any one has in his own hands not for the good of those who are under it, but for his own private separate advantage."[173] Indeed, the "publick good" can be an even higher criterion of legitimacy than conformity to positive law. In extraordinary circumstances the executive may act "without the prescription of the law, and sometimes even against it"; but such action is a legitimate exercise of "prerogative" *only* when it has been undertaken in an emergency and "for the publick good."[174] Consideration of the "publick good" can thus make the decisive difference in the people's decision whether to obey or to resist executive action. Resistance becomes justified (and even morally obligatory) when such action violates the "publick good."

As I suggested earlier, Locke defined the "publick good" as the preservation of property (which, again, includes life, liberty, and estate), so far as it was consistent with the preservation of the entire community; and the chief end of government was therefore the preservation of property (broadly understood).[175] The New England clergy, both before and during the Revolutionary period, and often in the context of interpreting the "politicks of St. Paul," also identified the "publick good" with the preservation of property and defined the end of government in this way.[176] Moreover, when the ministers cited a "secular" source to authorize these (and other) political views, the honor usually went to "Locke on Government." Of course, these political views are not uniquely Lockean; but they do represent essential elements of Locke's political theory, which in turn fits integrally and uniquely within a framework of "theological commitments" that the clergy generally shared. The Lockean connection here, then, is substantive.

Let me put this into the methodological framework I outlined earlier in the book. On the one hand, the consistency between the political theory in the *Second Treatise* and Locke's exegesis of Romans 13 reinforces the interpretation of the theistic Locke. On the other hand, the connection between Lockean and clerical thought in this area is established on the basis of three kinds of evidence: (1) internal-textual: conceptual and linguistic similarities between Locke and the clergy in regard both to political theory and to the exegesis of Romans 13; (2) external-textual: the clergy's tendency to cite (as well as quote and closely paraphrase, with or without attribution) "Locke on Government" far more frequently than any other "secular" source to support the "politicks of St. Paul" in terms of political theory; (3) circumstantial: the clergy's "exceedingly high" esteem for Locke's "Scripture commentary."

It is worth recalling another link in the substantive connection, which is strengthened by the Lockean exegesis of the "politicks of St. Paul." The law which binds the magistrate (as well as the subject) in the pursuit of the "publick good" is the positive law of the society only insofar as that positive law conforms to the law of nature. Once again theistic epistemology informed the political thought of both Locke and the New England clergy.[177] The revealed teaching in Romans 13 and the law of nature apprehended by reason together contributed to a single political theory—and the same political theory—in both Lockean and clerical thought.

In any case, neither Locke, as political theorist or "Scripture commentator," nor the New England ministers exempted anyone from obedience to rulers so long as the rulers themselves acted strictly in the "character" of magistrates, that is, so long as they served the "publick good" and acted within the law. But rulers who used the public sword for their own private advantage, abrogating law and perverting the end of magistracy itself, were to be regarded as "private persons" who had initiated a "state of war" against society, and were therefore to be resisted by force.[178] Whether this distorts or clarifies St. Paul's political teaching is a question best left to theologians and biblical historians. What matters here is, first, that Locke and the clergy offered essentially the same interpretation of Romans 13, drawing from it the same liberal political conclusions, and, second, that many ministers liked to support those conclusions in the terms of "Mr. Locke's doctrine."

IV. "Who Shall Be Judge?":
Political Judgment as a Requisite for Salvation

How do you persuade a majority of common men and women to risk all—life, liberty, and estate—for a political ideal or cause? The answer depends on historical circumstances, not the least of which is the character of the people involved. My own sense of the American Revolution is that it had something to do with putting the fear of God into the colonists who bled for it. Religion, in one form or another, has always been premium fuel for the fires of revolution and counter-revolution. The faithful are the willing fodder for *jihad*. Even today, religion still has unsurpassed power to kindle blood-letting "enthusiasm" on a mass scale, and to induce great numbers of people to seek the eternal blessings of martyrdom. The carnage in the Persian Gulf, which, as I write, has been underway for nearly a decade, proves the point. So one solution to the recruitment problem is this: Persuade the believer that his or her soul is at stake and you have created, in terms of motivation if not military prowess, a fearsome and dependable combatant.

This solution makes certain demands upon the political movement in question. First, believers can be persuaded only by fellow believers whose authority they respect, namely, their religious leaders, or clergy, who therefore play a prominent and strategically indispensable role. We know that this was true of the New England clergy in the American Revolution.[179] Second, the ideology of the movement cannot be essentially secular or, if you will, "bourgeois," since neither the religious leaders nor those whom they lead would accept it as such and the generals would soon find themselves short of troops. The ideology, then, must make primary reference to the objects of religion —God, the soul, salvation, etc. Furthermore, an atheistic—or nontheistic—political theory would be of little use to the clergymen who formulate and convey the triggering ideology to the people. If not explicitly theocratic, the political theory must at least fit—as Locke's did—within Rossiter's "scriptural spoon."

The critical moment in the mobilization of the people comes when they are persuaded that they can and must take radical political action: God allows and demands it. The ideological preparation for this takes time. In the American Revolution, and in the decades preceding it, this preparation was usually accomplished in church, with the clergy preaching the right, duty, and competence of the people to make and act upon the most consequential political judgments. The ministers often supplemented their biblical justifications for this view by citing the "secular" authority of "the great Mr. Locke." We might be content to regard this simply as a matter of convenience—like the formal connection, a textually correct use of Locke's political theory without reference to its broader interpretive context. But if we trace the roots of this political argument in both Lockean and clerical thought, we arrive at the same religious source, namely, private, individual judgment as a requisite for salvation. The substantive Lockean connection thus informs one of the most important ideological aspects of American Revolutionary thought: persuading the common people to fight.

At the foundation of theistic liberalism lies the duty (and therefore the right) every person owes to God to judge for himself in matters pertaining to his salvation. Lockean individualism is in the first instance, and so long as the theistic philosophical framework is intact, a doctrine of individual responsibility. As we've seen, Locke believed that man's first concern should be for his "eternal estate." [180] "Man's first care should be for his soul," and for its immortal destiny "in the world to come." [181] Yet Locke also maintained that each individual has the enduring responsibility to discover and to do what is pleasing to God. "Regarding his salvation, every man has the supreme and final power of judging for himself" (this is one of the keys to the liberal political doctrine of religious toleration). [182] Practicing what he preached, Locke undertook his arduous exegesis of St. Paul's Epistles to the Romans precisely because it was his "duty and interest" to study scripture and to draw his own conclusions about the requisites of salvation. [183] No wonder he discovered a "liberal" Apostle!

This notion of individualism has ties to Lockean epistemology as well as to Lockean politics. In the first place, the irreducibly subjective nature of human understanding complements the judicial responsibility of the individual before God. We cannot "know by other men's understandings," wrote Locke. Our "understandings" are "no less different than our palates."[184] But our "understandings" are crucially important. "If I must believe for myself [with respect to the requisites of salvation], it is unavoidable that I must understand for myself,"[185] and thus necessary that I be free to search and interpret scripture as best I can. It is interesting to note that while Locke viewed human understanding as "the most excellent part of [God's] workmanship,"[186] the New England Clergy, too, regarded the understanding as "the leading faculty of the soul."[187] And in both cases, it was the vital role of the understanding, and of its free exercise, in the pursuit of salvation that earned it the highest esteem and that conferred legitimacy exclusively upon the Lockean-liberal politics of toleration.

Theistic epistemology propels the doctrine of individual judgment into Lockean political theory. Each man must judge for himself, by the study of scripture, the content of God's law. But the law of nature, for Locke and the clergy, is also the law of God. And if the "obligations of the law of nature" are "drawn closer" in civil society and constitute the basis of all legitimate "municipal laws,"[188] then individual judgment must extend from the religious to the political context. Thus, in the final political reckoning, "*the people shall be judge*" and, indeed, "*every man is judge* for himself."[189]

Theistic individualism decisively informs the theory of revolution in the *Second Treatise*, and the critical concept, again, is judgment, individual and divine. On the one hand, each individual—"any single man," says Locke—must judge for himself whether circumstances warrant obedience or resistance to the commands of the civil magistrate; we are all qualified, entitled, and morally obliged to evaluate the conduct of our rulers in relation to that "Law antecedent and paramount to all positive laws of men," and to gauge our actions accordingly. This political judgment, moreover, is not simply or primarily a right, but, like self-preservation (which undoubtedly is involved here), a duty to God. As such it is a judgment that men "cannot part with" according to "God and Nature."[190] On the other hand, in deciding whether or not to resist, each individual's judgment is itself judged by God, that is, by the "Tribunal that cannot be deceived" and "will be sure to retribute to every one according to the mischiefs he hath created to his fellow-subjects." The individual, then, must ultimately answer to God for the quality and social consequences of his political judgment.[191]

While commonly depicted as primarily a theory of economic and political rights, Lockean individualism is actually derived from the theistic doctrine of individual responsibility. Duties to God are first; and they authorize all rights. Men must have liberty to do what God requires them to do, and only political arrangements that provide such liberty are deemed legitimate. Without a liberty to judge in matters of religion, as well as in politics, the individual is denied the status of a moral, responsible agent. Liberty is therefore "indispensable to morality" and, as such, a requisite for salvation.[192] Accordingly, men are irrevocably *obliged* to exercise political judgment *and* to defend their liberty—both civil and religious—as much as they value their souls. Liberty, then, is not merely literally but above all normatively central in the Lockean triad of "life, liberty, and estate."

The theistic doctrine of individual judgment, culminating in the call for socially responsible, popular political judgment, constitutes a vital link in the substantive Lockean connection in American Revolutionary thought. The clerical teaching, before and during the Revolutionary period, included this Lockean understanding of individualism as an essential constituent; it stressed the indispensability of private judgment in religious matters, often with explicit reference to Locke himself; and it drew the Lockean political conclusions. For example, Elisha Williams made a "plea for religious liberty" in 1744, offering "a short sketch of what the celebrated Mr. Locke . . . has largely demonstrated." Williams defined "Christian liberty" as "the right of private judgment" and called it the "most valuable of all our rights." This right was "unalienable" and, indeed, "an original right of human nature." Yet the source of this right, and of its "unalienable" character, lay in the individual's duty to God to act as a moral, religious agent. "No action is a *religious* action without understanding and choice in the agent."[193]

Duty to God thus infused liberty with compelling normative force by making the unhindered exercise of judgment a necessary precondition for achieving moral status in the eyes of God. As Jonathan Mayhew argued in 1748, in a sermon devoted to "the right and duty of private judgment" in matters pertaining to religion, "it is the duty of Christians to assert their right of private judgment, in opposition to all that are for usurping authority over them." Mayhew, moreover, transcribed at length "the words of Mr. Locke" to secure an epistemological argument intended to show that "God has given us abilities to judge even of ourselves what is right, and requires us to improve them." And duties precede rights. Private judgment in religious matters is a right—Mayhew called it "the natural right and privilege of every man"—because "the Christian religion . . . enjoins it upon us as a duty." For Mayhew, "God has not only given us liberty to examine and judge for ourselves, but has expressly *required* us to do it." [194]

Almost thirty years later, in the aftermath of Lexington and Concord, Samuel Baldwin strove to inspire his congregation with Revolutionary ardor. "The cause of liberty is the cause of God," he declared, as he pleaded for "the right of judgment in matters purely religious." British military operations now posed a material threat to that right. The colonists, therefore, were morally obliged—it was a duty to God —to defend it with force of arms. [195]

The primacy of individual judgment received frequent affirmation in many sermons from the years separating Williams and Baldwin. All men have a "right as moral agents and accountable creatures to think and act for themselves in things that relate to their own eternal salvation." [196] Every Protestant "according to his abilities should search the scriptures and judge whether the things which his minister delivers be according to this rule." [197] Each individual has "a natural, unalienable right to think and see for himself"; [198] for "as every man must answer for himself at the great and last day, so every one ought to be left at liberty to judge for himself here." [199] "Christian liberty" means that "every Christian has and must have a right to judge for himself the true sense and meaning of all gospel truths." [200] As a prerequisite for moral agency and salvation, it is "not only the right but the duty of men to defend that liberty." To renounce "liberty of private judgment in matters of religion" would "destroy the foundation of all religion" and "must therefore be a violation of the law of nature." [201]

There are many more examples of this doctrine in the clerical writings from the Revolutinary period,[202] as well as in some of the most prominent "secular" writings from that time.[203] In each case the author affirmed it to be the duty and therefore the right of every person to make his or her own judgments in matters of religion. The New England view of moral law, natural or revealed, characteristically reserved the final interpretation for the individual.[204] So did Locke, who was, in fact, personally committed to the principle of private judgment, and whose commitment did not go unnoticed by members of the New England clergy.

As in Lockean thought the ministers' affirmation of the primacy of individual judgment in religious matters registered in their political doctrine as the legitimation of popular political judgment on the most consequential questions of obligation and revolution. The theoretical reasons for this development in Lockean thought, as discussed above, applied with equal force in the clerical teaching, and colonial experiences accelerated the process. Local ecclesiastical controversies during the middle of the eighteenth century, and above all the perceived connection between revenue "innovations" such as the Stamp Act on the one hand and the perennial efforts to establish "prelatical tyranny" under an American Episcopate on the other,[205] encouraged the ministers to recognize the essential interdependence of civil and religious liberty in practical terms.

In his 1773 Massachusetts Election Sermon, Charles Turner declared that "religious liberty is so blended with civil that if one falls it is not to be expected that the other will continue."[206] Also that year Simeon Howard warned that "the destruction of civil liberty is generally fatal to *religions*"; therefore, "from a regard to religion, men are *obliged* to defend their liberty from encroachments, though the attack should not immediately affect religion."[207] Peter Whitney made the same argument in 1774, warning his congregation that "religious liberties are always endangered when the civil are invaded."[208] And the General Association of Congregationalist Ministers described and defended "the cause of America" as "the cause of civil liberty, which if taken away, we fear would involve the ruin of religious liberty."[209] Such statements as these, when taken in context, strongly suggest that from the clerical point of view, private judgment, the essence of liberty as such, had to be extended from religion to politics—and defended with equal vigor in both spheres—for the sake of religion itself.

The emergence of the doctrine of popular political judgment in the sermon literature deserves close attention for three reasons. First, it is probably the most significant conceptual development in a century of clerical political thought. It is, in any case, the only exception I could find to the rule that if direct references to specific events and personalities were deleted, "the dating of a sermon would not be easy on the basis of internal evidence alone." [210] Second, the doctrine is rooted in theological commitments similar to Locke's; and the clerical expression of it, according to both internal and external evidence in the sermon literature, is quintessentially Lockean. It is, therefore, a prime example of the substantive Lockean connection. Finally, the emergence of this doctrine in the clerical teaching represents a decisive moment in the ideological preparation of the people. As such it testifies to the importance of the substantive Lockean connection in the making of the American Revolution.

The clerical affirmation of faith in the people's right, duty, and competence to judge how well they are governed, and to obey or to resist their rulers accordingly, appeared in response to the "common question"—in Locke's words, from section 240 of the Second Treatise: "Who shall be judge whether the Prince or Legislative act contrary to their trust"? And the trend in the clerical writings was increasingly, and often explicitly, toward Locke's unequivocal position—again from section 240: "The people shall be judge." This development, however, did not occur under the pressures of a revolutionary situation, merely as a matter of political expediency or for propaganda purposes. It actually began much earlier, in the 1730s; and it was essentially completed by Jonathan Mayhew in 1750.

In 1705 Joseph Easterbrooke was "certain" that "the people are not competent judges of the actions of magistrates." He alluded to "mysteries of state, to the bottom of which the people are not able to dive." [211] Nathaniel Stone warned, in 1720, that "the people, through ignorance and want of judgment, may think that amiss in rulers which is not so." Thus, like Easterbrooke, Stone believed that the people lacked the competence to render informed political opinions.[212] John Barnard concurred in this political exclusion of the people. In 1734 he declared that "every man has resigned up his own private thought about right and wrong, in civil [though not in religious] matters, to the public judgment of the ruler."[213]

Barnard's brand of conservatism, however, was clearly on the wane. By 1736 the people had already acquired greater political potency in the eyes of the New England Clergy. In that year Edward Holyoke proclaimed that "all forms of government originate from the people"; hence, "doubtless they may be changed whensoever the body of the people choose to make such an alteration in their state." Holyoke called this the underlying principle of the Glorious Revolution, the legitimacy of which not even the most inveterate Tories would dare publicly to call into question.[214]

In 1740 William Cooper echoed some of the reservations of Easterbrooke and Stone concerning the political wisdom of the people, but he confessed to being "too deep in the principles of liberty" to side with Barnard on the question of right. For Cooper, "every people are left to judge for themselves" in fundamental political matters, "to frame such a constitution as may best answer the ends of government for them, and to alter and change that too at discretion, and by common consent."[215] Nathaniel Appleton also feared that "the common people are not always able to judge what is just and righteous in a public administration." Nevertheless, "everyone can feel when he is oppressed and injured, or done justly by." Thus, "although the ignorance of the people should make them very cautious" in judging their governors, "it is by the manner of their administration that they must regulate their thought of them."[216]

By 1750 the reluctance with which Cooper and Appleton had endorsed the political judgment of the people had given way to the more optimistic assessment of the people's abilities that would henceforth prevail in the clerical teaching. The most important early statement of this position came (as we might expect) from Jonathan Mayhew, and the relevant passage from his *Discourse Concerning Unlimited Submission* should be recorded at length.

To say that subjects in general are not proper judges when their governors oppress them and play the tyrant, and when they defend their rights, administer justice impartially, and promote the public welfare, is as great a treason as ever man uttered. 'Tis treason, not against one single man, but against the state—against the whole body politic; 'tis treason against mankind; 'tis treason against common sense; 'tis treason against God. And this impious principle lays the foundation for justifying all the tyranny and oppression that ever any prince was guilty of. The people know for what end they set up and maintain their governors, and they are the proper judges when their governors execute their trust as they ought to do it.[217]

Mayhew thus fixed the people's right, duty, and competence to make and act upon fundamental political judgments in a religious framework, arming what might be called popular sovereignty with the supreme authority.

The doctrine of popular political judgment was an article of faith for the ministers and their congregations by the time they received news of the Stamp Act. Andrew Eliot, in 1765, declared that the "people are generally capable of knowing when they are well used."[218] A year later William Patten cited "the great Mr. Locke in his essay on government," transcribing the whole of section 240 in support of the claim that the people are the proper judges of whether "the Prince or the Legislative betrays its trust."[219] In 1768 Richard Salter asserted that the people have a sense of their "constitutional as well as natural rights," and "know when they are well served."[220] And in a 1769 election sermon which, by the reckoning of the Boston Weekly Newsletter, had found its way into "the hands of so many people in this province,"[221] Jason Haven proclaimed that "men have a natural right to determine for themselves in what way, and by whom, they will be governed." To illustrate this essential principle of Revolutionary ideology, Haven transcribed section 240 of "Locke on Government" in its entirety.[222]

John Tucker cited "Locke on Government" three times in his 1771 election sermon, arguing that "the people . . . are the proper judges of the civil constitution they are under."[223] In 1773 from the same pulpit, Charles Turner asserted that *the people have a right to judge of the conduct of government, and its tendency,*" and that they are "capable of judging in things of such a nature."[224] The following year Gad Hitchcock read from Proverbs 29, 2: "When the righteous are in authority, the people rejoice; but when the wicked beareth rule, the people mourn." For Hitchcock, "the passage correctly supposes the people to be judges of the good or ill effects of administration," and he called this "the principle from which the British nation acted" in 1688.[225] Dan Foster expressed the same sentiments in his *Short Essay on Civil Government*, a pamphlet that summarized the substance of six sermons he delivered in 1774. The people, Foster insisted, are "the original of civil power," and they are "the proper judges whether the power they invest their king with be used well or ill."[226]

In 1774 Peter Whitney of Massachusetts delivered a sermon on the occasion of the public fast. Whitney asserted that "the people must be judge of the good or ill conduct of their rulers" and called it "the highest popery to affirm otherwise." He cited the election sermons of Andrew Eliot, Jason Haven, and Charles Turner, and made repeated appeals to scripture; but the only "secular" authority invoked on behalf of his thesis was "the great Mr. Locke."[227]

Finally, in the Massachusetts election sermon delivered less than two months before the Continental Congress declared the nation's independence from Great Britain, Samuel West cited Locke and restated this essential thesis of the Revolution: "If it be asked, Who are the proper judges to determine when rulers are guilty of tyranny and oppression? I answer, the public."[228]

In sum, by the time of the Stamp Act, every churchgoing New Englander took for granted (without having to read) the political theory that would ultimately be used to justify the Revolution itself and understood this theory to have a religious sanction. The clergy had implanted the Lockean ideological dynamite in the political consciousness of the people long before it had occasion to explode. Moreover, the ministers' affection for "Locke on Government," as evinced by internal and external evidence in their writings, could well be attributed not merely to the relevance and utility of Locke's argument in their immediate circumstances, but more fundamentally to the clergy's informed appreciation for the theistic framework of "religious preoccupations" and "theological commitments" within which that argument was essentially embedded. At the very least the ministers must have felt more comfortable with Locke, a fellow believer, en route to the "eternal estate" than on the civic humanist road to political salvation.

Locke, then, was the political line of the American Revolution, as it was laid down from the New England pulpit; and from the clerical perspective, this was the theistic Locke. This substantive Lockean connection has eluded the republican reinterpretation of the founding doctrine because of the revisionists' failure to deal adequately with Locke's thought. The strategic importance of the New England clergy in the Revolutionary movement makes this a serious omission from the Revolution's ideological history. The ministers persuaded the people to take radical, courageous political action, or at least justified such action to the satisfaction of the faithful. Yet the clergy's indispensable contribution to the Revolution—not to mention the equally indispensable contributions of those who heeded the ministers' call to arms—cannot be fully understood without reference to Locke and, indeed, to the Locke of theistic liberalism.

6

History, Myth, and the Secular Salvation
of American Liberalism

In a sense the American founding is a myth, and the founding doctrine is a mythologized record of factual events in political history. But this myth is more, not less, than fact; it is the story in which the facts of the Republic's conception and birth reside, punctuating the narrative that endows them with meaning. As such, the founding is a myth in the exalted sense of Plato's noble lie, or royal fiction, or however we translate that ancient idea.[1] And the founding doctrine is the testament of American ideals, values, and norms; it is the Republic's self-understanding of its origins, purposes, and national distinctions between good and bad, right and wrong.

Plato would be critical of both the content of the myth and Americans' related propensity to amend it. In democratic America, historians—or any citizens who are so inclined—periodically do the work that ought to be done, once and for all, only by philosopher-kings. We are only fooling ourselves, whereas Plato thinks we should be fooled by experts. But Plato's grave concern for the integrity and sanctity of founding doctrine in general is justified regardless of his verdict in particular cases, because any society's opinion of itself and the world—its myth—says so much about that society as well as about the quality of life that is possible within it.

I have argued that an underlying premise of the American myth, the source of the related notions of religious toleration and limited government, and a powerful ideological force in preparing Americans for the Revolution was the religious obligation of individuals to "search scripture" or study the law of nature for knowledge of the requisites of salvation. Individuals must resist moral paternalism and judge for themselves in matters pertaining to the "eternal estate." I have also argued that, for historical and theoretical reasons, this religious obligation made political liberty and free inquiry, as well as the exercise of popular political judgment, necessary, not merely optional, in civil society (as they are integral, not ad hoc, in Lockean liberalism). It is therefore legitimate and even necessary for Americans to scrutinize the myth itself—the scripture of the American Genesis—and to interpret its content as best they can. Americans are faithful to their myth so long as they continue to examine it, in good faith, thereby keeping it alive.

This is the intrinsic source of the greatness as well as the vulnerability of the American myth (and of liberal-democratic doctrine in general): It places its own fate, and thus the fate of the Republic, into the hands of the people. For this reason Plato's understanding of the vital centrality of a founding doctrine in the moral and political life of a society is particularly relevant in the study of American Revolutionary thought. It reminds us of the seriousness of the undertaking, while freedom of inquiry—itself one of the most cherished ideals of liberalism—may induce a kind of carelessness in which we forget that we are inquiring into something that is sacred and inseparable from the welfare of the nation. We should therefore tread freely and critically, but responsibly (that is, conscious of the potential impact of our research and the uses to which it might be put), through America's royal fiction. It is fittingly ironic that in the Lockean-liberal contribution to the political thought of the American Revolution, responsibility was the primal justification for political freedom.

Even if the founding is a fiction (in the Platonic sense), the founders themselves were real enough (though idealized by posterity); and they left two observable legacies from which we can obtain a fair estimate of their ideals, purposes, and moral distinctions. First, we know much of what they said, at least when they wrote it down; and in those days, before telegraphy, photography, and, ultimately, television changed the world, the written word dominated and shaped public discourse in general and expressed the prevailing spirit of the age.[2] So the founding generation wrote a great deal, leaving us a rich literary record of the formation of the American myth; and much of the original documentation is still intact and available to study. In addition, we have the institutional results of their work by which to gauge the nature of their intentions. Much of that is still intact, too; and it could say more than all the pamphlets and sermons combined.

The written and institutional legacies suggest that the Lockean-liberal spirit played a very important role in the formation of the American myth and, ideologically, in the making of the American Revolution. This book has anchored Lockean liberalism in the written record, primarily from the Revolutionary years. But the spirit in these writings is consistent with the institutional continuity which the founding generation sought to preserve and improve through the colonial, Revolutionary, and Constitutional periods. This was a political tradition of lawful, limited government, the consent of the governed, religious toleration and the separation of church and state, the sovereign judgment of the people—in sum, a tradition embracing a *combination* of principles which, it seems, *only* liberalism, integrally and by definition, justifies and requires in the organization of political life.

It seems that if we deny the significant historical "presence" and efficacy of the Lockean-liberal spirit in the founding era, we could explain the institutional outcome of the Revolution only by treating it as essentially an unanticipated (and unwanted) consequence, a kind of radical deviation from the objectives of the Revolution itself. But then we would still have to account for "the unvarnished doctrine of the Americans," as set forth, prolifically, in their writings from the Revolutionary period. Of course, these two legacies have republican content, too. The days of *Locke et praeterea nihil* in the American myth are gone forever. But *omnia praeter Lockem* is also untenable. The deliberalization of the American Revolution has no basis in history or political theory; civic republicanism was not the ubiquitous, exclusive, and determinative antiliberal worldview of the American Revolution, any more than it is the panacea for whatever ails the Republic two centuries later.

By the same token, although the understanding of Lockean liberalism that I have sought to establish both in Locke's texts and in the Revolutionary writings should not be blamed for the ills of American modernity, it cannot cure them either. Theistic liberalism is not an ideology for our times. This is where the study of history brings to light a substantive problem for contemporary political theory. (The highway between disciplines runs both ways.) Here is the situation: Liberals take the moral and prudential superiority of their Lockean political ideals (constitutionalism, toleration, etc.) as given— or, as the American myth says, self-evident. The religious premise of Locke's entire argument, however, is not at all self-evidently true.[3] From the modern perspective theistic liberalism seems almost like a contradiction in terms. The compelling question for political theory, then, is whether those Lockean-liberal ideals and institutions can be preserved and persuasively justified independently of their theistic foundation.

To put it more bluntly: Can we—to borrow Locke's words—take away God without dissolving all? Locke himself did not think so. That is precisely why his liberal politics found sanctuary, and flourished, in colonial and Revolutionary New England. But this is the late twentieth century. It is a very different world. Above all, religion in America is not what it was at the founding. We are not pious puritans. We do not have Locke's faith—his "religious preoccupations" and "theological commitments." That is not Jonathan Edwards, Jonathan Mayhew, or the Black Regiment fleecing the flock from America's electronic pulpit. And aside from the atheists, people generally do not feel threatened by "prelatical tyranny" (though perhaps they should). So we do have to depart from the theistic Locke in order to make a persuasive case for liberalism today.

It helps to have historical legitimacy. The recovery of the Lockean connection in the political thought of the American Revolution should help to defend the liberal tradition in America. You can call yourself the "L-word" and still be deemed an American, with authentic ideological ties to the founding fathers (who might have been amazed to see today's Tories claim a monopoly on American patriotism). Theirs was a distinctively *liberal* republicanism. Knowing this, we can see how the antiliberal rhetoric of some of our leading politicians encourages the Republic to reject its own first principles and how republican historiography, whatever its intentions, has encouraged this dangerous trend.

But the historical recovery of the Lockean connection is not enough to counter the present danger. Much more needs to be done—theoretical work, politics, education. We know where the liberal tradition came from, and that it played a vital role in American Revolutionary thought, shaping the liberal republic. But traditions do not have a life of their own. They must be sustained by living commitments. People must give them life, continuously, or they expire—especially when they are under attack. Fragments may be exhumed during the next Dark Ages, like the fragments of the ancient wisdom that relit the world. But this would not save us or our children.

Liberals, in any case, confront the kind of task that Plato's brothers imposed upon Socrates. They must justify their ideals without reference to the hereafter.[4] Now Socrates would have examined these ideals and said to the liberal, "Never." (Or he would have gotten the liberal to say it for him—which may explain what happened to Socrates.) Moreover, Plato's brothers were not liberals. So Socrates will not save the liberal tradition in America—although the classical perspective will help us to understand it better.

So where do liberals turn to justify, preserve, and improve liberal ideals and institutions, now that the theistic Locke has been honorably retired? Although that question lies beyond the scope of this book, I shall venture to offer briefly some tentative suggestions. For example, liberals could point to two centuries of secularization and conclude that most Americans, liberal or not, no longer require or even desire theological justification for their politics in the way that the Revolutionary generation did. I think this is true; but it begs, rather than answers, the question. It does not provide liberalism with an alternative justification.

Liberalism could look to itself, that is, to its own heroes, as well as to contemporary scholars who seek to revitalize the tradition, for assistance.[5] Liberals, moreover, should avoid parochialism and reach out to other traditions, so long as the latter respect and share the essential political ideals. This would enrich the source of ideas; and it makes good political sense, too. Let us briefly consider two of the more promising possibilities.

Liberals could give some thought to libertarianism, which is currently something of a force in the United States, with its own "beltway" think tank, a presidential candidate in 1988, and some fine scholars devoted to the cause. There does seem to be a basis for an alliance here. The liberal has something very important in common with the libertarian: Both accept the genetically liberal ideal of limited government. But these perspectives on government are not exactly the same. Unlike the libertarians, liberals do not insist that the government which governs least necessarily governs best. And this must be regarded as a distinction with a difference.

Liberals instinctively resist extremes—in this case, governments which govern most as well as those which govern least. Ironically, this is something that liberals and traditional conservatives (as opposed to American neoconservatives of the "New Right") have in common. In contrast, the libertarian view tends to be extreme, uncompromising, predictable—in essence, ideological. Defending the virginity of the market against political seduction—indeed, against virtue—takes priority over all other considerations. Thus, when pressed for justice, which in the real historical world requires some modification of market output, libertarianism responds, in effect, with the question, "Am I my brother's keeper?"

This sounds like the bourgeois Locke, the ideological champion of insatiably acquisitive, self-interested materialism. It is also what the republican revisionists found so distressing in modern America and associated with "Lockean liberalism." The ironies abound. Libertarians praise the bourgeois Locke, whom the revisionists wish to bury; but both sides are committed to this skewed, devitalized understanding of Locke's liberalism. Republicanism, moreover, defends virtue against commerce, while libertarianism does precisely the opposite. And republicans and libertarians work with mutually exclusive profiles of "Cato," the hero they share: "essentially anti-capitalistic" on the one hand, the "spirit of capitalism" on the other.[6] The republican revision, however, was wrong about Locke's liberalism and Cato's republicanism, both as political theories and as historical-ideological forces in the making of the American Revolution; and libertarianism commercializes the spirit of both of those doctrines.

If free to choose, or forced to choose, the liberal would prefer to be with Robert Nozick and the libertarians than with Sir Robert Filmer or the authoritarians of the right or left.[7] Liberals may be uneasy with politics, but so far they have at least been able to recognize the basic distinctions in the American political environment. Libertarians, however, have been suffering from a kind of political dyslexia. They have supported candidates who are also supported by the neo-theocratic right, which represents the real antithesis of liberalism and libertarianism alike. They seem to believe that the Invisible Hand (which now operates out of the Cato Institute!) will sort things out in the end, saving them from the enthusiasm of their evangelical partners. But liberals, again, must now seek justification for their ideals and institutions without reference to theology—religious or economic. Moreover, they must balance and reconcile property on the one side with the demand for justice on the other. Liberals and libertarians can and should work together, intellectually and politically. But liberalism will not flourish within the narrow ideological confines of libertarianism. And it must not give in to its own most selfish instincts.

Another possible source of ideas for liberals is civic republicanism. Like liberalism itself, republicanism is an undeniably important part of the American myth. But we should not embrace the republican alternative without due regard for the hazards of virtue and the mitigating influence of liberalism. Machiavelli is an awesome thinker, but a scary one, too—and more often right than wrong. He prescribes the truth that works, which is strong medicine. The Machiavellian cure could kill the patient—without saving its "lost soul." Or it could restore virtue to the body politic at the cost of freedom. As Pocock himself observed in the penultimate paragraph of the *Machiavellian Moment*, "the ideal of virtue is highly compulsive."

Pocock is absolutely right on another point, too: Locke is no kind of classical or Machiavellian republican.[8] But that is precisely why Americans are so fortunate to have had the spirit of Lockean liberalism in the founding of their republic. Numa—the ideal Machiavellian lawgiver—would have rejected the reasonableness of Christianity.[9] And Machiavelli himself surely would have declined to subordinate the prince to the law of nature or to anything except the survival of the state and the steady growth of its power.

This suggests that Machiavellian republicanism offers no moral or theoretical justification for the American Revolution or for its Constitutional outcome. It also suggests that an account of Revolutionary thought that "stresses Machiavelli at the expense of Locke,"[10] besides being historically untenable, tends to deny the legitimacy of the Revolution itself. Neither the American Revolution nor its institutional settlement, then, can be explained or justified without reference to the spirit of Lockean liberalism. Nevertheless, republicanism is also a part of that explanation, if not the justification, so the work required to clarify the meaning of American republicanism should be worth the effort.

We should begin by calling a truce in the war between republicanism and liberalism. The antithesis between these two traditions is neither historically nor theoretically sound. Moreover, if there were such an antithesis, it would not be between virtue and commerce (since republicans and liberals like "honest commerce"), but between virtue and liberty (since republicanism ultimately makes the cultivation and enforcement of virtue the responsibility of the state and an explicit priority over the freedom of the individual).

In any case, *American* republicanism in the Revolutionary years was a distinctively *liberal* republicanism because it was embedded in a political and intellectual tradition which included a vital and essential Lockean-liberal component. Republicanism and liberalism *coexisted* at the founding, and coexistence must have modified both points of view. So rather than dwell upon abstract antitheses, or seek our lost virtue in a Machiavellian founding, we might now wish to consider the *constructive interactions* between these two doctrines. These interactions produced the American Revolution and the founding of the Republic. The secular justification for liberal politics will be at least partly available in the American myth.

Notes

When more than one page is listed for a specific source, or more than one section (§) in a citation of Locke's *Two Treatises of Government*, the ordering of pages or of sections reflects the order in which they are quoted or referred to in the text. In some cases, the page or section from which I quote is cited, followed by additional pages or sections that contain relevant supportive passages. Pages and sections, therefore, are not always listed in ascending order.

1
The Historiographic Revolution:
The Rise of "Cato" and the Decline of Locke in
American Revolutionary Thought

1. J. G. A. Pocock, *The Machiavellian Moment* (Princeton University Press, 1975), p. 509. See the discussion of Pocock's work, below, especially at note 67.

2. Judith N. Shklar, "Gone with the Wind," *The New Republic* (March 21, 1988), p. 41. Shklar's dispassionate analysis of John Calhoun's defense of the slaveholding minority in his *Disquisition on Government* should persuade the democratic critics of liberalism to think twice before jumping onto the bandwagon of American republicanism: "With his obsession with corruption and his martial tones, Calhoun was closer to the 'republican' writers of the Revolutionary period than to his own contemporaries, or to Madison. . . . He is, therefore, a writer who should not be ignored by those who are currently resuscitating that 'republican' tradition in the hope of finding a pure and native source for public virtue and solidarity. As a defender of slavery as a positive good, especially when compared to the disorders of liberal capitalism, Calhoun was surely an authentic heir to the 'republican' ethos of antiquity. That he was shallow, and a menace to the real welfare of his country, is also relevant. At the very least Calhoun tells us something about the implications of republicanism in the modern world. In its emphasis on martial discipline, social cohesion, political

agreement, and conformity as requirements for public policy, republicanism now is a threat to personal freedom and justice. It is after all not true that we have had no experience of established ideologies of solidarity in the 20th century."

3. Merle Curti, "The Great Mr. Locke, America's Philosopher," *Huntington Library Bulletin* 11 (1939). John C. Miller, *Origins of the American Revolution* (originally published by Little, Brown, 1943; revised printing by Stanford University Press, 1966), p. 171.

4. Vernon L. Parrington, *Main Currents in American Thought* (Harvest Books, 1927), v. 1, p. 193. Miller, *Origins of the American Revolution*, p. 170. Miller writes: "It is not too much to say that during the era of the American Revolution, the 'party line' was John Locke."

5. Louis Hartz, *The Liberal Tradition in America* (Harcourt, Brace and World, 1955).

6. J. G. A. Pocock writes: "It is clear that the textbook account of Augustan political thought as *Locke et praeterea nihil* badly needs revision." Pocock, "Machiavelli, Harrington, and English Political Ideologies in the Eighteenth Century," in *Politics, Language, and Time* (Atheneum, 1971), p. 107. Stanley Katz agrees: "*Locke et praeterea nihil*, it now appears, will no longer do as a motto for the study of eighteenth-century Anglo-American political thought." Katz, "The Origins of American Constitutional Thought," in *Perspectives in American History* 3 (1969), p. 474. For similar enunciations of the revisionist battle cry, in Latin, see Robert Shalhope, "Toward a Republican Synthesis: The Emergence of an Understanding in American Historiography," *William & Mary Quarterly* 29 (1972), pp. 49, 59; and Nathan O. Hatch, *The Sacred Cause of Liberty* (Yale University Press, 1977), p. 57 n. 5.

7. Katz, "The Origins of American Constitutional Thought," p. 486. Here Katz is endorsing the views of historian J. R. Pole.

8. John Dunn, "The Politics of Locke in England and America in the Eighteenth Century," in John Yolton (ed.), *John Locke: Problems and Perspectives* (Cambridge University Press, 1969), p. 80.

9. Pocock, *The Machiavellian Moment*, p. 424.

10. Bernard Bailyn, *The Ideological Origins of the American Revolution* (Harvard University Press, 1967), and other works cited below. Pocock, *The Machiavellian Moment*, and other works cited below. Shalhope, "Toward a Republican Synthesis," pp. 49–80. In 1981 Pocock, in discussing Bailyn's work and referring to Shalhope's article, announced—with approval—that "it has become usual to accord paradigmatic status to 'the republican synthesis' in the historiography of America." I do not believe that Pocock has withdrawn this endorsement, even though Shalhope himself expressed some reservations in a subsequent article. J. G. A. Pocock, "*The Machiavellian Moment* Revisited," *Journal of Modern History* 53 (March 1981), pp. 49–50. Shalhope, "Republicanism and Early American Historiography," *William & Mary Quarterly* 39 (1982), pp. 334–356. Lance Banning prefers the term "republican hypothesis" in "Jeffersonian Ideology Revisited: Liberal and Classical Ideas in the New American Republic," *William & Mary Quarterly*, v. 43, 1 (January 1986), p. 3.

11. J. G. A. Pocock, "Virtue and Commerce in the Eighteenth Century," *Journal of Interdisciplinary History* 3 (Summer 1972), pp. 119–134.

12. For reasons set forth below (chapter 2, at note 13; chapter 3, note 105), this study of early American political thought stops at 1776. Thus it makes no claims concerning liberalism and republicanism in the post-Revolutionary, Constitutional era. That subject has been most lucidly expounded by Thomas L. Pangle in his very recent book, *The Spirit of Modern Republicanism: The Moral Vision of the American Founders and the Philosophy of Locke* (University of Chicago Press, 1988). Pangle's learned study "is centered on *The Federalist Papers*," an examination of which "points us back to a renewed examination of the major treatises and essays of John Locke" (p. 2). In his view, and contrary to currently fashionable opinion, Locke's political philosophy "expresses most fully the dominant, though by no means uncontested, theoretical strand in the American Constitutional founding" (p. 3). The same can be said of Lockean thought, as I endeavor to show throughout this book, in the ideology and political thought of the earlier, Revolutionary period.

I approach Locke's texts differently than Pangle does, however, and thus interpret Locke's liberalism differently, too. (Readers interested in the methodological issue should compare chapter 4, at notes 134–140, and especially note 137, with Pangle's statement of method on page 3 of his book.) But according to the criteria of interpretation I develop below (chapters 1 and 4), my interpretation of Locke's political philosophy does not generally depend upon impugning the textual credentials of competing interpretations. So perhaps the elements in Lockean thought which I emphasize were most relevant in the Revolutionary climate, whereas those elements stressed by Pangle were most salient during the Constitutional era, with its different political-theoretical agenda. In any case, my differences with Pangle concerning the interpretation of Locke's political philosophy did not detract from the pleasure of serving on a panel with him—and debating these issues—three years ago.

13. Pangle, *The Spirit of Modern Republicanism*, p. 29. The rest of Pangle's critique is quite relevant to arguments later in my book: "Contemporary scholars read the classic and early modern texts of political philosophy in a spirit which is not only alien, but also inferior in seriousness, to the spirit of eighteenth-century readers. The American statesmen and publicists of the eighteenth century searched the pages of Plutarch, of Locke, of Trenchard and Gordon for guidance toward the permanent truth as regards God, human nature, and politics; they did not read these earlier authors in order to find evidence for linguistic contexts or conceptual 'paradigms.' This means that they read and studied with a passion, a need, and hence a seriousness, that is lacking in our contemporary scholars. One ought not therefore to be surprised to find that the most thoughtful men of the eighteenth century read more carefully and understood more profoundly the texts of previous political theorists." Elsewhere (p. 35), Pangle calls the "misreading of the major sources . . . a grave failing" of the republican revision.

14. The reader will note that this goal does not include an attempt to demonstrate Locke's "influence" on the American Revolutionists. A thousand technically correct citations of Locke (or of any other source) in a Revolutionary pamphlet would not authorize a claim of influence. In short, there's no way to measure influence, however much it may have occurred. But we can still determine whether the Revolutionists held Lockean-liberal ideas about politics, provided we understand

the nature of Lockean-liberal political ideas and can recognize them on sight in the Revolutionists' writings. For further discussion, see chapters 2 and 3, below.

15. Shalhope, "Toward a Republican Synthesis," p. 58. Bailyn, *Ideological Origins*, pp. 35–36.

16. Bailyn, *Ideological Origins*, p. 52. The context is Bailyn's analysis of Jonathan Mayhew's famous sermon, *A Discourse Concerning Unlimited Submission and Non-Resistance to the Higher Powers* (1750). For a discussion of Bailyn's analysis, see chapter 4, below, at note 44. I discuss Mayhew's sermon in some detail in chapter 5, below.

17. C. B. Macpherson, *The Political Theory of Possessive Individualism* (Oxford University Press, 1962; reprint, Oxford Paperbacks, 1965), pp. 213, 220–221, 199.

18. Ibid., p. 270.

19. Ibid., p. 257.

20. Ibid., pp. 224, 258.

21. Ibid., pp. 237, 221.

22. On Strauss's method, see chapter 4, below.

23. Leo Strauss, *Natural Right and History* (University of Chicago Press, 1953), p. 234 n. 106.

24. Richard Ashcraft, "The *Two Treatises* and the Exclusion Crisis: The Problem of Lockean Political Theory as Bourgeois Ideology," in J. G. A. Pocock and Richard Ashcraft (eds.), *John Locke* (University of California Press, 1980), p. 27.

25. Strauss, *Natural Right and History*, p. 234.

26. Ibid., pp. 242, 246. Leo Strauss, *What Is Political Philosophy?* (The Free Press of Glencoe, Ill., 1959), p. 49: Here Strauss says that "Locke took over the fundamental scheme of Hobbes and changed it in only one point. He realized that what man primarily needs for his self-preservation is less a gun than food, or more generally, property. Thus the desire for self-preservation turns into the desire for property, for acquisition, and the right to self-preservation becomes the right to unlimited acquisition." "Acquisitiveness," for Strauss, is Locke's "immoral or amoral substitute for morality."

27. Strauss, *Natural Right and History*, p. 246. On Locke's "caution," and his hidden meaning, see pp. 207–209, 220–221. Also, see below, chapter 4, for a discussion of Strauss's "esoteric" reading of the classic texts.

28. Ibid., p. 246.

29. John Patrick Diggins, *The Lost Soul of American Politics: Virtue, Self-Interest, and the Foundations of Liberalism* (Basic Books, 1984), p. 19.

30. Ibid., chapter 1 ("Who's Afraid of John Locke?").

31. Louis Hartz, "The Rise of the Democratic Idea," in John P. Roche (ed.), *Origins of American Political Thought* (Harper Torchbooks, 1967), p. 68.

32. Hartz, *The Liberal Tradition in America*, p. 26. See also Diggins, *The Lost Soul of American Politics*, p. 5.

33. Hartz, *The Liberal Tradition in America*, pp. 3–4, 24.

34. Ibid., pp. 35, 66, 67.

35. Hartz, "The Rise of the Democratic Idea," p. 69. See also Diggins, *The Lost Soul of American Politics*, p. 5.

36. Hartz, *The Liberal Tradition in America*, pp. 5–6.

37. Ibid., p. 140.

38. Carl Becker, *The Declaration of Independence* (Vintage Books, 1958), p. 27.

39. Ibid., pp. 72–73.

40. Ibid., pp. 79, 24.

41. Dunn, "The Politics of Locke," pp. 46, 79. Daniel Boorstin, *America and the Image of Europe: Reflections on American Thought* (Meridian Books, 1960), pp. 65–80.

42. Garry Wills, *Inventing America: Jefferson's Declaration of Independence* (Vintage Books, 1979), pp. 183, 201, 205, 217, 239, 315, 368.

43. Ronald Hamowy, "Jefferson and the Scottish Enlightenment: A Critique of Garry Wills's *Inventing America: Jefferson's Declaration of Independence*," in *William & Mary Quarterly* 36 (1979), p. 523.

Hamowy's thorough, well–documented critique devastates the Scottish Enlightenment model of interpretation and makes it difficult to take Wills's book seriously. For example, Wills stresses Hutcheson, and the Scottish Enlightenment thinkers in general, over Locke—indeed, to the exclusion of Locke. But, as Hamowy points out, Wills fails to mention that Hutcheson was closer to Locke than to Hume and the others on such crucial issues as natural law and the right of resistance, or that in this regard Hutcheson explicitly acknowledged his debt to Locke (pp. 508–511). Moreover, Wills fails to produce a single Jeffersonian reference to Hutcheson, while he "minimizes, misinterprets, or disregards every piece of evidence supporting Jefferson's familiarity with Locke's political views and their role in providing the argument in the Declaration" (pp. 512, 514).

This and more lead Hamowy to conclude (p. 523): "Wills's book is so speculative and so unfocused . . . that the unwary reader may be overwhelmed by the author's seeming erudition and lulled into accepting his conclusions. In a word, Wills talks a pretty good game. But the moment his statements are subjected to scrutiny, they appear a mass of confusions, uneducated guesses, and blatant errors of fact. *Inventing America* falls into the category of 'impressionistic' intellectual history, where breadth of coverage substitutes for scholarly substance. . . . Future scholars may feel called upon to consult *Inventing America* when investigating Jefferson's intellectual roots, for completeness' sake if for no other reason. They will there find that Wills has invented a new Jefferson influenced by a Scottish moral philosophy which Wills has seriously misconstrued."

Diggins also questions Wills's argument: The "relevance" of Scottish Enlightenment philosophy "to the predicament of the colonists . . . is unclear. For Scottish writers were either silent or ambiguous on a question of vital importance to the colonists: the right of resistance. The idea that government arises from a rationally willed social contract was precisely what Scottish philosophy questioned and rejected." Diggins, *The Lost Soul of American Politics*, p. 33.

44. Wills, *Inventing America*, pp. 244, 254–255. See below, note 103.

45. Ibid., pp. 229, 230–231.

46. John Locke, *Two Treatises of Government*, rev. ed., edited by Peter Laslett (Mentor Books, 1965), *Second Treatise*, §§87, 123.

47. Bernard Bailyn, *Pamphlets of the American Revolution* (Harvard University Press, 1965). Pages 749–752 contain tables of contents for volumes two, three, and four, which have not been published. The four volumes together would contain seventy-two pamphlets.

48. Bailyn, *Ideological Origins*, pp. 33–40, 43, 53–54. See also Bernard Bailyn, *The Origins of American Politics* (Vintage Books, 1970). On the "commonwealthmen," see Caroline Robbins, *The Eighteenth Century Commonwealthman* (Harvard University Press, 1959). For an earlier study of these "classical republicans," see Zera S. Fink, *The Classical Republicans: An Essay in the Recovery of a Pattern of Thought in Seventeenth-Century England* (Northwestern University Press, 1945).

49. Isaac Kramnick, *Bolingbroke and His Circle: The Politics of Nostalgia in the Age of Walpole* (Harvard University Press, 1968).

50. Bailyn, *Ideological Origins*, p. 51.

51. Ibid., p. 45.

52. On the conspiracy theory, see Ibid., pp. 94–95, 119–120, 138, 144–159. Also Bailyn, *Origins of American Politics*, pp. 11–14, 136; Gordon S. Wood, *The Creation of the American Republic* (University of North Carolina Press, 1969), pp. 16, 22–23, 30–36, 40–43.

53. Bailyn, *Ideological Origins*, pp. 55–93.

54. Pocock, *The Machiavellian Moment*, pp. 506–509; "Virtue and Commerce," p. 121. Isaac Kramnick, "Republican Revisionism Revisited," *The American Historical Review*, v. 87, no. 3 (June 1982), pp. 630–631, 632. Diggins, *The Lost Soul of American Politics*, pp. 9–10, 19. See chapter 4, below, for a discussion of the meaning of "virtue" in *Cato's Letters*.

55. Bailyn, *Origins of American Politics*, p. 56.

56. Bailyn, *Ideological Origins*, p. 35; *Origins of American Politics*, p. 41 (emphasis added).

57. Ibid., pp. ix–x.

58. Dunn, "The Politics of Locke," pp. 46, 79, and passim.

59. Ibid., p. 79.

60. Ibid., p. 77. See also Esmond Wright, "Men with Two Countries," *The Development of a Revolutionary Mentality* (Library of Congress, 1972), p. 153: "The authority Locke supported was that of the British Parliament."

61. Dunn, "The Politics of Locke," p. 77.

62. Ibid., pp. 79 (and n. 1), 80.

63. John Dunn, "The Identity of the History of Ideas," *Philosophy* (April 1968).

64. See, for example, Ronald E. Pynn, "The Influence of John Locke's Political Philosophy on American Political Tradition," *North Dakota Quarterly*, v. 42, no. 3 (Summer 1974), p. 56. Also, Wills, *Inventing America*, p. 170; and Hamowy's critique in "Jefferson and the Scottish Enlightenment," p. 505. Hamowy writes: "Wills goes far beyond the conclusions warranted by a careful reading of Dunn's article."

65. Wood, *The Creation of the American Republic*.

66. Pocock, "Virtue and Commerce," pp. 121–122; *The Machiavellian Moment*, pp. 545, 507.

67. Pocock, *The Machiavellian Moment*, p. 509.

68. Ibid., p. 424.

69. Pocock, "Virtue and Commerce," p. 127.

70. Ibid., p. 124.

71. J. G. A. Pocock, *Politics, Language, and Time*, p. 144.

72. See, for example, Hatch's account of the political thought of the New England clergy. Hatch cites the seminal literature of the republican revision, invokes the Latin slogan, and then writes about his subject without mentioning a single clerical reference to Locke, even when the argument he is considering in a particular sermon is supported only by a citation of "Locke on Government." Compare Hatch, *The Sacred Cause of Liberty*, p. 72 (text and n. 45), with Simeon Howard, *A Sermon Preached to the Ancient and Honorable Artillery Company in Boston* (1773), in Charles S. Hyneman and Donald S. Lutz (eds.), *American Political Writings of the Founding Era* (Liberty Press, 1983), v. 1, pp. 187–188 (pp. 8–9 in the 1773 edition cited by Hatch). I discuss this and other aspects of Hatch's book in greater detail below, in chapters 4 and 5. See also note 6 above.

73. Pocock, *The Machiavellian Moment*, p. 507. Dorothy Ross, "The Liberal Tradition Revisited and the Republican Tradition Addressed," in John Higham and Paul Conkin (eds.), *New Directions in American Intellectual History* (The Johns Hopkins University Press, 1979), p. 117.

74. Pocock, "Civic Humanism and Its Role in Anglo-American Thought," in *Politics, Language, and Time*, p. 81.

75. Pocock, *The Machiavellian Moment*, p. 361.

76. Ibid., p. 384. Pocock (ed.), *The Political Works of James Harrington* (Cambridge University Press, 1977), p. 15.

77. Pocock, *The Machiavellian Moment*, p. 419; "Virtue and Commerce," p. 121.

78. Pocock, "Virtue and Commerce."

79. Pocock, *The Machiavellian Moment*, p. 433.

80. Pocock, "Virtue and Commerce," p. 120.

81. Bailyn, *Ideological Origins*, pp. 35–36.

82. Pocock, *The Machiavellian Moment*, p. 468.

83. Ibid., pp. 547, 507; "Virtue and Commerce," pp. 121–122.

84. Pocock, "Virtue and Commerce," p. 123; *The Machiavellian Moment*, pp. 507, 509; *Politics, Language, and Time*, p. 104. Hartz and Pocock go to opposite extremes; thus both fall wide of the mark. Hartz's thesis, however, is rooted in a comparative sociohistorical analysis which seems more substantial than Pocock's analysis of language paradigms.

85. Pocock, "Virtue and Commerce," p. 120; *Politics, Language, and Time*, p. 103. See J. H. Hexter, "Republic, Virtue, Liberty, and the Political Universe of J. G. A. Pocock," in *On Historians* (Harvard University Press, 1979), pp. 293–303.

86. For example, Pocock, "Virtue and Commerce."

87. J. G. A. Pocock, "The Myth of John Locke and the Obsession with Liberalism," in J. G. A. Pocock and Richard Ashcraft (eds.), *John Locke* (University of California, 1980), pp. 17–18; *Politics, Language, and Time*, p. 144.

88. Pocock, "The Myth of John Locke," pp. 3–24.

89. The implications are discussed in chapter 4, below.

90. Pocock, *The Machiavellian Moment*, pp. 527, 436, 424.

91. Ibid., p. 424 (emphasis added). Pocock often depicted civic republicanism as an antiliberal (or anti-Lockean) tradition of thought. He liked to emphasize the discontinuity and tension between the "two vocabularies" of republicanism and liberalism—their "different values," and "different strategies of speech and argument." Pocock, "Virtues, Rights, and Manners: A Model for Historians of Political Thought," in *Political Theory*, v. 9, no. 3 (August 1981), p. 356. Pocock, "*The Machiavellian Moment* Revisited, " p. 55.

Not all historians see a clear distinction, let alone an antithesis, between liberalism and republicanism. For instance, Lance Banning notes that the similarities between the two "are as clear as their ultimate incompatibilities," since "the same thinkers contributed to both. Liberalism and classical republicanism both insisted upon a definition of the individual in terms of his autonomy. Both linked liberty with property. There were many points of contact and even confusion." Banning, "Jeffersonian Ideology Revisited," p. 12 n. 30. On the relationship between liberalism and republicanism, see chapters 4 and 6, below.

92. Wood, *The Creation of the American Republic*, p. 418.

93. John Dunn, *The Political Thought of John Locke* (Cambridge University Press, 1969; 1st paperback edition, 1982), p. 222.

94. Nathan Tarcov, *Locke's Education for Liberty* (University of Chicago Press, 1984), p. 127. I hedge my reliance on Dunn precisely where Tarcov qualifies his endorsement: Dunn's emphasis on the Calvinist notion of the calling does not inform my interpretation. See below, at note 102, and chapter 4, note 69.

95. Henry C. Van Schaack, *The Life of Peter Van Schaack, LL.D.* (D. Appleton, 1842). The documents cited by Dunn are on pp. 54–58. Those which complete the story are on pp. 257–263. All are either letters or personal notes written by Peter Van Schaack himself.

96. Ibid., p. 261.

97. The idea of a "design" or "conspiracy" against liberty is crucial, according to Bailyn, in the Americans' "peculiar inheritance of thought." Yet this concept was an important part of Locke's theory of revolution long before Cato wrote about it. For Locke, only "a sedate settled design upon another man's life puts him in a state of war with him against whom he has declared such an intention." See note 52, above, for citations of Bailyn and Gordon Wood; Locke, *Second Treatise*, §§16, 225, 230.

98. H. C. Van Schaack, *The Life of Peter Van Schaack, LL.D.*, p. 263.

99. Ibid., p. 259.

100. Dunn, *The Political Thought of John Locke*, p. 222.

101. Dunn, "The Politics of Locke," pp. 79 (text and n. 1), 80.

102. Dunn, *The Political Thought of John Locke*, pp. xi–xii.

103. John Locke, *Essay Concerning Human Understanding*, edited by P. H. Nidditch (Oxford University Press, 1975), p. 646 (bk. 4, ch. 12, §11), emphasis added; *A Letter on Toleration*, edited by J. W. Gough (Clarendon Press, 1968), p. 131 ("Man's first care should be of his soul," and of its immortal destiny "in the world to come"). Cf. Wills, at notes 44–45, above.

104. Locke, *Second Treatise*, §6.

105. Ibid., §§135, 12.

106. Dunn, *The Political Thought of John Locke*, pp. 87, 93, 12.

107. For Locke, man's primary concern should be for his salvation, but "regarding his salvation, every man has the supreme and final power of judging for himself"; "the care, therefore, of every man's soul belongs to himself, and is to be left to him" (*Letter on Toleration*, pp. 131, 125, 91). The right and duty of individual judgment are irrevocably extended to the political sphere when Locke insists, on the one hand, that "the obligations of the law of nature . . . are drawn closer" in civil society and, on the other hand, that the people's decision whether or not the ruler has forfeited their obedience by violating the "law antecedent and paramount to all positive laws" is a "judgment they cannot part with" according to "God and Nature" (*Second Treatise*, §§135, 168). On the competence of the people to exercise political judgment on the most consequential political issue, revolution, see *Second Treatise*, §240. For the extrapolation of the moral justification for violent resistance from the divinely imposed suicide taboo, see *First Treatise*, §176; *Second Treatise*, §§6, 23, 135, 168, 17, 18, 155. See chapters 4 and 5, below, where the derivation of Locke's political radicalism from theistic principles is treated in detail.

108. Locke, *A Letter on Toleration*, p. 135.

109. Sheldon Wolin, *Politics and Vision: Continuity and Innovation in Western Political Thought* (Little, Brown, 1960), pp. 24–25.

110. Winthrop S. Hudson, "John Locke—Preparing the Way for the Revolution," *Journal of Presbyterian History*, v. 42, no. 1 (March 1964), pp. 21, 22. Modern interpreters, Hudson writes, seem unable to "avoid the temptation to equate references to the 'civil order' and 'natural law' with secularism. But neither John Milton's contemporaries nor those of Locke would have made this mistake. And certainly the 'pietists' of the Revolutionary generation in America, as heirs of the older Puritan tradition, would not have read Locke in this way."

111. Tarcov, *Locke's Education for Liberty*, p. 210: "Finding nothing decent or inspiring in the interpretations of Locke that are offered to them, students of our political culture have gone off seeking 'non-Lockean' elements in our heritage. They should discover, instead, the 'non-Lockean' elements in Locke."

112. Locke's chapter 5 ("Of Property") in the *Second Treatise* is the locus classicus of possessive individualism, the stronghold of the bourgeois Locke. Yet I have found only two citations of chapter 5 in the American writings, and only one of these (*Boston Evening Post*, April 2, 1750) was correct. John Lathrop, a minister, quoted Locke, also citing "Locke on Government, Chapter Five" as the source (*A Discourse Preached December 15, 1774. . .* , Evans 13370, p. 27). The transcribed passage, however, was §140 (10–11) from chapter 11 ("Of the Extent of the Legislative Power").

Most of the Locke citations in the Revolutionary writings (which were, again, by far the most numerous of all citations of nonbiblical sources) came from the sections of the *Second Treatise* that deal with the extent of legislative power; the difference between tyrants and magistrates; the right, duty, and competence of the people to judge the conduct of government; and the dissolution of government and consequent reversion of sovereignty to the people. In other words, the Revolutionists cited Locke as an authority on constitutional politics and revolution.

113. Pynn, "The Influence of John Locke's Political Philosophy," p. 53.

114. Bailyn once claimed to have reached that "ultimate stage of maturity in historical interpretation where partisanship is left behind." At the Hegelian moment of the republican synthesis, he announced his arrival at the "ultimate mode of interpretation," where "all the earlier assumptions of relevance, partisan in their nature, seem crude, and fall away, and in their place there comes a neutrality, a comprehensiveness . . . lacking in earlier interpretations. . . . Now the historian . . . is no longer a partisan. He has no stake in the outcome. He can now embrace the whole event, see it from all sides." Bailyn, "The Central Themes of the American Revolution," in Kurtz and Hutson, eds., *Essays on the American Revolution* (University of North Carolina Press, 1973), p. 15; *The Ordeal of Thomas Hutchinson* (Harvard University Press, 1974), pp. 32, ix.

2 A Discourse on Method

1. H. Trevor Colburn, *The Lamp of Experience* (University of North Carolina Press, 1965), p. 199. For a discussion of Colburn's important contribution to the revisionist movement, see Robert Shalhope, "Toward a Republican Synthesis: The Emergence of an Understanding in American Historiography," *William & Mary Quarterly* 29 (1972), pp. 57, 59, 67–68.

2. John Dunn, "The Politics of John Locke in England and America in the Eighteenth Century," in John Yolton (ed.), *John Locke: Problems and Perspectives* (Cambridge University Press, 1969), p. 69.

3. Daniel Boorstin, *America and the Image of Europe: Reflections on American Thought* (Meridian Books, 1960), p. 73.

4. Colburn, *The Lamp of Experience*, pp. 199, 200–232. I do not include orders placed with booksellers, or the post–1776 library catalogs.

5. Garry Wills, *Inventing America: Jefferson's Declaration of Independence* (Vintage Books, 1979), pp. 169–170; Dunn, "The Politics of Locke," p. 70; J. G. A. Pocock, "The Myth of John Locke and the Obsession with Liberalism," in Pocock and Richard Ashcraft (eds.), *John Locke* (University of California, 1980), p. 21. See also Donald S. Lutz, "The Relative Influence of European Writers on Late Eighteenth-Century American Political Thought," *The American Political Science Review*, v. 78, no. 1 (March 1984), p. 196.

6. David Lundberg and Henry F. May, "The Enlightened Reader in America," *American Quarterly*, v. 28, no. 2 (special issue: Summer 1976), pp. 262–293. I have been helped here (and elsewhere) by Ronald Hamowy's excellent article, "Jefferson and the Scottish Enlightenment: A Critique of Gary Wills's *Inventing America: Jefferson's Declaration of Independence*," *William & Mary Quarterly* 36 (1979).

7. Bernard Bailyn, *Pamphlets of the American Revolution* (Harvard University Press, 1965), pp. 1–203.

8. This is Lutz's definition. "The Relative Influence of European Writers," p. 191.

9. *Massachusetts Spy*, March 14, 1771. In this issue of the *Spy*, "The Whisperer" claimed that since "both the legislative and the prince have acted contrary to their trust, resistance is . . . not only necessary to save us from a state of lasting slavery

as a nation, but it has absolutely become the duty of every individual." To support this radical position, he transcribed, word for word, sections 228 through 231 of the *Second Treatise*, but he did not use quotes, and there was no mention whatsoever of Locke or "Locke on Government."

10. See note 24, below.

11. Lutz, "The Relative Influence of European Writers."

12. Ibid., p. 196.

13. Ibid., pp. 192–193. Lutz has confirmed my interpretation of his data for the Revolutionary period in personal correspondence. See Bernard Bailyn, *The Ideological Origins of the American Revolution* (Harvard University Press, 1967), p. 1.

14. Lutz, "The Relative Influence of European Writers," p. 193.

15. Ronald E. Pynn, "The Influence of John Locke's Political Philosophy on American Political Tradition," *North Dakota Quarterly*, v. 42, no. 3 (Summer 1974), p. 53.

16. Joseph Galloway, *A Candid Examination of the Mutual Claims of Great Britain and Her Colonies* (1775), pp. 10–11.

17. Ibid., pp. 49–50.

18. John Locke, *Two Treatises of Government*, rev. ed., edited by Peter Laslett (Mentor Books, 1965), *First Treatise*, §1.

19. Locke, *Second Treatise*, §1.

20. "To the Author of a Pamphlet Entitled *A Candid Examination of the Mutual Claims of Great Britain and Her Colonies*," *Pennsylvania Journal* (March 8, 1775), reproduced in Peter Force (ed.), *American Archives*, fourth series, v. V, pp. 85–91.

21. Both of Galloway's quotations from the *Second Treatise* appear on p. 4 of his *Candid Examination*.

22. John Adams, quoted by Carl Becker in *The Declaration of Independence* (Vintage Books, 1958), pp. 119–120.

23. There is a peculiar similarity between Galloway and Leo Strauss when it comes to quoting Locke. See Strauss's interpretation of Locke in *Natural Right & History* (The University of Chicago Press, 1953); John Yolton's penetrating critique of Strauss in "Locke on the Law of Nature," *Philosophical Review* (October 1958); and the discussion of this issue in chapter 4, below.

24. Some examples of unattributed paraphrasing that meet these conditions are William Patten, *A Discourse Delivered at Hallifax* (Boston, 1766), p. 9 (§77 of the *Second Treatise*); Judah Champion, *Election Sermon* (Connecticut, 1776), p. 7 (§§77 and 123 of the *Second Treatise*); John Allen, *The American Alarm* (Boston, 1773), p. 32 (§138 of the *Second Treatise*).

25. Dorothy Ross, "The Liberal Tradition Revisited and the Republican Tradition Addressed," in John Higham and Paul Conkin (eds.), *New Directions in American Intellectual History* (The Johns Hopkins University Press, 1979), p. 117.

26. J. G. A. Pocock, *The Machiavellian Moment* (Princeton University Press, 1975), p. 507.

27. See chapter 4, below. Also, see Thomas L. Pangle, *The Spirit of Modern Republicanism: The Moral Vision of the American Founders and the Philosophy of Locke* (University of Chicago Press, 1988), p. 30. On Pangle, see chapter 1, above, note 12.

28. See chapter 1, above, for discussion of Pocock's paradigm.

29. James Otis, *The Rights of the British Colonies Asserted and Proved* (Boston, 1764), in Bailyn, *Pamphlets of the American Revolution*, pp. 436–437. These matters —Otis, natural law, the clergy—are taken up in detail in subsequent chapters. Also, see the statement by Peter Oliver, at note 48, below.

30. John Locke, *A Paraphrase and Notes on the Epistle of St. Paul to the Romans*, in *The Works of John Locke* (London, 1823; reprinted in Germany by Scientia Verlag Aalen, 1963), v. 8. See chapter 5, below, for details of the Lockean exegesis of the "politicks of St. Paul."

31. Nathan O. Hatch, *The Sacred Cause of Liberty* (Yale University Press, 1977), p. 57 n. 5. See above, chapter 1, note 72, and below, chapters 4 and 5. The New England clergy cited Locke more frequently than any other nonbiblical source. Hatch, however, fails to mention *any* of the numerous Locke citations in the clerical writings from the colonial and Revolutionary periods, even when the argument he is considering in a particular sermon is supported exclusively by a citation of "Locke on Government." He simply cites Bailyn and Pocock, repeating the slogan that interpretations which stress *Locke et praeterea nihil* badly need revision, and moves completely to the other extreme.

32. Ezra Stiles, quoted in Herbert D. Foster, "International Calvinism through Locke and the Revolution of 1688," *American Historical Review*, v. 32, no. 3 (April 1927), p. 475.

33. On the education of the New England clergy, and the availability and teaching of Locke's works at Harvard and Yale, see note 43, below. For Locke's renown as a "Scripture commentator," see note 32, above. We also know that Locke's "unanswerable" *Letter on Toleration* enjoyed high favor in clerical circles; it became the first American edition of any of Locke's writings, the work of the senior class at Yale in 1742. Moreover, Locke's *Essay Concerning Human Understanding* was immensely influential throughout the eighteenth century—even Pocock acknowledges this. And one minister actually "borrowed" Locke's title, *The Reasonableness of Christianity*, for his own distinctively Lockean assault on the misguided purveyors of deism and natural religion. See Clinton Rossiter, *Seedtime of the Republic* (Random House, 1953), p. 491 n. 111; Alice M. Baldwin, *The New England Clergy and the American Revolution* (Duke University Press, 1928), p. 60. Pocock, "The Myth of John Locke," pp. 169–170. Jonathan Dickinson, *The Reasonableness of Christianity* (1732). And see note 5, above.

34. Merrill Jensen, *Tracts of the American Revolution: 1763–1776* (Bobbs-Merrill, 1967), p. xiii.

35. Moses Coit Tyler, *The Literary History of the American Revolution: 1763–1783* (The Facsimile Library, 1941), v. 1, p. 7.

36. Elaine K. Ginsberg, "The Patriot Pamphleteers," in Everett Emerson (ed.), *American Literature, 1764–1789: The Revolutionary Years* (University of Wisconsin Press, 1977), p. 20. Homer L. Calkin, "Pamphlets and Public Opinion during the American Revolution," *Pennsylvania Magazine of History and Biography* 64 (1940), p. 24.

37. Dora Mae Clark, *British Opinion and the American Revolution* (Yale University Press, 1930), p. 4.

38. Ginsberg, "The Patriot Pamphleteers," p. 19. Calkin, "Pamphlets and Public Opinion during the American Revolution," p. 28.

39. Tyler, *The Literary History of the American Revolution: 1763–1783*, v. 1, p. 21.

40. Ibid., p. 19.

41. The Resolutions of the North Carolina Provincial Council, December 24, 1775, in *American Archives*, v. IV; pp. 306–307.

42. Charles J. Stille, *The Life and Times of John Dickinson* (Historical Society of Pennsylvania, 1891), p. 31.

43. Dunn, "The Politics of Locke," pp. 69–70. Claude M. Newlin, *Philosophy and Religion in Colonial America* (Philosophical Library, 1962), pp. 24, 25, 21. Martha Louise Counts, "The Political Views of the Eighteenth-Century New England Clergy, as Expressed in Their Election Sermons" (Ph.D. diss., Columbia University, 1956), pp. 275–279.

44. Counts, "Political Views," pp. 29, 105.

45. Ibid., pp. 275–279 (appendix B). Lester Douglas Joyce, *Church and Clergy in the American Revolution* (Exposition Press, 1966), p. 80: "Election sermons, the great moulders of public opinion, were delivered before the colonial governors and the entire law-making bodies and, afterward, published and circulated throughout the country."

46. "Even though the preachers of election sermons constitute only a small proportion of all of the New England clergy, nevertheless these ministers represented the entire group in several ways. Some came from small towns, others from cities. Some were young, others were old. Some had ideas in keeping with the majority of the civil rulers, others held views that clashed with those of the magistrates. The majority were Congregationalists, but a few were Baptists or Episcopalians. Sometimes the legislature selected prominent clergymen [to deliver the annual election sermon] but at other times it chose inferior and insignificant men. Therefore . . . these two hundred and forty-nine ministers reflected in their sermons the various changes which took place in the political thinking of the New England clergy." Counts, "Political Views," p. 6.

47. Extract of a letter from John Adams to a friend, dated February 18, 1776, in *American Archives*, fourth series, v. IV, pp. 1183–1184.

48. The most revealing testimony comes from some of the Revolution's staunchest foes, men who fought hard to uphold the authority of Parliament. Thomas Hutchinson, the last civilian royal governor of Massachusetts, bitterly complained that the "prayers and preaching of many of the clergy . . . inflame the minds of the people and instill principles repugnant to the fundamental principles of government." Harrison Gray, urging his countrymen to "lay down the weapons of rebellion" and to "submit to the wise, lenient" government of Great Britain, charged that "many of the dissenting clergy have so far prostituted their sacred office in assisting the cause of opposition." Peter Oliver, the last chief justice of Massachusetts under colonial rule, denounced the "Black Regiment," whose "prayers and sermons were interlaced

with scandal against the laws and the government." Oliver eventually concluded that "it was in vain to struggle against the Law of [James] Otis and the Gospel of his Black Regiment." And an anonymous Bostonian, in a secret communication to a top government official in London, praised the loyalty of the "members of the Church of England" in Massachusetts, but had this to say about the non-Anglican clergy: "[T]he pulpits groan with the most wicked, malicious and inflammatory harangues, spiriting their godly hearers to the most violent opposition to Government; persuading them that if they would rise as one man to oppose those arbitrary schemes, God would assist them to sweep away every 'ministerial tool' . . . from the face of the earth; that now was the time to strike . . . ; together with a long string of such seditious stuff, well-calculated to make them run into every degree of extravagance and folly, which if I see aright, they will have leisure enough to be sorry for."

Hutchinson and Oliver, quoted in Baldwin, *The New England Clergy and the American Revolution*, pp. 98 (text and n. 46), 113 (text and nn. 21–22), 122 n. 1. Harrison Gray, *A Few Remarks upon Some of the Votes and Resolutions of the Continental Congress . . . by a Friend to Peace and Good Order* (Boston, 1775), Evans 14074, pp. 20, 7. The anonymous letter is in *American Archives*, fourth series, v. 1, p. 301.

Testimonials to the importance of religion and of the New England clergy in the American Revolution are legion. For a sampling across time and the political spectrum, see the following: Edmund Burke, "Speech in Support of Resolutions for Conciliation with the American Colonies," March 22, 1775, in Elliot R. Barkan (ed.), *Edmund Burke on the American Revolution: Selected Speeches and Letters*, 2d ed. (Peter Smith, 1972), p. 84. Governor Thomas Pownall, before the House of Commons, February 8, 1769, in Thomas Curson Hansard's *Parliamentary History of England* (London: Johnson Reprint Corporation, 1966), pp. 498–499. Cortlandt Skinner in a letter to his brother, dated December 1775, in *American Archives*, fourth series, v. IV, p. 363. Ambrose Serle, in a letter to the earl of Dartmouth (November 8, 1776), in B. F. Stevens (ed.), *Facsimiles of Manuscripts in European Archives Relating to America, 1773–1783* (Mellifont Press, 1970), v. 24, no. 2045. Claude H. Van Tyne, "Influence of the Clergy, and of Religious and Sectarian Forces, on the American Revolution," in *American Historical Review*, v. 19, no. 1 (October 1913). Sidney E. Ahlstrom, *A Religious History of the American People* (Yale University Press, 1972), p. 361. Joyce, *Church and Clergy in the American Revolution*, pp. 34, 39. And no list is complete without the authoritative works of Perry Miller: for instance, *The New England Mind: From Colony to Province* (Harvard University Press, 1953); *The New England Mind: The Seventeenth Century* (Harvard University Press, 1939); *Errand into the Wilderness* (Harvard University Press, 1956).

49. Stille, *The Life and Times of John Dickinson*, pp. 29, 31.

50. John Dunn, *The Political Thought of John Locke* (Cambridge University Press, 1969; 1st paperback edition, 1982), pp. xi–xii.

51. Joyce, *Church and Clergy in the American Revolution*, pp. 34, 39.

52. Jonathan Mayhew, *Discourse Concerning Unlimited Submission and Non-Resistance to the Higher Powers* (Boston, 1750), in John Wingate Thornton (ed.), *The Pulpit of the American Revolution* (1860; reprint Burt Franklin, 1970), p. 88.

53. See notes 57 and 58, below.

54. C. H. Van Tyne, "Influence of the Clergy," pp. 44, 54.

55. Stille, *The Life and Times of John Dickinson*, p. 31.

56. Jesse Lemisch, "What Made Our Revolution," *The New Republic* (May 25, 1968).

57. Bailyn, *Pamphlets of the American Revolution*, pp. xiii, xv–xvi, 749–752.

58. Thomas R. Adams, *American Independence: The Growth of an Idea—a Bibliographic Study* (Brown University Press, 1965), pp. xi–xiii.

59. See note 57, above.

60. In 1764 there were twenty-three newspapers published in America. By 1775 the number had reached thirty-eight—an increase of 60 percent. Tyler argued that the distinction between the newspaper essay and the pamphlet was only "mechanical": John Dickinson's series of "Letters from a Pennsylvania Farmer" appeared in several newspapers before being printed between the covers of a single pamphlet; Stephen Hopkins's great protest against the Stamp Act appeared first in a pamphlet —*The Rights of the Colonies Examined*—and was subsequently published in a number of newspapers. Pamphlets and newspapers thus, upon occasion, functioned interchangeably. Nevertheless, pamphlets and newspapers were different media, suitable for different purposes. Pamphlets provided the space in which to fit rounded constitutional arguments, detailed political treatises, and sermons with a political thrust. Newspapers demanded more concise exposition but allowed an author to "hit and run" in response to the most immediate developments.

Newspapers, in any event, were "'immense moral and political engines' that advanced opinions as well as reported occurrences." In the American Revolution, the service of the press "to political thought was as imposing as its service to political action." As a Boston Tory complained: The press had made it possible for "the peasants and their housewives in every part of the land . . . to dispute on politics and positively to determine upon our liberties."

See Arthur M. Schlesinger, *Prelude to Independence* (Alfred A. Knopf, 1958), p. 296; Rossiter, *Seedtime of the Republic*, p. 330; the Reverend Samuel Miller, quoted in Stephen Botein, "Printers and the American Revolution," in Bernard Bailyn and John B. Hench (eds.), *The Press and the American Revolution* (American Antiquarian Society, 1980), p. 11; Tyler, *The Literary History of the American Revolution: 1763–1783*, v. 1, p. 17.

61. Edmund Morgan has demonstrated how the official documents and resolutions from the Revolutionary period can shed new light upon received opinions. In the formal statements of the colonial assemblies, Morgan contends, "it is scarcely possible to discern a trace of the ideas which the Americans are supposed to have adopted during the period under discussion." Specifically, Morgan has found that the problematical distinction between internal and external taxation, though widely believed to have been essential to the American argument, was never a part of the official colonial case against the Stamp Act, but was rather an ad hoc theoretical device used by America's friends in England in order to induce the Rockingham Ministry to support the Repeal. "The pressures of politics undoubtedly dissuaded the

friends of the colonies from giving publicity to the colonial declarations, and probably led them to cooperate with Rockingham in adopting a distinction which the
colonists themselves would never have allowed."

Morgan's substantive point is that the colonists did not jump "like grasshoppers
from one unworkable constitutional theory to another," but consistently denied Parliament the right to impose any kind of taxes whatsoever. The distinction they are
charged with having abandoned under pressure by 1767 is a distinction that they
had never adopted in the first place. Morgan's methodological point is that this important insight into Revolutionary thought would not have been possible without a
close reading of the "*official* colonial position" (emphasis added).

See Edmund S. Morgan, "Colonial Ideas of Parliamentary Power," in Jack Greene
(ed.), *Reinterpretation of the American Revolution* (Harper & Row, 1968), pp. 151–
180. The "Tory Libel," which charges that the colonists' political theory consisted
of a series of "strategic retreats" from one indefensible position to another, comes
from Arthur M. Schlesinger, *New Viewpoints in American History* (Alfred A. Knopf,
1922), p. 179. Charles McIlwain also criticizes Schlesinger in *The American Revolution: A Constitutional Interpretation* (Cornell University Press, 1923).

62. Shalhope, "Toward a Republican Synthesis," p. 58. Bailyn, *Ideological Origins*,
pp. 35–36.

3   The Lockean Response to British "Innovations"

1. Ebenezer Bridge, *Election Sermon* (Massachusetts, 1767), Evans 10569, p. 46.

2. "Election sermons, the great moulders of public opinion, were delivered before
the colonial governors and the entire law-making bodies and, afterward, published
and circulated throughout the country." Lester Douglas Joyce, *Church and Clergy in
the American Revolution* (Exposition Press, 1966), p. 80.

3. Gad Hitchcock, *Election Sermon* (Massachusetts, 1774), in Charles Hyneman
and Donald Lutz (eds.), *American Political Writings of the Founding Era* (Liberty Press,
1983), v. I, pp. 288, 300.

4. *Pennsylvania Gazette*, July 18, 1774. *Pennsylvania Gazette*, postscript to 2386,
September 16, 1774. Samuel Langdon, *Election Sermon* (Massachusetts, 1775), in
John Wingate Thornton (ed.), *The Pulpit of the American Revolution* (1860; reprint
Burt Franklin, 1970), pp. 257–258 (n. a), 237. On the "asylum" granted in New
England to the "tyrannicides, Whalley, Goffe, and Dixwell," see Ibid., p. xx. Joseph
Perry, *Election Sermon* (Connecticut, 1775), pp. 8–9.

5. William Gordon, *A Discourse Preached December 15, 1774. . .* , in Thornton,
Pulpit of the American Revolution, pp. 215–216, 210 (emphasis added).

6. Ibid., p. 196. Thornton notes this review of Gordon's sermon by "a friend to
peace and good order."

7. Edmund S. Morgan, "The American Revolution: Revisions in Need of Re-
vising," in Morgan (ed.), *The American Revolution: Two Centuries of Interpretation*
(Prentice-Hall, 1965), p. 175; Paul Conkin, *Self-Evident Truths* (Indiana University
Press, 1974), p. 109.

8. See the discussions of Bernard Bailyn and J. G. A. Pocock in chapter 1, above, particularly at notes 55, 57, 66, 83 (and corresponding text). See also Nathan O. Hatch, *The Sacred Cause of Liberty* (Yale University Press, 1977). Consider Hatch's causal claim on behalf of "country" ideology: "Ministers of contrasting theologies defended the Revolution with the full force of religious persuasion *because* certain aging religious symbols common to both were revitalized as they became infused with the potent connotations of Real Whig or 'country' ideology" (p. 13, emphasis added).

9. John C. Miller, *Origins of the American Revolution* (Little, Brown, 1943; revised printing by Stanford University Press, 1966), p. 35.

10. Ernest Barker, "Natural Law and the American Revolution," in *Traditions of Civility* (Cambridge University Press, 1948), pp. 298–299.

11. Memorial of Governor Shute to the King (1723), in Merrill Jensen (ed.), *English Historical Documents* (Oxford University Press, 1962), v. IX: American Colonial Documents to 1776, p. 261.

12. Governor Belcher to the Board of Trade (1732), in *English Historical Documents*, v. IX, p. 266.

13. Governor Glen quoted by Claude H. Van Tyne, *The Causes of the War of Independence* (Riverside Press, 1922), pp. 46–47.

14. Ibid.

15. Jack P. Greene, "The Role of the Lower Houses of Assembly in Eighteenth-Century Politics," in Greene (ed.), *Reinterpretation of the American Revolution* (Harper and Row, 1968), p. 109.

16. The Stamp Act Congress: Petition to the King, in Edmund S. Morgan (ed.), *Prologue to Revolution* (University of North Carolina Press, 1959), p. 65. See also Silas Downer, *A Discourse* (Providence, 1768), Evans 10886, p. 6. The Massachusetts House of Representatives (in Morgan, *Prologue to Revolution*, p. 57) used natural rights to reserve exclusively to itself the power to levy taxes in 1765: "All Acts made, by any Power whatever, other than the General Assembly of this Province, imposing Taxes on the Inhabitants are Infringements of our *inherent* and *unalienable* Rights, as men and British Subjects."

17. Lord North, quoted by Van Tyne, *The Causes of the War of Independence*, p. 396. *English Historical Documents*, v. IX, pp. 700, 771, 773.

18. J. G. A. Pocock, *The Machiavellian Moment* (Princeton University Press, 1975), p. 507; "Virtue and Commerce in the Eighteenth Century," *Journal of Interdisciplinary History*, vol. 3 (Summer 1972), pp. 121–122.

19. Gordon Wood describes republican ideology as "essentially anti-capitalistic" in *The Creation of the American Republic* (University of North Carolina Press, 1969), p. 418. Lance Banning offers a different view in "Jeffersonian Ideology Revisited: Liberal and Classical Ideas in the New American Republic," *William & Mary Quarterly* 43 (January 1986), p. 12 n. 30. See chapter 4, below.

20. John Dickinson, in his second *Letter from a Farmer* (pp. 8, 9), wrote: "Never did the British Parliament, till the period above mentioned, think of imposing duties in America for the purpose of raising a revenue. . . . This I call an innovation, and

a most dangerous innovation." See the preambles to the Revenue Act of 1764 (the "Sugar Act"), the Stamp Act of 1765, and the (Townshend) Revenue Act of 1767, in *English Historical Documents*, IX, pp. 543, 656, 701.

21. *The Examination of Dr. Benjamin Franklin before an August Assembly (Parliament), Relating to the Repeal of the Stamp Act* (Edes & Gill, 1766), p. 1.

22. *Newport Mercury*, March 24, 1764. Rhode Island Resolves of 1765 and Connecticut Resolves of 1765, in Morgan, *Prologue to Revolution*, p. 51, 55.

23. See below, at notes 85, 86.

24. Oxenbridge Thacher, *The Sentiments of a British American*, in Bernard Bailyn (ed.), *Pamphlets of the American Revolution* (Harvard University Press, 1965), p. 491.

25. The term "salutary neglect" is a little misleading insofar as it suggests a condition devoid of political conflict. The century prior to the American Revolution was actually marked by bitter and seemingly endless contention between the colonial assemblies and the royal governors. "Neglect" refers only to the fact that during this period, Parliament did not intervene in that conflict in a substantial way. And Parliament's neglect was "salutary" for the colonies, according to Colonel Isaac Barre, insofar as "they flourished not by our care but by our neglect."

Barre said this in the House of Commons, as he argued against the proposed Stamp Act. Charles Townshend, a strong supporter of the Stamp Act, had complained that "these Americans, children planted by our care, nourished up by our indulgence, . . . and protected by our arms," would now refuse to help the mother country to defray the cost of her benevolence. Barre replied to Townshend: "They planted by your care? No! Your oppressions planted them in America. . . . They nourished up by your indulgence? They grew by your neglect of them. . . . They protected by your arms? They have nobly taken up arms in your defence. . . ."

Incidentally, it was in this speech, which was widely reported in the colonial newspapers, that Barre inadvertently furnished a name for a secret organization of American patriots when he described Americans as "those Sons of Liberty."

See *Proceedings and Debates of the British Parliaments Respecting North America, 1754–1793*, v. 2, pp. 13, 16; *English Historical Documents*, v. 9, pp. 660–661.

26. See, for example, John Bulkley, *Election Sermon* (Connecticut, 1713), Evans 1598, p. 29. Jeremiah Wise, *Election Sermon* (Massachusetts, 1729), Evans 1342, p. 8. Alice M. Baldwin, *The New England Clergy and the American Revolution* (Duke University Press, 1928), p. 39.

27. Jonathan Mayhew, *A Discourse Concerning Unlimited Submission and Non-Resistance to the Higher Powers*, in Thornton, *Pulpit of the American Revolution*, pp. 43, 89.

28. Commission to Sir Edmund Andros as Governor of the Dominion of New England (April 7, 1688), in *English Historical Documents*, v. IX, p. 239.

29. Van Tyne, *The Causes of the War of Independence*, pp. 45, 347.

30. Edward Rawson and Samuel Sewall, *The Revolution in New England Justified* (Boston, 1691), p. 7. See also *A Narrative of the Proceedings of Sir Edmund Androsse and his Complices* (Boston?, 1691).

31. *The Revolution in New England Justified*, p. 6.

32. Ibid.

33. Theodore B. Lewis, "A Revolutionary Tradition, 1689–1774," *New England Quarterly* 46 (1973), pp. 436–438, and passim. Samuel Cooke, *Election Sermon* (Massachusetts, 1770), in Thornton, *Pulpit of the American Revolution*, pp. 176–178.

34. Benjamin F. Wright, *American Interpretations of Natural Law* (Harvard University Press, 1931), p. 38.

35. The story of the "Jerseymen" is told by Edward Countryman, in "Out of the Bounds of Law: Northern Land Rioters in the Eighteenth Century," in Alfred F. Young (ed.), *The American Revolution: Explorations in the History of American Radicalism* (Northern Illinois University Press, 1976), pp. 37–69. The justificatory tract containing the transcription from the *Second Treatise* is in *New Jersey Archives*, first series, v. VII (1746–1751), p. 30; the transcription itself is on p. 42, where John Locke is referred to as "a very learned and worthy author."

36. *Newport Mercury*, August 31–September 7, 1767.

37. Judah Champion, *Election Sermon* (Connecticut, 1776), p. 16. On p. 7, Champion closely paraphrases (without attribution) §§77 and 123 of Locke's *Second Treatise*. And on p. 8 he transcribes, without quotes, §23 (1–4), where Locke writes: "This *Freedom* from Absolute, Arbitrary Power, is so necessary to, and closely joined with, a Man's Preservation, that he cannot part with it, but by what forfeits his Preservation and Life together." A footnote at this point in the sermon tells us to consult "Locke on Government."

38. Dickinson, *Letters from a Farmer* (no. 7), p. 35.

39. Hampden, "The Alarm" (no. 5), October 27, 1773, p. 2.

40. *Pennsylvania Gazette*, postscript to no. 2075, September 29, 1768.

41. *Newport Mercury*, January 3, 1774.

42. William Hicks, *On The Nature and Extent of Parliamentary Power Considered* (Philadelphia, 1768), Evans 10985, p. 2. Hicks claimed to have written this pamphlet prior to the repeal of the Stamp Act in 1766.

43. John Lathrop, *A Discourse Preached December 15, 1774*, Evans 13370, p. 27. Lathrop's footnote says "See Locke on Government, Chapter 5," which is the chapter "Of Property"; but the quotation itself is from chapter 11, "Of the Extent of the Legislative Power." I am using Locke, *Two Treatises of Government*, rev. ed., edited by Peter Laslett (Mentor Books, 1965). See above, chapter 1, note 112.

44. *Proceedings and Debates of the British Parliaments Respecting North America, 1754–1793*, v. II, p. 323 (Speech of March 7, 1766). Thomas Curson Hansard's *Parliamentary History of England* (Johnson Reprint Corporation, 1966), v. XVI (1765–1771), pp. 180–181. Camden's speech was reprinted in the *Newport Mercury* (June 6, 1774). It also appeared much earlier, though incorrectly attributed to Lord Chatham (William Pitt), in the *New York Mercury*, supplement to no. 843 (December 30, 1767), and in the *Newport Mercury* (January 4–11, 1768).

45. *Pennsylvania Gazette*, postscript to no. 2075, September 29, 1768.

46. *Massachusetts Spy*, December 12, 1771.

47. *Report of the Record Commissioners: Boston Town Records*, p. 98.

48. *Massachusetts Spy*, March 30, 1775. Arthur M. Schlesinger called the series of articles signed "From the County of Hampshire" the "ablest sustained reply" to the Tory, Daniel Leonard. He suggested that Joseph Hawley, a member of the

Massachusetts House of Representatives, might have been the author of these articles. Schlesinger, *Prelude to Independence: The Newspaper War on Britain, 1764–1776* (Alfred A. Knopf, 1958), p. 221 n. 42.

49. John Allen, *The American Alarm* (Boston, 1773), pp. 32, 8.

50. Camden's Speech of March 7, 1766, in *Proceedings and Debates of the British Parliaments*, v. II, p. 323; *Parliamentary History of England* v. XVI, p. 180. See below, for a discussion of the Declaratory Act.

51. Lord Mansfield's Speech of March 7, 1766, in *Proceedings and Debates of the British Parliaments*, v. II, p. 321.

52. Locke, *Second Treatise*, §142 (emphasis added).

53. Camden's Speech of March 7, 1766, in *Proceedings and Debates of the British Parliaments*, v. II, p. 323.

54. Samuel Adams, in Randolph Adams, *Political Ideas of the American Revolution* 3d ed. (Barnes & Noble, 1958), p. 148.

55. Camden's Speech of February 3, 1766, *Proceedings and Debates of the British Parliaments*, v. II, p. 127.

56. Randolph G. Adams, *Political Ideas of the American Revolution*, p. 144.

57. Barker, "Natural Law and the American Revolution," pp. 284, 317.

58. Van Tyne, *The Causes of the War of Independence*, pp. 233–234.

59. Joseph Warren, *An Oration Delivered March the 5th, at the Request of the . . . Town of Boston . . . to Commemorate the Bloody Tragedy* (Edes and Gill, 1772), p. 10.

60. Morgan, *Prologue to Revolution*, p. 55.

61. Petition to the King from the Stamp Act Congress, in Ibid., p. 65.

62. Pitt's [Lord Chatham's] Speech in the House of Lords, January 20, 1775 (pp. 104–105 in John Dickinson's *Farmer's Letters*).

63. Peter Force (ed.), *American Archives*, fourth series, v. 4, pp. 833–834.

64. Locke, *Second Treatise*, §174 (4–7). An Address Read at the Annual Meeting of Merchants in Philadelphia, April 25, 1768, in the *Newport Mercury*, June 9–16, 1768.

65. Locke, *Second Treatise*, §§85, 192.

66. *Essex Gazette*, March 19–26, 1771.

67. *Parliamentary History*, v. XVI, p. 178. Grenville, the Prime Minister, called these words of Camden "a libel upon Parliament."

68. John Tucker, *Election Sermon* (Massachusetts, 1771), in Hyneman and Lutz, *American Political Writings of the Founding Era*, v. 1, pp. 162–163.

69. [Anonymous], *A Discourse to the Sons of Liberty . . . in Boston* (Providence, 1766), p. 6.

70. Downer, *A Discourse . . .* , pp. 9–10.

71. Massachusetts Resolves of 1765, in Morgan's *Prologue to Revolution*, p. 56 (emphasis in the original).

72. *Boston Evening Post*, May 4, 1772. According to Arthur M. Schlesinger, "Junius Americanus" was the pen name of Arthur Lee, "a crony of John Wilkes and a correspondent of Samuel Adams." See Schlesinger, *Prelude to Independence*, p. 139.

73. *Parliamentary History*, v. XVI, p. 178.

74. See notes 30–32, above, and corresponding text.

75. Morgan, *Prologue to Revolution*, pp. 58, 59, 62.

76. Locke, *Second Treatise*, §138.

77. Ibid., §139.

78. Ibid., §222. Representation actually seems to be a condition for civil society, according to Locke. After noting (§90) the disadvantages of absolute monarchy, which is "inconsistent with civil society," Locke maintained (§94) that "the people . . . could never be safe nor at rest, *nor think themselves in civil society,* till the legislature was placed in collective bodies of men, call them Senate, Parliament, or what you please" (Locke's emphasis).

79. Locke, *Second Treatise*, §§87, 123.

80. Petition of the Virginia House of Burgesses to the House of Commons (December 18, 1764), in *English Historical Documents*, v. IX, pp. 667–668.

81. James Otis, *The Rights of the British Colonies Asserted and Proved* (Massachusetts, 1764), in Bailyn's *Pamphlets of the American Revolution*.

82. *The Examination of Dr. Benjamin Franklin*, p. 12.

83. Camden's Speech of February 3, 1766, *Proceedings and Debates of the British Parliaments*, v. II, pp. 127–128.

84. *Newport Mercury*, May 9–16, 1768. The speaker also quoted (twice) §174 (lines 8–9) of the *Second Treatise*. "Political power [is] where men have property in their own disposal."

85. Morgan, *Prologue to Revolution*, pp. 57, 60, 63, 67.

86. [Anonymous], *Pennsylvania Journal*, March 13, 1766.

87. Thomas Whately, *The Regulations Lately Made Concerning the Colonies and the Taxes Imposed upon Them, Considered* (London: 1765).

88. Soame Jenyns, *The Objections to the Taxation of Our American Colonies . . . Considered* (London, 1765).

89. James Otis, *Considerations on Behalf of the Colonists in a Letter to a Noble Lord* (London: Edes and Gill, 1765), p. 6.

90. Carl Becker, *The Declaration of Independence* (Vintage Books, 1958), p. 133.

91. Ibid., pp. 133–134.

92. Wright, *American Interpretations of Natural Law*, p. 341.

93. John Dunn, "The Politics of Locke in England and America in the Eighteenth Century," in John Yolton (ed.), *John Locke: Problems and Perspectives* (Cambridge University Press, 1969), p. 70.

94. Otis, *The Rights of the British Colonies Asserted and Proved*, in Bailyn, *Pamphlets of the American Revolution*, pp. 436–437.

Lord Mansfield, a staunch advocate of parliamentary sovereignty, warned the House of Lords that Otis's writings "may be called silly or mad, but mad people, or persons who have entertained silly and mad ideas, have led the people to rebellion and overturned empires." *Parliamentary History*, v. 16, p. 172.

Patrick Riley explains some of the differences between Locke and Grotius on natural law, in *Will and Political Legitimacy* (Harvard University Press, 1982), p. 90. John C. Miller called natural law "the first line of defense of colonial liberty." According to Miller, "what Americans particularly relished in John Locke was his emphasis upon natural law." Miller, *Origins of the American Revolution*, pp. 173, 171.

95. Daniel Dulany, *Considerations on the Propriety of Imposing Taxes in the British Colonies* (Maryland, 1765), in Bailyn, *Pamphlets of the American Revolution*, p. 611 (emphasis added).

96. Ibid., p. 612.

97. Ibid., p. 615.

98. Ibid., p. 616.

99. Edmund S. Morgan, "Colonial Ideas of Parliamentary Power," in Greene, *Reinterpretation of the American Revolution*, p. 174–175.

100. Dulany, *Considerations on the Propriety of Imposing Taxes*, p. 611: "I am upon a question of *propriety*, not of power."

101. Locke, *Second Treatise*, §140 (emphasis added).

102. Dunn, "The Politics of Locke," p. 64.

103. Locke, *Second Treatise*, §138.

104. *Pennsylvania Gazette*, postscript to 2075, September 29, 1768.

105. My conclusions concerning the textual "presence" of Locke and of republican sources in the American writings are supported by the results of Donald S. Lutz's survey of that literature, specifically for the period 1760 to 1776, which Lutz defines as the Revolutionary era. Lutz has confirmed my interpretation of his findings in personal correspondence. See Lutz, "The Relative Influence of European Writers on Late Eighteenth-Century American Political Thought," *The American Political Science Review*, v. 78, no. 1 (March 1984), pp. 196, 192–193. See discussion above, chapter 2, at notes 11–14.

Bernard Bailyn adopts virtually the same definition of the Revolutionary period. He opens the seminal text of the republican revision of the founding doctrine with John Adams's famous observation (made in a letter to Thomas Jefferson) that the Revolution "was effected from 1760 to 1775." Bailyn, *The Ideological Origins of the American Revolution* (Harvard University Press, 1967), p. 1 (epigraph).

106. Robert Shalhope, "Toward a Republican Synthesis: The Emergence of an Understanding in American Historiography," *William & Mary Quarterly* 29 (1972), p. 58. Bailyn, *Ideological Origins*, pp. 35–36.

107. John Trenchard and Thomas Gordon, *Cato's Letters* (3d corrected ed., 1733; reissued by Russell & Russell, 1969), v. 3, letter 97, p. 272.

108. Wood, *The Creation of the American Republic*, p. 418. Bailyn, *Ideological Origins*, p. 35. Extreme libertarianism, which stresses the priority of the individual over *all* other considerations and embraces the laissez-faire model of capitalism, is indeed the antithesis of civic republicanism, which stresses virtue over commerce, or the subordination of private to public interests. But the republican revision wants to have it both ways—and so do contemporary libertarians. See chapters 4 and 6, below.

109. John Locke, *Second Treatise*, §§87, 123.

110. Aristotle, *Politics*, translated by Ernest Barker (Oxford University Press, 1970–71), p. 332. Pocock, "Virtue and Commerce," p. 120.

111. Trenchard and Gordon, *Cato's Letters*, v. 3, letter 97, p. 272.

112. Becker, *The Declaration of Independence*, pp. 72–73.

113. Barker, "Natural Law and the American Revolution," p. 289.

114. *Boston Evening Post*, May 4, 1772 (emphasis added). The Locke quotation is from §139 of the *Second Treatise*.

115. *Pennsylvania Gazette*, June 8, 1774.

116. Morgan, *Prologue to Revolution*, p. 155 (emphasis added).

117. John Adams, *The Works of John Adams* (Little, Brown, 1856), v. 10, pp. 185, 187–188, 288. Lester Douglas Joyce quotes Adams on the fear of an American Episcopate as "a force in bringing about the Revolution: 'It is difficult to this day to realize how much the opposition of the colonists to the Church of England had to do with bringing about the Revolution. But although the fact is not always noticed by historians, *there was probably no other one cause which exerted such an influence.* The feeling of opposition was not so much religious as political. It was proposed to introduce bishops in America to be accepted by the government as they were in England. This meant a hierarchy under foreign domination.' And, according to Adams, it was in discussing this very subject that the colonists were first led to question the supremacy of Parliament." Joyce, *Church and Clergy in the American Revolution*, pp. 58–59. See also Baldwin, *The New England Clergy and the American Revolution*, p. 91 n. 23; Becker, *The Declaration of Independence*, p. 120.

118. John Patrick Diggins, *The Lost Soul of American Politics: Virtue, Self-Interest, and the Foundations of Liberalism*, (Basic Books, 1984), p. 33. Clinton Rossiter, *Seedtime of the Republic* (Random House, 1953), pp. 231–233. Baldwin, *The New England Clergy and the American Revolution*, pp. 90, 92, 169. Thornton, *Pulpit of the American Revolution*, p. 44: "It was Dr. Mayhew who suggested to James Otis the idea of committees of correspondence . . .—a thing of vital importance."

119. Jonathan Mayhew, *The Snare Broken* (May 23, 1766), in Frank Moore (ed.), *The Patriot Preachers of the American Revolution* (New York, 1862), p. 25. John Adams called Mayhew a "transcendent genius." Adams, *Works*, v. 10, p. 288.

120. Ebenezer Baldwin's appendix to Samuel Sherwood's *Sermon*, delivered August 31, 1774 (New Haven), p. 57. "From the County of Hampshire, no. 2," *Massachusetts Spy*, February 16, 1775. *Pennsylvania Gazette*, postscript 2379, July 27, 1774.

121. *Massachusetts Spy*, December 22, 1774.

122. *Newport Mercury*, October 3, 1774.

123. *Pennsylvania Gazette*, June 8, 1774. *Massachusetts Spy*, October 9, 1770 (reporting the proceedings of the Grand Jury of Philadelphia: September 24, 1770).

124. "The British American, no. 7" (July 14, 1774), in *American Archives*, v. 1, p. 541. See also the declaration of the South Carolina Provincial Congress (March 26, 1776), in *American Archives*, v. 5, pp. 609–615.

125. Charles F. Mullett, *Fundamental Law and the American Revolution* (Octagon Books, 1966), p. 170.

126. "To the Inhabitants of Virginia, from a Planter" (April 6, 1776) in *American Archives*, v. 5, pp. 798–800. The author warns that any retreat from resisting the principle of the Declaratory Act "immediately draws after it an endless train of miseries."

127. Locke, *Second Treatise*, chapter 11. Note the literal centrality of the issue in Locke's title for the *Second Treatise*. "An Essay Concerning the True Origins, Ex-

tent, and End of Civil Government." On the American side, see "From the County of Hampshire, no. 1," *Massachusetts Spy*, February 9, 1775. The author quotes Parliament's assertion of illimitable authority from the Declaratory Act and says: "This is the Question. And to this claim is our opposition made."

128. *Pennsylvania Gazette*, August 4, 1768.

129. Ibid., §§134, 135.

130. Ibid., §§149, 240.

131. Ibid., §§135, 138–140.

132. Ibid., §142.

133. Rossiter, *Seedtime of the Republic*, p. 491 n. 111. Alice M. Baldwin, *The New England Clergy and the American Revolution*, p. 60.

134. John Locke, *A Letter on Toleration*, edited by J. W. Gough (Clarendon Press, 1968), pp. 69, 67. Locke, *Scritti Editi e Inediti Sulla Tolleranza*, edited and translated by Carlo Viano (Turin, 1961), pp. 90, 91. This is Locke's 1667 *Essay Concerning Toleration*, an early version of the definitive *Letter on Toleration*.

135. "A Watchman" (December 24, 1774), in *American Archives*, v. I, pp. 1063–1065.

136. Hampden, *The Alarm*, p. 2: The author quotes from the Declaratory Act and says, "This Act declares that you have no property of your own, for as Mr. Locke justly observed, 'what property have they in that which another may by right take when he pleases to himself'; and Parliament declares it has this right. This Act, therefore, declares to all the world that you are slaves, the live-stock of the people of Great Britain."

"A Friendly Address to the Freemen, from Epaminondas," *Connecticut Courant*, March 27, 1775: The author transcribes §136 (1–5) of the *Second Treatise* to denounce the Declaratory Act.

"From the County of Hampshire, no. 2," *Massachusetts Spy*, February 16, 1775. "From the County of Hampshire, no. 7," *Massachusetts Spy*, March 30, 1775: The author transcribes §138 (lines 1–17) and §139 (lines 1–3) to support an argument against the Declaratory Act.

Letter of Charles Garth (London: March 5, 1766), reporting the use of Locke by the opponents of the Declaratory Act in the debate on that act in Parliament, in *Maryland Historical Magazine*, v. VI, no. 3 (September 1911), pp. 287–305, and especially 291–292.

Camden's Speech to the House of Lords (March 7, 1766), in Hansard's *Parliamentary History of England*, v. XVI, pp. 180–181. Camden's speech, in which he read aloud from the *Second Treatise*, was reprinted in the *Newport Mercury*, June 6, 1774. It also appeared much earlier, but incorrectly attributed to Lord Chatham, in the *New York Mercury*, supplement to no. 843, December 30, 1767, and in the *Newport Mercury*, January 4–11, 1768.

These citations are samples of external evidence of the formal Lockean connection with respect to the Declaratory Act. Virtually every piece of internal evidence introduced in this chapter, insofar as it concerns the limits of civil authority, also testifies against the Declaratory Act, either by name or by implication. The substantive Lockean connection in the political thought of the New England clergy echoes this hostility to political absolutism, but traces the roots of constitutionalism back to fundamental theological conceptions in both Lockean and clerical thought. See chapter 5, below.

137. Ronald E. Pynn, "The Influence of John Locke's Political Philosophy on American Political Tradition," *North Dakota Quarterly*, v. 42, no. 3 (Summer 1974), p. 53.

138. Esmond Wright, for example, maintains that "the authority Locke supported was that of the British Parliament." Wright, "Men with Two Countries," in *The Development of a Revolutionary Mentality* (Library of Congress, 1972), p. 153. Similar confusion is revealed by Pocock's decision to count Locke among the "adversaries" of the ideology of the American Revolution and Bailyn's assertion that Locke's "ideas would scarcely have supported" the argument in Jonathan Mayhew's *Discourse Concerning Unlimited Submission*. Pocock, *The Machiavellian Moment*, p. 424; Bailyn, *Ideological Origins*, p. 52; and see below, chapter 4, at note 44.

139. The following anonymous contribution appeared in the *Massachusetts Spy* (July 30, 1772): "Please to publish the following extract from Mr. Locke. It is of the utmost importance that every man should be rightly informed of the difference between a lawful governor and a tyrant, how far and when he has a right to resist, and when he must bear. I heartily recommend the passage to the repeated and serious perusal of your readers." The author then transcribed §§202 (1–28) and 203–210 (entire) from the *Second Treatise*. See also: "From the County of Hampshire to the Inhabitants of Massachusetts-Bay, no. 9" (April 13, 1775), in *American Archives*, v. 2, pp. 329–334. Here the author uses §230 of the *Second Treatise* to show how civil rulers cease to be the "ordinance of God."

140. "William Temple" wrote: "I shall leave it to the consideration of every lover of liberty, and recommend it to them to read Mr. Locke's chapter on the dissolution of government." He then transcribed §§227 (19–26) and 228–230 (entire) from the *Second Treatise*. *Newport Mercury*, July 30, 1764. James Otis quoted from §§149, 211, 212, 222 of the *Second Treatise* in *The Rights of the British Colonies Asserted and Proved*, in Bailyn, *Pamphlets of the American Revolution*, pp. 429, 434–435. An anonymous contributor to the *Massachusetts Spy* (August 27, 1772) quoted "the incomparable Mr. Locke" to determine "who shall be judge whether the Prince acts contrary to his trust," and then transcribed all of §§240–243 from the *Second Treatise*. Untitled broadside by "Somers" (March 8, 1775), in *American Archives*, v. 5, pp. 121–123. "From the County of Hampshire, no. 9," in *American Archives*, v. 2, pp. 329–334 (citing §222 of the *Second Treatise*). William Patten cited "the great Mr. Locke in his essay on government," transcribing the whole of section 240 to show that the people are the proper judges of whether "the Prince or the Legislative betrays its trust." Patten, *A Discourse Delivered at Hallifax* (Boston, 1766), Evans 10440, pp. 17–18 n.

These and other citations call into question Clinton Rossiter's assertion that Locke's "discussion of 'the dissolution of government' was hardly used at all" by the colonial authors. In fact, it was one of their favorite arguments. Rossiter, *Seedtime of the Republic*, pp. 358–359.

141. *Massachusetts Spy*, July 23, 1772. "Mucius Scaevola" transcribes §163 (8–26)

of the *Second Treatise* in an attack against Governor Hutchinson's misuse of prerogative. See also Gad Hitchcock's distinctively Lockean understanding of prerogative
in his *Election Sermon*, in Hyneman and Lutz, *American Political Writings during the
Founding Era*, v. I, pp. 298–299. Compare with Locke, *Second Treatise*, chapter 14.

142. *Massachusetts Spy*, August 22, 1771. This edition of the *Spy* opens with a
verbatim transcription of chapter 18 ("Of Tyranny") from the *Second Treatise*, in its
entirety.

143. *Report of the Record Commissioners: Boston Town Records* (1772), pp. 95–96.
The principle of religious toleration is stated explicitly in the terms of "Mr. Locke,"
who "has asserted, and proved beyond the possibility of contradiction on any solid
ground, that such toleration ought to be extended to all whose doctrines are not
subversive of society." The reader is advised to "see Locke's Letters on Toleration."

144. James Otis, *The Rights of the British Colonies Asserted and Proved*, in Bailyn,
Pamphlets of the American Revolution, p. 440. Referring to §§4 and 11 of the *Second
Treatise*, Otis calls natural liberty "this gift of God," which "cannot be annihilated."

145. Letter from "A Virginian" to the editors of the *Pennsylvania Gazette*, appearing in a postscript to issue 2075, September 29, 1768.

146. Letter to Mr. Alexander Purdie, from A. B., April 12, 1776, in *American
Archives*, v. V, pp. 860–862. The author presents a quotation from §212 of the *Second Treatise* to support the argument for independence: "'Besides the overturning
from without, governments are dissolved from within when the legislature is altered,'
are the words of Mr. Locke. We have not only altered the legislature, but exercised
the judicial, the executive, and every other power of independent sovereignty. . . .
We shall be obliged to call ourselves (what, for some months, we have really been)
independent."

147. *Boston Gazette*, November 18, 1765. This article, written by "John Locke,"
consists entirely of verbatim transcriptions from the *Second Treatise*, covering a wide
range of topics, in the following order: §§192 (17–27), 193 (8–9), 194 (19–23),
195 (1–11), 202 (24–27, 1–7), 204 (1–4), 208 (3–5, 9–14), 209 (4–17), 210 (1–9,
13–23).

148. See above, chapter 1, note 112.

149. *Report of the Record Commissioners: Boston Town Records* (1772), p. 96: "The
essential natural rights" and "the means of preserving those rights" cannot be re-
nounced upon entrance into society because "the very great end of civil government
from the very nature of its institution is for the support, protection, and defence of
those very rights, the principal of which . . . are life, liberty, and property." General Court of Massachusetts (1776), *American Archives*, v. 4, p. 833: "When kings,
ministers, governors, or legislators, instead of exercising the powers entrusted with
them according to the principles, forms, and proportions stated by the constitution,
and established by the original compact, prostitute those powers to the purposes of
oppression, to subvert instead of supporting a free constitution, to destroy instead of
preserving the lives, liberties, and properties of the people, they are no longer to be
deemed magistrates vested with a sacred character, but become public enemies, and
ought to be resisted."

150. See, for example: "The Political Maxims of America" (anonymous), in the

Massachusetts Spy, November 5–8, 1770: "The people always have a right to judge of the conduct of their rulers, and reward them according to their deeds." "Mucius Scaevola" to the *Massachusetts Spy*, June 27, 1771: When kings and governors "leap the bounds of the law and set up their will for the rule of government, they are no longer lawful rulers but tyrants, and the people have a right to reduce them to their private station and punish them for betraying the trust reposed in them." The Preceptor, *Social Duties of the Political Kind* (Boston, 1772), in Hyneman and Lutz, *American Political Writings during the Founding Era*, v. I, p. 181: Under the heading, "Political Duties of the People"—"The people are the fountain of power and authority, the original seat of majesty. . . . If they shall find the power they have conferred abused by their trustees, their majesty violated by tyranny or usurpation, . . . then it is their right, and what is their right is their duty, to resume that delegated power and call their trustees to account." The General Court of Massachusetts (1776), in *American Archives*, v. 4, p. 833: "It is a maxim that in every government there must exist, somewhere, a supreme, sovereign, absolute, and uncontrollable power; but this power resides, always, in the body of the people."

151. The Preceptor, *Social Duties of the Political Kind* (see note 150, above). General Court of Massachusetts (see note 149, above). John Dickinson, *Essay on the Constitutional Power of Great Britain over the Colonies in America* (extract), *Massachusetts Spy*, January 12, 1775: "Submission may sometimes be a less evil than opposition, and therefore a duty. . . . But when submission becomes inconsistent with and destructive of the public good, the same veneration for and duty to the divine authority commands us to oppose."

152. *The Political Maxims of America* (anonymous), in the *Massachusetts Spy*, November 5–8, 1770: "Rulers were instituted to be servants to the people and ministers of God for good; but if instead of servants they become masters, and instead of ministers for good they are ministers for evil, they are no longer rulers according to their institution. . . . The people always have a right to judge of the conduct of their rulers, and reward them according to their deeds."

153. "Mucius Scaevola" (see note 150, above). The General Court of Massachusetts (see note 149, above). Benjamin Church, *Oration Delivered at Boston, March 5, 1773*, in Hezekiah Niles, *Principles and Acts of the Revolution in America* (A. S. Barnes & Co., 1876), p. 35: "When rulers become tyrants, they cease to be kings." *The Political Maxims of America* (see note 152, above). "Amicus Constitutionis," in the *New York Journal*, October 19, 1775: "Rebellion is a traiterous taking up of arms against the king, in the regular discharge of his important trust. . . . But when the king . . . violates the constitution . . . he unkings himself, and is liable to be deposed. Nay, he, in a sense, deposes himself," and does himself become a rebel. "The Whisperer," in the *Massachusetts Spy*, March 14, 1771: "When kings grow lawless, tyrants they commence; and to obey 'em argues want of sense." See also the General Court of Massachusetts (note 150, above).

154. "Amicus Constitutionis" (note 153, above). Josiah Quincy, *Observations on the Act of Parliament*. . . . (Boston: 1774), Evans 13561, p. 22: "Tyrants are rebels against the first laws of Heaven and Society. To oppose their ravages is an instinct of nature—the inspiration of God in the heart of man." "Pacificus to Tranquillus,"

in the *Pennsylvania Gazette*, September 14, 1774: "I readily agree with you, Sir, that the crime of rebellion is of the deepest dye, and in every civil war, doubtless one side or the other are rebels; but if that be the only government pleasing to God or useful to man, which maintains the peace, safety, and happiness of the people, and if no good reason can be assigned to induce any rational creature to become a member of that community which denies these blessings to its members, then I ask, who are the rebels in any contest of the kind, the governors who abuse the trust reposed in them, and exercise the delegated power of the people to their hurt, or the governed, who attempt to protect themselves against the abuse of that power? If subjection is only due to a legal exertion of power, and if power ought only to be employed for the good of the community, then he alone is chargeable with rebellion who uses the power he possesses to the hurt of the people, and not the people who oppose every illegal exertion of that power. The happiness and good of the people is the only law by which every contest between the supreme magistrate and the people is or ought to be tried; and the party transgressing against that law are the rebels against the constitution." To the Printer from A Free Man, *New York Constitutional Gazette*, September 9, 1775: "Rebellion is the resisting of the *just* and *lawful* power of government; and if so, it is no rebellion to resist an *unjust* and *usurped* power; for it would then be rebellion to resist rebellion, and there would be no just defence against the exorbitant power of rulers. . . . They are rebels who arm against the constitution, not they who defend it by arms." The relevant passages from the *Second Treatise* are in §§226 and 227.

155. "To the People of Pennsylvania, from Salus Populi" (March 1776), in *American Archives*, v. 5, pp. 96–99: It is never "the interest of any civil society to exalt any set of religious tenets above all others or to unite the church and state. Most of the wars which deluged the world in blood . . . arose from this false policy. The priesthood of any sect in religion, with sorrow I repeat it, can easily be made the tools of tyranny and arbitrary power." Compare with Locke, *A Letter On Toleration*, pp. 145, 141.

156. Pocock, "Virtue and Commerce," p. 124.

157. Pocock, *The Machiavellian Moment*, p. 424.

158. Pynn, "The Influence of John Locke's Political Philosophy on American Political Tradition," p. 56. Pynn notes a "lack of Lockean citations" in the Revolutionists' writings, which he then attributes to their "disgust for the ambiguity in Locke and a distrust for his thought." The analysis of the formal connection, however, shows that any "disgust" and "distrust" for Locke is strictly in the head of the revisionist, and that it is very probably based on a fundamental misunderstanding of Lockean thought. The analysis also suggests that Pynn failed to look closely at the writings from the Revolutionary period before proclaiming the absence of Locke.

4 Historiography and the Interpretation of Political Theory

1. C. B. Macpherson, *The Political Theory of Possessive Individualism* (Oxford University Press, 1962; reprint, Oxford Paperbacks, 1965). Leo Strauss, *Natural Right and History* (University of Chicago Press, 1953).

2. John Patrick Diggins, *The Lost Soul of American Politics: Virtue, Self-Interest, and the Foundations of Liberalism* (Basic Books, 1984), p. 19.

3. Robert Shalhope, "Toward a Republican Synthesis: The Emergence of an Understanding in American Historiography," *William & Mary Quarterly* 29 (1972), p. 58. Bernard Bailyn, *The Ideological Origins of the American Revolution* (Harvard University Press, 1967), pp. 35–36.

4. Shalhope, "Toward a Republican Synthesis," p. 58.

5. John Trenchard and Thomas Gordon, *Cato's Letters*, v. 3, letter 105, p. 335. I am using the two-volume Russell & Russell 1969 reissue of the four-volume third corrected edition of 1733. Unfortunately, the pagination is confusing; each of the four volumes begins with "page one." Therefore, the volume number in my citations refers to the number assigned by "Cato" himself. I also include the number of the cited letter to dispel any remaining confusion.

6. Niccolò Machiavelli, *The Discourses*, edited by Bernard Crick (Penguin Books, 1979), pp. 111–112, 132; *The Prince*, translated by George Bull (Penguin Classics, 1983), pp. 90–91, 96–97, 100.

7. Trenchard and Gordon, *Cato's Letters*, v. 1, letter 31, p. 238.

8. Jeffrey Isaac, "Liberalism vs. Republicanism: A Reinterpretation" (paper presented at the annual meeting of the American Political Science Association, New Orleans, 1985; quoted with the author's permission), p. 15.

9. John Patrick Diggins, "Comrades and Citizens: New Mythologies in American Historiography," *The American Historical Review* (June 1985), pp. 635, 647–648.

10. J. G. A. Pocock, "The Myth of John Locke and the Obsession with Liberalism," in J. G. A. Pocock and Richard Ashcraft (eds.), *John Locke* (University of California Press, 1980), pp. 3–24. See the discussion above, chapter 1.

11. Leo Strauss, *Thoughts on Machiavelli* (University of Chicago Press, 1958), pp. 59, 120, 173.

12. Pocock once criticized Strauss's interpretation of Machiavelli directly, thus bravely incurring the wrath of Stauss's "well-armed guardians" who assert that "all Strauss's critics are pathetically incompetent." He noted the "methodological assumptions that tend to place Strauss's procedure beyond the reach of criticism— which is, of course, to make it critically worthless." Pocock sought to distinguish criticism and demystification of Strauss's argument from "blasphemy and impertinence," preferring to treat Strauss as a scholar, brilliant but fallible, and not as an "oracle." Accordingly, he viewed Strauss's work on Machiavelli as "marvelously perceptive in some ways, as well as marvelously wrong-headed in others." See the "Exchange on Strauss's Machiavelli" between Pocock and Harvey C. Mansfield, Jr., in *Political Theory*, v. 3, no. 4 (November 1975), pp. 372–405. See below, for a discussion of Strauss's method.

13. J. G. A. Pocock, *The Machiavellian Moment* (Princeton University Press, 1975), pp. 424, 545.

14. Leo Strauss, *What Is Political Philosophy?* (The Free Press, 1959), p. 49. In his *Thoughts on Machiavelli* (p. 282), Strauss concludes that *The Prince* and *The Discourses* "are both republican." What, then, is Locke, through whom Machiavelli became "victorious?"

15. Strauss, *Thoughts on Machiavelli*, p. 9; *What Is Political Philosophy?*, p. 40;

"Niccolo Machiavelli," in *History of Political Philosophy*, 2d edition, edited by Leo Strauss and Joseph Cropsey (University of Chicago Press, 1973; 1981), pp. 271–292.

16. I find Sir Isaiah's analysis of Machiavelli most compelling. Isaiah Berlin, "The Originality of Machiavelli," in *Against the Current* (Viking Press, 1980).

17. John G. Gunnell, *Political Theory: Tradition and Interpretation* (Winthrop Publishers, 1979), p. 67.

18. John G. Gunnell, "The Myth of the Tradition," *The American Political Science Review* (March 1978), p. 131, 132.

19. Trenchard and Gordon, *Cato's Letters*, v. 2, letter 40, pp. 54–55.

20. Ibid., p. 56.

21. Trenchard and Gordon, *Cato's Letters*, v. 3, letter 75, p. 76. See also v. 1, letter 33, pp. 256–257, 262–263; v. 2, letter 40, pp. 50–51; v. 2, letter 44, p. 77; v. 3, letter 96, pp. 262–263.

22. Trenchard and Gordon, *Cato's Letters*, v. 2, letter 42, p. 70.

23. Trenchard and Gordon, *Cato's Letters*, v. 1, letter 31, p. 238; v. 2, letter 42, p. 70; v. 2, letter 40, pp. 50–51, 56.

24. Thomas Hobbes, *Leviathan*, edited by C. B. Macpherson (Pelican Classics, 1980), pp. 223, 186. Trenchard and Gordon, *Cato's Letters*, v. 2, letter 39, p. 47; v. 2, letter 44, p. 78.

25. Pocock, *The Machiavellian Moment*, pp. 524, 436. Thomas L. Pangle tackles this issue from a slightly different angle in *The Spirit of Modern Republicanism: The Moral Vision of the American Founders and the Philosophy of Locke* (University of Chicago Press, 1988), p. 30. On Pangle's work, see above, chapter 1, note 12.

26. Pocock, *The Machiavellian Moment*, p. 397.

27. Ibid., pp. 471, 472.

28. Gordon S. Wood, *The Creation of the American Republic* (University of North Carolina Press, 1969), p. 418.

29. Lance Banning, "Jeffersonian Ideology Revisited: Liberal and Classical Ideas in the New American Republic," *William & Mary Quarterly* 43 (January 1986), p. 12 n. 30. Edmund Morgan, "The American Revolution: Revisions in Need of Revising," in Morgan (ed.), *The American Revolution: Two Centuries of Interpretation* (Prentice-Hall, 1965), p. 175; Paul Conkin, *Self-Evident Truths* (Indiana University Press, 1974), p. 109. See above, chapter 3.

30. Isaac, "Liberalism vs. Republicanism," pp. 3, 42, 35.

31. Jesse Goodale, "J. G. A. Pocock's Neo-Harringtonians: A Reconsideration," *History of Political Thought* (Summer 1980), p. 251. Trenchard and Gordon, *Cato's Letters*, v. 2, letter 38, p. 39. Pangle notes (*The Spirit of Modern Republicanism*, pp. 32–33) that "Cato rails, not against free enterprise, but against the obstacle to unrestricted free enterprise—state or state-sponsored ownership of property, monopoly, and exclusion of business privileges." Cato's "radically libertarian character," he argues, "is quite incompatible with the closed society presupposed by a genuinely classical or virtuous republicanism."

Here again the republican synthesis displays an inadequate understanding of the terms it employs as well as a serious but unacknowledged difference among its founders. Wood calls American republicanism "essentially anti-capitalistic" (note 28, above), and Pocock treats it as the doctrine which stresses the normative priority of other-regarding virtue over commerce and self-interest. Bailyn, on the other hand, describes Cato as the principal spokesman for the "extreme libertarianism" of the Revolutionary worldview (*Ideological Origins*, p. 35). Yet "extreme libertarianism" celebrates the uninhibited pursuit of self-interest in the socioeconomic context of laissez-faire capitalism.

32. Trenchard and Gordon, *Cato's Letters*, v. 1, preface, p. liv–lv.

33. Thomas Paine, *Common Sense* (Penguin, 1983), pp. 68–69.

34. Trenchard and Gordon, *Cato's Letters*, v. 3, letter 80, p. 120; letter 85, pp. 159, 162.

35. Jesse Lemisch, "What Made Our Revolution," *New Republic* (May 25, 1968).

36. Trenchard and Gordon, *Cato's Letters*, v. 3, letter 80, p. 120; letter 85, pp. 159–163.

37. Bailyn, *Ideological Origins*, chapter 3, pp. 55–93.

38. Trenchard and Gordon, *Cato's Letters*, v. 4, letter 115, p. 82; v. 1, letter 33, pp. 255–263; v. 2, letter 40, pp. 50–51. Hobbes, *Leviathan*, p. 161.

39. Benjamin R. Barber, *Strong Democracy: Participatory Politics for a New Age* (University of California Press, 1984), pp. 14–15, 21, 22, 102–103.

40. Ibid., p. 21 n. 24.

41. Bailyn, *Ideological Origins*, p. 34; J. G. A. Pocock, "Virtue and Commerce in the Eighteenth Century," *Journal of Interdisciplinary History* 3 (Summer 1972), p. 120. If I am right about Cato, it is worth noting that in its way, Hobbes's *Leviathan* contains the most "radical social and political thought of the English Civil War and Commonwealth period."

42. Pocock, *The Machiavellian Moment*, p. 509. Pocock endorses Bailyn's interpretation of Revolutionary political thought, claiming that it "altogether replaces" the Hartzian model.

43. For instance, compare the following: Locke, *Second Treatise*, §§6, 23, 135, 168, with Trenchard and Gordon, *Cato's Letters*, v. 2, letter 59, pp. 214, 216 and v. 2, letter 60, p. 228; *Second Treatise*, §§168, 240, 241, with *Cato's Letters*, v. 2, letter 59, p. 217; *Second Treatise*, §§168, 176, 241, 242, with *Cato's Letters*, v. 2, letter 59, pp. 217–218, 222–223; and *Second Treatise*, §§208, 223, 225, 230, with *Cato's Letters*, v. 2, letter 59, pp. 224, 225.

44. Bailyn, *Ideological Origins*, p. 52. See chapter 1, above, at note 16.

45. Simeon Howard, *A Sermon Preached to the Ancient and Honorable Artillery Company in Boston* (1773), in Charles S. Hyneman and Donald S. Lutz (eds.), *American Political Writings of the Founding Era* (Liberty Press, 1983), v. 1, p. 187. Howard twice reaffirms the distinction between liberty and license (pp. 196, 208).

46. Bailyn, *Ideological Origins*, p. 28 n. 7.

47. Locke, *Two Treatises of Government*, rev. ed., edited by Peter Laslett (Mentor Books, 1965); *Second Treatise*, §§6, 22, 57, 202. Gordon Wood discusses the distinction between liberty and license in colonial political thought in *The Creation of the American Republic*, p. 23. This distinction appeared in a number of sermons before and during the American Revolutionary period. See, for example, Jared Eliot, *Election Sermon* (Connecticut, 1738), p. 15 (on p. 27 Eliot calls Locke "a great writer,"

and in a footnote he tells us to "see Locke on Government"). Elisha Williams (writing as "Philalethes"), *A Seasonable Plea for the Liberty of Conscience and the Right of
Private Judgment in Matters of Religion, Without Any Control from Human Authority*
(Boston, 1744), pp. 2–5 (this sermon is full of transcriptions, citations, and para-
phrases from "Locke on Government," as well as high praise for the "celebrated Mr.
Locke"). Nathanael Hunn, *Election Sermon* (1747), p. 14. Nathaniel Niles, *Two Dis-
courses on Liberty* (from sermons, 1774), in *American Political Writings of the Founding
Era*, p. 271. John Carmichael, *A Self-Defensive War Lawful* (Lancaster, 1775), p. 30.
John Joachim Zubly, *The Law of Liberty: A Sermon in American Affairs, Preached at
the Opening of the Provincial Congress of Georgia* (Philadelphia, 1775), p. 6. Samuel
West, *On the Right to Rebel Against Governors* (Massachusetts Election Sermon of
1776), in *American Political Writings during the Founding Era*, pp. 415, 436, 442 (West
quotes Locke on p. 413).

48. Locke, *Second Treatise*, §§57, 22. For the crucial but often overlooked difference between the Hobbesian and the Lockean conceptions of liberty, see Sterling P.
Lamprecht, *The Moral and Political Philosophy of John Locke* (Russell & Russell, 1962),
pp. 99–102.

49. Locke, *Second Treatise*, §6. On the importance and implications of man's
status as the creature of God in Locke's political theory, see A. W. Sparkes, "Trust
and Teleology: Locke's Politics and His Doctrine of Creation," *Canadian Journal of
Philosophy*, v. 3, no. 2 (December 1973), pp. 263–273.

50. John Dunn, "Consent in the Political Theory of John Locke," *The Historical
Journal*, v. 10, no. 2 (1967), p. 158.

51. Locke, *Second Treatise*, §§6, 23, 135, 168.

52. Dunn, "Consent in the Political Theory of John Locke," pp. 156–157, 170.
Locke, *First Treatise*, §86.

53. Locke, *Second Treatise*, §22.

54. Ibid., §17.

55. Ibid., §23.

56. Ibid., §17.

57. Ibid., §§18, 155.

58. Ibid., §§220, 239.

59. Howard, *A Sermon*, p. 191.

60. Ibid., pp. 201–202, 187.

61. Ibid., p. 203.

62. Ibid., p. 195.

63. Nathan O. Hatch, *The Sacred Cause of Liberty* (Yale University Press, 1977),
pp. 63 (text and n. 21), 13, 72.

64. Locke, *Second Treatise*, §57.

65. Ibid., p. 72 n. 45.

66. Howard, *A Sermon*, p. 188 (p. 9 in the 1773 text cited by Hatch).

67. Ibid., p. 187 (p. 8 in the 1773 text cited by Hatch).

68. Nathan Tarcov, *Locke's Education for Liberty* (University of Chicago Press,
1984), p. 210.

69. John Dunn, *The Political Thought of John Locke* (Cambridge University Press,

1969; 1st paperback edition, 1982), pp. xi–xii. As I indicated above (chapter 1, at note 102), it is the generally theistic, rather than the specifically Calvinist, nature of Locke's thought that I emphasize in my interpretation. My reliance on Dunn, then, is hedged in precisely the area where Nathan Tarcov also qualifies his endorsement of Dunn's work. Except for the emphasis he places on the Calvinist notion of the calling in Locke's thought, writes Tarcov, Dunn offers "one of the most sensitive and careful interpretations of Locke." Tarcov, *Locke's Education for Liberty*, p. 127.

70. Herbert D. Foster, "International Calvinism through Locke and the Revolution of 1688," *American Historical Review*, v. 32, no. 3 (April 1927), p. 487. George Santayana, *Some Turns of Thought in Modern Philosophy* (Charles Scribner, 1933), pp. 13–14: According to Santayana, "probably the most important" presupposition in Locke's mind was his "confident and sincere" Christian faith.

71. John Locke, *Essay Concerning Human Understanding*, edited by Peter H. Nidditch (Oxford University Press, 1975), p. 622 (bk. 4, ch. 10, §7).

72. Lamprecht, *The Moral and Political Philosophy of John Locke*, p. 84.

73. John Locke, *Scritti Editi e Inediti Sulla Tolleranza*, edited and translated by Carlo Viano (Turin, 1961), p. 86. This is Locke's 1667 *Essay Concerning Toleration*, an early version of the definitive *Letter on Toleration* (cited in note 83, below).

74. Locke, *Essay Concerning Human Understanding*, p. 74 (bk. 1, ch. 3, §12).

75. John Locke, *Essays on the Law of Nature*, edited by W. von Leyden (Clarendon Press, 1954), first essay, p. 111.

76. Locke, *Essays on the Law of Nature*, first essay, p. 119.

77. Locke, *The Reasonableness of Christianity*, in *The Works of John Locke* (London, 1823; reprinted in Germany by Scientia Verlag Aalen, 1963), v. 7, p. 150.

78. Locke, *Essay Concerning Human Understanding*, p. 281 (bk. 2, ch. 21, §70), 273 (bk. 2, ch. 21, §60).

79. Ibid., p. 69 (bk. 1, ch. 3, §6).

80. Ibid., p. 352 (bk. 2, ch. 28, §8).

81. John Stuart Mill, *On Liberty* (ed. Bobbs-Merrill, 1956), p. 60.

82. "Locke is a hedonist," says Strauss (*Natural Right and History*, p. 249). For Locke's "Christian hedonism," see Richard I. Aaron, *John Locke*, 2d ed. (Clarendon Press, 1955), p. 257; Donald J. Devine, "John Locke: His Harmony between Liberty and Virtue," *Modern Age*, v. 22, no. 3 (Summer 1978), p. 249; Locke, *The Reasonableness of Christianity*, p. 150. Compare with Hobbes, *Leviathan*, p. 200. See the discussion of Wills in chapter 1, above.

83. John Locke, *A Letter on Toleration*, edited by J. W. Gough (Clarendon Press, 1968), p. 135. Gerald Runkle, *A History of Political Theory* (The Ronald Press, 1968), p. 254.

84. John Locke, *A Vindication of the Reasonableness of Christianity*, in *The Works of John Locke*, v. 7, p. 161; *A Letter on Toleration*, p. 135.

85. Mill, *On Liberty*, pp. 36–39, 63.

86. Locke, *A Letter on Toleration*, p. 65.

87. Ibid., pp. 77, 123.

88. Ibid., p. 77.

89. Locke, *A Letter on Toleration*, p. 69.

90. Ibid., p. 77. Locke, in a treatise which excluded Catholics from religious toleration, prudently refrained from using the term "excommunication" to describe the expulsion of the hopelessly wayward from a religious society.

91. Ibid., p. 69.

92. Devine, "John Locke: His Harmony between Liberty and Virtue," p. 250.

93. Ibid., pp. 145, 141.

94. Locke's Journal entry for August 23, 1676, available in *Essays on the Law of Nature*, p. 275.

95. Locke, *A Letter on Toleration*, pp. 85–87.

96. Ibid., p. 71.

97. Ibid.

98. Pocock, "The Myth of John Locke and the Obsession with Liberalism."

99. Locke, *Essay Concerning Human Understanding*, p. 69 (bk. 1, ch. 3, §6).

100. Tarcov, *Locke's Education for Liberty*, pp. 2–5.

101. Locke, *Scritti Editi e Inediti Sulla Tolleranza*, pp. 90, 91.

102. Locke, *A Letter on Toleration*, p. 65.

103. Ibid., p. 131.

104. Ibid., pp. 125, 91; John Locke, *An Essay for the Understanding of St. Paul's Epistles by Consulting St. Paul Himself*, in *The Works of John Locke*, v. 8, p. 22; Raymond Polin, "John Locke's Conception of Freedom," in John Yolton (ed.), *John Locke: Problems And Perspectives* (Cambridge University Press, 1969), p. 16.

105. Locke, *A Letter on Toleration*, p. 67.

106. *Essays on the Law of Nature*, first essay, p. 119.

107. J. W. Gough, *John Locke's Political Philosophy* (Clarendon Press, 1964), p. 17.

108. Lamprecht, *The Moral and Political Philosophy of John Locke*, pp. 25, 26.

109. See above, notes 71, 73, 77, 79, 80.

110. Locke, *Essay Concerning Human Understanding*, pp. 687 (bk. 4, ch. 17, §23), 694 (bk. 4, ch. 18, §7), 695 (bk. 4, ch. 18, §9).

111. Locke, *The Reasonableness of Christianity*, p. 139.

112. John Locke, *Some Thoughts Concerning Reading and Study for a Gentleman*, in *The Works of John Locke*, v. 3, p. 296 (cited by Devine, "John Locke: His Harmony between Liberty and Virtue," p. 248). Locke makes a very similar argument in *Some Thoughts Concerning Education*, in *The Works of John Locke*, v. 9, p. 176, §185.

113. Locke, *The Reasonableness of Christianity*, pp. 141, 142–143, 147. Also, *The Works of John Locke*, v. 9, p. 377. Compare with Mill, *On Liberty*, pp. 59–63: ". . . I think it is a great error to persist in attempting to find in the Christian doctrine that complete rule for our guidance which its Author intended it to sanction and enforce, but only partially to provide. I believe, too, that this narrow theory is becoming a grave practical evil, detracting greatly from the moral training and instruction which so many well-meaning persons are now at length exerting themselves to promote. . . . [A] large portion of the noblest and most valuable moral teaching has been the work, not only of men who did not know, but of men who knew and rejected, the Christian faith."

114. Lamprecht, *The Moral and Political Philosophy of John Locke*, p. 23. Locke, *The Reasonableness of Christianity*, p. 145.

115. Lamprecht, *The Moral and Political Philosophy of John Locke*, pp. 66, 26, 27.

116. Sidney E. Ahlstrom, *A Religious History of the American People* (Yale University Press, 1972), p. 353.

117. Lamprecht, *The Moral and Political Philosophy of John Locke*, pp. 23–24.

118. John Yolton, *John Locke and the Way of Ideas* (Oxford University Press, 1956), pp. 174, 204, 182.

119. Devine, "John Locke: His Harmony between Liberty and Virtue," p. 248.

120. Strauss, *Natural Right and History*, pp. 220, 226.

121. Ibid., p. 249. For Locke "tacitly" following "the lead given by Hobbes," see pp. 221, 222, 229, 231, 249, 250.

122. Ibid., p. 203.

123. Ibid., pp. 74–75. See Devine's critique in "John Locke: His Harmony between Liberty and Virtue."

124. M. F. Burnyeat, "Sphinx Without a Secret," *New York Review of Books* (May 30, 1985), p. 30.

125. Strauss, *Natural Right and History*, pp. 203 n. 48, 219 (Locke's " 'partial law of nature' ").

126. John Yolton, "Locke on the Law of Nature," *Philosophical Review* (October 1958), pp. 484–486, 489. The passage under discussion here and at the previous note is from John Locke's *Second Vindication of the Reasonableness of Christianity*, in *The Works of John Locke*, v. 7, p. 229 (emphasis added).

127. Locke, *Essays on the Law of Nature*, sixth essay, pp. 189, 187.

128. Locke, *Essay Concerning Human Understanding*, pp. 352 (bk. 2, ch. 28, §8), 698 (bk. 4, ch. 19, §4). S. B. Drury, "John Locke: Natural Law and Innate Ideas," *Dialogue*, v. 19, no. 4 (December 1980), p. 533. Patrick Riley illuminates this issue in *Will and Political Legitimacy* (Harvard University Press, 1982), pp. 87–91.

129. Even Sir Ernest Barker, a sympathetic interpreter of Locke, secularizes Locke's law of nature. Barker likens Locke's natural-law theory to the theories of Grotius, Pufendorf, Hobbes, and Spinoza and calls it a "modern and secular theory." But James Otis knew better. See Barker's "Natural Law and the American Revolution," in his *Traditions of Civility* (Cambridge University Press, 1948), p. 313; also, my discussion of Otis and Locke's theory of natural law in chapter 3, above.

130. Locke, *The Reasonableness of Christianity*, p. 143.

131. Locke, *First Treatise*, §§3–4, 16, 112.

132. Locke, *Second Treatise*, §31.

133. Locke, *A Letter on Toleration*, p. 65.

134. Leo Strauss, *Persecution and the Art of Writing* (Free Press, 1952), p. 25; *What Is Political Philosophy?* pp. 221–232. Joseph Cropsey (ed.), *Ancients and Moderns: Essays on the Tradition of Political Philosophy in Honor of Leo Strauss* (Basic Books, 1964), p. viii. For the esoteric method applied to Locke, see Strauss, *Natural Right and History*, pp. 207–209, 220–221.

135. Richard Rorty, "That Old-Time Philosophy," *The New Republic* (April 4, 1988), p. 29: "Straussians typically do not countenance alternative, debatable interpretations of those writings, but rather distinguish between their own 'authentic understandings' and others' 'misunderstandings.' " Also, see Burnyeat's critique in "Sphinx Without a Secret."

136. Ibid. And see note 12, above, for Pocock's views on the esoteric method.

137. Ruth W. Grant considers Strauss's method in relation to Locke in her important study of Locke's liberalism. She notes Strauss's citation of *The Reasonableness of Christianity*, which seems to justify the esoteric method. But she also cites— and seems more persuaded by—"the many places where Locke emphasizes both that proper writing should clearly and consistently state the author's meaning without metaphor, analogy, or rhetorical flourish and that a reader should approach a work looking for the plain sense of the language and for its chain of logical argument. While Locke took extraordinary care to conceal the fact that he was the author of the political views he published, he often emphasized that the best writing made the author's views directly accessible to the reader and minimized the possibility of confusion or misinterpretation."

Grant concludes that, Strauss to the contrary, Locke did not deliver the essence of his teaching exclusively between the lines of his texts. Nor did he purposely introduce "apparently contradictory statements" in order "to indicate some deeper unifying thought" which, if stated openly, might have provoked the hostility of his contemporaries. Grant's straightforward (yet penetrating) approach to Locke's texts is not without irony: Her book is based on a doctoral thesis that won the Leo Strauss Award from the American Political Science Association in 1985.

See Ruth W. Grant, *John Locke's Liberalism* (University of Chicago Press, 1987), pp. 8–9 (at note 6). The passages cited by Grant that cast doubt upon the applicability of the esoteric approach to Locke's texts are: John Locke, *Conduct of the Understanding*, 2d ed., edited by Thomas Fowler (Burt Franklin, 1971), §§20, 29, 32, 42; *Essay Concerning Human Understanding*, pp. 475–524 (bk. 3, ch. 9–11); *An Essay for the Understanding of St. Paul's Epistles by Consulting St. Paul Himself*, p. 21. And see *PS*, v. 18, no. 4 (Fall 1985), p. 978.

138. Martin Seliger, *The Liberal Politics of John Locke* (Praeger, 1969), pp. 58, 33. Ruth Grant sees a close resemblance between her approach to Locke and Seliger's. See Grant, *John Locke's Liberalism*, p. 7 n. 4.

139. Ibid., pp. 33–34. For Locke's "mitigation" of Hobbes, see Strauss, *What Is Political Philosophy?* p. 49.

140. Seliger, *The Liberal Politics of John Locke*, p. 34. On pp. 35–36, Seliger raises this telling objection to the claim that Locke, fearing persecution, sought to conceal his true thoughts on sensitive subjects by writing "between the lines": "Must it not be asked [of Straussian interpreters] what the concealment of a radical political teaching amounts to if revolution is openly advocated, and in a way that gives the whole philosophical show away for all to see? . . . Clearly, the question which needs answering is whether the philosophical foundation of an argument was more offensive than its most poignant practical conclusion."

141. Lamprecht, *The Moral and Political Philosophy of John Locke*, p. 99: "Liberty he considered indispensable to morality; for if either matter or even God controls men altogether by an external power, there can be no such thing as duty or obligation."

142. John Locke, *The Correspondence*, edited by E. S. de Beer (Clarendon Press, 1976), v. 4, letter 1592, pp. 625–626 (emphasis added). Also available in *The Works of John Locke*, v. 9, p. 305.

143. Seliger, *The Liberal Politics of John Locke*, p. 60 (emphasis added).

144. Locke, *Second Treatise*, §§135, 12. Winthrop S. Hudson, "John Locke—Preparing the Way for the Revolution," in *Journal of Presbyterian History*, v. 42, no. 1 (March 1964), p. 21.

145. Locke, *Essays on the Law of Nature*, first essay, p. 111; *Second Treatise*, §§172, 135, 176. Dunn, "Consent in the Political Theory of John Locke," p. 182: "In the last resort, the judge of the legitimacy of a practice can only be God."

146. Locke, *Second Treatise*, §§240, 168, 176 (lines 39–45).

147. Seliger, *The Liberal Politics of John Locke*, p. 33.

148. Locke, *Essay Concerning Human Understanding*, p. 646 (bk. 4, ch. 12, §11).

149. See citations at note 104, above.

150. Locke, *A Letter on Toleration*, p. 135.

151. Strauss, *Natural Right and History*, p. 246 (emphasis added).

152. On this topic, see Richard L. Bushman, *From Puritan to Yankee* (Harvard University Press, 1967).

153. Hudson, "John Locke—Preparing the Way for the Revolution," pp. 21, 22.

154. Ahlstrom, *A Religious History of the American People*, p. 353. Ezra Stiles, an influential cleric writing as president of Yale in the critical year 1775, praised Locke's "new method of Scripture commentary, by paraphrase and notes," which had made his "reputation as a Scripture commentator exceedingly high with the public." Stiles is quoted in Foster, "International Calvinism through Locke and the Revolution of 1688," p. 475. See chapter 5, below, for a look at Locke's "Scripture commentary."

155. Martha Louise Counts, "The Political Views of the Eighteenth-Century New England Clergy as Expressed in Their Election Sermons" (Ph.D. diss., Columbia University, 1956), p. 258.

156. See above, chapter 1, note 112.

5 Theistic Liberalism in the Teaching of the New England Clergy

1. Carl Becker, *The Declaration of Independence* (Vintage Books, 1958), p. 27.

2. See chapter 2, above.

3. Clinton Rossiter, *Seedtime of the Republic* (Random House, 1953), pp. 40, 53, 237.

4. John Dunn, *The Political Thought of John Locke* (Cambridge University Press, 1969; 1st paperback edition, 1982), pp. xi–xii.

5. Donald S. Lutz, *The Origins of American Constitutionalism* (Louisiana State University Press, 1988), p. 140; "The Relative Influence of European Writers on Late Eighteenth-Century American Political Thought," *American Political Science Review*, v. 78, no. 1 (March 1984).

6. Samuel Lockwood used the phrase, "the politicks of St. Paul," in his *Election Sermon* (Connecticut, 1774), p. 11. Ezra Stiles, an influential cleric writing as president of Yale in the critical year 1775, praised Locke's "new method of Scripture commentary, by paraphrase and notes," which had made his "reputation as a Scripture commentator exceedingly high with the public." Stiles, quoted by Herbert D.

Foster, "International Calvinism through Locke and the Revolution of 1688," *American Historical Review*, v. 32, no. 3 (April 1927), p. 475. As noted in chapter 2, above, I regard Stiles's remark as an extremely important piece of "circumstantial" evidence.

7. Perry Miller, "The Puritan State and Puritan Society," in John P. Roche (ed.), *Origins of American Political Thought* (Harper Torchbooks, 1967), p. 92. Alice M. Baldwin, *The New England Clergy and the American Revolution* (Duke University Press, 1928), pp. 29–30 n. 22.

8. John Wise, quoted in Claude M. Newlin, *Philosophy and Religion in Colonial America* (Philosophical Library, 1962), p. 49. Baldwin, *The New England Clergy*, p. 28.

9. Jared Eliot, *Election Sermon* (Connecticut, 1738), p. 27 (Eliot refers to "a great writer" and says in a note, "See Locke on Government"). Baldwin, *The New England Clergy*, p. 42.

10. Jared Eliot, quoted in Newlin, *Philosophy and Religion*, pp. 67–69.

11. John Locke, *Essay Concerning Human Understanding*, edited by Peter H. Nidditch (Oxford University Press, 1975), p. 698 (bk. 4, ch. 19, §4).

12. John Barnard, *Election Sermon* (Massachusetts, 1734), Evans 3745, pp. 2, 3, 11, 7. Locke, *Essay Concerning Human Understanding*, pp. 46 (bk. 1, ch. 1, §5), 552 (bk. 4, ch. 3, §20). Barnard's theory of government, however, differed from Locke's in this crucial way: Locke trusted the people; Barnard did not. See note 213, and the discussion in section IV, below.

13. Eliphalet Williams, *Election Sermon* (Connecticut, 1769), Evans 11533, p. 17; William Cooper, *Election Sermon* (Massachusetts, 1740), Evans 4498, p. 6. In addition, see John Barnard, *Election Sermon*, pp. 11, 13, 16; Charles Chauncey, *Election Sermon* (Massachusetts, 1747), Evans 5919, p. 10; Stephen White, *Election Sermon* (Connecticut, 1763), Evans 9538, p. 6; Ebenezer Bridge, *Election Sermon* (Massachusetts, 1767), Evans 10569, p. 15; Richard Salter, *Election Sermon* (Connecticut, 1768), Evans 11062, p. 8.

14. John Locke, *Two Treatises of Government*, rev. ed., edited by Peter Laslett (New York: Mentor Books, 1965), *Second Treatise*, §135.

15. Chauncey, *Election Sermon*, p. 9.

16. Andrew Eliot, *Election Sermon* (Massachusetts, 1765), Evans 9964, p. 17.

17. John Tucker, *Election Sermon* (Massachusetts, 1771), in Charles Hyneman and Donald Lutz (eds.), *American Political Writings during the Founding Era* (Liberty Press, 1983), v. I, p. 161.

18. Samuel West, *Election Sermon* (Massachusetts, 1776), in *American Political Writings of the Founding Era*, v. I, p. 416.

19. Eliphalet Williams, *Election Sermon* (Connecticut, 1769), Evans 11533, p. 42.

20. Peter Whitney, *The Transgression of a Land Punished by a Multitude of Rulers, Considered in Two Discourses, Delivered July 14, 1774* (Boston, 1774), Evans 13769, pp. 18–19.

21. Jonathan Mayhew, *Discourse Concerning Unlimited Submission and Non-Resistance to the Higher Powers* (Boston, 1750), in John Wingate Thornton (ed.), *The Pulpit of the American Revolution* (1860; reprint Burt Franklin, 1970), pp. 84, 87.

22. Daniel Shute, *Election Sermon* (Massachusetts, 1768), in *American Political Writings during the Founding Era*, v. I, p. 126.

23. Charles Turner, *Election Sermon* (Massachusetts, 1773), Evans 13053, p. 31.

24. John Lathrop, *Artillery-Election Sermon* (Boston, 1774), Evans 13371, pp. 7–8.

25. West, *Election Sermon*, pp. 435, 432.

26. Locke, *First Treatise*, §§3–4, 16, 112.

27. Rossiter, *Seedtime of the Republic*, p. 491 n. 111; Baldwin, *The New England Clergy*, p. 60. For general (and sometimes explicit) statements of the Lockean position on toleration, see, for example, Peter Clark, *Election Sermon* (Massachusetts, 1739), Evans 4350, pp. 18–19; Charles Chauncey, *The Only Compulsion Proper to Be Made Use of in Affairs of Conscience and Religion* (Boston, 1739), Evans 4349, pp. 9–11; Elisha Williams (writing as "Philalethes"), *A Seasonable Plea for Religious Liberty* (1744), Evans 5520, pp. 50, 7, 8; Isaac Backus, *A Seasonable Plea for Liberty of Conscience* (Boston, 1770), pp. 11–12; Izrahiah Wetmore, *Election Sermon* (Connecticut, 1773), pp. 29, 31. And see Newlin's discussion of Mayhew in *Philosophy and Religion*, p. 195.

28. John Locke, *A Letter on Toleration*, edited by J. W. Gough (Clarendon Press, 1968), p. 65.

29. Chauncey, *The Only Compulsion*, p. 9.

30. Moses Dickinson, *Election Sermon* (Connecticut, 1755), Evans 7407, pp. 23–24.

31. Thomas Foxcroft, *Some Seasonable Thoughts on Evangelical Preaching* (Boston, 1740), Evans 4510, p. 8.

32. Locke, *Essay Concerning Human Understanding*, p. 694 (bk. 4, ch. 18, §7). See discussion in chapter 4, above.

33. John Locke, *Some Thoughts Concerning Reading and Study for a Gentleman*, in *The Works of John Locke* (London, 1823; reprinted in Germany by Scientia Verlag Aalen, 1963), v. 3, p. 296; cited by Donald J. Devine, "John Locke: His Harmony between Liberty and Virtue," *Modern Age*, v. 22, no. 3 (Summer 1978), p. 248. See also Locke, *Some Thoughts Concerning Education*, in *The Works of John Locke*, v. 9, p. 176, §185. And see chapter 4, above.

34. Charles Chauncey and Jared Eliot, quoted in Newlin, *Philosophy and Religion*, pp. 194, 94, 67–69. Locke, *Essay Concerning Human Understanding*, pp. 687 (bk. 4, ch. 17, §24), 694 (bk. 4, ch. 18, §8), 695 (bk. 4, ch. 18, §10), 698 (bk. 4, ch. 19, §4).

35. John Locke, *The Reasonableness of Christianity*, in *The Works of John Locke*, v. 7, pp. 139–140.

36. Ibid., pp. 140, 143.

37. Newlin, *Philosophy and Religion*, p. 25.

38. Samuel Johnson, quoted in Ibid., pp. 53–54.

39. Locke, *The Reasonableness of Christianity*, p. 5.

40. Ibid., p. 135.

41. Ibid., p. 139.

42. Ibid., pp. 146, 157.

43. Ibid., p. 145. See chapter 4, above.

44. John Bulkley, quoted in Newlin, *Philosophy and Religion*, pp. 55–56.

45. Gad Hitchcock, quoted in Ibid., pp. 206–208. Newlin says, "To account for man's slowness in the acquisition of knowledge, Hitchcock made use of the epistemology of John Locke"—specifically, Locke's refutation of innatism.

46. Ibid., pp. 206–208.

47. Jonathan Dickinson, quoted in Ibid., pp. 58–60. How much proof do we need? Interestingly, Newlin did not connect Locke and Dickinson, in terms of the titles or of the contents of their books.

48. Locke, *The Reasonableness of Christianity*, p. 140.

49. Ibid., p. 145.

50. Newlin, *Philosophy and Religion*, pp. 205–208.

51. Peter Clark, quoted in Ibid., p. 201.

52. Locke, *The Reasonableness of Christianity*, pp. 149–150, 140.

53. Ibid., p. 143.

54. Ibid., p. 140.

55. Locke, *Essay Concerning Human Understanding*, pp. 687 (bk. 4, ch. 17, §24), 694 (bk. 4, ch. 18, §8), 695 (bk. 4, ch. 18, §10).

56. Jared Eliot, quoted in Newlin, *Philosophy and Religion*, pp. 67–69.

57. Locke, *Essay Concerning Human Understanding*, p. 698 (bk. 4, ch. 19, §4).

58. Charles Chauncey, quoted in Newlin, *Philosophy and Religion*, pp. 194, 92.

59. Jared Eliot, quoted in Ibid., pp. 67–69.

60. Samuel West, Ibid., p. 202.

61. Locke, *Essay Concerning Human Understanding*, p. 698 (bk. 4, ch. 19, §4).

62. Referring to Trenchard and Gordon, coauthors of *Cato's Letters* (which the republican synthesis has proclaimed the textbook of American republicanism), Pocock notes "a high degree of correlation in the early eighteenth century between neo-Harringtonian republicanism and deism." J. G. A. Pocock, *The Machiavellian Moment* (Princeton University Press, 1975), p. 476. In addition, see Pocock, "Machiavelli, Harrington, and English Political Ideologies in the Eighteenth Century," in *Politics, Language, and Time* (Atheneum, 1971), pp. 134–135.

On p. 507 of *The Machiavellian Moment*, Pocock refers parenthetically to the "deist modes of American religion" in speaking about the influence of "country" ideology on the Revolutionary generation. Deism would account for the clergy's alleged susceptibility to the influence of "neo-classical politics" (i.e., republicanism). But I find far more Lockean liberalism than civic republicanism in clerical thought and very little deism—which, I suppose, is precisely the point of the substantive Lockean connection.

63. See citation at note 6, above.

64. Baldwin, *The New England Clergy*, pp. xii, 7–8.

65. Nathan Hatch dismisses Baldwin, and Locke, in a single footnote. He begins by citing the seminal works of the republican synthesis—Bailyn, Pocock, etc.—to justify writing an account of clerical thought without reporting even one of the many references to Locke (see chapter 4, above). As for Baldwin, her conclusions, "which point to *Locke et praeterea nihil*, need considerable revision." Baldwin's interpretation, however, is not monolithically Lockean, while Hatch's account, which points

to *omnia praeter Lockem*, completely overlooks or disregards the most frequently cited nonbiblical source of political theory in the sermon literature. Hatch, *The Sacred Cause of Liberty* (Yale University Press, 1977), p. 57 n. 5.

66. Baldwin, *The New England Clergy*, pp. 22–23.

67. Ibid., pp. 29–30 n. 22.

68. Bernard Bailyn, *Ideological Origins of the American Revolution* (Harvard University Press, 1967), pp. 220–222. Becker, *The Declaration of Independence*, pp. 101–102, 106–107.

69. Baldwin, *The New England Clergy*, pp. 17–18.

70. Newlin, *Philosophy and Religion*, p. 204.

71. Ibid., p. 4.

72. G. Bulkley, *Will and Doom* (1692), preface, p. 94, quoted by Baldwin, *The New England Clergy*, p. 17 n. 21.

73. Ebenezer Pemberton, *Election Sermon* (Massachusetts, 1710), p. 29.

74. John Bulkley, *Election Sermon* (Connecticut, 1713), Evans 1598, p. 17.

75. Anonymous clerical pamphlet, in Baldwin, *The New England Clergy*, p. 17 n. 21.

76. Mayhew, *Discourse Concerning Unlimited Submission*, p. 95.

77. Jonathan Mayhew, *Election Sermon* (Massachusetts, 1754), Evans 7256, p. 20.

78. Baldwin, *The New England Clergy*, p. 19.

79. Tucker, *Election Sermon*, pp. 160, 171, 164. Locke, *Second Treatise*, §202.

80. Lathrop, *Artillery-Election Sermon* (Boston, 1774), p. 17.

81. Ibid., pp. 7–8.

82. Locke, *Essay Concerning Human Understanding*, pp. 692 (bk. 4, ch. 28, §5), 694 (bk. 4, ch. 28, §8).

83. West, *Election Sermon*, p. 414.

84. John G. Buchanan, "Drumfire from the Pulpit: Natural Law in the Colonial Election Sermons of Massachusetts," *American Journal of Legal History* 12 (1968), p. 244.

85. Baldwin, *The New England Clergy*, pp. 22–23.

86. Locke, *Essay Concerning Human Understanding*, p. 265 (bk. 2, ch. 21, §§49, 50).

87. See John Yolton's introduction to his edition of Locke's *Essay Concerning Human Understanding* (J. M. Dent & Sons, 1961), pp. ix–xv. (All other citations of the *Essay* in this book are of the Nidditch edition, as fully cited in note 11, above.)

88. Locke, *Essay Concerning Human Understanding*, pp. 692 (bk. 4, ch. 28, §5), 694 (bk. 4, ch. 28, §8).

89. Locke, *First Treatise*, §6; *Second Treatise*, §195.

90. Locke, *The Reasonableness of Christianity*, pp. 111–112.

91. For Locke, see the discussion in the following section.

92. George H. Sabine, *A History of Political Theory*, 4th ed., revised by Thomas Landon Thorson (Dryden Press, 1973), pp. 177, 187, 335–339.

93. Ibid., p. 177.

94. Ibid., p. 338.

95. Quentin Skinner, *The Foundations of Modern Political Thought* (Cambridge

University Press, 1978 paperback edition), v. II, p. 213; also p. 15. Skinner surveys the use of Romans 13 to support passive obedience throughout both volumes of this valuable work.

96. West, *Election Sermon*, v. I, p. 427.

97. Ibid., p. 427.

98. Ibid., p. 427; Stephen Johnson, *Some Important Observations Occasioned by . . . the Public Fast* (sermon delivered December 15, 1765; published in Newport, 1776), Evans 10346, pp. 26–27.

99. Jeremiah Wise cited Romans 13—"He is a minister of God to thee for good" —to show that "civil authority is not designed for destruction but for protection" of persons in their "estates, liberties and lives. This is the end that rulers should aim at." *Election Sermon* (Massachusetts, 1729), Evans 3242, p. 8. See also Elisha Williams (writing as "Philalethes"), *A Seasonable Plea for Religious Liberty*, pp. 26–27.

100. See note 5, above.

101. Benjamin Stevens, *Election Sermon* (Massachusetts, 1761), Evans 9017, p. 33 n.

102. Skinner, *Foundations*, v. I, pp. 209–210.

103. Locke, *An Essay for the Understanding of St. Paul's Epistles by Consulting St. Paul Himself*, in *The Works of John Locke*, v. 8, p. 16.

104. Ibid., p. 4.

105. Mayhew, *Discourse Concerning Unlimited Submission*, pp. 54–55, 68–69. Diggins notes that Mayhew "often ended his sermons by citing 'the incomparable Locke.'" John P. Diggins, *The Lost Soul of American Politics: Virtue, Self-Interest, and the Foundations of Liberalism* (Basic Books, 1984), p. 33.

106. Skinner, *Foundations*, v. II, p. 227.

107. Christopher Morris, *Political Thought in England: Tyndale to Hooker* (Oxford University Press, 1953), p. 148.

108. Edmund Burke, "Speech in Support of Resolutions for Conciliation with the American Colonies," March 22, 1775, in Elliot R. Barkan (ed.), *Edmund Burke on the American Revolution: Selected Speeches and Letters*, 2d ed. (Peter Smith, 1972), p. 84.

109. Louis Hartz, *The Liberal Tradition in America* (Harcourt, Brace & World, 1955), pp. 5–6. See chapter 1, above.

110. Edward Rawson and Samuel Sewall, *The Revolution in New England Justified* (Boston, 1691), p. 1. See chapter 3, above.

111. *New England Courant*, May 7–14, 1722.

112. *New England Weekly Journal*, January 25, 1731.

113. Edward Holyoke, *Election Sermon* (Massachusetts, 1736), Evans 4026, pp. 12–13.

114. White, *Election Sermon*, p. 22; Salter, *Election Sermon*, p. 25; Johnson, *Some Important Observations*, p. 21.

115. Johnson, *Some Important Observations*, pp. 26–27. Johnson is a "Lockean" preacher because of his generous deployment of Locke citations.

116. Shute, *Election Sermon*, p. 126. See Locke, *First Treatise*, §§3–4.

117. West, *Election Sermon*, p. 414.

118. Samuel Lockwood, *Election Sermon* (Connecticut, 1774), Evans 13382, p. 15.

119. Charles Turner, *Election Sermon* (Massachusetts, 1773), pp. 9, 8. See also Elisha Williams, *A Seasonable Plea for Religious Liberty*, pp. 26–27. And see, for example, the following: Noah Welles, *Election Sermon* (Connecticut, 1764), Evans 9866, p. 24; Salter, *Election Sermon*, pp. 8, 10; Eliphalet Williams, *Election Sermon*, p. 13; Samuel Cooke, *Election Sermon* (Massachusetts, 1770), in *Pulpit of the American Revolution*, pp. 159, 162; Mark Leavenworth, *Election Sermon* (Connecticut, 1772), Evans 12430, p. 46.

120. Elisha Williams, *A Seasonable Plea for Religious Liberty*, pp. 26–27, 2–5, 7, 29–30.

121. Thornton, *Pulpit of the American Revolution*, p. 43.

122. John Adams, *The Works of John Adams* (Little, Brown, 1856), v. 10, p. 301.

123. Baldwin, *The New England Clergy*, p. 44. Claude H. Van Tyne, "The Influence of the Clergy, and of Religious and Sectarian Forces, on the American Revolution," *American Historical Review*, v. 19, no. 1 (October 1913), p. 50.

124. Mayhew, *Discourse Concerning Unlimited Submission*, pp. 51–52, 63.

125. See above, notes 105, 76, 21.

126. Mayhew, *Discourse Concerning Unlimited Submission*, pp. 60, 61.

127. Ibid., p. 61 (note b), 69, 74.

128. Ibid., p. 47.

129. Ibid., pp. 73–74. The distinction between tyrants and magistrates, grounded in the notion of rule for the common good, is ancient wisdom. Socrates made the point when he tangled with Thrasymachus in Plato's *Republic*: "No ruler, *insofar as he is acting as a ruler*, will study or enjoin what is for his own interest. All that he says and does will be said and done with a view to what is good and proper for the subject for whom he practices his art." In addition, Aristotle used this distinction to separate true from perverted forms of government: "Those constitutions which consider the common interest are *right* constitutions, judged by the standard of absolute justice. Those constitutions which consider only the personal interest of the rulers are all *wrong* constitutions, or *perversions* of the right forms. Such perverted forms are despotic. . . ." The "politicks of St. Paul," however, differs from the ancient wisdom in two ways. First, Plato and Aristotle did not theorize in a theological environment. Second, they did not use this distinction to illuminate the question of political obligation. Plato, *The Republic*, translated by Francis MacDonald Cornford (Oxford University Press, 1980), p. 24 (emphasis added). Aristotle, *Politics*, translated by Ernest Barker (Oxford University Press, 1970–71), pp. 112, 114. See below, note 173.

130. Mayhew, *Discourse Concerning Unlimited Submission*, pp. 94–95 (note a).

131. Ibid., p. 78.

132. Ibid., pp. 87 (note a), 79.

133. Ibid., pp. 78–79.

134. Ibid., p. 86 (note a), 79.

135. Ibid., p. 75, 88 (emphasis added).

136. Peter Laslett, introduction to Locke's *Two Treatises*, p. 60. See note 14, above.

137. Andrew Eliot, *Election Sermon*, pp. 42–43, 47–48.

138. Johnson, *Some Important Observations*, p. 25.

139. Ibid., pp. 22, 23.

140. Ibid., pp. 23–24. Locke, *Second Treatise*, §§220 (9–23), 239 (20–23).

141. Turner, *Election Sermon*, pp. 8, 9, 29, 31.

142. Whitney, *The Transgression of a Land*, pp. 10–11, 16–18 (emphasis added).

143. Ibid., pp. 16–18.

144. West, *Election Sermon*, pp. 424–425.

145. Ibid., pp. 425, 426.

146. Ibid., p. 421.

147. Ibid., pp. 421, 422.

148. Ibid., p. 423.

149. Ibid., p. 427.

150. Ibid., p. 427.

151. See, for example, Edward Barnard, *Election Sermon* (Massachusetts, 1766), Evans 10235, p. 38; Jonathan Lee, *Election Sermon* (Connecticut, 1766), Evans 10354, p. 15; Shute, *Election Sermon*, pp. 126–127; Eliphalet Williams, *Election Sermon*, pp. 12–13; Stephen Johnson, *Election Sermon* (Connecticut, 1770), Evans 11691, pp. 6–7; Tucker, *Election Sermon*, pp. 164–165; Gad Hitchcock, *Election Sermon* (Massachusetts, 1774), in *American Political Writings during the Founding Era*, v. I, p. 292; Lockwood, *Election Sermon*, pp. 13, 15–17.

152. Baldwin, *The New England Clergy*, p. 129.

153. See note 6, above.

154. Locke, *An Essay for the Understanding of St. Paul's Epistles*, p. 22.

155. Locke, *A Letter on Toleration*, p. 125.

156. John Locke, *A Paraphrase and Notes on the Epistle of St. Paul to the Romans*, in *The Works of John Locke*, v. 8, pp. 368, 367 (note b).

157. Ibid., p. 367 (note b).

158. Ibid., p. 367 (note b).

159. Locke, *Second Treatise*, §168. ("This judgment they cannot part with"; thus, it is inalienable. See the discussion of political judgment in section IV, below.)

160. See chapter 4, above.

161. Locke, *First Treatise*, §92. Compare this to Eliphalet Williams, *Election Sermon*, pp. 12–13; and Lockwood, *Election Sermon*, pp. 15–17.

162. Locke, *Second Treatise*, §§87, 123.

163. Ibid., §3 (emphasis added to the last five words).

164. Ibid., §§142, 165.

165. Ibid., §135.

166. Ibid., §131.

167. Ibid., §239.

168. Locke, *A Paraphrase and Notes*, p. 367 (note b).

169. See note 156, above.

170. Bailyn asserts that Locke's "ideas would scarcely have supported" Mayhew's argument in the *Discourse Concerning Unlimited Submission*. Bailyn, *Ideological Origins*, p. 52. See discussion in chapter 4, above, at note 44.

171. Locke, *Second Treatise*, §202.

172. Ibid., §200.

173. Ibid., §199. See note 129, above.

174. Ibid., §§160, 159, 166 (where Locke writes that "prerogative is nothing but the power of doing publick good without a rule").

175. Ibid., §§124, 85, 87, 123.

176. See, for instance, John Bulkley, *Election Sermon*, p. 29; Wise, *Election Sermon*, p. 8; Shute, *Election Sermon*, pp. 111–112; Hitchcock, *Election Sermon*, pp. 289, 294.

177. Locke, *Second Treatise*, §12. Shute, *Election Sermon*, p. 120. John Lathrop, *Innocent Blood Crying to God* (sermon of March 5, 1770, occasioned by the Boston Massacre), Evans 12094, p. 13.

178. Locke, *Second Treatise*, §155.

179. See chapter 2, above.

180. Locke, *Essay Concerning Human Understanding*, p. 646 (bk. 4, ch. 12, §11).

181. Locke, *A Letter on Toleration*, p. 131.

182. Ibid., p. 125.

183. Locke, *An Essay for the Understanding of St. Paul's Epistles*, p. 22.

184. Locke, *Essay Concerning Human Understanding*, pp. 8 (Epistle to the Reader), 101 (bk. 1, ch. 4, §23).

185. Locke, *An Essay for the Understanding of St. Paul's Epistles*, p. 22.

186. Locke, *Essay Concerning Human Understanding*, p. 693 (bk. 4, ch. 18, §5).

187. William Breitenbach, "The Consistent Calvinism of the New Divinity Movement," *William & Mary Quarterly*, v. 41, no. 2 (April 1984), p. 242.

188. Locke, *Second Treatise*, §§135, 12.

189. Ibid., §§240, 241. More ancient wisdom? See Aristotle, *Politics*, pp. 126–127 (§§14, 18). Or is it merely common sense? See Thomas Paine, *Common Sense* (Penguin, 1983), pp. 63–64: "[T]he good people of this country . . . have an undoubted privilege to inquire into the pretensions" of King and Parliament, "and equally to reject the usurpation of either."

190. Locke, *Second Treatise*, §168.

191. Ibid., §176.

192. Sterling P. Lamprecht, *The Moral and Political Philosophy of John Locke* (Russell & Russell, 1962), p. 99.

193. Elisha Williams, *A Seasonable Plea for Religious Liberty*, pp. 5, 7–8. Also available in Edmund S. Morgan (ed.), *Puritan Political Ideas: 1558–1794* (Bobbs-Merrill, 1965), especially pp. 286–287.

194. Jonathan Mayhew, *Seven Sermons* (Boston, 1748; London, 1750), available in Mayhew, *Sermons* (Arno Press and The New York Times, 1969), pp. 59, 37–38, 58, 52, 60 (emphasis added).

195. Samuel Baldwin, *A Sermon Preached at Plymouth* (delivered December 22, 1775; published in Boston, 1776), Evans 14657, pp. 21, 14.

196. Moses Dickinson, *Election Sermon*, pp. 23–24.

197. William Rand, *Convention Sermon* (Massachusetts, 1757), Evans 8014, p. 15.

198. Joseph Fish, *Election Sermon* (Connecticut, 1760), Evans 8598, pp. 13–14.

199. Edward Dorr, *Election Sermon* (Connecticut, 1765), Evans 9955, pp. 23–24.

200. John Tucker, *Convention Sermon* (Massachusetts, 1768), pp. 15–18. Baldwin, *The New England Clergy*, p. 108 n. 10.

201. Simeon Howard, *A Sermon Preached to the Ancient and Honorable Artillery Company in Boston* (1773), in *American Political Writings during the Founding Era*, v. I, pp. 203, 188–189.

202. See, for example, Amos Adams, *Religious Liberty* (sermon delivered December 3, 1767; published in Boston, 1768), Evans 10810, p. 7; Shute, *Election Sermon*, p. 120.

203. "The Centinel, no. 5," *The Pennsylvania Journal and Weekly Advertiser* (April 21, 1768). The authors (Francis Alison, John Dickinson, and George Bryan) defended "the Rights of private Judgment, and the indispensable Duty of every Christian to examine the Scriptures" against the threat of Episcopacy. In the next installment, they enlisted "Locke on Government" on behalf of liberty. "The Centinel, no. 6," *The Pennsylvania Journal and Weekly Advertiser* (April 28, 1768). These essays are available in *"The Centinel": Warnings of a Revolution*, edited by Elizabeth I. Nybakken (Associated University Presses, 1980).

204. Benjamin F. Wright, Jr., *American Interpretations of Natural Law* (Harvard University Press, 1931), p. 334.

205. On the dreaded American Episcopate, see discussion above, chapter 3, at notes 117–119. Thomas Paine understood the spirit of the times when he suggested that a Continental Congress should secure "freedom and property to all men, and *above all things* the free exercise of religion, according to the dictates of conscience." Paine, *Common Sense*, p. 97 (emphasis added).

206. Turner, *Election Sermon*, quoted by Van Tyne, "The Influence of the Clergy," p. 55.

207. Howard, *A Sermon Preached*, p. 203 (emphasis added).

208. Whitney, *The Transgression of a Land*, p. 61.

209. The General Association of Congregationalist Ministers (1774), quoted in Lester Douglas Joyce, *Church and Clergy in the American Revolution* (Exposition Press, 1966), p. 76.

210. Charles F. Mullett, *Fundamental Law and the American Revolution* (Octagon Books, 1966), p. 73. On the right and competence of the people to judge in political affairs, see Martha Louise Counts, "The Political Views of the Eighteenth-Century New England Clergy as Expressed in Their Election Sermons" (Ph.D. diss., Columbia University, 1956), p. 123. Also, Alice M. Baldwin, *The New England Clergy*, p. 129 n. 29.

211. Joseph Easterbrooke, *Election Sermon* (Massachusetts, 1705), Evans 1205, p. 21.

212. Nathaniel Stone, *Election Sermon* (Massachusetts, 1720), Evans 2180, p. 17.

213. John Barnard, *Election Sermon*, p. 45.

214. Holyoke, *Election Sermon*, pp. 12–13.

215. Cooper, *Election Sermon*, p. 10.

216. Nathaniel Appleton, *Election Sermon* (Massachusetts, 1742), Evans 4881, pp. 34–35.

217. Mayhew, *Discourse Concerning Unlimited Submission*, p. 87 n. See also Mayhew's *Election Sermon*, p. 14.

218. Andrew Eliot, *Election Sermon*, p. 45.

219. William Patten, *A Discourse Delivered at Hallifax* (Boston, 1766), Evans 10440.

220. Salter, *Election Sermon*, pp. 29–30.

221. *Boston Weekly Newsletter*, November 23, 1769.

222. Jason Haven, *Election Sermon* (Massachusetts, 1769), Evans 11289, pp. 9, 41–42.

223. Tucker, *Election Sermon*, p. 164.

224. Turner, *Election Sermon* (Massachusetts, 1773), Evans 13053, pp. 29, 7 n.

225. Hitchcock, *Election Sermon*, pp. 284, 294.

226. Dan Foster, *A Short Essay on Civil Government* (the substance of six sermons, prepared in October, 1774; published in Hartford, 1775), Evans 14036, pp. 70–71.

227. Whitney, *The Transgression of a Land*, pp. 16–18.

228. West, *Election Sermon*, pp. 423, 413.

6 History, Myth, and the Secular Salvation of American Liberalism

1. Plato, *The Republic*, translated by Francis MacDonald Cornford (Oxford University Press, 1980), p. 106.

2. Neil Postman, *Amusing Ourselves to Death: Public Discourse in the Age of Show Business* (Penguin Books, 1985). This small book contains much wisdom and truth. It sobers, enlightens, and prompts us to ask whether the spirit of the American founding could ever be nurtured, conveyed, and sustained through any medium *but* print. I suspect that Postman would say no. And since print has been surpassed by electronic forms of communication (especially television) as the dominant medium of our culture, one must worry that America has permanently lost touch with its founding spirit.

3. John Dunn says that the only Lockean argument still of interest "as a starting point for reflection about any issue of contemporary political theory is the theme of the *Letters on Toleration*, and in Locke's thought this rests firmly upon a religious premise." I believe that the notion of limited government is necessarily implied, and originated historically, in the argument for religious toleration. Dunn, *The Political Thought of John Locke* (Cambridge University Press, 1969; 1st paperback edition, 1982), pp. x–xi. See chapter 3, above, at note 134.

4. Plato, *The Republic*, p. 53.

5. John Stuart Mill is a key figure in the pantheon of liberal political philosophers. John Rawls may eventually enter the pantheon. His book, *A Theory of Justice* (Harvard University Press, 1972) is a modern classic, which has spawned its own interpretative industry. See also Thomas A. Spragens, Jr., *The Irony of Liberal Reason* (University of Chicago Press, 1981). Spragens identifies tendencies in liberalism which, ironically, threaten the humane values which liberalism itself has bequeathed to Western civilization. With the help of Wittgenstein and Freud, he begins "to

transcend the sources of liberal corruption and to resuscitate the humane essentials of the liberal tradition, properly understood" (p. viii).

6. The republican revision tries to have it both ways. Gordon Wood says American republicanism was "essentially anti-capitalistic," and Pocock's dialectic between virtue and commerce incorporates this view. Bailyn, however, calls John Trenchard and Thomas Gordon, coauthors of *Cato's Letters*, the "most important" spokesmen for "extreme libertarianism" in colonial America. Gordon S. Wood, *The Creation of the American Republic* (University of North Carolina Press, 1969), p. 418. Bernard Bailyn, *The Ideological Origins of the American Revolution* (Harvard University Press, 1967), p. 35. On this topic, see chapter 4, above, notes 28–31 and corresponding text; chapter 3, above, note 108. For a discussion of Pocock's paradigm, see chapter 1, above.

7. Robert Nozick, *Anarchy, State, and Utopia* (Basic Books, 1974). Nozick's book has become a kind of bible of American libertarianism. And the bourgeois Locke is one of its patron saints.

8. J. G. A. Pocock, *The Machiavellian Moment* (Princeton University Press, 1975), p. 424.

9. Niccolò Machiavelli, *The Discourses*, edited by Bernard Crick (Penguin Books, 1979), pp. 139–142.

10. Pocock, *The Machiavellian Moment*, p. 545.

Index

Steven M. Dworetz graduated from York College,
City University of New York, and received his Ph.D.
in political science from Rutgers University.
He teaches political science at
Wheaton College, Norton, Massachusetts.

Library of Congress Cataloging-in-Publication Data
Dworetz, Steven M.
The unvarnished doctrine : Locke, liberalism, and the American
Revolution / Steven M. Dworetz.
p.   cm.
Includes index.
ISBN 0-8223-0961-0
ISBN 0-8223-1470-3 (pbk)
1. Locke, John, 1632–1704.   2. Liberalism—United States—
History—18th century.   3. United States—History—Revolution,
1775–1783.   4. United States—Intellectual life—18th century.
1. Title.
JC 153.L87D86   1990
320.5'12'097309033—dc 20   89-35756